For my loved ones:
My late father Gavriel Kraus,
My mother Victoria, may she live long,
My sisters Liat and Livnat,
My brothers in law Moshe and Moran, My nephews Ronnie,
Ori, Omer, Jonathan, Ilay and Oriyan-Gavriel
Eliran Elkayam, Nofar & Refael
Eldar Bar Lev and Ofer, the children Arin, Ilay and Itay,
Gil Itzhak, Shelly Sinvani-Itzhak,
Esther Odel, San Oved & Reef (Gilit)
Ben Yanover & Rachel, Dudi, Keren, Yehonatan & Yoav

Special thanks:
David Dedi Itzhak

EUROVISION

Oved Kraus

Executive and Chief editor: Netanel Semrik, David Maayan & Oved Kraus

Translator and interior book designer:
David Maayan

Book cover designer:
Smadar Peled

Photos:
Uri Aloni, Ilan Ben Shachar in courtesy of the "Lahiton" archive,
Bruno Torricelli, David Paz and Eric Bachmann

In Memory of the late Uri Aloni

ISBN: 978-965-598-334-0
Printing date, January 2025

Table of Contents

Introduction

68 years spanning two centuries, crossing one millennium — are the most reliable evidence for the story of one of the oldest and perhaps most watched entertainment contests in the world. Since 1956 to the present day, the Eurovision song contest has come a long way with dramatic shifts in theme, essence and even in audience. The event, proved in order to unite the western part of Europe facing the Eastern-Communist Bloc, became a pan-European festival, which at one point was taken over by the outlying Eastern countries.

Does music and songs really matter most at Eurovision? Only several performers have been blessed to build a beautiful career thanks to their participation or win in this contest and even fewer are the songs that have received the audience's sympathy outside the circles of the Eurovision fans and supporters throughout generations.

In the 1970s, the event became a consensus in Europe. Millions of people were eagerly anticipating an annual evening in which the most beautiful song would be selected amongst the candidates, much like the "Miss Universe" competition, except here the ratings and popularity were much greater. Thus, the sense of belonging to the victory seems to have been stronger amongst the citizens of the winning country, even than the performers. As a result, even in most of the winning cases, these felt much prouder of the achievement than the singer who reached the coveted moment.

Throughout the 1970s, 1980s and 1990s, despite its classification and image as a low-quality music contest, to say the least, some big names in the music industry took part in it and while some of them try to deny it, the Eurovision is part of their career landscape. In the current millennium, the event has been painted in the colours of the LGBTQ community, which seems to have patronized the ESC, embracing it back in its turn, leading to a new fan base and momentum that seems to have strengthened the core of Eurovision in the 2000s. After years of taking a great interest and accumulating valuable information, which is actually the Eurovision timeline, I explored the possibility of writing a book that would consolidate the data, stories and anecdotes that make up the contest's full history.

When I first began to delve into this medley, I never imagined that the task of collecting and grouping the statistics, hundreds of songs, dozens of exciting moments, the winners who entered the pantheon, the greatest moments, as well as a quite a few embarrassments and entertaining incidents, would have such a magnetizing effect, like an endless pit full of secrets. After more than halfway through the process of collecting material

and writing, I realised that to turn it all into a book, I would have to put aside my other pursuits and be enslaved to complete the task: Nights became days and the book actually became a long, tedious but also fascinating documentation journey. Thousands of hours were spent recreating the history of the Eurovision Song Contest, along with personal stories, countless interviews and conversations I had with Eurovision heroes, before and behind the scenes (some of whom passed away while authoring this book), accumulating days, weeks, months and almost a quarter of a century, until the work was completed.

The contest's evolution is undeniable. It had always sought to shun politics, but somehow politics always adhered to it... It is mocked and criticized, not much importance is attached to it, but it is standing of over 60 years has made it clear it is impossible to live without. The facts speak for themselves. Despite countless attempts to cancel and ignore the Eurovision Song Contest, it was and still is the largest music show in the world, which to this day, in an age of multi-channels and social networks, is regularly watched, year after year, by hundreds of millions all over the globe. The purpose of this book is not to unravel the contest's secret, nor to analyse sociological or social phenomena and certainly not to open discussions on musical philosophies. The objective is to introduce the Eurovision's history, year by year, from 1956 until today, with all the data, numbers, and stories along the timeline.

It is intended, of course, for the world's tireless Eurovision fans, but also for the various performers who have been part of its history, for people in the mass media who seek to understand the phenomenon and look at numerical data, as well as for those who have never liked or heard of the Eurovision Song Contest and who might simply fall in love with its marvellous tradition.

I extend my gratitude to the good people who made it possible for this book to see the light of day: My brilliant partner, David Dedi Itzhak; the publisher, Netanel Semrik, who spent hours and days with me until the desired result and for which I am grateful; Osnat, Ariel, Kesem, Ayal and the Contento Now family who have greatly helpful; the one and only Uri Aloni who passed away on the eve of book's printing; Ilan Ben Shachar, the one man museum; The savant and knowledgeable Yuval Niv; Kobi Oshrat, Moti Dichne, Alex Giladi, Amnon Barkai, Frank Naef, Atilla Şereftuğ, Ossi Runne, Juan Carlos Calderón, Joy Fleming, Dolf van der Linden, Matts Olsson, Terry Wogan, Noel Kelehan and all the other performers, musicians, producers, and journalists from all over the world who spoke openly and generously with me and helped me fill this book with important and unprecedented information in its scope. Let us go on a journey...

Izhar Cohen and "Alphabeta", bringing Israel a historical win in Paris, 1978 >> Photo by: Uri Aloni, in courtesy of Ilan Ben Shachar and the Lahiton archive

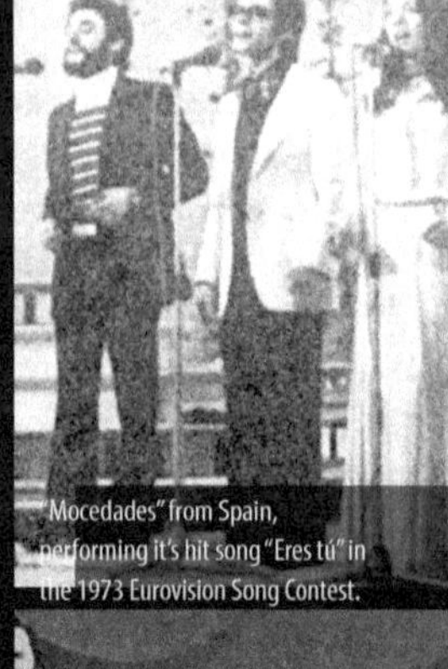

"Mocedades" from Spain, performing it's hit song "Eres tú" in the 1973 Eurovision Song Contest.

The renowned Nicola Di Bari from Italy, on stage in Edinburgh 1972 >> Photo by: Uri Aloni, in courtesy of Ilan Ben Shachar and the "Lahiton" archive

Anne-Marie David (1973 winner), along with the composer Claude Morgan >> Photo by: Uri Aloni, in courtesy of Ilan Ben Shachar and the "Lahiton" archive

"Teach-In", entitling the Netherlands to its fourth victory of the contest, 1975.

Séverine (the 1971 winner), achieving Monaco's sole victory of the contest >> Photo by: Uri Aloni, in courtesy of Ilan Ben Shachar and the "Lahiton" archive

Vicky Leandros amazes everyone with "Après toi" and wins the Eurovision of 1972 >> Photo by: Uri Aloni, in courtesy of Ilan Ben Shachar and the "Lahiton" archive

"Brotherhood of Man", reaching the most overwhelming win in the history of Eurovision, in 1976 >> Photo by: Uri Aloni, in courtesy of Ilan Ben Shachar and the "Lahiton" archive

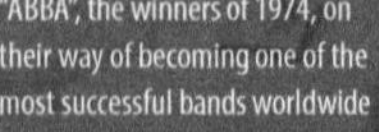

"ABBA", the winners of 1974, on their way of becoming one of the most successful bands worldwide

>> Photo by: Uri Aloni, in courtesy of Ilan Ben Shachar and the "Lahiton" archive

The Swiss Daniela Simmons, finishing second in 1986 >> Photo by: Eric Bachmann

Sandra Reemer as part of the duo "Sandra & Andres", reaching fourth place in 1972 >> Photo by: Uri Aloni, in courtesy of Ilan Ben Shachar and the "Lahiton" archive

>> Photo by: Uri Aloni, in courtesy of Ilan Ben Shachar and the "Lahiton" archive

Celine Dion celebrating her victory in Dublin, 1988. To her right, Nella Martinetti, who wrote the lyrics of the winning song with the composer and conductor Atilla Şereftuğ to her left >> Photo by: Bruno Torricelli

>> Photo by: Uri Aloni, in courtesy of Ilan Ben Shachar and the "Lahiton" archive

"The New Seekers" from the United Kingdom, missing the first place in 1972 >> Photo by: Uri Aloni, in courtesy of Ilan Ben Shachar and the "Lahiton" archive

Ofra Haza, making history on her journey to Munich with the song "Hay", in the cockpit >> Photo by: Uri Aloni, in courtesy of Ilan Ben Shachar and the "Lahiton" archive

1956-1959

THE EUROVISION SONG CONTEST TAKES ITS FIRST STEP

TThe Netherlands (2 wins) stood out in the second half of the 1950s, the first decade of the Eurovision Song Contest (the first took place in 1956). This decade had three solo female singers winning, whereas only one male singer. It was one of only two decades in which each year the event was held in different countries, therefore no country hosted it twice.

1956 – Lugano, Switzerland

"Teatro Kursaal" will go down in history as the first venue to ever host the Eurovision Song Contest. Who could have imagined it would still be important and watched by millions of viewers in this multi-channel era, deep into the next millennium..? Only seven countries gathered in Lugano, the ninth largest city in Switzerland, located right next to the Italian border of this wealthy little country. To ensure the show would run for more than half an hour, the organisers agreed that two entries will represent each country (Which is how it came to be that 14 songs were performed in the first ever Eurovision). Each competing country was recommended to conduct a preliminary song contest to select the entry that would represent them it in the event — thus making it even more festive. Denmark and Austria were also invited to take part in the inaugural Eurovision, but they missed the registration deadline and were therefore unable to participate. United Kingdom, the main country from which the musical phenomenon originated, was the most notable absentee (it simply did not enter the contest). This has taken place only once more, in 1958.

Each country diversified its entries with different singers and songs, ostensibly to take advantage of both opportunities. Only the host, Switzerland, had the same contestant singing twice, Lys Assia, who sang two Swiss songs — which turned out to be a trump card: Assia was the first ever singer to win the Eurovision Song Contest.

The theatre, a historic building that later became a casino, was designed specifically for the television broadcast by the Italian super-designer, Achille Sfondrini. But, while the cameras were definitely rolling, the most important thing was the radio broadcast that went out to hundred millions of listeners around the world who were curious to hear about this new wonder. It is important to keep in mind that the television set was a luxury back then and not a common commodity in every household.

Duo acts or bands were not allowed to participate in the first Eurovision, but only solo singer. The songs could be no longer than three minutes and thirty seconds (this was also shortened to only three minutes over the years), and they were accompanied by a large orchestra of 24 musicians, led by Fernando Paggi. Only four of the seven countries that participated came with their own conductors: Belgium, Luxembourg, Italy and France (with the renowned Franck Pourcel, who was France's almost-constant conductor, with its successful songs until 1972).

Lohengrin Filipello presented the contest in Italian and was in fact the only male presenter in the Eurovision's history, until Léon Zitrone joined in 1978. Oddly enough, both the victory of Switzerland and the presentation in Italian — formative events in the Eurovision's history — only happened rarely throughout the history of the contest. Italy's "Aprite le Finestre", performed by Franca Raimondi, came straight from the legendary Sanremo Festival and was the prominent candidate to win. Although this was not the case, the song became a huge hit in Italy. As mentioned, Lys Assia made history: "Refrain" will always be remembered as the first song to ever win the Eurovision Song Contest. Assia once told me that she had heard rumours about her first performance of another song that evening, "Das alte Karussell", being voted last place that evening... If that is true, Assia should enter the Guinness World Records as the only singer to win both first and last place in the same contest...

In terms of language, French was the dominant with seven songs being performed in it on stage (including the winning entry), much more than German (three performances). This dominance would accompany the event up until the end of the 20th century.

Due to unexpected delays in delivering the results, the artistic dance troupe which entertained the audience and viewers — while awaiting the juries' decision regarding the winner — was promptly asked to extend its performance.

This issue would also be subjected to many further upheavals until the voting system for the jury was put in place.

Two jury representatives arrived from each of the participating countries as delegation members and were asked to award 2 points to their favourite song (Luxembourg was the only country that did not send juries for unclear reasons, and the Swiss representatives were allowed to vote on their own behalf, which caused quite a bit of wonder among the other participants). The European Broadcasting Union decided, for some reason, that the procedure and the internal results should be a secret, therefore no one knew the place of any of the songs apart from the winner. This was to be the first and last time this voting system was used.

So, who finished second and last? Nobody really knows, although Simon Barclay published a full scoreboard of the 1956 Eurovision's results in his book "The Complete and Independent Guide to the Eurovision Song Contest 2010" – a table that has no reference or approval whatsoever. Walter Andreas Schwarz from Germany took second place, according to the author Jostein Pedersen, but this was never officially confirmed either. So, paradoxically, those who took second place along with another 12 songs — finished last too...

On two occasions in the history of the ESC there was no record of the contest. It happened for the first time, by coincidence, at the first event in 1956. The only recording to survive is of Lys Assia's repeat performance after winning. None of the rest survived in no broadcasting authority, not even in the local Swiss one.

In 1964, after a fire destroyed the archives of the Danish Broadcasting Union which hosted the Eurovision that year, the EBU decided that each host country would be obliged to provide three original video copies to its representatives at the end of the contest, which have since been kept at the EBU archives in Geneva.

1957 – Frankfurt, Germany

The second Eurovision Song Contest was crucial for the EBU, which made an immense effort to continue the new tradition and demonstrate to the Soviet Iron Curtain and its partners the unity of Western Europe. Switzerland refused to host the event for the second time in a row and so the lot fell on Germany, which saw hosting the contest as an opportunity to regain some of the prestige it had lost after the two world wars.

As the number of competing countries increased to 10, the one-time format in which each country was represented by two songs was abandoned from 1956 onwards. The graceful presentation of the contest's presenter, Anaid Iplicjian, who was one of the most respected stage actors in Germany and Austria, was fearfully made.

The event, which took place in Frankfurt 's state-of-the-art and luxurious (at the time) television studio, was held indefinitely, with no limit to the length of the songs.

The Italian entry performed by Nunzio Gallo, was considered a potential winner. "Corde della Mia Chitarra" came from the Sanremo Festival, but for some reason the Italian conductor, Armando Trovajoli, in an incomprehensible act of casuistry, extended the length of the song to five minutes (!), ruining its magic and leaving the incredible vocalist with no chance of success.

Lys Assia, the Swiss singer, would not settle for winning the previous year and went for another win, but she only finished eighth this time, despite being marked by many as a winning candidate with the entry, "L'enfant que j'étais". This is seen as the hatred of favourites by the juries and not for the last time in the contest, when they have almost always been vindictive towards those who have been candidates to win.

Denmark made double history: It was the only country to take advantage of the new rules that allowed more than one singer to perform on stage, and so the duo, Birthe Wilke and Gustav Winckler, were sent in.

At the end of their song, which, as expected, finished exceedingly high (third place), the couple kissed (in what was considered an extremely sensational act at the time). The kiss was so long that the director of the event nervously signalled the Danes to put an end to it....

In fact, few people were able to enjoy the sight of that formative moment, as the 1957 Eurovision was also a contest primarily aimed at radio listeners and less at television viewers, who were very few (both in 1957 and until the early 1960s).

Corry Brokken hit the jackpot and stole the spotlight by a mile with "Net Als Toen". Her fine vocal performance led to a sweeping victory for the Dutch, receiving points from all countries, something quite unusual in those days of Eurovision. Like Lys Assia, Brokken participated in the contest again (both were the only ones to represent their countries in a second consecutive Eurovision), but this time the Dutch competitor had the upper hand.

The German song was written by Ralph Maria Siegel, father of Ralph Siegel, the man who wrote more songs for the Eurovision than anyone else (Apparently, he grew up with the love and passion for the European contest). In any case, Siegel Sr. was one of the most respected composers and musicians in Germany, so the apple did not fall far from the tree.

After realizing that there is no point in concealing the juries' decisions, it was determined that 10 points would be openly awarded by each country (to be divided amongst all the selected songs). The juries' results would then be delivered to a special spokesperson, announcing them to the presenter and the entire audience, for the first time ever, via telephone. At the voting opening, in what would seem totally pathetic today, the presenter Iplicjian waited for the phone to ring, as it did with the first score from Bern, Switzerland. A particularly memorable moment was when the presenter asked the Danish spokesperson: "Ha, do you speak English?". He apparently did ...

1958 – Hilversum, The Netherlands

Corry Brokken's victory brought the third Eurovision to the Netherlands, which chose to host it in the northern city of Hilversum, the ultimate broadcasting centre of the Netherlands since the 1920s. The contest was held on a Wednesday at AVRO Studios, one of the most advanced television studios in Europe at the time. All of that made this Eurovision a television breakthrough, but it was quite characterless in many other respects.

For the first time, Sweden competed and thus set a grand and long-standing tradition in motion. Due to a labour dispute between the BBC, which was supposed to select the song that would represent the country that year, and various artistic unions, the United Kingdom was absent from the contest. Hence, oddly enough, in three years, the UK has missed a second Eurovision. These two events (1956 and 1958) were also the only ones in which there was not a single song in the English language.

To the left of the stage, the excellent orchestra, directed by Dolf van der Linden, was set up and provided musical transitions.

It was the first time the event had been opened, not by the presenter, Hannie Lips, but instead by an immediate transition to the first song.

As a whole, it seemed as though the presenter, Lips, considered her job a bother; she read from prompts and clumsily recited texts.

Domenico Modugno of Italy was considered favourite. "Nel blu dipinto di blu (Volare)" was major hit from the Sanremo Festival that preceded the Eurovision, and everyone was sure it would bring the Italians a sweeping victory. Modugno opened the contest, but it turned out at the end that a technical glitch had prevented it from being heard by certain countries. Therefore, in an unexpected turn of events, he had to perform his song yet again. It was poetic justice that the best and most successful song in the contest, was heard again, instead of the winning entry. "Volare" only finished third, but it has since become one of the world's best — known Italian songs.

Lys Assia insisted on returning to the ESC in another attempt to recapture her 1956 win. Unlike her 1957 failure, the Swiss singer was remarkably close to doing so with "Giorgio". It is difficult to grasp what the Jury saw in this lifeless and unrefined song, but there is no arguing with the results.

Assia ended up with three points less than the winner and finished her third Eurovision with honour.

The Netherlands was again represented by Corry Brokken, the previous year's winner (also for the third time in a row), however she came in last, earning her a rather questionable record as the only Eurovision singer to reach first and last place. Assia and Brokken made this contest unique because all the winners up until then performed in it.

No one was surprised by André Claveau's victory. The French was marked as a potential winner with "Dors, mon amour" and was awarded particularly high scores from Denmark, Italy and Austria — but with no points from the host (the Netherlands). This was France's first win, one of the strongest and highest quality competitors in the history of the Eurovision Song Contest.

The vote was tense and captivating: the presenter, Lips, addressed the participating countries in reverse order of appearance and from the outset, France's lead was evident, with Italy trailing it. Switzerland burst forward with a high number of points in the second half of the vote, settling in second place, with a point less than the French. The Italians, who voted last, tipped the scales by awarding 6 points to the French and only 4 to the Swiss.

1959 – Cannes, France

In the late 1950s, Eurovision was still considered an entertainment event rather than a national one. That is one of the reasons that led France to choose the resort town of Cannes to host the contest, rather than its capital, Paris.

The locals hosted the fourth ESC at the tourist-packed city's congress hall on the French Riviera, where a traditional International Film Festival also took place.

A slight change in the panel of juries of each country was reflected in a prohibition on the participation of composers and publishers in the voting.

For the first and only time in the history of Eurovision, the three songs that finished first were performed again at the end of the contest, which is probably attributed to the French tradition and did not reoccur.

Luxembourg was absent from for no particular reason, while Monaco made a debut that it would like to forget.

The United Kingdom returned after a year of absence and was referred to as "Great Britain" and not "United Kingdom", which it would be called from the following year to this day. Pearl Carr and Teddy Johnson finished second. The UK would be the runner-up for another fourteen times (more than any other country), making it the ultimate loser in the history of the contest.

Teddy Scholten scooped the Netherlands' second victory in the last three contests with the song "Een beetje".

Until its next victory, the Netherlands would have to wait a decade — and it will not be an exclusive victory either.

The favourite to win was, again, Domenico Modugno. Italy continued to bet on the Sanremo Festival winner, returning this time with another classic, "Ciao, ciao bambina" — which, like "Volare", was a major hit in Europe and around the world. However, Domenico Modugno and Eurovision were not a winning combination, to say the least. This time, too, the Italian failed and finished eighth, which he found insulting, although it was not the most humiliating position he would achieve at Eurovision, to which he returned next decade.

1956

Hosting Country: Switzerland

Hosting City: Lugano

Date: 24.5.1956

Location: Teatro Kursaal

Presenter: Lohengrin Filipello

Orchestra Conductor: Fernando Paggi

Chief Executive: Rolf Liebermann

Participating Countries: 7 (every country represented by 2 entries)

Voting: 2 Jury-members of each participating country attribute 2 votes for their favourite song.

Broadcaster: Radiotelevisione svizzera di lingua italiana (RTSI)

Director: Franco Marazzi

Interval act: Les Joyeux Rossignols & Les Trois Ménestrels

Duration: 1 hour and 40 minutes

Broadcast: To all participating countries and to United Kingdom (Wilfred Thomas), Denmark (Gunnar Hansen) and Austria (Wolf Mittler).

No.	Country	Song	Performing Artist	Lyrics	Composer	Conductor	Language	Commentator	Points	Place
01	The Netherlands	"De vogels van Holland"	Jetty Paerl	Annie M. G. Schmidt	Cor Lemaire	Fernando Paggi	Dutch	Piet te Nuyl	-	2
02	Switzerland	"Das alte Karussell"	Lys Assia	Georg Benz Stahl	Georg Benz Stahl	Fernando Paggi	German	Georges Hardy	-	2
03	Belgium	"Messieurs les noyés de la Seine"	Fud Leclerc	Robert Montal	Jean Miret, Jacques Say	Léo Souris	French	Janine Lambotte, Nand Baert	-	2
04	Germany	"Im Wartesaal zum großen Glück"	Walter Andreas Schwarz	Walter Andreas Schwarz	Walter Andreas Schwarz	Fernando Paggi	German	Wolf Mittler	-	2
05	France	"Le temps perdu"	Mathé Altéry	Rachèle Thoreau	André Lodge	Franck Pourcel	French	Michèle Rebel	-	2
06	Luxembourg	"Ne crois pas"	Michèle Arnaud	Christian Guitreau	Christian Guitreau	Jacques Lassry	French	Michèle Rebel	-	2
07	Italy	"Aprite le finestre"	Franca Raimondi	Pino Perotti	Virgilio Panzuti	Gian Stellari	Italian	Franco Marazzi	-	2
08	The Netherlands	"Voorgoed voorbij"	Corry Brokken	Jelle de Vries	Jelle de Vries	Fernando Paggi	Dutch	Piet te Nuyl	-	2
09	Switzerland	"Refrain"	Lys Assia	Émile Gardaz	Géo Voumard	Fernando Paggi	French	Georges Hardy	-	1
10	Belgium	"Le plus beau jour de ma vie"	Mony Marc	David Bee	Claude Alix	Léo Souris	French	Janine Lambotte, Nand Baert	-	2
11	Germany	"So geht das jede Nacht"	Freddy Quinn	Peter Mösser	Lotar Olias	Fernando Paggi	German	Wolf Mittler	-	2
12	France	"Il est là"	Dany Dauberson	Simone Vallauris	Simone Vallauris	Franck Pourcel	French	Michèle Rebel	-	2
13	Luxembourg	"Les amants de minuit"	Michèle Arnaud	Jacques Lassry	Simone Laurencin	Jacques Lassry	French	Michèle Rebel	-	2
14	Italy	"Amami se vuoi"	Tonina Torrielli	Mario Panzeri	Vittorio Mascheroni	Gian Stellari	Italian	Franco Marazzi	-	2

Hosting Country: Germany

Hosting City: Frankfurt

Date: 3.3.1957

Location: Großer Sendesaal des hessischen Rundfunks

Presenter: Anaïd Iplicjian

Orchestra Conductor: Willy Berking

Chief Executive: Rolf Liebermann

Participating Countries: 10

Voting: Every country has a Jury that awards its 10 points to one or more entries

Broadcaster: Arbeitsgemeinschaft der öffentlich-rechtlichen Rundfunkanstalten der Bundesrepublik Deutschland (ARD)

Interval act: -

Duration: 1 hour and 8 minutes

Broadcast: To all participating countries

No.	Country	Song	Performing Artist	Lyrics	Composer	Conductor	Language	Commentator	Spokesperson	Points	Place
01	Belgium	"Straatdeuntje"	Bobbejaan Schoepen	Eric Franssen	Harry Frekin	Willy Berking	Flemish	Nic Bal, Janine Lambotte	Bert Leysen	8	5
02	Luxembourg	"Amours mortes (tant de peine)"	Danièle Dupré	Jacques Taber	Jean-Pierre Kemmer	Willy Berking	French	Robert Beauvais	Pierre Bellemare	4	9
03	United Kingdom	"All"	Patricia Bredin	Alan Stranks	Reynell Wreford	Eric Robinson	English	Berkeley Smith, Tom Sloan	David Jacobs	6	7
04	Italy	"Corde della mia chitarra"	Nunzio Gallo	Giuseppe Fiorelli	Mario Ruccione	Armando Trovajoli	Italian	Bianca Maria Piccinino	Nunzio Filogamo	7	6
05	Austria	"Wohin, kleines Pony?"	Bob Martin	Kurt Svab, Hans Werner	Kurt Svab	Carl de Groof	German	-	Rudolf Fochler	3	10
06	The Netherlands	"Net als toen"	Corry Brokken	Willy van Hemert	Guus Jansen	Dolf van der Linden	Dutch	Piet te Nuyl	Siebe van der Zee	31	1
07	Germany	"Telefon, Telefon"	Margot Hielscher	Ralph Maria Siegel	Friedrich Meyer	Willy Berking	German	Wolf Mittler	Joachim Fuchsberger	8	4
08	France	"La belle amour"	Paule Desjardins	Francis Carco	Guy Lafarge	Paul Durand	French	Robert Beauvais	Claude Darget	17	2
09	Denmark	"Skibet skal sejle i nat"	Birthe Wilke & Gustav Winckler	Poul Sørensen	Erik Fiehn	Kai Mortensen	Danish	Gunnar Hansen	Svend Pedersen	10	3
10	Switzerland	"L'enfant que j'étais"	Lys Assia	Émile Gardaz	Géo Voumard	Willy Berking	French	Robert Beauvais	Mäni Weber	5	8

	Switzerland	Denmark	France	Germany	The Netherlands	Austria	Italy	United Kingdom	Luxembourg	Belgium	
Switzerland	■	2	–	1	–	–	1	–	1	–	Switzerland
Denmark	–	■	–	–	5	–	3	2	–	–	Denmark
France	–	2	■	6	1	–	–	2	4	2	France
Germany	–	–	6	■	–	–	1	–	–	1	Germany
The Netherlands	7	3	4	1	■	6	1	1	3	5	The Netherlands
Austria	–	–	–	–	1	■	–	2	–	–	Austria
Italy	–	1	–	–	2	–	■	2	1	1	Italy
United Kingdom	2	–	–	–	1	1	–	■	1	1	United Kingdom
Luxembourg	–	–	–	–	–	3	4	1	■	–	Luxembourg
Belgium	1	2	–	2	–	–	–	–	–	■	Belgium

1958

Hosting Country: The Netherlands
Hosting City: Hilversum
Date: 12.3.1958
Location: AVRO Studios
Presenter: Hannie Lips
Orchestra Conductor: Dolf van der Linden
Chief Executive: -
Participating Countries: 10
Voting: Every country has a jury that awards its 10 points to one or more entries
Broadcaster: Nederlandse Televisie Stichting (NTS)
Interval act: Metropole Orkest
Duration: 1 hour and 15 minutes
Broadcast: To all participating countries and to United Kingdom

No.	Country	Song	Performing Artist	Lyrics	Composer	Conductor	Language	Commentator	Spokesperson	Points	Place
01	Italy	"Nel blu dipinto di blu"	Domenico Modugno	Domenico Modugno, Franco Migliacci	Domenico Modugno	Alberto Semprini	Italian	Bianca Maria Piccinino	Fulvia Colombo	13	3
02	The Netherlands	"Heel de wereld"	Corry Brokken	Benny Vreden	Benny Vreden	Dolf van der Linden	Dutch	Siebe van der Zee	Piet te Nuyl	1	9
03	France	"Dors, mon amour"	André Claveau	Pierre Delanoë	Hubert Giraud	Franck Pourcel	French	Pierre Tchernia	Armand Lanoux	27	1
04	Luxembourg	"Un grand amour"	Solange Berry	Monique Laniece, Raymond Roche	Michel Eric	Dolf van der Linden	French	Pierre Tchernia	Pierre Bellemare	1	9
05	Sweden	"Lilla stjärna"	Alice Babs	Gunnar Wersén	Åke Gerhard	Dolf van der Linden	Swedish	Jan Gabrielsson	Roland Eiworth	10	4
06	Denmark	"Jeg rev et blad ud af min dagbog"	Raquel Rastenni	Sven Ulrik, Harry Jensen	Sven Ulrik, Harry Jensen	Kai Mortensen	Danish	Gunnar Hansen	Svend Pedersen	3	8
07	Belgium	"Ma petite chatte"	Fud Leclerc	André Dohet	André Dohet	Dolf van der Linden	French	Arlette Vincent, Nic Bal	Paule Herreman	8	5
08	Germany	"Für zwei Groschen Musik"	Margot Hielscher	Fred Rauch, Walter Brandin	Friedrich Meyer	Dolf van der Linden	German	Wolf Mittler	Claudia Doren	5	7
09	Austria	"Die ganze Welt braucht Liebe"	Liane Augustin	Günther Leopold, Kurt Werner	Günther Leopold, Kurt Werner	Willy Fantl	German	Wolf Mittler	Unknown	8	5
10	Switzerland	"Giorgio"	Lys Assia	Fridolin Tschudi	Paul Burkhard	Paul Burkhard	Italian /German	Theodor Haller, Pierre Tchernia	Mäni Weber	24	2

	Switzerland	Austria	Germany	Belgium	Denmark	Sweden	Luxembourg	France	The Netherlands	Italy	
Switzerland	■	–	–	2	–	4	5	3	6	4	Switzerland
Austria	2	■	–	1	–	1	1	3	–	–	Austria
Germany	–	1	■	1	–	1	–	2	–	–	Germany
Belgium	1	–	5	■	1	1	–	–	–	–	Belgium
Denmark	–	–	–	–	■	1	–	1	1	–	Denmark
Sweden	3	1	–	1	–	■	3	–	2	–	Sweden
Luxembourg	1	–	–	–	–	–	■	–	–	–	Luxembourg
France	1	7	1	1	9	1	1	■	–	6	France
The Netherlands	1	–	–	–	–	–	–	–	■	–	The Netherlands
Italy	1	1	4	4	–	1	–	1	1	■	Italy

1959

Hosting Country: France
Hosting City: Cannes
Date: 11.3.1959
Location: Palais des Festivals et des Congrès
Presenter: Jacqueline Joubert
Orchestra Conductor: Franck Pourcel
Chief Executive: -.
Participating Countries: 11
Voting: Every country has a jury that awards its 10 points to one or more entries
Broadcaster: Radiodiffusion-Télévision Française (RTF)
Director: Marcel Cravenne
Interval act: -
Duration: 1 hour and 13 minutes
Broadcast: To all participating countries and to Luxembourg

No.	Country	Song	Performing Artist	Lyrics	Composer	Conductor	Language	Commentator	Spokesperson	Points	Place
01	France	"Oui, oui, oui, oui"	Jean Philippe	Pierre Cour	Hubert Giraud	Franck Pourcel	French	Claude Darget	Marianne Lecène	15	3
02	Denmark	"Uh, jeg ville ønske jeg var dig"	Birthe Wilke	Carl Andersen	Otto Lington	Kai Mortensen	Danish	Sejr Volmer-Sørensen	Svend Pedersen	12	5
03	Italy	"Piove (Ciao, ciao bambina)"	Domenico Modugno	Dino Verde	Domenico Modugno	William Galassini	Italian	Renato Tagliani	Enzo Tortora	9	6
04	Monaco	"Mon ami Pierrot"	Jacques Pills	Raymond Bravard	Florence Veran	Franck Pourcel	French	Unknown	Claude Darget	1	11
05	The Netherlands	"Een beetje"	Teddy Scholten	Willy van Hemert	Dick Schallies	Dolf van der Linden	Dutch	Piet te Nuyl	Siebe van der Zee	21	1
06	Germany	"Heute Abend wollen wir tanzen geh'n"	Alice & Ellen Kessler	Astrid Voltmann	Helmut Zander	Franck Pourcel	German	Elena Gerhard	Hans-Joachim Raus-chenbach	5	8
07	Sweden	"Augustin"	Brita Borg	Åke Gerhard	Harry Sandin	Franck Pourcel	Swedish	Jan Gabrielsson	Roland Eiworth	4	9
08	Switzerland	"Irgendwoher"	Christa Williams	Lothar Löffler	Lothar Löffler	Franck Pourcel	German	Theodor Haller	Boris Acquadro	14	4
09	Austria	"Der K und K Kalypso aus Wien"	Ferry Graf	Günther Leopold	Norbert Pawlicki	Franck Pourcel	German	Elena Gerhard	Karl Bruck	4	9
10	United Kingdom	"Sing, Little Birdie"	Pearl Carr & Teddy Johnson	Syd Cordell	Stan Butcher	Eric Robinson	English	Tom Sloan, Pete Murray	Pete Murray	16	2
11	Belgium	"Hou toch van mij"	Bob Benny	Ke Riema	Hans Flower	Francis Bay	Flemish	Nic Bal, Paule Herreman	Bert Leysen	9	6

	Belgium	United Kingdom	Austria	Switzerland	Sweden	Germany	The Netherlands	Monaco	Italy	Denmark	France	
Belgium	■	2	–	–	–	3	1	1	–	2	–	Belgium
United Kingdom	2	■	2	3	–	–	5	2	–	1	1	United Kingdom
Austria	–	–	■	1	2	–	–	1	–	–	–	Austria
Switzerland	1	5	1	■	3	1	–	1	–	2	–	Switzerland
Sweden	–	–	–	–	■	–	3	–	–	1	–	Sweden
Germany	1	–	–	1	–	■	–	–	1	–	2	Germany
The Netherlands	3	1	3	–	–	2	■	1	7	–	4	The Netherlands
Monaco	–	–	1	–	–	–	–	■	–	–	–	Monaco
Italy	1	–	–	3	1	–	–	1	■	–	3	Italy
Denmark	–	2	2	1	4	–	1	1	1	■	–	Denmark
France	2	–	1	1	–	4	–	2	1	4	■	France

1960-1969

TOTAL FRENCH HEGEMONY

France was the Eurovision queen of the sixties (3 wins, or, if you will — 2 and a quarter wins).
The UK, Spain and Luxembourg (with 2 wins each) followed France's lead, all of which reached an enormous success in the European contest further on.

During this decade, no less than ten female soloists won, while only two male singers, and only one duo from Denmark, managed to reach first place. The event was held three times in London, UK, during this decade.

1960 – London, United Kingdom

The 1960 Eurovision grew to 13 participants. The Netherlands, last year's winner gave up hosting and the UK jumped at the opportunity. The Royal Festival Hall situated on the South Bank of the River Thames in London was a most worthy setting for the first Eurovision Song Contest held on the British Isles.

Katie Boyle inaugurated a long tradition as presenter of many contests and in her typical way, she did so with great grace and absolute professionalism. At the opening of the show, the performers were introduced by name and went on stage to bow to the audience — a tribute that was repeated in 1961 and 23 years later at the Eurovision in Munich. In the British tradition, for a second successive year, Bryan Johnson finished as the runner-up. The Swedish Siw Malmkvist settled for 10th place. Nine years later, she would return to Eurovision (representing Germany with "Primaballerina"). For the third time (after 1956 and 1958), the Belgian Fud Leclerc represented his country, and once again, he stayed far from the top.

Luxembourg, a future Eurovision empire, tried using the local German language, only to find out the hard way it was no golden goose and finished last. Norway, represented by Nora Brockstedt (A Norwegian musical legend), made its Eurovision debut with an excellent score (fourth place), which did not hint at the trials and tribulations that its performers would endure until eventually finishing first in 1985.

The most impressive performance was by Monaco's François Deguelt, undoubtedly the best of that evening, granting the principality its highest place thus far — third. The Netherlands, which gave up hosting, arrived with a strong impetus from the country's popular singer Rudi Carrell with "Wat een geluk", who was seen as a favourite to win the contest. The jury thought otherwise, and Carrel finished last but one, even though the Dutch song had been played in Europe for months on end.

Germany, with the hit "Bonne nuit ma chérie" and Wyn Hoop's fantastic performance, came in with high hopes only to finish fourth, alongside Norway.

The favourite to win the event was — yet again — Italy. The song "Romantica" was a tremendous success and sounded like a Eurovision winner. For some reason, Tony Dallara, its original signer, (perhaps affected by Domenico Modugno's failures) refused to participate and was replaced by singer-actor Renato Rascel. In addition, with a particularly poor orchestration that completely deviated from the original, one could reach the peculiar conclusion that the Italians did not really want to win... They ended up in the eighth place.

The circumstances paved the way for the second favourite, France. André Popp, the successful composer, teamed up with the star Jacqueline Boyer, and her winning performance resulted in a second French Eurovision victory. "Tom Pillibi" was a huge hit and is still considered an eternal Eurovision song. Boyer defended her title as the youngest woman to win the Eurovision until 1964.

The voting method was repeated, with points awarded in the opposite order of the songs' performances. United Kingdom took the lead almost from the start with a promising advantage over France, which steadily closed the gap until the last vote, when the locals had already been beaten by two points.

1961 – Cannes, France

Eurovision kept growing and reached a record of 16 participating countries. Spain, Yugoslavia and Finland made their debut, while no country withdrew from or returned to the contest, unlike the preceding year. Once more, France hosted Eurovision at the "Palais des Festivals et des Congrès" in Cannes, where the ping-pong of victories between the host and the Netherlands was interrupted by Luxembourg's first win in the contest. That grand prix started off a great tradition that would end 32 years later. Another history was made, with the event taking place for the first time on a Saturday night, which will be set as the perpetual date of the Eurovision Song Contest.

The presenter, just like two years before, was Jacqueline Joubert.

Lill Babs, the Swedish legend, built high hopes with "April, april", but despite the cheers and her highly confident performance, Babs finished last with only 2 points. The French Jean-Paul Mauric hit a series of off-key high notes at the end of his performance, which did not prevent him from being awarded 13 points and reaching the relatively high fourth place.

Norway marvelled at its great achievement of the previous year (fourth place) and again sent Nora Brockstedt, who finished seventh this time, which was fairly respectable, certainly regarding Norway's rankings in the years to come...

A year after reaching the humiliating last place, Luxembourg decided to use a winning formula and chose the notable chanteur Jean-Claude Pascal to represent the country, who delivered the performance of his life with "Nous, les amoureux", which gave the small principality, and rightfully so, its first win at the ESC.

Backed by their success in the local charts, "the Allisons" from the UK were quite confident and convinced that they would achieve the first place for an English language song (which would later become par for the course, especially in the 2000s), but this time again, the United Kingdom would only reach first place... after the winner. "Are You Sure" had a safe and exorbitant lead over Luxembourg until the halfway mark, when the exact opposite happened, and Jean-Claude Pascal found himself ranking at the bottom. Only then, the unbelievable happened and he was awarded all the points he needed.

For the umpteenth time, Italy was favourite for the win. The song "Al di là", originally performed by Emilio Pericoli, was considered a major success at the Sanremo Festival and around the world. Pericoli, who learned from his colleagues' failures on the European music stage, refused to perform and was replaced by the renowned Betty Curtis. Curtis was excellent, and she captivated the crowd, getting even the local audience to clap throughout the song and at the end her performance she received a big round of applause from the audience. Nevertheless, as the voting began, it was again apparent that the Italians could release gold-worthy songs, however they just could not find a similar success at Eurovision.

The scoreboard was equipped with a tracking arrow that each time pointed to the country that was awarded points. The 8 points given to Denmark by Norway certainly raised suspicions, although it had no significant impact at that time (two years later there would be a heavily disputed scandal).

The UK also received the highest score (8 points) from its competitor Luxembourg. The largest score ever to be awarded by this method is 9 points — which France received from Denmark in 1958 and Ireland from Belgium in 1970 (in both cases these points secured the grand prix for the receiving country).

The jury spokesperson for the UK was none other than 28-year-old Michael Aspel, a British television star, who went on to present countless television programmes as well as the UK's Eurovision pre-selection contest. Apropos the British people, time is of the utmost importance to them: The BBC cut off the broadcast from Cannes just before Jean-Claude Pascal was about to sing the winning song again, since the event was extended beyond the predetermined time frame.

1962 – Luxembourg City, Luxembourg

1962 Eurovision was characterised by fairly high-quality songs and it was evident that the contest was evolving and becoming a first-rate modern musical show. The host, Luxembourg, was proud to be the centre of Europe for one evening and its investment was evident in the exquisite programme.

"Villa Louvigny" in Luxembourg City was the unique building that hosted the event and it served as the Television Development Centre in Luxembourg before becoming the building affiliated with the renowned RTL.

All the countries from the preceding contest participated in Luxembourg.

Finland's Marion Rung entered with "Tipi-tii" and would return 12 years later with an utterly different song.

The new voting system that was introduced, led many countries to end up with the same number of points, so for the first time ever, not one point was attributed to the four countries that shared last place: Belgium, Spain, Austria and the Netherlands.

Belgium's Fud Leclerc very much wanted to mark his fourth participation in Eurovision (56, 58, 60, 62), but the nul points he received will be remembered as his greatest failure. Eleonore Schwarz, one of Austria's best-known opera singers, represented her country with an operetta-like performance, but it was made clear that the Opera does not belong to the Eurovision (21 years later, Turkish singer Çetin Alp would feel alike). Inger Berggren of Sweden finished seventh, but her performance of "Sol och vår" was unforgettable and the song became a considerable success in Europe. In the Swedish pre-selection contest, Berggren performed the song alongside Lily Berglund, but SVT (a year after the Lill-Babs — Siw Malmkvist scandal) decided to forgo Berglund and have Berggren sing alone — a decision that bear fruit this time around.

The hit par excellence of the 1962 Eurovision was, undoubtedly, the German entry "Zwei kleine Italiener", performed by Conny Froboess. Both the song and the performer became legends and people throughout Europe hummed and recited the story of the two Italians from Naples courting Tina and Maria... Eventually, Froboess was by far the true winner of this Eurovision, despite a rather moderate 6th place

The Dutch entry "Katinka", was a huge hit in Europe — but finished with no points. It is attributed by some to a technical glitch that darkened the screen during "De Spelbrekers"'s performance of the song.

Isabelle Aubret's victory caught no one by surprise: It was no secret that "Un premier amour" ("First love") was born to win Eurovision, especially since winning on an even year had become a habit for France, starting from 1958. Aubret delivered a touching and excellent performance made history and crowned France as the Eurovision queen, with three wins.

Yugoslavia's Lola Novaković finished fourth, which was her country's greatest achievement so far. Following the remarkable accomplishment (achieved again only 21 years later), Novaković was invited to a personal appreciation meeting with the president of Yugoslavia, Josip Broz Tito.

United Kingdom was the favourite to win. Ronnie Carroll's "Ring-A-Ding Girl" had already reached high on local hit parades across Europe and was played a lot both before and after the contest.

Once again, a song in the English language failed to win Eurovision, despite Carroll's confident performance and only reached fourth place.

Luxembourg's Camillo Felgen returned to Eurovision but had something to sell this time: "Petit bonhomme" was a ballad that became a massive hit played at every early 1960s French party, raising high hopes for a second consecutive win in the hearts of the locals. However, it was considered an almost impossible task in those years. Nonetheless, the third place it reached was a great achievement for the host.

The winning song from the Sanremo Festival, "Addio, addio", was the Italian entry, with the legendary composer Domenico Modugno and renowned performer Claudio Villa. Villa's impassioned performance raised hopes that, perhaps, Italy would do it this time — but 3 points and 9th place made it abundantly clear that what the general public loves in Europe does not necessarily fit the tastes of the Eurovision juries.

François Deguelt also returned to ESC, and it was a highly successful return as he represented Monaco and led it to second place with the ballad "Dis rien".

In order to liven up the intervals between songs and the voting results' announcement, the Luxembourgers invited French entertainer, Achille Zavatta (of Tunisian origin) to provide a funny and entertaining performance, following which he became immensely popular in the Francophone countries — although it did not prevent his unfortunate suicide in 1993.

To make the voting even more intense, EBU introduced a new voting system: each jury would select only three songs and attribute 3, 2 and 1 points to their three favourite songs. The scoreboard at the end raised many doubts concerning the effectiveness of this change. In any case, no one has been able to even get close to Aubret's crisp and clear victory, with 13 points between her and the runner up. France's third landslide victory made it an Eurovision Empire.

1963 – London, United Kingdom

Eurovision 1963 entered the history books as one of the finest and highest quality ever. How unfortunate it was that this particular event had rather poor conditions which failed to respect the occasion. France, the previous year's winner, announced that due to a severe fiscal crisis affecting its broadcasting service, it would not be able to host the contest. United Kingdom volunteered to host the event and held it at London's BBC Studios Centre. The centre, which was quite advanced in the 1960s and closed in 2013, was a unique multi-purpose studio designed for television shows and series, but it is doubtful whether it was suitable for a musical performance that would include an orchestra and live broadcast throughout Europe. The unprecedented and controversial decision made in collaboration between the British and the European Broadcasting Union members, was to pre-record performers and songs in advance — one of the greatest challenges of the contest: The live performances and singing. The British reasoning was the introduction of the innovative "boom" microphone, which had been used in suspense and drama series, but as mentioned, all these spectacular effects were irrelevant to this contest, and were indeed icing on the cake for the participants and the audience. For the second time, Katie Boyle, the eternal presenter, was the strong link of the British production. Eurovision 1963, characterised by famous performers, some of them music legends and others were noticeably big stars at the beginning or in the making. Even the number of unforgettable songs was the greatest so far. In fact, to this day, this specific event is considered a musical turning point in the Eurovision timeline. Annie Palmen was sent to save the Netherlands' honour, after receiving Nul Points in the previous Eurovision, but she herself fell into the pit, making her country the first and last participant to receive no points for two consecutive years. The name Carmela Corren might not sound familiar for music enthusiasts in the Holy Land, but the Israeli singer, discovered by Ed Sullivan, made a bold move when she represented Austria with her impressive vocal performance in English and German. Her respectable seventh place was a starting point for a decent career. Corren will always be remembered as the first Israeli singer to appear on the Eurovision stage, 10 years before Ilanit did so as an official representative of the State of Israel. Emilio Pericoli refused to appear in the 1961 Eurovision Song Contest, but two years later he relented and perhaps he knew why: "Uno per tutte", another classic Italian hit, finally fulfilled the Italian's expectations, threatening the first place for the first time right up to the last moment of the jury's announcement. Finally, it took third place, making the Italians incredibly pleased and hinting at the future to come. Few, if any, believed that Grethe and Jørgen Ingmann from Denmark would make their way amongst that year's big stars and amaze the audience with a win that seemed to come out of nowhere. "Dansevise" was not the best entry that evening, but the juries must have found it quite catchy, and, of course, the Danish victory was accompanied by a huge scandal that is still to be discussed. It is absurd that on the night of the first Nordic victory, the other Scandinavian representatives finished last with Nul Points, alongside the Netherlands. Norway experienced, for the first time, what would be its fate several more times: the bottom of the barrel, without any points. Sweden and Finland were also unsuccessful and would do their homework in the years to come. Unprecedentedly, Yugoslavia sent a Croatian representative to Eurovision and not just anyone, but the country's most popular star of the day, Vice Vukov. "Brodovi" only reached 11th place, yet Vukov's performance will be remembered in his country for many years. From the moment Esther Ofarim became known in Israel it was clear that she would prosper. When she left the country, no one expected it to happen this quickly, and that she would be part of the most important music contest in Europe, perhaps even in the globe. Ofarim, a great singer, reached her top status when she represented Switzerland with "T'en va pas" which was marked, from the outset, as a top candidate for victory. Esther's captivating and compelling performance made her a leading dark horse that was supposed to win. Had it not been for what happened at the end, Ofarim would have been the first Israeli winner at the ESC. Alain Barrière is by far the biggest name that has ever represented France in the Eurovision. The entry, "Elle était si jolie", which was one of the most well-known and beloved chansons, seemed to be a safe bet for France's second victory. However, as mentioned, there was an unspoken tendency not to choose the same country twice as winner. There is no other explanation why one of the most renowned and beloved songs to be performed on the Eurovision stage, by one of France's most popular singers of all time, has only reached fifth place. Another incredibly big star from the 1960s, Françoise Hardy, represented Monaco with the song "L'amour s'en va" — another musical masterpiece that shared, with great honour, fifth place with Alain Barrière. Luxembourg — a magnet for major names — also brought the biggest star that had ever represented it, Greek singer Nana Mouskouri. Indeed, in 1963 Mouskouri was not yet the legend she became in later decades, but her excellent vocals and magical voice were nevertheless noticed in "À force de prier" — another unforgettable performance in an outstanding event. The British took a step forward from the previous year's Luxembourg initiative, presenting Ola & Barbro in a virtuoso show that will be mainly remembered for their cycling stunts. It remains unknown whether the performance between the entries and the score announcements was live or pre-recorded, which did not make a difference to the great interest it aroused. Following the relative failure of the voting system's modification, and in the light of the protests of the countries that were not awarded points in Luxembourg the previous year, the EBU decided to implement another change, a kind of upgrade to the new system: Each jury, consisting of 20 members, would select five of its favourite songs (instead of three) and award them one to five points.

This did not prevent four countries from finishing with Nul Points once again. Another change: The voting was done in the order of the performances in the event. After the first vote Esther Ofarim received the full five points and Carmela Corren followed closely with 4. Those who fantasised about an Israeli struggle to the end witnessed Corren slowly falling out of the race, leaving behind her a duel between Ofarim and the Danish representatives. So far everything was fine. Norway was the fifth to announce its results: Roald Øyen announced that Switzerland had been awarded three points and Denmark two. Then, presenter Katie Boyle interrupted him and asked him to repeat the results in the entries' appearance order. For some unexplained reason, Øyen asked her to return to him later. Thus, the Norwegian vote was pushed off to the end, while a remarkably close race developed between Switzerland and Denmark, with Italy lurking behind. A severe judgement error occurred when Monaco awarded one point twice — which is prohibited in the rules of the contest — to the UK and to Luxembourg. The playful announcer from the Principality of Monte Carlo had to repeat his vote at the end of the contest and decided the UK would keep the point. But that was a minor scandal compared to what happened at the end: Luxembourg, which was supposed to close the vote, left Switzerland with 39 points, Denmark with 38 points and Italy with 34 points. Then, Katie Boyle returned to the Norwegians, who had clearly announced earlier that Denmark had been awarded 2 points and Switzerland 3 points (which actually guaranteed a sweet victory for Switzerland and Esther Ofarim), and had only to repeat their results on procedural and unclear grounds. But this time, much to the amazement of the audience, the vote changed: Denmark was awarded 4 points and Switzerland only one. Hardly anyone noticed this, except for the astonished Ofarim and the Swiss team, of course. Second place was quite respectable for the Israeli singer, but due to the incident — Ofarim did not return to the Eurovision stage — despite receiving many enticing offers over the years. None of this changed the fact that Denmark won, bringing ample respect to their country. Grethe and Jørgen Ingmann entered the history books as the first to bring victory in the European song contest to Scandinavia. The next ones to do so, were the members of... "ABBA".

1964 – Copenhagen, Denmark

The ninth Eurovision was the most glorious and invested to date in terms of equipment and organization. Denmark took hosting the European contest very seriously and held it in the magnificent Tivoli Concert Hall, which was opened in 1843 in the capital, Copenhagen. The 22-year-old Lotte Wæver (a well-known actor in Denmark) was the presenter. Despite her early age, Wæver went through the evening smoothly and left a great impression with a professional and fluent presentation. The Danes presented an invested stage with staircases and gleaming backdrop. The scoreboard was also considered to be particularly innovative, with a black line stretching alongside each country displaying the number of points it received. Kai Mortensen and the Danish Orchestra received a great deal of praise for their precision and seriousness. Undoubtedly, Eurovision 1964 set standards that all the next hosting countries would later have to live up to. Sweden, the host's close neighbour, was absent from the contest due to an artists' boycott of Swedish television, which came in the wake of the refusal to ensure that the winner of the (pre-selection) Swedish song festival — would be the one to sing at Eurovision. Hugues Aufray who was known as the "French Bob Dylan", joined the glorious line of renowned artists who represented Luxembourg with the hit: "Dès que le printemps revient", in a unique Mexican style, which became a major hit in France and its neighbours. Arne Bendiksen, one of the greatest Norwegian musicians of the 20th century and responsible for discovering many music stars and setting up successful bands, appeared as a soloist for the only time at Eurovision and — thanks to the maximum score he received from host Denmark — he slid to eighth place. Some claim it was the Danish repaying their neighbour, for the score that actually granted them their victory at the Eurovision 1963... Udo Jürgens, the Austrian singer, won sixth place, and two years later he would significantly improve his ranking. The French were optimistic that Rachel would give them their permanent every even-year victory since 1958, but the wall was too high this time. "Mallory's Song" was written by the team that created "Tom Pillibi," but lightning did not strike twice, and France finished fourth. Matt Monro hoped to be the one to finally win first place at Eurovision for the UK. "I Love the Little Things" joined the never-ending list of UK songs that stopped at second place. Again, the voting system took casualties: Four countries finished with Nul Points for the third successive year, this time Germany, Portugal, Yugoslavia and Switzerland. Romuald, one of the world's most famous French singers, began his romance with Monaco at Eurovision, where he reached a respectable third place. It would be the best achievement for the principality within the frame of its three appearances in the contest.

Portugal's reception was rather insulting. For their Eurovision debut, the Portuguese chose António Calvário with an old-fashioned chanson-style song. "Oração" was certainly not the worst song of the big night, but it failed to garner any points from the juries. Switzerland brought a first-rate Italian song, performed by Anita Traversi, who returned to Eurovision after 4 years, but the old-fashioned style that was right for the 1950s did not stand the test of time and she finished with Nul Points. It is not because of the negative points that Switzerland will be remembered from the 1964 Eurovision

Song Contest, but because of an angry protestor who tried to break onto the stage after Traversi performed her song, waved a sign and cried out against Franco and Salazar (rulers of Spain and Portugal). After a few embarrassing seconds, the organisers got him under their control as the camera wandered toward the scoreboard. This time even the most sceptical were willing to put all their money on Italy. After years of bitter disappointments and victories in the betting tables on the eve of the contest that failed when in the end, one of the most musical countries in Europe has finally won a landslide victory. Gigliola Cinquetti, who was not even 17 years old, was the youngest winner in Eurovision history until Sandra Kim broke her record in 1986. "Non ho l'età" is without a doubt one of the greatest songs in the history of ESC, a legend that has become a reality. An overwhelming and unprecedented victory of 49 points, almost three times higher than the runner-up, nothing like that has ever been seen before and will never happen again. The local audience's cheers at the end of the song said it all, they also realised that such a song had never been heard there before. Following the previous year's scandal, the EBU decided to appoint an executive supervisor, Miroslav Vilček, who would be involved in the process of reading and receiving voting results from each country. In fact, Vilček became voting director, the person who can stop the process at any stage and even ask about different issues concerning points which were or were not awarded. Although the EBU guidelines explicitly stated that the Supervisor would not intervene and harm the voting flow, if there was no reason to do so, Vilček's successors took advantage of the microphone that had been put in their hands and it seemed that sometimes they were merely demanding more attention... Another change was made, again to the voting system: this time it was decided that a jury of 10 members from each county would divide the points between three selected songs to receive 5 points, 3 points and 1 point. If the team only chose two songs then those would receive 6 and 3 points respectively, while if all of them choose one song it will be awarded 9 points. In any case, all the juries, without exception, awarded points to three songs, so there was no irregular situation created. From the beginning, there was no doubt about the winner: Gigliola Cinquetti rose to a most impressive victory in the old-fashioned era of points before 1975 and became a global star. Until this day the song "Non ho l'età" is the most associated with her. Italy was the first country in the Eurovision history from the previous millennium to lead the scoreboard at all stages of the vote, from the opening until its victory. Only Luxembourg (1965 and 1972), Ireland (1970) and Sweden (1974) compared to it. Eurovision 1964 could have remained a perfect souvenir if it were not for a fire that broke out in the offices of the Danish Broadcasting Union in the early 1970s, consuming a great deal of valuable archival material, including the master tape of the only Eurovision hosted by Denmark in the 20th century. A hectic search for the missing tape lasted for years: It is claimed that German Television has a copy, but, although there is a record of it in the archives — it was never found. The BBC also claimed it has a copy of the tape but when push came to shove, all they found was an empty box labelled, "Eurovision 1964". In the 1990s, about $ 1 million was offered by Eurovision enthusiasts to anyone who had a copy of the tape, but so far it has not been found. It may or may not be related, but in 1971, the EBU decided that the production team of the contest would entrust the master tape to an EBU representative at the conclusion of the event, which would be taken for safekeeping to the offices in Switzerland.

1965 - Naples, Italy

The 10th Eurovision set a record: 18 countries participated. The contest took place in Naples, the southern capital of the boot-shaped country and without a doubt a type of capital for Italian music — as the best of its stars are Neapolitan. This is even though the winner who brought the Eurovision to Italy was from Verona (Gigliola Cinquetti) and the presenter from Milan — the cultural antithesis to Naples. The stage was arranged with a relief of the contest's icon at the back — a setting that would be copied both in 1968 and 1992 (on the actual stage floor). Renata Mauro, a well-known Italian television personality, presented the contest with aplomb and introduced a contemporary style: presenting each song, performer and conductor. Teddy Scholten, winner of 1958, returned — this time as a commentator, which did not inspire Conny van den Bos very much, as she finished in eleventh place. The UK was sure that it would finally win with "I Belong," but even Kathy Kirby's brilliant performance failed, as usual, to bring them beyond the respectable second place. Conchita Bautista, who had a reputation as a well-known film actor and flamenco singer, returned to the contest; however, her unique style again was not going to bring Spain the Grand Prix and she left with her tail between her legs and Nul Points. Bautista was not alone. Once again: 4 countries finished with no points. Unexpectedly, Germany was among them: Ulla Wiesner's song was a major hit in her country, and under the guise of a love song, it was a protest song about how difficult life was in post-war Germany — especially with many hours of work and exhausting restorations. "Paradies, wo bist du?", as mentioned, received a score from hell.... For the fourth time, Belgium and Finland did not receive a single point, nor were they enlightened by any of the juries. Ireland, future queen of the Contest, made a rather successful debut at sixth place. Udo Jürgens of Austria, who had held that spot the year before, returned for the second time in a row, gaining Austria the excellent fourth place this time. Kirsti Sparboe, the rising Norwegian music star, registered a difficult rite of passage in Eurovision with only one point. Just like Simone de Oliveira, one of Portugal's greatest singers. Sweden sent its opera star Ingvar Wixell, known as "The Great Baritone". The entry "Annorstädes vals" was written by none other than one of Sweden's greatest poets — Alf Henrikson. To this day, Wixell's performance is considered in Sweden one of the marvellous and perhaps even of the highest musical quality, despite only reaching a moderate tenth place. France, who was used to winning the contest every second year, had not been victorious for three years. Guy Mardel impressed the audience with "N'avoue jamais" — an enormous hit in the Francophone countries, which definitely aimed for the crown, eventually finishing third. The main candidate for victory was Italy. Most bets in dicated that the Italian heartthrob Bobby Solo would take first place and bring two consecutive wins to the same country for the first time. "Se piangi, se ridi" is one of Italy's most famous love ballads and has long been a classic. Bobby Solo ultimately did not win the contest and, surprisingly, only finished fifth, but his successful performance was the starting point of a glorious career that many still talk about. Many eyebrows were raised surrounding Luxembourg's song "Poupée de cire, poupée de son" ("Wax Doll, Rag Doll"). Serge Gainsbourg — a controversial French artist, offered the adventurous Luxembourg the entry, performed by the then only 17-year-old France Gall (almost like Gigliola Cinquetti who had won the previous year). The novelty and audacity did their own: Despite the French girl's nervous and off-key performance — Luxembourg recorded its second victory at the end of the evening and the Jewish artist, Gainsbourg, rose to fame as a musical artist. As in Copenhagen, France Gall's song crossed continents and enjoyed unprecedented professional and commercial success. Incidentally, Alain Gor aguer, who conducted countless French songs for the ESC and never won, finished first, however not with his own country this time, but with Luxembourg. He deserved this victory, which was in large part due to his wonderful arrangement and utilization of the excellent Italian orchestra. The interval act between the entries and voting results featured Mario Del Monaco. Long before Luciano Pavarotti, the tenor from Florence was considered to be the greatest Italian opera singer. One extraordinary moment was During the votes, when Belgium was the first to award (under the new voting system) 6 and 3 points. Other than that, apart from a few moments, there was not much doubt as to Luxembourg's victory, with the UK and France breathing down its neck. parenthetically, the "Intervision" contest started the same year, led by Eastern European countries — counter to the Eurovision. Ultimately, this event was unable to compete with the traditional European singing contest and ended in the 1980s, when the Eastern European countries gradually joined the great Eurovision, changing it indefinitely.

1966 – Luxembourg City, Luxembourg

After France Gall's victory, Luxembourg was honoured to host the contest for a second time, and this time the well-maintained Villa Louvigny was chosen as the event venue. 1966 Eurovision was the most watched up until that year, when Eastern European countries, and most notably the Soviet Union, broadcast the event for the first time, alongside Morocco — the first Arab state to broadcast the Eurovision (and would become the only one to participate in it). Despite having a massive audience of nearly a quarter billion people, the excellent presenter, Josiane Chen demonstrated composure and professionalism. The producers made sure that there would be a dynamic stage, which was the first of its kind until then, and special close-up shots, especially in the local song. That year, the rule that formally required each country to sing in its official language came into effect, some believe that Sweden was the reason for this as their entry from the previous year was performed in English. This rule would later undergo upheavals and alterations. The Danish song "Stop — mens legen er go" will be remembered for two reasons: The dancers on stage who distracted the attention from the singer, Ulla Pia, and the fact that it would be Denmark's last appearance at Eurovision, until its return in 1978. Belgium reached a dignified fourth place, thanks to singer Tonia, proving again that its French-language songs are more successful than the Flemish versions. Luxembourg built-up grand expectations for French singer Michèle Torr to bring them a second consecutive win, but in 1966 there would be no back-to-back Eurovision, and despite the memorable close-up, Torr only finished in tenth place. In a rare coincidence, Sweden and Norway won places 2 and 3, respectively. Although they did not really pose a risk to the winning song, this was the pair of Scandinavian countries' best achievement until they won the contest (1974, 1984 and 1985). Norway was represented by Åse Kleveland, perhaps the most important cultural figure in her country and the 1986 Eurovision presenter. Sweden was represented by Lill Lindfors (in a duo with Svante Thuresson), who presented the ESC the year before Kleveland in 1985... The cluster of attractions and precedents at the 1966 Eurovision included Finnish conductor Ossi Runne's debut performance. He both wrote and composed the entry "Playboy" which finished in tenth place alongside the hosting country. Runne would return and conduct the Finnish songs for the next 23 years. Even if he had not won at Eurovision, Udo Jürgens would have made history for performing three consecutive times as Austria's representative. He advanced steadily in 1964 and 1965, until coming of age in Luxembourg, fulfilling the adage "third time lucky".

The entry "Merci, Chérie" became a classic and Jürgens entered the pantheon of Austrian music, starting up a tremendous career in Germany. Jürgens was considered a favourite to win even prior to the contest, hence no one was surprised that he caught the juries' attention on his way to a rare Austrian victory. Unlike previous years, only two countries did not receive points this time, and those were particularly painful downfalls: Yugoslavian Tereza Kesovija represented Monaco with "Bien plus fort" and many believed she would finish higher but, in the end, astonishingly, she received no points. Thus, Alain Goraguer, this entry's conductor, became the only winner (as a conductor) in Eurovision's history to experience Nul Points a year after winning the contest. "Dio, come ti amo" performed by Gigliola Cinquetti became a hit after the Sanremo Festival and was chosen to represent Italy at ESC. It was predicted to be a certain victory for Cinquetti, but the song's writer — Domenico Modugno — insisted on going to perform the song himself in Luxembourg. Modugno, perhaps the most renowned and greatest Italian singer of all times, had a burning desire to win the contest and the fact that despite performing in it with his greatest hits in the late 1950s he had not won — was difficult for him to accept. It was a terrible mistake: Modugno's performance was dull and old-fashioned, the song's magic was lost, and Italy ended with the unbelievable score of "Nul". This was a major blow to Domenico Modugno, and ever since this astounding failure Italy has not sent Sanremo Festival winning songs to the Eurovision Song Contest (apart from a rare case in 1972), which is a loss for everyone. The interesting fact is that Gigliola Cinquetti's version has become a cultural asset in Italian music as well as a worldwide hit, with cover versions in several languages. The Dutch Milly Scott made double history: She was the first black singer to ever perform on Eurovision stage and the first to use a portable microphone. "Fernando en Filippo" was a Dutch version of "Speedy Gonzalez", but although it is still considered an extremely popular song in the Netherlands to this day, Scott finished the contest at the bottom of the scoreboard. Scottish performer Kenneth McKellar took the stage with a traditional kilt and embraced his origin and nationalism. But, beyond everything, in the opinion of many, UK's "A Man without love", has perhaps the most beautiful lyrics ever written for the Eurovision Song Contest. Peter Callander's words still resound to this day: "A man without love is only half a man. And half a man is nothing". In defiance of Eastern Bloc viewers, the Luxembourgers chose a show featuring traditional American songs...

Another landmark was around the new Executive Supervisor of the contest, British Clifford Brown, who began a tumultuous term which was to end in 1977. For the first time, the audience was highly active, perhaps too active, during the score announcement process: Sneers and chuckles were heard in the gallery after Norway awarded its full 5 points to Sweden. Finland got the same reaction after giving 3 points to Denmark and 5 to Sweden. The crowd, it turns out, did not like the Scandinavian guile and did not spare its harsh criticism about Spain and Portugal exchanging the maximum score... However, there was thunderous applause when Luxembourg was awarded 5 points by... Sweden. The thunder was stolen by witty Michael Aspel, spokesperson for the United Kingdom: The presenter, Josiane Chen, greeted him with "Good night, London" and Aspel, without thinking twice, responded "Good morning, Luxembourg"... The latter did not stop there, and when he finished his vote, he wished the presenter, Chen, in French "Have a good sleep"... Altogether, it was an easy victory for Udo Jürgens who was awarded almost twice as much as his Scandinavian competitors, despite not receiving any points from the two countries that voted first and the three countries that voted last. After receiving the award from France Gall, Jürgens finished off with a particularly original greeting in paraphrasing his song: "Merci, Jury" ...

1967 – Vienna, Austria

1967 Eurovision was held in April and introduced a contemporary style, primarily in video photography instead of film, which was quite cutting-edge at the time. This would be the last black and white Eurovision, before the transition to colour broadcasts. This year there was an unexpected decline in the number of worldwide viewers and no country except for those participating in the contest broadcast it. The Austrians put a lot of effort into the classic event, literally: The opening of the Eurovision was accompanied by a classic waltz arrangement of "Merci, Chérie" that had won the previous year, bringing the event to Vienna. The presenter, Erica Vaal, challenged herself by wishing the contestants "good evening" in all the competing countries' languages. "Hofburg" Palace, the contest's venue, has a fascinating history: It was the royal family's home during the Austro-Hungarian Empire and serves today as residence of the President of Austria. The stage set up was unique and unprecedented: Behind the performers, along with other luxurious and lavish decor, were two mirrored walls that revolved during each performance. There were two strong favourites to win this time: In the lead, Vicky Leandros, a Greek singer who represented Luxembourg and had dazzled Europe with "L'amour est bleu". It was a splendid classic, composed by André Popp, which was supposed to win the contest, and Leandros performance was superb, however due to the wonders of Eurovision's scoring, the exceptional entry finished only fourth — which did not prevent it from becoming a massive success everywhere else, and on every stage before and after the big evening in Vienna. The second favourite to win was Noëlle Cordier of France. "Il doit faire beau là-bas" is one of the finest songs the French have ever sent to Eurovision, but Cordier's excellent performance brought France, once again, only to the third place — which it won more than any other country. Portugal's Eduardo Nascimento's performance was controversial. Many have claimed that Portugal's ruler, Salazar, deliberately sent the dark-skinned singer as a fig leaf counter to the backdrop of allegations against him regarding discrimination and racism policies in the country. In any case and despite only being awarded 3 points, Nascimento delivered an outstanding performance. This time, only one singer "won" nul Points and the dubious honour went to Géraldine Gaulier of Switzerland. Finland sent one of the country's most popular musicians — Fredi (Matti Siitonen), who was known for His overwhelming dimensions. "Varjoon — suojaan" came to Vienna with high hopes, but despite Fredi's vocal and dramatic abilities, the Finns only reached twelfth place. Inge Brück aspired to infiltrate the upper ranks with "Anouschka", and the German delegation who felt at home was extremely disappointed that Hans Blum's entry only reached the eighth place. "Ik heb zorgen" ("I Have Worries") was the Belgian song's name, but the outstanding performer, Louis Neefs, seemed to have no real cause for concern at the end of the contest, bringing the Belgians their highest accomplishment with a Flemish language song (seventh place). There seems to have been no contests in which the UK has not been marked or considered a favourite to win. The many times it reached second or just missed first place, crowned the British songs regular losers. Therefore, none of the experts rushed to bet on Sandie Shaw as Eurovision winner. The Dagenham native's unique and exceptional barefoot performance was magical and probably left no room for doubt: With a phenomenal 47-point victory and a more than two-fold difference from second place, "Puppet on A String" knocked out the contest, bringing a historic victory to the country from which the musical phenomenon had grown and evolved. And, this was achieved despite a 4-second technical glitch, during which Sandie's microphone did not work (at the beginning of the song) — but that did not seem to have any effect on the United Kingdom's crushing win. For the second time in a row, Spanish singer Raphael represent ed his country, and this time, "Hablemos del amor" was a major hit both in his country and in the South American countries. The third favourite to win, also a Francophone, came from Monaco. After his Eurovision victory with France Gall in 1965, the talented and provocative Serge Gainsbourg wanted to reap another achievement with the bold and controversial song "Boum-Badaboum". Perhaps if this song had been performed by another singer (who was not Minouche Barelli), it might have won, but it finally took fifth place, which was not disastrous — but it was a disappointment for the principality in terms of its elevated expectations. The surprise of the contest came from Ireland's Sean Dunphy: The catchy and charming "If I Could Choose" managed to reach second place and granted Ireland its best achievement at Eurovision in the 1960s. Before the voting results were announced, the outstanding Vienna Boys' Choir delivered a first-rate performance of the "Blue Danube" waltz that is so closely associated with the host country. There was a notable change to the voting system that went back to the system where 10 points were distributed by 10 member juries in each country. For the first time, the announcement of results was in English and French which became the contest's official languages, and each country received its score in the order of its appearance in the event. There has never been a case where one country has divided its 10 points into 10 different countries. Portugal practically broke the record by awarding points to no less than nine (!) countries. Spain, as expected, received from its Iberian neighbours most of the points that remained in the Portuguese hands (2). The Italian voting spokesperson was one of the country's biggest media figures — Mike Bongiorno.

The Executive Supervisor, Clifford Brown, stole the thunder, as usual, when time after time he corrected delays in recording of the results on the scoreboard. Brown embarrassed the presenter, Vaal, until she finally lost her patience, saying: "I cannot see the board behind me"... But the really embarrassing part for Erica Vaal was when she forgot to turn to one last country that was due to vote — Ireland. Vaal already announced the British winner and Clifford Brown did not miss the opportunity to rebuke the presenter and, of course, ask her to call on the Irish: "I'm so sorry," apologised the flustered presenter, and as if to rub salt in her wounds, Gay Byrne, the Irish spokesperson, said: "I thought we were going to be left out". Other than these anecdotes, the voting was clear-cut: The UK's victory was evident from the outset, only Spain and Yugoslavia did not award any points to the UK. When the voting was over, four prominent bulbs on the scoreboard announced the four countries that had finished first: The United Kingdom, Ireland, France and Luxembourg. For the first time, two English songs won the first two places and two songs in French came after. In a way, it was a revolution. Sandie Shaw took the stage to perform the song again, as the winner, and she was interrupted by the swarm of photographers who stormed the stage. The curtain fell on the last black and white Eurovision, and the proud winner, the UK, would be the first to produce it in full colour.

1968 – London, United Kingdom

1968 Eurovision started off a new era: It was the first time the contest was broadcast in colour and this history will be forever credited to the British and the BBC. France, the Netherlands, Germany, Switzerland and Sweden also enjoyed the full colour broadcast. The rest watched it in black and white. A record number of 25 countries broadcast the contest, including the entire Eastern European bloc without exception, which resulted in a record number of hundred millions of viewers. The host country did everything it could to win and be the first to have a back-to-back, so it decided to go for a safe victory: Not only did it recruit Bill Martin and Phil Coulter — two of the most talented songwriters in the UK and in the music world in general (writers of the winning 1967 Eurovision entry) — but the great sensation, that initially sounded like an impossible fantasy, actually came true and Cliff Richard agreed to represent his country in the European contest, thus raising the bar and level of interest in Eurovision to new, previously unseen numbers. Bringing Cliff Richard to the ESC can be compared to Beyoncé, Rihanna or Mariah Carey agreeing to appear in the Eurovision today. Cliff, one of the biggest music stars in the world, who at his peak, competed neck and neck with Elvis Presley for virtually equal popularity, was not only a favourite to win — but he was also the winner even before the contest began. Some betting agencies took Cliff out of the game, and the other participating artists, walked on eggshells around him at rehearsals. To complete the show, the English chose the "Royal Albert Hall", a temple of music and concerts (established in 1871 and considered one of the most prestigious halls in the world) as the venue to host the contest. Once again, the host set a particularly high bar. The legendary presenter, Katie Boyle, did it again with her usual grace and unshakeable air of authority and blended well with the impressive, professional landscape of the efficiently run contest. The relatively small stage was decorated with the Eurovision icon on its back. Another innovation brought by progress: A photograph of the performer was displayed on the back of the stage before the beginning of each song. It was a fruitful and interesting contest for the other participants as well: The Czech "Golden Voice", Karel Gott, represented Austria with the entry "Tausend Fenster" composed by none other than the 1966 Eurovision winner, Udo Jürgens. Luxembourg went for and old-fashioned style with a sweet duet by Chris Baldo & Sophie Garel, as did Monaco, and they both finished in a solid place in the middle. Sweden aimed extremely high when it sent its heart throb, Claes-Göran Hederström, who belted out
"Det börjar verka kärlek, banne mig". His excellent, rollicking performance took him to the fifth place. Although Cliff Richard had been marked as the indubitable winner, Isabelle Aubret was there to try to give him a run for his money. The latter had brought the Grand Prix to France (1962) and infinitely hoped to complete a rare two victories. "La source", written by the talented Guy Bonnet (who would represent his country as a singer more than once at the contest), was very well received and actually contended for first place before falling to third place, which is most strongly associated with France. Italy, which had been burned many times at the Eurovision, was represented by the popular Sergio Endrigo, but instead of sending "Canzone per te", winner of the Sanremo

Festival and a song that could undoubtedly reach a high place, they settled for the mediocre and dull entry "Marianne", written by Endrigo himself. As Cliff Richard took the stage, the screams of the fans could be heard. "Congratulations" was named at first "I think I love you", but a dispute between the songwriters led to the change of name. Norrie Paramor, the British super-producer who was the conductor of the General Orchestra and of the British song, formed a high-quality professional team with a clear focus on one place only. Cliff's performance left no room for doubt: he would be the winner. The Norwegians sent Odd Børre and his exceptional style: "Stress" is to this day considered one of the oddest and most original Eurovision entries. Ireland continued its marvellous momentum and Pat McGuigan with a superb song, "Chance of A Lifetime", delivered an outstanding performance, receiving a great round of applause from the local audience. He came in fourth place, with a song that in any other contest and on every other evening might well have won. It is doubtful that anyone even noticed Massiel, the proud young Spanish singer who came to London without any particular pretensions with the entry "La, La, La". This song, originally sung by Joan Manuel Serrat of Barcelona, has been associated with numerous myths and even more conspiracies. The Catalan singer insisted on performing the song at the London Eurovision in the Catalan language, which sparked the wrath of Spain's ruler Franco, who ordered that Serrat be replaced by another singer. After failing to find one, it was decided to let the inexperienced Massiel perform. This caused disagreements, there are many versions, and nobody knows what really happened that brought Spain its most sensational win in the history of Eurovision. It is not disputed that Massiel delivered an excellent performance that was worthy of a position at the top of the contest, but a victory? Highly questionable. Germany, too, hoped to finally reach a prestigious achievement: Wenche Myhre enthralled the crowd with a huge hit, "Ein Hoch der Liebe" that came in seventh, but more importantly: was awarded the maximum score (5) by the host, the UK. Yugoslavia closed the contest with one of the most nostalgic songs in the history of the country that broke up in 1991: "Jedan dan", which is considered a song that unites the Yugoslavs and expresses joy and optimism far and wide. The "Troubadours" duo, dressed in typical Dubrovnik costume, accompanied by a violin and mandolin, are to this day thought of as sweet nostalgia for everyone who lived in the Yugoslavia of those days. Instead of folklore, the British preferred to take advantage of the colour broadcast to present a promotional video of the City of London. It was the outset of the showing of films and promotional presentations, which has grown over the years to this day. Befitting the glamorous Eurovision, even the scoreboard was grand, with the names of the countries engraved in gold letters on a reddish background. The voting was the most climactic since 1963, with Belgium, Luxembourg and Switzerland boosting Isabelle Aubret to a promising lead over Cliff Richard and Massiel. Apropos Luxembourg, for the first and only time, The Semi-Francophone State delivered its results in the English language. The country that put Richard back in the race and gave him a push was actually Monaco which did not award France, its protectorate, even a single point! The latter established the United Kingdom's status, keeping it in a safe lead. Michael Aspel, the UK jury spokesperson who excelled over the years with his witty humour, spoke

to the presenter, Boyle, in French, who was not flustered and called him "Michelle"...
Before the last two votes, Spain began narrowing the difference from the UK to just 3 points. But then, Germany stupefied the local audience by awarding 6 points to Massiel and only 2 to Cliff, turning the scales and granting the Spanish singer a 29-point lead versus superstar Richard's 28 points.

Yugoslavia was the last to vote. The spokesperson for the North Macedonian jury chose to award 6 points to Ireland, 2 to Italy and 3 to Switzerland (its only points of the evening). A quite illogical vote that shocked the audience and the entire production team. Katie Boyle immediately noticed that the Yugoslavs had awarded 11 points instead of 10, offering hope that this might have been a mistake, and something would change, but the hope was shattered: 2 points were awarded to Switzerland, instead of 3, and the rest remained the same. The smoke lifted and Spain won. A sensation unparalleled in the history of Eurovision. So how did that happen? The voting analysis shows that those who gave Spain the highest score were France (4), Monaco (4), and Germany (6), who are not usually suspected of shady business. The question also arises as to why Spain did not award its main competitors, the UK and France, a single point? This was even though no other countries did so. Endless rumours and conspiracies, as mentioned, were thrown around. A decade ago, the Spanish television channel "La Sexta", aired a documentary centred around claims that two weeks prior to the event, Spain's ruler, Franco, sent a senior journalist from the Spanish Radio and Television Corporation (RTVE) to various broadcasting networks in Europe with one hand full of cash and the other holding enticing contracts to acquire series from these networks. Anything — in exchange for awarding points in the vote to bring Spain its long-awaited victory at Eurovision. Journalist José María Íñigo confirmed this, saying he had witnessed it. After the documentary aired, there was an uproar in Spain, Íñigo recanted and Massiel threatened to sue the station. In the end, this storm also subsided. No one imagined that a year after the victory in London, this scandal would only be an introduction for what would happen in Madrid....

1969 - Madrid, Spain

The 14th edition of the ESC will never be forgotten. The scandals surrounding the contest began with Spain's controversial win the previous year in London. In a defiant move, the Welsh service of the BBC decided that it wanted to participate in Eurovision and represent Wales (which is known as part of the United Kingdom). The Welsh even held a pre-selection contest, but the EBU curbed their enthusiasm, stating that Wales was not a sovereign country and that it was annexed to the United Kingdom when it came to participating in the contest. Austria also stirred the pot when it withdrew from the contest, presumably as a protest over the Franco-Spanish rule. Thus, only 16 countries participated, delivering the tightest and most suspenseful contest of all time. Unfortunately, the consequences of this suspense would induce a further reduction in the number of participants in the following year. 27 countries, the largest number ever, broadcast the contest and even Brazil aired it for the first time. The Spanish people stood behind their country for the Eurovision in Madrid, which was considered to be the most important and significant event for the nation during General Franco's reign. With its weakening image, it was important for the ruler of the country to present a better Spain to the world. And what better way was there to do so than on a stage in front of hundreds of millions of viewers? Franco can be lauded for recognising the opportunity and squeeze every drop of it. The best Spanish artists were recruited to design the stage, headed by Salvador Dali. The Madrid Opera House, "Teatro Real", was chosen to host the event and closed for all activities in the six months prior to the contest, so it could be adapted for the television broadcast. Another problem that the Spanish hosts had to deal with (and in the next decade Israeli television would have to face) was the colour broadcast. The new contest rules explicitly stated that the show would be broadcast in full colour, but Spain was not at all prepared to broadcast in colour and most of the state's television productions were aired in black and white. This was not a problem for Franco, who invested a fortune in order to produce a colour broadcast, what led to the establishment of a foundation for colour broadcasts over the entire country. However, since most Spanish citizens had black-and-white receivers and did not have a penny in their pockets to purchase a colour television set, Spanish television continued to broadcast in black and white until the second half of the 1970s. The chosen presenter was Laurita Valenzuela, an experienced and personable television figure, who could not have imagined to herself what kind of embarrassment she would face at the end of the evening. Alongside her, the Spanish Radio and Television Orchestra played under conductor, Augusto Algueró. Just like in 1968, there was a clear favourite for a win, and all bets were on her. It was Lulu, a major pop star in the UK and wife of singer Maurice Gibb of the "Bee Gees". With Alan Moorhouse's "Boom Bang-a-Bang", she was expected to cruise to victory in Madrid. Even before the start of rehearsals and the contest, the entry, and Lulu, had become a mega-hit in Europe and America. Lulu, who remembered very well what happened to Cliff Richard, took the stage and definitely did her best to ensure the performance would be remembered for years to come, managing to secure 18 points and the most justified first place in the world, however... A record number of five artists who had participated before in the contest returned to compete. Romuald (who represented Monaco in 1964 and returned to represent it in 1974), with "Catherine", failed to take Luxembourg back to the top. Like him, there was Louis Neefs of Belgium who recaptured the seventh place from 1967 with "Jennifer Jennings". The great Simone de Oliveira from Portugal delivered her second Eurovision performance (1965), but once again did not return home with a significant achievement. Norway's Kirsti Sparboe experienced an immense failure, after also participating in1965 and 1967. Her song "Oj, oj, oj, så glad jeg skal bli", tells the story: it finished in last place and was only awarded one point by its good neighbour, Sweden. Germany pinned high hopes on the Swedish singer, Siw Malmkvist, who represented the great country and did not even come close to winning Eurovision with "Primaballerina". Malmkvist, who had represented her own country in 1960, left the stage relatively disappointed again, with ninth place, despite giving a sweet performance that won her praise. The 12-year-old French boy, Jean Jacques who represented Monaco, which was desperate for a victory and tried every possible gimmick to achieve it, tried to steal the show. The way the young singer sang "Maman, Maman", placed him in a close competition during the first part of the contest and in third place throughout most of the evening, but towards the end he dropped out of the race and finished sixth. Today, incidentally, Jean Jacques is a rugby coach in his country. Italy, just like the previous year in London, sent the winner of the Sanremo Festival, Iva Zanicchi, one of the most famous singers in the country, but not with the song that had won the festival. "Zingara", one of the most glorious composition of Italian music, could have, undoubtedly, threatened the top places, but once again the Italians chose another song, which left them and Zanicchi at the bottom of the list. Tommy Körberg, a rising star from Sweden, will be remembered favourably from this Eurovision with "Judy, min vän", which has been translated into many languages and became a hit in Europe. In the contest itself, his decent performance only took him to the ninth place, which he tied with Germany. Throughout the rehearsals, the reporters marked Paola, the Swiss singer, as the only threat to the favourite, Lulu. "Bonjour, bonjour", which was remarkably successful in German-speaking countries, was a catchy and very fitting entry for the renewed spirit of Eurovision. In the end, Paola was the runner up, behind the victors, at fifth place with 13 points. Grand expectations were placed on the experienced shoulders of Salomé, who was counted on to be the first in history to bring a second consecutive win to her country in the European contest. "Vivo cantando" instilled hope. In a controversial decision by Augusto Algueró, the arrangement was almost completely changed, and this was not to the satisfaction of the performer. Despite everything and with a push from the home audience, Salomé managed to scrape up the 18 points that also gave her the win, like the other joint winners.

Dutch singer, Lenny Kuhr, aspired to finally bring her country back to the top of European music after years of disappointments and failures. With a guitar in her hands and a winning song, "De troubadour", she succeeded in the task and won the contest with 18 points. It should be noted that, according to the rule enacted immediately after the case of the four-way tie, the entry that received the highest number of points from a judging country — would be the winner. According to this rule, if it had been implemented before the contest, Lenny Kuhr would have been the exclusive winner, as she received 6 points from France. France itself yearned to win the Eurovision again after seven years of being close. In the Francophone country they thought it was time, with the stirring singer Frida Boccara and the song "Un jour, un enfant", which was made from winning material; and indeed, Boccara also reached the magic number 18 and was the fourth winner in the contest, tied with the other winners. According to the latest Eurovision score rule in the case of a tie (the song that received points from the most countries is the winner), Boccara (who received points from nine countries) would have been declared as the exclusive winner. Spain took advantage of the interval between the entries and announcement of the results, to show a propaganda film that mainly featured the industry of the country. It is unclear what caused the hosts to choose music reminiscent of that in horror films to accompany the images, which also included waterfalls and vistas from Madrid and its environs. The scoreboard was simple, relative to the rest of the set, and as usual, the Executive Supervisor, Clifford Brown, tried to steal the show during the voting announcements and stopped the procedures more than once, for no particular reason, except apparently, to steal attention and screen time. The vote was the tightest in history and the lead drifted between UK, France and Spain with Monaco also being in the picture of victory. The French put a spoke in the wheel with their extraordinary vote by giving no less than six points to the Netherlands thus placing it at the top. A moment before the curtain came down on the scoreboard, the Netherlands, Spain, and France were neck and neck with 18 points each, while the UK had one point less. Finland was the last to announce its votes and was expected to unravel the tangle. In practice, the Finns complicated the situation even more, awarding Lulu one point, tying it with the top three, which did not receive any points! Thus, Spain, the United Kingdom, the Netherlands, and France finished with the same number of points (18), in a precedent. What could be done? Valenzuela, the presenter, turned to Brown who did not hesitate before ruling: "We have four winners this year". The embarrassed Valenzuela was sure that Brown was joking and explained to the audience that there was an unusual situation — a tie. She turned to Brown again, who reiterated his astonishing and ridiculous answer. It turned out that the rules of the contest were not prepared for the event of a tie at the end of the voting, which was amended immediately after this contest and it was determined that the song that received the highest number of votes from a judging country would be the winner. Admittedly, a late fix. According to the quality and performance, there was no doubt that the victory should have been Lulu's. Even so, these were golden years for the UK, from 1967 to 1978, when it did not drop from the top five at Eurovision. Of course, the host was not prepared for four wins.... Three medals for the winners had been prepared in advance: One for the performer, one for the writer and one for the composer. Therefore, the other nine medals which were meant to be given out that evening, according to the rules of the ceremony, were only prepared after the contest and sent to the winners about two months later. Before the show ended, for the first and last time in the history of Eurovision, the four winning songs were performed again, in the order of their appearance in the contest. Several records were broken thanks to the four-way tie, or in contempt of it, depending on the point of view: France became the Eurovision queen with a fourth Grand Prix, the Netherlands gained its third victory, the British and Spanish gained their second wins. In fact, the top four countries with Eurovision achievements, won the contest in Madrid. Spain was the first to record a second consecutive win. Which, as of today, was also its last.

1960

Date: 29.3.1960
Location: Royal Festival Hall
Presenter: Katie Boyle
Orchestra Conductor: Eric Robinson
Chief Executive: -.
Participating Countries: 13
Voting: Every country has a Jury that awards its 10 points to one or more entries
Broadcaster: British Broadcasting Corporation (BBC)
Director: Innes Lloyd
Interval act: Eric Robinson's Orchestra
Duration: 1 hour and 45 minutes
Broadcast: To all participating countries and to Finland

No.	Country	Song	Performing Artist	Lyrics	Composer	Conductor	Language	Commentator	Spokesperson	Points	Place
01	United Kingdom	"Looking High, High, High"	Bryan Johnson	John Watson	John Watson	Eric Robinson	English	David Jacobs and Pete Murray	Nick Burrell-Davis	25	2
02	Sweden	"Alla andra får varann"	Siw Malmkvist	Åke Gerhard	Ulf Kjellqvist	Thore Ehrling	Swedish	Jan Gabrielsson	Tage Danielsson	4	10
03	Luxembourg	"So laang we's du do bast"	Camillo Felgen	Henri Moots	Henri Moots, Jean Roderès	Eric Robinson	Luxembourgish	Pierre Tchernia	Unknown	1	13
04	Denmark	"Det var en yndig tid"	Katy Bødtger	Sven Buemann	Vilfred Kjær	Kai Mortensen	Danish	Sejr Volmer-Sørensen	Svend Pedersen	4	10
05	Belgium	"Mon amour pour toi"	Fud Leclerc	Robert Montal	Jack Say	Henri Segers	French	Georges Désir, Nic Bal	Arlette Vincent	9	6
06	Norway	"Voi"	Nora Brockstedt	Georg Elgaaen	Georg Elgaaen	Øivind Bergh	Norwegian	Erik Diesen	Kari Borg Mannsåker	11	4
07	Austria	"Du hast mich so fasziniert"	Harry Winter	Robert Gilbert	Robert Stolz	Robert Stolz	German	Wolf Mittler	Emil Kollpacher	6	7
08	Monaco	"Ce soir-là"	François Deguelt	Pierre Dorsey	Hubert Giraud	Raymond Lefèvre	French	Pierre Tchernia	Unknown	15	3
09	Switzerland	"Cielo e terra"	Anita Traversi	Mario Robbiani	Mario Robbiani	Cédric Dumont	Italian	Theodor Haller	Boris Acquadro	5	8
10	The Netherlands	"Wat een geluk"	Rudi Carrell	Willy van Hemert	Dick Schallies	Dolf van der Linden	Dutch	Piet te Nuyl	Siebe van der Zee	2	12
11	Germany	"Bonne nuit ma chérie"	Wyn Hoop	Kurt Schwabach	Franz Josef Breuer	Franz Josef Breuer	German and French	Wolf Mittler	Hans-Joachim Rauschenbach	11	4
12	Italy	"Romantica"	Renato Rascel	Dino Verde	Renato Rascel	Cinico Angelini	Italian	Giorgio Porro	Enzo Tortora	5	8
13	France	"Tom Pillibi"	Jacqueline Boyer	Pierre Cour	André Popp	Franck Pourcel	French	Pierre Tchernia	Armand Lanoux	32	1

	France	Italy	Germany	The Netherlands	Switzerland	Monaco	Austria	Norway	Belgium	Denmark	Luxembourg	Sweden	United Kingdom	
France	■	–	1	2	1	5	1	5	3	4	1	4	5	France
Italy	–	■	–	1	–	2	–	–	1	–	1	–	–	Italy
Germany	4	–	■	–	–	2	2	–	2	–	–	1	–	Germany
The Netherlands	–	1	–	■	–	–	–	–	1		–	–	–	The Netherlands
Switzerland	–	1	–	–	■	–	2	1	–	–	1	–	–	Switzerland
Monaco	3	–	7	–	1	■	–	–	–	2	1	–	1	Monaco
Austria	–	1	–	–	–	–	■	–	1	2	–	–	2	Austria
Norway	2	–	–	1	4	–	1	■	1	2	–	–	1	Norway
Belgium	–	3	1	–	–	–	1	–	■	–	–	4	–	Belgium
Denmark	–	–	–	–	–	–	–	2	–	■	1	–	1	Denmark
Luxembourg	–	1	–	–	–	–	–	–	–	–	■	–	–	Luxembourg
Sweden	2	1	–	1	–	–	–	–	–	–	–	■	–	Sweden
United Kingdom	–	2	1	5	4	1	3	2	1	–	5	1	■	United Kingdom

1961

Hosting Country: France
Hosting City: Cannes
Date: 18.3.1961
Location: Palais des Festivals et des Congrès
Presenter: Jacqueline Joubert
Orchestra Conductor: Franck Pourcel
Chief Executive: -.
Participating Countries: 16
Voting: Every country has a Jury that awards its 10 points to one or more entries
Broadcaster: Radiodiffusion-Télévision Française (RTF)
Director: Marcel Cravenne
Interval act: Tessa Beaumont and Max Bozzoni
Duration: 1 hour and 45 minutes
Broadcast: To all participating countries

No.	Country	Song	Performing Artist	Lyrics	Composer	Conductor	Language	Commentator	Spokesperson	Points	Place
01	Spain	"Estando contigo"	Conchita Bautista	Antonio Guijarro	Augusto Algueró	Rafael Ferrer	Spanish	Federico Gallo	Diego Ramírez Pastor	8	9
02	Monaco	"Allons, allons les enfants"	Colette Deréal	Pierre Delanoë	Hubert Giraud	Raymond Lefevre	French	Robert Beauvais	Unknown	6	10
03	Austria	"Sehnsucht"	Jimmy Makulis	Leopold Andrejewitsch	Leopold Andrejewitsch	Franck Pourcel	German	Wolf Mittler	Emil Kollpacher	1	15
04	Finland	"Valoa ikkunassa"	Laila Kinnunen	Sauvo Puhtila	Eino Hurme	George de Godzinsky	Finish	Aarno Walli	Poppe Berg	6	10
05	Yugoslavia	"Neke davne zvezde"	Ljiljana Petrović	Miroslav Antić	Jože Privšek	Joze Privzek	Serb	Ljubomir Vukadinović (Televizija Beograd), Gordana Bonetti (Televizija Zagreb), Tomaž Terček (Televizija Ljubljana)	Unknown	9	8
06	The Netherlands	"Wat een dag"	Greetje Kauffeld	Pieter Goemans	Dick Schallies	Dolf van der Linden	Dutch	Piet te Nuyl	Siebe van der Zee	6	10
07	Sweden	"April, april"	Lill-Babs	Bo Eneby	Bobbie Ericsson	William Lind	Swedish	Jan Gabrielsson	Roland Eiworth	2	14
08	Germany	"Einmal sehen wir uns wieder"	Lale Andersen	Ernst Bader	Rudolf Maluck	Franck Pourcel	German	Wolf Mittler	Heinz Schenk	3	13
09	France	"Printemps, avril carillonne"	Jean-Paul Mauric	Guy Favereau	Francis Baxter	Franck Pourcel	French	Robert Beauvais	Armand Lanoux	13	4
10	Switzerland	"Nous aurons demain"	Franca di Rienzo	Émile Gardaz	Géo Voumard	Fernando Paggi	French	Theodor Haller, Robert Beauvais	Boris Acquadro	16	3
11	Belgium	"September, gouden roos"	Bob Benny	Wim Brabants	Hans Flower	Francis Bay	Flemish	Nic Bal, Robert Beauvais	Ward Bogaert	1	15
12	Norway	"Sommer i Palma"	Nora Brockstedt	Egil Hagen	Jan Wølner	Øivind Bergh	Norwegian	Leif Rustad	Mette Janson	10	7
13	Denmark	"Angelique"	Dario Campeotto	Aksel V. Rasmussen	Aksel V. Rasmussen	Kai Mortensen	Danish	Sejr Volmer-Sørensen	Ole Mortensen	12	5
14	Luxembourg	"Nous les amoureux"	Jean-Claude Pascal	Maurice Vidalin	Jacques Datin	Leo Chauliac	French	Robert Beauvais	Unknown	31	1
15	United Kingdom	"Are You Sure?"	The Allisons	John Allison, Bob Allison	John Allison, Bob Allison	Harry Robinson	English	Tom Sloan and Peter Murray	Michael Aspel	24	2
16	Italy	"Al di là"	Betty Curtis	Mogol Ervin Drake	Carlo Donida	Gianfranco Intra	Italian	Corrado Mantoni	Enzo Tortora	12	5

	Italy	United Kingdom	Luxembourg	Denmark	Norway	Belgium	Switzerland	France	Germany	Sweden	The Netherlands	Yugoslavia	Finland	Austria	Monaco	Spain	
Italy	■	–	–	4	–	4	–	1	–	–	1	1	–	–	1	–	Italy
United Kingdom	1	■	8	1	–	1	7	–	–	–	3	–	–	–	–	3	United Kingdom
Luxembourg	3	–	■	1	–	–	1	1	5	1	1	5	3	4	4	2	Luxembourg
Denmark	–	–	–	■	8	–	–	–	–	2	1	–	1	–	–	–	Denmark
Norway	–	–	–	1	■	5	–	–	–	–	–	1	2	–	–	1	Norway
Belgium	–	–	1	–	–	■	–	–	–	–	–	–	–	–	–	–	Belgium
Switzerland	2	2	–	–	–	–	■	–	–	4	2	1	–	2	2	1	Switzerland
France	–	2	1	–	–	–	–	■	4	1	–	–	1	–	2	2	France
Germany	–	–	–	1	–	–	–	–	■	1	–	–	–	1	–	–	Germany
Sweden	–	–	–	–	–	–	–	2	–	■	–	–	–	–	–	–	Sweden
The Netherlands	2	–	–	–	–	–	–	1	1	–	■	2	–	–	–	–	The Netherlands
Yugoslavia	–	1	–	1	–	–	1	2	–	–	1	■	–	3	–	–	Yugoslavia
Finland	2	2	–	1	–	–	–	1	–	–	–	–	■	–	–	–	Finland
Austria	–	1	–	–	–	–	–	–	–	–	–	–	–	■	–	–	Austria
Monaco	–	1	–	–	–	–	1	–	–	–	–	–	3	–	■	1	Monaco
Spain	–	1	–	–	2	–	–	1	–	1	1	–	–	–	1	■	Spain

1962

Hosting Country: Luxembourg
Hosting City: Luxembourg City
Date: 18.3.1962
Location: Villa Louvigny
Presenter: Mireille Delannoy
Orchestra Conductor: Jean Roderès
Chief Executive: -.
Participating Countries: 16
Voting: Every country has a Jury that attributes 3 points to its favourite song, 2 points to its second favourite and 1 point to its third favourite.
Broadcaster: Compagnie Luxembourgeoise de Télédiffusion (CLT)
Director: Jos Pauly & René Steichen
Interval act: Achille Zavatta
Duration: 1 hour and 24 minutes
Broadcast: To all participating countries

No.	Country	Song	Performing Artist	Lyrics	Composer	Conductor	Language	Commentator	Spokesperson	Points	Place
01	Finland	"Tipi-tii"	Marion Rung	Kari Tuomisaari, Jaakko Salo	Kari Tuomisaari, Jaakko Salo	George de Godzinsky	Finish	Aarno Walli, Erkki Melakoski	Poppe Berg	4	7
02	Belgium	"Ton nom"	Fud Leclerc	Tony Golan	Eric Channe	Henri Segers	French	Nicole Védrès, Willem Duys	Arlette Vincent	0	13
03	Spain	"Llámame"	Victor Balaguer	Miguel Portoles	Mario Selles	Jean Roderes	Spanish	Federico Gallo	Diego Ramírez Pastor	0	13
04	Austria	"Nur in der Wiener Luft"	Eleonore Schwarz	Bruno Uher	Bruno Uher	Bruno Uher	German	Ruth Kappelsberger	Emil Kollpacher	0	13
05	Denmark	"Vuggevise"	Ellen Winther	Sejr Volmer-Sørensen	Kjeld Bonfils	Kai Mortensen	Danish	Skat Nørrevig	Ole Mortensen	2	10
06	Sweden	"Sol och vår"	Inger Berggren	Ulf Källqvist	Åke Gerhard	Egon Kjerrman	Swedish	Jan Gabrielsson	Tage Danielsson[1]	4	7
07	Germany	"Zwei kleine Italiener"	Conny Froboess	George Buschor	Christian Bruhn	Rolf-Hans Müller	German	Ruth Kappelsberger	Klaus Havenstein	9	6
08	The Netherlands	"Katinka"	De Spelbrekers	Henny Hamhuis, Lodewijk Post	Joop Stokkermans	Dolf van der Linden	Dutch	Willem Duys	Ger Lugtenburg	13	0
09	France	"Un premier amour"	Isabelle Aubret	Roland Valade	Claude Henri Vic	Franck Pourcel	French	Pierre Tchernia	André Valmy	26	1
10	Norway	"Kom sol, kom regn"	Inger Jacobsen	Ivar Andersen	Kjell Karlsen	Øivind Bergh	Norwegian	Odd Grythe	Kari Borg Mannsåker	2	10
11	Switzerland	"Le retour"	Jean Philippe	Émile Gardaz	Géo Voumard	Cédric Dumont	French	Theodor Haller, Georges Hardy, Renato Tagliani	Alexandre Burger	2	10
12	Yugoslavia	"Ne pali svetla u sumrak"	Lola Novaković	Drago Britvić	Jože Privšek	Jože Privšek	Serb	Ljubomir Vukadinović, Gordana Bonetti, Tomaž Terček	Mladen Delić	10	4
13	United Kingdom	"Ring-A-Ding Girl"	Ronnie Carroll	Stan Butcher	Syd Cordell	Wally Stott	English	David Jacobs, Peter Haigh	Alex Macintosh	10	4
14	Luxembourg	"Petit bonhomme"	Camillo Felgen	Maurice Vidalin	Jacques Datin	Jean Roderes	French	Nicole Védrès	Robert Diligent	11	3
15	Italy	"Addio, addio"	Claudio Villa	Franco Migliacci	Domenico Modugno	Cinico Angelini	Italian	Renato Tagliani	Enzo Tortora	3	9
16	Monaco	"Dis rien"	François Deguelt	René Rouzaud	Henri Salvador	Raymond Lefèvre	French	Pierre Tchernia	Unknown	13	2

	Monaco	Italy	Luxembourg	United Kingdom	Yugoslavia	Switzerland	Norway	France	The Netherlands	Germany	Sweden	Denmark	Austria	Spain	Belgium	Finland	
Monaco	■	–	3	–	–	–	2	1	3	1	–	–	3	–	–	–	Monaco
Italy	–	■	2	–	1	–	–	–	–	–	–	–	–	–	–	–	Italy
Luxembourg	3		■	–	–	1	–	–	–	–	–	–	1	3	3	–	Luxembourg
United Kingdom	–	–	–	■	2	2	–	–	–	–	–	2	–	1	–	3	United Kingdom
Yugoslavia	–	3	–	–	■	–	–	3	–	–	2	–	–	–	1	1	Yugoslavia
Switzerland	–	–	–	–	–	■	–	–	–	2	–	–	–	–	–	–	Switzerland
Norway	–	–	–	–	–	–	■	2	–	–	–	–	–	–	–	–	Norway
France	1	2	1	1	3	3	3	■	–	3	3	–	2	2	2	–	France
The Netherlands	–	–	–	–	–	–	–	–	■	–	–	–	–	–	–	–	The Netherlands
Germany	2	–	–	2	–	–	–	–	2	■	–	1	–	–	–	2	Germany
Sweden	–	–	–	–	–	–	–	–	1	–	■	3	–	–	–	–	Sweden
Denmark	–	1	–	–	–	–	–	–	–	–	1	■	–	–	–	–	Denmark
Austria	–	–	–	–	–	–	–	–	–	–	–	–	■	–	–	–	Austria
Spain	–	–	–	–	–	–	–	–	–	–	–	–	–	■	–	–	Spain
Belgium	–	–	–	–	–	–	–	–	–	–	–	–	–	–	■	–	Belgium
Finland	–	–	–	3	–	–	1	–	–	–	–	–	–	–	–	■	Finland

1963

Hosting Country: United Kingdom

Hosting City: London

Date: 23.3.1963

Location: BBC Television Centre

Presenter: Katie Boyle

Orchestra Conductor: Eric Robinson

Chief Executive: -

Participating Countries: 16

Voting: Every country has a Jury that includes 20 members and gives 1-5 votes to its top 5 favourite songs

Broadcaster: British Broadcasting Corporation (BBC)

Director: Yvonne Littlewood

Intermediate performance: Ola & Barbro

Duration: 1 hour and 35 minutes

Broadcast: To all participating countries and Portugal

No.	Country	Song	Performing Artist	Lyrics	Composer	Conductor	Language	Commentator	Spoker of Results	Points	Place
01	United Kingdom	"Say Wonderful Things"	Ronnie Carroll	Norman Newell	Philip Green	Eric Robinson	English	David Jacobs, Michael Aspel	Pete Murray	28	4
02	The Netherlands	"Een speeldoos"	Annie Palmen	Pieter Goemans	Pieter Goemans	Eric Robinson	Dutch	Willem Duys	Pim Jacobs	0	13
03	Germany	"Marcel"	Heidi Brühl	Charly Niessen	Charly Niessen	Willy Berking	German	Hanns Joachim Friedrichs	Werner Veigel	5	9
04	Austria	"Vielleicht geschieht ein Wunder"	Carmela Corren	Peter Wehle	Erwin Halletz	Erwin Halletz	German/English	Hanns Joachim Friedrichs	Emil Kollpacher	16	7
05	Norway	"Solhverv"	Anita Thallaug	Dag Kristoffersen	Dag Kristoffersen	Øivind Bergh	Norweigen	Øivind Johnsen	Roald Øyen	0	13
06	Italy	"Uno per tutte"	Emilio Pericoli	Mogol, Alberto Testa	Tony Renis	-	Italian	Renato Tagliani	Enzo Tortora	37	3
07	Finland	"Muistojeni laulu"	Laila Halme	Börje Sundgren	Börje Sundgren	George de Godzinsky	Finish	Aarno Walli, Erkki Melakoski	Poppe Berg	0	13
08	Denmark	"Dansevise"	Grethe & Jørgen Ingmann	Sejr Volmer-Sørensen	Otto Francker	Kai Mortensen	Danish	Ole Mortensen	Unknown	42	1
09	Yugoslavia	"Brodovi"	Vice Vukov	Mario Nardelli	Mario Nardelli	Miljenko Prohaska	Croatian	Ljubomir Vukadinović; Gordana Bonetti; Saša Novak	Miloje Orlović	3	11
10	Switzerland	"T'en va pas"	Esther Ofarim	Émile Gardaz	Géo Voumard	Eric Robinson	French	Theodor Haller; Georges Hardy; Renato Tagliani	Alexandre Burger	40	2
11	France	"Elle était si jolie"	Alain Barrière	Alain Barrière, A. Migiani	Alain Barrière, A. Migiani	Franck Pourcel	French	Pierre Tchernia	Armand Lanoux	25	5
12	Spain	"Algo prodigioso"	José Guardiola	Camillo Murillo Janero	Fernando García Morcillo	Rafael de Ibarbia Serra	Spanish	Federico Gallo	Julio Rico	2	12
13	Sweden	"En gång i Stockholm"	Monica Zetterlund	Beppe Wolgers	Bobbie Ericsson	William Lind	Swedish	Jörgen Cederberg	Edvard Matz	0	13
14	Belgium	"Waarom?"	Jacques Raymond	Wim Brabants	Hans Flower	Francis Bay	Flemish	Herman Verelst and Denise Maes, Pierre Delhasse	Ward Bogaert	4	10
15	Monaco	"L'amour s'en va"	Françoise Hardy	Françoise Hardy	Françoise Hardy	Raymond Lefèvre	French	Pierre Tchernia	Unknown	25	5
16	Luxembourg	"À force de prier"	Nana Mouskouri	Pierre Delanoë	Raymond Bernard	Eric Robinson	French	Pierre Tchernia	Unknown	13	8

	United Kingdom	The Netherlands	Germany	Austria	Norway	Italy	Finland	Denmark	Yugoslavia	Switzerland	France	Spain	Sweden	Belgium	Monaco	Luxembourg	
United Kingdom	■	3	–	–	5	–	3	3	3	–	3	5	2	–	1	–	United Kingdom
The Netherlands	–	■	–	–	–	–	–	–	–	–	–	–	–	–	–	–	The Netherlands
Germany	–	–	■	–	2	–	–	–	–	–	–	–	–	–	3	–	Germany
Austria	4	–	–	■	–	–	4	1	–	–	2	–	3	2	–	–	Austria
Norway	–	–	–	–	■	–	–	–	–	–	–	–	–	–	–	–	Norway
Italy	2	1	–	–	3	■	2	5	4	5	–	3	–	3	5	4	Italy
Finland	–	–	–	–	–	–	■	–	–	–	–	–	–	–	–	–	Finland
Denmark	3	5	2	3	4	2	5	■	–	3		–	5	5	–	5	Denmark
Yugoslavia	–	–	–	–	–	–	–	–	■	–	1	2	–	–	–	–	Yugoslavia
Switzerland	5	–	4	5	1	5	–	4		■	–	4	1	4	4	3	Switzerland
France	–	4	1	2	–	4	–	–	5	4	■	1	–	1	2	1	France
Spain	–	–	–	–	–	–	–	–	2	–	–	■	–	–	–	–	Spain
Sweden	–	–	–	–	–	–	–	–	–	–	–	–	■	–	–	–	Sweden
Belgium	–	–	–	4	–	–	–	–	–	–	–	–	–	■	–	–	Belgium
Monaco	1	2	5	1	–	3	–	–	1	1	5	–	4	–	■	2	Monaco
Luxembourg	–	–	3	–	–	1	1	2	–	2	4	–	–	–	1	■	Luxembourg

1964

Hosting Country: Denmark

Hosting City: Copenhagen

Date: 21.3.1964

Location: Tivolis Koncertsal

Presenter: Lotte Wæver

Orchestra Conductor: Kai Mortensen

Chief Executive: Miroslav Vilček

Participating Countries: 16

Voting: Every country has a Jury that includes 10 members and gives 1 vote to their 3rd place song, 3 votes to their 2nd place song and 5 votes to their favourite song. If only 2 songs are selected, the favourite song gets 6 points and the 2nd best gets 3 votes, if only one song is selected — it gets 9 votes.

Broadcaster: Danmarks Radio (DR)

Director: Poul Leth Sørensen

Intermediate performance: Ballet-harlequinade

Duration: 1 hour and 34 minutes

Broadcast: To all participating countries and to Sweden

No.	Country	Song	Performing Artist	Lyrics	Composer	Conductor	Language	Commentator	Spoker of Results	Points	Place
01	Luxembourg	"Dès que le printemps revient"	Hugues Aufray	Jacques Plante	Hugues Aufray	Jacques Denjean	French	Robert Beauvais	Unknown	14	4
02	The Netherlands	"Jij bent mijn leven"	Anneke Grönloh	René de Vos	Ted Powder	Dolf van der Linden	Dutch	Ageeth Scherphuis	Pim Jacobs	2	10
03	Norway	"Spiral"	Arne Bendiksen	Egil Hagen	Sigurd Jansen	Karsten Andersen	Norweigen	Odd Grythe	Sverre Christophersen	6	8
04	Denmark	"Sangen om dig"	Mogens Dam	Mogens Dam	Aksel V. Rasmussen	Kai Mortensen	Danish	-	Pedro Biker	4	9
05	Finland	"Laiskotellen"	Lasse Mårtenson	Sauvo Puhtila	Lasse Mårtenson	George de Godzinsky	Finish	Aarno Walli, Erkki Melakoski	Poppe Berg	9	7
06	Austria	"Warum nur, warum?"	Udo Jürgens	Udo Jürgens	Udo Jürgens	Johannes Fehring	German	Willy Kralik	Walter Richard Langer	11	6
07	France	"Le chant de Mallory"	Rachel	Pierre Cour	André Popp	Franck Pourcel	French	Robert Beauvais	Jean-Claude Massoulier	14	4
08	United Kingdom	"I Love the Little Things"	Matt Monro	Tony Hatch	Tony Hatch	Harry Rabinowitz	English	David Jacobs, Tom Sloan	Unknown	17	2
09	Germany	"Man gewöhnt sich so schnell an das Schöne"	Nora Nova	Niels Nobach	Rudi von der Dovenmühle	Willy Berking	German	Hermann Rockmann	Lia Wöhr	0	13
10	Monaco	"Où sont-elles passées"	Romuald	Pierre Barouh	Francis Lai	Michel Colombier	French	Robert Beauvais	Unknown	15	3
11	Portugal	"Oração"	António Calvário	Francisco Nicholson, Rogério Bracinha	João Nobre	Kai Mortensen	Portuguese	Gomes Ferreira	Maria Manuela Furtado	0	13
12	Italy	"Non ho l'età"	Gigliola Cinquetti	Nicola Salerno	Mario Panzeri	Gianfranco Monaldi	Italian	Renato Tagliani	Rosanna Vaudetti	49	1
13	Yugoslavia	"Život je sklopio krug"	Sabahudin Kurt	Stevan Raičković	Srđan Matijević	Radivoj Spasić	Serb	Miloje Orlović, Gordana Bonetti, Tomaž Terček	Unknown	0	13
14	Switzerland	"I miei pensieri"	Anita Traversi	Sanzio Chiesa	Giovanni Pelli	Fernando Paggi	Italian	Theodor Haller, Georges Hardy, Renato Tagliani	Alexandre Burger	0	13
15	Belgium	"Près de ma rivière"	Robert Cogoi	Robert Cogoi	Robert Cogoi	Henri Segers	French	Paule Herreman, Herman Verelst	André Hagon	2	10
16	Spain	"Caracola"	LOS TNT (Edelweiss Croatto, Argentina Croatto, Hermes Croatto)	Fina de Calderón	Fina de Calderón	Rafael de Ibarbia Serra	Spanish	Federico Gallo	Julio Rico	1	12

	Luxembourg	The Netherlands	Norway	Denmark	Finland	Austria	France	United Kingdom	Germany	Monaco	Portugal	Italy	Yugoslavia	Switzerland	Belgium	Spain
Spain	–	–	–	3	–	5	1	–	–	–	–	–	–	–	–	■
Belgium	–	–	–	–	–	1	–	–	–	3	–	5	–	–	■	–
Switzerland	–	–	–	–	–	–	–	5	–	1	–	3	–	■	–	–
Yugoslavia	–	–	–	–	–	–	1	–	–	3	–	5	■	–	–	–
Italy	3	–	–	–	–	5	–	–	–	–	–	■	–	–	–	1
Portugal	–	–	–	–	–	–	3	–	–	–	■	5	–	–	1	–
Monaco	–	–	–	–	–	–	5	–	–	■	–	3	–	–	1	–
Germany	5	–	–	–	–	–	–	1	■	–	–	3	–	–	–	–
United Kingdom	–	1	–	–	3	–	–	■	–	–	–	5	–	–	–	–
France	3	–	–	–	–	–	■	1	–	5	–	–	–	–	–	–
Austria	–	–	–	–	–	■	3	1	–	–	–	5	–	–	–	–
Finland	–	–	1	–	■	–	–	3	–	–	–	5	–	–	–	–
Denmark	–	1	5	■	3	–	–	–	–	–	–	–	–	–	–	–
Norway	–	–	■	1	3	–	–	5	–	–	–	–	–	–	–	–
The Netherlands	3	■	–	–	–	–	–	1	–	–	–	5	–	–	–	–
Luxembourg	■	–	–	–	–	–	1	–	–	3	–	5	–	–	–	–

1965

Hosting Country: Italy

Hosting City: Naples

Date: 20.3.1965

Location: Sala di Concerto della RAI

Presenter: Renata Mauro

Orchestra Conductor: Gianni Ferrio

Chief Executive: Miroslav Vilček

Participating Countries: 18

Voting: Every country has a Jury that includes 10 members and gives 1 vote to their 3rd place song, 3 votes to their 2nd place song and 5 votes to their favourite song. If only 2 songs are selected, the favourite song gets 6 points and the 2nd best gets 3 votes, if only one song is selected — it gets 9 votes.

Broadcaster: Radiotelevisione Italiana (RAI)

Director: Romolo Siena

Intermediate performance: Mario del Monaco

Duration: 1 hour and 39 minutes

Broadcast: To all participating countries

No.	Country	Song	Performing Artist	Lyrics	Composer	Conductor	Language	Commentator	Spoker of Results	Points	Place
01	The Netherlands	"'t is genoeg"	Conny Vandenbos	Joke van Soest	Johnny Holshuyzen	Dolf van der Linden	Dutch	Teddy Scholten	Dick van Bommel	5	11
02	United Kingdom	"I Belong"	Kathy Kirby	Phil Peters	Peter Lee Sterling	Eric Robinson	English	David Jacobs, David Gell	Alastair Burnet	26	2
03	Spain	"¡Qué bueno, qué bueno!"	Conchita Bautista	Antonio Figueroa Egea	Antonio Figueroa Egea	Adolfo Ventas Rodríguez	Spanish	Federico Gallo	Pepe Palau	0	15
04	Ireland	"Walking the Streets in the Rain"	Butch Moore	Teresa Conlon, Joe Harrigan, George Prendergast	Teresa Conlon, Joe Harrigan, George Prendergast	Gianni Ferrio	English	Bunny Carr, Kevin Roche	Frank Hall	11	6
05	Germany	"Paradies, wo bist du?"	Ulla Wiesner	Barbara Kist, Hans Blum	Barbara Kist, Hans Blum	Alfred Hause	German	Hermann Rockmann	Lia Wöhr	0	15
06	Austria	"Sag ihr, ich lass sie grüßen"	Udo Jürgens	Udo Jürgens, Frank Bohlen	Udo Jürgens	Gianni Ferrio	German	Willy Kralik	Walter Richard Langer	16	4
07	Norway	"Karusell"	Kirsti Sparboe	Jolly Kramer-Johansen	Jolly Kramer-Johansen	Øivind Bergh	Norweigen	Erik Diesen	Sverre Christophersen	1	13
08	Belgium	"Als het weer lente is"	Lize Marke	Jaak Dreesen	Jef van den Berg	Gaston Nuyts	Flemish	Herman Verelst, Paule Herreman	Ward Bogaert	0	15
09	Monaco	"Va dire à l'amour"	Marjorie Noël	Jacques Mareuil	Raymond Bernard	Raymond Bernard	French	Pierre Tchernia	Unknown	7	9
10	Sweden	"Absent Friend"	Ingvar Wixell	Alf Henrikson	Dag Wirén	William Lind	English	Berndt Friberg	Edvard Matz	6	10
11	France	"N'avoue jamais"	Guy Mardel	Guy Mardel	Françoise Dorin	Franck Pourcel	French	Pierre Tchernia	Jean-Claude Massoulier	22	3
12	Portugal	"Sol de inverno"	Simone de Oliveira	Jerónimo Bragança	Carlos Nóbrega e Sousa	Fernando de Carvalho	Portuguese	Gomes Ferreira	Maria Manuela Furtado	1	13
13	Italy	"Se piangi, se ridi"	Bobby Solo	Mogol, Roberto Satti	Gianni Marchetti, Roberto Satti	Gianni Ferrio	Italian	Renato Tagliani	Daniele Piombi	15	5
14	Denmark	"For din skyld"	Birgit Brüel	Poul Henningsen	Jørgen Jersild	Arne Lamberth	Danish	Skat Nørrevig	Claus Toksvig	10	7
15	Luxembourg	"Poupée de cire, poupée de son"	France Gall	Serge Gainsbourg	Serge Gainsbourg	Alain Goraguer	French	Pierre Tchernia	Unknown	32	1
16	Finland	"Aurinko laskee länteen"	Viktor Klimenko	Reino Helismaa	Toivo Kärki	George de Godzinsky	Finish	Aarno Walli, Erkki Melakoski	Poppe Berg	0	15
17	Yugoslavia	"Čežnja"	Vice Vukov	Žarko Roje	Julio Marić	Radivoj Spasić	Croatian	Miloje Orlović, Mladen Delić, Tomaž Terček	Ljubo Jelčić	2	12
18	Switzerland	"Non, à jamais sans toi"	Yovanna	Jean Charles	Bob Calfati	Mario Robbiani	French	Theodor Haller, Georges Hardy, Giovanni Bertini	Alexandre Burger	8	8

	The Netherlands	United Kingdom	Spain	Ireland	Germany	Austria	Norway	Belgium	Monaco	Sweden	France	Portugal	Italy	Denmark	Luxembourg	Finland	Yugoslavia	Switzerland
Switzerland	-	5	-	-	-	-	-	-	1	-	-	-	-	-	3	-	-	■
Yugoslavia	-	-	-	3	-	-	-	-	1	-	5	-	-	-	-	-	■	-
Finland	-	-	-	-	-	-	-	-	-	3	1	-	-	-	5	■	-	-
Luxembourg	-	-	-	-	-	-	-	-	-	-	3	-	1	5	■	-	-	-
Denmark	-	5	-	-	-	-	-	-	-	3	-	-	-	■	1	-	-	-
Italy	-	1	-	5	-	3	-	-	-	-	-	-	■	-	-	-	-	-
Portugal	-	-	-	3	-	5	-	-	-	-	-	■	-	-	-	-	1	-
France	-	-	-	-	-	-	-	-	-	-	■	-	3	-	-	-	1	5
Sweden	-	3	-	-	-	-	-	-	-	■	-	-	-	5	1	-	-	-
Monaco	-	-	-	-	-	-	-	-	■	-	5	1	3	-	-	-	-	-
Belgium	-	6	-	-	-	-	-	■	-	-	-	-	3	-	-	-	-	-
Norway	5	1	-	-	-	-	■	-	-	-	-	-	-	-	3	-	-	-
Austria	-	-	-	-	-	■	1	-	-	-	-	-	-	-	5	-	-	3
Germany	-	-	-	-	■	-	-	-	-	3	-	1	-	-	5	-	-	-
Ireland	-	-	-	■	-	5	-	-	-	-	1	-	-	-	3	-	-	-
Spain	-	5	■	-	-	-	-	-	-	-	3	-	-	-	1	-	-	-
United Kingdom	-	■	-	-	-	3	-	-	-	-	1	-	1	-	-	-	-	-
The Netherlands	■	-	-	-	-	-	-	-	-	-	1	-	3	-	5	-	-	-

1966

Hosting Country: Luxembourg

Hosting City: Luxembourg City

Date: 5.3.1966

Location: Villa Louvigny

Presenter: Josiane Chen

Orchestra Conductor: Jean Roderès

Chief Executive: Clifford Brown

Participating Countries: 18

Voting: Every country has a Jury that includes 10 members and gives 1 vote to their 3rd place song, 3 votes to their 2nd place song and 5 votes to their favourite song. If only 2 songs are selected, the favourite song gets 6 points and the 2nd best gets 3 votes, if only one song is selected — it gets 9 votes.

Broadcaster: Compagnie Luxembourgeoise de Télédiffusion (CLT)

Director: Unknown

Intermediate performance: Les Haricots Rouges

Duration: 1 hour and 28 minutes

Broadcast: To all participating countries and to Soviet Union, Czechoslovakia, East Germany, Hungary, Poland, Romania and Morocco.

No.	Country	Song	Performing Artist	Lyrics	Composer	Conductor	Language	Commentator	Spoker of Results	Points	Place
01	Germany	"Die Zeiger der Uhr"	Margot Eskens	Hans Bradtke	Walter Dobschinski	Willy Berking	German	Hans-Joachim Rauschenbach	Werner Veigel	7	10
02	Denmark	"Stop — mens legen er go'"	Ulla Pia	Erik Kåre	Erik Kåre	Arne Lamberth	Danish	Skat Nørrevig	Claus Toksvig	4	14
03	Belgium	"Un peu de poivre, un peu de sel"	Tonia	Phil van Cauwenbergh	Paul Quintens	Jean Roderes	French	Paule Herreman, Herman Verelst	André Hagon	14	4
04	Luxembourg	"Ce soir je t'attendais"	Michèle Torr	Jacques Chaumelle	Bernard Kesslair	Jean Roderes	French	Jacques Navadic	Camillo Felgen	7	10
05	Yugoslavia	"Brez besed"	Berta Ambrož	Elza Budau	Mojmir Sepe	Mojmir Sepe	Slovenian	Miloje Orlović, Mladen Delić, Tomaž Terček	Dragana Marković	9	7
06	Norway	"Intet er nytt under solen"	Åse Kleveland	Arne Bendiksen	Arne Bendiksen	Øivind Bergh	Norwegen	Sverre Christophersen	Erik Diesen	15	3
07	Finland	"Playboy"	Ann-Christine Nyström	Ossi Runne	Ossi Runne	Ossi Runne	Finish	Aarno Walli	Poppe Berg	7	10
08	Portugal	"Ele e ela"	Madalena Iglésias	Carlos Canelhas	Carlos Canelhas	Jorge Costa Pinto	Portuguese	Henrique Mendes	Maria Manuela Furtado	6	13
09	Austria	"Merci, Chérie"	Udo Jürgens	Udo Jürgens, Thomas Hörbiger	Udo Jürgens	Hans Hammerschmid	German	Willy Kralik	Walter Richard Langer	31	1
10	Sweden	"Nygammal vals"	Lill Lindfors and Svante Thuresson	Björn Lindroth	Bengt Arne Wallin	Gert Ove Andersson	Swedish	Sven Lindahl	Edvard Matz	16	2
11	Spain	"Yo soy aquél"	Raphael	Manuel Alejandro	Manuel Alejandro	Rafael de Ibarbia Serra	Spanish	Federico Gallo	Margarita Nicola	9	7
12	Switzerland	"Ne vois-tu pas?"	Madeleine Pascal	Roland Schweizer	Pierre Brenner	Jean Roderes	French	Theodor Haller, Georges Hardy, Giovanni Bertini	Alexandre Burger	12	6
13	Monaco	"Bien plus fort"	Téréza	Jean-Max Rivière	Gérard Bourgeois	Alain Goraguer	French	François Deguelt	Unknown	0	17
14	Italy	"Dio, come ti amo"	Domenico Modugno	Domenico Modugno	Domenico Modugno	Angelo Giacomazzi	Italian	Renato Tagliani	Enzo Tortora	0	17
15	France	"Chez nous"	Dominique Walter	Jacques Plante	Claude Carrère	Franck Pourcel	French	François Deguelt	Jean-Claude Massoulier	1	16
16	The Netherlands	"Fernando en Filippo"	Milly Scott	Gerrit den Braber	Kees de Bruyn	Dolf van der Linden	Dutch	Teddy Scholten	Herman Brouwer	2	15
17	Ireland	"Come Back to Stay"	Dickie Rock	Rowland Soper	Rowland Soper	Noel Kelehan	English	Brendan O'Reilly, Kevin Roche	Frank Hall	14	4
18	United Kingdom	"A Man Without Love"	Kenneth McKellar	Peter Callander	Cyril Ornadel	Harry Rabinowitz	English	David Jacobs, John Dunn	Michael Aspel	8	9

	Germany	Denmark	Belgium	Luxembourg	Yugoslavia	Norway	Finland	Portugal	Austria	Austria	Spain	Switzerland	Monaco	Italy	France	The Netherlands	Ireland	United Kingdom	
Germany	■	–	1	–	–	–	–	–	–	–	–	5	–	1	–	–	–	–	Germany
Denmark	–	■	–	–	–	1	3	–	–	–	–	–	–	–	–	–	–	–	Denmark
Belgium	5	–	■	–	–	–	–	3	–	1	–	–	–	–	–	5	–	–	Belgium
Luxembourg	–	–	–	■	–	–	–	–	1	5	–	–	–	–	1	–	–	–	Luxembourg
Yugoslavia	5	–	–	–	■	–	1	–	–	–	–	–	–	–	–	–	–	5	Yugoslavia
Norway	1	–	–	–	–	■	–	–	3	3	3	–	–	5	–	–	–	–	Norway
Finland	–	3	–	–	–	3	■	–	–	–	–	–	–	–	1	–	–	–	Finland
Portugal	–	1	–	–	–	–	–	■	–	–	5	–	–	–	–	–	–	–	Portugal
Austria	–	–	5	5	5	–	–	1	■	–	1	3	5	3	3	–	–	–	Austria
Sweden	–	5		–	–	5	5	–	–	■	–	1	–	–	–	–	–	–	Sweden
Spain	–	–	–	–	1	–	–	5	–	–	■	–	–	–	–	–	–	3	Spain
Switzerland	–	–	–	1	–	–	–	–	5	–	–	■	3	–	–	–	3	–	Switzerland
Monaco	–	–	–	–	–	–	–	–	–	–	–	–	■	–	–	–	–	–	Monaco
Italy	–	–	–	–	–	–	–	–	–	–	–	–	–	■	–	–	–	–	Italy
France	–	–	–	–	–	–	–	–	–	–	–	–	1	–	■	–	–	–	France
The Netherlands	–	–	–	–	–	–	–	–	–	–	–	–	–	–	–	■	1	1	The Netherlands
Ireland	–	–	3	–	3	–	–	–	–	–	–	–	–	–	5	3	■	–	Ireland
United Kingdom	–	–	–	3	–	–	–	–	–	–	–	–	–	–	–	–	5	■	United Kingdom

1967

Hosting Country: Austria

Hosting City: Vienna

Date: 8.4.1967

Location: Großer Festsaal der Wiener Hofburg

Presenter: Erica Vaal

Orchestra Conductor: Johannes Fehring

Chief Executive: Clifford Brown

Participating Countries: 17

Voting: Every country has a Jury that shared its 10 votes among one or more entries

Broadcaster: Österreichischer Rundfunk (ORF)

Director: Herbert Fuchs

Intermediate performance: The Blue Danube by Wiener Sängerknaben

Duration: 1 hour and 49 minutes

Broadcast: To all participating countries

No.	Country	Song	Performing Artist	Lyrics	Composer	Conductor	Language	Commentator	Spoker of Results	Points	Place
01	The Netherlands	"Ring-dinge-ding"	Thérèse Steinmetz	Gerrit den Braber	Johnny Holshuyzen	Dolf van der Linden	Dutch	Leo Nelissen	Ellen Blazer	2	14
02	Luxembourg	"L'amour est bleu"	Vicky Leandros	Pierre Cour	André Popp	Claude Denjean	French	Jacques Navadic	Unknown	17	4
03	Austria	"Warum es hunderttausend Sterne gibt"	Peter Horton	Karin Bognar	Kurt Peche	Johannes Fehring	German	Emil Kollpacher	Walter Richard Langer	2	14
04	France	"Il doit faire beau là-bas"	Noëlle Cordier	Pierre Delanoë	Hubert Giraud	Franck Pourcel	French	Pierre Tchernia	Jean-Claude Massoulier	20	3
05	Portugal	"O vento mudou"	Eduardo Nascimento	João Magalhães Pereira	Nuno Nazareth Fernandes	Armando Tavares Belo	Portuguese	Henrique Mendes	Maria Manuela Furtado	3	12
06	Switzerland	"Quel cœur vas-tu briser?"	Géraldine Gaulier	Gérard Grey	Daneil Faure	Hans Möckel	French	Theodor Haller, Georges Hardy, Giovanni Bertini	Alexandre Burger	0	17
07	Sweden	"Som en dröm"	Östen Warnerbring	Patrice Hellberg	Marcus Österdahl, Curt Peterson	Mats Olsson	Swedish	Christina Hansegård	Edvard Matz	7	8
08	Finland	"Varjoon — suojaan"	Fredi	Alvi Vuorinen	Lasse Mårtenson	Ossi Runne	Finish	Aarno Walli	Poppe Berg	3	12
09	Germany	"Anouschka"	Inge Brück	Hans Blum	Hans Blum	Hans Blum	German	Hans-Joachim Rauschenbach	Lia Wöhr	7	8
10	Belgium	"Ik heb zorgen"	Louis Neefs	Phil van Cauwenbergh	Paul Quintens	Francis Bay	Flemish	Herman Verelst, Janine Lambotte	Ward Bogaert	8	7
11	United Kingdom	"Puppet on a String"	Sandie Shaw	Bill Martin, Phil Coulter	Bill Martin, Phil Coulter	Kenny Woodman	English	Rolf Harris, Richard Baker	Michael Aspel	47	1
12	Spain	"Hablemos del amor"	Raphael	Manuel Alejandro	Manuel Alejandro	Manuel Alejandro	Spanish	Federico Gallo	Margarita Nicola	9	6
13	Norway	"Dukkemann"	Kirsti Sparboe	Ola B. Johannessen	Tor Hultin	Øivind Bergh	Norweigen	Erik Diesen	Sverre Christophersen	2	14
14	Monaco	"Boum-Badaboum"	Minouche Barelli	Serge Gainsbourg	Serge Gainsbourg	Aimé Barelli	French	Pierre Tchernia	Unknown	10	5
15	Yugoslavia	"Vse rože sveta"	Lado Leskovar	Milan Lindič	Urban Koder	Mario Rijavec	Slovenian	Miloje Orlović, Mladen Delić, Tomaž Terček	Unknown	7	8
16	Italy	"Non andare più lontano"	Claudio Villa	Vito Pallavicini	Gino Mescoli	Giancarlo Chiaramello	Italian	Renato Tagliani	Mike Bongiorno	2	15
17	Ireland	"If I Could Choose"	Sean Dunphy	Wesley Burrowes	Michael Coffey	Noel Kelehan	English	Brendan O'Reilly, Kevin Roche	Gay Byrne	22	2

	The Netherlands	Luxembourg	Austria	France	Portugal	Switzerland	Sweden	Finland	Germany	Belgium	United Kingdom	Spain	Norway	Monaco	Yugoslavia	Italy	Ireland	
The Netherlands	■	–	–	–	–	–	–	–	–	–	1	–	–	–	–	–	1	The Netherlands
Luxembourg		■	–	–	–	–	–	2	–	1	2	1	–	1	1	3	2	Luxembourg
Austria	–	–	■	–	1	–	–	–	–	–	–	–	–	–	1	–	–	Austria
France	1	2	1	■	–	1	4	–	2	–	2	–	–	2	4	–	1	France
Portugal	–	–	–	1	■	1	–	–	–	–	–	1	–	–	–	–	–	Portugal
Switzerland	–	–	–	–	–	■	–	–	–	–	–	–	–	–	–	–	–	Switzerland
Sweden	–	–	–	–	1	–	■	1	–	–	–	–	2	–	1	–	2	Sweden
Finland	1	–	–	–	1	–	–	■	–	–	–	–	–	–	–	1	–	Finland
Germany	–	–	–	–	1	–	1	–	■	1	1	–	1	–	–	1	1	Germany
Belgium	–	–	–	–	1	–	–	3	1	■	1	–	–	–	1	–	1	Belgium
United Kingdom	2	5	3	7	1	7	1	2	3	3	■	–	7	3	–	2	1	United Kingdom
Spain	1	1	1	–	2	–	–	–	–	1	–	■	–	2	1	–	–	Spain
Norway	1	–	–	–	–	–	1	–	–	–	–	–	■	–	–	–	–	Norway
Monaco	–	–	2	1	–	–	1	–	–	–	–	5	–	■	–	1	–	Monaco
Yugoslavia	–	1	–	1	1	–	–	–	–	1	–	2	–	–	■	1	–	Yugoslavia
Italy	–	–	–	–	–	1	–	–	–	–	1	1	–	–	–	■	1	Italy
Ireland	–	1	3	–	1	–	2	2	4	3	2	–	–	2	1	1	■	Ireland

1968

Hosting Country: United Kingdom

Hosting City: London

Date: 6.4.1968

Location: Royal Albert Hall

Presenter: Katie Boyle

Orchestra Conductor: Norrie Paramor

Chief Executive: Clifford Brown

Participating Countries: 17

Voting: Every country has a Jury that shared its 10 votes among one or more entries

Broadcaster: British Broadcasting Corporation (BBC)

Director: Stewart Morris

Executive Producer: Tom Sloan

Intermediate performance: Sights from London

Duration: 1 hour and 37 minutes

Broadcast: To all participating countries and to Bulgaria, Czechoslovakia, East Germany, Hungary, Poland, Romania, Soviet Union and Tunisia.

No.	Country	Song	Performing Artist	Lyrics	Composer	Conductor	Language	Commentator	Spoker of Results	Points	Place
01	Portugal	"Verão"	Carlos Mendes	José Alberto Diogo	Pedro Vaz Osório	Joaquim Luís Gomes	Portuguese	Fialho Gouveia	Maria Manuela Furtado	5	11
02	The Netherlands	"Morgen"	Ronnie Tober	Theo Strengers	Joop Stokkermans	Dolf van der Linden	Dutch	Elles Berger	Willem Duys	1	16
03	Belgium	"Quand tu reviendras"	Claude Lombard	Roland Dero	Jo van Wetter	Henri Segers	French	Janine Lambotte, Herman Verelst	André Hagon	8	7
04	Austria	"Tausend Fenster"	Karel Gott	Walter Brandin	Udo Jürgens	Robert Opratko	German	Willy Kralik	Walter Richard Langer	2	13
05	Luxembourg	"Nous vivrons d'amour"	Chris Baldo & Sophie Garel	Jacques Demarny	Carlos Leresche	André Borly	French	Jacques Navadic	Unknown	5	11
06	Switzerland	"Guardando il sole"	Gianni Mascolo	Sanzio Chiesa	Aldo D'Addario	Mario Robbiani	Italian	Theodor Haller, Georges Hardy, Giovanni Bertini	Alexandre Burger	2	13
07	Monaco	"À chacun sa chanson"	Line & Willy	Roland Valade	Jean-Claude Oliver	Michel Colombier	French	Pierre Tchernia	Unknown	8	7
08	Sweden	"Det börjar verka kärlek, banne mej"	Claes-Göran Hederström	Peter Himmelstrand	Peter Himmelstrand	Mats Olsson	Sweden	Christina Hansegård	Edvard Matz	15	5
09	Finland	"Kun kello käy"	Kristina Hautala	Juha Vainio	Esko Linnavalli	Ossi Runne	Finish	Aarno Walli	Poppe Berg	1	16
10	France	"La source"	Isabelle Aubret	Henri Dijan, Guy Bonnet	Daniel Faure	Alain Goraguer	French	Pierre Tchernia	Jean-Claude Massoulier	20	3
11	Italy	"Marianne"	Sergio Endrigo	Sergio Endrigo	Sergio Endrigo	-	Italian	Renato Tagliani	Mike Bongiorno	7	10
12	United Kingdom	"Congratulations"	Cliff Richard	Bill Martin, Phil Coulter	Bill Martin, Phil Coulter	Norrie Paramor	English	Pete Murray	Michael Aspel	28	2
13	Norway	"Stress"	Odd Børre	Ola B. Johannessen	Tor Hultin	Øivind Bergh	Norweigen	Roald Øyen	Sverre Christophersen	2	13
14	Ireland	"Chance of a Lifetime"	Pat McGuigan	John Kennedy	John Kennedy	Noel Kelehan	English	Brendan O'Reilly, Kevin Roche	Gay Byrne	18	4
15	Spain	"La, la, la"	Massiel	Manuel de la Calva Ramón Arcusa	Manuel de la Calva Ramón Arcusa	Rafael Ibarbia	Spanish	Federico Gallo, José María Íñigo	Ramón Rivera	29	1
16	Germany	"Ein Hoch der Liebe"	Wenche Myhre	Carl J. Schäuble	Horst Jankowski	Horst Jankowski	German	Hans-Joachim Rauschenbach	Hans-Otto Grünefeldt	11	6
17	Yugoslavia	"Jedan dan"	Dubrovački trubaduri (Hamo Hajdarhodžić and Luci Kapurso)	Stijepo Stražičić	Đelo Jusić, Stipica Kalogjera	Miljenko Prohaska	Croatian	Miloje Orlović, Mladen Delić, Tomaž Terček	Snežana Lipkovska-Hadžinaumova	8	7

	Portugal	The Netherlands	Belgium	Austria	Luxembourg	Switzerland	Monaco	Sweden	Finland	France	Italy	United Kingdom	Norway	Ireland	Spain	Germany	Yugoslavia	
Portugal	■	–	–	–	–	–	–	–	–	–	–	–	2	–	3	–	–	Portugal
The Netherlands	–	■	–	–	–	–	–	–	–	–	1	–	–	–	–	–	–	The Netherlands
Belgium	1	–	■	–	–	–	–	–	1	1	3	1	–	–	1	–	–	Belgium
Austria	–	–	–	■	–	–	–	–	–	–	–	–	–	–	–	2	–	Austria
Luxembourg	–	1	–	1	■	–	1	–	–	1	–	1	–	–	–	–	–	Luxembourg
Switzerland	–	–	–	–	–	■	–	–	–	–	–	–	–	–	–	–	3	Switzerland
Monaco	–	2	–	–	1	–	■	–	3	–	–	1	–	1	–	–	–	Monaco
Sweden	1	1	–	–	–	–	–	■	1	–	–	2	6	4	–	–	–	Sweden
Finland	–	–	–	–	–	–	–	–	■	–	–	–	1	–	–	–	–	Finland
France	–	3	6	2	3	3	–	1	–	■	2	–	–	–	–	–	–	France
Italy	1	–	–	–	–	2	–	–	–	–	■	–	–	–	2	–	2	Italy
United Kingdom	1	2	2	–	1	4	5	3	2	4	1	■	–	1		2	–	United Kingdom
Norway	–	–	–	–	1	–	–	–	–	–	–	–	■	–	1	–	–	Norway
Ireland	1	1	1	4	1	–	–	4	–	–	–	–	–	■	–	–	6	Ireland
Spain	4		–	2	1	–	4	–	3	4	3	–	1	1	■	6	–	Spain
Germany	–	–	–	–	1	1	–	2	–	–	–	5	–	–	2	■	–	Germany
Yugoslavia	1	–	1	1	1	–	–	–	–	–	–	–	–	3	1	–	■	Yugoslavia

1969

Hosting Country: Spain

Hosting City: Madrid

Date: 29.3.1969

Location: Teatro Real

Presenter: Laurita Valenzuela

Orchestra Conductor: Augusto Algueró

Chief Executive: Clifford Brown

Participating Countries: 16

Voting: Every country has a Jury that shared its 10 votes among one or more entries

Broadcaster: Televisión Española (TVE)

Director: Ramón Díez

Intermediate performance: the film "La España diferente"

Duration: 1 hour and 46 minutes

Broadcast: To all participating countries and to Austria, Brazil, Chile, Czechoslovakia, East Germany, Hungary, Morocco, Poland, Romania, Soviet Union and Tunisia

No.	Country	Song	Performing Artist	Lyrics	Composer	Conductor	Language	Commentator	Spoker of Results	Points	Place
01	Yugoslavia	"Pozdrav svijetu"	Ivan & 4M	Milan Lentić	Milan Lentić	Miljenko Prohaska	Croatian	Miloje Orlović, Mladen Delić, Tomaž Terček	Gordana Bonetti	5	13
02	Luxembourg	"Catherine"	Romuald	André di Fusco	Paul Mauriat, André Borgioli	Augusto Algueró	French	Jacques Navadic	Unknown	7	11
03	Spain	"Vivo cantando"	Salomé	Aniano Alcalde	María José de Cerato	Augusto Algueró	Spanish	José Luis Uribarri, Miguel de los Santos	Ramón Rivera	18	1
04	Monaco	"Maman, Maman"	Jean Jacques	Jo Perrier	Jo Perrier	Hervé Roy	French	Pierre Tchernia	Unknown	11	6
05	Ireland	"The Wages of Love"	Muriel Day & The Lindsays	Michael Reade	Michael Reade	Noel Kelehan	English	Gay Byrne, Kevin Roche	John Skehan	10	7
06	Italy	"Due grosse lacrime bianche"	Iva Zanicchi	Carlo Daiano	Piero Soffici	Ezio Leoni	Italian	Renato Tagliani	Mike Bongiorno	5	13
07	United Kingdom	"Boom Bang-a-Bang"	Lulu	Peter Warne	Alan Moorhouse	Johnny Harris	English	David Gell, Michael Aspel and Pete Murray	Colin-Ward Lewis	18	1
08	The Netherlands	"De troubadour"	Lenny Kuhr	Lenny Kuhr	David Hartsema	Frans de Kok	Dutch	Pim Jacobs	Leo Nelissen	18	1
09	Sweden	"Judy, min vän"	Tommy Körberg	Britt Lindeborg	Roger Wallis	Lars Samuelson	Swedish	Christina Hansegård	Edvard Matz	8	9
10	Belgium	"Jennifer Jennings"	Louis Neefs	Phil van Cauwenbergh	Paul Quintens	Francis Bay	Flemish	Herman Verelst, Paule Herreman	Ward Bogaert	10	7
11	Switzerland	"Bonjour, Bonjour"	Paola Del Medico	Jack Stark	Henry Mayer	Henry Mayer	German/French	Theodor Haller, Georges Hardy, Giovanni Bertini	Alexandre Burger	13	5
12	Norway	"Oj, oj, oj, så glad jeg skal bli"	Kirsti Sparboe	Arne Bendiksen	Arne Bendiksen	Øivind Bergh	Norweigen	Sverre Christophersen, Erik Heyerdahl	Janka Polanyi	1	16
13	Germany	"Primaballerina"	Siw Malmkvist	Hans Blum	Hans Blum	Hans Blum	German	Hans-Joachim Rauschenbach	Hans-Otto Grünefeldt	8	9
14	France	"Un jour, un enfant"	Frida Boccara	Eddy Marnay	Emil Stern	Franck Pourcel	French	Pierre Tchernia	Jean-Claude Massoulier	18	1
15	Portugal	"Desfolhada portuguesa"	Simone de Oliveira	Ary dos Santos	Nuno Nazareth Fernandes	Ferrer Trindade	Portuguese	Henrique Mendes	Maria Manuela Furtado	4	15
16	Finland	"Kuin silloin ennen"	Jarkko & Laura	Juha Vainio	Toivo Kärki	Ossi Runne	Finish	Aarno Walli	Aarre Elo	6	12

	Yugoslavia	Luxembourg	Spain	Monaco	Ireland	Italy	United Kingdom	The Netherlands	Sweden	Belgium	Switzerland	Norway	Germany	France	Portugal	Finland	
Yugoslavia	■	–	1	–	–	–	–	–	–	1	–	–	–	–	3	–	Yugoslavia
Luxembourg	1	■	–	3	–	–	–	1	–	1	–	–	1	–	–	–	Luxembourg
Spain	1	2	■	3	1	–	–	–	–	3	–	1	3	2	2	–	Spain
Monaco	–	–	2	■	–	4	–	2	2	1	–	–	–	–	–	–	Monaco
Ireland	–	–	–	–	■	–	1	1	1	–	3	–	1	–	–	3	Ireland
Italy	1	–	–	1	1	■	–	–	–	–	–	–	–	–	1	1	Italy
United Kingdom	2	4			–	3	■	1	5	–	–	–	1	–	1	1	United Kingdom
The Netherlands	–	2	–	1	–	3	–	■	–	1	4	1	–	6	–	–	The Netherlands
Sweden	–	–	–	–	–	–	–	1	■	–	–	3	–	–	1	3	Sweden
Belgium	–	–	2	–	–	–	3	1	–	■	2	2	–	–	–	–	Belgium
Switzerland	2	–	–	–	3	–	2	–	–	1	■	1	2	–	–	2	Switzerland
Norway	–	–	–	–	–	–	–	–	1	–	–	■	–	–	–	–	Norway
Germany	3	–	2	–	–	–	–	–	–	1	–	1	■	1	–	–	Germany
France	–	1	–	2	4	–	4	2	1	–	1	–	1	■	2	–	France
Portugal	–	–	2	–	–	–	–	–	–	1	–	–	–	1	■	–	Portugal
Finland	–	1	1	–	1	–	–	1	–	–	–	1	1	–	–	■	Finland

Ilanit became one of the most popular singers in Europe's media (1973) >> Photo by: Uri Aloni, in courtesy of Ilan Ben Shachar and the "Lahiton" archive

Dutch "Mouth & MacNeal" jolly and cheerful in Brighton

Anna Vissi in her early career, representing Greece in 1980 Eurovision >> Photo by: Uri Aloni, in courtesy of Ilan Ben Shachar and the "Lahiton" archive

Romina Power and Al Bano on stage in 1976, the Hague >> Photo by: Uri Aloni, in courtesy of Ilan Ben Shachar and the "Lahiton" archive

Dutch "Mouth & MacNeal" jolly and cheerful in Brighton >> Photo by: Uri Aloni, in courtesy of Ilan Ben Shachar and the "Lahiton" archive

Corinne Hermès in a rare moment of smile, Munich 1983 >> Photo by: Uri Aloni, in courtesy of Ilan Ben Shachar and the "Lahiton" archive

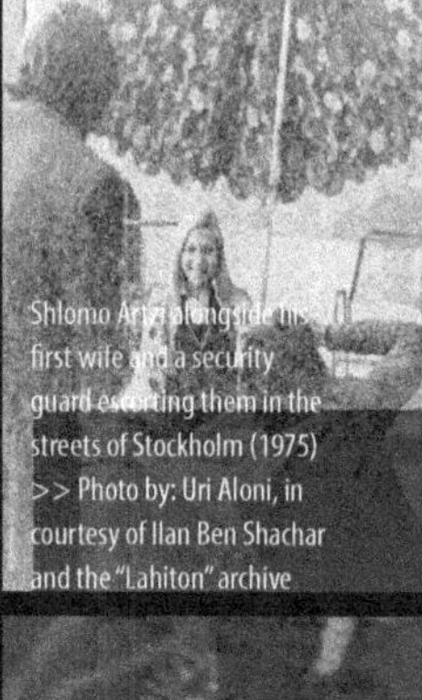

Shlomo Artzi alongside his first wife and a security guard escorting them in the streets of Stockholm (1975) >> Photo by: Uri Aloni, in courtesy of Ilan Ben Shachar and the "Lahiton" archive

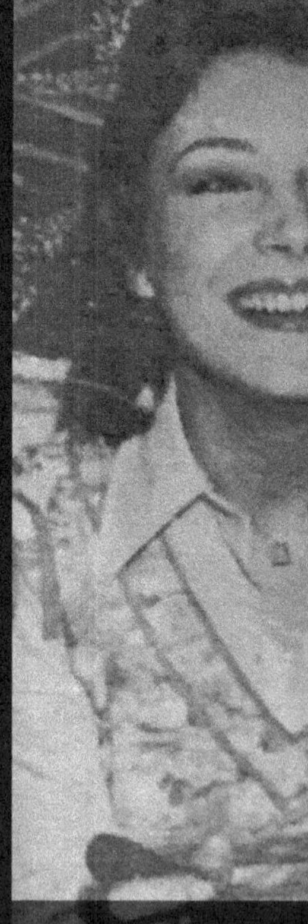

French Marie Myriam celebrating her birthday and victory of the 1977 contest.

>> Photo by: Uri Aloni, in courtesy of Ilan Ben Shachar and the "Lahiton" archive

Cliff Richard in an outstanding performance (1973) that was not enough for a victory. Uri Aloni, in courtesy of Ilan Ben Shachar and the "Lahiton" archive

Daniel Pe'er and Yardena Arazi successfully presenting the 1979 Eurovision held in Jerusalem >> Photo by: Uri Aloni, in courtesy of Ilan Ben Shachar and the "Lahiton" archive

Dutch "Teach In" celebrating its win, 1975 Eurovision >> Photo by: Uri Aloni, in courtesy of Ilan Ben Shachar and the "Lahiton" archive

"ABBA", winner of 1974 Eurovision, with "Forbes", last place in 1977 >> Photo by: Uri Aloni, in courtesy of Ilan Ben Shachar and the "Lahiton" archive

Vicky Leandros, 1972 Eurovision winner, in a souvenir photo with 1971 winner (Séverine) and Mary Roos, third place from the Edinburgh contest. >> Photo by Uri Aloni, in courtesy of Ilan Ben Shachar and the "Lahiton" archive

>> Photo by: Uri Aloni, in courtesy of Ilan Ben Shachar and the "Lahiton" archive

"Island", the first Cyprus representative, in 1981 Eurovision >> Photo by: Uri Aloni, in courtesy of Ilan Ben Shachar and the "Lahiton" archive

1970-1979

FROM "ABBA" TO HALLELUJAH

Luxembourg and Israel ruled the 1970s with two wins each. Five female singers won during this decade, but for the first time a prominent trend took over, with five of the last six winners of this decade belonging to bands! In the 1970s, the UK was again the most productive host, with the contest held on its land three times (Edinburgh, Brighton and London), compared to its one and only win...

1970 – Amsterdam, The Netherlands

After the 1969 farce, the 15th Eurovision was not festive, to say the least. Finland, Sweden, Norway and Portugal (despite having held a pre-selection) withdrew from the contest and left a rather poor number of participants: only a dozen. The main question was where would the event take place? In a discussion which sought to examine the issue at the EBU it was determined that after the last two Eurovisions were held in the United Kingdom and Spain (2 of the previous year's victors), it would be a toss-up between the Netherlands and France, when the Dutch would be the ones to receive the honour. Thus, in a relatively gloomy atmosphere, Dutch producer Warner van Kampen, was given a nearly impossible task. How could he extend this broadcast to fit a decent timeslot of an hour and a half? That is how the "postcards" between entries were born, clips that show the performers against a background of landscapes from their countries. Those with a sharp eye could notice that the Luxembourg and Monaco representatives were photographed, like the French entry, against the backdrop of Paris... And, apropos French, five of the twelve songs (almost half of the contest) were in this language! However, none of them finished among the top three. To add insult to injury, the entry that took last place was in French. The Amsterdam Convention Centre, founded in 1922 and renovated nine years before the contest, was chosen as the event venue. Utmost attention was given to the unique stage, designed by Roland de Groot: a semicircle, adorned with several curved horizontal metal bars and silver baubles that moved around. To this day, that stage is considered one of the five most magnificent stages seen at the Eurovision in the twentieth century. After a short four-minute-long promotional film of the Netherlands, the presenter, Willy Dobbe, introduced the entries and welcomed viewers in English, French and Dutch, in an introduction that lasted less than 30 seconds, and from that point the "postcards" and songs began. This model would continue to evolve in the years to come, abating the presenters' "burden" and adapting the contest to the style of television where pictures speak louder than words. While it was a drab and slightly depressing Eurovision, considering the circumstances, that did not prevent big names from participating and anonymous names from becoming major. For the first time since ESC came into existence, none of the participants were second timers, all this year's participants were "brand new". The host, the Netherlands, opened the event with "Waterman" by "Hearts of Soul", a trio of women singers, of which Stella, would appear twice in Eurovision. Their interesting vocal performance took the host to the seventh place with 7 points — more or less according to expectations.

Henri Dès won the 1969 Sopot Song Festival in Poland. A year later he was very hopeful to do the same for his country, Switzerland, at Eurovision. At the end of the day, the fourth joint place he reached was a great achievement for him and the beginning of a glorious career as a writer, composer and performer of children's songs, who is famous and successful to this day in all the French-speaking countries. Italy sent Gianni Morandi, a rising star in the country. The narrative is that the writer of the entry "Occhi di ragazza", the late Lucio Dalla — was one of the biggest musical icons in the boot-shaped country. It only reached eighth place, which was almost customary at Eurovision, to Italy's disappointment. Belgium reached the exact same place with its local icon — Jean Vallée, who wrote, composed and performed "Viens l'oublier" in his chanson style. Vallée's second attempt at taking the top of the European contest in 1978 would prove to be far more successful. "Marie-Blanche" was perhaps the most romantic song in the 1970 Eurovision. The performer, Guy Bonnet, one of the most talented musicians in France, perhaps was not in the fight for the first place, but he won the joint fourth place, and could certainly be satisfied with his performance that was accompanied by an enchanting piano score. As in 1968 and 1969, the bets were all only on the British who sent the popular Mary Hopkin, a "hit machine" who in retrospect greatly regretted her appearance in the contest and hated the song she performed, "Knock, Knock Who's There?" But in those days, the British song was the hottest thing on the European music scene, it was translated into many languages and sold like hotcakes. The beautiful Welsh singer's appearance did not hurt her chances, it looked like the UK had secured its third win in 4 years. During rehearsals Hopkin was slightly impatient, but on the evening of the show she took the stage with a smile, full of confidence, delivering a winning performance and conquering the audience. 26 points, twice as much as the country that finished in third place, were only enough to reach a most surprising second place. The British had been so confident in their victory that on the day of the event they had already handed out invitations to their victory party, which naturally did not take place in the end.... Luxembourg bet on a well-known international Dutch singer, David Alexandre Winter, who had great aspirations to win the Eurovision. In all the interviews and press conferences that preceded the big evening, Winter stated that only he could beat Mary Hopkin. The name of the song, "Je suis tombé du ciel" ("I Fell from Heaven"), predicted exactly what happened to him: he fell to the last place with Nul Points. The biggest name to participate in the 1970 contest, was, in fact, a singer who was relatively anonymous when he arrived, but in retrospect, it was a big gimmick: The story of Real Madrid's goalkeeper, who was forced to retire from football due to an accident and had started concentrating on music, captured many headlines in Europe. "Gwendolyne", was a hint of what was to come, and Julio Iglesias provided a taste of a high-quality, exciting stage performance that ended in fourth place alongside Switzerland and France. Germany, the great country and Music Empire, did not even come close to winning the Eurovision until the early 1970s. This time, the wonderful Katja Ebstein achieved the respectable third place for her country with the song "Wunder gibt es immer wieder" ("Miracles Keep Happening Again and Again"). And miracles did happen, but not for Katja Ebstein, rather for a high school student, from the war-ridden land of Northern Ireland. Those were exceedingly challenging times for poor and besieged Ireland, which had suffered tremendously from the frequent war between the British Empire and the Northern Irish underground which demanded independence. Dana, who, as a child, had experienced the pain of war, was selected by the Irish Broadcasting Authority to represent her country at the ESC in Amsterdam. It should be noted that their budget was so meagre that they could not afford the option of representation by well-known Irish artists who did not want to "go looking for trouble". Furthermore, Noel Kelehan, the immortal Irish conductor, was asked to stay home as they did not have the budget to fly him in with the extremely limited Irish delegation (the honour of conducting the Irish song was reluctantly accepted by Dolf van der Linden). "All Kinds of Everything", for some reason, did not attract the attention of the gambling agencies or of any of the reporters who were at rehearsals and showed nothing more than a little sympathy for the Irish girl. A sign of what was to come could be seen at the end of the dress rehearsal, when three Dutch orchestra players put their instruments down, stood up and applauded the Irish girl. On the evening of the show, Dana put on a passionate performance, perched on a bar stool, won the most audience applause, and it turned out, also the jurors' commendations.

The audience was treated to an artistic performance by the Don Lurio Dancers with their amazing moves on stage that enthralled the crowd. This time it was clear that there would be a ruling for any situation that might occur in a decision that would change in the years ahead, it was determined that if two or more songs finished with a tie, they would go on to a final, perform their entry again and then a jury (one of jurors would be from the first round) from every country would decide between them. This system has never been tested before. There was no doubt that Ireland and the UK would go head-to-head for the win. The winds of history blew strongly enough, when Belgium awarded no less than 9 points (out of a possible 10!) to Ireland, to everyone's amazement.

From that moment it was clear that whatever happened, Victory would be Dana's. This, despite the fierce competition from Mary Hopkin, who received points from 9 of the eleven countries, as opposed to Dana who received points from eight. Bottom line, the 32 points achieved by the Irish winner left no room for doubt. At the end of the vote, Dana took the stage to the clicking of the media cameras covering the event, which turned her into the Queen of Europe for one evening and, possibly for a lifetime, into — Queen of Ireland. When landing in Dublin, she was greeted like royalty and did not hide her excitement. She was asked to — and performed — "All Kinds of Everything" at the foot of the plane. For the average Irishman it was a festive day: "We have never won anything. Even the bread we want to eat we have not won … Dana enlightened our lives." One could say that the story of Dana's victory somewhat saved the prestige of Eurovision and gave it a positive and optimistic turn.

1971 – Dublin, Ireland

After the slump, the Eurovision Song Contest had come to at the beginning of its third decade, it was decided that a self-examination and reorganization had to be conducted. And, indeed, the EBU submitted to almost all requirements of the withdrawing countries (Sweden, Norway, Finland, Austria and Portugal), and completely changed the voting system, adding both cosmetic and organizational changes that gave it a facelift — On April 3rd, 1971, eighteen countries presented themselves in Dublin to participate in the most widely viewed Eurovision until that time. The whole of Ireland was festive, and it seemed that hosting the ESC was the topic of the day on every street corner in the capital Dublin in particular, and in the whole country in general. The proud and determined Irish, who knew that this contest was their window to the wider world and the opportunity to show off a bit of their country, besides the political and economic issues they were facing at the time, had many challenges to contend with. The venue was prone to problems from the outset, but the Irish refused to compromise: The small Gaiety Theatre was the country's most beautiful hall, but it could not accommodate more than a few hundred spectators at best. Additionally, they needed sufficient space for an orchestra and design a stage. In the end, the Irish managed to complete their task, although the presenter, Bernadette Ní Ghallchóir, did her job from a special booth in the stands and not on the stage... The love-hate relationship between the United Kingdom and Ireland was complex but fascinating. Even UK's greatest Irish critics admitted that without the BBC's assistance it was doubtful that the Irish RTE could have produced the complex televised event: All Irish television equipment was intended for black and white broadcasting, and the local network had never produced a bilateral broadcast at this level. In addition to providing cameras and other professional equipment, the British crews were intricately linked to the Irish production in all steps prior to the contest and during the actual broadcast. As part of the changes and innovations made prior to the 1971 edition, 6 participants from each country were allowed to take the stage (as opposed to one-third of the it in previous years); Each country had to produce a preliminary clip of the entry that represented them and broadcast the songs of the participating countries in two broadcasts close to the date of the event; each participant was also tasked with bringing a 30 second promotional video, showing the representative country, to be aired before its performance. The Eurovision became a festive event, not only in Ireland, but in every Irish community in the world. Thereupon, for the first time in history, ESC was broadcast in the United States — due to the immense pressure from other major Irish communities in New York and Massachusetts, which probably increased the numbers of viewers to close to a billion (!). Noel Kelehan, the legendary Irish conductor who was hurt after not being sent with Dana to the Eurovision in Amsterdam due to lack of funding, demonstratively refused to be the hosting orchestra's chief conductor, so the honour (and the baton) fell into the hands of Colman Pearce, who was the only conductor in the contest's history (together with the Israeli, Ziko Graziani in 1979), who conducted the contest orchestra — but not one entry that contested in it. Austria returned to Eurovision after a three-year break with the powerful Marianne Mendt, but not even the dramatic entry "Musik" and singing in the Viennese dialect — helped the country that opened the event abscond from the disappointing sixteenth place. A new participant entered the contest: Malta. "Marija l-Maltija" was the song that started a tradition that begun badly for the Maltese. Joe Grech, who sang in Maltese rather than English (as was expected), finished in last place, and thanks to the new system, not with Nul Points. Most of the betting agencies and journalists had pointed to Monaco as a definite and almost sure-fire favourite. This time, the bet turned out to be true: An all-French team starring an impressive (but anonymous) Séverine, gave the sovereign state the historic victory. "Un banc, un arbre, une rue", is still considered one of the highest quality entries in the history of the contest. Throughout rehearsals, the song that talks about the loss of innocence, attracted attention, and on the evening of the contest everything ran smoothly, en route to a big, one-time victory for Monte-Carlo. Peter, Sue and Marc — the legendary trio — performed four times as representatives of Switzerland at Eurovision. Each of the four times, in a different language. In "Les illusions de nos vingt ans", the trio asked in French for "The Illusions of their Twenties", and despite lofty expectations to be included at least in the top five, the Swiss only finished twelfth. In Amsterdam, Katja Ebstein, who brought Germany its greatest achievement — third place — was introduced to the world. The Germans saw an opportunity and sent their winning card again, hoping she could reach two places higher. "Diese Welt" was considered an extraordinarily strong competitor and was in the top five for every bet leading up to the big night. Ebstein's exceptional performance, was eventually able to bring it back to the very respectable third place, with 100 points. Spain's beautiful years continued in Dublin as well: this time the Spaniards sent Karina who was marked as well, during rehearsals, as a dark horse that could surprise. "En un mundo nuevo", was a hit in South American countries, and even though Karina's microphone malfunctioned in the first 5 seconds of performance, she did not stop giving Séverine a run for her money, until finishing in impressive second place — the third best achievement of all time for Spain. France sent Serge Lama, a household name in Francophone music. "Un jardin sur la terre" is a classic, remembered by many, but that evening, Lama dropped to tenth place — very disappointing for the country that had not declined from fourth place since 1966. Luxembourg, after having failed with Dutch singer David Alexandre Winter the previous year, made a rare decision to send a local singer. This had only happened eight times in Luxembourg's history at Eurovision, however "Pomme, pomme, pomme" was one of the most popular and most-played songs in the period before the contest in Europe, and afterwards. Monique Melsen, at the time a music teacher, wore a long, conservative attire for rehearsals, and as the week progressed, she decided, on the advice of the Irish production team, to wear a slightly showier outfit until at the actual evening of the event, to the amazement of her delegation, she performed in a particularly short skirt, which ultimately did not change the fact that she finished thirteenth. The story of the contest was that of Clodagh Rodgers. The Northern Irish singer, who was immensely popular in both England and Ireland, accepted the offer to represent the United Kingdom. The British took a calculated step: they believed that thanks to Rodgers's popularity, they could win the sympathy of the Irish. They were mistaken. Clodagh received many threats to her life from the Irish underground as well as a cold shoulder from the local production team during rehearsals. "Jack in the Box" had amazing potential for a third British win at Eurovision; Rodgers was wonderful, some of the local audience avoided applauding her and she eventually won fourth place. That very evening was the British broadcaster, Terry Wogan's (Irish Eurovision Icon) debut broadcast of the European contest, a position that he would return to in different variations until presenting the event in 1998 — and well after. The duo, Nikol and Hugo were selected to represent Belgium with "Goeiemorgen, morgen". However, a sudden illness that struck Nikol before rehearsals in the Irish Capital, forced the Belgians to rush and find a replacement duo, who would quickly learn the song, rushed to rehearsals and succeeded in accomplishing the feat… for Lily Castel & Jacques Raymond, finishing the evening in fourteenth place was equivalent to finishing in first place. Massimo Ranieri, the Italian vocalist, came to Dublin with a rich and distinguished resume. Ranieri (stage name for Giovanni Calone) brought his country its best achievement since 1965 — fifth place. The return of the Scandinavian countries rejuvenated the contest. Sweden began a tradition that would break records, being the first to send a band to Eurovision: "Family Four" (two men and two women — a familiar format that would repeat itself three years later) — that sang "Vita vidder" and positioned their country sixth. Their partner in this place, the Netherlands, with Saskia & Serge, introduced "Tijd" — which was particularly loved by the local audience. A year after Dana, Ireland took a complete change of direction with Angela Farrell and "One Day Love", a beautiful but slightly outdated musical piece, which was only deserving of eleventh place. Tonicha from Portugal was convinced that she would bring her country its best achievement. "Menina do alto da serra" swept the Portuguese pre-selection and the heart-warming appearance by the brunette singer from Beja, gave hope that Portugal would finally break through its own ceiling and reach the top five. Despite a superior performance, Tonicha finished ninth, being only 10 points away from the top players. The last to appear on stage was also the youngest performer in the contest — Norwegian Hanne Krogh. Under the honourable cloak of Arne Bendiksen (who wrote, composed, and also conducted "Lykken er"), with an umbrella in her hand and a conquering smile, the 15-year-old had hoped to achieve a little more than the penultimate place she eventually "won". 14 years later she would return to Eurovision — this time as the big winner. A traditional Irish operatic performance separated the entries and the voting results — the biggest innovation to the 1971 ESC. For the first time, one could see the local juries in the adjacent studio: Each country had a jury made up of two people, one over 25 years of age and the second, under 25. Each jury had a scoreboard that they controlled, with points from 1 to 5. The jury presented its score for each song for the public to see.

All the juries, similarly to a courtroom jury, were housed in a hotel away from the event centre to avoid any influence over them until the opening of the contest. The main advantages of the new method: The fact that the juries could be seen — was befitting for a television broadcast. With the results visible, nobody was worried about shady business in play, and of course, with this system, no country would end up with Nul Points. But there were also several drawbacks to this system, mainly: Juries who, out of a desire for their country to win, would give low scores to favourite entries, disinterest and lack of drama during the voting process. In any case, this method would only last for three consecutive Eurovision before going away. Among the juries, Gaetano Abela, the Maltese television representative who was the head of Malta's delegation from Eurovision 1991 to the early 2000s, was recognizable. Another novelty was a scoreboard with electronic numbers. One could say that this board was ahead of its time by several years. From the start of the vote, Monaco, who Spain unsuccessfully chased, stood out.

Of course, the Spanish had to make a minor scandal, awarding Monaco no more than 2 points (one point and one point-the lowest possible score), the only ones to do so. It felt as if they were just putting a spoke in the wheels of those who were standing between them and the victory, which is certainly possible. Nonetheless, even that did not manage to ruin Monaco's glorious Grand Prix. The victorious Séverine, who returned to the stage thrilled to receive the prize and sing the winning song again, acknowledged that she had never been to Monaco, except for the time she was filmed for the entry's clip ... That was also the reason that there was not much excitement in the principality following the honourable victory and that Séverine did not receive the welcome of a hero — she went directly from Dublin to Paris. It was just a victory recorded in the pages of history, which remains there, lacking any emotion or eminence.

1972 – Edinburgh, United Kingdom

The 1972 Eurovision was supposed to take place in Monaco. From the moment Séverine won, everyone was very curious to know how the event could take place in the affluent and closed off sovereign state. Since Monaco did not have a state broadcasting authority, the EBU sent a letter directly to Rainier III, Prince of Monaco, covering the conditions for hosting the European song contest in the Principality. The royal palace consulted and a few days later, a decision was made that the Sovereign State would not be able to produce the contest in its territory, not necessarily for financial reasons, but rather for logistical and security reasons. Before delivering its negative reply to the European authority, Monaco tried to bargain and negotiated with French television about organising the event in Cannes or Nice, bordering on the sovereign state. The French were willing to take on the hosting, but Monaco demanded that the broadcast and content of the event be under its control. France refused to take on hosting under these conditions, and the case was returned to the EBU. A month and a half prior to the contest, it was clear that both Spain, which had finished second the previous year, and Germany, which had finished third — would not be able to meet the conditions. As usual in these situations, the one to pick up the gauntlet on this challenge was the BBC, and the Eurovision was held, for the fourth time, in the UK, this time not in England — but in Edinburgh — the proud Scottish capital. "Usher Hall" situated in the cultural centre of Edinburgh, seats 3,000 and is known as one of the rarely preserved buildings in the Scottish capital as well as for its outstanding acoustics. The contest was presented in a conservative and orderly way by Moira Shearer, a well-known Scottish actor and dancer (she can be credited with pulling off the evening without making any mistakes or blunders). In December 1971, three months before the event, while on reserve duty in the Israeli army, Uri Aloni — the publisher, founder and executive editor of the Israeli magazine "Lahiton" — found out that Israel had been invited to participate in the 1972 Eurovision. However, the local broadcasting authority had turned the invitation down, for budgetary reasons. Aloni, who immediately realized the event's potential for the Israeli entertainment world in particular and the young country in general, placed an urgent call to Rebecca Bahiri, spokesperson of the Authority, and urged her to change the decision, promising that he would finance Israel's participation in the contest. A few days later Bahiri responded with a disappointing answer: "We are too late, registration for this year's Eurovision is closed". The Israeli audience, however, took comfort in a first and historic broadcast of the contest in the Holy Land. This is alongside countries like Iceland, Taiwan, Thailand, the Philippines, Hong Kong, Greece and Brazil — where it turns out, there is a loyal and dedicated Eurovision audience. The event's stage featured ornate lighting, a huge screen on the back of the stage designed to showing pictures of the singers who took the stage,

Germany opened the event in a flurry, with the highly confident singer, Mary Roos. "Nur die Liebe läßt uns leben" — did not advance the Germans — they placed third, for the third time in a row — but this kept them at the top of the European music scene. Roos would return to Eurovision 12 years later. For the first time, an Irish song was performed in Gaelic and not in English. Sandie Jones remains the only person to have ever done this, but it was not enough for more than a lowly fifteenth place, which made it clear to the Irish that it would be better to sing in its other popular official language (English). Jaime Morey's "Amanece", marked an uncharacteristic Spanish drop to the tenth place, despite expectations and the fact that the entry was written by Ramón Arcusa, who had some outstanding achievements at Eurovision, as well as being one of Spain's most esteemed musicians. The hot favourite to win was, almost as usual, the host: "The New Seekers" conquered the charts even before the contest with "Beg, Steal or Borrow", and they came to the rehearsals in Edinburgh full of confidence and optimism. In the Scottish capital, the English band gained an unprecedented amount of popularity. Besides the fact that the representative entry was played non-stop on the radio, a giant poster was hung in the airport of the Scottish capital greeting "The New Seekers". Absurdly, all the delegations arriving from overseas encountered the poster, which was rather insulting to them — whereas the English band actually arrived in Edinburgh by train and never saw the sign... Despite their remarkable performance in the contest, as it turns out, somebody else held the key to victory, and the hosts only finished in the second place, again. When the voting was over, the band left the hall disappointed and shocked by the fact that they did not win and returned immediately to the hotel where they were staying. Apropos the hotel, large groups of adoring fans gathered every evening under expectations and the fact that the entry was written by Ramón Arcusa, who had some outstanding achievements at Eurovision, as well as being one of Spain's most esteemed musicians. The hot favourite to win was, almost as usual, the host: "The New Seekers" conquered the charts even before the contest with "Beg, Steal or Borrow", and they came to the rehearsals in Edinburgh full of confidence and optimism. In the Scottish capital, the English band gained an unprecedented amount of popularity. Besides the fact that the representative entry was played non-stop on the radio, a giant poster was hung in the airport of the Scottish capital greeting "The New Seekers". Absurdly, all the delegations arriving from overseas encountered the poster, which was rather insulting to them — whereas the English band actually arrived in Edinburgh by train and never saw the sign... Despite their remarkable performance in the contest, as it turns out, somebody else held the key to victory, and the hosts only finished in the second place, again. When the voting was over, the band left the hall disappointed and shocked by the fact that they did not win and returned immediately to the hotel where they were staying. Apropos the hotel, large groups of adoring fans gathered every evening under "The New Seekers'" hotel room window. One of the group's singers, Marty Kristian, said that he received at the time about a hundred marriage proposals a week... Norway's entry "Småting", was the dark horse, according to the reporters who attended the rehearsals and fell in love with Grethe Kausland and Benny Borg. But the Norwegian duo, despite giving an enjoyable performance on the big evening, was disappointed, like the whole Nordic country, who perhaps expected a first victory and finished far from it in fourteenth place. Another country that hoped to win was Portugal, which sent Carlos Mendes again (he had performed in 1968) — with hopes that indeed vanished, but on the other hand, he reached seventh place. "A festa da vida" was one of Portugal's most successful songs and was also widely listened to in Spain. Poor Malta failed to rise from last place in 1971 and finished again, in exactly the same spot — a negative record — nothing like this had been seen before. "L-imħabba" by Helen and Joseph, performed in Maltese, remained behind all the other entries, and Malta took a three-year break to regroup and erase the disgrace. Austria's "Milestones" band brought with it a new, rhythmic spirit with "Falter im Wind" and finished fifth, with its head held high. The great Eurovision success did not satisfy the Austrians who saw themselves as favourites to win and were convinced that a different scoring method would have made them victorious. Therefore, they announced at the end of the contest that they would no longer participate in Eurovision until the scoring method was changed. Another strong favourite to win was Italy. Sanremo Festival winner, Nicola Di Bari, brought "I giorni dell'arcobaleno", which is considered a sequel to the famous song "L'arce di noe", also performed by him. Di Bari received the most attention during rehearsals with his charming and romantic song, and there was an impression that Italy was on its way to a second win. Many Italians were present in the hall, watching and cheering on Nicola's performance, but the juries thought otherwise. The sixth place that he reached made it clear that the Italian classics, despite remaining in the consciousness of the music world for many years, were not appreciated by the ESC juries in real-time. Another singer who returned to the contest after a tough failure in 1966 (last place with Nul Points for Monaco), was Tereza Kesovija, The Croatian, who proudly represented her country, Yugoslavia, this time. Nikica Kalogjera composed and conducted "Muzika i ti", Tereza delivered with a sweeping performance, and in the end, the Yugoslavs settled for ninth place. On an evening of so many favourites and discoveries, Sweden had hoped to get into the top five, with the help of the band that had represented it at the previous Eurovision. This time, "Family Four" performed Härliga sommardag" (a contrast to the wintery entry it sang the previous year) and only reached 13th place. Despite everything, Sweden would continue its band tradition for the next two years. Monaco did not make much of an effort to defend its title and win another victory. Local singers, Anne-Marie Godart and Peter MacLane gave a dull performance of "Comme on s'aime". The sixteenth place, two from last, definitely reflected the disappointment, including that of Séverine — the previous year's winner — who preferred to leaf through the programme during the entry that represented the country she had won for the previous year.... The topic of the day was Vicky Leandros. The Greek singer who had performed one of the most beautiful songs in Eurovision's history in 1967 "L'amour est bleu" and who "only" reached fourth place, was called up to the Luxembourg flag again, this time not willing to settle for less than what she eventually achieved. Vicky came to rehearsals anticipating a tough fight with the British and Nicola Di Bari, but from day to day she positioned herself as the main candidate for victory. "Après toi" was written by Yves Dessca, who broke a personal record and is to this day the only writer in the history of Eurovision to win twice in a row (doing so for two different countries). Leandros soared to new heights thanks to "Après toi" and the German crew and made a name for herself in Europe and Canada with the cross-border hit. An impressive and flawless performance fostered the expectation of the win to come. Unexpectedly, the last song of the evening was the surprise of the contest. Sandra Reemer and Dries Holten, who performed as the Sandra and Anders duo, captivated the crowd with "Als het om de liefde gaat" and won the most generous applause, which probably influenced the juries who positioned the Dutch duo very firmly in the race for the first place, propelling them into fourth place. While the juries calculated the results, the audience watched a typical Scottish show: a local orchestra that played traditional music at Edinburgh Castle. For the Scots, it was a wonderful opportunity to market their culture to 400 million viewers. Yet again, a tedious and tension-free voting system was applied, which, although it created an unprecedented situation where there was no equal number of points shared by any countries in the placing, what had been considered the last treat of the Eurovision, had lost its dramatic effect almost entirely. Starting from the first set of results, there was no doubt

that Luxembourg would be the winner and indeed it was a loud and clear victory to Vicky Leandros, with 128 points, 14 above her opponent in second place, the United Kingdom. However, the Spanish voted scornfully once again: This country's jury team continued the tradition of giving the lowest score to the country that was the candidate to win (in hope that this would hurt their chances for the first place, leaving the way open for Spain). Thus, unbelievably, Luxembourg, the UK and Italy only got 2 points (1 + 1) from the Spaniards, who convinced everyone that they had decided on their vote before they left home. None of this stopped Vicky Leandros from finally smiling and relieving her tension, to perform "Après toi" again and win Luxembourg's third victory in its history, second only to France. Furthermore, Luxembourg became the only country in the history of the contest, with two of its victories (1965 and 1972) apparent from the first all the way through to the last vote.

1973 – Luxembourg City, Luxembourg

Eurovision 1973 constituted an all-time record in many ways. Luxembourg, which had struggled over the years to manifest its presence and excellence in the European contest and to use it as an invaluable opportunity to market the small principality to the world (in a survey conducted in the 1980s by RTL, 81% of respondents around the globe said they learned about the existence of Luxembourg solely from the Eurovision), hosted the event at the state-of-the-art Grand Theatre, in Luxembourg City. Until then, Eurovision events were held without concern about terrorist incidents and the formal security atmosphere was relatively sleepy. Until 1973, no one had given any thought to security and safety at all, despite the loophole calling out to terrorists in the form of, god forbid, an attack with exposure to a billion people. It is doubtful that those who wholeheartedly approved Israel's participation in the Eurovision thoroughly understood the implications this would have. Six months prior to the event in Luxembourg, 11 Israelis were massacred at the 1972 Olympics in Munich. Since then, all the red lights were on with preparations made accordingly, at every international event attended by Israelis. Consequently, for the first time, the ESC, which had been created in order to unify Western Europe, found itself deep in a political conflict against its will. Israel had the right to participate as it was a member of the EBU — although geographically it is not part of the Old Continent. Eurovision challenged the Luxembourgers, who were not at all accustomed to such problems, with the most difficult security issue the sovereign state had faced since its inception. "The tension of the security situation could already be felt at the registration for the event", publisher of the Israeli magazine "Lahiton", Uri Aloni, said. "At 1972 Eurovision in Edinburgh, I received a simple name tag, while in Luxembourg they have already demanded that it have a photo on it too, as part of the effort to reduce the possibility of a terrorist attack. Security personnel were constantly walking around the hall and the seventh floor at the 'Holiday Inn' where the Israeli delegation was staying, which became a sterile area". The hosts needed the guidance of the Israeli and German security forces. They would not take any risks and set strict and harsh rules, the likes of which had never been seen before in the European song contest. About a week before the event, with the arrival of the Israeli delegation and the opening of rehearsals, the "Grand Theatre" became a sterile territory, the Israeli flag was flown alongside the flags of all the other participating countries and any car that merely approached the area of the hall was stopped for questioning. Before the show opened, at the traditional audience briefing, the stage manager implored: "Please stay seated throughout the evening, do not get up, otherwise you might get shot". The only ones who had the opportunity to get up and move around freely during the evening were the artists, who sat in the special artists' stand set up in the corner of the hall where they awaited the final results. Before the Spanish singer's performance, one of the audience members who apparently wanted to get up and stretch his legs, was about to stand up, but when he was unequivocally screamed at by the chief security officer, he immediately sat back down. Beyond the security challenge, which Luxembourg ultimately carried out successfully, it was assisted by the BBC, who flew many crews out to the sovereign state, and actually produced a first-of-its-kind event held outside the United Kingdom. In fact, most locals were indifferent to the Eurovision. Well-known television personality, Helga Guitton, was chosen as presenter and gracefully did an incredibly decent job. Luxembourg certainly managed to renovate a spacious stage, adorned with a huge gold medal and for the first time the orchestra was set up in a three level, semi-circle, around the stage. It was a novelty that has never repeated itself since, partially due to how difficult it was for the conductors to control a scattered orchestra and of course the acoustics were also ruined, and this could be discerned in the television broadcast with the missing string instruments. The rule forcing every country to sing in its official language had been abolished, opening up a flood of English songs, which was used by the three Scandinavian delegates Finland, Norway and Sweden — that brought them their best results in years. Strangely, this Eurovision was only seen in Europe. No country outside the Old Continent broadcast the contest. However, it is estimated that nearly half a billion viewers watched it. Beyond that, this ESC was one of the most watched broadcasts on Europe's broadcasting channels, earning a record rating, which has not been matched to this day. The honour of opening the evening fell to Finland. The Jewish singer, Marion Rung, who had also participated in 1962, returned re-energised and the entry "Tom Tom Tom", which she decided to sing in English, came in at sixth place, the highest spot ever for the Finns (up to the end of the previous millennium) and gained great popularity in Europe. Nicole & Hugo were unlucky again: The Belgian duo who missed 1971 Eurovision by just days due to Nicole's illness returned to represent their country with "Baby, Baby" and despite their unusual costume and movements on stage, the Belgians finished last. Germany continued the tradition of representation by Scandinavian singers, this time by Danish singer Gitte with "Junger Tag", which marched to the eighth place. Arne Benediksen continued to dominate Norway. This time he formed a quartet called "The Bendik Singers" and the entry "It's Just A Game" broke a record for containing words in no less than 11 (!) languages. This international concoction took the Norwegians to the seventh place, which was extraordinarily successful for them. The Spanish golden age continued and this time there was no doubt that "Eres tú" sung by the Mocedades from the Basque city of Bilbao, would take the first place. There is no doubt that this is perhaps the greatest Spanish Eurovision entry of all time, even though it only came second to another great song, people treat it as though it is a winner in its own right. The first Spanish performance by a band captivated the hearts of the audience and this was the beginning of a tremendous career for "The Mocedades" which continues to this day. Hints of the future of the ESC could be seen in the performance by Swiss singer, Patrick Juvet (who also wrote a song for Mike Barnett). Although the successful pop singer sang "Je vais me marier, Marie" ("I´m Getting Married, Mary"), few knew that he was actually "bisexual", (which he acknowledged in his biography), a subject that has become commonplace and prevalent in a contest, which in the 2000s has become a kind of proud home for the LGBT community. Switzerland put a lot of faith in its star, but despite an optimistic performance, he only reached twelfth place. It was an outstanding Eurovision, partially due to the performer who only finished 15th, Zdravko Čolić of Yugoslavia. Čolić, known as the Balkan Tom Jones, is the all-time greatest Yugoslavian singer and tickets to his concerts are always sold-out months in advance. "Gori vatra" ("The Fire Is Burning"), is still burning today in the heart of every ex-Yugoslav, a classic that is one of the pillars of his Serbian-Bosnian performances. Massimo Ranieri visited Eurovision again, after a two-year hiatus and he will not remember 1973 fondly. "Chi sarà con te" only took him to thirteenth place and he would continue his remarkably successful musical journey at the Sanremo Festival. "Tu te reconnaîtras", performed by Anne-Marie David is perhaps the most successful entry in the history of Eurovision in several aspects. David, the French singer who emerged from nowhere to represent Luxembourg and won with her catchy song and impeccable performance, faced a difficult challenge. With very tough competitors, an orchestra that was missing the violins' voice (which played an especially important part in the song), and with no accompanists on stage (who were also missing), Anne-Marie took the stage to win and that is what she eventually did. Few people know, but on the day of the actual show, after lunch, Anne-Marie David's show dress was stained... The singer, frightened and in a hurry, began to walk around the streets of Luxembourg to urgently find a new dress. According to her, the sellers showed surprising indifference and she scolded them: "If you don't mind, I'm representing your country at Eurovision tonight" ... In the end Anne-Marie managed to purchase a red dress that went down in history. Sweden continued with the tradition of bands. The most interesting story happened at the Swedish Melodifestivalen, where their representative for the contest was selected: The second place was won by none other than the band... "ABBA". Who knows what would have happened if "ABBA" had actually won the 1973 local pre-select with a song of lower quality to the contest to compete against much stronger songs? In any case, "You're Summer", by "The Novas", became one of the most successful songs from the contest in Luxembourg and took fifth place. Sweden also made history when, for the first time, a woman — Monica Dominique — who did an excellent job, conducted the ESC orchestra. The stage was lit up during all the entries except the Dutch one. Ben Cramer, accompanied by an accordionist, wanted dark lighting and hoped to glean a good result with "De oude muzikant", a slightly nostalgic song that did not meet the pace and standards of that evening. There was a huge blow-up in the Irish delegation between the high-ranking singer — Maxi and the Dublin television heads, revolving around the pace and arrangement of "Do I Dream". Decca Records, the company that represented the singer, demanded that she should sing as she did on the studio recording, while the Irish television crew insisted that Maxi perform "Do I Dream" exactly as she had in the local pre-selection. On the day of the show itself, the Irish delegation decided to fly Tina Reynolds to Luxembourg and the latter actually landed at 6 pm, three hours before Eurovision began (!), to replace Maxi. But while Reynolds was in the air, the parties settled on a certain change in the refrain and Maxi performed as planned and took the tenth place. The disappointed Tina Reynolds, waited exactly a year to get onto the Eurovision stage, and this time not as a designated stand-in. After the embarrassment in 1968, the great Cliff Richard became obsessed with winning the ESC. After waiting five years, he decided it was time to take the European contest by storm again and also had an excellent entry "Power to All Our Friends". It was not a huge, sweeping hit like "Congratulations", but was still a definite favourite to win the contest, and everyone who watched the rehearsal were also willing to put money on it. Cliff managed everything: from the fact that he wanted to skip the traditional conductor shot at the opening of the song and open directly with himself, through a modern stance to the dance moves that completed the stage performance. Only him the performance on the big evening was simply perfect, and it was followed by the feeling that the UK would win again, and Cliff would finally close the circle. The juries awarded him 123 points, which should have been enough for first place, had it not been for that one-off evening in Luxembourg, where there were another two immortal songs... France, which was used to reaching respectable achievements at Eurovision, recorded a rare setback. "Sans toi" raised many expectations in Paris, and before the Eurovision event the local press reported that Martine Clémenceau would run neck and neck with Cliff Richard for the first place. In practice, as mentioned, it did not really work, and the French fell to the penultimate place which was very disappointing for them. "If I was afraid of any of the competitors, it was you", Anne-Marie David told Ilanit, Israel's representative at Eurovision, who was the last representative to perform that evening, in what was considered the most important moment of her life. Ilanit had an unreal week in Luxembourg. The Israeli singer was the most sought-after of the artists participating in the contest and was stubbornly and enthusiastically pursued by all the media which came to review the event. Ehud Manor wrote the adorable lyrics for "Ey Sham", and Boris Julich's arrangement in the song's recording in Munich was magnificent. The song composer argued with the producer, Shlomo Zach, during rehearsals. The latter rightly demanded that the song open powerfully with the refrain, thus increasing Ilanit's chances, but eventually settled for a quiet opening with the piano. Unaccompanied, wearing a Bedouin dress, with incredible composure, she performed the first Israeli entry ever in Eurovision in the most perfect way. The cheers from the local audience at the end said it all. The fourth place she won was a rare achievement, especially considering those who ranked before her. Incidentally, the Bedouin dress she wore was not an armoured dress — despite the rumours surrounding the issue. Israel's first performance in Eurovision was made possible — as stated — by Uri Aloni, Editor and founder of the Israel "Lahiton" magazine, who arranged the financing of Ilanit's and the song composer's flights, thanks to sponsorship on the cover of his popular weekly magazine by the tourism company "Daphna

Tours"...

Aloni himself refused to miss the first celebration of his creation and was the travel partner and roommate of promoter and producer Shlomo Zach. For the first time in history the artistic show included a clown. Spanish "Charlie Rivel" was given the stage, making him the most famous clown in Europe and setting him up afterwards for numerous appearances on the continent. In retrospect, it is not certain that such a show would even be approved for children today... The new voting system ended after this Eurovision. The decision was made, although this time, unlike the previous two, it was a remarkably close race that was only decided in the final round, with Luxembourg and the UK fighting an intriguing duel for first place. In the end, Anne-Marie David had the upper hand. Spain, with a solid finish, came second and Cliff Richard, despite his superb performance, only came in at third place. The artists were placed in a side room and sat next to each other, in neat rows without any tables, as would become customary in the future in every "green room", with Cliff Richard, (like in 1968) choosing to be alone again and not wait for the results with his colleagues. Among the juries, there was a former singer who had participated in Eurovision — Paola of Switzerland, perhaps the most famous person to serve as juror using this system. The person who "stole the show" from Paola was the other anonymous Swiss jury who was above her and behaved strangely and childishly (he waved his hands,made funny faces, and ridiculous gestures), which provoked the wrath of Executive Supervisor, Clifford Brown. The race between three of the best entries in the history of the contest, which competed with each other in the same year, is characterised by a high accumulation of points. Luxembourg's "Tu te reconnaîtras" accumulated 129 points out of 160 possible points and 81%, the highest ever until then, in any voting system. Luxembourg's fourth win made it the Eurovision queen. Helga received the winning singer, Vicky Leandros, with a warm hug and awarded her the grand prize, and Anne-Marie David performed once again the song that changed her life. The Luxembourg Orchestra also realised that it was not just another song and not just another evening, and they initiated playing the catchy refrain of "Tu te reconnaîtras" again (after the entry ended). Thus, ended a record evening in the history of Eurovision, a record that will never repeat itself.

1974 – Brighton, United Kingdom

1974 Eurovision, it may be said, was a kind of continuation of its predecessor. Those were the most beautiful years of the European contest, pinnacle years that most probably will never repeat themselves. Luxembourg, overly excited about its second consecutive win, could still meet the hosting costs, but the security impositions due to Israel's participation gave it no other choice than to relinquish the honour. The United Kingdom was the one to jump at the opportunity, a country that had hosted a fair amount of Eurovisions, regardless of its wins. The BBC understood the potential of the event and chose to host it at the "Brighton Dome" in the English resort town. The presenter, Katie Boyle, set a personal record, which will probably never be broken, as Eurovision presenter for the fourth time, and once again did an excellent job, which won her much praise. After 1973, when only the Scandinavian countries took advantage of the opportunity to sing in English, this time there were no less than 6 (!) songs in the English language (including the winning entry) as well as at least another four songs which were meant to be performed in English, but at the last moment, the delegations changed their minds and left their songs in their native languages. This trend would intensify in subsequent years until singing in a non-official language of each country was prohibited in 1977. Many celebrities crowded the stands in Brighton, and one that stood out, in particular, was Joan Collins, who was still in the early years of her fame, just before she starred in "Dynasty". Finland won the honour of opening the contest for the second year in a row, again in English, but in contrast to Marion Rung's achievement in 1973, Carita floundered with "Keep Me Warm" and found herself at the bottom of the rankings. The Australian pop singer, Olivia Newton-John, was called upon to represent her native country, the UK. Olivia, a rising star who would go on to become one of the biggest and most famous film's stars in the world four years later, thanks to "Grease", disliked the entry, "Long Live Love", to put it mildly ("I was never really happy with the song I had to sing"). Still, in the end, it became the entry that gave her international career a boost. She finished fourth, in a tie with three other countries, and overall, her Eurovision experience can be summed up positively. Peret, one of Spain's most well-known and beloved singers, delivered a traditional execution of "Canta y sé Feliz", which was extraordinarily successful in the Latin countries. The contestant who anticipated victory, drawing attention to herself during rehearsals, was Anne-Karine Strøm or Norway. This time, the "Bendik Singers" who participated in their second consecutive Eurovision, accompanied the soloist. Before the contest, her husband, Frode Thingnæs, who composed and conducted "The First Day of Love", carried out tough negotiations with the many recording companies that came to Brighton and the Norwegians indicated that they would be victorious. At the end of the day, and despite an exceptional performance by Anne-Karine, the pleasant Norwegian was astonished to find out that she had come last with only 3 points (a tie with four other countries). Greece premiered at Eurovision and sent one of the Mediterranean country's most famous singers, Marinella. "Krasi, Thalassa ke t' agori mou" a traditional Greek entry reached the eleventh place. Especially memorable is the scene from the British broadcast when commentator, David Vine, enthusiastically announced: "This is the bouzouki!" at the sight of the musical instrument so strongly associated with the Greeks. After Ilanit's remarkable success, the Israeli Broadcasting Authority decided to send the hottest name in local music — the "Poogy (Kaveret)" band (who competed to be sent to Brighton against other local Israeli artists "HaGashash HaHiver" and "The Parvarim"). The phenomenal seven, who had long been one of the greatest bands of all time in their country, were in a predicament: According to Eurovision rules, more than six performers were not allowed on stage at once. The late Avraham Deshe Pashanel, came up with the solution, giving the conductor's baton to Yonathan Recther, member of the band, thus solving the problem to everyone's satisfaction. "Natati La Khayay", which became a piece of Israeli history, and not only because of Eurovision, was a refreshing and contemporary song that was definitely a good fit for the seventh-place finish, with 11 points, 3 points less than the three fourth-place countries. The Israelis' performance was particularly memorable because of the sweater vests they wore, and it can certainly be said that they did not look expressly nervous on the stage in Brighton. Incidentally, the Eurovision was not broadcast live in Israel since it was held exactly on the evening of Passover (it was aired in full the next evening). The Eurovision band phenomenon impacted Yugoslavia as well: The Serbian "Korni Grupa" with their entry about the generation of 1942, also had an English version, which they played at the dress rehearsal. However, pressure from home had an influence, and in the end, the Yugoslavs performed "Moja generacija" in the Serbian language, which on the evening of the contest took them to twelfth place. Before their departure to Brighton, Belgrade Border Patrol officials refused to allow the band to leave Yugoslavia because the members' passport photos did not match their hairy appearances when they were about to go overseas. The band's manager went all the way up to the Yugoslav Interior Minister and warned him of an international scandal that would prevent the country from participating in the contest. He worked quickly to arrange the band's departure for England. 1974 Eurovision would not be remembered as a historical landmark, had it not been for a completely anonymous Swedish band that brought a new energy, "ABBA". Benny, Björn, Anni and Agnetha, with their glittery make-up, performed "Waterloo" in English — despite local pressure from Swedish television to perform the song in their native language. The show was stolen that evening by the Swedish conductor, Sven-Olof Walldoff, who took the stage dressed as Napoleon Bonaparte. He said that he did this for two reasons: the song's connection to the Battle of Waterloo where Napoleon lost and as a tribute to France, whose president had passed away that week. The Swedes had not been candidates for a win, and betting odds had them placed between fourth and tenth place. Even during rehearsals, there was no dramatic change in their odds and therefore their victory, which was indisputable almost from the moment the voting began, was quite surprising. Nevertheless, the Swedes did not make a sweeping win in Europe with sensational results. Of course, it did not prevent "ABBA" from becoming one of the biggest and most famous bands in the world. Luxembourg selected British singer, Ireen Sheer, to represent it in an attempt to reach a consecutive and unprecedented third win. "Bye Bye I Love You", was the first Eurovision entry written by German composer Ralph Siegel, who would over the years become "Mr. Eurovision", and the tied fourth place Luxembourg won was undoubtedly a good start. The candidate to win the contest was Monaco. The princedom that had already won in 1971 sent Romuald, who had already participated twice in ESC, to Brighton. The latter was at the peak of his career and was supposed to continue the French winning streak. "Celui qui reste et celui qui s'en va" was one of the most played songs in Francophone countries during that period, and the chansonnier was treated as the presumed winner during rehearsals. The gambling agencies also placed Romuald extremely high, with exceedingly high odds of winning, but in practice and despite a tremendous and thrilling performance, Monaco only finished in fourth place, which it considered a disappointment. Another disappointing candidate for victory was Belgium. Jacques Hustin composed the fabulous and unpretentious "Fleur de liberté". Overall, it seemed that three consecutive French-language songs had done their thing and the juries were looking for something else. The Belgians were only placed ninth, despite the song's exceptional success in France and Canada. One of the biggest surprises of the contest came from the Netherlands: "Mouth and MacNeal" duo, with their music box, which was a unique stage attraction, managed to secure third place for the Netherlands with their playful and energetic entry, "I See a Star". The duo took an indirect route to Brighton: Mouth, who had a fear of flying, preferred to make her way there by sea and land but not via air, a journey that took a full day instead of a one-hour flight. Irish singer, Tina Reynolds, was summoned to Luxembourg few hours before the 1973 contest to replace Maxi, who was in disarray with the delegation, but in the end, Reynolds did not perform. She was compensated in

Brighton: "Cross Your Heart" was one of the most beautiful songs in the event and finished in a tie for seventh place with the Israeli band "Kaveret". Two countries that were scheduled to participate at Eurovision were forced to withdraw close to the event date. Malta (for unknown reasons, but probably stemming from the conflict between the Maltese broadcasting network and the EBU) and France, who brought the impressive singer, Dani, to Brighton with the entry "La vie à vingt-cinq ans", which was supposed to have been a force to reckon with in the contest. But three days before the big moment, the president of the Republic, Georges Pompidou, passed away. France declared a period of mourning and his funeral took place precisely on the day of the Eurovision. Under these circumstances, the French had no choice but to withdraw from the contest. Dani remained in Brighton and watched the event, heartbroken. The incident also affected Anne-Marie David, the previous year's winner, who was supposed to give out the Grand Prix — but as a French citizen, was also in national mourning and therefore unable to attend the awards ceremony at the end of the evening. Hence, she also missed the chance of being in a historical photograph with "ABBA"... 1974 will forever be remembered as the year that a military revolution began because of Eurovision. No Portuguese will ever forget where he was when Paulo de Carvalho started singing "E Depois do Adeus". It was the sign and mark of the military revolution that took power in Portugal without a single shot being fired. Apparently, the revolutionaries chose the timing carefully, "Just when the whole country, and the security people, are watching our song in Eurovision", and thus de Carvalho entered Portuguese and European history. Nobody really cared about the fact that it finished last in a tie with Germany, Switzerland and Norway. Italy is also a player in one of the fascinating stories to come out of the 1974 Eurovision. A decade after her impressive win in Copenhagen, Gigliola Cinquetti returned to the European contest determined to achieve a double victory with "Sì" ("Yes"). But the story behind the song was based on a referendum held the same day in Italy: To allow or not allow married couples to divorce (Yes or no). Many conservatives protested that Cinquetti's entry was disguised propaganda intended to increase the camp of supporters of divorce, which led to the scandalous decision not to broadcast the Eurovision in Italy. In the end, a replay of the contest was aired, following the results of the referendum: Cinquetti was placed a close second to "ABBA", received 18 points, only six less than the Swedes, and despite the dignified but heart-wrenching second place — it was announced the same evening that at least Italy had said "Yes" and would allow its citizens the option to be released from the Catholic institution of marriage. In the interval between the entries and the result announcements, the audience was treated to a special guest appearance in the form of a film starring "The Wombles", characters from the most successful children's series on the British Isles. The film was so popular and successful that the theme song of the series, which accompanied the film, was added as a bonus musical track to the official 1974 Eurovision album. After three years, the EBU decided to revert to the old, known voting system, with each country awarding 10 points to one or more countries. A slight change was made to the system: In order to prevent various biases, all the nations would be ready and the presenter, Katie Boyle, would call on them entirely randomly, not allowing anyone to know what was really happening in the hall at that moment. Helga Vlahović from Zagreb announced Yugoslavia's votes, and 16 years later she presented the Eurovision in her own city. The result announcement process went smoothly, without any incidents, Sweden led in the first place, Italy a close second, but not close enough to jeopardise "ABBA's" victory. An interesting statistic: the Swedish did not even receive one point from the host, the UK, who embraced "ABBA" perhaps more than any other European country after the Eurovision. As the Swedes grew closer to victory, local broadcaster, Johan Sandström, became completely ecstatic, commenting, "Oy oy oy", in a shaky voice after every good score the band received. In Anne-Marie David's absence, the Director-General of the BBC, Sir Charles Curran, presented the grand prize to the winners. When "Waterloo" was performed again, the members of "ABBA" looked ahead, and it was clear that their victory at Eurovision was just their starting point.

1975 – Stockholm, Sweden

After the hangover from "ABBA's" victory, Sweden found itself in a peculiar situation: On one hand, the honour of hosting the 20th Eurovision had befallen it, and on the other hand, most of the nation's citizens protested vigorously against the contest being held in the capital, Stockholm. The government's imposition of harsh taxes along with social welfare policies brought many residents to the streets to protest against so much unnecessary money being spent on hosting the European song contest, as far as they were concerned. Many demonstrations took place, some even during the contest days and around the 'Stockholmholmsen' where the event was held, creating an unpleasant atmosphere that permeated the participants themselves. There was a feeling that the Swedes wanted it to end quickly, and they really did not enjoy the experience and consequences of hosting such an international event in their country. The climax of the protest was expressed by an alternative music festival that was held in Stockholm, at the exact same time as the ESC, where anybody could participate and present a song... The SVT also resented the production costs, which it considered exquisite, and as a protest withdrew from participating in the 1976 Eurovision held the next year in The Hague. The EBU did not remain indifferent to the protest. Once again, like other times when the Scandinavian countries "flexed their muscles", the EBU acquiesced and enacted new rules for the contest hosting, ensuring that the economic burden was distributed "more equally" between the other participants and not just the host. Presenter, Karin Falck, would also like to forget the big evening: Her presentation was dull, too official and utterly devoid of humour, while she got lost during the voting, making some embarrassing mistakes. The stage was also one of the most miserable in the history of the contest; it was reminiscent of a high school graduation ceremony in a community centre, more than an event which was watched by several million viewers. This Eurovision was not free of political incidents: Sweden refused to allow Chile to broadcast the contest, as a protest of Augusto Pinochet's reign. The host was reprimanded for this by the EBU, which would assume full authority in the future as to allowing non-participating countries to broadcast the contest. The security concerns that had started in 1973 culminated in Stockholm: in addition to Israel's participation — a real headache for the organisers — the German ultra-leftist terrorist group "Baader–Meinhof" threatened to carry out a terrorist attack in Stockholm during the contest. As a result, all the Swedish security forces were fully prepared, stretching their capabilities to the limit, preventing any possibility of an atrocity. In order not to take any risks, the organisers placed the Israeli delegation, which included singer Shlomo Artzi and his conductor, Eldad Shrem, in the isolated "Holiday Inn". Artzi was accompanied by his then-wife, Milka (the couple divorced in the 2000s) and the two went everywhere together (including nightclubs in the Swedish capital), accompanied by police and undercover security guards. On Saturday, the morning of the show, Shlomo Artzi was able to visit the Central Synagogue in Stockholm, and he even read from the Torah (Artzi was brought up in a religious home, and he laid tefillin until he was 17). Before he performed on the big evening, one of the production people went up to Artzi and shared his concerns with him that a PLO terrorist had managed to infiltrate the hall and intended to shoot him during his performance of the Israeli song. Was that true? It is doubtful, because the Swedes took all possible security measures, including sniffer dogs, and it seems that not even a fly could have entered the site of the event in Stockholm. Despite the problematic opening conditions, one must remember that Eurovision 1975 was the largest ever until then, in terms of participants, with no less than 19 participating countries. This record would be broken only three years later, in Paris. The opening of the contest caused a great deal of outrage in women's organisations around the world: The Swedes wanted to show a humorous film of the history of their people, through the Viking history, when the women were wrongfully treated. Evidence of this was in the opening short film in which a man pulled a young woman's hair, pulling her helplessly behind him. Then they showed a naked model, with the Swedish man portrayed as a vigorous athlete, alongside a naked woman. There is no doubt that such an opening would never be approved to be broadcast today. There were no filmed "postcards" shown between the songs; After the hangover from "ABBA's" victory, Sweden found itself in a peculiar situation: On one hand, the honour of hosting the 20th Eurovision had befallen it, and on the other hand, most of the nation's citizens protested vigorously against the contest being held in the capital, Stockholm. The government's imposition of harsh taxes along with social welfare policies brought many residents to the streets to protest against so much unnecessary money being spent on hosting the European song contest, as far as they were concerned. Many demonstrations took place, some even during the contest days and around the 'Stockholmholmsen' where the event was held, creating an unpleasant atmosphere that permeated the participants themselves. There was a feeling that the Swedes wanted it to end quickly, and they really did not enjoy the experience and consequences of hosting such an international event in their country. The climax of the protest was expressed by an alternative music festival that was held in Stockholm, at the exact same time as the ESC, where anybody could participate and present a song... The SVT also resented the production costs, which it considered exquisite, and as a protest withdrew from participating in the 1976 Eurovision held the next year in The Hague. The EBU did not remain indifferent to the protest. Once again, like other times when the Scandinavian countries "flexed their muscles", the EBU acquiesced and enacted new rules for the contest hosting, ensuring that the economic burden was distributed "more equally" between the other participants and not just the host. Presenter, Karin Falck, would also like to forget the big evening: Her presentation was dull, too official and utterly devoid of humour, while she got lost during the voting, making some embarrassing mistakes. The stage was also one of the most miserable in the history of the contest; it was reminiscent of a high school graduation ceremony in a community centre, more than an event which was watched by several million viewers. This Eurovision was not free of political incidents: Sweden refused to allow Chile to broadcast the contest, as a protest of Augusto Pinochet's reign. The host was reprimanded for this by the EBU, which would assume full authority in the future as to allowing non-participating countries to broadcast the contest. The security concerns that had started in 1973 culminated in Stockholm: in addition to Israel's participation — a real headache for the organisers — the German ultra-leftist terrorist group "Baader–Meinhof" threatened to carry out a terrorist attack in Stockholm during the contest. As a result, all the Swedish security forces were fully prepared, stretching their capabilities to the limit, preventing any possibility of an atrocity. In order not to take any risks, the organisers placed the Israeli delegation, which included singer Shlomo Artzi and his conductor, Eldad Shrem, in the isolated "Holiday Inn". Artzi was accompanied by his then-wife, Milka (the couple divorced in the 2000s) and the two went everywhere together (including nightclubs in the Swedish capital), accompanied by police and undercover security guards. On Saturday, the morning of the show, Shlomo Artzi was able to visit the Central Synagogue in Stockholm, and he even read from the Torah (Artzi was brought up in a religious home, and he laid tefillin until he was 17). Before he performed on the big evening, one of the production people went up to Artzi and shared his concerns with him that a PLO terrorist had managed to infiltrate the hall and intended to shoot him during his performance of the Israeli song. Was that true? It is doubtful, because the Swedes took all possible security measures, including sniffer dogs, and it seems that not even a fly could have entered the site of the event in Stockholm. Despite the problematic opening conditions, one must remember that Eurovision 1975 was the largest ever until then, in terms of participants, with no less than 19 participating countries. This record would be broken only three years later, in Paris. The opening of the contest caused a great deal of outrage in women's organisations around the world: The Swedes wanted to show a humorous film of the history of their people, through the Viking history, when the women were wrongfully treated. Evidence of this was in the opening short film in which a man pulled a young woman's hair, pulling her helplessly behind him. Then they showed a naked model, with the Swedish man portrayed as a vigorous athlete, alongside a naked woman. There is no doubt that such an opening would never be approved to be broadcast today. There were no filmed "postcards" shown between the songs; instead, all performers ware documented trying to draw themselves in the dressing room and signing their portraits in the end. The paintings undoubtedly have historical value and are collectables for every Eurovision lover: For years, the artists have asked what happened to their images, it turns out that the organisers did not allow the artists to take the pictures as a souvenir, so where are they? Some believe that at the end of the event, contest producer Roland Eiworth forgot them in the hall, and they were dumped in the garbage... Never until 1975 did song number one win the contest. The responses to the entry that is sung first, they claim, are very restrained by the juries who expect to give their best to the rest. Therefore, an entry that is performed last has a better chance — and this is although the last performance had never won until 1982... None of this mattered to the Netherlands, who came incredibly determined to win with "Ding-a-Dong" by the "Teach-In" band. A rhythmic and innovative pop song, of course in English (maximum utilization of the rule that no longer restricted any country to sing only in its official language) which was said, both during rehearsals and before the contest, to have a chance of reaching first place, but its chances of winning on the Eurovision evening were not high. The soloist, Getty Kaspers, and her band, with a captivating smile and outstanding performance — brought the Netherlands its fourth win at the ESC. The end of the song was unforgettable, when band member, Ruud Nijhuis, was meant to tap a small glass and produce the final ding from it. On the big night, Nijhuis broke the glass, he seemed surprised, but the incident went smoothly and did not affect the final result. After its win in 1969, France experienced a decline in its Eurovision status and was determined to return home to Paris with the Grand Prix. Many hopes were pinned on Nicole Rieu, to lead her country to its fifth victory. "Et bonjour à toi l'artiste" is one of the most charming musical pieces written for Eurovision, and Pierre Delanoë and Jeff Barnel can be thanked for that. Nicole was considered the strongest candidate to win, and all agencies placed her at the top of the betting table. But the heavy pressure put on her along with the not so brilliant arrangement of the music, which lost some of the emotional song's charm, resulted in a less than exhilarating performance in the decisive moment, and ultimately France was very disappointed to be placed fourth. Another candidate that created a fuss was Germany. In the local pre-select that year, the popular Israeli duo, Shuki and Aviva (Shuki Levi and Aviva Paz) also competed, finishing sixth — but awfully close to the top places. No one could compete with Joy Fleming's powerful performance. "Ein Lied kann eine Brücke sein" was not only a song of extremely high musical and vocal quality, but also constituted a real possibility for Germany to win at Eurovision finally. Once again, there was a problem with the musical arranger's and local orchestra's chemistry, including a hysterical and unsuccessful performance by Joy Fleming, but the person who ruined it all was the conductor and composer Rainer Pietsch, who took the stage while he was intoxicated, stomped his foot loudly and embarrassingly shouted out the rhythm before the song started... Later Pietsch again stole the show when he leapt in the air on the conductors' stand in a way that would not disgrace an Olympic athlete, thus vastly lowering Fleming's chances to win, slamming her down to the seventeenth place. The country who planned to return and win again was Luxembourg. RTL tried hard and this time hired a reliable British team: Phil Coulter and Bill Martin, who had been extraordinarily successful both at Eurovision and in general. With Pierre Cour's help, they created "Toi", an entry that had the formula for an ESC win. Cour, in a very courageous move, strongly recommended that his life partner, Geraldine, perform the song. The Irish singer, who was only 21 years old, and who had not known a word in French until that moment (he participated in the 1973 Irish pre-select), took the challenge with both hands. During rehearsals, her Anglo-Saxon accent grated on the French song, but when it became clear that the French were faltering slightly and the Germans were becoming lost, Geraldine seemed like not too bad an option for first place and her reasonable performance placed her fifth at the end of the night. The "Bendik Singers" dynasty continued their reign in Norway, this time it was the wonderful Ellen Nikolaysen singing a lovely ballad in English, which did not make it to the top scorers, but won her high praises for her music and a record deal. "Touch My Life (With Summer)", is one of the most beautiful songs Norway ever sent to

Eurovision and the second to last place, despite Nikolaysen's exciting performance, greatly short-changed the Nordic singer. During rehearsals, Peter Jacques, the Swiss arranger and conductor, demanded a xylophone. Indeed, it was the first time this charming instrument was witnessed at Eurovision, alongside a compelling performance by Simone Drexel with "Mikado", which surprisingly managed to reach sixth place. The group that was really convinced it was going to win was the famous British representatives: "The Shadows". "We've come here to win", said the band's soloist Hank Marvin very confidently and throughout the rehearsals, the British behaved arrogantly; They imparted the feeling that Eurovision was unimportant to them. They had good reason to do so: their popularity and the massive crowd of fans who waited outside the hall after every rehearsal, and also the fact that their song, "Let Me Be the One", was the most played before the contest and was a huge pop hit worldwide. During rehearsals, Marvin tended to get confuse the second line of the song and during the live broadcast, in front of millions of viewers, he was pleased with himself when he managed to sing the line correctly. He even shamelessly sneaked in the words: "I knew it"... After the dress rehearsal, their colleagues approached them and congratulated them on the anticipated victory, but no one expected the tsunami from the Netherlands. 138 points and four times the maximum 12 points led the UK to a frustrating second place. Israel continued to send its most famous singers to Eurovision. After Ilanit and "Poogy", it was Shlomo Artzi's turn. Although he was not yet the undisputed idol of the Millennium he would become, Artzi was one of Israel's top singers even back in the 1970s. He composed the music for Ehud Manor's lyrics, "At Va'Ani". The conductor Eldad Shrem obtained the lowest percentage of success in relation to the other Israeli conductors who won with Israeli songs more than once. He certainly was not the reason Israel only reached the eleventh place. After a strong start with 10 points from the Netherlands that sparked fantasies of significant achievement, it started receiving much lower votes from the rest of the countries that preferred other songs. It is impossible to say a bad word about Artzi's performance: it was professional, very precise and in good taste. But alone on the big stage, Artzi was lost and finished with disappointment: "Israel will never have a chance to win Eurovision", he said after the contest. Greece withdrew from the contest to protest the debut of Turkey, its bitter enemy. After broadcasting the ESC for quite a few years, the Turks decided to jump into the chilly water, and they were freezing. Semiha Yankı received the honour of singing and performed "Seninle Bir Dakika" which was composed by Kemal Ebcioğlu. Europe did not give Turkey a warm welcome, and like Malta in 1971 and 1972, the Turks were also pushed to the last place with only the three points they got from Monaco. Turkey would still go through a tough time until it broke out of the last place syndrome in the European contest, and to the credit of Turkey, it can be said that it was quite persistent in the matter and did not give up. Sophie Garel, who returned to Eurovision after her duet with Chris Baldo in 1968 (representing Luxembourg), performed one of the contest's most beautiful songs "Une chanson c'est une lettre", which represented Monaco. This French chanson, composed by master craftsman André Popp, did not get the score it deserved and at the end of the evening reached the thirteenth place. There was a big story surrounding Finland's song: "Pihasoittajat" band was marked as the dark horse of the race. "Old Man Fiddle", in English, is an American-style country song. They asked for the "postcard" clip to be shot on a farm but eventually settled for a bar. In order to provoke, or to attract attention, the Finns asked if they could bring no less than a cow or a calf on-stage during their performance... which would be tied to the fiddler. The Swedish organisers had a fit, the Finns would not give up, and the matter was brought before the EBU who explained to the Finnish representatives that there is no logical way to get a cow up onto the stage. After that, it was decided that no animals would be given the stage and used during Eurovision. Even without a cow on the stage, the Finnish song was very invigorating and prosperous, and it placed seventh, winning Douze Points twice — from Switzerland and Germany. The Swedes' hostility toward military rulers was reflected in their disgraceful attitude toward Duarte Mendes, the Portuguese representative. One year after the "Carnation Revolution" that began, as mentioned, with the performance of the song that represented the country at the 1974 Eurovision, Duarte Mendes arrived proudly with the entry "Madrugada" which is a song of praise to the military revolution that took place in the country. At first, Mendes wanted to take the stage dressed in his country's military uniform, but the organisers strongly opposed that. Mendes underwent very stringent security checks compared to the other singers participating in the contest, under the claim that he was carrying or was liable to carry a firearm and during one of the rehearsals he threatened and almost went home and cancelled Portugal's participation. In the end, he took the stage 'armed' with a carnation in the lapel of his jacket, everything went peacefully, and Mendes made an interesting statistic line: Song number 16, with 16 points and he ended in the sixteenth place... And in those days, there was one king of Spanish music: Whoever wanted to find fame and success had to go through Juan Carlos Calderon. The gifted musician from Madrid who discovered many of the most successful singers in the country, for the most part, found his discoveries in the Basque Country, which was known as a region that was rich in musical talent. This time, he selected a duo, Sergio & Estíbaliz, to perform the charming duet he wrote and composed, "Tú volverás". The Basque duo failed to recapture "The Mocedades" tremendous success, but in Spain, they were content with the tenth place. Lars Berghagen, the Swedish idol, is etched in the memories of Swedish children. In Sweden of the 1970s, every parent put their children to sleep to the sound of his "Teddybjörnen Fredriksson" song. Berghagen, who was married to Lill-Babs, also a local singer and a local idol in those days, wrote and composed "Jennie, Jennie" by himself. The song was performed in English, in the hope that it would help them recreate "ABBA's" achievement of the previous year in Brighton. But in this contest, there were much stronger competitors, and Berghagen settled for eighth place. The surprise of the event came from Italy. The duo made up of the dark-skinned Wess and light-skinned Dori Ghezzi, was not considered likely to be even among the top ten. But with low expectations and the song "Era" (written by Shel Shapiro), Italy surprised even the duo that represented it when it reached the third place in Eurovision with 115 points — an enormous achievement for the Italians which kept them at the top for a second consecutive year. All the Swedes could offer the viewers during the break between songs and the result, was static art photography which completely bored the audience. What should have stimulated the whole business was the new voting system (although longer than its predecessor, it turned out to be much more exciting and effective): A team of juries in each country would award points to 10 countries: 12 points to the best song, 10 to second-best, 8 to the next one, and so forth until it got down to 1 point. This method known as the "Douze Points" system, turned out to be a remarkable success and has lasted with minor changes, until this day. In the initial format, the results were given in the order of the countries appearing in the contest and not in the order of points, causing confusion and repeated mistakes. In 1980 the format was improved, and finally, the results were given in the order of points, from 1 to 12. At the opening of the contest, Luxembourg led, until the UK, which had led a close fight with the Netherlands for first place, took over. It was precisely at the moment when presenters are supposed to rise, that Karin Falck gave a terrible performance. The presenter read the results slowly and late, causing misunderstandings and quite a few breaks with the juries' telephone call centres. In addition, Falck insisted on using the term "votes" rather than "points", and the negative climax arose when the UK awarded Sweden 7 points, the presenter who was supposed to repeat the score in French, got stuck and asked in English: "Seven, how much is seven in French?".... The Israeli spokesperson, Yitzhak Shimoni also had an embarrassing moment, when he repeated himself three times, thinking he was not heard, with hysterical cries of "They can hear! They can hear! Talk already," in the background.... The amusing part of the vote was when Monaco gave Turkey its three first and historical points in the Eurovision, but the scoreboard did not respond. The presenter, Falck, spoke to the scoreboard, demanding: "Can I get three points for Turkey please?". One can get the sense of just how impressive the Dutch song was by the fact that it received points from all of the countries, a considerable achievement with the new system. For the second year in a row, the winner did not receive the prize from the previous year's winner... This time, "ABBA" were terribly busy with their new album and did not really consider the Eurovision in Stockholm. High hopes surrounded the "Teach-In" band after their victorious performance with the camera flashes of tens and hundreds of media people in the hall, but their dreams of being the next "ABBA" quickly wore off. There was great pandemonium on the stage after the winning song was performed, when journalists, photographers and those who were simply curious charged up to the stage, threatening to knock the backdrops on them, leaving the victors from the Netherlands pressed, but incredibly pleased.

1976 – The Hague, The Netherlands

"Teach-In's" win brought Eurovision to the Netherlands for the second time in the 1970s. The Dutch hosted the contest in The Hague, where the state government offices are located, in the magnificent convention centre. Once again it was Roland de Groot who designed the vast and spacious Dutch stage with a dynamic backdrop with alternating geometric shapes. In general, the Dutch organisation and hospitality were widely praised. Corry Brokken was the first Dutch singer to win first place in Eurovision (1957), and she became the first winner to become the event's presenter (that would only happen again in 1991 with Gigliola Cinquetti and Toto Cutugno of Italy). Brokken's presenting was hackneyed and did not leave much of a mark on the evening. The Dutch brought back the "postcards" format — short film clips that were played before each artist from a different country took the stage, before showing the clip an illustrated background with the 18 flags of participating countries was presented, to the sound of piano music. The hosts were not innocent of an attempt to gain a home advantage when the Dutch song finished and before the Norwegian song, the piano playing (which accompanied every "postcard" from beginning to end) began with the chorus of "The Party's Over", the entry that represented the locals... Nine songs (!), about half of the contest, were performed in English. In light of many protests about the sterilisation of entries from the identity and culture of each country, and the desire to sing in the international pop language in order to win, the practice would later be abolished in part of the 1977 Eurovision and entirely in 1978. Sweden withdrew from the contest, with the local broadcasting authority's official excuse being: "If we win, we have no money nor the possibility of hosting the contest the following year." Under the pressure of Swedish music lovers, once it had been decided that the hosting costs would be shared more equitably among all participants, Sweden returned to Eurovision in 1977. Enzo Guzman was selected to represent Malta with "Sing Your Song, Country Boy", but political disputes over the delegation's line-up led to the Maltese withdrawing (they would only return to the contest in 1991). Another country that very much wanted to participate was Liechtenstein. As early as 1969, the sovereign state had wanted to enter the ESC in Madrid but was refused, since it did not have a broadcasting service at all and mainly as it was not a member of the EBU. Seven years later, it attempted again, putting its hopes on the rising star, Biggi Bachmann with "My Little Cowboy". Despite a personal request from Prince Franz Josef II, the EBU again rejected the application outright for the same reason it refused in 1969. Since then, the principality has opened a local broadcasting company which is a member of the EBU and was able to participate in Eurovision. Four past participants returned for the second and third time to the contest: Matti Siitonen (Fredi) of Finland, Anne-Karine Strøm of Norway, Sandra Reemer from the Netherlands and Peter, Sue and Marc from Switzerland. After the Dutch victory with the opening song, the UK supposed that opening the event might not be such a big disaster. "Brotherhood of Man ", a band made up of two female and two male singers, won the UK pre-select in a battle with "Co-Co", which they closely defeated. In retrospect, of course, no one regretted it. "Save Your Kisses for Me" is a charming love song, whose end particularly makes it a trump card: "Save all your kisses for me...Even though you're only three". It is rare that the favourite is the winner, but part of dealing with the tension and routine of rehearsal and anticipation for the big evening is reflected in the forecasts: that projected a win for the British, which indeed occurred. The band's pleasant and calm manner should be noted. In an interview before the show, one of its members, Martin Lee, said: "We have no complaints, everything is fine, we just want to get on stage and sing". After a perfect and delightful performance, conducted by Alyn Ainsworth, the feeling in the hall was that they had reached the highlight of the evening already during the opening — which, ultimately, was true. "Brotherhood of Man" did not just win this Eurovision, it achieved an unprecedented result and the highest success rate of all times (above 80), based on the current system.

Switzerland, in which French, Italian and German are spoken, has been influenced by the use of English in Eurovision and converted its entry into the popular language as well. Peter, Sue and Mac returned to the ESC scene again with "Djambo, Djambo", a song about the sad clown who was on the stage with an old-fashioned music box. It seems like the attraction did not hurt the Swiss, who reached fourth place with 91 points. One of the favourites to win was Germany and for the first time, the prolific composer Ralph Siegel managed to win the German pre-select with the help of British musician Les Humphries. The latter founded "The Les Humphries Singers", a group of singers from around the world that gained tremendous popularity in Germany. The rhythmic and catchy "Sing Sang Song" seemed like a winning card, but, according to Siegel, Humphries ruined everything as he took the stand to conduct the orchestra and made arrogant victory signals to the camera, thus averting many points from the German song. Otherwise, it is impossible to explain how this song crashed to 15th place. Another reason may be found in the band's big shambles on the stage, and the English-German merger that did not work properly. Siegel would have to work hard to return and represent his country again, and it would pay off for both. Although Les Humphries was disappointed with the results, he did succeed in starting an affair that lasted several months. The IBA reverted Shlomo Artzi's failure to legendary producer Avraham Desha Pashanel. After succeeding in entering "Poogy" in Eurovision, it was now the turn of "The Chocolate girls (Chocolate Menta Mastik)". Yardena Arazi, Leah Lupatin and Ruti Holtzman were selected to represent Israel, and a private pre-select of three songs was held for them. In the opinion of most experts, the best and most solid entry in the pre-select was "Ze Tov" (composed by Roni Weiss to Eliuz Rabin's words), which was capable of reaching the top three at Eurovision, but the committee decided on "Emor Shalom" by Ehud Manor and Matti Caspi as the winner. There were no remarkably lofty expectations of this song, which surprised and managed to obtain 77 points and a respectable sixth place (where the band stayed almost throughout the voting process) thanks, in large part, to the professionalism and class of Arazi, Lupatin and Holtzman. It is doubtful that there was another conductor there that evening as talented as Matti Caspi, who graced the resume of the European contest with his presence in The Hague. Yardena, Ruti and Leah were a walking attraction in the Netherlands, both in and outside of rehearsals. The producer, Pashanel, with his keen sense of smell of talent, very quickly understood the 'vibe' and managed to organise them an extraordinarily successful tour overseas, following their good Eurovision performance. "Are you real?" Les Humphries asked Yardena Arazi, a question that led to a few months' long passionate affair between the two! Luxembourg very much wanted to return victoriously and to do so held a cut-throat pre-select contest in which Jürgen Marcus and Marianne Rosenberg — the hottest names of the time in German music competed against one another. Eventually, Marcus had the upper hand and a French song, written by Vline Buggy (Eurovision's 1973 winning songwriter) was tailored to him. The expectations were sky-high, but it turned out that big names were no longer impressive if the style was not innovative and attractive enough (only three countries awarded Jürgen Marcus points and Luxembourg finished in 14th. The event in The Hague created a huge star overnight, the Belgian Pierre Rapsat. "Judy et Cie", which he composed and performed, is to many the most exciting musical work of that year. Some thought that he would be the dark horse of the 1976 race, although at the end of the night the board only pointed to the eighth place: "Judy, the one who is forgotten from the moment the evening ends, but she may very well be the girl you end up marrying", made Rapsat an idol in Belgium, and he was dubbed "the local Jacques Brel". Rapsat also rose to fame in the neighbouring countries, but his life was cut short by cancer when he was just 53, in the early 2000s. Irish novelist Brendan Graham had his first Eurovision experience with "When" written by himself and composed by Red Vincent Hurley, one of Ireland's favourite singers. The rehearsals and betting agencies determined that Hurley would finish in the top five, but the Irish were disappointed to find that despite the exciting performance, the vote only took them to tenth place. The locals also made overly optimistic predictions: "The Party's

Over" by Sandra Reemer (who returned after a successful performance at the 1972 contest) was highly complimented and seemed to be a contender for the first place. In the end, despite the attractive Sandra, it was not enough to win for the second time in a row, and the Netherlands finished 9th. In 1976, it was the end of the line for the Bendik Singers: Anne-Karine Strøm, in her third Eurovision performance, was brave enough to return to the contest where she had finished last in 1974. Then, like at The Hague, her husband, Frode Thingnæs, wrote and composed her song and this time too, as in Brighton, Anne-Karine was one of those who were sure they were there to take the first prize. Perhaps as a tribute to the Dutch hosts, Anne-Karine sang about "Mata Hari", the Dutch artist who was convicted of spying in favour of Germany at the end of the First World War, a case that to this day is still considered a painful scar on the local history. The betting agencies in London actually ranked Anne-Karine in second place at one point, and during rehearsals, some journalists claimed that this time Anne-Karine would win. Even on the big evening, Anne-Karine managed to be the centre of focus with her golden outfit and gimmick, the sunglasses worn by her and her backup singers. You cannot say a bad word about Strøm's performance, which she chose to execute in English, but again this time she was 'betrayed' by the juries and finished last with seven points, were it not for... Greece created a big uproar, returning to Eurovision after a year of absence in protest over Turkey joining the contest, but the Greeks would not give up on an opportunity to settle scores: One and a half years after the Turkish invasion of Cyprus, Michael Fotiades wrote "Panagia Mou, Panagia Mou", lamenting the conquest of the island close to the heart of Greece. Turkey, as expected, responded by withdrawing furiously from the contest. Two years later, the two bitter enemies would learn to accept each other in the same Eurovision. Mariza Koch, an esteemed folk singer with a strong stage presence, composed the song she performed with all her heart. The excitement was also evident on the face of conductor Michalis Rozakis, and any Greek who saw this event will never forget it. Koch's performance in The Hague reached one of the highest places on the Greek National Pride Index. The daughter of the renowned filmmaker, Tyrone Power, the beautiful Romina, was embarking on her career when she joined the well-known Al Bano Carrisi. The two, who had a fascinating and sensational life story, made their first international move by representing Italy at Eurovision in The Hague with "We'll Live It All Again", which was half in English. The romantic duet that remembered so well because of the couple's tight, smiling dance on stage earned the Italians seventh place. After four years of absence, Austria returned to Eurovision with Waterloo and Robinson. "My Little World", also in English, was a breath of fresh air and received high acclaim from the local audience. The Austrians were surprised when they won fifth place, an achievement that they had not reached before the end of the twentieth century. The hot favourite to win, after the British, of course, was Italy's Mary Christy who represented Monaco. The Principality of Monte-Carlo again invested in the contest with the incredible composer, Georges Costa, (who was a relative of the girl wonder, Nikka Costa) and the arranger- conductor Raymond Donnez from France. Throughout the rehearsals many people crowded in to hear "Toi, la musique et moi" and Christie's performance at the defining moment was also excellent. It seemed Monaco would reach the top, but, as mentioned, being a favourite is not necessarily positive at Eurovision, and Mary was extremely disappointed to find herself at the end of the evening with 93 points and in third position (although this was Monaco's third-best achievement of all time). After Nicole's disappointing in Sweden, the French kept a low profile in The Hague, but they knew they had a winning card in their hands: Catherine Ferry, the young woman who had driven the Republic crazy with "Un, deux, trois" which for a long time in 1976 was the most played song in the country. Jean-Paul Cara and Tony Rallo (who also conducted the orchestra), were responsible for the catchy and fast-paced entry, which like its name, caught on and during rehearsals and joint the list of potential winners. Ferry's performance was simply perfect, and despite her early age, she was not nervous, but seemed utterly energised and ready for victory. The juries were also enthusiastic about Catherine and her song, and awarded her 147 points, with no country skipping Ferry, however, despite collecting enough points to have won every other Eurovision event, France could not compete with the popularity of the British song and finished second (yet the closest to first it could come). 1975 Eurovision shattered the myth that whoever opens the contest cannot win and the Eurovision at The Hague shattered the legend that whoever sings last has the highest chances of winning. Yugoslavia closed the list of songs with its well-known band "Ambasadori" from Sarajevo and vocalist Ismeta Dervoz-Krvavac. "Ne mogu skriti svoju bol" was one of the most treasured and loved songs in The Hague, that speaks also what would happen to this wonderful country 15 years later. Yet, what occurred after that, did not stand up to real-time: The European juries were not impressed with the Yugoslavs, and only awarded them 10 points that should have placed the "Ambasadoris" in the second to last place. But the Yugoslavia's luck had really run out: the 4 points that France had awarded them were not recorded on the scoreboard, Clifford Brown the Supervisor, did not realise it at the right time and the evening concluded with only 6 points on the scoreboard, at an unjust "equal" last place with Anne-Karine of Norway. Although the EBU admitted afterwards that an injustice had been done to the Yugoslavs, it was not possible to change their last place according to the dry rules. The Dutch introduced a novelty that, incomprehensibly, was not continued until the mid-2000s: While the local brass band played on the stage, the co-presenter, Hans van Willigenburg, walked around among the artists backstage in the "Green Room" and asked them to bet on a winner. Five artists were interviewed, including Ruti Holtzman, the Israeli, who praised all the songs and did not have a favourite, Braulio from Spain shared her opinion. Waterloo & Robinson from Austria bet on song number 18, "just because it's song number 18", which in the end was placed last... The only ones to really bet were the Belgian Pierre Rapsat who believed Monaco would win and Catherine Ferry of France who bet on the UK, and in the end, she was right. Despite the Yugoslav failure, the scoreboard was the most modern up to that point with the country names and scores completely lit up. After an insignificant Swiss lead at the opening, France and UK left the others far behind and fought a close duel, up to the halfway mark Catherine Ferry was in the lead by a slight difference. The one to turn the game was Greece, who placed the UK first, with 89 points versus France's 87 points. From there on, "Brotherhood of Man went from strength to strength, all the way to a glorious victory that had never been seen before. Some interesting anecdotes occurred during the Voting: Portugal received Douze Points (12 points) from France, which is the number of points that it received from all the other countries put together, which placed it... twelfth. Italy and Ireland demonstrated reciprocity by awarding each other 12 points. Monaco did not receive any points from France (despite Mary Christy's immense popularity) and the UK's lowest score (only 3 points) came from its neighbour, Ireland, to the awkward laughter from the audience and host Corrie Brokken. Speaking of Brokken, in the close race between the French and the British, the Dutch presenter could be heard groaning at the thrill of it all... The British won 7 Douze Points compared to France's 5 — one more than the song that won in 1975 received. Only Ireland in 1980 equalled it (in a Eurovision which included 20 countries), and Germany in 1982 passed it when it managed to obtain the maximum score from half of the participants (!). It was the UK's third victory, which gave them a firm foothold in the top four Eurovision Empires (France, Luxembourg and the Netherlands). It was the most magnificent and impressive among these, obviously in terms of numbers, but mostly, thanks to an entry that remains immortal to this day. For the third time in a row, a Eurovision band, with an English-language, pop-style song was the winner. Was it a new era, or was it still too early to eulogise the other styles and languages?

1977 – London, United Kingdom

1977 Eurovision was one of the biggest shows of misery related to the production of this event, especially being produced by the BBC. Despite a modern hall, an excellent orchestra, a brightly lit, arched, impressively large stage, the first scoreboard of its kind on which country flags were placed beside their names, and an extremely experienced presenter. How, despite all of this, would the EBU's 22nd Music Contest be remembered as a farce or uninspiring? Well, it seemed that the BBC had had its fill of Eurovision contest productions and no longer saw it as a professional challenge to refresh it and make the contest exciting. The event venue was perfect: On the banks of the River Thames, in one of the most famous and bustling areas in the UK and around the world, inaugurated In January 1977, Wembley Hall is officially adjacent to the mythological football Stadium. The 70's were a grey or even black era in the UK: The Labour Government had reached a dead end, and there were recurring labour disputes with workers' committees (who were then at the peak of their power and influence over what happened in the UK). The Eurovision was scheduled to take place on April 2nd, but two weeks before the big curtain went up, the BBC's foreign photographers decided to embark on a strike, the timing was perfect for them. They demanded to match their wages to those of the studio photographers and the means of extortion was perfect: preventing the Eurovision broadcast if their demands were not met. The management of the British Broadcasting Corporation refused to surrender and announced that they would postpone the Eurovision contest for two weeks, and later for a month. Meanwhile, huge pressure was put on the committee not to break the rules of the game and cause the biggest disgrace in BBC history. The CEO of the corporation even threatened to close and reopen, in order to put an end to the extortion and workers committees. After a while, both sides began to climb off their high horses and reached an agreement that would end the strike, allowing the Eurovision broadcast. The delay caused the contest to take place for the first time in May, on May 7th. What was considered an unusual and one-off delay became the usual month of the event in the 1980s. After being exhausted by the BBC's foreign photographers' war, director, Stewart Morris, had a brief passage of time to organise the event. Even so, two months after the "new" songs were played on the world's radio stations and some even managed to enter and exit the hit parades in their countries, many questioned the viability of holding the contest that year.

The production had to give up on a few things it was not able to prepare in such a brief time, including transition video clips. Thus, without wishing to do so, the British set up an interesting format, in retrospect, where the attention and camera moved among the audience between songs. Therefore, the significance of the broadcast accompanying the contest on behalf of each country was quite large this time. And again — Israel was the only outcast that did not send a broadcaster to the event, for financial reasons. In fact, it was Yitzhak Shimoni, the Israeli voting spokesperson, who only spoke during the voting stage, but it was a mockery. The artistic section before the voting process also amounted to a video starring Mr Acker Bilk and his Paramount Jazz Men. They hosted all the contestants at one of the clubs in London — not something likely to attract hundreds of millions of viewers to the screen. Tunisia created a minor commotion. It, and was supposed to make its debut in the Eurovision with a song in Arabic for the first time, on account of its membership in the EBU. Tunisia was scheduled to sing fourth, but apparently, after discovering that Israel would be performing on the exact same stage, in the same contest, the Tunisians withdrew, close to the contest date. Another country that withdrew in anger and slammed the door on the Eurovision for five years was Yugoslavia, due to the scandal with the points the previous year, which placed it in the last place although it had been awarded more points than the country that did finish last — Norway. At the beginning of the broadcast, a video was screened about England, Scotland, Wales and Northern Ireland that make up the British kingdom. When they moved to the presenter, Angela Rippon, she was searching for the right camera to look at... This was not the only issue in a series of ongoing problems, glitches, and it was evident that the professional British (both due to the strike and for other reasons), were taking it lightly this time and were not doing their best job, to say the least. After the Netherlands and the United Kingdom, Ireland hoped that song number one would bring it a triumph. "The Swarbriggs Plus Two" after a mediocre performance in 1975, arrived full of confidence with "It's Nice to Be In Love Again" and the truth is that nobody took them into account. In fact, after a brilliant performance (you could say almost perfect), the Irish were a major surprise, they sometimes touched on the top in the vote and finally finished with their heads held high, with 119 points in 3rd place. Michèle Torr very much wanted to represent France at Eurovision, but the talented musical country would not give the stage to Maurice Chevalier's relative. Torr had represented Luxembourg in 1966 and was disappointed when she only arrived tenth. This time, on behalf of Monaco, she came with a talented musical team led by conductor Yvon Rioland, who arranged the song "Une petite française". Torr's more mature performance would enter the contest's classics, and like Ireland — it would receive points from all the countries except for one. At the end of the evening, Torr could say she had a favourable experience, reaching the fourth place with 96 points. Two months before the original date of the London ESC, the EBU decided that "the English festivity" would have to end, and each country could only sing in its own language. The decision was made under the Francophone countries' pressure, which noticed how the hegemony was moving to English. The climax came when countries like Switzerland decided to sing in English alongside half of the participants (!). One complicated issue was the deciding factor: Germany, Belgium, the Netherlands, Austria, Switzerland, Sweden, and Finland had already recorded their versions for the contest in English. What could be done? In a no less controversial decision, the EBU captains ruled that only Germany and Belgium could, as an exception, sing in English, because their songs in the local pre-selection stage were sung in English, while the rest had recorded their entries in English after they were selected in their respective countries. Hence, the Netherlands, which had a not too shabby 9 to 1 chance with "De mallemolen" had to recalculate its track, and all the magic in Heddy Lester's song was lost with the performance in Dutch. Could Lester have gone further than the twelfth place in English? Probably yes, but these raindrops wet everyone else as well. The "Schmetterlinge" band, a continuation of the "Milestones" that succeeded in 1972 was convinced that "Boom Boomerang" would conquer Europe. There was indeed a lot of talk about the Austrian song which is a kind of disguised protest about the music world, which has become too industrial, too fast, compromising quality and making artists slaves (and this was 1977...). But the decision to prevent the Austrians from singing in English was to their detriment, the band's musical director and conductor, Christian Kolonovits, who took the conductors stand with a roguish appearance, wearing a leather jacket, claimed that there is a world of difference between the German and English versions. The "Schmetterlinge" band delivered a stunning performance, wearing white and black suits and masks on their backs, which they showed the audience when turned around. The dramatic look, which included the use of cards, hats and modern choreography, perhaps drew the attention slightly away from the song itself, and this is how the Austrians crashed down to second to the last place. Germany pinned its hopes on one of the world's best-known pop bands — "Silver Convention". The band that was founded in Munich and released several hits in the 1970s was the definite favourite for victory by the time they arrived in London. "Telegram" remained a strong candidate for the win even after rehearsals, but with a slight setback that predicted it would reach second place. The song about a device that at the time was sort of a "messaging app" was considered one of the 1970s' wonders ... The song's opening was accompanied by a telegram set attached to the piano that stood on the stage. The Germans decided to use local Ronnie Hazlehurst as the arranger and conductor and their performance was perfectly accurate (in English, which increased the feeling that this time Germany was perfectly capable of going all the way). Still, it is unclear why "Telegram" failed and was only awarded 56 points and finished 8th, far from the winners' struggle. Luxembourg came to London with many aspirations and a great appetite to win. As per tradition, an experienced French team, led by Pierre Cour ("Tom Pillibi", "L'Amour Est Bleu"), wrote "Frère Jacques" ("Brother Jack") — a bold disco song that preceded its time and suggested a special relationship: "Brother Jack, are you asleep (just like the opening of the traditional French song)?... Brother Jack, there are so much better things for you to do than pretending to be my big brother... Brother Jack, wake up and come sleep with me". Anne-Marie B, the sensual performer and actor by profession, was a media attraction, they enjoyed interviewing her, and she would bring Luxembourg back to the top of the Eurovision Contest after four years of not being in the top four positions. Ultimately, the controversial messages in the song and the disco style did not stand in Anne-Marie B's favour, who returned home with her tail between her legs after she placed sixteenth. Portugal continued with its display of patriotism, and the "Os Amigos" band members included Fernando Tordo and Paulo de Carvalho who had already participated in Eurovision in the past. "Portugal no coração" was one of the strongest candidates for the last place. Therefore, they were even a little pleased to finish fourteenth, with 18 points. The British host, as usual, a strong contender for the first places, chose the duo, Mike Moran and Lynsey de Paul, who wrote and composed "Rock Bottom" which reflected the depressing state of the country in those years, but was executed humorously with a catchy, flowing melody. With the excellent position of the two performers sitting back-to-back at two grand pianos, bets on the talented Moran and the beautiful de Paul skyrocketed, marking the UK as one of the three candidates to win. To his discontentment, Ronnie Hazlehurst took the stand to conduct the song with a walking stick in one hand and a newspaper in the other, mumbling something that was heard to be his dissatisfaction with his appearance... Apparently, the performers had made this an ultimate requirement for Hazlehurst, to the point of threatening to replace him with another conductor. The esteemed British musician preferred to endure the bizarre appearance because he believed in his feeling that "Rock Bottom" could win. What ultimately almost happened: The British led the vote safely after the halfway mark, but gradually weakened in the race and found themselves — for the tenth time (!) in second place, with a record for winning Douze Points six times, for a song that finished second. But for Lynsey de Paul, who expressed herself sharply towards the winning entry and did not accept the loss in a sporting spirit, the second place was not acceptable: "I do not care what song wins, as long as it is the best song in the contest, but the winning song was nothing, terrible, unbearable, and unprofessional". The English duo also boycotted the Eurovision after-party, held at the end of the contest. The event's sensation came from Greece. The country that had failed to make its mark in the two previous Eurovision Contests that it had participated in until then, also took on the band format and gambled on Paschalis, Marianna, Robert and Bessy. The wonderful chemistry of this band was just the appetiser for one of the most memorable songs of the evening at Wembley's "Mathima Solfège ", considered to this day a classic in Greece and is taught as necessary in music lessons in schools all over the country. When the Greeks arrived in London, the bookmakers placed them somewhere in the top ten, with 20 to 1 odd. Already at rehearsals, it was obvious that this was a dark horse and "Mathima Solfège" became viral. The votes soon came in, and Greece experienced its greatest achievement in its ESC history (which it was unable to recreate until just 15 years ago): fifth place, with 92 points, which made Pascalis, Marianna, Robert and Bessy heroes in Athens and they embarked on a successful tour of Europe. After "Poogy", Shlomo Artzi and "Chocolate Menta Mastik" failed to repeat the amazing achievement of 1973 (fourth place), Ilanit was selected by majority vote to return to Eurovision and represent Israel again. An absolute consensus about the national singer was not reached, and many artists protested: "It is okay to send Ilanit twice, do we have anyone else anyway?" (Shaike Levy); "In light of the results, I don't understand why they sent Ilanit twice" (Svika Pick);

After Ilanit was chosen it was time to select the song that would be performed in London — Kobi Oshrat put the song "Valentino" on the table which could have done wonders. But the Israeli Broadcasting Authority's electoral committee refused to use "Valentino" because of the Latin word that they believed abused their local language, and they preferred the song "Ahava hi Shir Lishnaim". Anything that Ilanit sang would sound beautiful and exciting, but Shlomo Zach, the producer and her ex-husband could feel in his bones that he did not have a winning card. The lyricist, Edna Peleg, following her victory at the Chile International Festival, believed that Ilanit could win. The composer and conductor, Eldad Shrem ("Eldad's arrangement was too complicated", concluded Noam Semel, the promoter, who was present in the concert hall) hoped to fix what had happened with Shlomo Artzi two years earlier. In the absence of a budget from the IBA, the producer, Zach, hired three local backing vocalists for a song, they were delighted with the opportunity to perform at Eurovision and learned their lines in a week. During rehearsals, Ilanit was highly complimented, and it seemed that "Ahava Hi Shir Lishnaim" could and would surprise, with the betting agencies predicting a place in the middle with odds of 16 to 1. On the big evening, Ilanit did not disappoint, she was excellent, and at the beginning of the voting segment, the Israelis thought they were dreaming: after hearing votes from two countries, Ilanit was in the lead, and after three votes she was in third place. But then came the big plunge, when seven countries did not award her any points; only Switzerland gave her a high score of 10. Ultimately, she finished in eleventh place. Ilanit was extremely disappointed and rightly so. It was a completely unnecessary performance for her: "There is no doubt that it was our worst performance at Eurovision and placing us eleventh was doing us a favour", said the Israeli actor Avraham Mor. Switzerland continued its line of successes with Peter Reber. The latter is part of the "Peter, Sue and Marc" trio, and after being 4th in 1976, he wrote and composed "Swiss Lady", which the members of the "Pepe Lienhard Band" performed admirably. For those who are superstitious, being song number 13, is not a good omen, to say the least. Sweden, which returned to Eurovision after a one-year absence, landed right in this position and the concerns were justified when it found itself at the bottom of the scoreboard at the end of the evening... "Forbes" came to London with an original tribute to the greatest band of all time, "The Beatles". The song about the British band was supposed to be performed in English, but the new rule, as mentioned, forced the Swedes to sing in their language, with only Germany volunteering to give them their only two points that evening. By the way, before the contest, "Forbes" was fortunate to participate in a heartening meeting and photoshoot with the great band "ABBA", but as mentioned, even that did not help the Swedes evade the horror of being last. Italy again attracted attention because of its performer, Mia Martini. As one of the most famous singers in one of the most musical countries in the world, she was successful with "Libera" outside of Eurovision owing to her unique presentation and her rough voice. Nevertheless, during the contest itself, she was disappointed to find that the European juries did not embrace her performance (33 points and 13th place).

"If we have a chance to win Eurovision, it's this time or never", Finnish Monica Aspelund said at her London press conference. "Lapponia" is indeed one of the best and most memorable Finnish songs in the ESC and Aspelund's vocal abilities, her performance and the accompaniment by her brother-in-law Kari Kuusamo on the piano left millions of Finns in front of their screens hoping for a historic win. Aspelund delivered the goods in regard to her excellent performance, and she received the evening's first Douze Points; it seemed that something big was about to happen to Finland. But as in the case of Israel, it was a fortuitous incident and Finland finished in tenth place with 51 points. The last two songs in the order of their appearance were the favourite and the winner. Belgium sent the Dutch group "Dream Express" made up of the three Maessen sisters (who made up "Hearts of Soul" which represented the Netherlands in 1970). Musician Luc Smets joined them and together they created a unique quartet on the stage that was mostly successful in Belgium, which has never won, or even been close to winning Eurovision. They pinned their hopes on "A Million in One, Two, Three", which was written and composed by Smets and hired the services of the British conductor, Alyn Ainsworth, who had conducted the "Brotherhood of Man's" brilliant victory the previous year. The song became a viral hit in almost every European country and the fact that it both competed in and won the Belgian pre-select in English, granted them the right to perform in this language, along with Germany. The two countries led the betting tables head and head. During rehearsals, the hegemony went to the Belgians who presented themselves on the big evening as the top candidates to win the contest, with attractive odds of 4 to 1. The Belgians' rhythmic and catchy song is definitely a typical hit for the hit parades of the time, and it should have overcome its competitors. What most probably hurt the Belgian's chances of victory was a complete symposium on the fact that the three singers, the Maessen sisters, did not wear bras, which made their nipples stand out which was seen through the clothing they chose for the event... Bianca Maessen, who was 27 that year, did not understand the turmoil: "We do not wear bras and besides, don't worry, our chests aren't as big as the British women's"... In the end, just to be safe, the cameras kept a safe distance from the performers and there were no close-ups of the Belgian song, lest, God forbid, the performers' breasts are revealed. Despite receiving Douze Points from the Netherlands and 10 points from the UK (the countries of the band members and the conductor, Ainsworth), "A Million in One, Two, Three" foundered with a disappointing score, with six countries not awarding it any points at all. Seventh place was not quite so bad compared to what Belgium had achieved hitherto in Eurovision, but given its grand expectations, this was considered a deep and profound disappointment. The band found it difficult to recover from this point, and its members dispersed in different directions, with solo careers that never really took off. Quietly, Marie Myriam from France took the stage for the last song, with no one really considering her a serious candidate that would interfere with the other favourites. France had exactly the same gambling odds as Israel — 16 to 1. Neither the journalists, the production, nor anyone who had randomly watched the rehearsals, had given Myriam a second look. "L'oiseau et l'enfant" a well-known familiar French chanson — some would say old-fashioned — was written by Jean-Paul Cara, who won second place at the 1976 Eurovision and arranged by the person who had won third place as Monaco's conductor that year, Raymond Donnez. With this team, there was undoubtedly high quality, and Marie Myriam also turned out to be quite the effective performer; with the orange floral dress, she did not move an inch from her position throughout the song and apparently knew how to stir the crowd and the juries. France was the first to receive points from all the countries, although it was only awarded 3 Douze Points (the lowest number to be awarded to a winner up until that time). However, it was enough to reach 136 points, and surpass its competitors by a convincing 14-point difference and to achieve the most surprising victory at Eurovision in years. The voting sequence itself was a massive fiasco for Angela Rippon, but mostly for the British Supervisor, Clifford Brown; that contest was his swan song. Afterwards, he ceased to serve as the EBU Supervisor at Eurovision and gave the floor to Frank Naef.

"He has enjoyed every moment", said the Jewish television broadcaster Pete Murray, who covered the broadcast for the BBC and it was as if he predicted evil for Brown: although he interfered with troublesome mistakes and corrections at almost every moment, there were four mistakes on the board, right under Brown's eyes, that were not corrected until the end of the voting sequence: Belgium, Finland, Israel, the United Kingdom, Germany, Austria and the Netherlands finished with several incorrect points that were obvious to everybody. Remember that at that time the Eurovision rules stated that the final result for each country was not the number of points it actually received but what was written on the scoreboard at the end of the evening. In 1976, Yugoslavia paid a high price coming last for no wrongdoing of its own. Fortunately, and wondrously, the places of the seven countries who were awarded an extra point, would not have been any different without that point. The comedy that was a nightmare for the presenter, Rippon, started with Ralph Inbar, the Israeli — Dutch television spokesperson who read the results for the Netherlands and began with typical Israeli audacity: "First of all, we think that Holland has 6 points up to now and not 5 points"... Inbar was right, the Netherlands had been awarded 3 points from Monaco and 3 points from Ireland, but there was a point missing from the board. The stunned Rippon responded in a rather annoyed and patronising way: "You've given our jurors a problem here". Inbar continued: "You know, we are counting here"... And the embarrassed Rippon smiled: "So are we... Why don't we let them sort out their problems, you give us your vote?" Inbar sent a unique "greeting" to his home country, announcing the award of 5 points to Israel in the Hebrew language. The phrase "We have a problem here again with our board," was a mantra repeated over and over by Rippon. Yitzhak Shim'oni who read the Israeli results forgot to award 4 points: "Yes, maybe I skipped it, Switzerland 4 points". The voting process was characterised by a fairly safe British lead and in the middle that momentum shifted to France which gradually opened up a gap from the locals and Ireland that was adjacent to the two. The French victory was already secured before the last three voters. Sir Charles Curran, President of the BBC, awarded the victory medal to Jean-Paul Cara, while Marie Myriam took her time getting to the stage, she kissed the rest of her colleagues in the 'green room', and she even reapplied her makeup, taking all the time in the world... The presenter, Angela Rippon, felt another wave of unpleasantness approaching, and her desperate calls for the winning French singer to take the stage were heeded. The overly excited Myriam marched up to accept the award from Curran. The previous year's winners, "Brotherhood of Man", could not be present that evening due to an earlier commitment, which they justly blamed on the technician strike which had caused the date of the contest to be changed twice. It was evident that Marie Myriam was incredibly surprised by the situation and the win was very unexpected. She had nothing to say, but she asked Charles Curran: "Where is the microphone I'm going to sing into?" with Angela Rippon directing her to the microphone: "All the fun in winning is that you get to sing your song again". All participating countries' flags were placed on the stage, and turned like a carousel, while Marie Myriam performed the winning song again, "L'oiseau et L'Enfant". In general, it was a dreadful evening for Angela Rippon, who received the harshest criticism from the public and the media in her country. Hours after the Eurovision, she was already in a helicopter en route to Essex County, where she had ... a horse-riding test. All of the UK followed Rippon's test, which she managed to pass successfully. On the night of her win, Marie Myriam forgot that it was her birthday.... the impresario made sure to remind it by giving her a birthday cake decorated in the three colours of the French flag: "I forgot the birthday... I did not sleep at all the night before the contest because the night before I dreamed that I started to sing and the microphones were silent. When I got on the stage, I trembled all over and tightened my hands to relax". Marie Myriam regained her composure and managed to go from a completely anonymous singer to one that was talked about throughout Europe in one night. Thanks to her, France was the victorious queen of Eurovision with five such wins. Unfortunately, it was precisely in the year that each country was forced to sing in its own language to avoid the contest being dominated by the English language (which was supposed to be for the benefit of the Francophone countries, especially France) that France celebrated its last victory in the contest to this day. Since 1988 there has not been a victorious French song (!). Thus, France's most unexpected Eurovision winner became a legend.

1978 – Paris, France

France restores the honour to the Eurovision: A year after surprisingly winning the contest in London, TF1 showed that it could do it far chicer than the satisfied British, featuring 20 countries (new record). Marie Myriam's victory made the locals' pride when they became kings of the Eurovision with five titles. In addition, the Francophone language rejuvenated (2nd, 3rd and 4th places) with a quarter of the contestants performing entries in French. The French were definitely hungry after 15 years of not hosting the most significant musical event in the world and presented a spectacular and meticulous production. "Palais des congrès de Paris", the glorious hall of congresses and events in Paris, hosted the event. For the first time, the French presented the "illuminated square stage", a format that will be repeated only in 1988 and the following years, with a bright and glittering background protruding from above and a dazzling disco ball. The attraction: An orchestra was rotating on the sides of the stage in the shape of a conch. Well-known French musical anchors could be spotted in the audience, among them Sylvie Vartan. The hosts made another history when for the first time, not one presenter was on stage but an excellent duo: Alongside Dénise Fabre was the fabulous Leon Citron. The chemistry between them, the lack of mistakes and supreme professionalism led to a perfect presentation — the best so far. The duo came up every five entries to introduce the next five. The rest of the time, they broadcast the contest to French television (this is efficiency). An opening film showing Paris brought the 700 million viewers into the unique atmosphere. After the opening remarks and explanation of the facilitators, it was possible to approach the business. Similar to the British the previous year, but for entirely different reasons, the French decided to abandon the 'postcards' — the videos documenting the artists in their countries — and innovatively accompany the performers behind the scenes, through the lift to the stage. At the end of each song, the previous performer waited at the back of the stage and shook hands with the next performer, before descending back to the 'Green Room'. Once again, Ireland was set to open the event. Colm Wilkinson, a supreme artist, actor and musician who has starred in major musicals around the world, was the Irish's hope. Wilkinson himself wrote and composed "Born to Sing" and was applauded and cheered, placing him at a respectable fifth place at the end of the evening. As per tradition, a record was produced with the entries that made up the ESC. Wilkinson's distribution company insisted on demanding royalties and unacceptable sums. Hence, unusually, on some Eurovision records, the Irish song was taken from the show itself (and some say it was much better than the original studio recording). Three times (besides Anne Karina in 1976) Norway "won" the last place. Until 1978, no country in the new system finished the evening with nul points. Jahn Teigen had the dubious honour and became the fifth Norwegian singer to return home with the last place, and with zero points out of 228 possible... "Mil Etter Mil" was very characteristic of the theatrical Teigen: A light-hearted and humorous presentation, but a rather bland song that on a relatively good evening musically, could not have survived the contest. But Teigen is not broken easily. "The singer who won 0 points at the 1978 Eurovision Song Contest" is a title that followed him for years, and thanks to his witty humour, he knew how to take it to his advantage, and make himself one of the biggest stars of his country. The "Ricchi e Poveri" band, which is responsible for one of the 1970s' major hits, "Che sarà", attracted a lot of attention in Paris The Italian representatives, who had an impressive resume of performances at the Sanremo Festival and many hits, once again tried to impress the Europeans. "Questo Amore" was performed correctly, but almost as usual, when it comes to Italian songs at the Eurovision — only the test of time made them appreciated. In the three-minute test, the Italians were once again stuck in a disappointing place (12). "Anna rakkaudelle tilaisuus", asked the Finnish Seija Simola, who was marked by many since the promos as a potential surprise of the evening. Despite the beautiful and delicate melody that was magnificently arranged (by the great

Ossi Runne) no one awarded this song any points. No one — except Norway, which gave the Finns two points, saving them from falling with it to the bottom. Portugal sent another band, "Gemini", who did a memorable act when the German-Jewish conductor, Thilo Krassman, humorously threw records on the camera that accompanied them to the stage. Only Italy (4) and Spain (1) managed to save "Dai li dou" from even greater shame than the five points it finally received. France wished to overtake Luxembourg in the France restores the honour to the Eurovision: A year after surprisingly winning the contest in London, TF1 showed that it could do it far chicer than the satisfied British, featuring 20 countries (new record). Marie Myriam's victory made the locals' pride when they became kings of the Eurovision with five titles. In addition, the Francophone language rejuvenated (2nd, 3rd and 4th places) with a quarter of the contestants performing entries in French. The French were definitely hungry after 15 years of not hosting the most significant musical event in the world and presented a spectacular and meticulous production. "Palais des congrès de Paris", the glorious hall of congresses and events in Paris, hosted the event. For the first time, the French presented the "illuminated square stage", a format that will be repeated only in 1988 and the following years, with a bright and glittering background protruding from above and a dazzling disco ball. The attraction: An orchestra was rotating on the sides of the stage in the shape of a conch. Well-known French musical anchors could be spotted in the audience, among them Sylvie Vartan. The hosts made another history when for the first time, not one presenter was on stage but an excellent duo: Alongside Dénise Fabre was the fabulous Leon Citron. The chemistry between them, the lack of mistakes and supreme professionalism led to a perfect presentation — the best so far. The duo came up every five entries to introduce the next five. The rest of the time, they broadcast the contest to French television (this is efficiency). An opening film showing Paris brought the 700 million viewers into the unique atmosphere. After the opening remarks and explanation of the facilitators, it was possible to approach the business. Similar to the British the previous year, but for entirely different reasons, the French decided to abandon the 'postcards' — the videos documenting the artists in their countries — and innovatively accompany the performers behind the scenes, through the lift to the stage. At the end of each song, the previous performer waited at the back of the stage and shook hands with the next performer, before descending back to the 'Green Room'. Once again, Ireland was set to open the event. Colm Wilkinson, a supreme artist, actor and musician who has starred in major musicals around the world, was the Irish's hope. Wilkinson himself wrote and composed "Born to Sing" and was applauded and cheered, placing him at a respectable fifth place at the end of the evening. As per tradition, a record was produced with the entries that made up the ESC. Wilkinson's distribution company insisted on demanding royalties and unacceptable sums. Hence, unusually, on some Eurovision records, the Irish song was taken from the show itself (and some say it was much better than the original studio recording). Three times (besides Anne Karina in 1976) Norway "won" the last place. Until 1978, no country in the new system finished the evening with nul points. Jahn Teigen had the dubious honour and became the fifth Norwegian singer to return home with the last place, and with zero points out of 228 possible... "Mil Etter Mil" was very characteristic of the theatrical Teigen: A light-hearted and humorous presentation, but a rather bland song that on a relatively good evening musically, could not have survived the contest. But Teigen is not broken easily. "The singer who won 0 points at the 1978 Eurovision Song Contest" is a title that followed him for years, and thanks to his witty humour, he knew how to take it to his advantage, and make himself one of the biggest stars of his country. The "Ricchi e Poveri" band, which is responsible for one of the 1970s' major hits, "Che sarà", attracted a lot of attention in Paris The Italian representatives, who had an impressive resume of performances at the Sanremo Festival and many hits, once again tried to impress the Europeans. "Questo Amore" was performed correctly, but almost as usual, when it comes to Italian songs at the Eurovision — only the test of time made them appreciated. In the three-minute test, the Italians were once again stuck in a disappointing place (12). "Anna rakkaudelle tilaisuus", asked the Finnish Seija Simola, who was marked by many since the promos as a potential surprise of the evening. Despite the beautiful and delicate melody that was magnificently arranged (by the great Ossi Runne) no one awarded this song any points. No one — except Norway, which gave the Finns two points, saving them from falling with it to the bottom. Portugal sent another band, "Gemini", who did a memorable act when the German-Jewish conductor, Thilo Krassman, humorously threw records on the camera that accompanied them to the stage. Only Italy (4) and Spain (1) managed to save "Dai li dou" from even greater shame than the five points it finally received. France wished to overtake Luxembourg in the number of victories and equal its rare achievement of two consecutive wins.

28-year-old Joël Prévost was recruited for the mission, and he was convinced that winning the contest would jump-start his career. He had every reason to be optimistic: "Il y aura toujours des violons" was winning material.

France restores the honour to the Eurovision: A year after surprisingly winning the contest in London, TF1 showed that it could do it far chicer than the satisfied British, featuring 20 countries (new record). Marie Myriam's victory made the locals' pride when they became kings of the Eurovision with five titles. In addition, the Francophone language rejuvenated (2nd, 3rd and 4th places) with a quarter of the contestants performing entries in French. The French were definitely hungry after 15 years of not hosting the most significant musical event in the world and presented a spectacular and meticulous production. "Palais des congrès de Paris", the glorious hall of congresses and events in Paris, hosted the event. For the first time, the French presented the "illuminated square stage", a format that will be repeated only in 1988 and the following years, with a bright and glittering background protruding from above and a dazzling disco ball. The attraction: An orchestra was rotating on the sides of the stage in the shape of a conch. Well-known French musical anchors could be spotted in the audience, among them Sylvie Vartan. The hosts made another history when for the first time, not one presenter was on stage but an excellent duo: Alongside Dénise Fabre was the fabulous Leon Citron. The chemistry between them, the lack of mistakes and supreme professionalism led to a perfect presentation — the best so far. The duo came up every five entries to introduce the next five. The rest of the time, they broadcast the contest to French television (this is efficiency). An opening film showing Paris brought the 700 million viewers into the unique atmosphere. After the opening remarks and explanation of the facilitators, it was possible to approach the business. Similar to the British the previous year, but for entirely different reasons, the French decided to abandon the 'postcards' — the videos documenting the artists in their countries — and innovatively accompany the performers behind the scenes, through the lift to the stage. At the end of each song, the previous performer waited at the back of the stage and shook hands with the next performer, before descending back to the 'Green Room'. Once again, Ireland was set to open the event. Colm Wilkinson, a supreme artist, actor and musician who has starred in major musicals around the world, was the Irish's hope. Wilkinson himself wrote and composed "Born to Sing" and was applauded and cheered, placing him at a respectable fifth place at the end of the evening. As per tradition, a record was produced with the entries that made up the ESC. Wilkinson's distribution company insisted on demanding royalties and unacceptable sums. Hence, unusually, on some Eurovision records, the Irish song was taken from the show itself (and some say it was much better than the original studio recording). Three times (besides Anne Karina in 1976) Norway "won" the last place. Until 1978, no country in the new system finished the evening with nul points. Jahn Teigen had the dubious honour and became the fifth Norwegian singer to return home with the last place, and with zero points out of 228 possible... "Mil Etter Mil" was very characteristic of the theatrical Teigen: A light-hearted and humorous presentation, but a rather bland song that on a relatively good evening musically, could not have survived the contest. But Teigen is not broken easily. "The singer who won 0 points at the 1978 Eurovision Song Contest" is a title that followed him for years, and thanks to his witty humour, he knew how to take it to his advantage, and make himself one of the biggest stars of his country. The "Ricchi e Poveri" band, which is responsible for one of the 1970s' major hits, "Che sarà", attracted a lot of attention in Paris The Italian representatives, who had an impressive resume of performances at the Sanremo Festival and many hits, once again tried to impress the Europeans. "Questo Amore" was performed correctly, but almost as usual, when it comes to Italian songs at the Eurovision — only the test of time made them appreciated. In the three-minute test, the Italians were once again stuck in a disappointing place (12). "Anna rakkaudelle tilaisuus", asked the Finnish Seija Simola, who was marked by many since the promos as a potential surprise of the evening. Despite the beautiful and delicate melody that was magnificently arranged (by the great Ossi Runne) no one awarded this song any points. No one — except Norway, which gave the Finns two points, saving them from falling with it to the bottom. Portugal sent another band, "Gemini", who did a memorable act when the German-Jewish conductor, Thilo Krassman, humorously threw records on the camera that accompanied them to the stage. Only Italy (4) and Spain (1) managed to save "Dai li dou" from even greater shame than the five points it finally received. France wished to overtake Luxembourg in the number of victories and equal its rare achievement of two consecutive wins.

28-year-old Joël Prévost was recruited for the mission, and he was convinced that winning the contest would jump-start his career. He had every reason to be optimistic: "Il y aura toujours des violons" was winning material.

France restores the honour to the Eurovision: A year after surprisingly winning the contest in London, TF1 showed that it could do it far chicer than the satisfied British, featuring 20 countries (new record). Marie Myriam's victory made the locals' pride when they became kings of the Eurovision with five titles. In addition, the Francophone language rejuvenated (2nd, 3rd and 4th places) with a quarter of the contestants performing entries in French. The French were definitely hungry after 15 years of not hosting the most significant musical event in the world and presented a spectacular and meticulous production. "Palais des congrès de Paris", the glorious hall of congresses and events in Paris, hosted the event. For the first time, the French presented the "illuminated square stage", a format that will be repeated only in 1988 and the following years, with a bright and glittering background protruding from above and a dazzling disco ball. The attraction: An orchestra was rotating on the sides of the stage in the shape of a conch. Well-known French musical anchors could be spotted in the audience, among them Sylvie Vartan. The hosts made another history when for the first time, not one presenter was on stage but an excellent duo: Alongside Dénise Fabre was the fabulous Leon Citron. The chemistry between them, the lack of mistakes and supreme professionalism led to a perfect presentation — the best so far. The duo came up every five entries to introduce the next five. The rest of the time, they broadcast the contest to French television (this is efficiency). An opening film showing Paris brought the 700 million viewers into the unique atmosphere. After the opening remarks and explanation of the facilitators, it was possible to approach the business. Similar to the British the previous year, but for entirely different reasons, the French decided to abandon the 'postcards' — the videos documenting the artists in their countries — and innovatively accompany the performers behind the scenes, through the lift to the stage. At the end of each song, the previous performer waited at the back of the stage and shook hands with the next performer, before descending back to the 'Green Room'. Once again, Ireland was set to open the event. Colm Wilkinson, a supreme artist, actor and musician who has starred in major musicals around the world, was the Irish's hope. Wilkinson himself wrote and composed "Born to Sing" and was applauded and cheered, placing him at a respectable fifth place at the end of the evening. As per tradition, a record was produced with the entries that made up the ESC. Wilkinson's distribution company insisted on demanding royalties and unacceptable sums. Hence, unusually, on some Eurovision records, the Irish song was taken from the show itself (and some say it was much better than the original studio recording). Three times (besides Anne Karina in 1976) Norway "won" the last place. Until 1978, no country in the new system finished the evening with nul points. Jahn Teigen had the dubious honour and became the fifth Norwegian singer to return home with the last place, and with zero points out of 228 possible... "Mil Etter Mil" was very characteristic of the theatrical Teigen: A light-hearted and humorous presentation, but a rather bland song that on a relatively good evening musically, could not have survived the contest. But Teigen is not broken easily. "The singer who won 0 points at the 1978 Eurovision Song Contest" is a title that followed him for years, and thanks to his witty humour, he knew how to take it to his advantage, and make himself one of the biggest stars of his country. The "Ricchi e Poveri" band, which is responsible for one of the 1970s' major hits, "Che sarà", attracted a lot of attention in Paris The Italian representatives, who had an impressive resume of performances at the Sanremo Festival and many hits, once again tried to impress the Europeans. "Questo Amore" was performed correctly, but almost as usual, when it comes to Italian songs at the Eurovision — only the test of time made them appreciated. In the three-minute test, the Italians were once again stuck in a disappointing place (12). "Anna rakkaudelle tilaisuus", asked the Finnish Seija Simola, who was marked by many since the promos as a potential surprise of the evening. Despite the beautiful and delicate melody that was magnificently arranged (by the great Ossi Runne) no one awarded this song any points. No one — except Norway, which gave the Finns two points, saving them from falling with it to the bottom. Portugal sent another band, "Gemini", who did a memorable act when the German-Jewish conductor, Thilo Krassman, humorously threw records on the camera that accompanied them to the stage. Only Italy (4) and Spain (1) managed to save "Dai li dou" from even greater shame than the five points it finally received. France wished to overtake Luxembourg in the number of victories and equal its rare achievement of two consecutive wins.

28-year-old Joël Prévost was recruited for the mission, and he was convinced that winning the contest would jump-start his career. He had every reason to be optimistic: "Il y aura toujours des violons" was winning material.

France restores the honour to the Eurovision: A year after surprisingly winning the contest in London, TF1 showed that it could do it far chicer than the satisfied British, featuring 20 countries (new record). Marie Myriam's victory made the locals' pride when they became kings of the Eurovision with five titles. In addition, the Francophone language rejuvenated (2nd, 3rd and 4th places) with a quarter of the contestants performing entries in French. The French were definitely hungry after 15 years of not hosting the most significant musical event in the world and presented a spectacular and meticulous production. "Palais des congrès de Paris", the glorious hall of congresses and events in Paris, hosted the event. For the first time, the French presented the "illuminated square stage", a format that will be repeated only in 1988 and the following years, with a bright and glittering background protruding from above and a dazzling disco ball. The attraction: An orchestra was rotating on the sides of the stage in the shape of a conch. Well-known French musical anchors could be spotted in the audience, among them Sylvie Vartan. The hosts made another history when for the first time, not one presenter was on stage but an excellent duo: Alongside Dénise Fabre was the fabulous Leon Citron. The chemistry between them, the lack of mistakes and supreme professionalism led to a perfect presentation — the best so far. The duo came up every five entries to introduce the next five. The rest of the time, they broadcast the contest to French television (this is efficiency). An opening film showing Paris brought the 700 million viewers into the unique atmosphere. After the opening remarks and explanation of the facilitators, it was possible to approach the business. Similar to the British the previous year, but for entirely different reasons, the French decided to abandon the 'postcards' — the videos documenting the artists in their countries — and innovatively accompany the performers behind the scenes, through the lift to the stage. At the end of each song, the previous performer waited at the back of the stage and shook hands with the next performer, before descending back to the 'Green Room'. Once again, Ireland was set to open the event. Colm Wilkinson, a supreme artist, actor and musician who has starred in major musicals around the world, was the Irish's hope. Wilkinson himself wrote and composed "Born to Sing" and was applauded and cheered, placing him at a respectable fifth place at the end of the evening. As per tradition, a record was produced with the entries that made up the ESC. Wilkinson's distribution company insisted on demanding royalties and unacceptable sums. Hence, unusually, on some Eurovision records, the Irish song was taken from the show itself (and some say it was much better than the original studio recording). Three times (besides Anne Karina in 1976) Norway "won" the last place. Until 1978, no country in the new system finished the evening with nul points. Jahn Teigen had the dubious honour and became the fifth Norwegian singer to return home with the last place, and with zero points out of 228 possible... "Mil Etter Mil" was very characteristic of the theatrical Teigen: A light-hearted and humorous presentation, but a rather bland song that on a relatively good evening musically, could not have survived the contest. But Teigen is not broken easily. "The singer who won 0 points at the 1978 Eurovision Song Contest" is a title that followed him for years, and thanks to his witty humour, he knew how to take it to his advantage, and make himself one of the biggest stars of his country. The "Ricchi e Poveri" band, which is responsible for one of the 1970s' major hits, "Che sarà", attracted a lot of attention in Paris The Italian representatives, who had an impressive resume of performances at the Sanremo Festival and many hits, once again tried to impress the Europeans. "Questo Amore" was performed correctly, but almost as usual, when it comes to Italian songs at the Eurovision — only the test of time made them appreciated. In the three-minute test, the Italians were once again stuck in a disappointing place (12). "Anna rakkaudelle tilaisuus", asked the Finnish Seija Simola, who was marked by many since the promos as a potential surprise of the evening. Despite the beautiful and delicate melody that was magnificently arranged (by the great Ossi Runne) no one awarded this song any points. No one — except Norway, which gave the Finns two points, saving them from falling with it to the bottom. Portugal sent another band, "Gemini", who did a memorable act when the German-Jewish conductor, Thilo Krassman, humorously threw records on the camera that accompanied them to the stage. Only Italy (4) and Spain (1) managed to save "Dai li dou" from even greater shame than the five points it finally received. France wished to overtake Luxembourg in the number of victories and equal its rare achievement of two consecutive wins.

28-year-old Joël Prévost was recruited for the mission, and he was convinced that winning the contest would jump-start his career. He had every reason to be optimistic: "Il y aura toujours des violons" was winning material.

In addition to Prévost's confident performance and the home advantage, the feeling was that France would fight for first place. In practice, the French were far from winning but were eventually the only participant to receive points from all countries, achieving third place and 119 points. Nevertheless, Joël Prévost has made a historic achievement for his country that has yet to be restored: France is the only country that was awarded points from all participating nations throughout three consecutive contests. As mentioned, this is an unprecedented record that there is no telling when or if it will happen again. In 1976, the "Co-Co" band was one step away from participating in the ESC but was defeated by "Brotherhood of Man", and the rest is history. Two years later, it was "Co-Co"'s time. With a glorious record of 11 years at the top, the betting agencies set lofty expectations for "The Bad Old Days" of the United Kingdom. During rehearsals, the British got better, much to the credit of conductor Alyn Ainsworth, the same one who brought

"Brotherhood of Man" to that victory. In colourful and unusual clothing, the British band came on stage smiling and motivated, giving an exceptional performance (when the band drummer using a megaphone, for the first time in the contest). The behind-the-scenes talk was about a British win in Paris, but European juries seemed to be fed up with British hegemony, leaving "Co-Co" with only 61 points and a resounding and disappointing 11th place (the UK's worst result ever at the Eurovision). Terry Bradford, a member of the British band, took the relative failure in stride: "There is no bitterness in our hearts. When we heard the Israeli song - we knew it would be the winner." Another participant who spoke loudly about winning was Switzerland. The fragile Carole Vinci excited everyone in the rehearsals, and "Vivre" was noticed by directors of record companies that landed in the French capital. Alain Morisod and Pierre Alain (the songwriters) had already dreamed of the money they would make and the closing of a 22-year cycle, but even after Vinci did her thing on stage, the Swiss did not prevail in the voting and finished 10th. The one who arrived very mature and goal-oriented to the Eurovision in Paris, was the Belgian 'Belmondo', Jean Vallée. After experimenting in 1970, Vallée returned more experienced, with live performance being his best expertise. "L'amour ça fait chanter la vie" is a Francophone classic at its best, written by Vallée. The conductor Jean Musy already had a fourth place in his resume with France in 1975, but this time aimed much higher. The bets were on Vallée reaching the top five, but journalists and production people were exposed to the Belgian's strong side with the start of rehearsals. On the big night, a momentary upheaval turned him from another performer with chances to win, into the hot favourite, when he electrified the Palais des Congrès. The crowd went wild, applauding minutes after the performance ended. Indeed, the votes' opening made it clear that the Belgian entry could make history, leading after three votes, but in a legendary two-way battle, Jean Valla surrendered. Nevertheless, this could not nullify the record he achieved for his country in the European contest (second place and 125 points). The law that requires every country to sing in its own language prevented many countries from singing in English. The Netherlands was the one to pay the price: "'t Is OK" was recorded in English and became a successful hit in Europe. but the Dutch were forced to sing a version in their language, what left them with only 37 points and 13th place, even though Israel chose to award them the full 12 points. Tough years indeed for a nation that was a true Eurovision empire. The British Ireen Sheer had already represented Luxembourg in 1974 and was chosen this time to represent Germany. "Feuer" was also one of the entries that could go all the way. Sheer's white dress and shiny make-up left an impression, and the Germans scored 84 points and sixth place, their best since 1972. For the third year in a row, Monaco surpasses itself and sends potent classics. Olivier Toussaint, who wrote Michèle Torr's successful entry in 1977, decided not only to write again but to move to the forefront and perform "Les Jardins de Monaco" alongside Caline. It was evident that Monaco would go far and might even win thanks to the return of French sovereignty and the memorable hit. Monaco received 107 points and achieved the fourth and most honourable place in a second consecutive year, all this only one year before retiring from the contest for many years ("Les Jardins de Monaco" was and remained one of the favourite songs in the Eurovision history). In London, Greece was the surprise of the evening. The task placed on the shoulders of the comedian-singer, Tania Tsanaklidou, was burdensome: Recreate the success from 1977 and finish higher than Turkey. For the first time, the two countries participated in the contest together, after years of mutual boycotts. "Charlie Chaplin" is not a typical Greek song, but a humorous and brave performance that is a kind of homage to one of the greatest comedians in history. The excellent arrangement of the conductor Haris Andreadis and Tsanaklidou's graceful performance did not manage to recreate Pascalis, Marianna, Robert and Bessy's achievement. Still, it brought 66 points and a respectable 8th for the Greeks, and most importantly for them — 64 points more than Turkey, which finished in penultimate place with the "Nazar" band. After 12 years, Denmark returned to the contest. Its return was pretty refreshing with the sympathetic band "Mabel" which included singer Mike Tramp (who went on to have a glorious singing career) and Andy Kulmbak, who stole the thunder with a giant heart drum — one of the most memorable views of 1978 Eurovision in general and Denmark's history in the Eurovision. "Boom Boom" was an attraction in rehearsals, and it seemed that the Danes could, after a long absence, reach one of the first places. But for some reason, despite a playful performance, "Mabel" did not penetrate the juries' armour. Above all, the "Baccara" girls were the clear and unequivocal candidates to win the Paris ESC. Just a year earlier, "Yes Sir, I Can Boogie" turned the world upside down and was the icing on the cake at every party. The Spanish duo, riding on the waves of success and other hits, decided to go on Eurovision's adventure. Musical director Rolf Soja led the move, the same one who created the golden hits and wrote "Parlez-vous français?", which bears a striking and suspicious resemblance to their massive hit. Luxembourg jumped on the bargain and had already polished its National Theatre stages for the 1979 contest since the betting agencies had closed the possibility of putting money on "Baccara" at some point. Added to the well-known fact that favourites rarely win the Eurovision was the hatred and aversion of the juries towards the betting tables and the feeling that they are trying to "determine" for them. The "Baccara" girls arrived in Paris with self-importance, inaccessible and arrogant, which upset many of the participants. "Parlez-vous français?" was sold in record stores and after the duo's appearance, it seemed that the vote was only formal. The slap that the Luxembourg representatives received will not be forgotten for a long time: Although Italy, Portugal and of course Spain gave "Douze Points" to Baccara, the other countries were not impressed with the favourites and sent them home with a downcast face and seventh place. In Israel, profound lessons were learned from the relative failures in the previous contest: Instead of a committee, the Eurovision entry would be chosen from the big and successful song festival that produced many hits. No one imagined that this decision would make such a significant history and so fast. In fact, the Israeli production people hoped that Hedva Amrani and "Belev Echad" would go to Paris and try to win, but Izhar Cohen stirred things up with "A-Ba-Ni-Bi" (ingenious writing by Ehud Manor with a chorus on the purity of "Bet language" — a children's language game where each syllable of the word is repeated with a bet preceding the consonant) and travelled unpretentiously to the French capital. Israel was ranked so low in the betting tables that Israeli television, in one of its biggest failures of all time, decided to order only two hours of satellite time and save the last twenty minutes of the broadcast "because no matter who wins, it's a waste of extra satellite time." In rehearsals, the Israelis were a rare bird: A song with a modern and rare rhythm, a young movement on stage choreographed by Shlomo Rosmarin, and a repetitive chorus in the Bet-language. On his way to the stage, Cohen smiled, and when he reached out to the "Baccara" girls who were waiting on the side of the stage, he received a cold handshake from them while they were not even looking at him and were busy analysing their performance. When he settled for the big moment of his life with the "Alphabeta group", Cohen conquered the stage and thanks to Rosmarin's outstanding choreography, he brought 'something new' to the hundreds of millions watching. The feeling in the Israeli camp was good, but still ... Who even thought of winning? Ehud Manor, the songwriter, a modest and socialising man, sat in the 'Green Room' with jeans and sandals. When the results started coming in, and the Israeli victory became tangible, Manor stripped the song composer's husband from his suit, and so he was seen "in his best clothes" when he later received the award as the winning song's writer. At first, it was a close race between Israel and Belgium, until a sudden streak of five douze points from Turkey (!), Germany, Switzerland, the Netherlands and the biggest competitor: Belgium, an unprecedented situation and established the Israeli victory (the 18th entry wins for the second year in a row, which will be repeated in 1982). The question that remained open was whether "A-Ba-Ni-Bi" could break the record of "Brotherhood of Man" and reach the highest score in history, but Sweden prevented it, being the only country that did not award any points to Israel. Björn Skifs was the Swedish representative in Paris. The young and messy singer, unwilling to put up with the rules, showed up for rehearsals with "Det blir alltid värre framåt natten" and performed it in English, contrary to the laws that require him to sing in the official language of his country. The EBU issued a public warning that the Swedish entry would be disqualified if Skifs sang it in English. As the Swedish singer continued to insist and sing in English, tensions escalated in the run-up to the event, resulting in an explicit threat from the Swedish delegation to its representative: "Sing in Swedish, or there will be consequences". Skifs absorbed the situation, sat down at the piano and in front of hundreds of millions spoke to the audience: "Sorry kept you waiting, but here is the top of the bill" ... When he started singing, he forgot his song's first lines and improvised with unclear murmurs of words... He later regained his composure, finished in 14th place, and perhaps got off the situation easy, although he learned his lesson and became one of Sweden's most esteemed artists. Between the entries and the results, the French provided a fine musical break with jazz artists Stephane Grappelli and Oscar Peterson, but the icing on the cake was the renowned Jewish violinist Yehudi Menuhin. Unlike the previous year, the French scoreboard was bright and efficient. No faults, smooth flow of results and complete control of the presenters — a hundred and eighty degrees from 1977. Following a series of glitches and problems, it was time for Clifford Brown to retire from his position as general supervisor of the contest. In his place was the director of special programs at the EBU, Frank Naef, in a temporary appointment that became permanent for 14 years. Israel and Belgium conducted a two-way race until the latter voted. From that moment on, Israel opened a fantastic lead, which shrank only towards the end, but not significantly. When Yitzhak Shimoni came up with the Israeli results, it was already evident, even theoretically, that his representatives would be in the first place. When he was done, the Jewish presenter Leon Citron greeted him in Hebrew: "Many thanks to Jerusalem for the cooperation." The end of voting darkened the board, while only the word Israel, and the substantial number of points it achieved, shone with precious light. Little Israel, which is located outside of Europe, is the big winner of the Eurovision — the most prominent music contest in the world — and is the country that everyone talked about that evening. As a tribute to Israel, a Star of David shone on the back of the stage, when Marie Myriam, captains of the EBU and seniors from French television waited for the writers, the "Alphabeta group" and Izhar Cohen who seemed to be walking on a cloud. Shlomo Zach also won the prestigious gold medal of victory and walked liked a groom on his wedding day. However, the people of Israel did not get to witness any of this, since the broadcast was interrupted seconds before Luxembourg gave Israel its sixth douze points and public outrage knew no bounds and rightly so. In distress, the Israelis sought the rest of the broadcast on a Jordanian station, which also televised the event, but it was interrupted there for other reasons: As the sensational Israeli victory became more apparent, the Jordanians panicked and broadcast slides with flowers. In their nightly news, the Jordanians said that Belgium (which finished second) is the Eurovision winner... The event was also broadcast to four other Arab countries: Algeria, Morocco, Tunisia and Dubai. In all these countries, except Dubai, the Israeli entry was not broadcast, but the results until the winning song's re-performance were aired. In an attempt to atone for the colossal failure, Israeli television broadcast the missing minutes of the Eurovision the next evening, including the moment of winning and awarding the prizes. An anonymous hand hid the Paris Eurovision tape from the IBA archives. How unfortunate that such a great moment was doomed. All this, of course, did not matter to Izhar Cohen. When he went up to perform "A-Ba-Ni-Bi" again, he did not know what was coming... That night Israeli Prime Minister Menachem Begin sent a telegram to the Israeli delegation in France: "You have gladdened the heart of the people and exalted the horn of Israel among the nations". Izhar Cohen and his band were not ready for what happened at the traditional after-party for the Eurovision Song Contest in Paris: "Clothes were torn, gold watches fell to the floor, women's shoe heels were dislodged," journalist Tamar Golan reported. A possibly antisemitic incident was provided by the announcer of the French national radio station: "We were unable to play the Israeli song for you... We did not think it would win, so we did not get it in advance. Besides, I had no idea Israel was in Europe; I assumed it was in Asia."

In Israel itself, thousands crowded near the Great Soliman's house (Izhar's father) in Giv'atayim, and tens of thousands celebrated the historic victory that is still considered one of the most exciting moments in the history of the State of Israel. However, there was no time to digest the amazing achievement, since another history was now on the agenda: Hosting the big event in Jerusalem.

1979 – Jerusalem, Israel

Izhar Cohen's big victory in 1978 in Paris had many consequences. The biggest one — hosting the 1979 ESC in Israel. How can a country with a young ten-year-old television authority that still broadcast in black and white, controlled by committees with electronic equipment that is mostly obsolete and outdated in most other European broadcasters, withstand a wide international production? Furthermore, it was an enormous financial burden for a country that was not accustomed to projects of this kind. The EBU felt uncomfortable with the Israeli victory. Beyond the political and security inconveniences in organizing the contest in Israel, it would be the first time the ESC would be held in the Asian continent... Arab countries exerted heavy pressure to boycott Israel, despite the peace treaty with Egypt that calmed hostility between the peoples. For Arabs and Muslims, the contest in Jerusalem was a red rag. Turkey tried to withstand the pressure, with a pre-elimination in which Maria Rita Epik won with "Seviyorum", which received compliments and was supposed to give Turkey the best position in its history at the Eurovision. Maria Rita Epik was shocked to discover two weeks before the dream of her life came true, while Turkey's name was already on the official logo and transitional clips were ready, that her country had raised a white flag in the face of threats from Arab countries and withdrew from the contest. The Turks would justify their retirement by stating that Israel had changed the event's location from Tel Aviv to Jerusalem and could not agree to that, but this was absurd since the fact of holding the ESC in Jerusalem was known to everyone six months before. Epik herself protested and was furious at the opportunity of her life being taken from her, and she retired from her singing career, while still teaching music in Istanbul. The Maghreb countries (Morocco, Algeria and Tunisia), which were used to broadcast the European contest, also boycotted the event, along with Jordan. Nonetheless, these facts were not supposed to ruin Israel's largest international celebration since its inception. The challenges were not only expressed in boycotts and expulsions: The decision to hold the contest in Israel was not smooth nor quick, obtaining the budgets was an arduous task, and the Broadcasting Authority had no idea how to make the giant production. After financial matters were settled and the EBU was given a lull notice, there were about six months left to prepare for the most-watched television event in the world. The decision that turned out to be the most ingenious was appointing Mr. Alex Gilady as the event's producer. Gilady, who began his television career as a journalist and esteemed sports broadcaster, continued to climb the ladder to the position of director of the sports department at the Israeli television and was discovered to be a brilliant media person, not to mention a prodigy. In 1977 he edited and produced one of the most complicated television broadcasts in Israel: Egyptian President Anwar Sadat's visit to Jerusalem (even then the international broadcast networks set their eyes on him). History entrusted Gilady with broadcasting unforgettable moments in Israeli sports: The Munich massacre, the winning of Maccabi Tel Aviv in the 1977 FIBA European Champions Cup and the historic ball game that same year against the Soviet sports giant CSKA Moscow. When Israel won the 1978 ESC in Paris, and it was clarified that the contest would take place in Israel the next year, there was no doubt for IBA director Arnon Zuckerman and CEO Yitzhak Livni that Alex Gilady would be the one to produce the most important television event ever in Israel. Gilady had a bellyful professionally for the local television that began broadcasting in 1968: "The establishment of television in Israel was disgraceful. The rest of the world had already started broadcasting in colour. If you have already decided to set up something new, why rely on the old? All the equipment brought here was from the junkyards of other televisions globally, and it was just awkward. To my delight, the Eurovision Song Contest in Jerusalem was one of the catalysts that pushed the start-up nation to start broadcasting, no-frills, in colour." In addition to Gilady, the professional decisions were made by Arnon Zuckerman and director Yossi Tzemach.

Izhar Cohen's big victory in 1978 in Paris had many consequences. The biggest one — hosting the 1979 ESC in Israel. How can a country with a young ten-year-old television authority that still broadcast in black and white, controlled by committees with electronic equipment that is mostly obsolete and outdated in most other European broadcasters, withstand a wide international production? Furthermore, it was an enormous financial burden for a country that was not accustomed to projects of this kind. The EBU felt uncomfortable with the Israeli victory. Beyond the political and security inconveniences in organizing the contest in Israel, it would be the first time the ESC would be held in the Asian continent... Arab countries exerted heavy pressure to boycott Israel, despite the peace treaty with Egypt that calmed hostility between the peoples. For Arabs and Muslims, the contest in Jerusalem was a red rag. Turkey tried to withstand the pressure, with a pre-elimination in which Maria Rita Epik won with "Seviyorum", which received compliments and was supposed to give Turkey the best position in its history at the Eurovision. Maria Rita Epik was shocked to discover two weeks before the dream of her life came true, while Turkey's name was already on the official logo and transitional clips were ready, that her country had raised a white flag in the face of threats from Arab countries and withdrew from the contest. The Turks would justify their retirement by stating that Israel had changed the event's location from Tel Aviv to Jerusalem and could not agree to that, but this was absurd since the fact of holding the ESC in Jerusalem was known to everyone six months before. Epik herself protested and was furious at the opportunity of her life being taken from her, and she retired from her singing career, while still teaching music in Istanbul. The Maghreb countries (Morocco, Algeria and Tunisia), which were used to broadcast the European contest, also boycotted the event, along with Jordan. Nonetheless, these facts were not supposed to ruin Israel's largest international celebration since its inception. The challenges were not only expressed in boycotts and expulsions: The decision to hold the contest in Israel was not smooth nor quick, obtaining the budgets was an arduous task, and the Broadcasting Authority had no idea how to make the giant production. After financial matters were settled and the EBU was given a lull notice, there were about six months left to prepare for the most-watched television event in the world. The decision that turned out to be the most ingenious was appointing Mr. Alex Gilady as the event's producer. Gilady, who began his television career as a journalist and esteemed sports broadcaster, continued to climb the ladder to the position of director of the sports department at the Israeli television and was discovered to be a brilliant media person, not to mention a prodigy. In 1977 he edited and produced one of the most complicated television broadcasts in Israel: Egyptian President Anwar Sadat's visit to Jerusalem (even then the international broadcast networks set their eyes on him). History entrusted Gilady with broadcasting unforgettable moments in Israeli sports: The Munich massacre, the winning of Maccabi Tel Aviv in the 1977 FIBA European Champions Cup and the historic ball game that same year against the Soviet sports giant CSKA Moscow. When Israel won the 1978 ESC in Paris, and it was clarified that the contest would take place in Israel the next year, there was no doubt for IBA director Arnon Zuckerman and CEO Yitzhak Livni that Alex Gilady would be the one to produce the most important television event ever in Israel. Gilady had a bellyful professionally for the local television that began broadcasting in 1968: "The establishment of television in Israel was disgraceful. The rest of the world had already started broadcasting in colour. If you have already decided to set up something new, why rely on the old? All the equipment brought here was from the junkyards of other televisions globally, and it was just awkward. To my delight, the Eurovision Song Contest in Jerusalem was one of the catalysts that pushed the start-up nation to start broadcasting, no-frills, in colour." In addition to Gilady, the professional decisions were made by Arnon Zuckerman and director Yossi Tzemach.

This was the trio that determined the production of 1979 Eurovision, when figures like Yitzhak Shimoni, the designated television director, and Hanoch Hasson who aspired to get a role in the giant production, had to bend and accept the authority of Gilady, Israel's most talented television person. "My affair with Eurovision started in 1978 when we realised that the satellite broadcasting time booked for the contest in Paris was limited to two hours. When it became clear that we were going to win, the magnitude of the default became apparent. I was approached in panic and asked to use my connections with Kevin O'Malley from CBS to try to get satellite time that will be enough to complete the Eurovision broadcast, and the people of Israel could witness Izhar Cohen receive the first prize. Unfortunately, the brief alert and the fact that O'Malley needed a satellite at the time to broadcast a significant boxing match in the United States failed to prevent the disgrace". Even then, Gilady realised that he had to work alone and rely on himself if he wanted to succeed. According to him, Gilady did not review previous contests and did not look at tapes from other Eurovision events: "I had my vision, and I knew exactly what I wanted to do. I was not given this position to copy from others". At the time, it must be said, the EBU was not overly involved in the production content and contented itself with the position of the observer. Frank Naef has been to Israel several times, and Gilady defined the cooperation with the EBU members as remarkably successful in general. Gilady undertook the production on some key conditions: Each employee in the project will receive two tickets to the show (not a manageable condition since there were 400 workers, meaning that 800 tickets, about a third of the hall, was seized by television people), a conference team of "Kenes" company led by Daniel Ben Naim (who himself became a successful international producer) will be responsible for security in the nation's buildings (not at all a simple matter In Jerusalem of those days: "I knew that if the ushers of 'Binyenei HaUma' were responsible for security, 5,000 people would enter the hall and not 2,400..."); I wanted the broadcast would not be transmitted from a satellite truck but from a special control room to be set up on the 2nd floor of the hall (to enable normal and convenient workspace for a complicated production of this kind)". All of Gilady's conditions were met one by one: "We started the preparations on time. I do not remember any delays or problems. My model was the 1976 Montreal Olympics". First, the host city had to be chosen. Of course, politicians pressed for Jerusalem, but this issue was not closed or guaranteed in advance at all: "We thought of Eilat, Tiberias and Caesarea. Tel Aviv was not in the picture at all. We thought of bringing a different train of thought and holding the Eurovision in an open space, but we finally realised that the production was already overwhelmed with the burden of budget issues and "Binyenei HaUma" was the only place that met the criteria". The choice of presenters was also a prominent issue: "Arie Orgad wanted to present, but to me, from a television point of view, and I told him that to his face, he was a cold fish. Dan Shilon, whom I very much appreciated, was in the United States, and when Arnon Zuckerman approved Daniel Pe'er's candidacy, it was possible to check this one off. The problem was with the female side since the first condition was that she spoke French, which was not available. I received a phone call from producer Shai Nesher informing me that Yardena Arazi is a French speaker. That solved the issue, and so we decided to go with her. We were not wrong." As a highly meticulous person, Gilady needed to welcome foreign delegations: "Everyone was received at our International Airport as VIP guests. The Eurovision was a holy word in the country; everyone got involved and knew that the country's face and image are at stake". The choice of Ziko Graziani as conductor of the IBA Orchestra was not an issue: "There was no doubt as to who was the best in this field. Ziko deserved to conduct, and he did his job on the best side, with compliments and kind words the orchestra received from the foreign conductors. I came across all sorts of requests that until then were foreign to me from the musical field: A unique orchestra pit for Ziko and a Metronome. Until then, I did not know what a metronome was... In any case, the only one who used the metronome was the Israeli conductor Kobi Oshrat". Gilady, as usual, set a tough and uncompromising schedule for the meticulous and accurate execution of every detail in the prestigious production and the 400 workers who were under him followed his instructions perfectly: "Everything was on time, like clockwork. When there is a plan, a schedule and everyone knows what they are doing — you do not have to rely on luck for the result to be good and successful". Everyone who entered the gates of "Binyenei HaUma" on the eve of the show, received an unusual welcome for an event in the State of Israel: "After passing the magnetometer, people were accompanied by a host, received a special program and a lilac flower that was brought especially on the day of the event from a nursery in the Beit She'an Valley". The Eurovision stage in Jerusalem is still remembered as pioneering and one of the most beautiful in history: "This stage was spoken of for 20 years. Yes, today everything has been perfected and lost a bit of proportion compared to then, but the symbol on the back of the stage that changed shape and the different setting for each entry did their own". "I can, unfortunately, point out two mistakes. One was the camera at the beginning of the broadcast in front of Daniel Pe'er, and the other a slight entanglement of Pe'er with the text, when luckily Yardena Arazi got him out of it". The passages, led by Yoram Boker, also resonated: "It was Yossi Tzemach's idea, we chose themes for each country, and the truth is that we set a precedent here because for the first time we did not send the viewers to pictures and landscapes they know by heart, but we introduced new and interesting animated content." In terms of entries, Gilady did not have a clear favourite: "Practically all of the songs were great. It is said to this day that part of the success was the excellent collection of songs. In rehearsals, I heard more enthusiasm around our 'Hallelujah'. Apparently, it was the first taste on the way to the second consecutive victory. Anne Marie David decided to perform with a David Star and Micha Marah from Belgium with a 'hamsa' necklace. It did not help any of them "... One of the great successes of the event was the performance of the 'Shalom 79' band led by the late Gavri Levy: "They were outstanding and were talked about a lot after the event. A door to perform abroad opened up for them". Today, Gilady reveals that their spectacular dances were pre-recorded and not broadcast alive: "To be on the safe side, since no one knows what it will look like in the decisive moment, we asked to record the performance of the band 'Shalom 79' on Wednesday night, and they were perfect. This is what was broadcast on the big evening. We combined the recorded with the live, to simulate a feeling of as live a broadcast as possible". Gilady faced quite a few technical problems; the battle for credit is just one example. It was decided that the broadcast would end without a roll of credits, similar to the 1977 and 1978 contests, and this is where the buzz began: Who would still be mentioned, why and how much. "To set a personal example and prevent discussions and protests, the only credit given in the international broadcast in a foreign language was to director Yossi Tzemach while I gave up mine". However, a mile-long roller appeared at the end of the broadcast in Israel, with full credit to everyone engaged in the craft and contributed to the event. The conclusion for Gilady surpassed imagination: "The Eurovision was an enormous success; everything went great, especially the breath-taking ending that set us up for an unusual live drama. The most important thing for me is that we brought recognition to Israeli talent and to the fact that Israel is a fun place to visit — this was the feeling all the delegations returned home with". Gilady's success did not go unnoticed by the American NBC network, which got its hands on him and took Alex Gilady in as a special vice president. Later on, he made the unbelievable and was appointed as a member of the International Olympic Committee and the right-hand of the legendary former president Juan Antonio Samaranch. He later returned to Israel and received the tender to operate the second Television channel in the country, when he established "Keshet Broadcasting" from the ground up, but the board did not let him enjoy the fruits of the revolution he had created. The choice of director Yossi Tzemach also proved itself: Dov Ben-David was entrusted with the construction of the stage and left an unforgettable impression. It was somewhat reminiscent of the 1970 Eurovision stage, but the Israeli stage also had a bit of the wide and bright arc of the 1977 contest. The visibility was fantastic and won much praise and feedback. Two and a half months before the event, "Binyenei HaUma" became a fortified and preserved destination, dealing exclusively with Eurovision matters. Like 1976 in The Hague, the orchestra's position was at the bottom of the front of the stage, which could have disturbed the audience in the front rows and the overall picture. But it has been proven that an orchestra in front of the stage produces perhaps the best sound for the singer on stage. The IBA orchestra, consisting of 39 musicians, was well prepared for the event by the legendary music director and conductor Ziko Graziani. Although to the viewer and the listener it sounded like there was no balance between the strings and the wind instruments, Graziani and the orchestra won much praise for superior accuracy and especially for the advance preparation that facilitated the work in rehearsals. Those who received the most publicity were the percussionists Meir Israel and Alon Hillel, who were in the middle of the orchestra and were the most captured by the camera. The intended presenter, Yardena Arazi, consulted with producer Shlomo Zach, who at the same time offered her to be the lead singer of the Israel entry that year — "Hallelujah" ... "Because 'Hallelujah' might not win, and your presentation is certain —

go for the presentation". The initial exploration, which led to Daniel Pe'er's presentation, took place in the toiletter of the television building: While Pe'er was washing his hands, the television director Yitzhak Shimoni came in, stared at him and asked: "Danny, were not you an English teacher at the university?". Pe'er said yes. "Would you like to present the Eurovision Song Contest?" Pe'er did not refuse. Israel was festive, and the whole country spoke only of the contest. The entries were played nonstop on the radio stations. On television, almost every newscast opened with the preparations for an event that will turn the country, in one evening, into a centre to which hundreds of millions of viewers will look up. The production of the colour broadcast was also a novelty and a standard that had to be met. Almost everyone wanted to watch the full-colour Eurovision, so many purchased colour television sets. Those who did not, made sure to be invited (or invite themselves) to someone who did have such a television. For the first time, an Israeli narrator accompanied the broadcast: Sports broadcaster Yoram Arbel. Yitzhak Shimoni was honoured to lead the broadcast on the radio, so, for the first time, Dan Caner was the one to read the Israeli juries' results. Maybe it was a consolation prize for not receiving the contest presentation. Dudu Geva illustrated image and movement transitions. Yet, the stars were the pantomimes Yoram Boker and his band that included Hanoch Rosen, Uri Tenenbaum, Ezra Dagan and Irit Lavi-Dagan, who presented each country in parody. The Belgians took it badly and submitted an official objection to the EBU, Israeli television and the Israeli government concerning the clip about them. The video showed two Belgians, trying to move a table without success, each pulling in the opposite direction... Ezra Dagan (married to the singer Tzila Dagan, who competed at the 1979 Song Festival), met Irit Lavi on set and the two later became a married couple who live together to this day. Except for the Belgian incident, the pantomime clips were a considerable success, and Yoram Boker received letters of admiration and appreciation from hundreds of viewers in Europe. At 22:00 Israel time, the state held its breath. The ESC was broadcast all over Europe, and the opening film (accompanied by Cosma's theme — "Rabbi Jacob") brought tears of true excitement to every Israeli. Thirty-one years after the state's establishment and less than half a century after the end of World War II, the State of Israel, of the Jews, is hosting the most important event of the European continent. "In thy blood, live", the entry into "Yad Vashem", live for hundreds of millions, including tens of millions of Germans, which who knows how they felt at that very moment — were an emotional record in Israeli broadcasting. This was perhaps the most exciting opening film ever made at the beginning of the contest, not just from an Israeli perspective. At the end of the film, the beautiful stage was exposed for all to see and Yardena Arazi and Daniel Pe'er began their work. Manuela Bravo from Portugal was the first to perform "Sobe, sobe, balão sobe" and bring Portugal its best achievement since 1971, with the German-Jewish conductor Thilo Krassman being excited to represent Portugal and do so on Holy Land soil. The Italian band "Matia Bazar", winner of the Sanremo festival was no more successful than its predecessor in Paris ("Ricchi e Poveri") and "Raggio di luna" reached only 15th place. The Italians were the only ones to give up a conductor for the orchestra. The Danish Tommy Seebach was one of the Israeli audience's favourites. "Disco Tango" was known In Europe as well, and it was clear that this was Denmark's best chance to win since 1963. Accompanied by Debbie Cameron on stage and conducted by Allan Botschinsky, Tommy received 12 prestigious points from Israel, but in a year with so many good entries, even being 6th made satisfied Seebach. For the second year in a row, the Irish sent a singer who wrote and composed the entry he performed, and in Jerusalem, as in Paris, Cathal Dunne excited with "Happy Man" and reached the fifth place, placing his country at the top of European music. Finland was represented by the country's most famous female singer, Katri Helena. "Katson sineen taivaan" was recorded in English and was also a song played in Israel. The handsome Helena expected to lead Finland to the top ten and the 14th place she reached, definitely deprived her. The Finnish conductor, Ossi Runne, the veteran of the contest, complimented the Israeli orchestra and said it was the best orchestra he had ever conducted at the Eurovision. For Monaco, it was a farewell performance from the contest until returning a quarter of a century later. Jean Baudlot who wrote Monaco's two successful entries from 1977 and 1978 hoped to continue the sequence, with another big name, Jean Albertini, joining him to create "Notre vie c'est la musique", a typical and modern French disco song. The performer, Laurent Vaguener, was underwhelming and Monaco dropped to the 16th place. The entry "Sokrati" performed by Elpida, spread widely in Israel before the contest, was not loved only by the Israeli public. The Greeks came self-confident, feeling that this is their moment. In Europe, the Greek song was remarkably high in the betting tables and their delegation, which once barely included the singer and conductor, was big and fancy. One of Greek television's representative at the event repeatedly interrogated the production, until they asked why, and he replied: "We want to learn how to do it next year." But lofty expectations lead to great disappointment. Greece came on strong with 10 points from Portugal but did not last and Elpida finished in the same place as the Greeks in the previous year — the eighth (while Israel also awarding it 10 points). That did not prevent her from performing across the country and the song's producers from earning quite a few royalties. Incidentally, the entry's composer, Doros Georgiades, arrived in Israel on a ship after his mother made him promise not to fly since she was convinced that if he comes by plane, he will die... The Swiss were exceptional: For the third time, Peter, Sue and Marc performed on the Eurovision stage, accompanied by another trio, this time with an unforgettable rag and bone performance. When the Swiss landed in Israel with a rake, a bucket, hollow pipes, broken shutters, a dresser and a large bin — the Israeli border police interrogated them about all this equipment...

"Trödler und Co" is one of the most bizarre songs in the contest's history. During rehearsals, and on the big evening, the production required extraordinary creativity, to suffice and place all the Swiss rag and bone equipment and evacuate it in time (before the next entry starts). It ended well, with "Peter, Sue and Marc" giving the Israeli and European audiences a funny and memorable performance that ended in tenth place, with 60 points and one "douze points" from Austria. By the way, the Swiss performers submitted their resume to the media on... Paper garbage bags. The attraction was Swiss, but the real show came from Germany: Ralph Siegel and Bernd Meinunger returned with "Dschinghis Khan", a homage to the Mongol Empire's domination, an innovative disco and acrobatic performance by the German band that called itself, how original, "Dschinghis Khan"... With Norbert Daum's conducting, the Germans received the highest applause from the stands and thoughts of a first victory for the great country in Europe were undoubtedly realistic. The Germans collected a considerable amount of 4 Douze Points (from Italy, Monaco, France and Spain), which are 48 points, but the remaining countries chose to only award them only 38 points, bringing it to a total of 86 points which still carried the Germans to their best place since 1972 — the 4th. Israel walked on a dream in 1979, after Izhar Cohen's victory. Everyone wanted to be in the local Song Festival to participate in the first Eurovision in Israel and, perhaps, win. Kobi Oshrat that went through many hardships until he came to rest with "Hallelujah" when the band "Habibi" was supposed to perform the song (which in 1978 was not even selected for the festival...), but the band's lead singer Shlomit Aharon decided to retire at the last minute. Producer Shlomo Zach, who always manages to make eggs from an omelette, had to find other "Habibi" matches. As a soloist, he had no problem bringing Gali Atari, who was signed to his office anyway. In an unusual move, Zach gathered Yehuda Tamir, Shmuel Bilu and Reuven Gvirtz, who were, of course, grateful for the opportunity and formed one of the most beloved bands in Israel, "Milk and Honey". Like "A-Ba-Ni-Bi", "Hallelujah"'s path to winning the festival was difficult and tedious: Svika Pick and (once again) Hedva Amrani, gave a tough competition. At the end of the evening, Shlomo Zach smiled as his band beat the popular Pick by two points and Amrani by six points, while the "Sexta" band and talented Sherry also giving a close fight. Then, the composer was facing another problem: The entry's duration exceeded by almost half a minute from the Eurovision rules explicitly stating that it shall not exceed three minutes. Oshrat once again proved that he is in a league of his own, even when it comes to arrangements and improvisations, and prepared an updated version for the orchestra (faster and a little shorter). "Hallelujah" was a top bet in England and elsewhere, the second win for Israel seemed tangible. Nevertheless, the great fear of the unknown and the 'curse of the favourites' was like a cloud hanging over the Israeli delegation. Before the dress rehearsal, two traditional girls sneaked in with a note to "Milk and Honey": "Enter the stage on the right foot and say the verse 'Noah found favour in the eyes of the Lord' seven times and you will win the Eurovision". There was nothing to lose, and so all the band members including conductor Kobi Oshrat followed the suggestion. Gali Atari and the trio's performance was perfect, and the audience responded accordingly. A sense of victory was in the air. One thing disrupted the boundless joy: Kobi Oshrat insisted on a musical instrument that produces bells' sound; such was given to him during the song's recording. Yet, for the Eurovision itself, they brought him an inferior quality instrument that did not respond so much to Alon Hillel's drumming... After a very tense vote, Israel won the contest for the second consecutive time and was on top of the world. Like in 1978, entry number ten reached 125 points. However, in Paris, Belgium had to settle for second place while in Jerusalem "Milk and Honey" celebrated a great victory. Anne-Marie David, the winner of the 1973 ESC, was determined to do that again, this time for her country France. "Je suis l'enfant soleil" was marked by experts as qualified to do precisely what Marie Myriam did in 1977 — surprise and win against all odds. David attracted a lot of attention in Israel and won major credit and respect. Apparently, her performance got even better, and her voice remained clear and even more accurate. At certain moments in the contest, after Douze points from the Netherlands and Luxembourg, she clung to first place and finally settled for third with 106 points. Once again, France finished third, for the sixth time. It was well-known that Belgium was in trouble in odd-numbered years, especially since the law compelling it to sing in its official language. These years are the Flemish and their entries' turn, which rarely reach the French-language entries' achievements. After finishing second in Paris, it was clear that too many miracles had to happen for the actor Micha Marah and the song "Hey Nana" to recreate Jean Vallée's achievement. Marah hated the song and preferred another. But that was just the tip of the iceberg. "Hey Nana" was written by Marah's fiancée, Guy Beyers. On the evening of the Flemish pre-contest, Sandra Reemer, who had already represented the Netherlands, was present as a guest. As Micha Marah performed "Hey Nana", Reemer rose up: "It is an exact replica of the song I released a year ago, 'Auntie.'" Although both the songwriters and the production company denied the song was copied, they asked for legal confirmation that they were 'clean' and that it could be recorded and distributed. Such approval was not obtained and thus "Hey Nana" became the only entry in the history of ESC that never had a studio version... Although not being Jewish at all, Micha Marah was enthusiastic about a "Chai" necklace she saw on one of her visits to Israel, purchased it and wore it on the eve of the contest, which did not save her from reaching the last place, with only five points. Another resemblance to the previous year: Entry number 12 finished in the 19th place. After the failed attempt with "Baccara ", Luxembourg did not refrain from bringing big names that might storm to the Eurovision win: This time it was Jean Renard, one of the greatest musicians and producers in France, the man who kicked off Mike Brant's career and wrote major classic chansons for many others. Renard wrote and composed: "J'ai déjà vu ça dans tes yeux". Jeane Manson, the model from Ohio, who was in France at the time, was chosen to perform. She really wanted to sing and demonstrated pretty reasonable abilities in the field. Manson asked that only her body's upper part, which was exposed entirely up to her breasts, be filmed when only at the end of the performance, the camera revealed her golden cleavage and black dress. The gimmick was not enough, and despite an impressive performance, Luxembourg finished far from the top with only 44 points. The Netherlands once again fell into the English trap with "Colorado" by Sandra Reemer (lead singer of the "Xandra" band), who returned to the contest for the third time, that was recorded in an English studio version and was distributed in Europe, and garnering popularity and high chances of winning. Reemer came to Jerusalem as a favourite, but when rehearsals began, it became clear again that it was difficult to win in the Dutch language. "Colorado" and Sandra with the glowing triangles on her black dress, were a memorable moment that evening. The audience appreciated the performance, but the European juries disappointed the Netherlands with 12th place. The entry that everyone was wary of was the Swedish "Satellit". The talented Ted Gärdestad managed to get to the ESC after four attempts and a tough, high-quality pre-contest in his country, while he manages to subdue the favourite Py Bäckman. "We were intimidated by the Swedish song, it seemed like an outsider who could win", said the Israeli composer Kobi Oshrat. The Swedes themselves were sure that they would be returning to the high places for the first time since "ABBA" won in the 1974 contest. No one prepared Ted for the big crash and 17th place with only eight points. This was a setback to the career of the musician that "ABBA" admired and collaborated with. His manager Stig Anderson, who was "ABBA" 's director as well, accompanied him closely in Jerusalem, where he was given two gold albums from the representatives of the Israeli record company for the sales of "ABBA"'s records in Israel. Eerie coincidences: One of the questions addressed to Ted at a press conference was related to the high suicide rate in Sweden. After the failure in Jerusalem, Ted deteriorated, until he ended his life when he jumped from a moving train in 1994 and his funeral was barely attended by a small number of friends. Anita Skorgan returned to the contest after two years due to Norway's tendency to re-send the same singers. The wonderful Skorgan recorded "Oliver" in English, and it was a well-known and successful version of the song she eventually performed in Norwegian. Even in the original language, there were quite a few bets about this entry's potential to reach the top. Although this was not the case, Skorgan relented with 11th place, which was much better than the nul points her husband Jahn Teigen ended with a year earlier. After the shock of the "Co-Co" failure, the British continued, despite everything, to believe in the concept of the bands that would accompany them for several more years, this time with "black Lace" trying to get their country back to places it had been for more than a decade. "Mary Ann" was not one of the most substantial entries in the contest, and the British did not have much hope in it when they arrived in Israel with a ridiculously small delegation. Even the well-known conductor Alyn Ainsworth gave up the trip to Jerusalem because he did not believe in the song, leaving the baton in Ken Jones' hands. Similarly to the previous Eurovision: Song number 17 won seventh place with 73 points, precisely what happened to "Black Lace". A song about Jerusalem is always lovely, but the Austrian Christina Simon took "Heute in Jerusalem" to a slightly different place, with a very oppressive jazz rhythm remembered as one of the most boring entries at the contest. Simon was lucky to get five points (4 from Italy) that somehow evaded her from the last place. She consoled herself when a week after the event she married her partner, Peter Wolf, who also wrote the song. The children's gimmick is not a Spanish invention, but they have definitely improved it. After a few dry years, Spain was determined to win, exactly a decade after its last victory. Betty Missiego emigrated from Peru to Spain in 1972. Her noble performance, with her clear and unique voice, led her to represent the country at the ESC in Jerusalem with "Su canción". As if a good entry was not enough, she was escorted by four little children who posted posters of the word "thank you" in Hebrew, English, French and Spanish at the end of the song. It was predicted from early on that Spain could win and it indeed waged a very stubborn battle against Israel for first place, which ended in an Israeli victory. Betty Missiego did not feel bad with the second place: At the end of the contest, while "Milk and Honey" were performing "Hallelujah" again, Missiego sipped from a champagne bottle and enthusiastically joined the winning song's chorus. Noble, no doubt about it. After the stunning performance of the band "Shalom 79", all the participants, presenters and pantomimes took the stage, creating a spectacular image for a souvenir that mirrored the incredible success of the 1979 Eurovision and the satisfaction of its participants faithfully. What slightly damaged the perfect Israeli production was the outdated and awkward scoreboard. The acoustics in the results' reading often created hearing problems for the presenters, especially for Yardena Arazi. The 'Green Room' where the singers stayed, was not as spacious and compact as the one in Paris, but these were minor issues. When Frank Naef replaced Clifford Brown, everyone thought it was finally time for the vote to go smoothly, without any interventions that were mostly an attempt to get attention and sneak into the broadcast. After a smooth voting process in 1978, Frank also caught the 'attention syndrome' and had to remind of his existence... He asked to repeat points (even though the entire hall had heard how much was awarded and to whom) and even complicated the situation when he asked to return to Oslo after the Norwegian Sverre Christophersen said "good night" and hung up. When Vienna from Austria was accidentally connected during the attempts, the presenter Daniel Pe'er lost some of his composure: "Vienna, what are you doing here"? It was an odd and volatile voting procedure: From the beginning, a somewhat surprising duel developed between Israel and the UK, until the hosts opened a gap of more than 20 points after seven votes. The 'seven bad years' in the form of the next seven juries, which awarded Israel only 22 points, put it in a fragile third place, far away from the leaders Spain and France, with Germany, Denmark and Ireland threatening to distance "milk and honey" even from the top five. It was clear that only an exceptional sequence of "Douze Points" could save Israel. Sweden, which was the only one not to award any points to Izhar Cohen the previous year, opened the floodgates with 12 points, along with the UK and Norway which gave their full points to the host — Israel returned to lead. Eight points from Austria placed "Milk and Honey" with one point less than the Spaniards who were the last to vote! How ironic and insane it was that Spain, which was known for its scoring combinations in the late 1960s and early 1970s, was the one to decide. If it awards even one point to Israel, it will lose (The number of "Douze Points" received by each country will determine, when Israel had six and Spain only four). The stakes could not be higher, the audience was on its feet, and Yardena Arazi trembled in fear while addressing Madrid for the results: Ten points for Portugal (originally 6, but Arazi admitted that she "does not hear"), 8 for Italy and 7 for Greece. Arazi for some reason heard BELGE instead of GRECE and almost caused heart attacks in the crowd (since Belgium was after Israel on the list and it meant Israel does not get any points). "Germany 12 points" — the Spaniard distributed most of its points and then came the longest second in the life of everyone watching the event from the hall or the broadcast: "Israel... 10 points"... The crowd in the hall went wild! In the 'Green Room', "Milk and Honey" 's members started pouring champagne when the nervous Shlomo Zach asked them to stop since they should go receive the prizes in a moment. Once again, the final Eurovision scoreboard highlights one winner: Israel Compared to Izhar's 'Slide win', it was a challenging but sweet victory. Izhar Cohen awarded the Grand Prix, along with senior members of the EBU, and of course, the man of the evening: Director-General of the IBA, Yitzhak Livni. However, that very night Livni ended his job, and at midnight of the 4.1, Tommy Lapid replaced him. Procedurally, Lapid was supposed to get a real gift when he took office — awarding the prize of the most significant television production ever to be made in the country since its inception. Livni, who was the CEO throughout production and preparations, implored Lapid to indulgently let him be the one to take the stage and award the prize. Lapid, who was not interested in honours and titles, gallantly gave up for Livni and everyone was satisfied. The tedious award ceremony, in which EBU President Regis de Calder-Mattin almost stumbled, brought the following productions to spare this hassle from the viewer and settle for a more efficient and faster awarding. Daniel Pe'er and Yardena Arazi respectfully closed the successful broadcast, which was the longest so far and the first to air for over three hours. Kobi Oshrat took the podium with a big smile, exchanged hugs with Ziko Graziani (who was a member of the committee that disqualified "Hallelujah" from contending in the 1978 Song Festival) and conducted the winning song once again. Then, as if waking them from a sweet dream, the broadcast ended and landed the Israelis back to a reality in which they will wait almost two full decades for the next time of hosting the Eurovision.

1970

Date: 21.3.1970

Location: RAI Congrescentrum

Presenter: Willy Dobbe

Orchestra Conductor: Dolf van der Linden

Chief Executive: Clifford Brown

Participating Countries: 12

Voting: Every country has a Jury that shared its 10 votes among one or more entries

Broadcaster: Nederlandse Omroep Stichting (NOS)

Director: Theo Ordeman

Executive Producer: Warner van Kampen

Intermediate performance: The Don Lurio Dancers

Duration: One hour and 15 minutes

Broadcast: To all participating countries and to Austria, Chile, Greece, Norway, Poland and Portugal.

No.	Country	Song	Performing Artist	Lyrics	Composer	Conductor	Language	Commentator	Spoker of Results	Points	Place
01	The Netherlands	"Waterman"	Hearts of Soul	Pieter Goemans	Pieter Goemans	Dolf van der Linden	Dutch	Pim Jacobs	Flip van der Schalie	7	7
02	Switzerland	"Retour"	Henri Dès	Henri Dès	Henri Dès	Bernard Gérard	French	Theodor Haller, Georges Hardy, Giovanni Bertini	Alexandre Burger	8	4
03	Italy	"Occhi di ragazza"	Gianni Morandi	Sergio Bardotti, Gianfranco Baldazzi	Lucio Dalla	-	Italian	Renato Tagliani	Enzo Tortora	5	8
04	Yugoslavia	"Pridi, dala ti bom cvet"	Eva Sršen	Dušan Velkaverh	Mojmir Sepe	Mojmir Sepe	Slovenian	Milovan Ilić, Oliver Mlakar, Tomaž Terček	Dragana Marković	4	11
05	Belgium	"Viens l'oublier"	Jean Vallée	Jean Vallée	Jean Vallée	Jacques Say	French	Claude Delacroix, Herman Verelst, Nand Baert	André Hagon	5	8
06	France	"Marie-Blanche"	Guy Bonnet	André-Pierre Dousset	Guy Bonnet	Franck Pourcel	French	Pierre Tchernia	Unknown	8	4
07	United Kingdom	"Knock, Knock Who's There?"	Mary Hopkin	John Carter Geoff Stephens	John Carter Geoff Stephens	Johnny Arthey	English	David Gell, Tony Brandon, John Russel	Colin-Ward Lewis	26	2
08	Luxembourg	"Je suis tombé du ciel"	David Alexandre Winter	Eddy Marnay	Yves de Vriendt	Raymond Lefèvre	French	Jacques Navadic, Camillo Felgen	Unknown	0	12
09	Spain	"Gwendolyne"	Julio Iglesias	Julio Iglesias, Leo Johns	Julio Iglesias, Leo Johns	Augusto Algueró	Spanish	José Luis Uribarri, Miguel de los Santos	Ramón Rivera	8	4
10	Monaco	"Marlène"	Dominique Dussault	Henri Dijan	Eddie Barclay, Jimmy Walter	Jimmy Walter	French	Pierre Tchernia	Unknown	5	8
11	Germany	"Wunder gibt es immer wieder"	Katja Ebstein	Günter Loose	Christian Bruhn	Christian Bruhn	German	Marie-Louise Steinbauer, Wolf Mittler	Hans-Otto Grünefeldt	12	3
12	Ireland	"All Kinds of Everything"	Dana	Derry Lindsay, Jackie Smith	Derry Lindsay, Jackie Smith	Dolf van der Linden	English	Valerie McGovern, Kevin Roche	John Skehan	32	1

	The Netherlands	Switzerland	Italy	Yugoslavia	Belgium	France	United Kingdom	Luxembourg	Spain	Monaco	Germany	Ireland	
The Netherlands	■	–	3	3	–	–	1	–	–	–	–	–	The Netherlands
Switzerland	2	■	–	–	–	2	1	–	–	–	2	1	Switzerland
Italy	–	–	■	1	–	–	–	–	2	–	2	–	Italy
Yugoslavia	–	–	–	■	–	–	4	–	–	–	–	–	Yugoslavia
Belgium	–	–	–	–	■	3	–	1	–	–	–	1	Belgium
France	–	–	1	2	–	■	–	–	–	2	–	3	France
United Kingdom	3	2	2	4	–	2	■	2	–	4	4	3	United Kingdom
Luxembourg	–	–	–	–	–	–	–	■	–	–	–	–	Luxembourg
Spain	–	–	3	–	–	–	–	2	■	3	–	–	Spain
Monaco	–	1	–	–	1	2	–	–	1	■	–	–	Monaco
Germany	–	1	1	–	–	–	–	3	4	1	■	2	Germany
Ireland	5	6	–	–	9	1	4	2	3	–	2	■	Ireland

1971

Hosting Country: Ireland

Hosting City: Dublin

Date: 3.4.1971

Location: Gaiety Theatre

Presenter: Bernadette Ní Ghallchóir

Orchestra Conductor: Colman Pearce

Chief Executive: Clifford Brown

Participating Countries: 18

Voting: Each participating country was represented by two member juries (one aged 16 to 25 and the other 25 to 55) ranked the entries between one till five points.

Broadcaster: Raidió Teilifís Éireann (RTÉ)

Director: Tom McGrath

Intermediate performance: Bunratty Castle Entertainers

Duration: One hour and 47 minutes

Broadcast: To all participating countries and to Greece, Iceland and United States of America.

No.	Country	Song	Performing Artist	Lyrics	Composer	Conductor	Language	Commentator	members (Jury)	Points	Place
01	Austria	"Musik"	Marianne Mendt	Richard Schönherz, Manuel Rigoni	Richard Schönherz, Manuel Rigoni	Robert Opratko	German	Ernst Grissemann, Hubert Gaisbauer	Beatrix Neundlinger and Jochen Lieben	66	16
02	Malta	"Marija I-Maltija"	Joe Grech	Charles Mifsud	Joe Grech	Anthony Chircop	Maltese	Victor Aquilina	Spiro Sillato and Gaetan Abela	52	18
03	Monaco	"Un banc, un arbre, une rue"	Séverine	Yves Dessca	Jean-Pierre Bourtayre	Jean Claude Petit	French	Georges de Caunes	Unknown	128	1
04	Switzerland	"Les illusions de nos vingt ans"	Peter, Sue and Marc	Maurice Tézé	Peter Reber	Hardy Schneiders	French	Theodor Haller, Georges Hardy, Giovanni Bertini	Unknown	78	12
05	Germany	"Diese Welt"	Katja Ebstein	Fred Jay	Dieter Zimmermann	Dieter Zimmermann	German	Hanns Verres, Wolf Mittler	Unknown	100	3
06	Spain	"En un mundo nuevo"	Karina	Tony Luz	Rafael Trabucchelli	Waldo de Los Ríos	Spanish	Joaquín Prat, Miguel de los Santos	Noelia Afonso and Francisco Madariaga	116	2
07	France	"Un jardin sur la terre"	Serge Lama	Henri Djian, Jacques Demarny	Alice Dona	Franck Pourcel	French	Georges de Caunes	Unknown	82	10
08	Luxembourg	"Pomme, pomme, pomme"	Monique Melsen	Pierre Cour	Hubert Giraud	Jean Claudric	French	Jacques Navadic, Camillo Felgen	Unknown	70	13
09	United Kingdom	"Jack in The Box"	Clodagh Rodgers	David Myers	John Worsley	Johnny Arthey	English	Dave Lee Travis, Terry Wogan, John Russel	Gay Lowe and Jeremy Patterson-Fox	98	4
10	Belgium	"Goeiemorgen, morgen"	Lily Castel & Jacques Raymond	Phil van Cauwenbergh	Paul Quintens	Francis Bay	Flemish	Herman Verelst, Janine Lambotte, Nand Baert, André Hagon	Unknown	68	14
11	Italy	"L'amore è un attimo"	Massimo Ranieri	Giancarlo Bigazzi Gaetano Savio	Enrico Polito	Enrico Polito	Italian	Renato Tagliani	Unknown	91	5
12	Sweden	"Vita vidder"	Family Four	Håkan Elmquist	Håkan Elmquist	Claes Rosendahl	Swedish	Åke Strömmer, Ursula Richter	Eva Blomqvist and Putte Wickman	85	6
13	Ireland	"One Day Love"	Angela Farrell	Donald Martin, Ita Flynn	Donald Martin, Ita Flynn	Noel Kelehan	English	Noel Andrews, Kevin Roche	Vivienne Colgan and Ken Steward	79	11
14	The Netherlands	"Tijd"	Saskia & Serge	Gerrit den Braber	Joop Stokkermans	Dolf van der Linden	Dutch	Pim Jacobs	Jos Cléber & Unknown	85	6
15	Portugal	"Menina do alto da serra"	Tonicha	Ary dos Santos	Nuno Nazareth Fernandes	Jorge Costa Pinto	Portuguese	Henrique Mendes	Pedro Albergaria and Luís Filipe Costa	83	9
16	Yugoslavia	"Tvoj dječak je tužan"	Krunoslav Slabinac	Zvonimir Golob	Ivan Krajač	Miljenko Prohaska	Croatian	Milovan Ilić, Oliver Mlakar, Tomaž Terček	Miso Kukic and Zoran Krzisnik	68	14
17	Finland	"Tie uuteen päivään"	Markku Aro & Koivistolaiset	Rauno Lehtinen	Rauno Lehtinen	Ossi Runne	Finish	Heikki Seppälä, Matti Paalosmaa	Markku Veijalainen and Vieno Kekkonen	84	8
18	Norway	"Lykken er"	Hanne Krogh	Arne Bendiksen	Arne Bendiksen	Arne Bendiksen	Norweigen	Sverre Christophersen, Erik Heyerdahl	Sten Fredriksen and Liv Usterud	65	17

	Austria	Malta	Monaco	Switzerland	Germany	Spain	France	Luxembourg	United Kingdom	Belgium	Italy	Sweden	Ireland	The Netherlands	Portugal	Yugoslavia	Finland	Norway	
Austria	■	2+1	2+3	1+1	4+3	1+1	2+1	1+1	2+1	1+2	2+4	2+2	3+3	2+1	2+3	2+2	2+1	2+3	Austria
Malta	2+2	■	1+1	1+1	1+2	3+2	2+1	1+1	2+1	2+2	3+1	1+1	2+2	3+2	1+1	1+1	2+1	1+1	Malta
Monaco	2+2	3+2	■	5+5	5+5	1+1	4+4	2+2	5+3	5+5	2+2	5+5	5+4	4+5	4+4	5+5	3+4	5+5	Monaco
Switzerland	2+3	3+2	2+2	■	3+3	1+1	3+3	1+1	4+2	1+2	2+5	2+2	2+3	2+3	3+3	3+1	3+1	2+2	Switzerland
Germany	3+3	3+2	4+3	3+3	■	3+5	5+3	1+1	3+3	3+4	5+1	3+3	3+2	3+2	3+4	4+3	3+2	2+2	Germany
Spain	3+1	4+4	5+5	3+2	3+4	■	5+5	2+2	4+3	2+2	4+1	3+3	4+5	4+2	3+4	3+4	4+5	4+4	Spain
France	1+2	1+1	4+4	4+4	2+3	3+2	■	1+1	3+2	1+2	3+1	2+2	2+4	5+4	3+2	3+2	2+1	2+3	France
Luxembourg	1+1	4+3	3+3	2-1	1+1	2+2	3+2	■	2+4	2+1	2+1	1+1	3+2	1+2	3+3	2+2	2+3	2+1	Luxembourg
United Kingdom	3+1	4+4	4+4	4+2	2+3	1+1	4+4	2+2	■	4+4	1+2	2+3	4+3	2+3	3+4	4+2	3+3	3+3	United Kingdom
Belgium	1+2	1+1	3+2	3+1	1+1	1+1	2+3	1+1	4+2	■	2+1	2+3	2+2	4+2	4+2	2+1	2+4	2+2	Belgium
Italy	2+2	3+3	5+4	3+5	2+4	3+3	4+5	1+1	3+3	1+1	■	3+4	2+4	1+1	1+2	4+4	1+1	2+3	Italy
Sweden	3+4	2+2	2+2	4+5	2+2	1+1	2+3	1+1	3+2	3+3	3+3	■	2+1	5+4	2+1	3+3	3+1	3+3	Sweden
Ireland	5+2	3+3	3+3	1+2	2+2	2+3	3+4	1+1	3+3	1+2	5+1	1+1	■	3+2	2+2	2+3	3+1	3+1	Ireland
The Netherlands	1+5	1+1	3+3	2+3	2+2	3+2	4+3	1+1	2+3	1+1	1+1	3+3	3+2	■	4+5	3+2	5+1	4+4	The Netherlands
Portugal	2+2	1+2	3+3	1+1	2+3	5+5	4+4	3+2	4+2	2+2	3+1	1+1	2+1	3+2	■	3+3	3+2	3+2	Portugal
Yugoslavia	3+3	1+1	2+2	1+1	3+4	2+4	3+3	1+1	2+1	1+1	4+1	1+1	2+3	2+2	2+2	■	2+1	2+3	Yugoslavia
Finland	2+2	2+2	2+2	2+2	2+2	2+1	3+1	1+1	5+5	5+5	1+1	2+2	3+3	2+1	5+3	3+3	■	2+4	Finland
Norway	1+2	1+2	3+3	2+2	1+1	1+1	3+2	1+1	3+4	3+3	1+1	1+1	4+3	1+1	2+3	2+2	2+1	■	Norway

1972

Hosting Country: United Kingdom

Hosting City: Edinburgh

Date: 25.3.1972

Location: Usher Hall

Presenter: Moira Shearer

Orchestra Conductor: Malcolm Lockyer

Chief Executive: Clifford Brown

Participating Countries: 18

Voting: Each participating country was represented by two member juries (one aged 16 to 25 and the other 25 to 55) ranked the entries between one till five points.

Broadcaster: British Broadcasting Corporation (BBC)

Director: Terry Hughes

Executive Producer: Bill Cotton

Intermediate performance: Tattoo at Edinburgh Castle

Duration: One hour and 47 minutes

Broadcast: To all participating countries and to Greece, Brazil, Iceland, Israel, Hong Kong, Japan, Philipines, Chinese Taipei and Thailand.

No.	Country	Song	Performing Artist	Lyrics	Composer	Conductor	Language	Commentator	members (Jury)	Points	Place
01	Germany	"Nur die Liebe läßt uns leben"	Mary Roos	Joachim Relin	Joachim Heider	Paul Kuhn	Germany	Hanns Verres, Wolf Mittler	Unknown	107	3
02	France	"Comé-comédie"	Betty Mars	Frédéric Botton	Frédéric Botton	Franck Pourcel	French	Pierre Tchernia	Unknown	81	11
03	Ireland	"Ceol an Ghrá"	Sandie Jones	Liam Mac Uistín	Joe Burkett	Colman Pearce	Irish	Mike Murphy, Kevin Roche	Unknown	72	15
04	Spain	"Amanece"	Jaime Morey	Ramón Arcusa	Augusto Algueró	Augusto Algueró	Spanish	Julio Rico, Miguel de los Santos	Emma Cohen + Luis María Ansón	83	10
05	United Kingdom	"Beg, Steal or Borrow"	The New Seekers (Lyn Paul Peter Doyle, Paul Layton, Marty Kristian, Eve Graham)	Steve Wolfe, Graeme Hall, Tony Cole	Steve Wolfe, Graeme Hall, Tony Cole	David Mackay	English	Tom Fleming, Pete Murray, Terry James	Doreen Samuels + Robert Bruce Walker	114	2
06	Norway	"Småting"	Grethe Kausland & Benny Borg	Kåre Grøttum, Ivar Børsum	Kåre Grøttum, Ivar Børsum	Carsten Klouman	Norweigen	Roald Øyen + Erik Heyerdahl	Rachel Nord + Signe Abusdal	73	14
07	Portugal	"A festa da vida"	Carlos Mendes	José Niza	José Calvário	Richard Hill	Portuguese	Henrique Mendes + Amadeu Meireles	Pedro Sousa Macedo + Maria João Aquiar	90	7
08	Switzerland	"C'est la chanson de mon amour"	Véronique Müller	Catherine Desage	Véronique Mülle	Jean-Pierre Festi	French	Theodor Haller, Georges Hardy, Giovanni Bertini	Unknown	88	8
09	Malta	"L-imħabba"	Helen and Joseph	Albert Cassola	Charles Camilleri	Charles Camilleri	Maltese	Norman Hamilton	Mary Rose Mallia + Joe Zerafa	48	18
10	Finland	"Muistathan"	Päivi Paunu & Kim Floor	Juha Flinck	Juha Flinck, Nacke Johansson	Ossi Runne	Finish	Heikki Seppälä + Erkki Melakoski	Merita Merikoski + Åke Granholm	78	12
11	Austria	"Falter im Wind"	Milestones	Heinz Unger	Richard Schönherz, Manuel Rigoni	Erich Kleinschuster	German	Ernst Grissemann + Hubert Gaisbauer	Unknown	100	5
12	Italy	"I giorni dell'arcobaleno"	Nicola di Bari	Dalmazio Masini	Piero Pintucci, Nicola Di Bari	Gianfranco Reverberi	Italian	Renato Tagliani	Unknown	92	6
13	Yugoslavia	"Muzika i ti"	Tereza Kesovija	Ivan Krajač	Nikica Kalogjera	Nikica Kalogjera	Croatian	Milovan Ilić, Oliver Mlakar, Tomaž Terček	Vera Zlokovic + Veljko Bakasun	87	9
14	Sweden	"Härliga sommardag"	Family Four (Agneta Munther Marie Bergman, Berndt Öst, Pierre Isacsson)	Håkan Elmquist	Håkan Elmquist	Mats Olsson	Swedish	Bo Billtén, Björn Bjelfvenstam	Titti Sjöblom + Arne Domnérus	75	13
15	Monaco	"Comme on s'aime"	Anne-Marie Godart & Peter MacLane	Jean Dréjac	Raymond Bernard	Raymond Bernard	French	Pierre Tchernia	Unknown	65	16
16	Belgium	"À la folie ou pas du tout"	Serge & Christine Ghisoland	Daniël Nelis	Daniël Nelis, Bob Milan	Henri Segers	French	Herman Verelst, Arlette Vincent, Nand Baert, André Hagon	Unknown	55	17
17	Luxembourg	"Après toi"	Vicky Leandros	Yves Dessca, Klaus Munro	Mario Panas, Klaus Munro	Klaus Munro	French	Jacques Navadic, Camillo Felgen	Unknown	128	1
18	The Netherlands	"Als het om de liefde gaat"	Sandra & Andres (Sandra Reemer, Dries Holten)	Hans van Hemert	Dries Holten	Harry van Hoof	Dutch	Pim Jacobs	Jennifer Baljet + Cornelis Wagter	106	4

	Germany	France	Ireland	Spain	United Kingdom	Norway	Portugal	Switzerland	Malta	Finland	Austria	Italy	Yugoslavia	Sweden	Monaco	Belgium	Luxembourg	The Netherlands
The Netherlands	4+2	3+3	2+3	3+2	4+4	2+2	2+3	2+3	3+1	4+4	4+5	2+3	2+4	3+2	2+3	2+1	5+4	■
Luxembourg	4+3	4+4	3+3	4+1	3+5	5+1	5+5	4+3	1+1	2+4	2+3	4+2	4+4	3+2	2+2	3+3	■	3+4
Belgium	5+2	3+4	3+1	2+1	1+3	3+1	2+5	2+2	1+1	4+4	2+2	2+4	5+3	5+2	2+2	■	3+5	1+1
Monaco	4+4	3+3	3+2	4+4	4+5	2+2	2+2	3+3	2+1	2+3	2+3	4+2	5+4	3+2	■	3+1	4+3	2+3
Sweden	4+4	1+1	2+3	4+3	3+3	2+2	3+4	2+2	1+2	2=2	5+5	5+3	3+1	■	2+1	1+1	4+4	2+4
Yugoslavia	3+2	3+2	2+1	1+1	4+5	2+3	3+1	3+2	1+1	2+2	4+4	3+1	■	3+4	2+2	1+1	5+5	4+5
Italy	4+3	1+2	2+1	1+2	3+4	1+1	4+5	2+3	1+1	2+1	3+3	■	1+1	2+1	1+2	2+1	5+4	1+2
Austria	2+3	1+1	2+2	3+2	3+4	1+2	1+3	4+4	1+1	1+2	■	3+3	1+2	1+3	1+2	1+1	4+4	3+3
Finland	2+3	3+1	2+1	2+2	3+4	4+3	1+1	3+4	1+4	■	2+2	4+2	1+2	3+2	2+3	1+3	1+5	5+4
Malta	2+2	2+3	5+1	2+2	1+1	3+2	1+4	3+1	■	1+2	2+3	1+5	2+2	1+3	3+2	4+1	2+2	1+2
Switzerland	3+2	2+1	2+1	2+1	4+4	1+1	2+4	■	1+1	2+1	4+3	4+5	1+1	1+1	1+1	2+1	4+2	5+1
Portugal	3+3	1+1	2+2	3+3	3+1	2+3	■	1+1	1+1	2+2	4+1	2+5	2+3	3+1	1+1	2+1	5+2	3+2
Norway	2+4	4+3	2+4	3+5	5+5	■	1+1	4+3	1+1	4+2	2+3	3+3	2+2	2+3	3+3	1+1	3+5	4+4
United Kingdom	1+4	5+4	2+2	1+2	■	3+1	1+3	2+2	3+3	1+4	1+2	2+1	1+4	1+2	3+2	2+3	5+5	4+5
Spain	4+5	1+1	3+1	■	1+1	2+3	3+4	2+3	1+1	4+2	2+4	1+1	4+4	2+1	2+1	1+1	1+1	5+3
Ireland	2+4	2+3	■	2+3	2+4	3+3	3+4	2+4	3+1	2+1	3+3	2+1	4+1	4+1	2+2	3+1	4+5	5+3
France	3+5	■	2+1	2+3	5+4	2+1	2+2	3+2	1+1	2+1	4+2	2+3	2+2	2+1	2+1	1+2	5+5	3+3
Germany	■	2+3	2+2	4+3	3+5	2+2	2+1	2+2	2+1	2+2	3+3	2+2	3+4	2+3	2+2	1+1	4+5	2+4

Hosting Country: Luxembourg

Hosting City: Luxembourg City

Date: 7.4.1973

Location: Grand Théâtre

Presenter: Helga Guitton

Orchestra Conductor: Pierre Cao

Chief Executive: Clifford Brown

Participating Countries: 17

Voting: Each participating country was represented by two member juries (one aged 16 to 25 and the other 25 to 55) ranked the entries between one till five points.

Broadcaster: Compagnie Luxembourgeoise de Télédiffusion (CLT)

Intermediate performance: Charlie Rivel

Duration: 1 hour and 42 minutes

Broadcast: To all participating countries and to Greece, Austria, Iceland, Malta and Turkey.

1973

No.	Country	Song	Performing Artist	Lyrics	Composer	Conductor	Language	Commentator	Members (Jury)	Points	Place
01	Finland	"Tom Tom Tom"	Marion Rung	Bob Barratt	Rauno Lehtinen	Ossi Runne	English	Erkki Pohjanheimo	Kristiina Kauhtio, Heikki Sarmanto	93	6
02	Belgium	"Baby, Baby"	Nicole & Hugo	Erik Marijsse	Ignace Baert	Francis Bay	Flemish	Herman Verelst, Paule Herreman	Unknown	58	17
03	Portugal	"Tourada"	Fernando Tordo	Ary dos Santos	Fernando Tordo	Jorge Costa Pinto	Portuguese	Artur Agostinho	José Calvário, Teresa Silva Carvalho	80	10
04	Germany	"Junger Tag"	Gitte	Stephan Lego	Günther-Eric Thöner	Günther-Eric Thöner	German	Hanns Verres	Unknown	85	8
05	Norway	"It's Just A Game"	Bendik Singers (Anne Karine Strøm, Ellen Nikolaysen, Bjørn Kruse, Philip A. Kruse)	Bob Williams	Arne Bendiksen	Carsten Klouman	English, French, Italian, Spanish, Danish, German, Hebrew, Serb/Croatian, Finish, Irish and Norweigen.	John Andreassen	Inger Ann Folkvord, Johs. Bergh	89	7
06	Monaco	"Un train qui part"	Marie	Boris Bergman	Bernard Liamis	Jean-Claude Vannier	French	Pierre Tchernia	Unknown	85	8
07	Spain	"Eres tú"	Mocedades	Juan Carlos Calderón	Amaya Uranga, Roberto Uranga, Izaskun Uranga, Carlos Zubiaga, Javier Garay, José Ipiña	Juan Carlos Calderón	Spanish	Julio Rico	Teresa González, José Luis Balbín	125	2
08	Switzerland	"Je vais me marier, Marie"	Patrick Juvet	Pierre Delanoë	Patrick Juvet	Hervé Roy	French	Theodor Haller, Georges Hardy, Giovanni Bertini	Paola del Medico	79	12
09	Yugoslavia	"Gori vatra"	Zdravko Čolić	Kemal Monteno	Kemal Monteno	Esad Arnautalić	Serb	Milovan Ilić, Oliver Mlakar, Tomaž Terček	Dušan Lekić, Ivan Antonov	65	15
10	Italy	"Chi sarà con te"	Massimo Ranieri	Giancarlo Bigazzi	Enrico Polito, Gaetano Savio	Enrico Polito	Italian	Renato Tagliani	Unknown	74	13
11	Luxembourg	"Tu te reconnaîtras"	Anne-Marie David	Vline Buggy	Claude Morgan	Pierre Cao	French	Jacques Navadic	Unknown	129	1
12	Sweden	"You're Summer"	Nova (Claes af Geijerstam Göran Fristorp) & The Dolls	Lars Forssell	Monica Dominique, Carl-Axel Dominique	Monica Dominique	Swedish	Alicia Lundberg	Lena Andersson, Lars Samuelson	94	5
13	The Netherlands	"De oude muzikant"	Ben Cramer	Pierre Kartner	Pierre Kartner	Harry van Hoof	Dutch	Pim Jacobs	Unknown	69	14
14	Ireland	"Do I Dream"	Maxi	Jack Brierley, George F. Crosbie	Jack Brierley, George F. Crosbie	Colman Pearce	English	Mike Murphy	Unknown	80	10
15	United Kingdom	"Power to All Our Friends"	Cliff Richard	Doug Flett	Guy Fletcher	David McKay	English	Terry Wogan	Catherine Woodfield, Pat Williams	123	3
16	France	"Sans toi"	Martine Clémenceau	Anne Grégory	Paul Koulak	Jean Claudric	French	Pierre Tchernia	Adeline Estragnat, Danièle Heymann	65	15
17	Israel	"Ey Sham"	Ilanit	Ehud Manor	Nurit Hirsh	Nurit Hirsh	Hebrew	-	Raanan Rogel, Avner Bahat	97	4

	Finland	Belgium	Portugal	Germany	Norway	Monaco	Spain	Switzerland	Yugoslavia	Italy	Luxembourg	Sweden	The Netherlands	Ireland	United Kingdom	France	Israel	
Finland	■	5+4	3+2	3+3	3+3	3+2	3+3	3+3	4+3	1+1	4+2	4+3	3+2	3+2	4+5	2+2	2+3	Finland
Belgium	2+2	■	2+1	2+2	1+2	3+3	3+3	2+2	2+2	1+1	2+2	1+1	2+1	3+1	2+3	1+1	1+1	Belgium
Portugal	2+2	4+2	■	2+3	2+3	2+2	5+3	5+3	3+3	1+2	1+3	1+1	3+2	2+2	2+3	3+3	2+3	Portugal
Germany	1+1	2+3	4+2	■	1+3	3+2	4+5	2+5	2+2	2+1	3+4	3+3	2+3	3+3	3+2	3+4	2+2	Germany
Norway	4+4	3+2	3+2	3+3	■	4+3	3+3	5+2	3+3	3+2	4+3	1+2	2+1	2+1	2+1	4+2	5+4	Norway
Monaco	3+3	2+1	1+1	2+2	1+2	■	3+3	2+3	4+5	4+4	3+3	1+3	2+3	3+3	4+5	2+3	1+3	Monaco
Spain	1+2	3+5	4+5	4+5	1+3	5+4	■	3+5	5+4	5+5	4+4	2+5	5+5	5+5	2+2	4+5	3+5	Spain
Switzerland	2+2	2+1	2+1	2+2	3+4	2+3	3+4	■	3+3	1+3	3+3	1+2	3+5	3+4	3+4	1+1	1+2	Switzerland
Yugoslavia	3+2	1+2	2+1	2+2	1+1	3+2	4+4	3+3	■	1+1	1+3	1+1	2+2	3+2	2+2	2+2	2+2	Yugoslavia
Italy	1+1	3+2	2+1	3+2	3+2	4+1	3+2	3+4	2+3	■	2+3	3+2	2+2	3+1	3+2	2+3	2+2	Italy
Luxembourg	3+3	3+3	5+3	3+4	3+5	4+3	3+3	5+5	4+5	4+5	■	3+5	5+4	5+3	5+5	5+5	4+4	Luxembourg
Sweden	4+4	1+3	2+2	2+3	5+3	2+3	3+4	5+4	3+3	3+2	2+4	■	4+2	3+2	3+4	3+1	2+3	Sweden
The Netherlands	2+2	2+2	1+1	2+3	3+2	3+1	2+3	2+3	2+3	2+2	3+4	2+1	■	3+2	2+1	2+4	1+1	The Netherlands
Ireland	1+2	5+2	1+1	2+2	4+2	3+3	4+3	3+2	2+3	3+2	4+2	2+3	4+2	■	3+2	2+2	2+2	Ireland
United Kingdom	4+5	2+4	3+3	3+4	3+4	3+5	2+2	3+5	3+5	2+3	5+5	4+5	5+5	5+4	■	5+3	4+5	United Kingdom
France	2+2	2+1	1+1	2+2	2+2	2+3	2+3	2+2	5+2	1+1	2+1	3+2	3+2	3+2	3+2	■	1+1	France
Israel	3+3	3+3	3+2	3+4	2+3	4+3	2+2	3+3	4+3	4+3	3+5	3+3	3+3	3+4	2+3	3+2	■	Israel

1974

Hosting Country: United Kingdom

Hosting City: Brighton

Date: 6.4.1974

Location: The Dome

Presenter: Katie Boyle

Orchestra Conductor: Ronnie Hazlehurst

Chief Executive: Clifford Brown

Director: Michael Hurll

Executive Producer: Bill Cotton

Participating Countries: 17

Voting: Every country has a Jury that shared its 10 votes among one or more entries

Broadcaster: British Broadcasting Corporation (BBC)

Intermediate performance: The Wombles

Duration: One hour and 50 minutes

Broadcast: To all participating countries and to Austria, Denmark France, Iceland, Malta and Turkey.

No.	Country	Song	Performing Artist	Lyrics	Composer	Conductor	Language	Commentator	Spoker of Results	Points	Place
01	Finland	"Keep Me Warm"	Carita	Frank Robson	Eero Koivistoinen	Ossi Runne	English	Matti Paalosmaa	Aarre Elo	4	13
02	United Kingdom	"Long Live Love"	Olivia Newton-John	Valerie Avon & Harold Spiro	Valerie Avon & Harold Spiro	Nick Ingman	English	David Vine	Colin-Ward Lewis	14	4
03	Spain	"Canta y sé feliz"	Peret	Pedro Pubill Calaf	Pedro Pubill Calaf	Rafael de Ibarbia Serra	Spanish	José Luis Uribarri	Antolín García	10	9
04	Norway	"The First Day of Love"	Anne-Karine Strøm feat. Bendik Singers	Philip A. Kruse	Frode Thingnæs	Frode Thingnæs	English	John Andreassen	Sverre Christophersen	3	14
05	Greece	"Krasi, thalassa ke t' agori mou"	Marinella	Pythagoras	Giorgos Katsaros	Giorgos Katsaros	Greek	Mako Georgiadou	Mako Georgiadou	7	11
06	Israel	"Natati La Hayay"	"Poogy" (Gidi Gov, Alon O'learchik, Efraim Shamir, Itzhak Klepter, Meir Penigstein, Danny Sanderson)	Danny Sanderson, Alon O'learchik	Danny Sanderson	Yonathan Rechter	Hebrew	-	Yitzhak Shimoni	11	7
07	Yugoslavia	"Generacija '42"	Korni Grupa (Kornelije Kovač, Bojan Hreljac, Josip Boček, Zlatko Pejaković and Vladimir Furduj)	Kornelije Kovač	Kornelije Kovač	Zvonimir Skerl	Serb	Milovan Ilić, Oliver Mlakar., Tomaž Terček	Helga Vlahović	6	12
08	Sweden	"Waterloo"	ABBA (Benny Andersson, Anni-Frid Lyngstad (Frida), Agnetha Fältskog, and Björn Ulvaeus)	Stikkan Anderson	Benny Andersson, Björn Ulvaeus	Sven-Olof Walldoff	English	Johan Sandström	Sven Lindahl	24	1
09	Luxembourg	"Bye Bye I Love You"	Ireen Sheer	Michael Kunze	Ralph Siegel	Charles Blackwell	French	Jacques Navadic	Unknown	14	4
10	Monaco	"Celui qui reste et celui qui s'en va"	Romuald	Michel Jourdan	Jean-Pierre Bourtayre	Raymond Donnez	French	Pierre Tchernia	Sophie Hecquet	14	4
11	Belgium	"Fleur de liberté"	Jacques Hustin	Jacques Hustin	Jacques Hustin	Pierre Chiffre	French	Georges Désir, Herman Verelst	André Hagon	10	9
12	The Netherlands	"I See a Star"	Mouth & MacNeal	Gerrit den Braber	Hans van Hemert	Harry van Hoof	English	Willem Duys	Dick van Bommel	15	3
13	Ireland	"Cross Your Heart"	Tina Reynolds	Ted O'Neill (AKA) Paul Lyttle	Ted O'Neill (AKA) Paul Lyttle	Colman Pearce	English	Mike Murphy	Brendan Balfe	11	7
14	Germany	"Die Sommermelodie"	Cindy & Bert	Kurt Feltz	Werner Scharfenberger	Werner Scharfen-berger	German	Werner Veigel	Ekkehard Böhmer	3	14
15	Switzerland	"Mein Ruf nach dir"	Piera Martell	Pepe Ederer	Pepe Ederer	Pepe Ederer	German	Theodor Haller, Georges Hardy, Giovanni Bertini	Michel Stocker	3	14
16	Portugal	"E depois do adeus"	Paulo de Carvalho	José Niza	José Calvário	José Calvário	Portuguese	Artur Agostinho	Henrique Mendes	3	14
17	Italy	"Sì"	Gigliola Cinquetti	Mario Panzeri, Daniele Pace, Lorenzo Pilat, Corrado Conti	Mario Panzeri, Daniele Pace, Lorenzo Pilat, Corrado Conti	Gianfranco Monaldi	Italian	Rosanna Vaudetti	Anna Maria Gambineri	18	2

	Finland	Luxembourg	Israel	Norway	United Kingdom	Yugoslavia	Greece	Ireland	Germany	Portugal	The Netherlands	Sweden	Spain	Monaco	Switzerland	Belgium	Italy
Italy	–	2	3	–	3	2	–	–	–	–	–	–	–	–	–	–	■
Belgium	–	1	–	1	1	1	–	–	1	–	1	–	–	2	1	■	1
Switzerland	–	–	–	–	1	–	–	–	1	2	–	5	–	1	■	–	–
Monaco	–	1	–	1	–	–	–	1	–	–	–	–	3	■	–	–	4
Spain	–	1	–	–	–	1	–	2	–	1	–	1	■	2	–	–	2
Sweden	–	–	1	1	–	–	2	2	–	–	3	■	–	1	–	–	–
The Netherlands	–	–	2	–	–	–	4	–	–	–	■	3	1	–	–	–	–
Portugal	–	–	2	–	–	1	1	–	–	■	1	1	2	1	–	–	1
Germany	–	1	–	–	2	–	–	–	■	–	1	2	1	2	1	–	–
Ireland	1	3	1	–	1	–	–	■	–	–	1	1	–	1	–	–	1
Greece	–	1	–	–	1	–	■	–	1	–	2	–	–	–	–	5	–
Yugoslavia	–	2	–	–	4	■	–	–	–	–	3	1	–	–	–	–	–
United Kingdom	1	–	2	–	■	–	–	1	–	–	–	–	–	–	1	–	5
Norway	–	–	–	■	–	–	–	2	–	–	1	2	2	1	–	2	–
Israel	2	2	■	–	–	–	–	1	–	–	1	2	–	1	–	–	1
Luxembourg	–	■	–	–	–	–	–	2	–	–	–	1	1	2	–	3	1
Finland	■	–	–	–	1	1	–	–	–	–	1	5	–	–	–	–	2

1975

Hosting Country: Sweden

Hosting City: Stockholm

Date: 22.3.1975

Location: Stockholmsmässan

Presenter: Karin Falck

Orchestra Conductor: Mats Olsson

Chief Executive: Clifford Brown

Executive Producer: Roland Eiworth & Bo Billten

Participating Countries: 19

Voting: Every participating country has a jury (11 members) that gives 1-8 points and then 10 and 12 points to its favourite song

Broadcaster: Sveriges Radio (SR)

Intermediate performance: The World of John Bauer

Duration: 2 hours and 13 minutes

Broadcast: To all participating countries and to Austria, Denmark, Greece and Iceland.

No.	Country	Song	Performing Artist	Lyrics	Composer	Conductor	Language	Commentator	Spoker of Results	Points	Place
01	The Netherlands	"Ding-a-dong"	Teach-In (Getty Kaspers, Ard Weeink, Chris de Wolde, John Gaasbeek, Koos Versteeg, Rudi Nijhuis)	Will Luikinga, Eddy Ouwens	Dick Bakker	Harry van Hoof	English	Willem Duys	Dick van Bommel	152	1
02	Ireland	"That's What Friends Are For"	The Swarbriggs	Tommy Swarbrigg, Jimmy Swarbrigg	Tommy Swarbrigg, Jimmy Swarbrigg	Colman Pearce	English	Mike Murphy	Brendan Balfe	68	9
03	France	"Et bonjour à toi l'artiste"	Nicole Rieu	Pierre Delanoë, Jeff Barnel	Pierre Delanoë, Jeff Barnel	Jean Musy	French	Georges de Caunes	Marc Menant	91	4
04	Germany	"Ein Lied kann eine Brücke sein"	Joy Fleming	Michael Holm	Rainer Pietsch	Rainer Pietsch	German and English	Werner Veigel	Ekkehard Böhmer	15	17
05	Luxembourg	"Toi"	Geraldine	Pierre Cour, Bill Martin, Phil Coulter	Bill Martin, Phil Coulter	Phil Coulter	French	Jacques Navadic	Unknown	84	5
06	Norway	"Touch My Life (With Summer)"	Ellen Nikolaysen	Svein Hundsnes	Svein Hundsnes	Carsten Klouman	English	John Andreassen	Sverre Chris-tophersen	11	18
07	Switzerland	"Mikado"	Simone Drexel	Simone Drexel	Simone Drexel	Peter Jacques	German	Theodor Haller, Georges Hardy, Giovanni Bertini	Michel Stocker	77	6
08	Yugoslavia	"Dan ljubezni"	Pepel in kri (Ditka Haberl Oto Pestner, Tadej Hrušovar Palmira Klobas, Ivan Mojzer Nada Žqur)	Dušan Velkaverh	Tadej Hrušovar	Mario Rijavec	Slovenian	Milovan Ilić, Oliver Mlakar, Tomaž Terček	Dragana Marković	22	13
09	United Kingdom	"Let Me Be the One"	The Shadows (Bruce Welch John Farrar, Hank Marvin Brian Bennett)	Paul Curtis	Paul Curtis	Alyn Ainsworth	English	Pete Murray	Ray Moore	138	2
10	Malta	"Singing This Song"	Renato	Mary Iris Mifsud	Sammy Galea	Vince Tempera	English	Norman Hamilton	Unknown	32	12
11	Belgium	"Gelukkig zijn"	Ann Christy	Mary Boduin	Mary Boduin	Francis Bay	Flemish and English	Willem Duys, Paule Herreman	Ward Bogaert	17	15
12	Israel	"At Ve Ani"	Shlomo Artzi	Ehud Manor	Shlomo Artzi	Eldad Shrem	Hebrew	-	Yitzhak Shimoni	40	11
13	Turkey	"Seninle Bir Dakika"	Semiha Yankı	Hikmet Münir Ebcioğlu	Kemal Ebcioğlu	Timur Selçuk	Turkish	Bülend Özveren	Bülent Osma	3	19
14	Monaco	"Une chanson c'est une lettre"	Sophie Garel	Boris Bergman	André Popp	André Popp	French	Georges de Caunes	Carole Chabrier	22	13
15	Finland	"Old Man Fiddle"	Pihasoittajat (Anja Karlsson, Hannu Karlsson, Seppo Sillanpää, Henrik Bergendahl, Harry Lindahl, Kim Kuusi)	Arthur Ridgway Spencer, Hannu Karlsson	Kim Kuusi	Ossi Runne	English	Heikki Seppälä	Kaarina Pönniö	74	7
16	Portugal	"Madrugada"	Duarte Mendes	José Luís Tinoco	José Luís Tinoco	Pedro Vaz Osório	Portuguese	Júlio Isidro	Ana Zanatti	16	16
17	Spain	"Tú volverás"	Sergio & Estíbaliz	Juan Carlos Calderón	Juan Carlos Calderón	Juan Carlos Calderón	Spanish	José Luis Uribarri	José María Íñigo	53	10
18	Sweden	"Jennie, Jennie"	Lasse Berghagen	Lasse Berghagen	Lasse Berghagen	Lars Samuelson	English	Åke Strömmer	Sven Lindahl	72	8

	The Netherlands	Ireland	France	Germany	Luxembourg	Norway	Switzerland	Yugoslavia	United Kingdom	Malta	Belgium	Israel	Turkey	Monaco	Finland	Portugal	Spain	Sweden	Italy	
The Netherlands	■	8	5	8	10	12	6	8	12	12	3	12	4	10	10	7	12	12	1	The Netherlands
Ireland	6	■	6	–	–	4	7	1	6	4	12	–	–	–	1	4	3	10	4	Ireland
France	8	12	■	–	–	–	3	–	8	7	2	7	1	7	–	12	8	8	8	France
Germany	–	–	–	■	8	–	–	–	–	3	–	–	–	–	–	–	4	–	–	Germany
Luxembourg	12	10	3	–	■	–	–	7	3	5	–	6	5	–	5	8	6	4	10	Luxembourg
Norway	2	–	–	–	–	■	–	–	–	–	–	–	–	2	–	–	–	–	7	Norway
Switzerland	7	1	10	6	2	1	■	–	5	6	8	–	7	5	4	2	–	–	12	Switzerland
Yugoslavia	3	4	–	2	–	–	–	■	–	–	5	–	–	–	–	1	–	7	–	Yugoslavia
United Kingdom	4	3	12	10	12	7	8	12	■	8	10	10	–	12	7	5	10	5	3	United Kingdom
Malta	1	–	8	–	5	2	4	2	–	■	7	1	2	–	–	–	–	–	–	Malta
Belgium	5	–	–	7	–	–	–	3	–	–	■	–	–	–	–	–	–	–	2	Belgium
Israel	10	1	1	1	1	5	2	–	1	–	1	■	6	–	3	–	–	6	2	Israel
Turkey	–	–	–	–	–	–	–	–	–	–	–	–	■	3	–	–	–	–	–	Turkey
Monaco	–	–	–	3	4	–	–	–	2	1	–	2	–	■	2	3	–	–	5	Monaco
Finland	–	5	–	12	6	10	12	5	4	–	–	8	–	8	■	–	1	3	–	Finland
Portugal	–	–	2	–	–	–	–	–	–	–	–	–	12	–	–	■	2	–	–	Portugal
Spain	–	7	–	5	–	3	5	4	–	–	4	4	3	4	8	–	■	–	6	Spain
Sweden	–	–	7	–	7	8	1	6	7	2	–	3	8	6	6	6	5	■	–	Sweden
Italy	–	6	4	4	3	6	10	10	10	10	6	5	10	1	12	10	7	1	■	Italy

1976

Hosting Country: The Netherlands

Hosting City: The Hague

Date: 3.4.1976

Location: Nederlands Congresgebouw

Presenter: Corry Brokken

Second Presenter: Hans van Willigenburg

Orchestra Conductor: Jan Steulen

Chief Executive: Clifford Brown

Director: Theo Ordeman

Executive Producer: Fred Oster

Participating Countries: 18

Voting: Every participating country has a jury (11 members) that gives 1-8 points and then 10 and 12 points to its favourite song

Broadcaster: Nederlandse Omroep Stichting (NOS)

Intermediate performance: The Dutch Swing College Band

Duration: 2 hours and 12 minutes

Broadcast: To all participating countries and to Turkey, Iceland and Denmark.

No.	Country	Song	Performing Artist	Lyrics	Composer	Conductor	Language	Commentator	Spoker of Results	Points	Place
01	United Kingdom	"Save Your Kisses for Me"	Brotherhood of Man (Martin Lee, Nicky Stevens, Sandra Stevens Lee Sheriden)	Tony Hiller, Lee Sheriden, Martin Lee	Tony Hiller, Lee Sheriden, Martin Lee	Alyn Ainsworth	English	Michael Aspel	Ray Moore	164	1
02	Switzerland	"Djambo, Djambo"	Peter, Sue and Marc	Peter Reber	Peter Reber	Mario Robbiani	English	Theodor Haller, Georges Hardy, Giovanni Bertini	Michel Stocker	91	4
03	Germany	"Sing Sang Song"	Les Humphries Singers	Kurt Hertha	Ralph Siegel	Les Humphries	German/English	Werner Veigel	Ekkehard Böhmer	12	15
04	Israel	"Emor Shalom"	"Chocolate, Menta, Mastik"	Ehud Manor	Matti Caspi	Matti Caspi	Hebrew	-	Yitzhak Shimoni	77	6
05	Luxembourg	"Chansons pour ceux qui s'aiment"	Jürgen Marcus	Fred Jay, Vline Buggy	Jack White	Jo Plée	French	Jacques Navadic	Jacques Harvey	17	14
06	Belgium	"Judy et Cie"	Pierre Rapsat	Eric van Hulse	Pierre Rapsat	Michel Bernholc	French	Georges Désir, Luc Appermont	André Hagon	68	8
07	Ireland	"When"	Red Hurley	Brendan J. Graham	Brendan J. Graham	Noel Kelehan	English	Mike Murphy	Brendan Balfe	54	10
08	The Netherlands	"The Party's Over"	Sandra Reemer	Hans van Hemert	Hans van Hemert	Harry van Hoof	English	Willem Duys	Dick van Bommel	56	9
09	Norway	"Mata Hari"	Anne Karine Strøm	Philip A. Kruse	Frode Thingnæs	Frode Thingnæs	English	Jo Vestly	Sverre Christophersen	7	17
10	Greece	"Panagia mou, Panagia mou"	Mariza Koch	Michael Fotiades	Mariza Koch	Michalis Rozakis	Greek	Mako Georgiadou	Irini Gavala	20	13
11	Finland	"Pump-Pump"	Fredi & Ystävät	Pertti Reponen	Matti Kalevi Siitonen	Ossi Runne	English	Vesa Nuotio	Erkki Vihtonen	44	11
12	Spain	"Sobran las palabras"	Braulio	Braulio Antonio García Bautista	Braulio Antonio, García Bautista	Juan Barcons	Spanish	José Luis Uribarri	José María Íñigo	11	16
13	Italy	"We'll Live It All Again"	Al Bano & Romina Power	Romina Power, Albano Carrisi	Detto Mariano	Maurizio Fabrizio	Italian and English	Silvio Noto	Rosanna Vaudetti	69	7
14	Austria	"My Little World"	Waterloo & Robinson	Gerhard Heinz	Gerhard Heinz	Erich Kleinschuster	English	Ernst Grissemann	Jenny Pippal	80	5
15	Portugal	"Uma flor de verde pinho"	Carlos do Carmo	Manuel Alegre	José Niza	Thilo Krassman	Portuguese	Eládio Clímaco	Ana Zanatti	24	12
16	Monaco	"Toi, la musique et moi"	Mary Christy	Gilbert Sinoué	Georges Costa	Raymond Donnez	French	Jean-Claude Massoulier	Carole Chabrier	93	3
17	France	"Un, deux, trois"	Catherine Ferry	Jean-Paul Cara	Tony Rallo	Tony Rallo	French	Jean-Claude Massoulier	Marc Menant	147	2
18	Yugoslavia	"Ne mogu skriti svoju bol"	Ambasadori	Slobodan Đurašović	Slobodan Vujović	Esad Arnautalić	Serb	Milovan Ilić, Oliver Mlakar, Tomaž Terček	Sandi Čolnik	6	18

	United Kingdom	Switzerland	Germany	Israel	Luxembourg	Belgium	Ireland	The Netherlands	Norway	Greece	Finland	Spain	Italy	Austria	Portugal	Monaco	France	Yugoslavia
United Kingdom	■	12	8	12	8	12	3	10	12	12	10	12	4	10	12	10	7	10
Switzerland	12	■	5	4	1	7	1	6	10	2	7	4	–	8	7	4	6	7
Germany	–	2	■	–	2	1	–	–	–	–	–	2	–	–	–	–	2	3
Israel	6	7	3	■	7	5	4	2	7	–	8	1	10	6	2	1	–	8
Luxembourg	–	–	–	–	■	6	6	5	–	–	–	–	–	–	–	–	–	–
Belgium	7	6	–	1	–	■	–	4	6	–	12	–	8	3	8	8	5	–
Ireland	10	–	1	3	3	–	■	–	–	8	–	5	12	2	–	6	3	1
The Netherlands	–	4	4	8	4	4	2	■	1	7	–	3	2	4	6	2	–	5
Norway	–	–	–	–	–	–	–	3	■	–	–	–	–	–	4	–	–	–
Greece	–	–	–	–	–	2	–	–	–	■	4	–	5	–	1	–	9	–
Finland	2	–	6	6	–	–	5	1	4	–	■	6	–	7	–	7	–	–
Spain	3	–	–	–	–	–	–	–	–	1	–	■	3	–	–	3	1	–
Italy	1	8	–	2	–	–	12	–	3	10	6	–	■	1	10	–	10	6
Austria	4	3	10	10	5	3	10	7	2	6	5	8	–	■	–	5	–	2
Portugal	–	–	–	–	6	–	–	–	–	4	1	–	1	–	■	–	12	–
Monaco	5	5	7	7	12	8	8	8	5	–	2	7	7	5	3	■	–	4
France	8	10	12	5	10	10	7	12	8	5	3	10	6	12	5	12	■	12
Yugoslavia	–	1	2	–	–	–	–	–	–	3	–	–	–	–	–	–	*4	■

* The 4 points France awarded to Yugoslavia were not recorded on the board during the voting process.

Hosting Country: United Kingdom

Hosting City: London

Date: 7.5.1977

Location: Wembley Conference Centre

Presenter: Angela Rippon

Orchestra Conductor: Ronnie Hazlehurst

Chief Executive: Clifford Brown

Director: Stewart Morris

Participating Countries: 18

Voting: Every participating country has a jury (11 members) that gives 1-8 points and then 10 and 12 points to its favourite song

Broadcaster: British Broadcasting Corporation (BBC)

Intermediate performance: Mr. Acker Bilk and his Paramount Jazz Men

Duration: 2 hours and 13 minutes

Broadcast: To all participating countries and to Denmark, Greenland, Iceland, Turkey and Yugoslavia.

No.	Country	Song	Performing Artist	Lyrics	Composer	Conductor	Language	Commentator	Spoker of Results	Points	Place
01	Ireland	"It's Nice to Be in Love Again"	The Swarbriggs Plus Two (Tommy Swarbrigg, Jimmy Swarbrigg, Nicola Kerr, Alma Carroll)	Tommy Swarbrigg, Jimmy Swarbrigg	Tommy Swarbrigg, Jimmy Swarbrigg	Noel Kelehan	English	Mike Murphy	Brendan Balfe	119	3
02	Monaco	"Une petite française"	Michèle Torr	Jean Albertini	Paul de Senneville, Olivier Toussaint	Yvon Rioland	French	Georges de Caunes	Carole Chabrier	96	4
03	The Netherlands	"De mallemolen"	Heddy Lester	Wim Hogenkamp	Frank Affolter	Harry van Hoof	Dutch	Ati Dijckmeester	Ralph Inbar	*36	12
04	Austria	"Boom Boom Boomerang"	Schmetterlinge	Lukas Resetarits	Schurli Hernstadt, Willi Resetarits, Herbert Zöchling-Tampier	Christian Kolonovits	German	Ernst Grissemann	Jenny Pippal	13*	17
05	Norway	"Casanova"	Anita Skorgan	Dag Nordtømme	Svein Strugstad	Carsten Klouman	Norweigen	John Andreassen	Sverre Christophersen	18	14
06	Germany	"Telegram"	Silver Convention (Penny McLean, Ramona Wulf, Rhonda Heath)	Michael Kunze	Sylvester Levay	Ronnie Hazlehurst	English	Werner Veigel	Ekkehard Böhmer	56*	8
07	Luxembourg	"Frère Jacques"	Anne-Marie B	Pierre Cour, Guy Béart	Pierre Cour, Guy Béart	Johnny Arthey	French	Jacques Navadic	Jacques Harvey	17	16
08	Portugal	"Portugal no coração"	Os Amigos (Paulo de Carvalho, Fernanda Piçarra, Luísa Basto, Edmundo Silva, Ana Bola, Fernando Tordo)	Ary dos Santos	Fernando Tordo	José Calvário	Portuguese	Júlio Isidro	Ana Zanatti	18	14
09	United Kingdom	"Rock Bottom"	Lynsey de Paul & Mike Moran	Lynsey de Paul / Mike Moran	Lynsey de Paul / Mike Moran	Ronnie Hazlehurst	English	Pete Murray	Colin Berry	122*	2
10	Greece	"Mathima solfege"	Pascalis Arvanitidis, Marianna Toli, Robert Williams, Bessy Argyraki	Sevi Tiliakou	Giorgos Hatzinasios	Giorgos Hatzinasios	Greek	Mako Georgiadou	Naki Agathou	92	5
11	Israel	"Ahava hi Shir Lishnaim"	Ilanit	Edna Peleg	Eldad Shrem	Eldad Shrem	Hebrew	-	Yitzhak Shimoni	50*	11
12	Switzerland	"Swiss Lady"	Pepe Lienhard Band (Pino Gasparini, Pepe Lienhard, Bill von Arx, Georges Walther, Mostafa Kafa'I Azimi)	Peter Reber	Peter Reber	Peter Jacques	German	Theodor Haller, Georges Hardy, Giovanni Bertini	Michel Stocker	71	6
13	Sweden	"Beatles"	Forbes (Peter Forbes Roger Capello, Claes Bure, Peter Björk, Anders Hector and Chino Mariano)	Sven-Olof Bagge	Claes Bure	Anders Berglund	Swedish	Ulf Elfving	Sven Lindahl	2	18
14	Spain	"Enséñame a cantar"	Micky	Fernando Arbex	Fernando Arbex	Rafael de Ibarbia Serra	Spanish	Miguel de los Santos	Isabel Tenaille	52	9
15	Italy	"Libera"	Mia Martini	Luigi Albertelli	Salvatore Fabrizi	Maurizio Fabrizio	Italian	Silvio Noto	Mariolina Cannuli	33	13
16	Finland	"Lapponia"	Monica Aspelund	Monica Aspelund	Aarno Raninen	Ossi Runne	Finish	Jean-Claude Massoulier	Kaarina Pönniö	51*	10
17	Belgium	"A Million in One, Two, Three"	Dream Express (Bianca Maessen, Patricia Maessen, Stella Maessen, Luc Smets)	Luc Smets	Luc Smets	Alyn Ainsworth	English	Luc Appermont, Patrick Duhamel	An Ploegaerts	70*	7
18	France	"L'oiseau et l'enfant"	Marie Myriam	Marie Myriam	Jean-Paul Cara	Raymond Donnez	French	Georges de Caunes	Marc Menant	136	1

	Ireland	Monaco	The Netherlands	Austria	Norway	Germany	Luxembourg	Portugal	United Kingdom	Greece	Israel	Switzerland	Sweden	Spain	Italy	Finland	Belgium	France	
Ireland	■	8	1	5	12	5	8	1	12	10	12	8	12	4	8	–	3	10	Ireland
Monaco	5	■	–	8	1	6	1	6	7	12	2	6	10	8	12	5	2	5	Monaco
The Netherlands	3	3	■	–	–	–	–	–	1	1	1	7	–	1	–	–	10	8	The Netherlands
Austria	–	5	–	■	2	–	–	–	–	3	–	–	–	–	–	1	–	–	Austria
Norway	–	–	–	–	■	–	3	2	2	–	–	–	1	–	5	–	5	–	Norway
Germany	1	1	3	2	–	■	2	8	8	8	5	–	5	5	6	–	–	1	Germany
Luxembourg	2	–	–	–	–	–	■	–	–	–	–	–	–	7	–	8	–	–	Luxembourg
Portugal	–	2	2	–	–	1	–	■	–	–	–	4	–	–	3	–	–	6	Portugal
United Kingdom	–	12	7	12	7	10	12	12	■		8	–	8	3	2	4	12	12	United Kingdom
Greece	–	10	10	4	4	4	6	10	5	■	3	1	7	12	1	6	6	3	Greece
Israel	7		5	3	5	–	–	–	–	–	■	10	3	6	–	–	1	2	Israel
Switzerland	6	–	–	10	10	–	5	4	4	6	4	■	–	–	4	10	8	–	Switzerland
Sweden	–	–	–	–	–	2	–	–	–	–	–	–	■	–	–	–	–	–	Sweden
Spain	–	–	6	1	–	7	7	–	3	4	–	3	–	■	7	7	7	–	Spain
Italy	8	6	–	–	–	3	–	3	–	–	–	2	–	2	■	2	–	7	Italy
Finland	12	–	4	6	8	–	–	–	–	2	7	5	2	–	–	■	–	4	Finland
Belgium	4	–	12	–	6	8	4	7	10	5	6	–	4	–	–	3	■	–	Belgium
France	10	4	8	7	3	12	10	5	6	7	10	12	6	10	10	12	4	■	France

1978

Hosting Country: France
Hosting City: Paris
Date: 22.4.1978
Location: Palais des Congrès
Presenters: Denise Fabre, Léon Zitrone
Orchestra Conductor: François Rauber
Chief Executive: Frank Naef
Director: Bernard Lion
Participating Countries: 20
Voting: Every participating country has a jury (11 members) that gives 1-8 points and then 10 and 12 points to its favourite song
Broadcaster: Télévision Française 1 (TF1)
Intermediate performance: Stéphane Grappelli and Oscar Peterson, Yehudi Menuhin, Kenny Clarke, Niels-Henning Ørsted Pedersen
Duration: 2 hours and 27 minutes
Broadcast: To all participating countries and to Algeria, Czechoslovakia, Dubai, East Germany, Hong Kong, Hungary, Iceland, Japan, Jordan, Morocco, Poland, Soviet Union, Tunisia and Yugoslavia.

No.	Country	Song	Performing Artist	Lyrics	Composer	Conductor	Language	Commentator	Spoker of Results	Points	Place
01	Ireland	"Born to Sing"	Colm C. T. Wilkinson	Colm C. T. Wilkinson	Colm C. T. Wilkinson	Noel Kelehan	English	Larry Gogan	John Skehan	86	5
02	Norway	"Mil etter mil"	Jahn Teigen	Kai Eide / english lyric by David Cooper	Kai Eide	Carsten Klouman	Norweigen	Bjørn Scheele	Egil Teige	0	20
03	Italy	"Questo amore"	Ricchi e Poveri (Marina Occhiena, Angela Brambati, Angelo Sotgiu, Franco Gatti)	Sergio Bardotti	Dario Farina, Mauro Lusini	Nicola Samale	Italian	Tullio Grazzini	Mariolina Cannuli	53	12
04	Finland	"Anna rakkaudelle tilaisuus"	Seija Simola	Reijo Karvonen, Seija Simola	Reijo Karvonen	Ossi Runne	Finish	Erkki Toivanen	Kaarina Pönniö	2	18
05	Portugal	"Dai li dou"	Gemini (Fatima Padinha, Teresa Miguel, Tozé Brito, Mike Seargent)	Carlos Quintas	Vítor Mamede	Thilo Krassman	Portuguese	Eládio Clímaco	Isabel Wolmar	5	17
06	France	"Il y aura toujours des violons"	Joël Prévost	Didier Barbelivien	Gérard Stern	Alain Goraguer	French	Léon Zitrone & Denise Fabre	Marc Menant	119	3
07	Spain	"Bailemos un vals"	José Vélez	Manuel de la Calva and Ramón Arcusa	Manuel de la Calva and Ramón Arcusa	Ramón Arcusa	Spanish	Miguel de los Santos	Matías Prats	65	9
08	United Kingdom	"The Bad Old Days"	Co-Co (Terry Bradford, Josie Andrews, Cheryl Baker, Keith Hasler, Paul Rogers)	Stephanie de Sykes & Stuart Slater	Stephanie de Sykes & Stuart Slater	Alyn Ainsworth	English	Terry Wogan	Colin Berry	61	11
09	Switzerland	"Vivre"	Carole Vinci	Pierre Alain	Alain Morisod	Daniel Janin	French	Theodor Haller, Georges Hardy, Giovanni Bertini	Michel Stocker	65	10
10	Belgium	"L'amour ça fait chanter la vie"	Jean Vallée	Jean Vallée	Jean Vallée	Jean Musy	French	Claude Delacroix, Luc Appermont	André Hagon	125	2
11	The Netherlands	"'t Is OK"	Harmony (Rosina Louwaars, Donald Lieveld, Ab van Woudenberg)	Toon Gispen, Dick Kooiman	Eddy Ouwens	Harry van Hoof	Dutch	-Willem Duys	Dick van Bommel	37	13
12	Turkey	"Sevince"	Nilüfer & Nazar	Hulki Aktunç	Dağhan Baydur, Onno Tunç	Onno Tunç	Turkish	Bülend Özveren	Meral Savcı	2	19
13	Germany	"Feuer"	Ireen Sheer	John Möring	Jean Frankfurter	Jean Frankfurter	German	Werner Veigel	Ute Verhoolen	84	6
14	Monaco	"Les jardins de Monaco"	Caline & Olivier Toussaint	Jean Albertini, Didier Barbelivien	Paul de Senneville, Olivier Toussaint	Yvon Rioland	French	Léon Zitrone & Denise Fabre	Carole Chabrier	107	4
15	Greece	"Charlie Chaplin"	Tania Tsanaklidou	Yiannis Xantoulis	Sakis Tsilikis	Haris Andreadis	Greek	Mako Georgiadou	Unknown	66	8
16	Denmark	"Boom Boom"	Mabel	Mabel	Mabel	Helmer Olesen	Danish	Jørgen de Mylius	Bent Henius	13	16
17	Luxembourg	"Parlez-vous français?"	Baccara	Frank Dostal, Peter Zentner	Rolf Soja	Rolf Soja	French	Jacques Navadic	Jacques Harvey	73	7
18	Israel	"A-Ba-Ni-Bi"	Izhar Cohen and Alphabeta group (Reuven Erez, Lisa Gold Rubin, Nehama Shutan, Ester Tzuberi, Itzhak Okev)	Ehud Manor	Nurit Hirsh	Nurit Hirsh	Hebrew	-	Yitzhak Shimoni	157	1
19	Austria	"Mrs. Caroline Robinson"	Springtime	Walter Markel, Gerhard Markel	Walter Markel, Gerhard Markel, Norbert Niedermayer	Richard Österreicher	German	Ernst Grissemann	Jenny Pippal	14	15
20	Sweden	"Det blir alltid värre framåt natten"	Björn Skifs	Peter Himmelstrand	Peter Himmelstrand	Bengt Palmers	Swedish	Ulf Elfving	Sven Lindahl	26	14

	Ireland	Norway	Italy	Finland	Portugal	France	Spain	United Kingdom	Switzerland	Belgium	The Netherlands	Turkey	Germany	Monaco	Greece	Denmark	Luxembourg	Israel	Austria	Sweden	
Ireland	■	12	–	3	–	5	–	–	7	10	–	10	5	–	10	–	10	–	6	8	Ireland
Norway	–	■	–	–	–	–	–	–	–	–	–	–	–	–	–	–	–	–	–	–	Norway
Italy	10	6	■	–	1	4	8	6	1	1	–	1	2	8	2	–	3	–	–	–	Italy
Finland	–	2	–	■	–	–	–	–	–	–	–	–	–	–	–	–	–	–	–	–	Finland
Portugal	–	–	4	–	■	–	1	–	–	–	–	–	–	–	–	–	–	–	–	–	Portugal
France	6	3	10	2	2	■	5	8	6	8	6	4	10	5	8	8	1	5	12	10	France
Spain	–	–	–	7	–	–	■	–	8	2	4	7	–	4	6	12	2	6	7	–	Spain
United Kingdom	3	–	–	–	6	2	3	■	2	4	2	6	8	7	3	–	5	2	5	3	United Kingdom
Switzerland	–	5	1	1	–	7	4	2	■	7	8	–	6	2	–	3	8	1	10	–	Switzerland
Belgium	12	7	6	6	4	12	2	12	10	■	5	–	3	12	12	–	7	7	4	4	Belgium
The Netherlands	–	–	5	–	–	–	–	3	–	–	■	–	4	1	–	5	6	12	–	1	The Netherlands
Turkey	–	1	–	–	–	–	–	1	–	–	–	■	–	–	–	–	–	–	–	–	Turkey
Germany	1	–	3	12	7	–	10	–	3	5	7	8	■	10	7	1	–	3	–	7	Germany
Monaco	4	4	7	8	5	1	–	10	5	6	10	5	7	■	4	10	–	8	1	12	Monaco
Greece	7	–	2	5	8	10	7	–	4	–	–	–	–	–	■	4	4	10	3	2	Greece
Denmark	–	–	–	–	–	6	–	–	–	–	1	–	–	–	–	■	–	4	2	–	Denmark
Luxembourg	2	–	12	–	12	–	12	7	–	3	3	2	–	6	1	7	■	–	–	6	Luxembourg
Israel	8	8	8	10	10	8	6	5	12	12	12	12	12	3	5	6	12	■	8	–	Israel
Austria	–	–	–	–	3	–	–	–	–	–	–	3	1	–	–	2	–	–	■	5	Austria
Sweden	5	10	–	4	–	3	–	4		–	–	–	–	–	–	–	–	–	–	■	Sweden

1979

Hosting Country: Israel

Hosting City: Jerusalem

Date: 31.3.1979

Location: International Conventions Center

Presenters: Yardena Arazi and Daniel Peer

Orchestra Conductor: Itzchak (Ziko) Graziani

Chief Executive: Frank Naef

Director: Yossi Zemach

Executive Producer: Alex Giladi

Participating Countries: 19

Voting: Every participating country has a jury (11 members) that gives 1-8 points and then 10 and 12 points to its favourite song

Broadcaster: Israeli Broadcasting Authority (IBA)

Intermediate performance: Shalom '79 dancing group (managed by Gavri Levy)

Duration: 2 hours and 59 minutes

Broadcast: To all participating countries and to Hong Kong, Iceland, Romania, Turkey and Yugoslavia.

No.	Country	Song	Performing Artist	Lyrics	Composer	Conductor	Language	Commentator	Spoker of Results	Points	Place
01	Portugal	"Sobe, sobe, balão sobe"	Manuela Bravo	Carlos Nóbrega e Sousa	Carlos Nóbrega e Sousa	Thilo Krassman	Portuguese	Fialho Gouveia	João Abel Fonseca	64	9
02	Italy	"Raggio di luna"	Matia Bazar (Carlo Marrale, Antonella Ruggiero, Giancarlo Golzi, Piero Cassano, Aldo Stellita)	Giancarlo Golzi, Salvatore Stellita	Carlo Marrale, Piero Cassano, Antonella Ruggiero	-	Italian	Rosanna Vaudetti	Paola Perissi	27	15
03	Denmark	"Disco Tango"	Tommy Seebach	Keld Heick	Tommy Seebach	Allan Botschinsky	Danish	Jørgen de Mylius	Bent Henius	76	6
04	Ireland	"Happy Man"	Cathal Dunne	Cathal Dunne	Cathal Dunne	Proínsias O'Duinn	English	Mike Murphy	David Heffernan	80	5
05	Finland	"Katson sineen taivaan"	Katri Helena	Veikko 'Vexi' Salmi	Matti Kalevi Siitonen	Ossi Runne	Finish	Anja-Maija Leppänen	Kaarina Pönniö	38	14
06	Monaco	"Notre vie c'est la musique"	Laurent Vaguener	Jean Albertini, Didier Barbelivien	Paul de Senneville, Jean Baudlot	Gérard Salesse	French	Marc Menant	Carole Chabrier	12	16
07	Greece	"Sokrati"	Elpida	Sofia Tsotou	Doros Georgiades	Lefteris Halkiadakis	Greek	Mako Georgiadou	Unknown	69	8
08	Switzerland	"Trödler und Co"	Peter, Sue, Marc, Pfuri, Gorps and Kniri (Peter Reber, Sue Schell, Marcel Dietrich, Pfuri Baldenweg, Anthony Fischer, Kniri Knaus)	Peter Reber	Peter Reber	Rolf Zuckowski	German	Theodor Haller, Georges Hardy, Giovanni Bertini	Michel Stocker	60	10
09	Germany	"Dschinghis Khan"	Dschinghis Khan (Louis Hendrik, Potgieter, Wolfgang Heichel, Henriette Heichel-Strobel Edina Pop, Steve Bender Leslie Mándoki)	Bernd Meinunger	Ralph Siegel	Norbert Daum	German	Ado Schlier, Gabi Schnelle	Lotti Ohnesorge	86	4
10	Israel	"Hallellujah"	Gali Atari and "Milk and Honey" (Reuven Gvirtz, Yehuda Tamir and Shmuel Bilu)	Shimrit Or	Kobi Oshrat	Kobi Oshrat	Hebrew	Yoram Arbel	Dan Kaner	125	1
11	France	"Je suis l'enfant soleil"	Anne-Marie David	Hubert Giraud	Eddy Marnay	Guy Mattéoni	French	Marc Menant	Fabienne Égal	106	3
12	Belgium	"Hey Nana"	Micha Marah	Guy Beyers	Charles Dumolin	Francis Bay	Flemish	Luc Appermont, Paule Herreman	An Ploegaerts	5	19
13	Luxembourg	"J'ai déjà vu ça dans tes yeux"	Jeane Manson	Jean Renard	Jean Renard	Hervé Roy	French	Jacques Navadic	Jacques Harvey	44	13
14	The Netherlands	"Colorado"	Xandra	Ferdi Bolland, Gerard Cox	Rob Bolland	Harry van Hoof	Dutch	Willem Duys	Ivo Niehe	51	12
15	Sweden	"Satellit"	Ted Gärdestad	Kenneth Gärdestad	Ted Gärdestad	Lars Samuelson	Swedish	Ulf Elfving	Sven Lindahl	8	17
16	Norway	"Oliver"	Anita Skorgan	Philip A. Kruse	Anita Skorgan	Sigurd Jansen	Norweigen	Egil Teige	Sverre Christophersen	57	11
17	United Kingdom	"Mary Ann"	Black Lace (Alan Barton, Colin Routh, Terry Dobson, Steve Scholey)	Peter Morris	Peter Morris	Ken Jones	English	John Dunn	Colin Berry	73	7
18	Austria	"Heute in Jerusalem"	Christina Simon	André Heller	Peter Wolf	Richard Oester-reicher	German	Max Schautzer	Jenny Pippal	5	18
19	Spain	"Su canción"	Betty Missiego	Fernando Moreno	Fernando Moreno	José Luis Navarro	Spanish	Miguel de los Santos	Manuel Almendros	116	2

	Portugal	Italy	Denmark	Ireland	Finland	Monaco	Greece	Switzerland	Germany	Israel	France	Belgium	Luxembourg	The Netherlands	Sweden	Norway	United Kingdom	Austria	Spain	
Portugal	■	6	–	–	2	5	–	4	4	–	10	5	3	3	3	6	–	7	6	Portugal
Italy	8	■	–	–	8	–	–	–	–	–	–	–	–	–	–	3	–	–	8	Italy
Denmark	–	–	■	2	–	3	12	1	10	12	6	7	4	8	1	–	3	3	4	Denmark
Ireland	5	5	5	■	6	–	10	6	6	3	–	10	7	–	8	5	4	–	–	Ireland
Finland	–	7	–	–	■	–	7	8	5	–	5	–	6	–	–	–	–	–	–	Finland
Monaco	1	2	4	–	–	■	–	–	–	–	3	–	–	–	–	–	–	–	2	Monaco
Greece	10	–	1	4	–	7	■	7	2	10	4	1	5	7	2	–	–	2	7	Greece
Switzerland	–	–	7	1	10	2	2	■	7	4	7	–	–	–	–	8	–	12	–	Switzerland
Germany	2	1	12	5	3	12	–	–	■	6	12	4	1	2	6	–	8	–	12	Germany
Israel	12	–	6	12	12	8	4	5	–	■	1	2	8	1	12	12	12	8	10	Israel
France	6	10	–	–	1	10	8	10	–	5	■	6	12	12	5	7	6	5	3	France
Belgium	–	–	2	–	–	–	–	–	1	–	–	■	–	–	–	–	2	–	–	Belgium
Luxembourg	7	–	–	3	4	4	5	3	–	–	2	–	■	4	–	2	10	–	–	Luxembourg
The Netherlands	–	–	8	10	5	–	3	–	3	7	–	3	–	■	4	4	–	4	–	The Netherlands
Sweden	–	–	–	6	–	–	1	–	–	1	–	–	–	–	■	–	–	–	–	Sweden
Norway	3	3	–	3	–	6	–	–	–	2	–	8	2	6	10	■	7	1	1	Norway
United Kingdom	4	8	10	7	7	1	–	2	8	–	–	–	–	5	–	10	■	6	5	United Kingdom
Austria	–	4	–	–	–	–	–	–	–	–	–	–	–	–	–	–	1	■	–	Austria
Spain	–	12	3	–	–	–	6	12	12	8	8	12	10	10	7	1	5	10	■	Spain

1980-1989

LOGAN ENTERS THE HISTORY BOOKS, CÉLINE DION IS DISCOVERED

Ireland managed to do what no other country has been able in the diverse decade of the 1980s: Win twice at the Eurovision Song Contest. Johnny Logan, the Irish singer responsible for both victories (and for the second place in mid-1984 as writer and composer), is to this day the only artist to have won the contest twice as a performer. Only four female singers made their debut (including Céline Dion), with three bands, one duo and one Johnny Logan (who won twice) making up the list of winners of the decade. In 1980, Israel gave up hosting in favour of the Netherlands, making it the last country not to host the contest after winning it to date. With two victories this decade, Ireland was also the country to host the event twice — more than any other in the 1980s.

1980 – The Hague, The Netherlands

Few know, but there was a step between the cancellation of the 1980 contest and the historic end of the European Song Contest forever. The 25th Eurovision, the Silver Eurovision, the first of the 1980s, was supposed to be held in Israel. After the "Hallelujah" victory, the local broadcasting authority gathered a meeting announcing that they would host the ESC again, borne along by the national enthusiasm and government support. Shlomo Lahat, Tel Aviv's mayor, offered to host the contest in his city, as did the mayor of Haifa, Arie Gorel, who promised to adjust the "Romema" Hall to the event. Over time, it became clear that the IBA was not prepared for the possibility, and the government was reluctant to put its hand in the empty pocket. CEO Tommy Lapid, who has never accounted for anyone, was shocked to learn at the preparatory meeting for the contest that the cost of holding another Eurovision in Israel is equal to the IBA's budget for an entire year... Days passed, a decision had to be made, and the die was cast as Lapid was swimming in the pool on Saturday morning: With his body wading in the water, he decided to renounce the hosting. Israel is not the first to give up hosting, but as of today, it is the last to take this step. Lapid had enough trouble within the hornet's nest of the IBA, and according to him, he persuaded his colleague from the Netherlands to take this dubious honour from him ... This was not exactly the case: When Israel announced that it was waiving the hosting, the news came unexpected for the EBU, and Spain was quickly approached but refused. The UK, as well, was no longer enthusiastic about producing the Eurovision. It turned out that the distance between producing the contest and permanently cancelling it was closer than ever: "We decided to hold the Eurovision Song Contest in the Netherlands because if we had not taken it upon ourselves, it would have brought an end to the whole contest", said Karl Anklar, director of the Dutch Broadcasting Authority, in an astonishing statement. Indeed, the Netherlands' agreement to take on the challenge at short notice saved the Eurovision. The Dutch prepared the hall that hosted the 1976 contest in The Hague. Based on that backdrop, artist Roland de Groot also designed the 1980 Eurovision stage. The meagre budget allocated to the event, the fleeting time and the amount of work forced the hosts to think outside the box and show extraordinary creativity and so it was. The opening video started at the beach, continued presenting the Netherlands and The Hague and moved on to the hall and presenter Marlous Fluitsma. The Dutch came up with an unusual idea: A representative from each nation will present his country's entry in his language. Norway selected Åse Kleveland, who brought her country its greatest achievement at the ESC at the time (third place in 1966) and had already prepared herself for the role of presenter, which she received six years later. The rest of the countries used local representatives or the broadcasters themselves (they went down to the stage and presented their country's entry to their audience). This format was one-time and stemmed, most likely, from the inability and lack of time to prepare other passages. The event's date was set precisely for the eve of the Israeli Memorial Day "Yom HaZikaron". Was this a retaliatory action by the EBU against the IBA? There is no telling. In any case, not only did Israel not host the contest as is tradition, but it was also the first winner in the history of the Eurovision not to defend its title, being absent from The Hague. Austria reorganised and was one of the contenders to win the contest with "Du bist Musik". Although the "Blue Danube" was far from the first places, it achieved Austria's best ranking in four years, the 8th. Turkey returned after a year of absence and sent its local superstar — Ajda Pekkan, one of Turkey's greatest singers and actors. The song "Pet'r Oil" was a massive hit in Arab countries and Israel. It received 12 whole points from the other Muslim country that participated in the contest, which helped the Turks accumulate 23 points and reach 15th place — their best achievement thus far. The Greek pre-contest was stormed by an anonymous Cypriot singer named Anna Vissi, who marvelled at her performance and was accompanied in The Hague by the "Epikouri" band (which included her sister Lia Vissi) that finished second in the same pre-contest. It was Vissi's first but certainly not last experience on the Eurovision stage, but in her debut, she had to settle for 13th place. Luxembourg hired the excellent services of the German Ralph Siegel and Bernd Meinunger. They set a precedent as the only writers to have two songs competing in the same Eurovision (they also wrote the German entry). "Papa pingouin" was a whole show on the stage, with a backup singer and three other singers standing behind the performing duo Sophie & Magaly disguised as penguins. Fifty-six points and ninth place were far from the Luxembourgers' expectations but were at least a better achievement than in Jerusalem. Israel's absence has opened the door to history: For the first time, the Arabic language was sung and heard on the Eurovision stage. It happened thanks to Morocco's participation. Samira Bensaïd, a promising singer at the beginning of her career, was sent to her first European experience with "Bitaqat Hub". With the help of the French arranger and conductor Jean Claudric, she adapted her performance for the European orchestra. Italy was the only one to award points to Morocco, 7 points that led to Morocco's ranking in the penultimate place (the same place the conductor Claudric had reached seven years earlier with France). King Hassan was furious at the result, took it as humiliation and decided that his country would no longer participate in the contest. One of Bensaïd's most memorable international appearances was in the Vatican, alongside the Israeli singer Rinat Gabay. One of the favourites to win was Paola from Switzerland, who returned to the ESC after 11 years (then was 5th). This time, "Cinéma", written by Peter Reber (who also conducted the entry), contained the right elements for victory: Paola's polished performance, a great arrangement of Reber and a rich and moving melody. The Swiss gave a close fight and received two 'Douze Points', from Ireland and Finland, finishing in a respectable fourth place — the best result her country has achieved in four years. The Sámi protest in Norway was at the heart of the song "Sámiid ædnan" representing the nation in The Hague. The Sámis claim constant discrimination in the country, and Sverre Kjelsberg chose to host Mattis Hætta, a 'Sámi' who arrived in traditional attire. The viewers will probably never forget his joining to the chorus. Despite the interest aroused by the entry, it only reached 15th place. After the remarkable success with "Dschinghis Khan", Ralph Siegel solidified his status as a hit's writer. "Theater", which he created with Bernd Meinunger, was specifically designed for singer Katja Ebstein, who made a comeback after winning third place twice in a row — in 1970 and 1971 — and was willing to make the leap to top of the table. Wearing gloves with small clowns on his fingers, Siegel accompanied Ebstein on the piano, who gave the performance of her life and garnered tremendous applause from the audience. Katja did improve from the third place, yet only to the second — with 128 points — Germany's best score till then, but still no victory. The British pre-contest was incredibly close, with two competitors tying after a tough competition. Eventually, the decision fell in favour of "Prima Donna", which promised to restore the UK's honour after two relative failures. With "Love Enough for Two" it kept its word and became 3rd. The Netherlands' was a strong candidate to win, with Maggie MacNeal also returning to the contest after participating in 1974. The juries could not ignore the powerful "Amsterdam" and awarded the maximum score three times, raising hopes for an overwhelming victory. But then it slowed down, and MacNeal did not get high points, until settling for fifth place. In 1970, Ireland managed to win the ESC for the first time with Dana, on Dutch soil. Ten years later, Johnny Logan marked the same goal. "What's Another Year", written by Shay Healy, matches the phenomenal Irish singer, who performed sitting on a chair and captured European audience's heart. The applause and Logan's shy smile made it clear that a new star had been born. Indeed, at the end of the evening, Logan was crowned King of Ireland, which enjoyed its second Eurovision win. Healy stated that he wrote the winning entry in... A bus, while going through a challenging period in his life: "My mother passed away, and my father was depressed. I divided my time between hospitals and my family, and while riding the bus, I heard a conversation between two guys when one of them said: 'so what? What's another year?' The sentence was caught in my head, and within five stations the song was ready". Johnny Logan's father,

Patrick O'Hagan, who lived with his family in Australia, was announced of his son's win at the contest on the beach when a friend drew his attention: "Hey, one of your guys, an Irishman, won first place in the Eurovision Song Contest tonight". Patrick, who almost fainted, knew that the only Irishman who participated in the Eurovision halfway around the world was none other than... His son. Belgium was incredibly original with a song called... "Euro-Vision". The "Telex" band and vocalist Michelle Moers with an old-fashioned stills camera in his hand, in a tribute to the contest they participated in. The same format of 1976 returned in 1980, when Hans van Willigenburg interviewed the performers in the 'Green Room', while an a multi-ccolor band was dancing on stage. How unfortunate that this nice and intriguing custom was not adopted in the following years either. It was already mentioned that the Dutch tried quite hard to be creative, what was evident during the results as well, when Fluitsma, the presenter, exchanged several types of telephones in which she allegedly talked to the juries' centres that provided her with the results. The scoring system, which came into use in 1975, finally straightened out in 1980, when the order of reading the results was no longer in the order of participation in the contest, but in ascending order of points, from 1 to 12. After a strong Dutch opening and a momentary German lead, Ireland took first place and held it securely until the end, leaving everyone behind and Johnny Logan celebrating with 7 full marks of twelve points. The absence of the "Milk and Honey" band from the Grand Prix awarding ceremony was jarring when the Irish star took the stage. Excited Logan performed "What's Another Year" in tears of joy and ended a dream evening for him. The Dutch concluded the broadcast with Johnny Logan whistling the ESC theme music in a video on the Dutch beach, inviting viewers to Ireland next year. It turns out that the Dutch pre-recorded all the performers on the beach doing the same act and finally placed the winner. Creativity indeed.

1981 – Dublin, Ireland

Johnny Logan's thrilling victory brought the Eurovision back to Dublin after ten years. The Irish saw the event as an excellent opportunity to promote the country and invested huge sums that far exceeded the Netherlands' budget in producing 1980. The "RDS Simmonscourt" in Dublin was much larger and more spacious than "The Gaiety Theatre" where the contest took place in 1971. the "Stage of Circles", which changed colours at a dizzying pace, was the Irishmen's attraction and the orchestra returned to the front of the stage (left to the audience). The amiable presenter, Doireann Ní Bhriain, carried out the task by herself after the Irish, like the Dutch, preferred to abnegate the format of two presenters that had been so successful in Paris and Jerusalem. After a relatively silent year in the Netherlands (A Eurovision without Israel and with Morocco), hundreds of security personnel accompanied the event when the concerns came from intra-European terrorist incidents. This was the last ESC held on the early date of April 4th, when next ones were held later, deep into May. A record number of seven repeat performers participated in the Dublin contest, one of them being Marty Brem from Austria, who arrived for a second consecutive performance after 1980, settling for only 17th place this time. Jean-Claude Pascal, 1961 Eurovision winner and the one who brought Luxembourg its first victory, decided to return to the contest after 20 years with an entry written by Jean-Claude Petit (who conducted the winner of the last Eurovision that was held in Dublin — Séverine for Monaco) and try to be the first returning singer to win. In his way of receiving the coveted ticket to Dublin stood the Israeli singer Riki Gal, who claims to this day that her entry was better than Pascal's and that only his connections with a senior RTL official led him to beat her. Either way, "C'est peut-être pas l'Amérique" was considered a serious contender to win, but the disappointed Pascal failed to recreate his 1961 achievement and was left heartbroken. Tommy Seebach and Debbie Cameron from Denmark wanted to emulate the immense success from Jerusalem and "Krøller eller ej" received Douze Points from Belgium and placing them 11th. The brown-skinned Cameron caused a scandal at the end of the contest, claiming a BBC technician approached her after the event, telling her that the results were "rigged", and that technicians from the British Broadcasting Corporation deliberately sabotaged songs from Denmark, Israel and Germany. Aside from the fact that it is puzzling as the contest was held in Ireland rather than the UK (where the corporation is situated), no support has been found for this claim. Maxi, who represented Ireland in 1973, returned with all her might as part of the local "Sheeba" band that hoped to recreate Johnny Logan's victory and at times it seemed attainable. "Horoscopes" was relatively successful, and it manifested in the form of the fifth place. Cheryl Baker experienced the failure with "Co-Co" in 1978 but returned as part of the "Bucks Fizz", who arrived in Dublin with little concern and much faith. Only Israel and the Netherlands gave their full points to the British "Making Your Mind Up", but it was the only entry in the contest to receive points from all the participating countries, which was eventually enough for a sweet victory on Irish soil. The British were not the only favourites, but they pulled out their trump card during their rhythmic song, precisely in a line that says "But if you want to see some more": The band members whipped off the girls' dresses, only to reveal short skirts underneath. Apparently, some gimmicks can work within reason. Peter, Sue and Marc returned to the Eurovision for the fourth time. After singing for Switzerland in French (1971), English (1976) and German (1979), the Italian language came in 1981 with their most powerful entry, "Io senza te", co-written by the talented Nella Martinetti and Peter Reber. Switzerland topped the betting charts and was set to win. It received the number of "Douze Points" that evening (5), an unprecedented number for a song that finished only fourth and was left with a tremendous sense of missing out. Peter, Sue and Marc were so disappointed that they swore to never perform at the ESC, although they kept trying to return to it. Björn Skifs (the seventh performer to come back to the contest in 1981 after previous performances), who was very problematic in 1978, won the "Melodifestivalen" in Sweden and to the displeasure of local television executives, he was chosen to represent their country for the second time in Dublin in 1981. In the same manner, as in Paris, he closed the list of 20 entries, and in Dublin as well he criticised the EBU for the style of the contest and the fact that singing in English was forbidden, but unlike the troubles he did in 1978, he was a 'good boy' this time, did not create any unnecessary dramas, performed "Fångad i en dröm" correctly and received the full mark from France. After taking over the German niche and being so close to victory in The Hague, Ralph Siegel and Bernd Meinunger stormed for the first place with "Johnny Blue", a touching ballad about Johnny the blind boy mocked by kids and eventually became a revered musician adored by millions. Lena Valaitis, a Lithuanian singer, was the best choice for gracefully delivering the German song that was so close to victory but finished, once again, only second. Israel returned to the contest after a year of absence with a miserable pre-contest full of playbacks. "Habibi" band came to the Eurovision refusing twice when it could have sung "A-Ba-Ni-Bi" and "Hallelujah", both of which eventually won the grand prize. Shuki Levy, now a prosperous musician and businessperson in the United States, composed "Halayla" and the experienced and professional band believed in its power to bring Israel a third Eurovision win. The bets also pointed to "Habibi" as possible winners, but Israel finished eventually only 7th, a very disappointing achievement in those days. Incidentally, Shlomit Aharon (with a professional and beautiful performance) was in her ninth month of pregnancy, a concern for the organisers, who ordered an ambulance and a midwife to the hall, in case she gave birth. For the first time in 15 years, Ossi Runne did not hold Finland's baton: Riki Sorsa, a huge star from Helsinki, brought the first Eurovision reggae entry ("Reggae OK") which was a tremendous success in his country and chose Henrik Otto Donner as the conductor. Runne, the gentleman, complied with Finnish television's request, travelled to Dublin to narrate the event as a commentator and watched as Sorsa crashed with his expectations to the depths of the 16th place. For the first time, France was represented by a singer from Tahiti, a territory that was under French control. Jean Gabilou was selected with "Humanahum" written by the duo that brought the Grand Prix in 1977, Joe Gracy and Jean-Paul Cara. The expectations of Gabilou were sky high, and the French were very hungry to win. The song was the first in contest's history to open with a church organ. With this repertoire, France was in the picture throughout almost the entire voting with 4 'Douze Points' and finished third for the seventh time. Finn Kalvik from Norway reached an all-time low when for only the second time in the new method's history, an entry received nul points and yet again, it was the Norwegian song. Unpleasant, but the Norwegians took the matter in good spirits and the head of their delegation, Harold Tusberg, said at the end of the contest:

"Who remembers who came second or third – people will remember us!". But this was nothing compared to the bitter fate that befell the Portuguese representative Carlos Paião, an extremely popular singer in Portugal responsible for many local hits, that performed with "Playback" in a very colourful performance on stage (with his backup singers moving like robots) and fell into the 18th place. In August 1988, he died in a severe car accident on his way to a concert. The Belgian Emly Starr wanted to be the first Flemish singer to reach the top places of the Eurovision with the disco entry "Samson" which received wide acclaim in Europe and was surprisingly appreciated by the various betting agencies. Despite a clean performance, Starr was disappointed to find that the Flemish barrier could once again not be broken, and Belgium would not reach the top of the rankings. Cyprus, in its Eurovision debut, was the one to steal the show in rehearsals. "Monika" by the "Island" band looked terrific in the preparations, and suddenly the betting agencies started to place the Cypriots even before Switzerland, the big favourite, making it a spectacular entrance into the contest. Everyone was expecting to witness the Cypriots. Although not disappointing with an outstanding performance that garnered the loudest applause, they were deceived to find out that bringing home the Grand Prix on their first ESC is probably too much to ask. After receiving zero points from the first five countries to vote, Israel came to the rescue with the first five historical points, which opened the floodgates that led "Island" to the honourable sixth place. Dublin City Ballet provided a spectacular performance to traditional local music's sounds, in what is still considered one of the most successful intervals in the history of the contest. The voting process provided quite a few interesting moments: The scoreboard went crazy and added 300 points to Ireland during the Luxembourg vote; Dan Kaner started reading the Israeli results with 12 points instead of 1 and Helga Vlahović from Yugoslavia culminated when she answered the presenter's question if she could deliver the results: "I don't have it". The audience burst out laughing, and Frank Naef was exasperated. Vlahović called back half a minute later, this time with the results, and read them nervously. Nine years later, she will find herself on the other side, as the presenter of the only Eurovision held in Yugoslavia, before its dissolution. France stormed in with 3 "Douze Points" out of the first 4 countries to vote but was weakened by the host Ireland's surprising lead. Halfway through, the UK more or less took pole position and seemed to be on the way to victory, until an incredible set of points for Switzerland brought it to the top at the right timing, with Germany lurking behind too. Two votes before the end and UK, Switzerland and Germany stabilised with 120 points each! It was the Swiss's turn to vote, which were the only ones not to award any points to Germany and bounced the British with 8 points to a safe leading position. The decision was in the hands of Sweden, who admittedly gave its maximum score to Germany, but eight more points for the British ensured the "Bucks Fizz"'s victory, leaving Lena Valaitis disappointed. Thus, the United Kingdom has celebrated its fourth Eurovision victory, with Johnny Logan awarding the Grand Prix to the winning band, with a bright backdrop on the stage. The UK will host the contest for the seventh time (a record that they will keep breaking in the future). The Irish hosts were actually content with the English victory: It turns out that band member Michael Nolan emigrated with his family at the age of three from Ireland to England and the band member Cheryl Baker's grandmother was also a pure Irish... Despite the many compliments on the organisation, tension and interest, numerous criticisms were heard about the level of entries and their inferior quality. For the Eurovision, it seems, a problem of identity and quality has arisen, with niche music stations such as MTV being set up around the world, broadcasting music and diminishing the importance of the contest.

1982 – Harrogate, United Kingdom

For the seventh time in 26 years of Eurovision, the United Kingdom produced the contest.

Like in 1977, so 1982: the BBC's enthusiasm for hosting the contest was long gone.

After four times of holding it in London, the British sought added value elsewhere and surprisingly chose Harrogate, the anonymous spa town in North Yorkshire.

How anonymous was Harrogate?

It was not lost on the British, when the opening of the contest's broadcast showed a map of Europe with the question "Where is Harrogate?" popping-up on screen out of the various countries' positions — in all their languages. This was followed by a video that illustrated the concept of a 'picturesque town'.

Things could not get more exciting in Harrogate. It felt like each one of the 75,000 town residents spoke only about the Eurovision, which was the most significant event in the place's history.

Harrogate is known for hosting a traditional international flower show; thus, each contestant was shot standing by beautiful flowers at the end of their country's promotional video, before performing their entry.

The International Centre in Harrogate was completed not long before the event, so it was postponed to almost May.

The 2000-seat auditorium was inaugurated on the show's eve, but the small stage, tiny in Eurovision terms, could not be ignored.

The reason was the decision to divide the stage into two parts.

In one part, the stage was designed with a glossy floor crossed by light strips with a rotating fixture at the back — somewhat reminiscent of the 1967 "Mirrors" stage in Vienna.

The left part was given to the broad BBC orchestra, positioned on two floors and conducted by Ronnie Hazlehurst.

Before each entry, the camera clung to each country's broadcast booth, where the commentator waved the viewers before showing the introductory video.

When the Austrian commentator's turn arrived, one of the British band "Bardo"'s production people was suddenly found in the booth, instead of the Austrian broadcaster who was probably busy with something else.

The legendary commentator, Terry Wogan, caught it and shared the anecdote with the viewers as he rolled with laughter: "I recognise that face. He is not Austrian! That's Harry"… The French television channel TF1 decided that the Eurovision has become a low-level song contest; ergo, it was not interested in participating in it.

The EBU granted the rights to another television channel in the country, but it was late in choosing an entry, and so France was absent from the ESC for the first time in its history (if Danny's retirement, three days before the 1974 Brighton contest due to the Republic's president Pompidou's death, is not considered).

In the Greek pre-contest, Themis Adamantidis won the candidacy with "Sarantapente Kopelies", but the Greek television production failed miserably, as it was a remake of an ancient Greek song and according to the known rules, a Eurovision entry must be completely original.

Adamantidis was supposed to take the stage second in Harrogate, but when the EBU learned of the renewed but not new song, Greece was removed from the contest, fined and allowed to return only the following year.

Anita Skorgan and her husband Jahn Teigen made a rather brave move when they returned to the ESC. It mattered less for Skorgan, that did not finish last (not that her two performances in the contest were too successful) but Teigen finished last with nul points in 1978, and after Finn Kalvik reached the same result the previous year, the duo was under tremendous pressure not to fail.

"Adieu" was an exciting duet between the couple and Norway was relieved when it scored 40 points. Incidentally, one of Norway's most prominent stars was in the "Red Squares" band in the sixties and performed in Israel, where he fell in love and even learned a few words in the local language. To the surprise of many, Teigen discovered that when he wants to express himself privately to himself, he uses... Hebrew words.

He did the same when all the Eurovision participants sat down to watch the pre-show before the dress rehearsal. Teigen, who heard the songs, graded each with a word in Hebrew... He anticipated many problems with Israeli entry in his homeland, for reasons that will be conveyed later. The main favourite was the host UK. "One Step Further" by the "Bardo" duo excited the kingdom and was loved by many.

The betting agencies placed "Bardo" at the top with a ratio of 5 to 8, and despite an acrobatic performance and a memorable opening by Sally Ann and Stephen Fischer, the slightly outdated arrangement they were thrust upon by the orchestra (the studio version had all sorts of innovative musical effects that gave the song the brilliance that made it a favourite) brought them only to the seventh place.

British cultural figures protested the song, as it included several syntax and speech errors in the English language, which is quite unacceptable in the kingdom.

The Finnish representative Kojo was controversial with the entry "Nuku pommiin", in a hard rock style that had not been heard before on the Eurovision stage and dealt with a protest against the dangerous nuclear capabilities of several European countries.

It remains unclear whether this was the reason for the last place and zero points Finland ended with, but absurdly enough, an almost similar style awarded it its first victory in 2006, and in 2007 when it hosted the contest in Helsinki, the "Teapacks" band, representing Israel, performed an anti-nuclear protest entry...

Switzerland completed three good years at the top with Arlette Zola and "Amour on t'aime", which came 3rd, but absurdly did not even threaten the first place, while the previous year's "Io senza te" took pole position two votes before the end and eventually finished fourth. A year after being favourite after rehearsals, Cyprus, the new participant, surprised again and sent Anna Vissi, who represented Greece in the 1980 contest.

Two years later, Vissi was already a big star in Greece and her native Cyprus. She wrote and composed her songs, and "Mono i agape" was chosen to represent the small island with high hopes. From her arrival in Harrogate, "Mono i agapi" captured the listeners' hearts, claiming that she would be the winner if the juries went for a ballad.

The song was translated into numerous languages, including a Hebrew version by Ilana Avital "Lama Atsuv Li". At the end of the evening, she could breathe easy after receiving 12 points from Norway and the Netherlands, finishing in the fifth place with her head held high, giving Cyprus its best Eurovision achievement until 1997.

Elisabeth Andreassen and Kikki Danielsson, the "Chips" duo, represented Sweden with the entry "Dag efter dag". The contest's organisers avoided a quite much embarrassment when an Irish band with a similar name finished second in Dublin's pre-contest. If it had won, there would have been two bands with the same name at the Eurovision in Harrogate.

The good friends, Andreassen and Danielsson, would probably not have believed that evening had they been told that three years later, they would be on opposite sides of the barricades, competing against each other for the Grand Prix in a close and insane race.

Stella has already participated in two Eurovisions: She represented the Netherlands as a member of "Hearts of Soul" in 1970, Belgium with "A Million in One, Two, Three" in 1977, which was considered a favourite, and returned to Harrogate, in French, as a soloist, to attempt at a Belgium victory with "Si tu aimes ma musique", which opened with a ballerina doll floating in a small music box. Stella's performance was captivating, and the results corresponded: She was the only participant to receive points from all the countries, but not a single Douze Points, which is a rarity. Finishing fourth, she brought Belgium its fifth-best achievement at the Eurovision to date. Israel's desire to recreate its late 1970s achievements was filled with real hopes when the popular Avi Toledano was chosen for the mission.

Although "Hora" struggled to beat Yardena Arazi and the "Izolirband" band in the Pre-contest, it arrived in Harrogate full of confidence, with feedback and praises coming from everywhere. The arranger and conductor Nancy Brandes was facing a real problem:

Everyone was sure he was a woman because of his first name and to clarify, he added the name "Silviu". However, this did not end Brandes' troubles when in rehearsals, the presenter called him "Sylvia Nancy Brandes"… The Israeli performance was enthralling and passionate; Toledano was terrific, but his companions were a bit off-key. One of them even kicked down the condenser, which did not prevent the audience from cheering loudly for the Israeli entry, a definite favourite that aroused much interest among the record companies lurking in the Harrogate venue's hallways.

One thing was not told to Toledano: The word "Hora" means "whore" in some of the Scandinavian languages …It may have affected Denmark and Norway, which awarded Israel only one point, but Sweden (10 points) and Finland (12 points) rather fancied the Israeli entry. Turkey and Ireland were the only ones not to give Israel any points. At the last minute, Germany made Toledano runner-up, straight from the fourth place, with a second Douze Points he received that evening. Toledano was 61 points away from first place, an unprecedented margin between the winner and the second place.

The performance by Bill van Dijk, an incredibly famous actor and singer in the Netherlands, caused a great deal of resentment when he sang "Jij en ik" accompanied by no less than five women (including the drummer) on stage, while he had controversial contact with two of them, including several acts that induced discomfort for the production.

This chauvinistic or feminist spectacle (a matter of perspective) did not flourish in the contest and received only 8 points.

UK, Cyprus, Belgium and Israel were considered favourites, but from rehearsals, it was obvious that Germany brought the most unique entry:

A 17-year-old girl sitting on stage with a white guitar and a black dress, singing with a soft voice and just asking for a little peace and tranquillity in the world.

Once again, Ralph Siegel and Bernd Meinunger wrote "Ein Bißchen Frieden", knowing that it was now or never after two consecutive second-place finishes.

Siegel himself accompanied his discovery on the piano, alongside two guitarists and a harpist. The day before the big show, producer Shlomo Zach told Israeli arranger Nancy Brandes:

"If you want to win, she needs to be thrown out the window (pointing at Nicole)"…

From the other side, Ralph Siegel was afraid of the evil eye and declared that Israel is the favourite, to keep Nicole out of the spotlight as much as possible.

The German was the last to perform that evening, and as she finished singing, she knew that no one would be able to take the victory away from her.

Sure enough, Germany had its first Eurovision victory like no other country before:

Nine Douze Points (out of 17 possible!), only four countries gave it less than 10 points and a record margin from the runner-up. The possibility of surpassing the UK's success rate since 1976 was thwarted by its two closest neighbours: Austria which gave it only one point and Luxembourg, not awarding it any points.

In an interview for the "60 Years of Eurovision" documentary, Nicole said that "most important for me, it was the point that a German girl with a song about peace got 12 points from Israel. Ralph took my hand and said, 'that's incredible'. The first time Germany gets 12 points from Israel, and we know our history. That was… wow".

The voting process went smoothly this time, with the scoreboard displaying the country's name and its flag (a format started by the British in 1977 and became permanent only from 1985) when the nation submitting the results was lit.

After two votes, Israel led with 20 points, and Avi Toledano started fantasising about a victory. But then, Germany's crazy run began, leaving the other competitors far behind, and from Douze Points to Douze points, Ralph Siegel was seen hugging his treasure, Nicole, with tears of joy.

When the winner was announced, Jan Leeming, the excellent presenter, invited the songwriters Siegel and Meinunger to the stage and after a few seconds announced that "they are not here", while these were standing behind her… Leeming looked back, recovered and corrected herself: "They are here!"…

Nicole received the Grand Prix and proved once again that she could keep her calm despite her early age even in such a great moment when she sang "Ein Bißchen Frieden" again in four different languages (German, English, French and Dutch).

First victory for Germany, in the hope that the message of peace and brotherhood will permeate everyone.

1983 - Munich, Germany

Munich was festive when Germany finally hosted the ESC after Nicole's brilliant victory in Harrogate. Twenty participants (Greece, France and Italy returned, whereas Ireland retired due to a television technicians' strike, who were unable to hold a pre-contest) gathered at the Rudi-Sedlmayer-Halle, where the 1972 Munich Olympics basketball tournament took place. Marlene Charell, a German virtuoso living in France, was chosen to present the event but did not stop there: she took care of the flower arrangements that adorned the stage before announcing each entry and starred in the intervals between the songs and voting results that included traditional German dances. But as the saying goes "enough is as good as a feast" and quite a few things went wrong. Charell made countless mistakes during the voting. She insisted on reading the results in three languages (English, French and German) and just as in the 1979 contest in Jerusalem, the voting lasted about an hour that seemed endless. But her most embarrassing error occurred in the Norwegian entry performance: Charell was apparently confused by the cards she held and did not know the name of the Norwegian conductor, Sigurd Jansen, which she had to announce for him to go up to the podium. In a failed improvisation, Charell called "Johannes Skorgen" — a hybrid between a common Scandinavian name and the last name of the Norwegian entry's co-performer… Jansen went on stage smiling, but definitely not amused, as he was robbed from the credit he was supposed to receive live in front of hundreds of millions. For the first time, Eurovision was broadcast to Australia, which fell in love with the contest and even began participating in it in 2015. At the opening of the broadcast, beautiful views from Germany were presented, and the entrance to the hall revealed the energetic and invested stage that included rough lighting squares in the back. The orchestra, conducted by Dieter Reith, garnered much praise for its efficiency and professionalism. The Germans copied the Israeli idea of bringing all the artists to the stage, but while in Jerusalem in 1979 it was done after the "Shalom 79" band's performance, in Munich the scene was chosen for the contest's beginning before the entries' performances. Guy Bonnet, a gifted pianist and excellent singer, was one of the four favourites that year. "Vivre" is one of the most beautiful works ever performed at the Eurovision Song Contest. This French classic eventually placed the singer who returned to the contest after 13 years, in the top ten. The Norwegians sent Jahn Teigen and Anita Skorgen for the second time in a row. The two even surpassed the result they achieved at Harrogate, returning incredibly pleased with the tenth place they reached with "Do Re Mi" (this was Teigen's last appearance in the contest). "Sweet Dreams" saw themselves as favourites: The British entry "I'm Never Giving Up" was one of the most impressive performances in the big night, but not among the contest's best entries. Turkey and Spain made history (from the wrong side) when they finished together with nul points and since then — neither of them finished last, but both reached together to the 19th place… while the Turks came with the strange performance of opera singer Çetin Alp (With the song "Opera"), accompanied by the "The Short Waves" band — Spain insisted on sending Remedios Amaya, a wonderful flamenco singer, but a far from suitable act for the Eurovision. Amaya took the stage barefoot and delivered "¿Quién maneja mi barca?" ("Who sails my boat?") in a loud performance. Ultimately, Amaya's ship sank into the abyss with no points...

16-year-old Carola was one of two surprises in Munich. Despite two stomach-dropping seconds in which her microphone did not work (is this a virtue for success? These mishaps accompanied Carola to the third place she reached in Munich and the Grand Prix she won 8 years later in Rome), the Swedish girl took over the entry "Främling" and with her colourful voice, delivered a tremendous performance. Riccardo Fogli arrived at the contest about six months after winning the Sanremo Festival. Had he gone to the event with the song he won the well-known local festival "Storie di tutti i giorni" with, he would have undoubtedly found himself at the top of the betting tables. But "Per Lucia" was nothing more than a mediocre song that did not stand out in Munich. The spark that eventually brought the Eurovision victory to Yugoslavia a few years later started in 1983 thanks to local pop idol Daniel Popović (who surprisingly beat the favourite Lepa Brena at the Yugoslav pre-contest). "Džuli" swept Europe, and it was clear that he would lead the race to the first prize. The Yugoslavs stormed Munich and in an aggressive PR campaign, showered bottles of wine, posters and all possible information on Daniel on all the delegations. As stated, right up until the last minute the Yugoslavs were at the top of several betting tables and were expecting the historic victory that eventually, despite a proper fight, did not come. Even without winning, the final result was Yugoslavia's best so far: fourth place and 125 points, with five Douze Points. Ralph Siegel, who brought Germany's first victory, wanted to write a winning entry for his country once again, but the Hoffman brothers who were selected to represent the hosts had other plans. Germany was certainly among the favourites to win and threaten the first place, which indeed happened in practice for the first half of the voting process. The song "Rücksicht", one of the most charming entries Germany ever sent, finally ended the evening in the top 5. Ralph Siegel contented himself with a glorious reception he held for all the Eurovision delegations, in which the delegates finished off over 2000 glasses of natural orange juice... Belgium sent an entry with only 11 words, "Rendez-vous", performed by the duo of dancers, "Pas de Deux": "Rendez-vous, but that's the limit, and I clam up". At least in Flemish, it is longer... This song will go down in history as the entry with the fewest words ever to participate in the contest. There was a tremendous pre-contest in Israel, which included an unforgettable fight between Ofra Haza, who won, and Yardena Arazi. The latter claimed that her loss, by just one single point, was due to an error in the calculation of the score and that the head of the juries' in Tel Aviv, Rafi Ginat, confessed to her that there indeed was an error in counting the votes in the first Hebrew city, which prevented her from going to Munich (Ginat responded: "Nonsense, it never happened"). The meaning of participating in the Eurovision on German soil and in the city in which the Munich massacre victims lost their lives in 1972 Olympics was well comprehended in the Holy Land. Ofra was amazing all along. Her beautiful voice attracted all the experts and the rehearsals viewers determined: "Hi" will be the winning entry. The Israeli delegation arrived in Munich with tremendous emotional baggage.

The song's author, late Ehud Manor, visited Germany for the first time and felt uncomfortable: "I have never been to Germany and although having a few opportunities to go there in the past, I rejected them all. I was afraid and did not want this encounter. While writing the song "Hi"'s lyrics, my mind and heart reeled with thoughts about us reaching a dangerous situation in which many of us started doubting our right to live as a free people in our country. But the most prominent thought was that if the song wins the pre-contest, it will be performed by Ofra Haza on German soil in Munich. I felt that on such land, Israel's representative should not be singing about nights of love and butterflies in the sun, but deliver a song of hope, of aspiration for a better future to the 500 million Europeans, a piece that will celebrate our lives as a people and nation, while recognising our current hardships, out of self-criticism, and emphasising the word 'still' in the line 'I am still alive'". Dorin Frankfurt was responsible for designing the performers' costumes. Her choice will be remembered forever: the five backup singers (Dina Rosemarin, Shlomo Maman, Shlomit Hillel, Peretz Talmor and Yuval Lurie) wore yellow, while Ofra was all white. "Alive, alive, alive, the people of Israel are alive" on German soil, in Munich, a few metres from where Adolf Hitler convened his headquarters, 38 years after the terrible Holocaust, was a sight that no Israeli who watched this contest could ever forget. Six months before her tragic death, Ofra recounted her experiences from Munich: "Throughout the week there, I kept my cool, content with the opportunity I was given to sing on such a stage and most importantly to raise the stature of the people of Israel. I was excited but positive, and when I took the stage, I felt like a fireball waiting to erupt, thinking about the encounter I had with Holocaust survivors who asked me to think about them while singing and of course, my visit to the Dachau concentration camp extremely affected me. I was very calm during the voting, I knew I had done my best, and that wheatear I won or lost would be more politically related than musically. More than that first place, it was important to convey the message on German soil: the people of Israel are alive". From the moment she landed in Germany, Ofra Haza became the star of the event. The magnificent Hilton Hotel in the Bavarian city became the place to be for Israelis, Jews, people from the music industry, journalists and fans who wanted to see Haza up close. At all receptions, Ofra was the life of the party. It turns out that the entry "Hi" conquered Europe as its English and French versions stormed the continent and on one of her days off, Ofra Haza took the time to record the German version of "Hi", written by Bernd Meinunger, in Ralph Siegel's studio, Betzalel Aloni, Haza's shrewd manager, well-understood which way the wind was blowing and arrived in Munich equipped with a stock of records that included "Hi" in several languages. Music company executives circled him and fought over the signing of Ofra Haza. The beginning of rehearsals was not easy for the Israeli delegation, but as the week wore on, and with director Rainer Bertram (who said that "Ofra is my favourite"), things got better. On the big evening, Haza's performance was unforgettable. The cold-headed Ofra enchanted, the applause lasted for numerous seconds, like an eternity, the most of all the entries. At that moment, she was indeed the winner. But then arrived Corinne Hermès. She went on stage to sing one last song and stirred everything up. Hermès had everything a winning entry needed at the time: an exciting ballad, effective use of French and a dramatic performance that captivated viewers. This emotional and winning slow song, from the moment it was selected, through the rehearsals until the victory — stood out as the joker of the contest. Unlike Ofra who smiled at the audience before beginning her performance, Corinne Hermès kept a stern face. Was it nervousness, or was she acting? It is unclear, but Corinne certainly delivered the performance of her life and brought Luxembourg its fifth victory. A justified one, admittedly. Even during the voting, Hermès was upset and nervous — compared to her Israeli rival who stayed rather calm. The points awarding was disappointing for Israel: Ofra expected to sweep Europe but received only two Douze Points, from Austria and the Netherlands, while Turkey and Cyprus did not give her points at all. Greece and Italy awarded an exceptionally low score and left Ofra without the possibility to win. The voting opened with Luxembourg receiving only one Douze Points, while not receiving any points twice. A surprise? Not for long. "Si la vie est cadeau" started accumulating points. Whenever a potential competitor such as Sweden, Yugoslavia or Israel came close — the Luxembourgers shook them off again with another Douze Points. Being the last to vote, Luxembourg had to maintain a 16-point safety margin from the second place, before its turn to award points. Towards the end, it opened a huge gap that was sufficient. Eventually, when the smoke cleared, only 6 points separated Ofra Haza and Corinne Hermès. Ofra received three times 10 points, after which Corinne received 12. If the situation were reversed only twice, Israel would have celebrated a third title. Thus, close and cruel, the 1983 Eurovision ended in a rather predictable and disappointing way for Israeli eyes. The one who again saw the Promised Land and did not get to enter was Avi Toledano, with quite an accomplishment of two successive years in the second place, as a performer and composer. Without a doubt, the Eurovision established Toledano as a popular singer in Israel and enhanced his economic situation beyond recognition when his two songs, "Hora" and "Hi", were bestsellers on the continent.

Another Israeli consolation was that the producer of the winning entry was none other than Haim Saban, who got deep in the US music industry and proudly accompanied Corinne Hermès to her impressive victory. Despite his historic achievement, the Yugoslav Daniel repeatedly lost his temper and cursed during the voting and could not control his disappointment at the first place that eluded him. For the first time in the new system, there was a tie between three pairs of countries. Turkey and Spain finished with 0 points; Austria received 10 points once, which was enough for it to overtake Norway despite the draw between them; but an amazing phenomenon was the absolute draw between Finland and Italy: the two received the exact same points, in the exact same division and thus shared the eleventh place. Another historical incident: Greece did not award any points to its sister Cyprus. Insiders point out that the source is in the conflict of Greek television with Stavros Sideras and Constantina Konstantinou (performers of the Cypriot entry) and the imposition of an embargo on the song in a one-time occurrence. That evening, Corinne Hermès was the Princess of Europe, and Luxembourg was once again crowned the Eurovision Queen. After the victory she finally allowed herself to smile. Corinne proudly performed the winning entry, the presenter Marlene Charell closing the event with a banal request from the winning singer: "Luxembourg, may I ask you please to take your place and sing again your song? I think everybody wants to hear it again"... At the gala dinner held for the contestants at the end of the Eurovision, Corinne Hermès refused to stand up in honour of Bavarian Prime Minister Franz Josef Strauss and have her picture taken with him. The latter was offended and was finally photographed with Ofra Haza and the previous year's winner, Nicole.

1984 – Luxembourg City, Luxembourg

Luxembourg, the Eurovision queen, hosted, for the last time, the contest it had won five times. The opening video expressed the sense of pride, including melodies of Luxembourg's winning entries over the years with "L'amour est bleu" by Vicky Leandros, which did not win the Eurovision but became one of the biggest hits in its history. The production left the event's presentation in the hands of Désirée Nosbusch, the youngest presenter in the ESC history — only 19 years old. Despite her language skills and light, humorous performance, she was quite a bit childish, in a way that overstepped the contest's formality a bit. Israel could not participate as it was set on the eve of the local Memorial Day. Therefore, the Eurovision was not broadcast live to the Holy Land, but only on the following Friday night and in part (only the entries were televised). The day after the event, excerpts from the contest and a brief discussion in the television's Independence Day studio special hosted by Yaron London were broadcast. Even before the date that would prevent Israel from participating was announced, the promoter Shlomo Zach planned to send "Balalaika" by Ilanit to Luxembourg. The song, which expressed the longing of the Soviet Union's Jews who were prevented from immigrating to the Jewish state, was supposed to bring Ilanit to the European contest for the third time, with good chances of finishing in the top five. The video passages were made by pantomimes, which humorous videos about each country. The contest was held at the same venue as the well-remembered 1973 Eurovision — the "Grand Theatre". Roland de Groot designed the stage. Much resemblance to the 1976 and 1980 stages, which the Dutch was responsible for as well, was noticed. Yet, this was the most impressive of all, leaning on three lighted pillars, with vertical stripes in the background and the number 4 highlighted, with a backdrop of glowing squares at the back. Owing to the stage's size, the orchestra that was in the back of the stage in 1973, moved to the bottom front, much like in 1975, 1976, 1979 and 1980. The betting agencies assumed the winner would come from Spain, Ireland or Italy. The Spaniards, a year after their nul points (Remedios Amaya), learned their lesson: Spain sent the contemporary "Bravo" the terrific entry "Lady, Lady", which restored the nation's respect with the third place — its best achievement in the eighties. Four years after his marvellous win, Johnny Logan did not feel confident enough to return as a performer. However, he believed that perhaps by writing an entry for his good friend Linda Martin, he could achieve another Eurovision title. "Terminal 3" was the most talked-about song in rehearsals and Linda was wonderful, including on the big night when everyone was convinced that the contest would return to Dublin. Martin did go hard for the victory and was close to the first place, but Portugal, the last to vote, awarded her only 2 points and the superb Irish singer contented with being runner-up. After lean years, Italy looked straight at the possibility of victory with the popular duo Alice and Franco Battiato, the winners of 1981 Sanremo Festival, enchanted with "I treni di Tozeur". They also impressed in the decisive moment with fantastic vocal chemistry on stage. But Italy, as befits Italy, could not live up to its expectations and the duo finished just 6th. The first entry to perform won the contest no more than twice, and when Sweden was placed there, no one took the possibility of it threatening first place at all seriously. The contempt for the "Herreys" trio was great. Their win in the Swedish pre-contest came as a surprise. They were considered inexperienced, and many doubted their ability to go through the Eurovision safely. Until the big night, "Diggi-Loo Diggi-Ley" was not considered an entry that could win the coveted prize, but a determined performance, with gold boots and contemporary choreography, spoke to the juries' taste and opinion, which gave the Swedes five Douze Points (Sweden also received points from all the participants) and one of the most surprising victories in the history of the contest. Another Scandinavian surprise came from Denmark, which brought the duo Kirsten and Søren, known as "Hot Eyes", into the open. The Danish performance was exciting and refreshing, "Det' lige det" was the second entry in the contest to receive points from all countries, which was enough for a respectable fourth place, the Danes' best achievement since winning in 1963. Luxembourg won the Eurovision five times being represented by a non-local singer. This time was no different, with Sophie Carle from France and the entry "100% d'amour", that was not worth more than the tenth place it won. The only technical fault in the event happened in the local song when the voice was muted for few seconds. Vladimir Cosma, one of France's most renowned composers and the one who wrote the famous melodies for the popular film "Rabbi Jacob", composed "Autant d'amoureux que d'étoiles" for Annick Thoumazeau. Maribelle's "Ik hou van jou" from the Netherlands was not so successful in Luxembourg but became one of the Eurovision fans' favourite ballads that was also included in several collections. Mary Roos returned to the contest after 12 years, with a hunger for recreating her success (third place). "Aufrecht geh'n" raised hopes in Germany and Mary's performance was excellent, but what worked for 1972, did not cut it this time.

Before the voting, Frank Naef seemed to be lurking around the corner for the young presenter Nosbusch, but she navigated the procedure very nicely and performed it flawlessly. The scoreboard, which displayed only the countries' names in yellow on a black background, changed to blue after the first half. Incidentally, one of the Spanish jury members was none other than the illustrious former Real Madrid basketball player, Rafael Rullán. In the first part, the pole position was divided between Ireland, Spain and Denmark when halfway through Sweden emerged from behind and safely took the surprising lead, increasing its advantage from voting to voting. But before the end, Ireland came back with some big points and created a completely opened situation before Portugal split the final votes: Sweden 141, Ireland 135. The Swedes were on their feet, exchanging concerned glances, but before becoming hysterical, Ireland received only 2 points, and the case was closed. Not long after that, the fresh winners got only 4 points, meaning that if Portugal had awarded Douze Points to the Irish — they would have won, but the possibility remains unimportant speculation. The content and surprised "Herreys" celebrated their victory, with Corinne Hermès awarding them the prize. Hermès's face made it clear that her year was not a particularly good one and that she would like to return, like any ESCs' winner, to her big moment. The excitement was especially evident on the three brothers, who performed "Diggi-Loo Diggi-Ley" half in Swedish and half in English, in a shaky voice, singing off-key at times. But after they won, who cares …

1985 – Gothenburg, Sweden

After the bitter memories of the dull 1975 Eurovision hosted by the Swedes, the EBU was naturally concerned about the contest's return to the Scandinavian country. But unlike that ESC Sweden reluctantly hosted under the yoke of heavy protests due to its financial cost, this time the state of mind was completely different: the country supported, rejoiced at the opportunity and the whole of Gothenburg joined in for the 30th Eurovision hosting, and rather successfully. The impressive production had many fathers and was led by one mother, Lill Lindfors, arguably the greatest presenter of all time. The singer, runner-up of the 1966 contest, stormed the stage from the opening with a performance of "Musik ska byggas utav glädje", a special song written for the event, proving that her singing talent never left. Lindfors led the contest with a winning combination of all the right ingredients: tasteful humour, seriousness at the right level, a captivating smile, mastery and no mistakes. The national Remembrance of the Dead in the Netherlands prevented the latter's participation. Another missing country was Yugoslavia, whose anniversary of state leader Josip Broz Tito's death fell on the contest's date (although the Yugoslavs selected an entry, apparently not being coordinated with the date). No less than 13 artists returned to the contest when a special guest was invited to the "Scandinavium" (the spacious hosting hall): the first Eurovision winner (1956), Lys Assia, who sat in the audience alongside the musician Ralph Siegel.

Two prominent candidates plotted the victory: the UK, which was hungry to return the grand prize to London after four years, and Israel, which aspired to a third victory after a year of absence, two almosts (in 1982 and 1983) and a high-quality pre-contest. British Vikki Watson wrote and composed "Love Is" (Her conductor John Coleman had already won in 1981) and for the first time since Olivia Newton-John in 1974, the British chose a soloist who, like the Australian at the time, came in fourth with a quiet and up-to-date pop entry — one of the kingdom's best. Israel bet on Izhar Cohen, the 1978 Eurovision winner, with "Olé, Olé" composed by Kobi Oshrat (1st with Hallelujah – 1979). The Israeli delegation felt great: Cohen was the best candidate for winning the big evening, and rehearsals only reinforced the sentiment. The betting agencies placed Izhar high up with an excellent ratio. It seemed that only a serious mishap could prevent him from bringing — again — the Eurovision to Jerusalem and becoming the first singer in history to win the contest twice. Not one fault, but a series of puzzling mishaps have significantly thwarted the Israeli dream. Inexplicably, Swedish director and producer Steen Priwin decided that the Israeli entry would be performed at the back of the stage and not in the centre. Israeli producer Shlomo Zach tried to argue, but without success. In the moment of truth, an act of devil made all the backing band's microphones fail, which not only marred the volume of the song's chorus but also highlighted the voice of the only one whose microphone remained open: Tali Sinay (now Riklis), who was shouting rather than singing. Before his big break as a lead singer, the singer Adam was among the backing band's members. With and despite the mishaps that undoubtedly deprived Israel of at least 30 points if not more, Izhar Cohen managed to get 12 points from France (Israel will have to wait another six years for its next Douze Points) and reach the fifth and disappointing place for him. This was the first but not last time that there was a radical change in the bon-ton towards Israel. The delegation felt a cold and sometimes alienated attitude — compared to the warm reception in the years before. A senior EBU member of those years admitted that "for us, Israel's victory is a big headache and not a desirable scenario. The political issues and the fact that this is a country with border conflicts outside of Europe raises many problems and requires security for the contest, which if it were not for Israel, would not have been in such volume". Linda Martin, the previous year's almost winner, was now the Irish commentator and kept her fingers crossed for the charming Maria Christian and talented Brendan Graham who wrote "Wait Until the Weekend Comes", the entry that kept Ireland at the top (sixth place). This hinted at Graham's future success in the Eurovision. For years, Lia Vissi was in her successful little sister Anna's shadow. She had a lot of mileage in the contest: in 1979 Lia accompanied Elpida to the event in Jerusalem, and a year later she was with her sister Anna in Amsterdam. This time, she decided to move to the front of the stage and represent her country Cyprus but did not quite succeed with "To katalava arga" (ended with an equal number of points to Greece, represented by Takis Biniaris and seldom these did not award each other Douze Points). Kirsten and Søren continued their Eurovision journey with Denmark, now with Søren's 9-year-old daughter who ran around the stage and probably caused headaches for some of the spectators. "Sku' du spørg' fra no'en?" was less successful than their previous entry and finished 11th. Spain sent its best to Gothenburg — Paloma San Basilio, the Latin Grammy winner, who is extremely popular in the Spanish and South American music world. The renowned Juan Carlos Calderón wrote her "La fiesta terminó" and failed to recreate his past achievements at the contest. The stage did not suit Paloma San Basilio, whose celebration in the European Singing Contest ended before it even started. Spain received 12 points from Turkey, but it was not enough for more than the 15th place. Michel Bernholc conducted the orchestra in the 1983 Luxembourg victory, and he hoped to do the same with France's Roger Bens, but "Femme dans ses rêves aussi" ("Woman in Her Dreams Too") left the victory in their dreams and France, again, in the mediocre tenth place. Turkey bet on "MFÖ", the popular trio in the country (included Mazhar, Fuat and Özkan) wanted to surpass the last places wall that was Turkey's lot in the contest with the rhythmic "Didai didai dai". Switzerland awarded them Douze Points and the UK gave them eight points, but these were swallows that did not make the summer for the great Muslim country. The heart goes out to Belgium's Linda Lepomme. "Laat me nu gaan", was one of the most beautiful and melancholy entries in the contest, a lovely melody that deserved much more than the last place. There was also a disgraceful failure for the Portuguese Adelaide Ferreira, who came as one of the top candidates with "Penso em ti, eu sei" and did not catch on despite Ferreira's impressive performance. Portugal continued to eat humble pit and finished in the penultimate place. Germany was the black horse of the 1985 Eurovision with the band "Wind" (will return in 1987 and 1992) and "Für alle", which on the big evening entered into the hearts of Europeans and led throughout most of the voting. The Germans ended up in second place, and it was a closure for the late Rainer Pietsch, the conductor in the 1975 contest's horror show, who was calm this time and did a wonderful job with the Swedish orchestra. Al Bano and Romina Power returned to the ESC after nine years. "Magic Oh Magic" composed by Dario Farina and the Jew Michael Hoffmann received 3 Douze Points (the most except the winner) and was at times in second place but pushed back to the 7th place like in their first appearance in 1976. Hanne Krogh, who finished second to last at the 1971 Eurovision, joined her friend Elisabeth Andreassen (a native of Gothenburg who felt at home), who had already represented Sweden in 1982. The two put together the "Bobbysocks!" duo, bounced on stage with "La det swinge (Let it Swing)" by Rolf Løvland, which sounded completely different than the usual of the country that had undergone mostly failures and embarrassments in the contest's history. Therefore, no one dared to bet on the pair of girls as possible winners, despite their excellent entry and declaration that they would be happy to bring Norway back to the top, for the first time since 1966. As the rehearsals advanced, Norway started to be considered a strong competitor, maybe even for the top. "Bobbysocks!" came to the big night with all their might and delivered a perfect performance. At the start of the voting, Norway received the first Douze points and made it clear that it would wipe the slate clean. It accumulated another 7 Douze Points (!) during the evening, but this was along with four countries that gave it a low score and three that did not award it any points. This led to a close struggle that started with Germany's lead, continued in a triple battle with Sweden and ended in a pretty clear Norwegian victory. Only 123 points were given to Norway, the lowest number scored by a winning entry in the new scoring system, but enough to make tens of thousands of Norwegians take to the streets and celebrate one of the happiest moments in the history of their country. Sweden did not give up on a second consecutive win and brought Lasse Holm and Ingela Forsman, the best creators in the Swedish Arsenal, for the mission. These wrote "Bra vibrationer", which was performed with perfection and determination by the fiery Kikki Danielsson. Danielsson's performance was the best and most impressive of all that evening, instantly making Sweden the biggest favourite to defend its title. The audience applause, and not just due to the home advantage, lasted for long seconds. Kikki occasionally led the vote, but a very weak score eventually left her in the third place, still a considerable achievement for the Swedish singer who got into serious drinking problems in the following years. One of the most interesting and arguably the most musical entries came from Luxembourg. The small principality turned to Ralph Siegel again, which created "Children, Kinder, Enfants", a repeated chorus performed in an impressive vocal performance by six professional singers including Ireen Sheer, with her third Eurovision appearance. The entry was officially catalogued in French, but other languages could be heard in the repeating chorus (which borderline broke the rules). The quality piece was not a sure recipe for victory but was rather far from it, and yet the performance conducted by the German Norbert Daum is remembered to this day. The most memorable moment from the event in Gothenburg has nothing to do with one of the entries or the Voting: with the end of the acoustic guitar show that preceded the points awarding, the acclaimed presenter Lindfors took the stage, and her dress was caught on a part of the set, leaving her with only underwear... She immediately folded another dress from her body and clarified that the alleged embarrassment was nothing more than humour: "I just wanted to wake you up a little "... The act as it turns out caused discomfort among senior EBU officials, and in conservatives from Sweden strongly criticised the naughty presenter. The voting was fascinating, emotional, and breathtaking. Germany took the lead almost to the end, before losing the first place to Sweden, due to an exceedingly small score in the second part of the voting. In 1982, Kikki Danielsson and Elisabeth Andreassen were part of the "Chips" duo that represented Sweden. But now, the two best friends found themselves on both sides of the barricade (with Andreassen representing Norway and Danielsson Sweden) and to reinforce the story, they both fought head-to-head with pretty equal chances (drama at its best). The mutual appreciation was also expressed with the 12 points the neighbours awarded each other and their thanks to each other in the green room. John Inman, the British television star (who starred in the comedy "Are You Being Served?"), was part of the British jury's panel, which chose to award its full points to the Norwegians. When Switzerland delivered its results, an unforgettable moment took place, and when it announced 12 points for Turkey, the audience burst into the hall with huge roars and applause. The embarrassed Turks knew that it was schadenfreude: Germany did not get a single point, and so Sweden temporarily jumped to first place. The lead moved from Sweden to Norway 4 votes before the end, and after two Douze Points, while its rivals did not get significant points, the Norwegians realised that no one could take this victory from them. The winners' joy was endless. When Krogh and Andreassen took to the stage bouncing and happy, the presenter Lindfors did not forget to tease them about past failures: "I am very glad it happened, after so many times you were last, you deserve it "... Elizabeth and Hanne performed excitedly "La det swinge", gave the signal for the big celebrations in Oslo and ended one of the most successful and enjoyable Eurovisions of all time.

1986 – Gothenburg, Sweden

No Eurovision victory has ever been received as enthusiastically as in Norway, except for maybe Israel in 1978, with the spontaneous scenes of uncontrollable joy, but in the Nordic country, it has become a real cult. Many Norwegians considered hosting the contest to be the country's most important event in the 20th century. Hence, it was no problem for one of the world's wealthiest economies to set an unprecedented record budget, and Norwegian television behaved accordingly. With an unlimited open wallet, director John Andreassen and producer Per Selstrom could fulfil any fantasy they had in mind. Arguably, the conditions at their disposal were a gold mine for the production. The first weighty decision was about the host city. The capital Oslo was the natural choice for the first Eurovision Norway holds on its soil, however, increasingly pushed for Bergen, to highlight the city's musical connection to the greatest musician in Norwegian history, Edvard Grieg. The decision provoked resentment, Oslo and Trondheim's mayors refused to accept the fact the contest would not take place in their cities, yet Bergen nonetheless won the great honour. In the town where it is said it rains 366 days a year, the "Grieghallen" (named after the renowned musician) is situated, and in honour of the Eurovision, it was converted into a Viking-era ice palace. The cost of making the replica, along with the intricate neon lighting scene, was astronomical. The honour of presenting the contest fell to Åse Kleveland, the singer who gave Norway its greatest achievement until winning in Gothenburg: third place in the 1966 Eurovision. Kleveland was not only an artist but also a public figure with strong political connections, which helped her get the coveted position. This completed a rare streak in which performers who finished in 2nd and 3rd places at the 1966 contest (Lill Lindfors and Åse Kleveland) presented it in 1985 and 1986. But this is where the similarity between the two faded: while Lindfors recorded both quality and entertaining presentation — Kleveland remained formal, rigid and a bit arrogant. However, her full authority and control over the event cannot be diminished. In the opening, Kleveland mimicked Lindfors and entered the hall performing the song "Welcome to Music". This tradition, of a singing presenter, would carry on in 1987 as well (where it will end). Kleveland's moves were quite heavy and not for nothing — her precious diamond-studded dress weighed about 15 pounds! Norwegian journalists jokingly claimed that a Eurovision could be produced solely with the dress's cost. Kleveland desperately wanted to keep it, but Norway's strict rules left the dress deep in the local broadcasting association's cellars. To illustrate the event's importance, the Norwegian royal family lined up in a very respectable composition in the "Grieghallen" stands, including the Crown Prince Harald, Prince Haakon Magnus, Crown Princess Sonja and Princess Märtha Louise. Speaking of Princess Sonja, the contest's organizers were flabbergasted when champagne was splashed on her as she entered the hall! The contest's opening time was at risk due to the chaos that ensued, but everything worked out eventually. The princess's champagne splatter's fate is unknown...

The presenter's opening words illustrated the event's nature: "For those of you who have followed Norway's course through the history with the Eurovision Song Contest, you will know that it has been quite thorny in fact… so imagine the pleasure we feel today, being able to welcome 700 million viewers to Norway and to Bergen". Italy and Greece withdrew from the contest for assorted reasons: the date fell on a Greek holiday, and the Italians decided not to participate in the ESC in Bergen. The task to bring the Eurovision back to Switzerland exactly 30 years after the first Eurovision in which Lys Assia won fell on the lovely Daniela Simmons's shoulders. Atilla Şereftuğ, a gifted musician and Turkish immigrant who paved the uneasy path to the heart of Swiss bourgeois society, proved his skills in composing "Pas pour moi", a charming French-language entry that was seen as the contest's potential winner. The Swiss did their best and finished with 140 points — 17 more than the winning song in 1985, which in the end was only enough for second place. Şereftuğ sobbed claiming that such an opportunity would not return, and such an entry was not written every day. Maybe he, too, could not have imagined the lightning that would strike him again two years later. It is said that dogs and children are irresistible. Belgium, which has never won the contest, felt that this was their moment, with "J'aime la vie", a rhythmic pop entry in French that was remarkably similar to the style of "Voyage, voyage" and such. But the icing on the cake was the performer — Sandra Kim, who told everyone she was 15 but was in fact only 13 (!). All this was not felt with the dress, hair styling and especially the determined and relaxed performance of the girl from Liège who surpassed her competitors swept Europe and won the Grand Prix with 176 points, the most a winning entry as ever won till then. Luxembourg returned to the origins, with the writer Alain Garcia who won the 1983 Eurovision and musician Rolf Soja, responsible for the "Baccara" duo's thriving career. The entry "L'amour de ma vie" was entrusted to Canadian singer Sherisse Laurence, thanks to whom the ESC was the first broadcast live to her home country, Canada. Laurence opened the contest, and in any Eurovision without the Swiss and Belgian songs, she would have also won. Ultimately, she successfully finished the event in third place. Unfortunately, this was the last time the principality reached the top three since in the coming years it will slip away from the top until retiring from the contest altogether. Three entries in French got the top places that year (for the first time since 1962), none of which was France. Even with conductor Jean-Claude Petit, who won with Séverine and Monaco in 1971, the quartet of "Cocktail Chic" singers did not live up to expectations, and "Européennes" landed in 17th place, the Republic's lowest ever. Israel also had a slump. The local 1986 pre-contest featured great songs such as "Nagni li balalaika" by Doron Mazar, "Halevay" by Boaz Sharabi (last place and one point...), "Svhil ha'bricha" by Rita and "Le'chaim" by Haim Moshe. From all of these, "Yavo Yom" was selected, written by Moti Giladi and Yoram Zadok. Giladi, who until then had been a successful entertainer, decided to sing on his own and added the children's star Sarai Zuriel, who certainly excelled in singing. The song's studio version, which was played in full playback in Israel, sounded reasonable (perhaps since among the performers in the original recording was none other than... Yardena Arazi), but this entry was never tested live, as in Bergen. There were many confrontations in the delegation between Zuriel and one of her backing singers, Sima Amiel, whose voice in the chorus was critical to the song's success. For some reason, in the final, Amiel was not heard, but Zuriel's off-key singing was. Rehearsals sounded reasonable, but the delegation had a bad feeling. They were willing to take the 'failures' of Shlomo Artzi (1975) and Ilanit (1977) who came 11th. In the decisive moment, it was a miserable performance for Giladi and especially for Zuriel, who sang off-key during the first verse and chorus, when she came around only in the second verse. Giladi seemed extremely excited about the occasion and realised that the European singing contest is nothing like shows in local halls. "As soon as the Israeli team left the stage, we knew there was a disaster", said renowned director Tzedi Tzarfati, responsible for setting up the Israeli performance. The result was accordingly: France and Norway awarded the duo one point, and Switzerland saved Israel from the last place with five points. The shock of the disgraceful failure in the contest was the topic of the day in Israel, and when Sarai Zuriel's career was supposed to reach new heights, it suffered a severe blow. Israel owes not finishing last to the Greek singer Elpida, who represented Cyprus this time. The same Elpida who delighted at the 1979 contest in Jerusalem with "Sokrati", was the only returning artist, who came back to the ESC with a look and shape that did not remind that 1979 singer at all. Her voice was no longer the same either and "Tora zo" plunged to the last place, with British conductor Martyn Ford holding the baton from the middle: he reached the fifth place with Anna Vissi in 1982 (the best Cypriot achievement at the time) and the last place with Elpida. In light of Israel and Cyprus's failures, the one that celebrated the best position in its ESC experience was Turkey. The smooth victory of "Klips ve Onlar" in the Turkish pre-contest hinted that "Halley" had something a Turkish entry never had before: a European style utterly devoid of oriental mannerism, and the result were not long in coming when the Turks, which were used to finishing in the last places, jumped to the ninth place with 53 points, receiving Douze Points from Yugoslavia and an unforgettable moment being placed 2nd after two votes. Ireland continued improving with one of the well-remembered entries that year, "You Can Count On Me", performed properly by the pop band "Luv Bug", which brought the Irish back to a prominent place at the top — the fourth. At the same time, the host Norway and Ketil Stokkan contented with the 12th place. Iceland debuted with "Gleðibankinn". The "ICY" band captivated the ice country to the small screen and hoped to bring honour, but it did not go easy, and Iceland was not able to go beyond the 16th place. The girls from "Frizzle Sizzle" of the Netherlands performed "Alles heeft ritme" barefoot on stage. On the other hand, the well-known Swedish composer Lasse Holm decided that he also wanted to sing and joined Monica Törnell in "E' de' det här du kallar kärlek?" that achieved the top five. After closing this circle, he stopped participating in the contest, except once in which he wrote the entry "Eloise "for the "Arvingarna" band in 1993. It was not a good evening for Israel, as the Israeli Timna Brauer that represented Austria with "Die Zeit ist einsam" also experienced: Brauer was the second Israeli singer to represent the Austrians, after Carmela Corren and at least she was comforted by surpassing her origin country by one place (18th). Brauer's history is far more fascinating than her participation in the Eurovision Song Contest: her father, Arik Brauer, was a well-known international artist who lived in Israel's artists' colony of Ein Hod. Her Yemeni maternal grandfather had the honour of driving the carter who led the Visionary of the State of Israel, Binyamin Ze'ev Herzl, during his visit to the Holy Land.

The voting was pretty dull this time since almost from the start, Belgium took first place and opened a huge and frustrating margin over Switzerland, followed by a hopeless chase. Sandra Kim received only 5 Douze Points, just like her Swiss rival, but clinched it with an unprecedented 10-point cluster (nine times!). She also received points from all countries, with only Israel, Germany, Austria, Sweden and Norway awarding it less than 10 points — and a total of 176 points. This record number reflected a 77 per cent success rate. For two successive years, entry number 10 finished second, and number 13 reached the first place. Who said that 13 brings bad luck? Although Sandra Kim was not in suspense as her victory was pretty clear from the beginning of the voting, her excitement was evident, especially when she took the stage to receive from Rolf Løvland and the duo "Bobbysocks!", with sparkling eyes, the award that would change her life. After performing "J'aime la vie" again, Kim received a tremendous and unparalleled onslaught of photographers. Flashes will still accompany her long after.

1987 - Brussels, Belgium

Sandra Kim brought the Eurovision to Belgium, one of the veteran contestants which — like the previous winner Norway — had a rocky road until reaching the coveted moment. However, unlike the hysteria and euphoria in the Scandinavian country, things were relatively calm in Belgium, and there was no over-enthusiasm for hosting the contest. The Belgians aspired to demonstrate unity in a country divided between Flemish and Walonians (French), but this aspiration quickly shattered beyond expectation into a wave of conflicts and disputes over almost anything and everything related to the production. At one point, it was not possible to go on, and the Flemish wing of Belgian television withdrew from the organisation taking half of the budget along... The French side sought to continue preparations and produce the contest alone, which required changes to the Belgian constitution and financial support from advertising sponsorships. Every odd year, Belgium is represented by a Flemish song, and so the local pre-contest was conducted in complete disconnection from the Eurovision held in that same country... This was reflected in a fairly simple show, mostly copied from Bergen: The Belgian production wanted the French-Belgian singer Viktor Lazlo to be the presenter at all costs. The latter had very tough conditions: Beyond appropriate salary conditions, she also demanded to perform her big hit "Breathless", at the opening of the event. Thus, Lazlo became the third consecutive presenter to start the contest singing. Holding the ESC in Brussels was also a kind of compromise between the two factions that make up the country. The Walonians wanted Liege, and the Flemish wanted Antwerp. Finally, as mentioned, the choice of the capital of Belgium was a kind of middle ground. It was the largest contest by then, with 22 participants. If Monaco, Malta and Morocco were to take part, it would have been a Eurovision with all the countries that ever participated. The possibility of the Soviet Union joining the party was very realistic and was proposed by various sources from the Soviet Ministry of Culture, which of course caused great excitement among in the EBU. Ultimately, despite President Mikhail Gorbachev's will in Perestroika, the matter was not event brought to the communist party members' confirmation on the count of it being considered too 'radical' and 'dangerous'... The 1987 Eurovision was marked by international stars who also came to try their luck on the European singing contest stage. Norwegian Kate Gulbrandsen was one of them, with an entry written by Hanne Krogh (half of the "Bobbysocks!" duo) and Rolf Løvland (composer of the song "La det swinge"), a promising group that made it to the higher positions with "Mitt liv" (Ninth place). Seyyal Taner from Turkey, with a glorious global resume that includes films in the US and a successful singing career in her country, arrived in Brussels greatly confident. Taner could not have imagined in her darkest dreams that "Şarkım Sevgi Üstüne" would crash down to the last place with zero points, the worst combination that happened to Turkey until that year. In the Israeli pre-contest, two songs could have been phenomenally successful in Brussels and challenge the crown: "Dai li dai" by Ilana Avital and especially "Casino Olami" by Miki Kam. Surprisingly and unexpectedly, Avi Kushnir and Nathan Datner won with "Shir Habatlanim" composed by Zohar Laskov. Among the other participants in that pre-contest were Haim Moshe, Arik Sinay, Svika Pick, Etti Ankri, Duo Datz, Izhar Cohen, Vardina Cohen and Dudu Fisher. Not for nothing did Datner state after winning the ticket to Brussles: "The fact that we won Dudu Fisher in a singing contest will enter the history books".

Shimon Parnas, a member of the Israeli pre-contest selection committee in 1987, said after "Habatlanim"'s victory: "We laughed when we first heard this song. We decided to put it in as a joke. We never imagined that it would go to the Eurovision". Israel did not process the fact that two comedians are set to represent the country in Europe. The Minister of Education, Itzhak Navon, threatened to resign if the two appeared in the Eurovision in Belgium, a threat that remained unfulfilled. Leading up to the event, Israel was prepared for a downfall. However, when they landed in Belgium, a pleasant surprise awaited the duo: it turns out that "Hopa Hule" became a hit in Belgium and the Israeli pair turn into a big deal. Datner and Kushnir delivered a very respectable performance, and their final position relieved Israel which returned to the higher places in the contest: 8th. Two delegations from the same Eurovision had a close relationship — the Israeli and its Icelandic counterpart. So much so that they stayed in adjoining rooms at the "Ramada" Hotel and spent time together sharing meals as well as long conversations. Gary Lux returned for the third time to represent Austria, in a two-year cluster (after 1983 and 1985), this time with "Nur noch Gefühl" which was supposed to bring him to a high position. His excellent performance was only enough for 8 points and the 20th place. His consolation: next year Austria will miss this score… Host Belgium was convinced that Liliane Saint-Pierre had a winning entry in hand: "Soldiers of Love", with the video showing children disguised as soldiers from a deck of cards, made a wish that the only soldiers in the world would be spreading love rather than holding weapons. This utopian dream corresponded with the German victory in 1982, but despite the good pace and home advantage, the Belgians were disappointed to find themselves only 11th. There was a big story behind Sweden, which introduced the one who would climb to the top of the local music world, Lotta Engberg. But her participation was not the main story of the Swedish delegation. The entry "Fyra bugg och en Coca Cola" contained two hidden commercials: The first was "Fyra bugg", a highly popular gum in the country until the 80s, but it was clear the hidden advertisement for the world-famous drink was crossing a line for the EBU. The compromise proposal made eventually and accepted by the songwriters Christer Lundh, and Michael Wendt was to change the name of the entry to "Boogaloo" and omit the hidden publicity, which allowed Engberg to perform in the contest. Yet Engberg faced another problem in the form of her pregnancy: According to the Swedish singer's doctors, she was supposed to deliver on the night of May 9th, 1987, less than 24 hours before the event. With expert advice and lots of exercises, Engberg managed to speed up the end of her pregnancy and successfully gave birth to her eldest son about three weeks before the contest. Umberto Tozzi & Raf were big names in the Italian music industry of the 1980s.

The two introduced a new and refreshing style from the boot-shaped country: "Gente di mare" was a commercially successful song that established Tozzi and Raf's status as leading artists in their country. They also brought Italy its best achievement in the contest since 1975 (third place, with 5 Douze Points, a first of its kind cluster for the Italians). The graceful Marcha returned the Netherlands to the top of the Eurovision with "Rechtop in de wind", one of the most remembered entries of that year. Denmark with "En lille melodi" by Anne-Cathrine Herdorf reached the same number of points as the Dutch (83). "Plastic Bertrand", the Belgian pop artist, was recruited by Luxembourg. There is no doubt that "Amour, amour" is a quite rare black spot in Bertrand's resume, that mostly succeeded in his country and France, but would rather forget his unfortunate evening in Brussels, where he degenerated Luxembourg to the worst place in its history so far — 21. This was the symptom of the most failed Eurovision of the French-speaking nations when for the first time, there was not a single entry from this language among the top 13 (!) in general and in the top five in particular. The UK experienced the worst ranking in its history so far: 13th place (which it could only dream of today). Rikki, a taxi driver from Scotland, surprised and represented the British in the Brussels contest with "Only the Light". He proudly noted that he does not intend to change his profession and that "the passengers I pick up in the taxi are my best audience". Whoever marked 20 Eurovision appearances was the lovable Finnish conductor Ossi Runne, who started his career in 1966 and went countless types of artists and entries. Vicky Rosti's "Sata salamaa" was 15th and her backing band "Boulevard", will take centre stage to represent Finland the following year. Yugoslavia continued its consistent attempts to win the contest and this time, it seemed ready with "Novi Fosili", one of the country's well-known bands led by the bouncy soloist Sanja Doležal. "Je sam za ples" reached an extremely prominent level of popularity and publicity for a Yugoslav song and its English version became remarkably successful in Western Europe. The Yugoslavs led the voting in the first round and eventually finished honourable among the top 4. The one who took the lead from Yugoslavia for a brief time in the vote was Germany, who again gambled on the band "Wind", which achieved second place in 1985 and returned after two years to do more, this time with the super co-writers, Ralph Siegel and Bernd Meinunger. These created "Lass die Sonne in dein Herz" and scored 141 points that led the Germans to be runner-up once again. But with all due respect to Ralph Siegel, the 1987 title was reserved for Johnny Logan. The 1980 Eurovision winner decided it was time to go back and win it again, three years after he attempted to do so as the songwriter for Linda Martin. "Hold Me Now" is an evident winning entry from the first listen. Logan's perfect and moving performance closed the story of the contest in Brussels even before it began. The betting gates were locked on Logan before the big night when no entry approached its chances for reaching first place. Upon his arrival in Brussels, there was a phenomenon of worship for Logan. The only fear was that the complacency and him being such a definite favourite would harm him in the voting, as many songs have undergone in the past. But no one is Johnny Logan — "Hold Me Now" brought the whole house down and woke the indifferent Belgian crowd up. It received 8 Douze Points, took the lead from Germany halfway through the voting and had a clear victory with 172 points.

As usual, Terry Wogan created another two amusing scandals: The BBC broadcaster called the Turkish Seyyal Taner's band 'ugly bunch', forcing the embarrassed British delegation to invite the Turks to a compensatory dinner in the Belgian capital. Wogan also did not spare Norwegian Kate Gulbrandsen: "She looks like they put her in an electrical outlet". The voting process went smoothly and exemplary, with a temporary Yugoslav lead, that became Germany's and finally Ireland's, which widened the margin until the spectacular win, their overall third. In the end, the gap between Ireland and Yugoslavia (which led the first part of the voting) was 80 points (!). The late manager, Yehuda Talit, who represented the Israeli duo, claimed that a representative from the Yugoslav delegation approached him to agree with him on an exchange of points between the countries: each country would award the second seven points. In practice, Israel did give Yugoslavia 7 points but did not receive a single point from it... Israeli director Ralph Inbar reread the Dutch results and gave Israel "three points" in Hebrew language. Inbar was also responsible for the only mistake during the Voting: he awarded Cyprus points twice — 2 and 10. Frank Naef, the legendary inspector, was alert, made Ralph aware of his mistake and the latter apologised and clarified that the 10 points are for Germany. As mentioned, the tension left the voting halfway through, when it was clear that Ireland and Johnny Logan were on their way to victory. Sandra Kim was respectfully invited to the stage, and Johnny received the Grand Prix. A local ballet company managed to hand out flowers to the winners while in motion, and the Australian-born Irish phenomenon thrilled Europe again with "Hold Me Now". After his victory, Johnny Logan became the only singer in history to win the Eurovision twice. To this day, he stays unparalleled.

1988 – Dublin, Ireland

The Eurovision hosting was entrusted to Ireland for the third time, and as in the previous two times, it was a first-class national event for the small country. Eurovision 1988 is considered one of the best of all time all round: the level of the entries, the two presenters, the production, the stage, the investment, the level of interest and the unprecedented thriller at the end of the voting. The 1988 contest stage is appraised as the most impressive of the twentieth century: against a black background, wide and illuminated squares were spread throughout the wide stage (which changed colours in each entry). Michael Grogan and Paula Farrell were responsible for the spectacular design. Due to its size, they stole many seats in the hall and significantly reduced the amount of audience. This was also why the production chose dark lighting and hardly spotlighted the stands, perhaps to create the illusion — which succeeded by the way — that there is a much larger audience than there is. An introductory opening to each song was first shown, followed by a beautiful video (starring each artist) shot amidst Ireland's landscapes. Michelle Rocca and Pat Kenny are, without a doubt the best pair of presenters in the history of the contest. The two were simply perfect, the chemistry between them was great, and they marvellously combined light and entertaining presentation with authoritative mastery. Their presentation in the voting moments should be taught in schools for Eurovision presenters. Ireland wanted to start a tradition in which a tribute is made to the previous year's winner at the beginning of the show when Johnny Logan took the stage to perform "Hold Me Now" and added another song that was perhaps a bit redundant, but Johnny was almost always "the best show in town". The events' successful director, Declan Lowney, has served as head of the Young Television programmes division at the Irish Television and undoubtedly had a part in the Eurovision production getting younger, also in terms of the audience invited to the show, that was mostly made up of a younger age group. Two big favourites and an additional three comprised the list of nominees for the win. Scott Fitzgerald of Glasgow was the betting crown's jewel, the entry "Go" written for him by the well-known Julie Forsyth (daughter of Bruce Foresight who was present at the hall) was supposed to recreate the last UK win from 1981 in... Dublin. Fitzgerald was not at his peak in rehearsals but surpassed himself when push came to shove. His performance received loud and sincere applause from the local audience who usually avoids applauding the hated neighbour's entries... The tense and dramatic voting was on a roller coaster. The UK was not so much in the picture for the first place, but Scott took the lead towards the last voting part and was in an almost certain position of winning it, which was robbed of him in the final minute by a single point. Instead of returning to his country as the big winner, he was pushed to the margins of UK's distinguished history in the contest with second place for the 11th time (!). A decade after its last significant achievement at the Eurovision Song Contest and two decades after its last victory, Spain counted on the band "La Década" ("the Decade") to bring the Eurovision back to Madrid, a country with a respectful tradition in the European contest. "La chica que yo quiero (Made in Spain)" is a Spanish disco song with hints of flamenco and a Latin spirit that was well received in the days leading up to the event and was very strongly considered a possible winner in rehearsals. But without a single Douze Points and a most disappointing score, the Spaniards returned home ashamed with being only 11th. France was determined to regain hegemony when it came to Dublin with a major name, Gérard Lenorman. "Chanteur de charme" and the experienced and popular artist's sweeping performance should have granted France at least the battle for the top if not the Grand Prix itself, but it seemed that even Lenorman could not re-ignite the French magic that worked so well and beautifully in the sixties and seventies. He received the last Douze Points of the evening from Yugoslavia which placed him only tenth. After the failure in Brussels, Luxembourg chose its emerging star Lara Fabian, who fitted the entry "Croire", written by Alain Garcia and Jacques Cardona, like a glove. This was the song supposed to bring Luxembourg back to the ESC's top after five weak years. After receiving 90 points and 3 Douze Points (from Finland, Switzerland and host Ireland), Lara Fabian's fourth place was a springboard that made "Croire" the most successful Eurovision entry from Dublin in terms of plays and sales. This would also be the last time Luxembourg reached the top four in the contest until its retirement in 1993. Atilla Şereftuğ was confident in 1986 that he had a winning entry in hand until Belgian prodigy Sandra Kim emerged and left him runner-up. Two years later, in 1988, the composer Şereftuğ came up with an even better formula, which came to him quite by chance: "One morning I woke up, sat down at the piano with the idea in my head and within three minutes I created 'Ne partez pas sans moi', went to my studio and recorded a first version". Daniela Simmons was destined to perform the song but hesitated, and meanwhile, he was recommended to give an opportunity to a 20-year-old anonymous Canadian singer named ... Céline Dion. The rest is history. Dion did not bring too much sophistication: her performance was fixed, not to say frozen, she hardly moved from her niche on stage, her hair arrangement now greatly embarrasses her looking back, and Dions' outward appearance did not arouse extraordinary excitement. But Céline just proved how great of a singer she is, period. While rehearsing in Dublin, it was made clear that Dion would fight for the victory and lead the struggle for the top: "I did not think that of any song in this contest that could win us, this entry was written to win the Eurovision", said Atilla Şereftuğ and rightfully so: Switzerland led most of the voting, and although losing the lead to the British towards the end and everything seemed lost, God seemed to want Dion's victory, and it was achieved, as mentioned, by a single point. Yardena Arazi had already participated twice in the contest: as part of the "Chocolate Menta Mastik" Trio (was 6th in the 1976 ESC in The Hague) and the presenter of 1979 Eurovision in Jerusalem. Even when the presenter Pat Kenny introduced her, he did not forget this and said, "I have been taking advice from Yardena Arazi because she did this very job in 1979 when Israel hosted the song contest". Since then, Arazi nurtured her solo career and had a rough road attempting to reach a third Eurovision: in 1982 she finished second to Avi Toledano, in 1983 was missing one point to beat Ofra Haza and in 1985 lost to Izhar Cohen in a triple race where Yigal Bashan was also present. "Od nagi'a", is considered to this day one of the biggest misses (it would have undoubtedly had a fantastic chance of winning in Gothenburg that year). After being Singer of the Year so many times, Yardena refused to compete again, and the Israeli television decided to hold a private pre-contest for her with four songs, from which "Ben Adam", written by Ehud Manor, was elected.

Arazi received conditions like no other Israeli artist who went to the Eurovision before. It seemed that the IBA was doing everything to please the popular singer, who was accompanied by no less than Yehuda Tamir and Reuven Gvirtz (two members of the "Milk and Honey" band, 1979 Eurovision winners), alongside the talented brothers Yehuda and Haim Hager and Iris Shemi ("Sexta"). Arazi became the only artist to present the contest and then participated in it. Opposite cases have happened, such as Corry Brokken from the Netherlands, Lill Lindfors from Sweden and Åse Kleveland from Norway. "Ben Adam" was never a contender for victory but was given a good place after the favourites. A fortune-teller thought otherwise and told Yardena Arazi that entry number nine would win when Israel was supposed to perform ninth. However... less than a month before the contest, Cyprus strangely found out that the song chosen to represent it at the event by Greek singer Yiannis Dimitrou had already participated in the 1984 Cypriot pre-contest and is therefore disqualified from Dublin. The discovery raised questions: Why did the Cypriots remember this at such an advanced stage? How did they not notice in real-time what almost every inhabitant of the small island already knew?

It should be noted that the Cypriot entry appeared on records that included the Eurovision songs. Cyprus' retirement left the contest with 21 participants. So Yardena Arazi became entry number eight when the winner was number nine, Céline Dion from Switzerland (which proved that the fortune-teller was eventually right...). In any case, the contest's makeup artist did not do well, to say the least with Yardena Arazi and robbed her of one of her winning cards: her clean and beautiful face. On the big evening itself, Yardena's excitement was apparent, and her performance can be summed up as no more than reasonable. Israel collected points from here and there and was only 8 points away of a considerable achievement – 3rd place. Finally, it was pushed to the seventh place with 85 points.

Tommy Körberg returned to the contest after 19 years more experienced and a greater artist who has already starred on international stages in the successful musical "Chess". Py Bäckman, Sweden's Tina Turner, wrote him "Stad i ljus" that many gambled on as the race's black horse. Körberg did marvel at the rehearsals and was considered the strongest candidate, but devil's work — Tommy caught severe flu at the worst timing: on the day of the event... By a joint decision of the Swedes and the Irish production, Körberg did not attend the dress rehearsal (mandatory for all participating artists) and was replaced by non-other than… Py Bäckman, who brought hints of blues and jazz to the song.

Meanwhile, the best doctors worked to prepare Körberg for the show (which finally sang with a high fever and a burning throat). The performance he managed to deliver was considered almost a miracle but sounded far less than his true abilities, which affected Sweden's low position. Dublin's big surprises came from Denmark and Norway. Kirsten and Søren led the Danes to an excellent third place (when at the end of the song, a cardboard guitar was thrown to the head of conductor Henrik Krogsgaard in one of the bizarre moments of the Eurovision), while Karoline Krüger managed to exceed the expectations with "For vår jord" written by Anita Skorgan and led Norway to the top 5. The Turkish "MFÖ" returned after three years with "Sufi" which conquered Turkey and lasted in the charts for months. Turkey did not finish last, but despite 8 points from Israel (which did not receive back a single point), it was at the bottom part of the table. Another singer who was ill and celebrated his 28th birthday on the eve of the contest was Gerard Joling, the singer from Alkmaar with the high-quality voice.

"Shangri-La" was one of Dublin's favourite songs, but Joling's performance quality was affected by the flu, and he failed to qualify higher than ninth place for The Netherlands. The Eurovision in Ireland was highly organised and characterised by high-level entries and close and tight competition for the juries' hearts. The German representatives Maxi & Chris Garden, mother and daughter, came to Ireland with grand ambitions with a "Lied für einen Freund" (written by Ralph Siegel and Bernd Meinunger), suffered from a rare mishap. Siegel believed that the mother and daughter gimmick, the two pianos and the powerful entry could bring Germany its second win. Even Nicole, Germany's only Eurovision winner at the time, felt that something good could happen and agreed to be a commentator on the German broadcast from Dublin. The rehearsals were excellent, but at the decisive moment, in the first minute of the performance, there was a malfunction in the two's microphones, and they were not heard in the hall. Germany's attempts to appeal were halted, as the two were not heard in the courtroom — but were seen and heard well on the television broadcast. After listening to the performance together, it was decided that the malfunction did not affect the quality of Maxi & Chris Garden's appearance. At the end of the evening, Nicole could be calm: from the 14th place, even the mother and daughter of the Garden family were not able to outdo her in the history books. Europe shuddered at Austria for electing Chancellor Kurt Waldheim, despite his known Nazi past. The Austrians were abominated, and it seemed that the Europeans were just waiting for the opportunity to leave them with nul points at the Eurovision, which that came when Wilfried Scheutz, a good singer who, to put it mildly, did not fit the contest with an entry that did not match ("Lisa Mona Lisa"), and a very grouchy performance fell to the last place and returned to Vienna without points. Italy sent a big star, Luca Barbarossa, who hoped to recreate Umberto Tozzi and Raf's achievement in Brussels. "Vivo (Ti scrivo)" was a great entry that failed to thrive in Dublin. Italians might not remember that 12th place, but they could definitely not forget the monologue in Italian by presenter Michelle Rocca after Barbarossa's performance, in which she sent a greeting to her Italian family and boasted that she was originally Italian. At the end of her remarks, colleague Pat Kenny brilliantly said: "that was Michelle, looking for a job on Italian television"... Dora from Portugal, another artist who returned to the contest after two years, was convinced that she was going to break the glass ceiling of her country in the ESC. "Voltarei" was very impressive in rehearsals and there were betting agencies determined that a Portuguese victory is a reasonable possibility but blessed is he who expects nothing: only five points and 18th place were all the shocked Dora which said at the end of the show, paraphrasing her song: "I will never return to the Eurovision". Yugoslavia had to patiently wait, being the last to perform with "Srebrna krila". The Yugoslavs felt good when at the end of the dress rehearsal voting they found themselves in the winning position (which is, of course, random and nothing professional should be drawn from it) and longed to recreate it in the big moment. "Mangup" continued the pop line that Yugoslavia chose and was indeed the only one that evening to bring an entry of this style to Dublin. The Yugoslavs received 3 Douze Points, and despite this considerable number, a weak ending sent them straight to the 6th place. The final stamp on the 1988 Eurovision being one of the best and most important of all was also given in the voting process. For the first time, the artists received a much wider space in the Green Room, which was no longer an overly crowded room, but a lavish hangar where drinks and appetisers are served to the delegations while eagerly awaiting results. But the final word was the transition from the awkward scoreboard, to an utterly animated scoreboard, which included a new computer system. The presenters, Rocca and Kenny, asked the audience to keep their fingers crossed that the system would not crash — although it, of course, had backups — and it worked perfectly, without any glitches. In doing so, the Irish set a wonderful precedent that would only get better in the years to come. Usually, Eurovision presenters changed their dress between the entries and the results stages, but Michelle Rocca took it a step further when she took the stage with a new and weird hairstyle, which was parodied by Israeli singer Boaz Sharabi (who played her) and Matti Caspi (who played Pat Kenny), in the music video of their song "Shalom Aleichem". Each country's jury panel was grown from 11 to 16, to expand the canvas and give the public more representation in deciding on the winning entry and fit much more diverse tastes. It was the first step, on the way to making the voting completely public in some years, instead of a small and professional team. In the Spanish team, one could also find, among others, Laura Valenzuela, presenter of the 1969 contest, along with many well-known actors. This team awarded the host Ireland, represented by the "Jump the Gun" band with "Take Him Home", its only Douze Points. The voting itself was the most dramatic and suspenseful ever. In fact, the winner remained unknown until the last minute, a situation that would be repeated before the end of the twentieth century only in 1991, 1993 and 1998.

The unprecedented division of Douze Points reveals to that extent the level of the entries was equal: Only three times did Switzerland receive the maximum score (the fewest for a winner since Marie Myriam's victory in 1977), equivalent to the amount the UK, Denmark, Luxembourg and Yugoslavia were awarded. After a relatively drowsy lead by Switzerland, things suddenly moved when the UK emerged from behind with an impressive set of points and opened a margin over its competitor. The 12 points received from Italy put Scott Fitzgerald at the top with 133 points, against Céline Dion's 118, with three votes left. It should be noted that only one country — the Netherlands — had not awarded points to the British up to this point. The Scottish already shed tears of glory as he believed no one could take it away from him, while Dion looked like a tragic character. France pushed the Swiss' foot into the grave by awarding them only one point. At that moment, 9 points for the British in one of the three remaining votes would have closed the deal, but surprisingly, the United Kingdom did not receive a single point from France. Even then, the

Swiss believed that anything was still possible: "René Angélil was a hopeless optimist", Atilla Şereftuğ said of Céline Dion's manager and partner: "Even though we were in the most difficult position of the voting, he kept whispering in my ears that there was a chance, that if such and such happens, we will win. To his credit, his prediction, which seemed to be a bit detached from reality in those moments, was on point". Portugal, the penultimate jury, added to the tension when it awarded Switzerland a Douze Points that brought it back to life, compared to only 3 points for the UK. Still, Scott Fitzgerald was in a better position: 136 points for him, compared to 131 for Céline Dion.

The decision fell to the well-known Slovenian Television woman, Miša Molk, responsible for reading Yugoslavia's results. "I have to tell you that we employed Agatha Christie to write the script for tonight", joked the excellent presenter Pat Kenny. Indeed, Miša delivered and awarded only 6 points to Switzerland — enough to temporarily pass the UK by one point, but this was on the condition that Scott would not get any point, which did not make sense given the fact that only two nations, the Netherlands (the British were particularly angry, as Fitzgerald was quite popular in this country) and France had given zero points to the British until then. Céline Dion sobbed and, but Molk continued with 7 points for the Netherlands, 8 for Germany and 10 for Norway. Hundreds of millions held their breath waiting for Ljubljana Yugoslav's words, to know who the winner is: "And finally, France"… Céline Dion was informed of her incredible victory. From that moment, she could not stop crying, all the way back to the stage that gave her a first and important push to a tremendous career as one of the best, most prosperous and successful singers in the world. It was a huge win for composer Atilla Şereftuğ who, with a massive entry, stubbornly and creatively managed to bring his country a victory it had not seen in 33 years and assimilate into Swiss society, through the front door. Scott Fitzgerald saw how in a one-point difference, the fame was taken from him and the cameras suddenly left him, instantly turning him into the second fiddle, who was the certain winner, finished runner-up and forgotten. Indeed, Scott's career did not reach his goals, and he bears to this day the scars of the victory robbed from him in the cruellest way possible. Incidentally, if the UK had received one more point, from France or Yugoslavia that did not award it any, it would have won despite the tie, since between it and Switzerland there was a total tie in the number of Douze Points, but the British got 10 points more times so the victory would go to them. A story of one point... This was also the second time Yugoslavia snatched the glory from the UK: the same happened in 1968 when the Yugoslavs were the last to vote and skipped Cliff Richard who lost by a point to Massiel from Spain. It may not be a coincidence, then, that Céline Dion, herself, is the last singer to win the Eurovision with an entry in French (the most dominant language in the early years of the contest). This was only the second victory for Switzerland, the first Eurovision winner to close the circle and after 1956, return the contest founded on its soil — home.

1989 – Lausanne, Switzerland

Switzerland waited 33 years to host once again the contest established in its country. The 1956 event in Lugano did not resemble what the Eurovision Song Contest became — the number one music show in the world and the most-watched event in the world as of 1989. Céline Dion brought the Eurovision to Switzerland and did everyone a big favour: it was a wonderfully maintained event, in which all participants returned filled with stories and pleasures from one of the most beautiful and touristy countries in the world. The event's management and production ran without any error, as characterised by the neutral state's punctual and meticulous nature. Lausanne was chosen as the host. The "Palais de Beaulieu" hall, located in the historic building where conferences and fairs are held in the French-speaking city, was tastefully designed and turned for one evening into the most visited place in Europe. The event's presenters were Lolita Morena-Matthäus (who was married to the German football star Lothar Matthäus) and the sports broadcaster Jacques Deschenaux. The two did an excellent job, but the reviews stated it was a robotic, overly square presentation, without any gimmicks or a sense of humour. The orchestra (one of the best in the contest's history) was entrusted with one of Switzerland's most talented musicians — Benoit Kaufman, who was chosen over Atilla Şereftuğ (who brought the Swiss the victory with the song he wrote a year before). Céline Dion received her well-deserved respect and performed with impressive entrance to the hall "Ne partez pas sans moi", thanks to which the contest came to Lausanne, and then played "Where Does My Heart Beat Now" for the first time, which became her first successful song in English. It was a contest with many favourites when until the delegations arrived in Lausanne, it was impossible to discern who was leading in the predictions for the win. It seemed that no Eurovision before had ever been so 'open' in terms of possibilities when on the eve of the contest no one suggested an absolute winner. Whoever impressed in rehearsals and led the overall impression was the UK. After the tight loss in Dublin, the "Live Report" band with lead singer Ray Caruana ("one of the best singers in the country", British broadcaster Terry Wogan said of him) and "Why Do I Always Get it Wrong?" slightly outpaced their competitors in the betting agencies, but they eventually fell into the traditional honey trap of the UK the Eurovision — the second place... "We lost to a much inferior and lower-quality song than ours", said the frustrated Caruana, who can at least boast of having received the most amount of Douze Points on the big night — five...

12-year-old Gili Netanel managed to overtake Avi Toledano in the Israeli pre-contest. Toledano's "Dayenu" could have unquestionably excelled in Lausanne, but the Israeli juries were convinced that the boy from Rishon Le-Zion would conquer Europe because of his age and talent. "Derech Hamelech" written and composed by Shaike Paikov, might have been successful at a children's festival, but the melody was not strong enough for the Eurovision. Galit Borg sang alongside Gili, and the duo was allotted to bring the contest back to Jerusalem after a decade. When the Eurovision entries were, as per tradition, screened about two weeks before the event, it became clear that Israel was not the only one to think of the Sandra Kim trick when France displayed an even younger participant than Gili: 11-year-old Nathalie Pâque. Suddenly, Gili was not the only child in the contest, and Israel's most reliable card fell out of its hands. In Lausanne, the bad energies started taking over the Israeli delegation: Shaike Paikov did not create a calm atmosphere, to say the least, Galit Borg contracted the flu, and Gili caught a cold. Shlomo Zach's tension was felt. The old hand, recruited to strengthen the delegation, knew that Israel was not on the path to the top. Somehow, things finally worked out with a pretty reasonable performance by Gili Netanel. The allegations of off-key singing and stage fright were nothing more than urban myths, Netanel was perfectly fine and was not wrong or sang off-key or (in anything, Galit turned out as a not-too significant reinforcement). The onslaught and exaggerated criticism of the boy was cruel; overall, the 12th place was not Gili's fault, rather than the fact that "Derech Hamelech" was not such a good song. Guy Mattéoni was convinced that Nathalie Pâque would upgrade "J'ai volé la vie" and pick up the grand prize, but the 11-year-old French girl learned first-hand that being a child and knowing how to sing was not enough, but a great song was also needed, which she did not have. Israel and France's relative failures were a badge of honour for the Eurovision in terms of preferring the song's quality over the gimmick. Following the children's performances, the EBU put things in order and ruled that participation in the contest will be possible in the future only for those over 16. Italy once again honoured the occasion with Anna Oxa and Fausto Leali, winners of the Sanremo Festival. "Avrei voluto", a charming duet of the two, was not appreciated enough and was definitely deprived, finishing in tenth place. All this did not stop veteran Laeli and Oxa from soaring in popularity and success in Italy and abroad.

There was a great commotion around the Turkish entry "Bana Bana". The distinctly oriental style granted it great sympathy in Europe, which in the late 1980s connected with oriental sounds (Ofra Haza for example). Group "Pan" was in high demand in pre-event interviews, and Turkish immigrants also flocked to Lausanne to support the band that might bring their country a historic victory. The Turks' performance was astonishing and elevated the generally indifferent and polite Swiss audience. This is mainly appropriated to the Turkish composer Timur Selçuk, whose performance as conductor of the orchestra (who manifested a rare choreography for a conductor) no one will ever forget... despite the excellent Turkish performance, the juries did not like "Bana Bana" and gave it only five insulting points. Despite the profound disappointment of the previous year from the penultimate place, Portugal believed it had their best entry ever this time: "Conquistador" by the "Da Vinci" band was indeed a great pop song that raised many hopes in the Iberian country that had never reached the top five in the Eurovision. They were also deprived and finished only in 16th place, despite a memorable performance. There was much talk about Tommy Nilsson from Sweden as a potential winner. The singer with the best voice in the Scandinavian country had everything needed for winning: an excellent entry ("En dag"), backing singers from the highest level, some of which successful pop singers on their own (Vicki Benckert, Anke Bakker and Jerry Williams) and the excellent conductor Anders Berglund. Nilsson was the experts and journalists' favourite, so it was not surprising that he came in fourth and honourable place, Sweden's third-best achievement in the eighties. Birthe Kjær, the most famous singer in Denmark, came with all her grace and experience to add the first place in the ESC to her glorious resume. Søren Bundgaard in a second successive appearance, this time as accompanist and composer of the entry "Vi maler byen rød", was also responsible for the rabbits pulled from the Danish hat: the lead singer Kjær invited conductor Henrik Krogsgaard at the end of the second verse to join the band, leaving the baton in the hands of the local orchestra's conductor Benoit Kaufman to replace him.

The Danes' impressive performance led to a recreation of their previous year's achievement in Dublin, third place. Another Scandinavian performer who will fondly remember this Eurovision is Anneli Saaristo, with the Spanish guitars and Latin rhythm. "La dolce vita" also made Finland a threat for the crown. Saaristo was praised for her performance, and Finland got its best position since 1973 and the second best in its history in the contest (in the twentieth century) — seven. It was also the farewell performance of the conductor Ossi Runne from the ESC, after 22 times in which he was entrusted with arranging and conducting the Finnish entry. But not everything was rosy for the Scandinavian representatives: For the first time, Iceland felt the bitter taste of the last place and the nul points that accompanied it. Daníel Ágúst Haraldsson, dressed in church clothing got lost with "Það sem enginn sér" ("What No One Sees"), and indeed — no one saw this entry worthy of points. Although it was definitely not a bad song, on an evening like this where there are so many good entries, someone had to pay the price. The host Switzerland decided to pay homage to its official fourth language, the ancient Romansh, spoken by a maybe little more than ten thousand people. The excellent Marie Louise Werth led the "Furbaz" and felt that "Viver senza tei" could replicate Céline Dion's victory, and so she told the local media. But winning the Eurovision twice in a row is a nearly impossible task, and although they delivered on the big evening, the Swiss parted from the title with 13th place.

Dieter Bohlen, the other half of the successful duo "Modern Talking", decided that he wants to take over the Ralph Siegel's little paradise, as Germany's Mr. Eurovision. In the first stage, he defeated Ralph in the German pre-contest times and was puffed-up in rehearsals in Lausanne. Bohlen wrote no less than two strong, high-quality entries for the contest. "Flieger" was played endlessly in Germany, and in rehearsals, many eyes were set on Bohlen, and the song performed by the girl idol from the biggest country in Europe, Nino de Angelo, sounded like the one with the right magic. The points, however, did not smile upon the Germans, who sank in 14th place. Dieter found solace in a song he had fewer expectations from: After the last place in 1988, Austria hoped that Bohlen (who wrote "Nur ein Lied" and chose the exciting and excellent Thomas Forstner to perform it), would erase the great shame. Austria's respect did return, fifth place and 97 points, its best since 1972.

For the second consecutive time, Yugoslavia had to wait nervously for its performance, as it was set to be the last one. The "Riva" band from Zadar hardly won the local pre-contest with "Rock Me". Composer Rajko Dujmić made the song almost unrecognizable with the changes he made to it. Still, there is no arguing with the results: "Rock Me" came to Lausanne with big ambitions, and although Yugoslavia was not really considered a possible winner, Emilija Kokić led her band to the performance of their lives. Israel was the first to award the Yugoslav Douze Points and so did three additional countries. Almost from the outset, "Riva" led and did not lose its advantage until the end, ensuring a historic first victory for their nation that was soon to be disbanded. This made Yugoslavia the first Eastern European to win the continental singing contest. Interval acts rarely captivate the viewers, but it happened thanks to Guy Tell, a virtuoso imitating the well-known Wilhelm Tell, who could shoot an arrow from a bow right inside an apple above the head. Tell delivered a performance for the books, when he shot with remarkable accuracy at apples in various situations, including a crazy stunt in which he placed the apple on his head and was depended on 17 arrows being fired at each other until hitting the inside of the apple lying on his head. Terry Wogan claimed that what was shown to the audience was an excerpt from the dress rehearsal and that in the live broadcast the arrow did not really hit the apple. The voting began with an Austrian lead, but a Yugoslav cluster of points kicked "Riva" to the first place, which they did not drop from until the end. At certain moments Denmark and Austria got a little closer to the leader, but the latter always reopened the necessary margin. Towards the end, the British favourites started gaining momentum and got close to Yugoslavia, but nothing more. Spain continued the tradition of including celebrities on its jury panel: this time it was renowned telenovela actor Antonio Banderas and Spain's national football team coach Javier Clemente. The Spanish team did not award any points to the winner Yugoslavia and gave its Douze Points to Italy. The Yugoslavs guaranteed their victory when they received one sweet little point from Germany, which determined that the UK could not catch up. In the end, only seven points separated "Riva" and "Live Report", which did not matter for the winners from Zadar and the eternal loser — the UK. The Yugoslav joy knew no bounds: in 1989, first cracks began to burst in the unity of the divided country heading for a brutal and bloody war between the republics that make it up. For one rare and beautiful evening, the Yugoslavs were able to commemorate a tremendous achievement that came close to the last two years of their existence as a single entity. "Riva" rejoiced and celebrated, Emilija Kokić shed tears of excitement and could tell her grandchildren that she had received the honourable award from Céline Dion. "Rock Me" was performed in English, a surprising victory, which closed the successful and refined evening in Lausanne.

1980

Hosting Country: The Netherlands

Hosting City: The Hague

Date: 19.4.1980

Location: Nederlands Congresgebouw

Presenter: Marlous Fluitsma

Second Presenter: Hans van Willigenburg

Orchestra Conductor: Rogier van Otterloo

Chief Executive: Frank Naef

Director: Theo Ordeman

Executive Producer: Fred Oster

Participating Countries: 19

Voting: Every participating country has a jury (11 members) that gives 1-8 points and then 10 and 12 points to its favourite song

Broadcaster: Nederlandse Omroep Stichting (NOS)

Intermediate performance: The Dutch Rhythm Steel and Show Band

Duration: 2 hours and 17 minutes

Broadcast: To all participating countries.

No.	Country	Song	Performing Artist	Lyrics	Composer	Conductor	Language	Commentator	Spoker of Results	Points	Place
01	Austria	"Du bist Musik"	Blue Danube (Wolfgang Weiss, Marty Brem, Marc Berry, Sylvia Schramm, Rena Mauris)	Klaus Peter Sattler	Klaus Peter Sattler	Richard Österreicher	German	Günther Ziesel	Jenny Pippal	64	8
02	Turkey	"Pet'r Oil"	Ajda Pekkan	Şanar Yurdatapan	Atilla Özdemiroğlu	Atilla Özdemiroğlu	Turkish	Bülend Özveren	Başak Doğru	23	15
03	Greece	"Autostop"	Anna Vissi and the Epikouri	Rony Sofu	Jick Nacassian	Jick Nacassian	Greek	Mako Georgiadou	Unknown	30	13
04	Luxembourg	"Papa pingouin"	Sophie & Magaly	Pierre Delanoë, Jean-Paul Cara	Ralph Siegel, Bernd Meinunger	Norbert Daum	French	Jacques Navadic	Jacques Harvey	56	9
05	Morocco	"Bitaqat Hub"	Samira Bensaïd	Malw Rawan	'Abd Al-'Ati Amyna	Jean Claudric	Arabic	-	Kamal Irassi	7	18
06	Italy	"Non so che darei"	Alan Sorrenti	Alan Sorrenti	Alan Sorrenti	Del Newman	Italian	Michele Gammino	Mariolina Cannuli	87	6
07	Denmark	"Tænker altid på dig"	Bamses Venner (Flemming 'Bamse' Jørgensen, Mogens Balle, Arne Østergaard, Bjarne Gren Jensen)	Flemming 'Bamse' Jørgensen	Bjarne Gren Jensen	Allan Botschinsky	Danish	Jørgen de Mylius	Bent Henius	25	14
08	Sweden	"Just nu!"	Tomas Ledin	Tomas Ledin	Tomas Ledin	Anders Berglund	Swedish	Ulf Elfving	Arne Weise	47	10
09	Switzerland	"Cinéma"	Paola	Peter Reber, Véronique Müller	Peter Reber	Peter Reber	French	Theodor Haller, Georges Hardy, Giovanni Bertini	Michel Stocker	104	4
10	Finland	"Huilumies"	Vesa-Matti Loiri	Veikko 'Vexi' Salmi	Aarno Raninen	Ossi Runne	Finish	Heikki Harma	Kaarina Pönniö	6	19
11	Norway	"Sámiid ædnan"	Sverre Kjelsberg & Mattis Hætta	Ragnar Olsen	Sverre Kjelsberg [and uncredited Mattis Hætta]	Sigurd Jansen	Norweigen	Knut Aunbu	Roald Øyen	15	16
12	Germany	"Theater"	Katja Ebstein	Bernd Meinunger	Ralph Siegel	Wolfgang Rödelberger	German	Ado Schlier	Unknown	128	2
13	United Kingdom	"Love Enough for Two"	Prima Donna (Kate Robbins, Lance Aston, Sally Ann Triplett, Jane Robbins, Danny Finn and Alan Coates)	Stuart Slater, Stephanie de Sykes	Stephanie de Sykes, Stuart Slater	John Coleman	United Kingdom	Terry Wogan	Ray Moore	106	3
14	Portugal	"Um grande, grande amor"	José Cid	José Cid	José Cid	Jorge Machado	Portuguese	Isabel Wolmar	Teresa Cruz	71	7
15	The Netherlands	"Amsterdam"	Maggie MacNeal	Alex Alberts	Frans Smit, Robert Verwey, Sjoukje Smit-van't Spijker	Rogier van Otterloo	Dutch	Pim Jacobs	Kaarina Pönniö	93	5
16	France	"Hé, hé, m'sieurs dames"	Profil (Martine Havet, Jean-Claude Corbel, Martine Bauer, Francis Rignault, Jean-Pierre Izbinski)	Richard de Bordeaux, Richard Joffo	Sylvano Santorio	Sylvano Santorio	French	Patrick Sabatier	Fabienne Égal	45	11
17	Ireland	"What's Another Year"	Johnny Logan	Shay Healy	Shay Healy	Noel Kelehan	English	Larry Gogan	David Heffernan	143	1
18	Spain	"Quédate esta noche"	Trigo Limpio (Luis Carlos Gil, Patricia Fernández and Iñaki de Pablo)	José Antonio Martin	José Antonio Martin	Javier Iturralde	Spanish	Miguel de los Santos	Alfonso Lapeña	38	12
19	Belgium	"Euro-Vision"	Telex (Michel Moers, Dan Lacksman, Marc Moulin)	Michel Moers, Dan Lacksman, Marc Moulin	Michel Moers, Dan Lacksman, Marc Moulin	-	French	Jacques Mercier, Luc Appermont	Jacques Olivier	14	17

	Austria	Turkey	Greece	Luxembourg	Morocco	Italy	Denmark	Sweden	Switzerland	Finland	Norway	Germany	United Kingdom	Portugal	The Netherlands	France	Ireland	Spain	Belgium	
Austria	■	–	1	–	3	4	5	1	4	5	6	4	6	3	3	4	10	4	1	Austria
Turkey	3	■	–	–	12	8	–	–	–	–	–	–	–	–	–	–	–	–	–	Turkey
Greece	5	–	■	1	–	2	2	–	–	–	4	–	3	1	8	–	4	–	–	Greece
Luxembourg	1	1	–	■	–	–	4	6	–	3	7	–	8	–	–	7	8	3	8	Luxembourg
Morocco	–	–	–	–	■	7	–	–	–	–	–	–	–	–	–	–	–	–	–	Morocco
Italy	2	6	2	–	–	■	3	10	8	6	2	7	4	12	1	2	2	10	10	Italy
Denmark	–	–	4	–	2	–	■	–	6	7	1	5	–	–	–	–	–	–	–	Denmark
Sweden	–	8	10	10	6	5	–	■	5	–	–	2	–	–	–	–	–	1	–	Sweden
Switzerland	6	2	–	5	7	3	8	2	■	12	10	10	7	6	10	–	12	2	2	Switzerland
Finland	–	–	–	–	–	–	–	–	–	■	5	–	–	–	–	1	–	–	–	Finland
Norway	–	–	–	–	4	–	–	–	–	–	■	6	–	–	2	3	–	–	–	Norway
Germany	8	10	–	3	10	12	7	5	7	2	–	■	10	8	12	10	5	12	7	Germany
United Kingdom	7	5	–	8	8	–	10	12	10	4	–	3	■	7	7	5	6	8	6	United Kingdom
Portugal	–	4	5	4	–	10	6	8	2	1	8	1	–	■	5	6	7	–	4	Portugal
The Netherlands	12	12	6	12	–	–	–	3	3	10	–	8	2	4	■	12	1	5	3	The Netherlands
France	–	3	7	2	1	–	1	4	1	–	3	–	5	–	4	■	3	6	5	France
Ireland	10	–	12	7	–	1	12	7	12	8	12	12	12	5	6	8	■	7	12	Ireland
Spain	4	7	8	6	5	6	–	–	–	–	–	–	–	2	–	–	–	■	–	Spain
Belgium	–	–	3	–	–	–	–	–	–	–	–	–	1	10	–	–	–	–	■	Belgium

1981

Hosting Country: Ireland

Hosting City: Dublin

Date: 4.4.1981

Location: RDS Simmonscourt

Presenter: Doireann Ní Bhriain

Orchestra Conductor: Noel Kelehan

Chief Executive: Frank Naef

Director: Ian McGarry

Executive Producer: Noel D. Greene

Participating Countries: 20

Voting: Every participating country has a jury (11 members) that gives 1-8 points and then 10 and 12 points to its favourite song

Broadcaster: Raidió Teilifís Éireann (RTÉ)

Intermediate performance: "Timedance" performed by Planxty featuring dance performance by the 'Dublin City Ballet'

Duration: 2 hours and 31 minutes

Broadcast: To all participating countries.

No.	Country	Song	Performing Artist	Lyrics	Composer	Conductor	Language	Commentator	Spoker of Results	Points	Place
01	Austria	"Wenn du da bist"	Marty Brem	Werner Böhmler	Werner Böhmler	Richard Österreicher	German	Ernst Grissemann	Jenny Pippal	20	17
02	Turkey	"Dönme Dolap"	Modern Folk Üçlüsü & Ayşegül (Doğan Çanku, Şelami Karaibrahimgil and Ahmet Kurtaran)	Ali Kocatepe	Ali Kocatepe	Onno Tunç	Turkish	Bülend Özveren	Başak Doğru	9	19
03	Germany	"Johnny Blue"	Lena Valaitis	Bernd Meinunger	Ralph Siegel	Wolfgang Rödelberger	German	Ado Schlier	Unknown	132	2
04	Luxembourg	"C'est peut-être pas l'Amérique"	Jean-Claude Pascal	Sophie Makhno, Jean-Claude Pascal, Jean-Claude Petit	Sophie Makhno, Jean-Claude Pascal, Jean-Claude Petit	Joël Rocher	French	Jacques Navadic, Marylène Bergmann	Jacques Harvey	41	12
05	Israel	"Halayla"	"Habibi" (Shlomit Aharon, Yuval Dor, Kiki Rothstein and Ami Mandelman)	Shlomit Aharon, Yuval Dor	Shuki Levy	Eldad Shrem	Hebrew	-	Dan Kaner	56	7
06	Denmark	"Krøller eller ej"	Tommy Seebach & Debbie Cameron	Keld Heick	Tommy Seebach	Allan Botschinsky	Danish	Jørgen de Mylius	Bent Henius	41	11
07	Yugoslavia	"Lejla"	Seid Memić "Vajta"	Ranko Boban	Ranko Boban	Ranko Rihtman	serb	Mladen Popović, Oliver Mlakar, Tomaž Terček	Helga Vlahović	35	15
08	Finland	"Reggae OK"	Riki Sorsa	Olli Ojala	Jim Pembroke	Henrik Otto Donner	Finish	Ossi Runne	Annemi Genetz	27	16
09	France	"Humanahum"	Jean Gabilou	Joe Gracy	Jean-Paul Cara	David Springfield	French	Patrick Sabatier	Fabienne Égal	125	3
10	Spain	"Y sólo tú"	Bacchelli	Amado Jaén	Amado Jaén	Juan Barcons	Spanish	Miguel de los Santos	Isabel Tenaille	38	14
11	The Netherlands	"Het is een wonder"	Linda Williams	Bart van de Laar	Cees de Wit	Rogier van Otterloo	Dutch	Pim Jacobs	Flip van der Schalie	51	9
12	Ireland	"Horoscopes"	Sheeba (Irene McCoubrey, Marion Fossett, Frances Campbell)	Joe Burkett	Jim Kelly	Noel Kelehan	English	Larry Gogan	John Skehan	105	5
13	Norway	"Aldri i livet"	Finn Kalvik	Finn Kalvik	Finn Kalvik	Sigurd Jansen	Norweigen	Knut Aunbu	Sverre Christophersen	0	20
14	United Kingdom	"Making Your Mind Up"	Bucks Fizz (Bobby G, Mike Nolan, Jay Aston, Cheryl Baker)	Andy Hill	John Danter	John Coleman	English	Terry Wogan	Colin Berry	136	1
15	Portugal	"Playback"	Carlos Paião	Carlos Paião	Carlos Paião	Shegundo Galarza	Portuguese	Eládio Clímaco	Margarida Andrade	9	18
16	Belgium	"Samson"	Emly Starr	Kick Dandy, Penny Els	Kick Dandy, Giuseppe Marchese	Giuseppe Marchese	Flemish	Luc Appermont, Jacques Mercier	Walter De Meyere	40	13
17	Greece	"Feggari kalokerino"	Yiannis Dimitras	Yiannis Dimitras	Yiannis Dimitras, Yiorgos Niarchos	Yiorgos Niarchos	Greek	Mako Georgiadou	Tatiana Darra	55	8
18	Cyprus	"Monika"	Island (Alexia Vassiliou, Areti Kassapi, Haralbidou, Aristos Moskovakis, Roger Lee, Doros Georgiadis)	Stavros Sideras	Doros Georgiadis	Michalis Rozakis	Greek	Fryni Papadopoulou	Unknown	69	6
19	Switzerland	"Io senza te"	Peter, Sue and Marc	Peter Reber, Nella Martinetti	Peter Reber	Rolf Zuckowski	Italian	Theodor Haller, Georges Hardy, Giovanni Bertini	Michel Stocker	121	4
20	Sweden	"Fångad i en dröm"	Björn Skifs	Björn Skifs and Bengt Palmers	Björn Skifs and Bengt Palmers	Anders Berglund	Swedish	Ulf Elfving	Bengteric Nordell	50	10

	Austria	Turkey	Germany	Luxembourg	Israel	Denmark	Yugoslavia	Finland	France	Spain	The Netherlands	Ireland	Norway	United Kingdom	Portugal	Belgium	Greece	Cyprus	Switzerland	Sweden	
Austria	■	6	–	–	–	1	–	–	5	6	–	–	–	–	–	–	–	–	–	2	Austria
Turkey	–	■	–	1	–	–	3	5	–	–	–	–	–	–	–	–	–	–	–	–	Turkey
Germany	5	12	■	3	8	8	2	7	8	12	3	6	4	7	12	10	5	8	–	12	Germany
Luxembourg	10	–	5	■	3	–	–	4	3	1	–	–	–	–	4	–	–	–	6	5	Luxembourg
Israel	8	–	–	4	■	–	–	6	–	–	7	7	8	4	5	–	–	–	4	3	Israel
Denmark	–	1	1	7	–	■	–	–	4	3	2	–	–	5	2	12	–	–	–	4	Denmark
Yugoslavia	–	4	–	–	–	–	■	8	–	–	–	2	1	–	–	5	2	3	10	–	Yugoslavia
Finland	–	–	–	2	–	–	–	■	1	2	5	5	–	–	1	–	–	–	5	6	Finland
France	12	–	12	12	7	2	4	10	■	–	6	4	5	1	10	3	8	7	12	10	France
Spain	–	10	–	–	6	–	–	–	–	■	4	3	10	–	3	–	–	–	2	–	Spain
The Netherlands	3	5	3	–	4	7	–	–	2	7	■	–	–	6	7	2	3	2	–	–	The Netherlands
Ireland	7	3	6	10	10	12	5	–	6	5	10	■	–	–	–	1	10	12	1	7	Ireland
Norway	–	–	–	–	–	–	–	–	–	–	–	–	■	–	–	–	–	–	–	–	Norway
United Kingdom	4	8	4	5	12	10	10	3	7	8	12	10	3	■	6	8	6	4	8	8	United Kingdom
Portugal	–	–	8	–	–	–	–	–	–	–	–	–	–	–	■	–	1	–	–	–	Portugal
Belgium	1	7	–	–	1	6	8	2	–	–	–	–	–	3	–	■	7	5	–	–	Belgium
Greece	6	–	2	6	–	–	1	–	–	10	–	1	2	8	–	6	■	6	7	–	Greece
Cyprus	–	–	–	–	5	3	6	–	–	–	8	8	7	10	–	7	12	■	3	–	Cyprus
Switzerland	2	2	7	8	–	4	12	12	10	4	1	12	12	12	8	–	4	10	■	1	Switzerland
Sweden	–	–	10	2	–	5	7	1	12	–	–	–	6	2	–	4	–	1	–	■	Sweden

1982

Hosting Country: United Kingdom

Hosting City: Harogate

Date: 24.4.1982

Location: Harrogate International Centre

Presenter: Jan Leeming

Orchestra Conductor: Ronnie Hazlehurst

Chief Executive: Frank Naef

Director: Michael Hurll

Executive Producer: Michael Hurll

Participating Countries: 18

Voting: Every participating country has a jury (11 members) that gives 1-8 points and then 10 and 12 points to its favourite song

Broadcaster: British Broadcasting Corporation (BBC)

Intermediate performance: Pictures from Yorkshire and Castle Howard

Duration: 2 hours and 12 minutes

Broadcast: To all participating countries and to France and Greece.

No.	Country	Song	Performing Artist	Lyrics	Composer	Conductor	Language	Commentator	Spoker of Results	Points	Place
01	Portugal	"Bem bom"	Doce (Lena Coelho, Fatima Padinha, Laura Diogo, Teresa Miguel)	António Pinho, Tozé Brito, Pedro Brito	António Pinho, Tozé Brito, Pedro Brito	Luis Duarte	Portuguese	José Fialho Gouveia	Unknown	32	13
02	Luxembourg	"Cours après le temps"	Svetlana (Claire de Loutchek)	Michel Jouveaux	Cyril Assous	Jean Claudric	French	Marylène Bergmann	Jacques Harvey	78	6
03	Norway	"Adieu"	Jahn Teigen & Anita Skorgan	Herodes Falsk	Jahn Teigen	Sigurd Jansen	Norweigen	Bjørn Scheele	Erik Diesen	40	12
04	United Kingdom	"One Step Further"	Bardo (Sally Ann Triplett, Stephen Fischer)	Simon Jefferis	Simon Jefferis	Ronnie Hazlehurst	English	Terry Wogan	Colin Berry	76	7
05	Turkey	"Hani?"	Neco	Olcayto Ahmet Tuğsuz	Olcayto Ahmet Tuğsuz, Faik Tuğsuz	Garo Mafyan	Turkish	Ümit Tunçağ	Başak Doğru	20	15
06	Finland	"Nuku pommiin"	Kojo	Juice Leskinen	Jim Pembroke	Ossi Runne	Finish	Erkki Toivanen	Solveig Herlin	0	18
07	Switzerland	"Amour on t'aime"	Arlette Zola	Pierre Alain	Alain Morisod	Joan Amils	French	Theodor Haller, Georges Hardy, Giovanni Bertini	Michel Stocker	97	3
08	Cyprus	"Mono i agapi"	Anna Vissi	Anna Vissi	Anna Vissi	Martyn Ford	Greek	Fryni Papadopoulou	Anna Partelidou	85	5
09	Sweden	"Dag efter dag"	Chips (Elisabeth Andreassen, Kikki Danielsson)	Monica Forsberg	Lasse Holm	Anders Berglund	Swedish	Ulf Elfving	Arne Weise	67	8
10	Austria	"Sonntag"	Mess (Michael Scheikl, Elisabeth Engstler)	Rudolf Leve	Michael Mell	Richard Österreicher	German	Ernst Grissemann	Tilia Herold	57	9
11	Belgium	"Si tu aimes ma musique"	Stella	Jo May	Fred Bekky, Rony Brack, Bobott	Jacques Say	French	Jacques Mercier, Luc Appermont	Jacques Olivier	96	4
12	Spain	"Él"	Lucía	Ignacio Román	Francisco Cepero	Miguel Angel Verona	Spanish	Miguel de los Santos	Marisa Naranjo	52	10
13	Denmark	"Video, Video"	Brixx (Jens Brixtofte, Steen Ejler Olsen, John Hatting, Torben Jacobsen, Bjørn Holmgaard Sørensen)	Jens Brixtofte	Jens Brixtofte	Allan Botschinsky	Danish	Jørgen de Mylius	Hans Otto Bisgaard	5	17
14	Yugoslavia	"Halo, halo"	Aska (Snežana Mišković Snežana Stamenković, Izolda Barudžija)	Miro Zec	Aleksandar Ilić	Zvonimir Skerl	Serb	Mladen Popović, Oliver Mlakar, Tomaž Terček	Miša Molk	21	14
15	Israel	"Hora"	Avi Toledano	Yoram Tahar-Lev	Avi Toledano	Nansi Silviu Brandes	Hebrew	-	Yitzhak Shimoni	100	2
16	The Netherlands	"Jij en ik"	Bill van Dijk	Liselore Gerritsen	Dick Bakker	Rogier van Otterloo	Dutch	Pim Jacobs	Flip van der Schalie	8	16
17	Ireland	"Here Today Gone Tomorrow"	The Duskeys (Nina Duskey, Dan Duskey, Sandy Kelly, Barbara Ellis)	Sally Keating	Sally Keating	Noel Kelehan	English	Larry Gogan	John Skehan	49	11
18	Germany	"Ein Bißchen Frieden"	Nicole	Bernd Meinunger	Ralph Siegel	Norbert Daum	German	Ado Schlier	Unknown	161	1

	Portugal	Luxembourg	Norway	United Kingdom	Turkey	Finland	Switzerland	Cyprus	Sweden	Austria	Belgium	Spain	Denmark	Yugoslavia	Israel	The Netherlands	Ireland	Germany	
Portugal	■	7	–	4	5	2	1	–	6	–	–	–	–	–	1	4	2	–	Portugal
Luxembourg	6	■	7	6	3	7	–	–	–	2	8	5	4	–	5	7	10	8	Luxembourg
Norway	–	6	■	–	–	–	–	4	4	6	2	2	–	–	–	–	6	10	Norway
United Kingdom	4	12	6	■	10	4	5	3	–	12	–	1	2	6	2	1	7	1	United Kingdom
Turkey	–	8	3	–	■	1	3	–	–	3	–	–	–	–	–	2	–	–	Turkey
Finland	–	–	–	–	–	■	–	–	–	–	–	–	–	–	–	–	–	–	Finland
Switzerland	2	2	4	12	2	–	■	6	2	10	12	–	7	10	10	10	8	–	Switzerland
Cyprus	5	4	12	3	–	8	8	■	–	5	3	7	–	5	7	12	–	6	Cyprus
Sweden	7	3	8	5	–	3	4	–	■	8	5	4	8	2	–	5	3	2	Sweden
Austria	–	–	–	10	7	–	–	7	–	■	6	8	6	4	4	–	5	–	Austria
Belgium	8	5	5	2	6	5	2	8	7	4	■	10	10	7	6	3	4	4	Belgium
Spain	–	1	–	–	8	6	7	10	–	–	4	■	–	1	8	–	–	7	Spain
Denmark	3	–	–	–	–	–	–	–	1	–	–	–	■	–	–	–	1	–	Denmark
Yugoslavia	–	–	–	–	4	–	–	1	12	–	1	–	3	■	–	–	–	–	Yugoslavia
Israel	10	10	1	1	–	12	10	2	10	7	7	6	1	3	■	8	–	12	Israel
The Netherlands	–	–	–	–	–	–	–	–	3	–	–	–	–	–	–	■	–	5	The Netherlands
Ireland	1	–	2	7	1	–	6	5	5	–	–	3	5	8	3	–	■	3	Ireland
Germany	12	–	10	8	12	10	12	12	8	1	10	12	12	12	12	6	12	■	Germany

1983

Hosting Country: Germany

Hosting City: Munich

Date: 23.4.1983

Location: Rudi-Sedlmayer-Halle

Presenter: Marlene Charell

Orchestra Conductor: Dieter Reith

Chief Executive: Frank Naef

Director: Rainer Bertram

Executive Producers: Christian Hayer, Gunther Lebram

Participating Countries: 20

Voting: Every participating country has a jury (11 members) that gives 1-8 points and then 10 and 12 points to its favourite song

Broadcaster: Arbeitsgemeinschaft Rundfunkanstalten Deutschland (ARD)

Intermediate performance: Marlene Charell and her dancing group

Duration: 2 hours and 56 minutes

Broadcast: To all participating countries and to Iceland, Australia, Ireland, Soviet Union, Hong Kong, Romania, Hungary and Czechoslovakia.

No.	Country	Song	Performing Artist	Lyrics	Composer	Conductor	Language	Commentator	Spoker of Results	Points	Place
01	France	"Vivre"	Guy Bonnet	Fulbert Cant	Guy Bonnet	François Rauber	French	Léon Zitrone	Nicole André	56	8
02	Norway	"Do Re Mi"	Jahn Teigen	Jahn Teigen, Herodes Falsk	Anita Skorgan, Jahn Teigen	Sigurd Jansen	Norweigen	Ivar Dyrhaug	Erik Diesen	53	10
03	United Kingdom	"I'm Never Giving Up"	Sweet Dreams (Bobby McVay, Carrie Grey, Helen Kray)	Ron Roker, Jan Pulsford, Phil Wigger	Ron Roker, Phil Wigger, Stephan Genovese	John Coleman	English	Terry Wogan	Colin Berry	79	6
04	Sweden	"Främling"	Carola Häggkvist	Monica Forsberg	Lasse Holm	Anders Ekdahl	Sweden	Ulf Elfving	Agneta Bolme-Bör-jefors	126	3
05	Italy	"Per Lucia"	Riccardo Fogli	Riccardo Fogli, Vincenzo Spampinato	Maurizio Fabrizio	Maurizio Fabrizio	Italian	Paolo Frajese	Paola Perissi	41	11
06	Turkey	"Opera"	Çetin Alp & the Short Waves	Aysel Gürel	Buğra Uğur	Buğra Uğur	Turkish	Başak Doğru	Fatih Orbay	0	19
07	Spain	"¿Quién maneja mi barca?"	Remedios Amaya	Isidro Muñoz	José Miguel Évoras	José Miguel Évoras	Spanish	José-Miguel Ullán	Rosa Campanero	0	19
08	Switzerland	"Io così non ci sto"	Mariella Farré	Nella Martinetti	Thomas Gonzenbach, Remo Kessler	Robert Weber	Italian	Theodor Haller, Georges Hardy, Giovanni Bertini	Michel Stocker	28	15
09	Finland	"Fantasiaa"	Ami Aspelund	Kaisu Liuhala	Kari Kuusamo	Ossi Runne	Finland	Erkki Pohjanheimo	Solveig Herlin	41	11
10	Greece	"Mou les"	Christie Stasinopoulou	Sofia Fildissi	Antonis & Mimis Plessas	Mimis Plessas	Greek	Mako Georgiadou	Irini Gavala	32	14
11	The Netherlands	"Sing Me a Song"	Bernadette	Martin Duiser	Piet Souer	Piet Souer	Dutch	Willem Duys	Flip van der Schalie	66	7
12	Yugoslavia	"Džuli"	Daniel (Milan Popović)	Mario Mihaljević	Daniel (Milan Popović)	Radovan Papović	Croatian	Mladen Popović, Oliver Mlakar, Tomaž Terček	Unknown	125	4
13	Cyprus	"I agapi akoma zi"	Stavros & Constantina (Stavros Sideras, Constantina Konstantinou)	Stavros Sideras	Stavros Sideras	Michalis Rozakis	Greek	Fryni Papadopoulou	Anna Partelidou	26	16
14	Germany	"Rücksicht"	Hoffmann & Hoffmann (Michael Hoffmann, Günter Hoffmann)	Volker Lechtenbrink	Michael Reinecke	Dieter Reith	German	Ado Schlier	Carolin Reiber	94	5
15	Denmark	"Kloden drejer"	Gry Johansen	Flemming Gernyx, Christian Jacobsen, Billy Cross	Flemming Gernyx, Christian Jacobsen, Lars Christensen	Allan Botschinsky	Danish	Jørgen de Mylius	Bent Henius	16	17
16	Israel	"Hay"	Ofra Haza	Ehud Manor	Avi Toledano	Nansi Silviu Brandes	Hebrew	-	Yitzhak Shimoni	136	2
17	Portugal	"Esta balada que te dou"	Armando Gama	Armando Gama	Armando Gama	Mike Seargent	Portuguese	Eládio Clímaco	João Abel Fonseca	33	13
18	Austria	"Hurricane"	Westend (Gary Lux, Hans Christian Wagner, Bernhard Rabitsch, Peter Vieweger, Patricia Tandien)	Heli Deinboek, Heinz Nessizius	Peter Vieweger	Richard Öster-reicher	German	Ernst Grissemann	Tilia Herold	53	9
19	Belgium	"Rendez-vous"	Pas de Deux (Dett Peyskens, Hilde Van Roy, Walter Verdin)	Paul Peyskens, Walter Verdin	Walter Verdin	Freddy Sunder	Flemish	Luc Appermont, Jacques Mercier	An Ploegaerts	13	18
20	Luxembourg	"Si la vie est cadeau"	Corinne Hermès	Alain Garcia	Jean-Pierre Millers	Michel Bernholc	French	Valérie Sarn	Jacques Harvey	142	1

	France	Norway	United Kingdom	Sweden	Italy	Turkey	Spain	Switzerland	Finland	Greece	The Netherlands	Yugoslavia	Cyprus	Germany	Denmark	Israel	Portugal	Austria	Belgium	Luxembourg	
France	■	3	–	–	10	–	–	10	6	7	2	3	4	4	–	1	3	–	–	3	France
Norway	–	■	5	3	–	6	–	–	–	–	8	–	–	1	8	4	6	3	7	2	Norway
United Kingdom	5	5	■	12	2	5	–	8	–	5	5	–	6	3	5	–	2	10	–	6	United Kingdom
Sweden	6	12	8	■	8	7	2	5	10	10	3	1	7	12	10	8	4	8	5	–	Sweden
Italy	7	–	–	2	■	4	3	–	1	2	–	8	1	–	–	6	7	–	–	–	Italy
Turkey	–	–	–	–	–	■	–	–	–	–	–	–	–	–	–	–	–	–	–	–	Turkey
Spain	–	–	–	–	–	–	■	–	–	–	–	–	–	–	–	–	–	–	–	–	Spain
Switzerland	–	1	–	–	7	–	1	■	–	–	–	7	–	–	–	–	–	6	1	5	Switzerland
Finland	1	2	6	–	–	3	–	4	■	8	–	–	–	7	–	7	–	2	–	1	Finland
Greece	3	–	–	–	–	–	12	–	5	■	–	–	12	–	–	–	–	–	–	–	Greece
The Netherlands	2	7	1	6	4	2	–	12	3	–	■	5	5	2	4	3	–	4	2	4	The Netherlands
Yugoslavia	–	8	12	–	1	12	10	–	12	6	7	■	8	6	12	10	–	1	12	8	Yugoslavia
Cyprus	–	4	–	–	–	–	–	1	–	–	–	6	■	5	1	5	–	–	4	–	Cyprus
Germany	10	10	7	8	6	–	–	2	4	1	10	–	–	■	3	–	8	7	6	12	Germany
Denmark	–	–	2	7	–	1	4	–	–	–	–	–	–	2	■	–	–	–	–	–	Denmark
Israel	8	6	10	5	3	–	6	7	7	3	12	10	–	10	7	■	10	12	10	10	Israel
Portugal	4	–	–	1	–	–	5	6	2	–	6	2	–	–	–	–	■	–	–	7	Portugal
Austria	–	–	3	4	5	10	–	–	–	4	4	4	3	–	6	2	5	■	3	–	Austria
Belgium	–	–	4	–	–	–	8	–	–	–	–	–	–	–	–	–	–	1	■	–	Belgium
Luxembourg	12	–	–	10	12	8	7	3	8	12	1	12	10	8	2	12	12	5	8	■	Luxembourg

1984

Hosting Country: Luxembourg

Hosting City: Luxembourg City

Date: 5.5.1984

Location: Grand Theatre

Presenter: Désirée Nosbusch

Orchestra Conductor: Pierre Cao

Chief Executive: Frank Naef

Director: Rene Steichen

Executive Producer: Hubert Terheggen

Participating Countries: 19

Voting: Every participating country has a jury (11 members) that gives 1-8 points and then 10 and 12 points to its favourite song

Broadcaster: RTL Télévision (RTL)

Intermediate performance: Prague Theatre of Illuminated Drawings

Duration: 2 hours and 14 minutes

Broadcast: To all participating countries and to Iceland, Soviet Union, Romania, Hungary, East Germany, Czechoslovakia, Australia, Jordan, Tunisia and Morocco.

No.	Country	Song	Performing Artist	Lyrics	Composer	Conductor	Language	Commentator	Spoker of Results	Points	Place
01	Sweden	"Diggi-Loo Diggi-Ley"	Herreys (Per Herrey, Louis Herrey, Richard Herrey)	Britt Lindeborg	Torgny Söderberg	Curt-Eric Holmquist	Swedish	Fredrik Belfrage	Agneta Bolme Börjefors	145	1
02	Luxembourg	"100% d'amour"	Sophie Carle	Jean-Michel Beriat, Patrick James	Jean-Pierre Goussaud	Pascal Stive	French	Valérie Sarn, Jacques Navadic	Jacques Harvey	39	10
03	France	"Autant d'amoureux que d'étoiles"	Annick Thoumazeau	Charles Level	Vladimir Cosma	François Rauber	French	Léon Zitrone	Jacques Harvey	61	8
04	Spain	"Lady, Lady"	Bravo (Luis Vilar, Yolanda Hoyos, Esteban Santos)	Amaya Saizar	Miguel Blasco	Eddy Guerin	Spanish	José-Miguel Ullán	Matilde Jarrín	106	3
05	Norway	"Lenge leve livet"	Dollie de Luxe (Ingrid Bjørnov, Benedicte Adrian)	Benedicte Adrian, Ingrid Bjørnov	Benedicte Adrian, Ingrid Bjørnov	Sigurd Jansen	Norweigen	Roald Øyen	Egil Teige	29	17
06	United Kingdom	"Love Games"	Belle and the Devotions (Kit Rolfe, Laura James, Linda Sofield)	Paul Curtis and Graham Sacher	Paul Curtis and Graham Sacher	John Coleman	English	Terry Wogan	Colin Berry	63	7
07	Cyprus	"Anna Maria Lena"	Andy Paul	Andy Paul	Andy Paul	Pierre Cao	Greek	Pavlos Pavlou	Anna Partelidou	31	15
08	Belgium	"Avanti la vie"	Jacques Zegers	Jacques Zegers	Henri Seroka	Jo Carlier	French	Jacques Mercier, Luc Appermont	Jacques Olivier	70	5
09	Ireland	"Terminal 3"	Linda Martin	Johnny Logan	Johnny Logan	Noel Kelehan	English	Gay Byrne	John Skehan	137	2
10	Denmark	"Det' lige det"	Hot Eyes (Kirsten Siggaard, Søren Bundgaard)	Keld Heick	Søren Bundgaard	Henrik Krogsgaard	Danish	Jørgen de Mylius	Bent Henius	101	4
11	The Netherlands	"Ik hou van jou"	Maribelle	Peter van Asten, Richard de Bois	Peter van Asten, Richard de Bois	Rogier van Otterloo	Dutch	Ivo Niehe	Flip van der Schalie	34	13
12	Yugoslavia	"Ciao, amore"	Vlado & Isolda (Vlado Kalember, Izolda Barudžija)	Milan Perić	Slobodan Bućevac	Mato Došen	serb	Mladen Popović, Oliver Mlakar, Tomaž Terček	Snežana Lipkovska-Hadžinaumova	26	18
13	Austria	"Einfach weg"	Anita	Walter Müller	Brigitte Seuberth	Richard Österreicher	German	Ernst Grissemann	Tilia Herold	5	19
14	Germany	"Aufrecht geh'n"	Mary Roos	Michael Kunze	Michael Reinecke	Pierre Cao	German	Ado Schlier	Ruth Kappelsberger	34	14
15	Turkey	"Halay"	Beş Yıl Önce, On Yıl Sonra (Nilgün Onatkut, Mehmet Horoz Artakan Unuvar, Esma Erden)	Ülkü Aker	Selçuk Başar	Selçuk Başar	Turkish	Başak Doğru	Fatih Orbay	37	12
16	Finland	"Hengaillaan"	Kirka	Jussi Tuominen	Jukka Siikavire	Ossi Runne	Finish	- Heikki Seppälä	Solveig Herlin	46	9
17	Switzerland	"Welche Farbe hat der Sonnenschein?"	Rainy Day (Rose Rengel, Frank Müller, Gerry Braukmann)	Günther Loose	Günther Loose	Mario Robbiani	German	Bernard Thurnheer, Serge Moisson, Ezio Guidi	Michel Stocker	30	16
18	Italy	"I treni di Tozeur"	Alice & Franco Battiato	Franco Battiato Rosario "Saro" Cosentino	Franco Battiato Giusto Pio	Giusto Pio	Italian	Antonio De Robertis	Mariolina Cannuli	70	6
19	Portugal	"Silêncio e tanta gente"	Maria Guinot	Maria Guinot	Maria Guinot	Pedro Vaz Osório	Portuguese	Fialho Gouveia	Unknown	38	11

	Sweden	Luxembourg	France	Spain	Norway	United Kingdom	Cyprus	Belgium	Ireland	Denmark	The Netherlands	Yugoslavia	Austria	Germany	Turkey	Finland	Switzerland	Italy	Portugal	
Sweden	■	6	6	4	10	7	12	7	12	12	10	4	12	12	3	8	10	6	4	Sweden
Luxembourg	–	■	–	7	–	–	7	–	5	5	–	8	–	–	4	–	–	3	–	Luxembourg
France	2	–	■	–	2	6	3	10	–	–	12	–	8	–	–	–	4	7	7	France
Spain	10	8	10	■	6	4	6	3	7	7	2	2	6	–	12	–	3	8	12	Spain
Norway	8	7	–	–	■	–	–	1	3	–	–	–	–	2	–	6	2	–	–	Norway
United Kingdom	3	1	–	3	8	■	2	2	8	1	4	1	2	7	1	4	–	10	6	United Kingdom
Cyprus	4	–	1	–	–	–	■	–	4	10	–	12	–	–	–	–	–	–	–	Cyprus
Belgium	–	12	12	2	3	–	–	■	–	–	8	–	3	4	5	10	–	1	10	Belgium
Ireland	12	5	3	10	4	8	10	12	■	3	7	–	10	10	10	7	12	12	2	Ireland
Denmark	5	3	8	6	12	12	5	8	10	■	3	6	4	5	2	5	1	5	1	Denmark
The Netherlands	–	2	7	8	–	1	–	–	6	–	■	5	–	–	–	–	5	–	–	The Netherlands
Yugoslavia	–	–	2	–	–	3	8	–	–	–	–	■	–	3	8	2	–	–	–	Yugoslavia
Austria	–	–	–	–	–	–	–	–	1	4	–	–	■	–	–	–	–	–	–	Austria
Germany	–	–	4	–	7	2	–	6	–	2	5	–	1	■	–	–	–	2	5	Germany
Turkey	6	–	–	–	–	5	–	4	2	–	1	10	–	–	■	3	6	–	–	Turkey
Finland	7	–	5	1	5	–	4	–	–	6	–	3	5	1	6	■	–	–	3	Finland
Switzerland	1	–	–	–	–	10	1	5	–	8	–	–	–	–	–	1	■	4	–	Switzerland
Italy	–	10	–	12	1	–	–	–	–	–	–	–	7	6	7	12	7	■	8	Italy
Portugal	–	4	–	5	–	–	–	–	–	–	6	7	–	8	–	–	8	–	■	Portugal

Hosting Country: Sweden

Hosting City: Gothenburg

Date: 4.5.1985

Location: Scandinavium

Presenter: Lill Lindfors

Orchestra Conductor: Curt-Eric Holmquist

Chief Executive: Frank Naef

Director: Steen Priwin

Executive Producer: Steen Priwin

Participating Countries: 19

Voting: Every participating country has a jury (11 members) that gives 1-8 points and then 10 and 12 points to its favourite song

Broadcaster: Sveriges Television (SVT)

Intermediate performance: Guitars Unlimited with Swedish Evergreens

Duration: 2 hours and 47 minutes

Broadcast: To all participating countries and to The Netherlands, Iceland, Poland, Yugoslavia, Australia and Soviet Union.

No.	Country	Song	Performing Artist	Lyrics	Composer	Conductor	Language	Commentator	Spoker of Results	Points	Place
01	Ireland	"Wait Until the Weekend Comes"	Maria Christian	Brendan J. Graham	Brendan J. Graham	Noel Kelehan	English	Linda Martin	John Skehan	91	6
02	Finland	"Eläköön elämä"	Sonja Lumme	Veli-Pekka Lehto	Petri Laaksonen	Ossi Runne	Finish	Heikki Harma & Kari Lumikero	Annemi Genetz	58	9
03	Cyprus	"To katalava arga"	Lia Vissi	Lia Vissi	Lia Vissi	Haris Andreadis	Greek	Themis Themistokleous	Annemi Genetz	15	17
04	Denmark	"Sku' du spørg' fra no'en?"	Hot Eyes (Kirsten Siggaard, Søren Bundgaard)	Keld Heick	Søren Bundgaard	Wolfgang Käfer	Danish	Jørgen de Mylius	Bent Henius	41	11
05	Spain	"La fiesta terminó"	Paloma San Basilio	Juan Carlos Calderón	Juan Carlos Calderón	Juan Carlos Calderón	Spanish	Antonio Gómez	Matilde Jarrín	36	15
06	France	"Femme dans ses rêves aussi"	Roger Bens	Didier Pascalis	Didier Pascalis	Michel Bernholc	French	Patrice Laffont	Clémentine Célarié	56	10
07	Turkey	"Didai didai dai"	MFÖ (Mazhar Alanson, Fuat Güner, Özkan Uğur)	Mazhar Alanson Fuat Güner, Özkan Uğur	Mazhar Alanson Fuat Güner, Özkan Uğur	Garo Mafyan	Turkish	Başak Doğru	Fatih Orbay	36	14
08	Belgium	"Laat me nu gaan"	Linda Lepomme	Bert Vivier	Pieter Verlinden	Curt-Eric Holmquist	Flemish	Luc Appermont, Jacques Mercier	An Ploegaerts	7	19
09	Portugal	"Penso em ti, eu sei"	Adelaide	Adelaide, Luís Fernando	Tozé Brito	José Calvario	Portuguese	Eládio Clímaco	Maria Margarida Gaspar	9	18
10	Germany	"Für alle"	Wind (Rainer Höglmeier, Petra Scheeser, Sami Kalifa, Willi Jakob, Alexander 'Ala' Heiler)	Hanne Haller	Hanne Haller	Reiner Pietsch	German	Ado Schlier	Christoph Deumling	105	2
11	Israel	"Oleh Oleh"	Izhar Cohen	Hamutal Ben-Zeev	Kobi Oshrat	Kobi Oshrat	Hebrew	-	Yitzhak Shimoni	93	5
12	Italy	"Magic Oh Magic"	Al Bano & Romina Power	Cristiano Minellono	Dario Farina, Michael Hoffmann	Fiorenzo Zanotti	Italian	Rosanna Vaudetti	Beatrice Cori	78	7
13	Norway	"La det swinge"	Bobbysocks! (Hanne Krogh, Elisabeth Andréassen)	Rolf Løvland	Rolf Løvland	Terje Fjærn	Norweigen	Veslemøy Kjendsli	Erik Diesen	123	1
14	United Kingdom	"Love Is…"	Vikki WATSON	James Kaleth and Vikki Watson	James Kaleth and Vikki Watson	John Coleman	English	Terry Wogan	Colin Berry	100	4
15	Switzerland	"Piano, piano"	Mariella Farré & Pino Gasparini	Trudi Müller-Bosshard	Anita Kerr	Anita Kerr	German	Bernard Thurnheer, Serge Moisson, Ezio Guidi	Michel Stocker	39	12
16	Sweden	"Bra vibrationer"	Kikki Danielsson	Ingela Forsman	Lasse Holm	Curt-Eric Holmquist	Swedish	Fredrik Belfrage	Agneta Bolme-Börjefors	103	3
17	Austria	"Kinder dieser Welt"	Gary Lux	Michael Kunze	Mick Jackson, Geoff Bastow	Richard Österreicher	German	Ernst Grissemann	Chris Lohner	60	8
18	Luxembourg	"Children, Kinder, Enfants"	Margo, Franck Olivier, Diane Solomon, Ireen Sheer, Chris & Malcolm Roberts	Bernd Meinunger, Jean-Michel Bériat	Ralph Siegel	Norbert Daum	French	Valérie Sarn	Frédérique Ries	37	13
19	Greece	"Miazoume"	Takis Biniaris	Takis Biniaris	Takis Biniaris	Haris Andreadis	Greek	Mako Georgiadou	Synia Kousoula	15	16

1985

	Ireland	Finland	Cyprus	Denmark	Spain	France	Turkey	Belgium	Portugal	Germany	Israel	Italy	Norway	United Kingdom	Switzerland	Sweden	Austria	Luxembourg	Greece
Greece	–	10	8	–	6	12	–	–	7	–	2	–	1	4	3	–	5	–	■
Luxembourg	–	–	–	–	1	3	–	–	–	10	6	12	7	8	2	5	4	■	–
Austria	3	–	–	5	–	3	–	–	–	–	7	6	12	2	1	4	■	8	–
Sweden	10	10	–	5	–	6	–	–	–	8	2	–	12	4	1	■	3	–	–
Switzerland	–	2	3	–	–	4	12	–	–	–	7	–	6	10	■	8	1	–	–
United Kingdom	5	7	–	–	4	2	8	–	–	1	5	–	12	■	–	6	10	–	–
Norway	12	–	–	6	–	–	1	–	–	8	10	–	■	7	5	12	2	4	–
Italy	–	7	3	2	–	10	–	–	–	–	5	■	6	8	–	4	–	1	–
Israel	8	1	–	–	–	3	–	–	–	7	■	4	12	2	–	6	10	5	–
Germany	4	–	–	6	–	–	2	–	–	■	7	–	12	5	1	6	10	3	–
Portugal	–	–	–	1	2	3	–	–	■	7	5	12	–	6	4	–	–	10	–
Belgium	–	–	–	3	–	–	1	■	–	10	–	2	12	6	5	7	4	–	–
Turkey	7	3	–	–	12	1	■	7	2	–	–	8	–	10	6	4	–	–	–
France	–	–	–	10	–	■	–	–	–	8	12	5	2	6	–	7	1	4	–
Spain	2	6	–	–	■	–	3	–	–	10	8	12	1	5	–	2	–	–	7
Denmark	–	–	–	■	–	–	–	–	–	10	4	1	12	5	6	8	7	2	–
Cyprus	1	6	■	3	1	4	–	–	–	12	5	10	–	–	2	–	–	–	8
Finland	6	■	–	–	8	5	2	–	–	10	–	6	4	7	3	12	–	–	–
Ireland	■	6	1	–	2	–	7	–	–	4	8	–	12	5	–	10	3	–	–

Hosting Country: Norway

Hosting City: Bergen

Date: 3.5.1986

Location: Grieghallen

Presenter: Åse Kleveland

Orchestra Conductor: Egil Monn-Iversen

Chief Executive: Frank Naef

Director: John Andreassen

Executive Producer: Per Selstrom

Participating Countries: 20

Voting: Every participating country has a jury (11 members) that gives 1-8 points and then 10 and 12 points to its favourite song

Broadcaster: Norsk rikskringkasting (NRK)

Intermediate performance: "Bergensiana" performed by Sissel Kyrkjebø and Steinar Ofsdal

Duration: 2 hours and 44 minutes

Broadcast: To all participating countries and to Greece, Romania, Poland, East Germany, Australia, Canada and Soviet Union.

1986

No.	Country	Song	Performing Artist	Lyrics	Composer	Conductor	Language	Commentator	Spoker of Results	Points	Place
01	Luxembourg	"L'amour de ma vie"	Sherisse Laurence	Frank Dostal, Alain Garcia	Rolf Soja	Rolf Soja	French	Valérie Sarn	Frédérique Ries	117	3
02	Yugoslavia	"Željo moja"	Doris Dragović	Zrinko Tutić	Zrinko Tutić	Nikica Kalogjera	Croatian	Mladen Popović, Ksenija Urličić, Miša Molk	Enver Petrovci	49	11
03	France	"Européennes"	Cocktail Chic (Catherine Bonnevay, Francine Chanterau, Martine Latorre, Dominique Poulain)	Georges Costa, Michel Costa, Daniel Costa	Georges Costa, Michel Costa	Jean-Claude Petit	French	Patrice Laffont	Patricia Lesieur	13	17
04	Norway	"Romeo"	Ketil Stokkan	Ketil Stokkan	Ketil Stokkan	Egil Monn-Iversen	Norweigen	Knut Bjørnsen	Nina Matheson	44	12
05	United Kingdom	"Runner in the Night"	Ryder (Maynard Williams, Dudley Phillips, Paul Robertson, Andy Ebsworth, Geoff Leach, and Rob)	Maureen Darbyshire	Brian Wade	-	Spanish	Terry Wogan	Colin Berry	72	7
06	Iceland	"Gleðibankinn"	ICY (Helga Möller, Eiríkur Hauksson, Pálmi Gunnarsson)	Magnús Eiríksson	Magnús Eiríksson	Gunnar Þórðarsson	Icelandic	Þorgeir Ástvaldsson	Guðrún Skúladóttir	19	16
07	The Netherlands	"Alles heeft ritme"	Frizzle Sizzle (Karin Vlasblom, Laura Vlasblom, Mandy Huydts, Marjon Keller)	Peter Schön	Peter Schön, Rob Ten Bokum	Harry van Hoof	Dutch	Leo van der Goot	Joop van Zijl	40	13
08	Turkey	"Halley"	Klips ve Onlar (Candan Erçetin Sevingül Bahadır, Gür Akad Derya Bozkurt, Emre Tukur)	İlhan İrem	Melih Kibar	Melih Kibar	Turkish	Gülgün Baysal	Ümit Tunçağ	53	9
09	Spain	"Valentino"	Cadillac (José María Guzmán Daniel J. Louis, Pedro A. Sanchéz)	José María Guzmán	José María Guzmán	Eduardo Leiva	Spanish	Antonio Gómez Mateo	Matilde Jarrín	51	10
10	Switzerland	"Pas pour moi"	Daniela Simmons	Nella Martinetti	Atilla Şereftuğ	Atilla Şereftuğ	French	Bernard Thurnheer, Serge Moisson, Ezio Guidi	Michel Stocker	140	2
11	Israel	"Yavo Yom"	Sarai Zuriel and Moti Giladi	Moti Giladi	Yoram Zadok	Yoram Zadok	Hebrew	-	Yitzhak Shimoni	7	19
12	Ireland	"You Can Count On Me"	Luv Bug (June Cunningham, Hugh Cunningham, Max Cunningham, Majella Grant, Ricky Meyler)	Kevin Sheerin	Kevin Sheerin	Noel Kelehan	English	Brendan Balfe	John Skehan	96	4
13	Belgium	"J'aime la vie"	Sandra Kim	Rosario Marino	Jean Paul Furnémon, Angelo Crisci	Jo Carlier	French	Patrick Duhamel, Luc Appermont	Jacques Olivier	176	1
14	Germany	"Über die Brücke geh'n"	Ingrid Peters	Hans Blum	Hans Blum	Hans Blum	German	Ado Schlier	Christoph Deumling	62	8
15	Cyprus	"Tora zo"	Elpida	Peter Yiannakis, Fivos Gavris	Peter Yiannakis	Martyn Ford	Greek	Neophytos Taliotis	Anna Partelidou	4	20
16	Austria	"Die Zeit ist einsam"	Timna Brauer	Peter Cornelius	Peter Janda	Richard Öster-reicher	German	Ernst Grissemann	Tilia Herold	12	18
17	Sweden	"E' de' det här du kallar kärlek?"	Lasse Holm & Monica Törnell	Lasse Holm	Lasse Holm	Anders Berglund	Swedish	Ulf Elfving	Agneta Bolme-Börjefors	78	5
18	Denmark	"Du er fuld af løgn"	Lise Haavik	John Hatting	John Hatting	Egil Monn-Iversen	Danish	Jørgen de Mylius	Bent Henius	77	6
19	Finland	"Never the End"	Kari Kuivalainen	Kari Kuivalainen	Kari Kuivalainen	Ossi Runne	Finish	Heikki Harma and Kari Lumikero	Solveig Herlin	22	15
20	Portugal	"Não sejas mau para mim"	Dora	Guilherme Inês, Zé Da Ponte, Luís Manuel de Oliveira Fernandes	Guilherme Inês, Zé Da Ponte, Luís Manuel de Oliveira Fernandes	Colin Frechter	Portuguese	Fialho Gouveia	Margarida Andrade	28	14

	Luxembourg	Yugoslavia	France	Norway	United Kingdom	Iceland	The Netherlands	Turkey	Spain	Switzerland	Israel	Ireland	Belgium	Germany	Cyprus	Austria	Sweden	Denmark	Finland	Portugal	
Luxembourg	■	5	8	12	8	1	8	–	–	2	4	7	10	12	8	10	10	2	4	6	Luxembourg
Yugoslavia	2	■	–	–	7	5	7	3	3	–	1	3	4	–	12	1	1	–	–	–	Yugoslavia
France	–	–	■	3	–	–	–	–	–	7	–	–	–	–	–	–	3	–	–	–	France
Norway	–	–	4	■	–	4	2	–	–	6	–	6	5	6	6	–	–	5	–	–	Norway
United Kingdom	4	–	10	6	■	–	–	6	2	4	2	–	–	5	2	3	8	8	10	2	United Kingdom
Iceland	–	–	–	–	–	■	5	2	6	–	–	–	–	–	4	–	2	–	–	–	Iceland
The Netherlands	1	2	–	–	–	–	■	7	1	–	8	–	–	10	1	–	–	–	3	7	The Netherlands
Turkey	6	12	–	–	2	–	6	■	–	8	3	–	6	8	–	2	–	–	–	–	Turkey
Spain	7	4	6	–	1	2	–	8	■	1	–	5	3	–	–	7	–	3	1	3	Spain
Switzerland	12	6	7	5	5	3	12	10	4	■	12	10	12	–	5	4	12	4	7	10	Switzerland
Israel	–	–	1	1	–	–	–	–	–	5	■	–	–	–	–	–	–	–	–	–	Israel
Ireland	3	8	3	2	–	8	–	5	12	–	6	■	2	–	–	12	7	12	8	8	Ireland
Belgium	10	10	12	8	10	10	10	12	10	10	5	12	■	1	10	6	6	10	12	12	Belgium
Germany	8	1	–	–	12	–	–	–	–	–	–	8	7	■	–	8	5	7	2	4	Germany
Cyprus	–	3	–	–	–	–	–	–	–	–	–	1	–	–	■	–	–	–	–	–	Cyprus
Austria	–	–	–	–	–	–	–	–	–	–	–	2	1	2	–	■	–	–	6	1	Austria
Sweden	5	7	2	7	3	12	3	–	7	12	–	–	–	4	–	5	■	6	5	–	Sweden
Denmark	–	–	5	10	6	7	4	–	5	3	10	4	–	7	7	–	4	■	–	5	Denmark
Finland	–	–	–	–	–	6	1	1	–	–	–	–	–	8	3	3	–	–	■	–	Finland
Portugal	–	–	–	4	4	–	–	4	8	–	7	–	–	–	–	–	–	–	1	■	Portugal

1987

Hosting Country: Belgium

Hosting City: Brussles

Date: 9.5.1987

Location: Palais du Centenaire

Presenter: Viktor Lazlo

Orchestra Conductor: Jo Carlier

Chief Executive: Frank Naef

Director: Jacques Bourton

Executive Producer: Michel Gehu

Participating Countries: 22

Voting: Every participating country has a jury (11 members) that gives 1-8 points and then 10 and 12 points to its favourite song

Broadcaster: Radio Télévision Belge Francophone (RTBF)

Intermediate performance: Mark Grauwels

Duration: 2 hours and 59 minutes

Broadcast: To all participating countries and to Poland, Hungary, Australia, Soviet Union and Jordan

No.	Country	Song	Performing Artist	Lyrics	Composer	Conductor	Language	Commentator	Spoker of Results	Points	Place
01	Norway	"Mitt liv"	Kate Gulbrandsen	Rolf Løvland, Hanne Krogh	Rolf Løvland	Terje Fjærn	Norweigen	John Andreassen and Tor Paulsen	Roald Øyen	65	9
02	Israel	"Shir Habatlanim"	Natan Datner and Avi Kushnir	Zohar Laskov	Zohar Laskov	Kobi Oshrat	Hebrew	-	Yitzhak Shimoni	73	8
03	Austria	"Nur noch Gefühl"	Gary Lux	Stefanie Werger	Kenneth Westmore	Richard Österreicher	German	Ernst Grissemann	Hans Leitinger	8	20
04	Iceland	"Hægt og hljótt"	Halla Margrét	Valgeir Guðjónsson	Valgeir Guðjónsson	Hjálmar Ragnarsson	Icelandic	Knut Bjørnsen	Nina Matheson	28	16
05	Belgium	"Soldiers of Love"	Liliane Saint-Pierre	Liliane Keuninckx (Liliane Saint-Pierre)	Gyuri Spies, Marc de Coen	Freddy Sunder	Flemish	Luc Appermont and Claude Delacroix	An Ploegaerts	56	11
06	Sweden	"Boogaloo"	Lotta Engberg	Christer Lundh	Mikael Wendt	Curt-Eric Holmquist	Swedish	Fredrik Belfrage	Jacob Dahlin	50	12
07	Italy	"Gente di mare"	Umberto Tozzi & Raf	Giancarlo Bigazzi	Umberto Tozzi, Raf	Gianfranco Lombardi	Italian	Rosanna Vaudetti	Antonio De Robertis	103	3
08	Portugal	"Neste barco à vela"	Nevada	Alfredo Azinheira	Alfredo Azinheira, Jorge Mendes	Jaime Oliveira	Portuguese	Maria Margarida Gaspar	Ana Zanatti	15	18
09	Spain	"No estás solo"	Patricia Kraus	Patricia Kraus	Rafael Martínez, Rafael Trabucchelli	Eduardo Leiva	Spanish	Beatriz Pécker	Matilde Jarrín	10	19
10	Turkey	"Şarkım Sevgi Üstüne"	Seyyal Taner & Lokomotif	Olcayto Ahmet Tuğsuz	Olcayto Ahmet Tuğsuz	Garo Mafyan	Turkish	Gülgün Baysal	Canan Kumbasar	0	22
11	Greece	"Stop"	Bang (Thanos Kalliris, Vasilis Dertilis)	Thanos Kalliris, Vasilis Dertilis	Thanos Kalliris Vasilis Dertilis	Yiorgos Niarchos	Greek	Dafni Bokota	Synia Kousoula	64	10
12	The Netherlands	"Rechtop in de wind"	Marcha	Peter Koelewijn	Peter Koelewijn	Rogier van Otterloo	Dutch	Willem van Beusekom	Ralph Inbar	83	5
13	Luxembourg	"Amour, amour"	Plastic Bertrand	Roger Jouret, Alec Mansion	Roger Jouret, Alec Mansion	Alec Mansion	French	Valérie Sarn	Frédérique Ries	21	4
14	United Kingdom	"Only the Light"	Rikki (Richard Peebles)	Richard Peebles	Richard Peebles	Ronnie Hazlehurst	English	Terry Wogan	Colin Berry	47	13
15	France	"Les mots d'amour n'ont pas de dimanche"	Christine Minier	Marc Minier	Gerard Curci	Jean-Claude Petit	French	Patrick Simpson-Jones	Lionel Cassan	44	14
16	Germany	"Lass die Sonne in dein Herz"	Wind (Andi Lebbing, Petra Scheeser, Christiane von Kutzsenbach, Sami Kalifa, Alexander 'Ala' Heiler)	Bernd Meinunger	Ralph Siegel	Laszlo Bencker	German	Lotti Ohnesorge and Christoph Deumling	Gabi Schnelle	141	2
17	Cyprus	"Aspro-mavro"	Alexia	Maria Papapaulou	Andreas Papapaulou	Jo Carlier	Greek	Fryni Papadopoulou	Anna Partelidou	80	7
18	Finland	"Sata salamaa"	Vicky Rosti & Boulevard	Veli-Pekka Lehto	Petri Laaksonen	Ossi Runne	Finish	Erkki Toivanen	Solveig Herlin	32	15
19	Denmark	"En lille melodi"	Anne-Cathrine Herdorf & Bandjo	Jacob Jonia	Helge Engelbrecht	Henrik Krogsgaard	Danish	Jørgen de Mylius	Bent Henius	83	6
20	Ireland	"Hold Me Now"	Johnny Logan	Johnny Logan	Johnny Logan	Noel Kelehan	English	Marty Whelan	Brendan Balfe	172	1
21	Yugoslavia	"Ja sam za ples"	Novi fosili (Sanja Doležal, Rajko Dujmić, Vladimir Kočis-Zec, Marinko Colnago, Nenad Šarić)	Stevo Cvikić	Rajko Dujmić	Nikica Kalogjera	Croatian	Ksenija Urličić and Miša Molk	Ljiljana Tipsarević	92	4
22	Switzerland	"Moitié, moitié"	Carol Rich	Jean-Jacques Egli	Jean-Jacques Egli	-	French	Bernard Thurnheer, Serge Moisson, Ezio Guidi	Michel Stocker	26	17

	Norway	Israel	Austria	Iceland	Belgium	Sweden	Italy	Portugal	Spain	Turkey	Greece	The Netherlands	Luxembourg	United Kingdom	France	Germany	Cyprus	Finland	Denmark	Ireland	Yugoslavia	Switzerland
Switzerland	6	8	–	–	–	–	7	–	–	–	–	10	–	5	2	1	4	–	3	12	–	■
Yugoslavia	–	–	–	–	4	–	12	–	–	–	5	8	–	2	–	7	10	1	–	6	■	3
Ireland	2	5	–	–	–	–	12	–	–	–	–	6	–	3	10	7	8	–	4	■	1	–
Denmark	3	–	–	–	–	7	–	–	–	–	6	2	–	4	–	12	10	–	■	5	8	1
Finland	5	7	–	–	3	–	4	–	–	–	–	2	–	1	–	10	6	■	8	12	–	–
Cyprus	3	–	–	–	5	7	1	–	–	–	12	–	–	2	–	6	■	–	–	8	10	4
Germany	7	8	–	10	4	–	12	2	–	–	–	–	–	5	–	■	3	1	–	6	–	–
France	4	10	–	–	–	3	–	–	–	–	7	6	12	8	■	5	–	–	–	1	2	–
United Kingdom	–	4	–	–	8	–	1	–	–	–	5	3	2	■	6	10	–	–	7	12	–	–
Luxembourg	–	–	–	–	5	–	4	–	–	–	7	8	■	1	12	6	–	2	–	10	–	3
The Netherlands	4	3	–	–	–	–	–	–	–	–	5	■	–	–	1	10	2	8	6	12	–	7
Greece	–	–	7	6	–	–	–	5	10	–	■	3	–	–	4	–	12	1	8	–	2	–
Turkey	–	–	–	–	4	2	8	–	–	■	–	7	–	3	6	–	–	–	1	10	12	5
Spain	3	–	–	4	7	–	12	8	■	–	5	–	–	–	1	–	–	2	–	10	6	–
Portugal	–	10	–	–	–	7	12	■	–	–	–	2	–	3	5	–	–	4	1	8	6	–
Italy	7	–	1	–	6	3	■	–	–	–	8	10	–	4	5	–	–	–	2	12	–	–
Sweden	10	4	–	–	–	■	1	–	–	–	6	–	–	5	–	7	2	3	8	12	–	–
Belgium	7	6	–	4	■	1	5	–	–	–	2	–	3	–	–	10	–	–	–	12	8	–
Iceland	–	5	–	■	–	8	3	–	–	–	1	–	–	–	4	12	6	–	7	–	10	2
Austria	4	1	■	–	3	–	6	–	–	–	–	–	5	2	10	–	–	–	7	12	8	–
Israel	–	■	–	–	2	12	3	–	–	–	–	5	–	10	–	8	–	–	6	4	7	1
Norway	■	2	–	4	5	–	–	–	–	–	–	–	–	–	1	3	6	10	7	8	12	–

1988

Hosting Country: Ireland

Hosting City: Dublin

Date: 30.4.1988

Location: RDS Simmonscourt Pavilion

Presenters: Pat Kenny

Michelle Rocca

Orchestra Conductor: Noel Kelehan

Chief Executive: Frank Naef

Director: Declan Lowney

Executive Producer: Liam Miller

Participating Countries: 21

Every participating country has a jury (16 members) that gives 1-8 points and then 10 and 12 points to its favourite song

Broadcaster: Raidió Teilifís Éireann (RTÉ)

Intermediate performance: Hothouse Flowers performing "Don't Go"

Duration: 2 hours and 50 minutes

Broadcast: To all participating countries and to Cyprus, Poland, Hungary, Australia, Soviet Union, United States of America, Jordan.

No.	Country	Song	Performing Artist	Lyrics	Composer	Conductor	Language	Commentator	Spoker of Results	Points	Place
01	Iceland	Sókrates""	Beethoven (Stefán Hilmarsson, Sverrir Stormsker)	Sverrir Stormsker	Sverrir Stormsker	-	Icelandic	Hermann Gunnarsson	Guðrún Skúladóttir	20	16
02	Sweden	"Stad i ljus"	Tommy Körberg	Py Bäckman	Py Bäckman	Anders Berglund	Swedish	Bengt Grafström	Maud Uppling	52	12
03	Finland	"Nauravat silmät muistetaan"	Boulevard (Kyösti Lajhi, Juha Lanu, Jari Njeminen, Tommi Tepsa, Erkki Korhonen, Jari Puhakka)	Kirsti Willberg	Pepe Willberg	Ossi Runne	Finish	Erkki Pohjanheimo	Solveig Herlin	3	20
04	United Kingdom	"Go"	Scott Fitzgerald	Julie Forsyth	Julie Forsyth	Ronnie Hazlehurst	English	Terry Wogan	Colin Berry	136	2
05	Turkey	"Sufi"	MFÖ (Mazhar Alanson, Fuat Güner, Özkan Uğur)	Mazhar Alanson	Mazhar Alanson, Fuat Güner, Özkan Uğur	Turhan Yükseler	Turkish	Bülend Özveren	Canan Kumbasar	37	15
06	Spain	"La chica que yo quiero (Made in Spain)"	La Década (Carmelo Martínez José Subiza, Cecilia Blanco, Ana Nery Fragoso, Manolo Aguilar, Manuel Santistéban)	Francisco Dondiego	Enrique Peiró	Javier de Juan	Spanish	Beatriz Pécker	Matilde Jarrín	58	11
07	The Netherlands	"Shangri-La"	Gerard Joling	Peter de Wijn	Peter de Wijn	Harry van Hoof	Dutch	Willem van Beusekom	Joop van Os	70	9
08	Israel	"Ben Adam"	Yardena Arazi	Ehud Manor	Boris Dimidstein	Eldad Shrem	Hebrew	-	Yitzhak Shimoni	85	7
09	Switzerland	"Ne partez pas sans moi"	Céline Dion	Nella Martinetti	Atilla Şereftuğ	Atilla Şereftuğ	French	Bernard Thurnheer, Serge Moisson, Ezio Guidi	Michel Stocker	137	1
10	Ireland	"Take Him Home"	Jump the Gun (Eric Sharpe Ciaran Wilde, Roy Taylor Brian O'Reilly, Peter Eades)	Peter Eades	Peter Eades	Noel Kelehan	English	Mike Murphy	John Skehan	79	8
11	Germany	"Lied für einen Freund"	Maxi & Chris Garden	Bernd Meinunger	Ralph Siegel	Michael Thatcher	German	Nicole and Claus-Erich Boetzkes	Corry von Kiel	48	14
12	Austria	"Lisa Mona Lisa"	Wilfried Scheutz	Klaus Kofler, Wilfried Scheutz, Ronnie Herboltzheimer	Klaus Kofler, Wilfried Scheutz, Ronnie Herboltzheimer	Harald Neuwirth	German	Ernst Grissemann	Tilia Herold	0	21
13	Denmark	"Ka' du se hva' jeg sa'?"	Hot Eyes (Kirsten Siggaard, Søren Bundgaard)	Keld Heick	Søren Bundgaard	Henrik Krogsgaard	Danish	Jørgen de Mylius	Bent Henius	92	3
14	Greece	"Clown"	Afroditi Frida	Dimitris Saksilis	Dimitris Saksilis	Haris Andreadis	Greek	Dafni Bokota	Fotini Giannou-latou	10	17
15	Norway	"For vår jord"	Karoline Krüger	Erik Hillestad	Anita Skorgan	Arild Stav	Norway	John Andreassen	Andreas Diesen	88	5
16	Belgium	"Laissez briller le soleil"	Reynaert	Joseph Reynaerts, Philippe Anciaux	Joseph Reynaerts, Dany Willem	Dany Willem	French	Pierre Collard-Bovy and Luc Appermont	Jacques Olivier	5	19
17	Luxembourg	"Croire"	Lara Fabian	Alain Garcia	Jacques Cardona	Régis Dupré	French	Valérie Sarn	Jean-Luc Bertrand	90	4
18	Italy	"Vivo (Ti scrivo)"	Luca Barbarossa	Luca Barbarossa	Luca Barbarossa	-	Italian	Daniele Piombi	Mariolina Cannuli	52	12
19	France	"Chanteur de charme"	Gérard Lenorman	Gérard Lenorman, Claude Lemesle	Gérard Lenorman	Guy Mattéoni	French	Lionel Cassan	Catherine Ceylac	64	10
20	Portugal	"Voltarei"	Dora	José Niza, José Calvário	José Niza, José Calvário	José Calvário	Portuguese	Margarida Andrade	Maria Margarida Gaspar	5	18
21	Yugoslavia	"Mangup"	Srebrna krila (Lidija Asanović, Mustafa "Muc" Ismailovski, Slavko Pintarić, Vlatka Pokos, Vlatka Grakalić, Barbara Vujević)	Rajko Dujmić, Stevo Cvikić	Rajko Dujmić	Nikica Kalogjera	Croatian	Mladen Popović, Oliver Mlakar, Marjeta Kersič Svetel	Miša Molk	87	6

	Iceland	Sweden	Finland	United Kingdom	Turkey	Spain	The Netherlands	Israel	Switzerland	Ireland	Germany	Austria	Denmark	Greece	Norway	Belgium	Luxembourg	Italy	France	Portugal	Yugoslavia	
Iceland	■	1	–	–	–	–	4	–	–	–	–	–	4	–	–	–	–	1	2	8	–	Iceland
Sweden	3	■	–	2	–	–	8	–	–	5	–	–	8	–	12	1	3	10	–	–	–	Sweden
Finland	–	–	■	–	–	–	=	3	–	5	–	–	8	–	12	1	3	10	–	–	–	Finland
United Kingdom	1	5	10	■	12	10	–	10	5	7	10	10	10	6	5	12	8	12	–	3	–	United Kingdom
Turkey	–	4	–	1	■	5	1	8	–	–	8	–	–	–	–	–	4	–	6	–	–	Turkey
Spain	2	–	–	–	5	■	–	2	6	–	–	8	1	8	2	6	6	8	–	–	4	Spain
The Netherlands	–	–	–	6	6	–	■	7	7	2	6	–	–	12	–	–	12	5	–	–	7	The Netherlands
Israel	6	–	6	4	–	6	3	■	10	1	5	2	–	3	–	10	5	3	10	10	1	Israel
Switzerland	7	12	5	10	10	8	10	4	■	10	12	–	–	10	8	4	1	7	1	12	6	Switzerland
Ireland	–	7	2	3	2	12	6	–	4	■	7	6	7	–	7	5	–	–	4	5	2	Ireland
Germany	8	–	–	5	1	3	–	5	–	6	■	–	6	–	4	–	–	–	–	2	8	Germany
Austria	–	–	–	–	–	–	–	–	–	–	–	■	–	–	–	–	–	–	–	–	–	Austria
Denmark	10	3	4	–	–	1	12	6	1	4	4	12	■	–	10	7	–	–	12	6	–	Denmark
Greece	–	–	–	–	3	–	–	–	–	–	–	–	–	■	–	–	–	–	7	–	–	Greece
Norway	5	8	7	12	–	–	7	1	–	8	1	3	5	7	■	3	–	4	–	7	10	Norway
Belgium	–	–	–	–	–	–	–	–	–	–	–	–	–	–	–	■	–	–	5	–	–	Belgium
Luxembourg	4	10	12	7	–	–	5	–	12	12	–	1	2	2	6	8	■	2	–	4	3	Luxembourg
Italy	–	–	8	–	4	7	–	–	8	–	2	5	–	–	3	–	2	■	8	–	5	Italy
France	–	2	3	–	8	2	2	–	3	–	3	7	3	5	1	2	10	–	■	1	12	France
Portugal	–	–	–	–	–	4	–	–	–	–	–	–	–	–	1	–	–	–	–	■	–	Portugal
Yugoslavia	12	6	1	8	7	–	–	12	2	3	–	4	12	4	–	–	7	6	3	–	■	Yugoslavia

1989

Hosting Country: Switzerland

Hosting City: Lausanne

Date: 6.5.1989

Location: Palais de Beaulieu

Presenters: Jacques Deschenaux, Lolita Morena

Orchestra Conductor: Benoit Kaufman

Chief Executive: Frank Naef

Director: Alain Bloch, Charles-André Grivet

Executive Producer: Raymond Zumsteg

Participating Countries: 22

Every participating country has a jury (16 members) that gives 1-8 points and then 10 and 12 points to its favourite song

Broadcaster: SRG SSR idée suisse (SRG SSR)

Intermediate performance: Guy Tell

Duration: 3 hours and 13 minutes

Broadcast: To all participating countries and to Poland, Hungary, Australia, Soviet Union, Romania, Canada, Japan and Jordan.

No.	Country	Song	Performing Artist	Lyrics	Composer	Conductor	Language	Commentator	Spoker of Results	Points	Place
01	Italy	"Avrei voluto"	Anna Oxa & Fausto Leali	Franco Ciani, Fabrizio Berlincioni	Franco Fasano	Mario Natale	Italian	Gabriella Carlucci	Pepi Franzelin	56	10
02	Israel	"Derech Hamelech"	Gili (Netanel) & Galit (Borg)	Shaike Paikov	Shaike Paikov	Shaike Paikov	Hebrew	-	Yitzhak Shimoni	50	12
03	Ireland	"The Real Me"	Kiev Connolly & The Missing Passengers	Kiev Connolly	Kiev Connolly	Noel Kelehan	English	Ronan Collins and Michelle Rocca	Eileen Dunne	21	18
04	The Netherlands	"Blijf zoals je bent"	Justine Pelmelay	Cees Bergman, Geertjan Hessing, Aart Mol, Erwin van Prehn, Elmer Veerhoff	Jan Kisjes	Harry van Hoof	Dutch	Willem van Beusekom	Joop van Os	45	15
05	Turkey	"Bana Bana"	Pan (Hazal Selçuk, Arzu Ece, Sarper Semiz, Vedat Sakman)	Timur Selçuk	Timur Selçuk	Timur Selçuk	Turkish	Bülend Özveren	Canan Kumbasar	5	21
06	Belgium	"Door de wind"	Ingeborg	Stef Bos	Stef Bos	Freddy Sunder	Flemish	Luc Appermont and Jacques Mercier	An Ploegaerts	13	19
07	United Kingdom	"Why Do I Always Get It Wrong?"	Live Report (Ray Caruana, John Beeby, Brian Hodgson, Maggie Jay, Mike Bell, Peter May)	Brian Hodgson, John Beeby	Brian Hodgson, John Beeby	Ronnie Hazlehurst	English	Terry Wogan	Colin Berry	130	2
08	Norway	"Venners nærhet"	Britt Synnøve Johansen	Leiv N. Grøtte	Inge Enoksen	Pete Knutsen	Norweigen	John Andreassen	Sverre Christophersen	30	17
09	Portugal	"Conquistador"	"Da Vinci" (Iei Or, Pedro Luís Neves, Ricardo, Joaquim Andradé, Dora Fidalgo, Sandra Fidalgo	Pedro Luís Neves	Ricardo Landum	Luís Duarte	Portuguese	Ana Zanatti	Margarida Andrade	39	16
10	Sweden	"En dag"	Tommy Nilsson	Ola Håkansson, Tim Norell	Alexander Bard, Ola Håkansson, Tim Norell	Anders Berglund	Swedish	Jacob Dahlin	Agneta Bolme-Börjefors	110	4
11	Luxembourg	"Monsieur"	Park Café (Maggie Parke, Rom Heck, Gast Waltzing, Rainer Kind, Serge Vesque, Ander Schmit)	Maggie Parke, Yves Lacomblez, Bernard Loncheval	Maggie Parke, Gast Waltzing	Benoît Kaufman	French	Valérie Sarn	Agneta Bolme-Börjefors	8	20
12	Denmark	"Vi maler byen rød"	Birthe Kjær	Keld Heick	Søren Bundgaard	Henrik Krogsgaard	Danish	Jørgen de Mylius	Bent Henius	111	3
13	Austria	"Nur ein Lied"	Thomas Forstner	Joachim Horn-Bernges	Dieter Bohlen	-	German	Ernst Grissemann	Tilia Herold	97	5
14	Finland	"La dolce vita"	Anneli Saaristo	Turkka Mali	Matti Puurtinen	Ossi Runne	Finish	Heikki Harma	Solveig Herlin	76	7
15	France	"J'ai volé la vie"	Nathalie Pâque	Sylvain Lebel	Guy Mattéoni, G. G. Candy	Guy Mattéoni	French	Lionel Cassan	Marie-Ange Nardi	60	8
16	Spain	"Nacida para amar"	Nina	Juan Carlos Calderón	Juan Carlos Calderón	Juan Carlos Calderón	Spanish	Tomás Fernando Flores	Matilde Jarrín	88	6
17	Cyprus	"Apopse as vrethume"	Fani Polymeri & Yiannis Savvidakis	Efi Meletiou anastazio	Marios Meletiou	Haris Andreadis	Greek	Neophytos Taliotis	Anna Partelidou	51	11
18	Switzerland	"Viver senza tei"	Furbaz (Marie Louise Werth, Ursin Defuns, Gion Defuns, Giusep Quinter)	Marie Louise Werth	Marie Louise Werth	Benoît Kaufman	Romansh	Bernard Thurnheer, Thierry Masselot, Ezio Guidi	Michel Stocker	47	13
19	Greece	"To diko sou asteri"	Marianna Efstratiou	Villy Sanianu	Yannis Kyris, Mariana Efstratiou	Giorgos Niachros	Greek	Dafni Bokota	Fotini Giannoulatou	56	9
20	Iceland	"Það sem enginn sér"	Daníel Ágúst Haraldsson	Valgeir Guðjónsson	Valgeir Guðjónsson	-	Icelandic	Arthúr Björgvin Bollason	Erla Björk Skúladóttir	0	22
21	Germany	"Flieger"	Nino de Angelo	Joachim Horn-Bernges	Dieter Bohlen	-	German	Thomas Gottschalk	Gabi Schnelle	46	14
22	Yugoslavia	"Rock Me"	Riva (Emilija Kokić, Dalibor Musap, Nenad Nakić, Zvonjimir Zrilić, Bosko Colić, Aleksandra Kalafatovic)	Stevo Cvikić	Rajko Dujmić	Nikica Kalogjera	Croatian	Oliver Mlakar and Marjeta Keršič Svetel	Dijana Čulić	137	1

	Italy	Israel	Ireland	The Netherlands	Turkey	Belgium	United Kingdom	Norway	Portugal	Sweden	Luxembourg	Denmark	Austria	Finland	France	Spain	Cyprus	Switzerland	Greece	Iceland	Germany	Yugoslavia	
Italy	■	–	–	–	–	–	–	–	7	–	–	–	–	10	–	12	6	2	4	–	7	8	Italy
Israel	1	■	7	3	–	–	2	–	–	5	–	5	–	5	–	–	–	7	–	5	3	7	Israel
Ireland	–	–	■	–	7	3	–	3	–	–	2	–	–	–	–	–	–	–	–	–	4	2	Ireland
The Netherlands	10	–	3	■	–	–	3	–	–	–	1	–	4	4	7	6	–	–	1	–	6	–	The Netherlands
Turkey	–	–	–	–	■	–	–	–	–	–	–	–	–	–	–	1	–	–	–	–	–	4	Turkey
Belgium	–	–	5	5	–	■	–	2	–	–	–	–	–	–	–	–	–	–	–	1	–	–	Belgium
United Kingdom	6	7	4	7	1	–	■	12	12	10	12	1	8	6	12	10	2	–	2	–	12	6	United Kingdom
Norway	–	2	–	2	5	8	–	■	–	2	–	6	–	–	4	–	–	1	–	–	–	–	Norway
Portugal	–	–	–	–	4	2	–	1	■	3	7	–	6	2	–	8	–	–	6	–	–	–	Portugal
Sweden	–	6	–	–	–	6	4	8	8	■	6	12	12	–	2	5	8	3	8	2	8	12	Sweden
Luxembourg	–	–	–	–	–	–	–	–	–	–	■	–	–	–	5	3	–	–	–	–	–	–	Luxembourg
Denmark	5	1	10	12	6	4	10	10	2	12	4	■	7	12	6	–	–	–	–	10	–	1	Denmark
Austria	12	8	–	–	3	12	–	–	–	7	–	4	■	1	–	2	10	8	12	8	5	5	Austria
Finland	–	10	8	6	10	–	–	–	1	4	4	–	3	■	10	7	3	–	–	–	–	10	Finland
France	3	5	6	4	–	–	–	5	–	1	8	3	5	3	■	–	7	–	5	–	2	3	France
Spain	8	–	–	–	2	7	7	4	–	–	10	–	–	8	8	■	4	10	10	–	10	–	Spain
Cyprus	2	3	1	–	–	–	6	–	6	–	–	8	2	–	–	–	■	4	7	12	–	–	Cyprus
Switzerland	4	4	–	10	8	–	8	–	3	–	–	2	1	–	–	–	–	■	–	7	–	–	Switzerland
Greece	–	–	–	1	–	1	5	6	10	–	–	–	–	–	1	4	12	12	■	4	–	–	Greece
Iceland	–	–	–	–	–	–	–	–	–	–	–	–	–	–	–	–	–	–	–	■	–	–	Iceland
Germany	7	–	2	–	–	5	1	–	5	6	–	7	–	–	–	–	1	6	3	3	■	–	Germany
Yugoslavia	–	12	12	8	12	10	12	7	4	8	5	10	10	7	3	–	5	5	–	6	1	■	Yugoslavia

Israeli band "Poogy" waiting in a buffet in Brighton 1974 >> Photo by: Uri Aloni, in courtesy of Ilan Ben Shachar and the "Lahiton" archive

Ireland's "Sheeba" after a successful home performance in Dublin (1981)

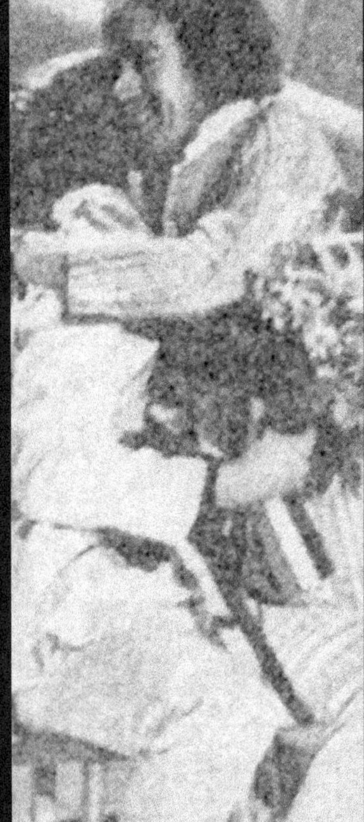

Johnny Logan wins 1 — on stage with Shay Healy in The Hague, 1980 >> Photo by: Uri Aloni, in courtesy of Ilan Ben Shachar and the "Lahiton" archive

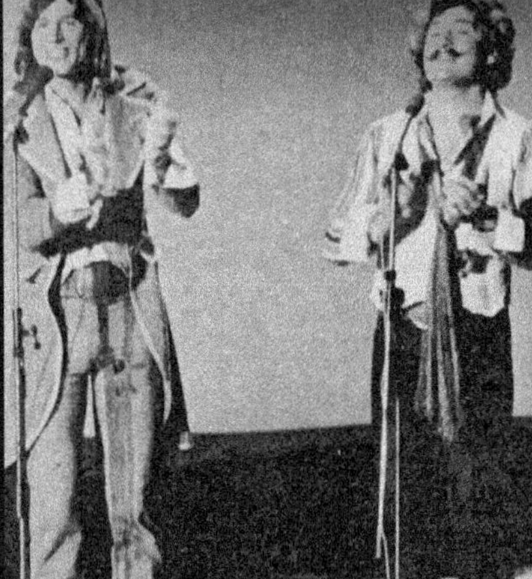

Waterloo & Robinson greatly succeeded in The Hague in 1976 >> Photo by: Uri Aloni, in courtesy of Ilan Ben Shachar and the "Lahiton" archive

The duo Sergio & Estibaliz, Spain's representative in 1975 Stockholm >> Photo by: Uri Aloni, in courtesy of Ilan Ben Shachar and the "Lahiton" archive

Debbie Cameron and Tommy Seebach represented Denmark three times in the contest >> Photo by: Uri Aloni, in courtesy of Ilan Ben Shachar and the "Lahiton" archive

"The Shadows" were only runners-up in 1975 Eurovision >> Photo by: Uri Aloni, in courtesy of Ilan Ben Shachar and the "Lahiton" archive

Wess & Dori Ghezzi from Italy — 1975 Eurovision' surprise

\>> Photo by: Uri Aloni, in courtesy of Ilan Ben Shachar and the "Lahiton" archive

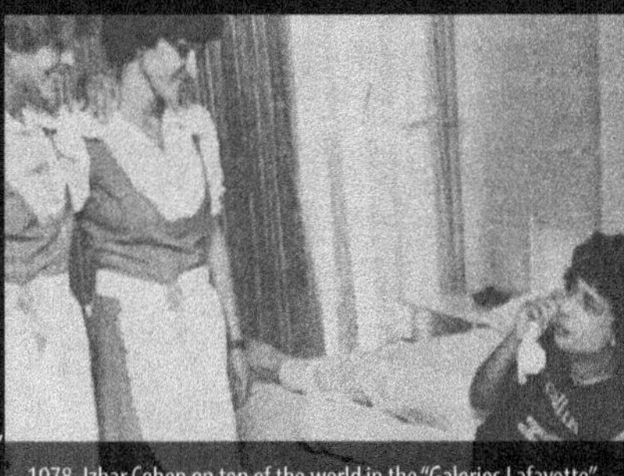

1978, Izhar Cohen on top of the world in the "Galeries Lafayette" hotel in Paris >> Photo by: Uri Aloni, in courtesy of Ilan Ben Shachar and the "Lahiton" archive

1976, "Chocolate Menta Mastik" girls from Israel waving in The Hague >> Photo by: Uri Aloni, in courtesy of Ilan Ben Shachar and the "Lahiton" archive

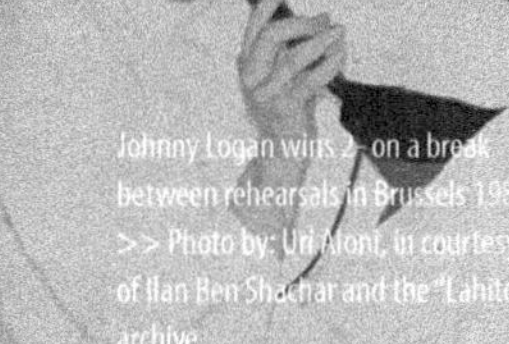

Johnny Logan wins 2 - on a break between rehearsals in Brussels 1987 >> Photo by: Uri Aloni, in courtesy of Ilan Ben Shachar and the "Lahiton" archive

"Bucks Fizz" performing the winning entry of the 1981 Eurovision >> Photo by: Uri Aloni, in courtesy of Ilan Ben Shachar and the "Lahiton" archive

1973, Ilanit delivering a tremendous performance in Luxembourg >> Photo by: Uri Aloni, in courtesy of Ilan Ben Shachar and the "Lahiton" archive

\>> Photo by: Uri Aloni, in courtesy of Ilan Ben Shachar and the "Lahiton" archive

Anne-Marie David in her happiest moments, 1973 Eurovision >> Photo by: Uri Aloni, in courtesy of Ilan Ben Shachar and the "Lahiton" archive

1990-1999

IRELAND ABOVE ALL

An ultimate dominance for Ireland in the 1990s which is unlikely to happen again: A decade record of four wins (three in a row!), another second place (1997) and third place (1990). It should also be noted that Sweden came in first place twice. Seven solo singers have completely returned the female dominance to the contest, with only Toto Cutugno from Italy being the only solo singer to win, alongside an Irish duo and a Norwegian band. Naturally, the flood of Irish wins brought the Eurovision Song Contest to be held four times in Ireland.

1990 – Zagreb, Yugoslavia

Just before passing away, Yugoslavia won an almost final honour: hosting the most significant event in Europe and not just any — the Eurovision that opens the last decade of the millennium. These were hectic times in the divided country, in which the sounds of war were already bubbling up. The debate over the location did not go smoothly: the heads of state television demanded that the event be held in the Serbian capital Belgrade while the Zagreb Television division believed that since a Croatian band achieved the victory, it should take part in their territory. The fact that Croatia's capital was much more musically connected than any other city in the country, in addition to the "Lisinski" Hall, which is considered the most fitting for hosting events of this magnitude, Zagreb was chosen. The Yugoslav state television and Zagreb television were responsible for the production when Goran Radman was the executive producer. Eurovision is usually a record event for the country and serves as a springboard for those engaged in it. But this was an exception when this production would not be considered anything to boast about in the portfolio of whoever took part. Helga Vlahović Brnobić and Oliver Mlakar were chosen as presenters. The latter was correct and lacked a sense of humour, while Vlahović, which is remembered for one of the most bizarre moments in the 1981 Eurovision voting, did not excel, to put it mildly, and sometimes did not manage to control her patriotic instincts, especially during the votes. The local press's negative reaction about their selection as presenters, claiming the production should have chosen younger hosts, led the two to retire in the week before the event! The production quickly hired Rene Medvešek and Dubravka Marković, but political interventions halted the move, the clock was turned back, and the original duo returned to its position. The format chosen by the Yugoslavs was remarkably similar to that of the 1978 Eurovision: the presentation's opening, the performance of several songs and the presenters returning to the stage to announce the next entries with unnecessary information. 1990 was declared the 'Year of European Tourism'. The European Union, in collaboration with the EBU, used the contest to convey the message, and so each country sent tourism materials that became a promotional video when Switzerland had the best one. How divided Yugoslavia was could be learned from the way it presented itself: At the opening of each video, the comic and animated cat "Eurocat" (the event's mascot) appeared in five seconds in which it was supposed to demonstrate the character of each country illustratively. In the Yugoslavian one, the cat looked in the mirror and saw six different figures, symbolising the six republics that consist the country and clashed: Serbia, Croatia, Bosnia, Montenegro, North Macedonia and Slovenia. The best thing that can be said about the production is the brilliant and colour changing stage, tastefully designed, that definitely impressed. The local orchestra was no more than reasonable. The artistic pieces were related to the host city's music and landscapes and a tourist homage to the whole country. Malta hoped to return to the contest after a 15-year absence, but the dry law stipulated that the maximum number of participants should not exceed 22 countries, and so although it had already chosen an entry, the lovely little country stayed out of the ESC. This law did not last and towards 1992, passed from the world. Even before the presenters said their first word, serious sound issues repeated in different variations during the contest were discovered from the event's opening. This Eurovision was tarnished from the opening entry: unofficial approvals to use a partial playback in addition to the orchestra were introduced. Since the definitions on the subject were vague, Spain (the opening country of the night) could allow itself to use a playback throughout the song "Bandido", by the exotic girls' duo "Azúcar Moreno". Conductor Eduardo Leyva turned pale when it became clear that the playback was playing from the middle. The Salazar sisters noticed that their entry started from the wrong place, left the stage in protest and returned behind the scenes with particularly nervous gestures towards the helpless stage workers. A few seconds later, the music was stopped to the amazement of the audience. Only the band's guitarist signalled the audience to applaud, thus releasing some of the immense embarrassment. There is no telling how such a thing can occur. But in any case, the Spaniards' act paid off — they went up again to perform "Bandido", this time with the playback playing from the beginning, the orchestra was synchronised, and at the end of the evening, Spain could smile when it finished in the top 5. Every cloud has a silver lining, and "Bandido" became one of the most successful Spanish songs in the world since, and the "Azúcar Moreno" duo grew highly popular in Spain and South American countries. Before the big night, the betting rates pointed to one notable favourite: Emma from the UK. The 15-year-old Welshwoman took advantage of the rule stating that a performer may compete if they turned 16 or turns 16 in the year in which contest takes place. Since she was born in 1974, she managed to sneak into the event. "Give a Little Love Back to the World", was supposed to provide the UK with a victory after two frustrating years as the runner-up, but as many times before, the juries despise the favourites. With the help of veteran and 1976 Eurovision winner Alyn Ainsworth, Emma received only one Douze Points from Belgium and was finally disappointed to find herself in the sixth place. Another candidate who was set for greatness was Céline Carzo from Luxembourg. "Quand je te rêve" is a French song that was winning material, but Luxembourg, which always made sure to choose quality and talented performers, entrusted this wonderful entry in the hands of Carzo, who in the moment of truth could not withstand the pressure. Her performance was disappointing and inaccurate, what ruined the small Principality's chances of a 6th Eurovision victory. After the last place in 1989, there were no particular expectations from the Icelandic duo "Stjórnin", except for the desire not to finish again with nul points. "Eitt lag enn" became the Eurovision surprise and rightly so: the Icelandic performance was clear and excellent, with an exceptional rhythm, and to their amazement, they found themselves competing for the first prize at certain stages. They finally finished fourth, with 124 points, the best in the Icelandic history at the time, second to date only to Selma's achievement in 1999. It was a year of peace and hope in Europe: the EU expanded, communist rule collapsed like a house of cards in the east of the continent, and the Berlin Wall fell, uniting Germany. Three songs were specially written for the contest in this spirit: Norwegian Ketil Stokkan returned to the ESC with "Brandenburger Tor" which described how most Europeans felt when they watched the stunning images from Berlin, where the wall between East and West fell. Despite an excellent performance, Stokkan returned to Norway with the penultimate place. Ralph Siegel moved the audience to tears with "Frei zu leben" he wrote with Michael Kunze, a charming duet performed by the Croatian Daniel Kovac (who felt at home) and Chris Kempers, addressing boundless love, without walls, hand in hand. The ninth place did not matter at all to the Germans who were proud of the song and performance. Austria also did not ignore what was happening to its close neighbour, and the wonderful Simone Stelzer also touched with "Keine Mauern mehr", a pop entry that opens with the words: "This is a time to be together, for one year". Indeed, a unique, conciliatory and hopeful atmosphere. The Israeli Broadcasting Authority repeated Yardena Arazi's format from 1988, but the audience did not even get to choose the performer Rita's entry, who was selected to represent Israel at the ESC. Seemingly, a worthy choice of a wonderful singer who took over the local market and became a complete consensus, but "Shara Barkhovot" written by the talented Tzruya Lahav to Rami Kleinstein's composition, was all but a Eurovision entry. Despite a great and emotional performance, including prostrating on the stage's floor with her cut-out black dress, Rita realised that the many compliments she received from the media (quite a few European journalists believed she was the best singer in the contest and could win thanks to her impressive vocals) could not save the Israeli singer from falling to the unpleasant 18th place. The Swiss Egon Egemann asked for special permission to sing in English "Musik klingt in die Welt hinaus". He was encouraged by the fact that his single in this language gained momentum and became a song played in numerous countries before the contest. But the rules did not bend for Egemann, who had to be the third to perform his entry in German on the big evening and despite the violin in hand, a good performance and a Douze Points from Greece and Denmark — finished only 11th.

Serge Gainsbourg has always attracted attention since he led France Gall to victory in 1965 with "Poupée de cire, poupée de son". Gainsbourg finally got the break from his country France and wrote "White and Black Blues", a ground-breaking song performed by Joëlle Ursull (the first brown-skinned to represent France in the contest) with anti-racist messages: "White and black, Africa, my love, I have you in my skin... When someone talks to me about skin colour, I have the blues which sends shivers down my spine... I feel as if I'm in a tale by Edgar Allan Poe". Few knew how to digest this unique French entry, but apparently, the juries greatly appreciated it: Ursull managed to reach the second and most honourable place, France's best achievement since winning in 1977!

Moreover, Ursull received 6 (!) Douze Points (twice more than the winner) — the largest number France has ever received in one Eurovision. The host Yugoslavia displayed Tajči, considered by many to be among the most beautiful and attractive women in the divided country. "Hajde da ludujemo" maintained the Yugoslavian pop line in the contest (might have gone a little far in its boldness), Tajči received Douze Points from Turkey and Israel and could be quite content from the seventh place, in one of Yugoslavia's last three Eurovision appearances. Liam Reilly was confident that "Somewhere in Europe" (a song that speaks in the spirit of the event about every possible tourist attraction across the old continent) was a trump card that could grant Ireland a fourth Eurovision win. Truthfully, from the moment he arrived in Zagreb and during rehearsals, more people believed that Ireland would be the winner. The satisfied Reilly, conducted by veteran Noel Kelehan, delivered a captivating performance singing and playing the piano and was indeed a significant factor in the race to top when he led in many voting stages. But then, in a brutal finish, the prize was taken from him, and he finished in third place, with equal number of points as the runner-up. Ossi Runne, the legendary conductor of Finland who retired after 22 times in which he conducted entries of his country, was invited to be a commentator and watched his successor Olli Ahvenlaht (who discovered that this position is not so simple). The "Beat" band performed the Finnish entry in Swedish (which is allowed, since Swedish is an official language in the country), but it did not pay off too well when Finland came in first, but from the end, with 8 points. Throughout the 1980s, Italy sent big names into the Eurovision, but none of them managed to scrape even a close battle for victory in the European contest. Until the colourful Toto Cutugno arrived ... No one could set the rules for Cutugno, and he decided to do almost everything by himself. It was his condition to take on the challenge that many of his good colleagues failed. He wrote and composed "Insieme: 1992", a song that hints at both the year in which Europe will unite and the Olympics to be held in Barcelona, Spain. Because Italian television was not generous with the budget, Toto Cutugno chose the Slovenian band "Pepel in kri" (which represented Yugoslavia at the 1975 ESC) as his backing band (a highly successful choice). Cutugno faced a problem when initially, his entry lasted close to 4 minutes, and he had to shorten it to perform and compete in Zagreb. The gifted Italian found a solution and the performance was thrilling, wonderful and perfect. For years, the Italians were favourites thanks to incredible songs and performances, but it was never to the jurors' liking. This time, Cutugno broke the clichés, all countries awarded him points except Iceland and Norway, with Spain, Portugal and Cyprus giving him Douze Points and the Grand Prix returned to Italy. Cutugno provided two entertaining anecdotes: At the end of his performance, the Italian said the word "toda" (thank you) in Hebrew... Someone misled him and told him this is how they say thank you in the local language. After his victory was cleared with 149 points, his friends from the delegation sprayed him with champagne. However, Toto did not know where to burry himself when the drink splashed on his head began to melt the colour of his hair, dripping directly on his white suit... Cutugno could not evade the awkward moment, as the camera was on him several hundreds of millions of people witnessed it... It was Italy's second victory at the ESC, 26 years after Gigliola Cinquetti in Copenhagen. After Yugoslavia received 12 points from Turkey during the vote, the presenter Vlahović expressed hope: "This is exactly how it started last year", and after Sweden awarded only one point to the locals, the cheeky presenter cynically muttered: "Thank you very much". A funny yet embarrassing incident occurred when the presenters addressed the local Zadar, to get the Yugoslavian jury's results. Supposedly, it is clear that contact with the host country should be the easiest, with no glitches and communication difficulties that sometimes characterise a telephone connection with a distant nation. But the voice from the city of Zadar was reluctant to come... "How can this be", said Oliver Mlakar in Croatian while Helga Vlahović tried to excuse with humour: "This is the longest road, between Zagreb and Zadar"... finally Drago Čulina was reached. He tried to justify the funny disconnect in the local language, until moving on to read the results of the host country's jury panel. The lead in the voting was again divided between two countries: Italy safely led the table, until the pole position was reached by Ireland, which seemed to be on the right path to victory. However, towards the end, there was another reversal, and Italy regained the lead. With two countries left to deliver their results, only one point separated Ireland and Italy. Cyprus tipped the balance by awarding Italy the full points, while not giving the Irish any, sending Toto Cutugno to celebrate his country's second Eurovision title. Cutugno took the stage in euphoria, thanked everyone, following tradition, and closed one of the most boring and least successful Eurovisions in terms of production with "Insieme: 1992". Two and a half years later Yugoslavia would be disbanded and amidst the tears and grief, one evening will be remembered, from early May 1990, perhaps the last evening that this nation was, even if only ostensibly, united.

1991 - Rome, Italy

Toto Cutugno's victory at the 1990 Eurovision made headlines in Italy. After countless disappointments in the European contest and a sense of rejection, the Italians got some comfort with a second victory, allowing them to host the ESC for the second time on the boot-shaped country's land. The plan was to hold the event quite festively in San Remo, where the famous Italian festival is held every year, but half a year before the event, the Gulf War stirred everything up. Italy was part of the international force that fought in Iraq, which conquered Kuwait and sent missiles to Israel, and thus the preparations for the Eurovision were postponed for several precious months. For these and other reasons, it was decided to relocate the event to the "Studio 15 di Cinecittà" in the capital Rome. The studios, built especially during the Mussolini era to upgrade the local film industry, are considered to be world-class giants, so it was no problem to convert "Studio 15" into the venue of the contest, with a blue V-shaped square stage, an illustrated urban backdrop and the RAI (Italian Broadcasting Union) orchestra on the stage's side, conducted by the excellent musical director Bruno Canfora. As the contest's presenters, the only two artists to win the Eurovision for Italy were selected: Toto Cutugno, alongside Gigliola Cinquetti who won 27 years before, in Copenhagen. They were prominent and well-known names in the local music industry (and Europe) and are considered among the most famous and well-known Eurovision presenters. The problem: Cutugno had a broken English and minimal French, and Cinquetti as well, barely knew how to speak English and had very little French. There was a lot of work with the two instructors on the languages and pronunciation, and eventually, they safely cleared this hurdle. Instead of videos, the Italians originally chose to let each participating artist sing their favourite Italian song, and the performance became a singing postcard for each performance, before going on stage. Among the choices were two songs initially performed by Gigliola Cinquetti ("Non ho l'età" sung by "Baby Doll" from Yugoslavia and "Dio, come ti amo" sung by Dulce Pontes from Portugal) and one by Toto Cutugno ("L'italiano", performed by "Atlantis 2000" from Germany). The evening opened with Cutugno performing "Insieme: 1992", which gave him the victory in Zagreb, and Cinquetti (accompanied by Cutugno on piano) singing "Non ho l'età" which won the contest in Copenhagen (1964), giving life to Gigliola's promising career. The favourite was - again — a British representative. Samantha Janus (with "Message to Your Heart"), a 19-year-old with breathtaking beauty, sang about hungry children and the conscience of the world. Paul Curtis wrote her the entry, and as in Zagreb, the betting decisively pointed to his song as the winner, but as always, the 'curse of favourites' did not spare the British and despite an excellent performance by Janus and her three backing singers who looked just like her, as if they were taken directly from a beauty pageant (one of them, Kit Rolfe, participated in the 1984 ESC), the United Kingdom had to settle for only tenth place. The second favourite arrived ready and prepared for her big moment: Carola Häggkvist had her first run in the Eurovision at the age of 16 and despite a two-second technical glitch, managed to bring a third and honourable place to Sweden in 1983. Eight years later, with "Fångad av en stormvind", it was clear that she was headed towards her country's third victory. An appliance store owner in Sweden wanted to make the dime of his life and published in the local media that if

Carola wins the Eurovision, anyone who buys a television from him will get his money back… After making his big business, he sat in his armchair on the big evening, hoping Carola would not take the Grand Prix. It initially seemed that he was about to get what he wished for: Substantial sound issues accompanied the performance of "Fångad av en stormvind", that were well noticed in the hall, but not on the television broadcast. Presenter Gigliola Cinquatti asked Frank Naef whether Carola was eligible for a re-do, but Naef ordered the contest to continue as usual.

Nonetheless, the mighty Carola was tremendous, and despite experiencing problems of this kind for the second time, she made it all the way to a dramatic victory, with most of the voting stages trailing behind Israel, bypassing it towards the end and being dragged into a dramatic draw with France in the last vote. A third Eurovision title for Sweden and an appliance store that went bankrupt immediately after the ESC… The Netherlands withdrew from the contest because "Remembrance of the Dead" fell exactly on the event's day and it was Malta's chance to return after 16 years of absence. Georgina Abela and Paul Giordimaina with the duet "Could It Be" made it clear that this time their country will not be food for powder and reached (for the first time) two Douze Points (from Sweden and Ireland), en route to a respectable sixth place with 106 points. For the second successive year, France thought outside the box: it was now the turn of Amina, a singer of Tunisian descent, with "C'est le dernier qui a parlé qui a raison". Amina's unique style, which included oriental poetry and trills, spoke to the jury teams across the continent and France, which seemed to have lost its way at the contest throughout the 1980s, returned full force in the 1990s with a second consecutive runner-up finish, missing just one point to win. Israel returned to its pre-contest 'kdam' format and held a glorious event with a live orchestra at the International Convention Centre in Jerusalem. The invested format paid off: in both times the pre Eurovision was held in Jerusalem with a live orchestra, Israel won the ESC, while once again big names from the local industry came to the pre-contest (Adam, Uri Fineman, the popular "Tzeirey Tel-Aviv", Ilana Avital, Shimi Tavori, Shlomi Shabat and the "Puncher" band). The Rome ticket winners were Orna and Moshe Datz (Duo Datz) with "Kan", written by Uzi Chitman (in 1989, this wonderful song was not even qualified to the pre-Eurovision of that year). The Duo Datz left for Rome overly optimistic, having the experience and achievements of Kobi Oshrat and the world's sympathy — following the missiles that landed on Israel during the Gulf War. "Kan" captured the hearts of Rome and as the clock for the big night ticked, Israel was marked as one who could emerge from behind and snatch the victory. Orna and Moshe Datz's performance was perfect, no less, with Kobi Oshrat providing a spectacular arrangement to the Italian orchestra.

The vote's opening was promising: Douze Points from Yugoslavia, 12 surprising points from Turkey and another perfect score from Spain were the basis for the lead in almost all voting stages, except the final and most important stage. With Italy left to vote, Israel trailed by 7 points behind Sweden and an Italian Douze Points (which was promised to Duo Datz throughout the week, because they were the locals' favourites) would have given Israel the victory, but the host country skipped Israel, which remained in the third place — its lowest in an unforgettable evening where the Datz duo got it back to the top of European music. Overall, the Italian orchestra was particularly good, but two mishaps are well remembered: Sophia Vossou of Greece came with great self-confidence, alongside her husband and songwriter Andreas Mikroutsikos. "I anixi" was not only a successful album but its theme song evoked strong feelings in Greece that it could win the Eurovision. Despite the good performance of the professional Vossou, the horrible and terrible off-key playing of the Italian orchestra's older saxophonist could not be ignored. It significantly damaged the Greeks and was expressed in a 13th place finish. When the Danish entry ("Lige der hvor hjertet slår") began to play, right in front of the cameras, two violinists from the Italian orchestra started exchanging jokes, with one of the orchestra members staring at them angrily... Incidentally, the performer from Denmark is Anders Frandsen, a singer with remarkably high vocal qualities who failed in this Eurovision, took his own life in 2004. Thomas Forstner demonstrated the idiom: "rise like a rocket and fall like a stick". After being considered Austria's saviour, with the great top 5 in 1989 (a year after finishing Wilfried Scheutz's nul points), Forstner arrived in Rome with "Venedig im Regen" and stayed with no points. Austria remained zeroed, for the second time in 3 years and for Forstner, who has cultivated a promising career, it was a heavy blow. Sergio Dalma was already a big star in Spain when he competed in the contest and attracted his fans to Rome, most of whom did not have invites the big evening... "Bailar pegados" was the race's black horse, mainly thanks to Dalma's charming and exciting performance. After many years, Spain competed for first place and, like 1979, Israel and Spain fought a fascinating duel for victory, until France and Sweden emerged from behind. Dalma finished fourth, accumulating Douze Points from Switzerland and Cyprus.

Italy was also very much considered a favourite. Naturally, when the person representing it was none other than Peppino di Capri, one of the greatest Italian singers and one of the world's most famous performers, who agreed to sing for his country at the ESC after Toto Cutugno's victory. "Comme è ddoce 'o mare", was premiered at the Eurovision in the romantic Neapolitan dialect in an emotional performance by Peppino. Portugal and Finland awarded him Douze Points, which was enough for the seventh place. When the jurors work hard to deliver the results after the entries are performed, it is usually a recess for the viewers, who take advantage of the break for errands and arrangements. But whoever missed the performance by the Italian entertainer Arturo Brachetti, must have greatly regretted it. Brachetti imitated opera singer Maria Callas staged spectacular magic acts and changed clothes at a dizzying pace.

The Italian production could be content with this show. The voting session was characterised by the over-nervousness of Toto Cutugno who urged the announcers to hand over their points in his pleasant but aggressive way and gave hell to Frank Naef. Even before starting the voting, the Italian presenters addressed Naef but did not let him say a word... During the vote, Cinquetti and Cutugno made several mistakes in the countries' names and the number of points and Frank's intervention was greater than ever. As in every vote in which the points were read in three languages (Jerusalem 1979 and Munich 1983), this time too it was longer than usual. Israel started with a promising lead, but Austria led the turnaround in which Spain jumped to first place. After that, the pole position bounced from one to the other, when the nation that pushed Israel back to the top was none other than... Turkey. The Asian neighbour who never awarded the Israelis many points in the contest and usually do not even give it any points, amazed when it announced that its 12 points are going to Israel. This was the second and last time such a thing happened. Duo Datz realised they were headed to a historic achievement, since the last time Turkey awarded Israel Douze Points was in 1978 when Izhar Cohen with "A-Ba-Ni-Bi". After the Norwegian vote, Israel led with a promising advantage: 98 points compared to 87 for Spain, 84 for Sweden and 76 for France.

They Seemed to be on their way to an exciting victory, but the Israelis' troubles began when Yitzhak Shimoni read the results from Jerusalem: 10 points for Sweden and 12 for France, suddenly pinned the Swedes very close to Israel and made them their most real threat. Exciting sights were seen when Shimoni announced Israel's Douze Points to France: Amina stood up and approached Orna Datz with opened arms. The two shared a long hug, with the cameras flashing and capturing this extraordinary moment in which the barriers were broken in a beautiful fraternity. The Finnish jury (one of the panel's member was Ainu Laktinen, a survivor of the Finnish Civil War, that lived until the age of 106) reduced the margin between Sweden and Israel to just 2 points, and the Germans turned the tables when they awarded the Swedes the Douze Points that positioned them in the top, until the end of the voting. The Swedes' margin was cut to 4 thanks to the twelve points that Spain (Salomé, winner of 1969, was a member of the jury panel) gave to Israel, but the British, who awarded 10 to Israel, strengthened the Swedish lead with 12 to Carola. With a status quo score, Cyprus left the decision to the Italian vote, when Sweden is in an excellent position with 146 points, Israel 139 points and France 134. In fact, anyone who was familiar with the laws (and they were not many) knew that only Israel could catch up with Sweden since in case of a draw, the number of Douze Points each country received would determine (Sweden and France had equality in this category, in case the latter get the maximum score from Italy) followed by the times each country got 10 points (here Sweden had 5 of those compared to 2 of France) — which left only Duo Datz a window to win. The Israeli delegation was cautiously optimistic before the last vote, even though Orna already seemed disappointed and reconciled with the expected loss. As the Italian vote went on, the suspense grew bigger, the points started coming, and none of the top three was mentioned. When Malta got 10 points, the tension could be cut with a knife. Rosanna Vaudetti announced the 12 points to Amina who caught up with the Swedes, with 146 points each. For the first time since 1969 — a draw. But this time unlike then, Frank Naef very quickly resolved the issue: "Sweden won. Both countries received four times each the maximum score, but Sweden got five times ten points compared to twice France", so the race was decided and thus Carola became the third Swede to win the Eurovision After "ABBA" and "Herreys."

1992 – Malmö, Sweden

Following Carola's victory in Rome, the proud musical country — Sweden — received the honour of hosting the third Eurovision on its soil. This time, the Swedes chose the city of Malmö (after Stockholm and Gothenburg) and broke a record with 23 participating countries. The following year, the contest will continue to grow, up to various restrictions and conditions that will lead a split in the 2000s expanding it to semi-finals. Harald Treutiger, who excitedly narrated Carola's in Rome, was chosen as the presenter alongside him the Lydia Cappolicchio. Carola herself was honoured when, after a reminder of her win at the previous Eurovision, she was invited on stage to perform "All the Reasons to Live", a powerful song in English from the album "Much More", highlighting her supreme vocal abilities. The Eurovision stage was a fusion of these from 1968 (the Eurovision symbol on stage) and 1986 (Viking ships with a giant dragon-shaped surface above them), with the orchestra conducted by Anders Berglund on the right side of the stage.

Similarly to the previous year, there were no big surprises with the favourite and winner. The UK was considered a solid competitor for the prize; Malta came with a very strong entry; Ireland arrived confident with a song by Johnny Logan and Linda Martin as the performer; and Austria brought a piece by Dieter Bohlen, that could reach the supreme target. It was clear that the winner would be one of these four and so it was (with three of the four finishing in the top 3). Johnny Logan was a safe bet for the Eurovision: After impressive victories in 1980 and 1987 that made him the only singer in the contest's history to win it twice, he wanted to be the only one to do so both as a performer and as a writer. He almost succeeded in 1984, but the second place was like an old wound for the fantastic Linda Martin who believed that someday she would close a circle. She did it in Malmö: "Why Me?" sounded like the right entry from the very first moment it was selected to compete in the Eurovision, through the impressive rehearsals and until its very expected and quite clear victory. Logan made history, Martin took the loser image off her back and became the oldest singer to win the contest. The 'Second Place Curse' did not let go of the United Kingdom: Michael Ball arrived confident, wanting "One Step Out of Time" to be one step ahead of everyone. Ball delivered an excellent performance and felt he was on his way to the Grand Prix, but as usual, the British were missing something to get to the first place. Instead of becoming the fifth winner of his country, Michael Ball was added to the long British runners-up list (the 13th).

Malta, a country with low mileage in the contest, wanted to feel part of the top and when "Little Child" by the local diva Mary Spiteri was heard, it was evident that this was an entry that could get them extremely far in Malmö. The song's studio version was perfect, and it seemed that the task of the arranger and conductor, Paul Abela, of translating all this beauty into the orchestra would be extremely difficult. Yet not only did he stand up to the task, but he also did the unthinkable and the orchestration in Sweden even upgraded the song. Mary Spiteri was a hit in rehearsals, although Ireland and England were favourites. But there was always great interest around Spiteri, and she was the only one who garnered prolonged applause from the stage staff and professionals at the end of each of her rehearsals. On the big evening, Spiteri chose her least successful dress from the wardrobe she brought to Sweden.

Nevertheless, she delivered a phenomenal performance, after which it seemed like Malta was capable of stealing Ireland's victory. The start of the voting had good news for the Maltese, who were in a frenzy after leading over Ireland and the UK, but it did not last. Regardless, the 123 points and third place were enough to make Spiteri a legend in her country. A Kafkaesque scenario revolved around the selection of the Israeli entry: In a meagre pre-contest, three songs were close in the race for Malmö (with the ambition to improve the wonderful achievement of Duo Datz): The prodigy Ronen Bahunker amazed with "Jerusalem" which could have been Shaike Paikov's (the songwriter) big amendment after "Derech Ha'melech", but despite leading at times, he was 2 points shorter than the winner and settled for third place. One point separated Anat Atzmon (returned to the pre-contest again with the excellent "Hatikva") and the winner Dafna Dekel ("Ze Rak Sport"). Atzmon did not accept the harsh verdict and dragged Dafna Dekel to court claiming her song was 17 seconds longer than what the Eurovision rules state (3 minutes). With slim chances (many songs throughout history, including Israelis, won their local contest exceeding the duration rule and cutting them with their arrival of the Eurovision itself) and Dekel and the Israeli Mr Eurovision Shlomo Zach facing her, Atzmon ultimately failed in the legal proceedings and was left with reputational damage in her attempts to develop a musical career in the country (years later she confessed: "In retrospect, it looks idiotic to me"). Objectively, it seems that "Hatikva" could have broken through the top five barrier in Sweden, but Dafna travelled and left the speculations to the historians. "Ze Rak Sport" has reached its potential and despite Dekel's excitement in her performance, she passed the Eurovision test and can look back satisfied with the sixth place she got, with Israel getting 12 points from Yugoslavia. These were the last 12 points this country awarded before being disbanded and Its participation in Malmö was its last in the contest: The excellent "Extra Nena" presented an entry that could have undoubtedly won and was also Dafna Dekel's favourite. "Ljubim te pesmama" was supposed to run at the top, but Europe turned its back on Yugoslavia (13th place), due to the opening of its civil war and one of the most beautiful and unique countries in Europe, parted ways with the ESC. Spain made significant history in the contest when it was represented by Serafín Zubiri, a talented and blind musician from birth. There was a lot of sympathy for "Todo esto es la música" performed by Zubiri, who was accompanying himself on the piano, but sympathy is not enough and Serafín, who opened the evening and did not achieve more than the 14th place. Few believed that the Greek Cleopatra could finish higher than one of the last places with "Olou tou kosmou i Elpida" written for her by Christos Lagos, a rising star in the Greek music scene. Her situation did not get better when her rehearsals did not take off, but then came the voting that stirred everything up: The juries loved Cleopatra and gave her the sensational fifth place, considered the biggest surprise of the 1992 Eurovision. Following the achievement, Cleopatra released a successful album in her country. Experts thought Iceland was a black horse in the race, thanks to the duo "Heart 2 Heart" who performed "Nei eða já", whose single was extremely successful and garnered some good sales before the event in Malmö. Renowned British musician Nigel Wright, recognising the potential, united with the Icelanders and declared that he would conduct the entry that would win first place. Wright's country, the UK, was influenced by this and awarded Iceland 12 points, but was the only one. France continued to give the stage to the different voices in the country, this time with Kali and the entry "Monté la riviè", a song in an African rhythm that received Douze Points from Israel. Kali was far from fighting for the victory, but the recognition he gained in Malmö led to his great popularity in Europe which included plays and performances of the song which won the 8th place.

Host Sweden hoped to achieve much more with Christer Björkman, the first outspoken gay person to represent the country in a contest that over the years has become a symbol of the LGBTQ community. Despite the optimism, the Swedes crashed into the penultimate place, the worst 'achievement' for a Eurovision host since 1958. At least they could find comfort in the name of their song: "I morgon är en annan dag (Tomorrow is a New Day)". Daisy Auvray from Switzerland was not even supposed to be on stage in Sweden with her "Mister Music Man". Géraldine Olivier was the one to win the Swiss pre-contest with "Soleil, soleil", which was supposed to defy the first places. Strangely enough, only after the local event, the Swiss noticed that the entry did not comply with the rules and disqualified it outright, leaving Olivier frustrated and out of the Eurovision. Her runner-up, Auvray, was sent in her place to Malmö and thanks to 12 points from Iceland, was rescued from the last positions. Luxembourg's swan song, the empire that won more than any other in the contest until retiring from it, could already be heard in Malmö. "Sou fräi" performed by Marion Welter with vigorous energies on stage, was actually with zero points, on the way to the principality's biggest humiliation at the Eurovision (since David Alexandre Winter in 1970), but a lifeline came from the Netherlands, which were the last to vote and awarded it 10 points that saved it from the last place, where Finland fell. In 1991, Austria finished with nul points, as it did in 1988. Then came Dieter Bohlen to save the Austrians and restore their lost dignity a year later. And why would what worked so well in 1989 not work again in 1992? Dieter surpassed himself when he wrote "Zusammen geh'n" with the performance entrusted to rising star Tony Wegas. The Austrian entry skyrocketed in predictions, and Eurovision enthusiasts who listened to it clearly ruled: "Such a thing has never been heard here before." British broadcaster Terry Wogan defined it in his humorous and particular fashion: "It's Austria's best song since the Austro — Hungarian Empire"... Will Austria return the Grand Prix to Vienna, 23 years after Udo Jürgens' victory? The answer came in the form of bitter disappointment for Bohlen, who was sure he had a hit in hands, but the best thing that happened to him that night was 12 prestigious points he received from the winner Ireland, and nothing more.

Later, Bohlen will no longer write entries for the European contest. Mia Martini returned to the Eurovision after 15 years, with a scorched voice from cigarettes and fragile health. All this did not take away from her marvellous ability to deliver an exciting and thrilling performance on stage, which was precisely what happened with "Rapsodia". In the early predictions, the song was not considered to reach the higher positions, but following the Italian's unforgettable show, it even threatened Ireland's first place, en route to be 4th with 111 points (the fourth-best place for Italy since 1964). "Wind" held a fantastic second-place record in its two Eurovision appearances (1985 and 1987). Ralph Siegel, who was already runner-up with them in Brussels, believed with his shrewd and professional sense that it would be possible to make another successful round. The story of "Träume sind für alle da", is one of the most interesting: the song's chorus was written as a jingle for a tribute evening by Siegel's record company... When the chorus was played repeatedly, people approached him, saying that the jingle is not bad at all and why not make it into a hit? So did Siegel and winning the German pre-contest gave him an appetite. At the end, it seemed that this was one too many performances for the excellent German band (only 16th place). The calm and smooth voting did not come as a surprise: Malta started strong and took the lead before losing their advantage to Ireland, who held on to the first place until the end, despite Italy's efforts and the UK's attempts to catch up. For the first and last time in an era that restricts countries to singing in their official language, three English-language entries finished in the top three — another sign to the sad decline of the French language in a contest that was once its home turf. The UK, Malta and Italy received the maximum score four times, while winning Ireland settled for just three Douze Points (which is less than Linda Martin had when she finished second at the 1984 Eurovision). The legendary supervisor Frank Naef parted ways with the ESC, at its peak, after 14 years in which he made his mark in the contest and became a recognised icon. Martin's win was characterised by much joy and excitement, with most of the attention going (of course) to the songwriter Johnny Logan: "You did it again Johnny, for the third time", the host Cappolicchio enthusiastically enthused. Logan devoted himself to the microphone and the show, opening with a monologue and a warm greeting to his family and friends in Australia... Incidentally, in 2013 one television presenter claimed that Johnny Logan won the 1992 contest held in Malmö, "Well, of course, Johnny Logan won when he was disguised as a woman", responded Linda Martin, in humour or bitterness ...

1993 - Millstreet, Ireland

1993 was a turning point in the Eurovision timeline. Yugoslavia's dissolution created the first bang of 3 new participants: Croatia, Slovenia and Bosnia Herzegovina. With the war in the Balkans still bleeding and the fire unabated, the contest in Ireland was conducted in the spirit of support for countries seeking liberation from Greater Yugoslavia. Later, North Macedonia, Montenegro and Serbia will join them, while the dissolution of the Soviet Union will also create new states. The consequences will make the contest very political in the voting, with the Eastern countries awarding points to each other, pushing the Western countries — the founders of the ESC — to the table's margins. The entries will no longer have an exclusive meaning in the decision and only limiting measures in the second decade of the 21st century will slightly restore the balance. But even that will not prevent the Eurovision from becoming a show of which music is only one part of. A hint of what would come was already given in how the three new entrants arrived in the contest. It happened through a unique preliminary competition in Ljubljana, Slovenia's capital, called "Kvalifikacija za Millstreet". Croatia, Bosnia and Herzegovina, Slovenia, Slovakia, Romania, Hungary and Estonia competed for three tickets to the Grand Final. This specific contest, which aroused great interest in the Balkans, took place in Ljubljana's television studios, which were held especially for the extensive broadcast. The scoring stage was particularly tense, with Slovakia leading before the last vote, ahead of host Slovenia and Hungary. Cruelly enough, the Slovaks themselves turned the tables and led to the victory of the host Slovenia, with Bosnia second and Croatia passing Slovakia by one point. Frank Naef was the EBU representative at the event, and he received farewell gestures from Slovenian television. No one imagined that a few years later, these countries that had struggled for even entering the contest, would feel entirely at home in it. To overcome the flood of participants on the one hand and the integration of the newcomers, the EBU determined that those who finish in the 20th-25th places will be eliminated from the next Eurovision, making way for other countries and so on. This rule lasted until 1995 when the rules were changed again until the semi-final tradition began in 2004. On the night Linda Martin won the 1992 Eurovision, Noel Duggan, the owner of a huge Millstreet complex (a small town near Cork), called the RTÉ (Irish television) CEO and submitted a request that sounded detached from reality: to host the ESC in his complex in a town of 1500 inhabitants only... Initially, RTÉ refused to take it seriously and wanted to hold the event at the capital's famous "Point" theatre. However, political pressure, along with Duggan's promise that all the tedious expenses and set-up process would be on him and that local businesses would financially and logistically work together for the event — convinced the decision-makers to grant the hosting to Millstreet. It was an unprecedented technical and professional challenge for Irish television, in a remote and difficult area in terms of multilateral broadcasting. The open space that has become a magnificent indoor, used to be a... horse riding site. BBC broadcaster Nicholas Witchell announced near the opening of the event that "The Eurovision will be held in a cowshed in Ireland" and had to apologise after the storm caused by his remarks. In practice, there was no cowshed nor horses: a spacious rhombus-shaped stage with impressive construction above it, when the orchestra is on its side, the audience is slightly far away from it, but the camera operators had enough space to move around and achieve great shots. Bottom line, the Eurovision in Millstreet was a tremendous success. This contest had two big favourites: One of them was Croatia with a moving ballad "Don't Ever Cry" by "Put". Europe sympathised with Croatia, which was in wartime and it seemed that they were on the way to their victory, but the Croatian performance was eventually swallowed up amid the styles and big mess that the 25 entries create, and the juries just ignored it. 15th place without any Douze Points shocked the Croatian delegation (it should be remembered that they also won the ticket to Ireland, hardly). The second candidate came from the UK: Sonia, a well-known singer, had one goal — to win the first place. Nothing else mattered to her, and indeed, the pop star made an impression that the event was small for her, arriving confident in Millstreet. Her merry performance can only be admired. 164 points — just like "Brotherhood of Man" achieved in 1976 (but with 18 participants and not 25) were only enough for being just second and a possibility of victory that was stretched right up to the last vote. "Better the Devil You Know" was the biggest hit of this contest, but without winning first place, it was a small consolation for Sonia. The 1993 Eurovision was probably in a seance with the 1979 contest, regarding two voices from the past: Danish Tommy Seebach and Finish Katri Helena, both finishing in disappointing places. Belgium found itself in the last place, as in 1979 and 1985, with a melancholy and beautiful entry, "Iemand als jij" performed by Barbara Dex. Annie Cotton brought Switzerland and the French language back to the top with "Moi, tout simplement", which as its name implies, is a pretty simple song, which did not herald a new style but was strong and catchy enough to reach the respectable 3rd place. France reached was included in the final four ranking, with the exciting "Mama Corsica" by Partick Fiori, started a successful career thanks to the ESC. One of the most intriguing bands in this edition came from Sweden, "Arvingarna", with many hysterical fans who accompanied with encouragement and screams every step of the four boys, two of whom are brothers of the Larsson family. Beyond the rhythmic and excellent entry "Eloise", the attraction was in the accompanying performance by the singers' fathers at the back of the stage... The seventh place the Swedes reached was not so terrible, but the boys' band project supposed to bring a new line to Scandinavia did not flourish. Host Ireland firmly aimed for a second consecutive victory and assigned the task to Niamh Kavanagh, with the excellent song written by Jimmy Walsh, "In Your Eyes". In addition to the crowd's help, Kavanagh's perfect performance led to a rare achievement — a second successive win, something that lastly happened at the 1979 Eurovision with Gali Atari and "Milk and Honey". A seance much? Kavanagh received points from all countries (and a total of 187) and her victory was secured with the evening's last Douze Points. "Modern Times" sang "Donne-moi une chance" in French and German-Luxembourgish, but the magic of the principality expired, and if not for the 10 points it received at the very last moment from Malta, it would have finished last with only one point. The 20th place it finally established actually eliminated it from the next Eurovision, which was the catalyst for RTL's decision to retire definitively, entirely and probably permanently from participating in the contest. In addition to Croatia, the two other new entrants from Yugoslavia were also very disappointed: Slovenia had already failed in its first appearance, while the bombed-out and besieged Bosnia with the band "Fazla" reminded everyone of its sad reality: "The pain of the whole world is concentrated tonight in Bosnia." 12 points from Turkey were not enough for the Bosnians who were also upset to discover that life at the Eurovision is not as difficult as in war but is not paradise either. The Netherlands returned to the top with its pop star Ruth Jacott (the entry "Vrede" is one of the beloved versions sent by the Netherlands to the contest) and the 12 points she got from the host and winner Ireland, were evidence of this. Seven years have passed since the Israeli nightmare in Bergen, and it seemed that the only country that participates in the contest and is not located in Europe invited its defeat in Millstreet. In the pre Israeli contest, there were quality songs by Doron Mazar, David D'Or, Dorit Reuveni and Adam, but the choice was actually Sarah'le Sharon and her band... Of course, there was some magic in sending the sing-along champion to the Eurovision, but this tribute was costly. Not only does Sarah'le not speak to the average European, but also Shaike Paikov, which already in 1989 did not create a calm atmosphere in the delegation, was the songwriter. "Shiru" was a mediocre song that only a unique and supreme performance could bring it anywhere except the last positions. When the Israeli Mr Eurovision Shlomo Zach was asked about Sharon's chances and her band in the contest, he replied in his unique way: "What do I know? There could be 24 songs worse than that". But not only were there not, but the routine of the Israeli delegation also caused a lot of headache to the Irish production: Sarah'le Sharon wanted all the focus on her from the outset, sitting and playing the piano, and all the explanations of the Israeli delegation that it was too dull and killed the song and shooting — did not help.. Amid the chaos, the one who tried to instil calm was the conductor Amir Frohlich, who was perhaps one of the few who did a good job. To add fuel to the fire, the sixth backing singer, Varda Zamir (who was asked to stay out of the camera focus throughout the song) decided that as soon as Sarah'le Sharon joins the other four backing singers in the song's ending chord, she will do the same: "I deserved my seconds of glory as well", Zamir claimed. Despite using one sentence in the repeating chorus in English, the expected defeat has indeed arrived. Only 4 points and penultimate place, Israel's worst until then and the penalty: non-participation in the 1994 ESC. It will take it many years to recover from this Eurovision experience. The one who felt the opportunity to surprise and steal a victory at Millstreet was Norway.

17-year-old Silje Vige performed "Alle mine tankar", written by her father Bjørn-Erik Vige, with emotion and cordiality. She was the last performer, and in the chorus, the audience joined her with rhythmic applause and a massive ovation at the end. In the stands and behind the scenes, it felt like the young Norwegian was going to be a huge surprise. In the first quarter of the road, she was level on points with Ireland, but later cleared the way for the Titans' fight Niamh-Sonia, accumulating 3 Douze Points and reaching 120 points and a great position in the top 5 — Norway's third-best achievement of all time, as of 1993. The graceful presenter Fionnuala Sweeney navigated the voting well, with the new supervisor Christian Clausen, maintaining modesty and not interfering. Among the jurors of the various countries were the Croatian singer Maja Blagdan (who will participate in the 1996 contest), Bessy Argyraki (part of the Greek quartet who came fifth at the 1977 ESC) and Sergio y Estíbaliz (who represented Spain at the 1975 Eurovision). An unexpected mishap occurred when contact with Malta was lost, and it was decided that the Maltese vote would be given at the end, after Norway (which was supposed to be the last voter). As expected with so many participants, the beginning led to frequent leadership exchanges (Bosnia was in the lead after two votes, then Switzerland, with Norway also reaching first place). After a third of the way, Ireland took first place, but The UK did not give up and at one point skipped over the Irish and saw the victory coming closer. Yet, with the support of the home crowd, the host made a comeback. The Israeli spokesperson Danny Roup, who read his country's results, had the power to decide and determine a victory for Ireland, so the presenter Sweeney, who was very emotionally involved during the voting, expected, and she did not hide her desire for a local victory. When Roup only awarded five to the host, the full points to Sonia and said goodbye to the presenter with a "shalom" Hebrew greeting, Sweeney reacted with an angry cold and alienated "shalom" face... The Norwegians calmed the presenter when they awarded 12 points to Ireland, compared to 8 for the British, thus creating a significant (but erasable) margin of 11 points, before Malta went on air to dispel the fog around the winner. In fact, the Irish had one point missing to secure the victory, while any point for The UK that is not 12, was also worth a win. But Malta went on and on and did not award points to any of the contenders for the first place. When it was announced that Luxembourg got 10 points, even the voice of the presenter Sweeney choked. An analogous situation happened only at the 1988 Eurovision, which was also held in Ireland when then there was the decision between Switzerland and the UK, and the British lost... and once again, they were the big losers when the Douze Points went to Ireland, which finally celebrated a sweet moment. In the voice of Terry Wogan, the BBC man of Irish descent, there was complete solidarity with the country to which he allegedly broadcast the loss, but he admitted in a private conversation that in his heart he was very happy about the Irish victory. Had the vote been conducted as it should have and Malta's score had been considered at the stage it was supposed to be given and not at the end, Ireland would have secured its double long before the last vote. The big celebration held in the hall on Millstreet after winning did not resemble any other spontaneous joy in the contest's history. It was probably the sweetest Irish victory that put this sympathetic country on the map with the Eurovision Kingdom of Luxembourg and France. Soon, it will be in a league of its own.

1994 - Dublin, Ireland

This was not the first back-to-back Eurovision victory, but no country had ever hosted it year after year. The Irish rose to the challenge and broke another record in the European contest's history. After the interestingly choosing Millstreet in 1993, the hosts were solid and returned to the capital Dublin, while taking advantage of the intervals between the entries to present promotional videos showing the Irish capital's unique sites. The "Point" Theater was with an urban backdrop, and the back of the stage looked like an illustration of Manhattan. After one year, the 'two presenters' format returned: Cynthia Ní Mhurchú was excellent, but the thunder was stolen by the prominent male side of the show — Gerry Ryan, a local television star who was not easily convinced to present the contest. Ryan, who has a pompous speaking style (exaggerating the dramatic and full tone of every word or sentence) was ridiculed by the British broadcaster of Irish descent, Terry Wogan, during the broadcast to the Kingdom. After the Eurovision, Ryan continued his extensive media career in Ireland, but personal difficulties and a prolonged conflict with his ex-wife led to his sad decline which manifested itself in many weight problems that created medical issues. In 2010, he was found lifeless in his home in a mysterious cause of death. The elimination of Israel, Belgium, Turkey, Luxembourg, Denmark and Slovenia due to their low positions in 1993, emptied the Eurovision of traditional and interesting competitors, replaced by Hungary, Romania, Slovakia, Estonia, Lithuania, Russia and Poland (Italy withdrew for unclear reasons, returned for a short run in 1997 and disappeared from the contest again for many years). One favourite shone above all when the predictions pointed to Germany as a potential winner. "Wir geben 'ne Party" written by Ralph Siegel and Bernd Meinunger (the team responsible for Germany's sole victory at the 1982 contest) brought a new style of modern pop with an excellent arrangement by Norbert Daum and the graceful female trio "MeKaDo". Siegel was excited in rehearsals, enjoying the compliments and statements about him having the hottest entry on the one hand, but knowing that the contest had an unwritten rule stating that the favourites rarely win... and eventually? The girls' excellent performance was enough for the third place, bringing Germany back to the top after seven years. Another hot favourite was, almost as usual, The UK. Frances Ruffelle with "We Will Be Free (Lonely Symphony)" said that she very much hopes not to finish in the second place... Her wishes were fulfilled but not in the desired direction: despite a peaceful and confident performance ("I was very calm and not nervous for some reason", she told Terry Wogan after her appearance), she eventually found herself in the tenth and very disappointing position. Edyta Górniak from Poland made history when her entry "To nie ja!" became the amazing runner-up, the best result in history for a country participating in the Eurovision for the first time. But not everything went smoothly for Górniak, when in the dress rehearsal (watched by the juries), she performed the Polish song, "To nie ja!" In English. This provoked much protest and a demand to remove her immediately from the contest (The request was rejected). A week after the Górniak's great success, which made her a household name in Poland, an Israeli writer claimed that the singer had copied the song from him (the matter was never brought before a court). Friderika from Hungary also had a fantastic performance and an outstanding debut for her country at the Eurovision with the fourth place, being the first in the scoring system's history since 1975 to open the voting session with three consecutive Douze Points! One of the best entries that year came from France: Nina Morato undoubtedly brought a new and interesting style with the song "Je suis un vrai garçon" and reached the seventh place, once a location that was considered a failure for France but became a respectable place for them in 1994... The fact that only one entry was performed in the French language in this contest (that of France) reflected the downfall of the language that undisputedly dominated the contest before. And the winner, unbelievably, was again... Ireland. One pianist, one guitarist and an acoustic performance set the stage for Paul Harrington and Charlie McGettigan. They conquered Europe with "Rock 'n' Roll Kids", a ballad that achieved a historical and hysterical number of points — 226 and yet, did not receive any points from just one country — Greece. Being a rather dull Eurovision, the ones who stole the show and were perceived as its real winners were the "Riverdance", the Irish dance troupe that made an international premiere in the pre-voting break. That gave them worldwide fame in their way of becoming one of the best talked-about dance troupes in the world. This ESC did introduce a novelty in the voting process: for the first time, the speakers of results were not only heard but also seen. This caused some ridicules from the audience since quite a few of the announcers were simply not ready and prepared for their television appearance, and the bursts of laughter towards them were quite cruel. Although Hungary astonished in the opening with 36 points out of 36 possible, the picture became clear very quickly: Ireland moved to the lead, received eight Douze Points and created a significant margin of 60 points from second place. Third consecutive Irish win and sixth overall — an inconceivable statistic that will probably not return in the coming decades.

1995 - Dublin, Ireland

The 40th Eurovision Song Contest received a very moving tribute. At the show's opening, spotlights of the various winners from 1960 to the present were screened for four minutes, a nostalgia that aroused much interest and emotion. After breaking all possible records, becoming the Queen of the Eurovision Song Contest with six wins, having the biggest winning streak (3) and hosting the contest for three consecutive years, Ireland had its fill. Paul Harrington and Charlie McGettigan's victory left the hosting of the third successive Eurovision big question marks. With the help of RTÉ, the BBC brought up a revolutionary proposal with extraordinary political implications: to co-host the ESC in Belfast, Northern Ireland, with all its meanings. The EBU were enthusiastic about this possibility, which could have gathered unprecedented interest in the European contest, but the Irish finally decided to take over the production again, without the British's help. "This time we do not want to win", RTÉ officials told anyone who was prepared to listen and seemed to be honest... "The next Eurovision will be only funded by sponsors", claimed government officials, and indeed — Ireland was afraid of a fourth consecutive win that would force her to produce — for the fourth time in a row — this expensive giant production. The Irish Television CEO solemnly informed his EBU colleagues that they should not expect Ireland to host the contest again if they win. The choice of Eddie Friel and the entry "Dreamin" was a statement below the surface that this time they would settle for a nice spot in the middle. However, the Irish crowd did not care for the budget issues and fatigue. They wanted a victory. The betting agencies as well did not take a chance when it came to Ireland and set a ratio that placed Friel extremely high in the betting table — 1 to 6. In rehearsals, the organisers were very pressured when the crowd pushed Friel and the other participants considered the host a strong competitor. But another Irish win was illogical, and sanity did win (this nice entry scored 44 points), when on the first point Ireland received just after two votes, the local public reacted with great contempt. The Irish took every moment to celebrate, including Johnny Logan's birthday ("He will not say how old he is", claimed the excellent presenter Mary Kennedy) who was set in the hall, next to Dana — the first to break the dam and bring Ireland its first Eurovision win in 1970. There were days. Yet, there was a milestone that tested the future of the Eurovision: Norway challenged the contest with the melody "Nocturne". To comply with the rules, Petter Skavlan wrote to it a few words sung in an operatic style by the wonderful Gunnhild Tvinnereim. This was not the entry with the least number of lyrics ever (Belgium in 1983), but it was the most distinct as a tune led by the Irish violinist Fionnuala Sherry, member of the "Secret Garden" band, directed by the musician Rolf Løvland who also wrote the song. The big question was how the jurors would react to this attempt. Any achievement could question the Eurovision's rights and wrongs, including using instrumental tunes to recreate the success. Løvland, who also wrote the entry that granted Norway the 1985 ESC victory, came up with the formula once again and Oslo rejoiced and celebrated a second win after a decade. Ultimately, the following years proved that this was a one-off afflatus, and the Eurovision did not become a melodies contest. After criticism regarding the number of countries participating, it was decided to reduce the event to 23 countries when this time the last places were not eliminated from the following year. In the 1996 contest, there was an early mini contest in which all interested countries competed when the lowest positions did not take part in the Eurovision (this too will be changed). The one who crashed into the last place was Germany, with just one point for Cheyenne Stone. Those were tough years for the veteran contestant until Ralph Siegel was called again…
On the other hand, Spain rose back to the top, recreating last great achievement from 1979, second place, thanks to Anabel Conde and "Vuelve conmigo", one of the most successful entries remembered of Dublin event. Russia sent a mega Star — local pop king Philipp Kirkorov who finished with 17 points in the 17th place. Croatia achieved its best accomplishment in the contest

so far (6th), thanks to a marvellous performance by the "Magazin" band and the fantastic Lidija of the song "Nostalgija", which left a profound impression on the jurors and experts thanks to their vocal qualities. France's Nathalie Santamaria continued the French pop line which again succeeded and came in fourth place. The UK also brought something new and unprecedented — the rap entry "Love City Groove" (the name of the song and the performing band). The British entry was one of the most played before and after the contest but did not catch on at the big night. Jan Johansen was the absolute favourite with "Se på mig". The young and heart-conquering Swede did everything right in his performance, opened with an impressive lead, but succumbed to his Norwegian neighbours. Later on, he suffered from the fact that most favourites usually do not win the Eurovision. Third place, nonetheless, was definitely an achievement for the Swedes. The surprise of the contest was the Danish Aud Wilken, the singer of East German descent. The refined and precise performance of "Fra Mols til Skagen" (which before rehearsals was considered a potential last-place finisher), astonished with being included in the top five, while at some voting times it even reached higher positions. Slovenian Darja Švajger soared in the rehearsal's week to the top of the betting with "Prisluhni mi", which sounded like victory material. It was the Slovenians' hope for winning, but at no point did Darja threaten the top. She took comfort in the seventh place, the best her country has achieved. In Israel, the illusion was that the winner of the Eurovision would be the singer Liora. After a brilliant victory over Dana International (in which she scored 82 out of 84 possible points!), "Amen", written for her by Moshe Datz, sounded like Israel's best chance since 1991. Orna Datz was supposed to sing, but eventually gave up and whoever capitalised on the situation was another discovery by Shlomo Zach, Liora (who in one night rose from complete anonymity to the most talked-about singer in Israel). In Europe, the entry's betting ratio was around 9 to 1, not the highest, but close enough to fantasise about a possible win. The Israeli delegation tried to convince the Irish production, which vehemently refused (due to the country's fire laws), to allow Israel to place candles on the stage, as it had in the past. But this did not seem to be the issue, like Gadi Goldman's heavy and conservative arrangement, despite Liora's incredible performance that proved she was born to stardom. "Amen" was a great song, but if it had contended eight or ten years earlier, it could have won a landslide victory (at the end a rather disappointing eighth place for Israel). Among the various countries' jurors were the Polish Edyta Górniak and Alejandro Abad from Spain — both participated in the 1994 Eurovision. At the beginning of the voting, Sweden led by a promising margin with 34 points out of 36 and seemed to be on the safe way to the title, but then Norway surpassed it, creating a significant and indelible advantage, until its second victory in the history of the contest. "Secret Garden" theoretically won when the Israeli announcer Daniel Pe'er (one of the 1979 contest presenters) awarded Norway 10 points and with it the fame, with a 25 points margin that could not be closed in any way. Three consecutive Eurovision years in Ireland were over, but as the future will show — not forever.

1996 - Oslo, Norway

At the 1996 Eurovision in Oslo, the first seeds of the event's rejuvenation were sown, discharging from the button-down suit and becoming more casual. "Secret Garden"'s victory forced the artists and the organisers to think outside the box and find a new audience for the old contest. The Norwegians picked up the gauntlet and once again enjoyed unlimited economic means, which resulted in an expensive and exceptional production, highlighting virtual reality technology, introducing unique shooting angles, inspiring effects in the songs' shooting, and all on a colossal stage divided into three parts. The production sought to arouse great interest toward the contest and did so mainly thanks to the presenter, Morten Harket, lead singer of the "a-ha" band and one of the most famous Norwegian figures in the world. Alongside him was Ingvild Bryn who brought an innovative, young and light-hearted presentation. Another exciting innovation introduced by the Norwegians was a good luck message by politicians from each country for the entry that represented their nation. Among the well-known political figures was Portugal's Prime Minister and the future Secretary-General of the United Nations, António Guterres. As recalled, the EBU had decided to repeal the rule stating the 20-25 places finishers would not participate in the following Eurovision, being replaced by the countries awaiting their turn. But the alternative was worse: 29 countries sought to take part in the contest in Oslo, of which only 22 could do so alongside host Norway. The EBU decided that the 29 countries that wish to participate should hold a mini-Eurovision between them (The seven nations that finish last could not take part in Oslo).

The bizarre conditions of the tournament held in a closed and undocumented circle (intentionally) on a Friday afternoon, when all the participants listen (without seeing) to the entries and then score it in the usual Eurovision way — led to a disastrous result. In Israel, for example, no one from the IBA took this 'preliminary Eurovision' seriously. No one believed that Galit Bell's entry "Shalom olam" would stay at home and be excluded from the 22 selected entries. There was much criticism of the selection of the anonymous Bell, which enjoyed the public reactions to the colourful songwriter Lt. Col. Eyal Madani. Israel was shocked to find itself in the 28th place out of 29, only 12 Points and a humiliating disqualification from the ESC. The notice of the elimination caught Bell and her partner songwriter Eyal Madani on a trip to a family dinner on a Friday night, after another week of gruelling preparations for the event. The results were disastrous, as great Germany, the Eurovision's main sponsor was also eliminated. The techno entry "Planet of Blue" finished in the 24th place, 2 points less than the 22nd place that sent Finland to the contest. The EBU's luck was that Norway had the financial means to deal with the German money shortage, but it was impossible to count on that in the future. It was the first and only time in history that Germany was absent from the contest. Hungary was particularly unlucky, finishing with 26 points, just like Finland, but the latter received the highest score (8 points) from Greece, a score the Hungarians did not get, and so, unfortunately, they stayed in Budapest. The Finns' joy did not last: The energetic Jasmine and "Niin kaunis on taivas" were the crowd favourites in Oslo but ended the evening in the last place with only 9 points, with the only comfort being the fact that it was the highest score for a song that finished last since the new scoring system entered in 1975. The winner of the preliminary Eurovision that filtered the 22 participants was Sweden (it was learned in retrospect) with "Den vilda" by "One More Time". On the big night in Oslo, that victory did not repeat itself and Sweden, for the second consecutive year, placed third with 100 points. It was a contest without clear favourites. There were talks about Gina G from the UK (her entry "Ooh Aah ... Just a Little Bit" was the most remembered and most played from the contest), which came 8th and Miriam Christine from Malta ("In the Heart of a Woman" who had a fantastic betting ratio for winning, but Christine's overly excited performance on the big night sent her to the tenth place). The open race led to surprising rankings for several countries, led by Estonia which came in fifth place, and Portugal with its best achievement in the contest so far — 6th, thanks to the wonderful and energetic Lúcia Moniz. Maja Blagdan from Croatia also brought her country to new heights (fourth place, a record achievement for the Croats) while Lisa del Bo, a big star in Belgium, came full of expectations to break the 'Flemish curse' in the contest with "Liefde is een kaartspel" (which ended in the 16th and very disappointing place for her). Host Norway strongly believed in Elisabeth Andreassen's fourth appearance at the contest. "I evighet" was perhaps the most perfect and moving piece remembered from this evening, that put Andreassen in the exclusive club of performers who won both first (1985) and second (1996) place. The Breton, an ancient language still spoken in France and elsewhere, was introduced by Dan Ar Braz and his band ("Diwanit Bugale"), who put on a fascinating musical performance that was not enough to get to the top. So, who won? Unbelievable, but it was Ireland again. This time, it was Eimear Quinn's turn with the unique voice and the winning entry written for her by Brendan Graham, "The Voice". It was no great wonder since the Irish entry was considered a potential winner, but few believed the jurors would decide to send everyone on another trip to Dublin, for the fourth time in five years (!). In doing so, Ireland broke another record — 4 wins in one decade. It was also Ireland's last victory so far. It is waiting 25 years for another one, while still holding the title of Eurovision queen. Presenter Ingvild Bryn introduced the 'Blue Room', with the virtual scoreboard (divided into 2 parts and Bryn even demonstrated how she supposedly moves the two parts of the board with her hand...). The speakers of the countries' results were presented against an animated map of their country, while the only tangible thing on stage was, in fact, Ingvild. A scattering of points characterised the Voting: The leader Croatia succeeded in opening a surprising margin in the first quarter (despite not receiving the maximum score even once). The lead passed into Ireland's hands from the second quarter, which closed the deal very quickly, without any serious competitor challenging its seventh title. Belén Fernández, the Spanish juror, made a mistake twice when she awarded 2 points to "Czechoslovakia" and infuriated the Slovaks ... She also gave 6 points to the Netherlands (whom she called HOLAND and not the NETHERLANDS), which caused a chain of blunders (the presenter mistakenly gave these points to Poland), which was finally corrected by the quiet and efficient chief executive Christine Marchal-Ortiz. Norway recreated its third-highest achievement, second place by Elisabeth Andreassen (who brought her country the Grand Prix in 1985 as part of "Bobbysocks!") and set a strange record in the only and last time so far, with an entry that finished 2nd but did not receive a single Douze Points. Morten Harket wandered with the microphone behind the scenes and captured a particularly amusing moment: the amiable Austrian performer George Nussbaumer was talking to his mother on his mobile phone when Morten snatched the device and started chatting with the worried Austrian mother... "Mom, you spoke to Morten from the band 'a-ha'", Nussbaumer informed his mother, after receiving the phone back from the Norwegian star. Since she secured her victory at an early stage of the evening, Eimear Quinn had plenty of time to prepare for going back on stage and performing "The Voice" again. Brendan Graham celebrated a second win as a writer and the big nightmare of Irish television franchises has resurfaced: How do you host a fourth Eurovision in five years?!

1997 - Dublin, Ireland

If there was one thing the Irish could not stand anymore in 1997, it was hosting another Eurovision... It seemed that Ireland was fed up to their back teeth with the European contest. Four wins in five years, 4 productions to make in the same amount of time and all without getting into the financial costs and the need to be original every time all over again. Undoubtedly, the Irish wished they could be left alone and not host the ESC. It would be interesting to know whether they still feel so, 24 years later... The intervals between the entries suggested the mood in the country: Well-known artists such as Julio Iglesias and Céline Dion, who started in the Eurovision, greeted the participants, while in between, the last Irish Eurovision winners performed in an amusing situation where they are blaming each other for the victories that brought the contest to the country... Dublin passed the test with dignity, the 1997 Eurovision production was pretty good, but had nothing unique or exciting. In response to Morten Harket from Oslo, the Irish brought Ronan Keating alongside actor Carrie Crowley. The EBU decided to withdraw from the 1996 pre-qualification method, which caused great controversy and left harsh sentiment for some countries. Instead, they set a key to participation reflected in the countries' achievements in their last four Eurovision participations (the decision left Belgium, Finland and Slovakia out). Italy's return and Germany's automatic participation (as one of the contest's five main sponsors) increased the number of countries, again, to 25. Israel withdrew from the event scheduled for the eve of the Holocaust Remembrance Day (but was still broadcast it live), thus saving Bosnia, which was supposed to be left out due to its balance in the past four years. It was a totally predictable Eurovision: The winner was determined almost in advance, and no one had any doubt regarding her identity. The UK was hungry for its first win after 16 years when throughout the dry spell, the British finished four times in the second place and were favourites quite a few more times for a win that did not come. But this time, as mentioned, Katrina and "The Waves" took no prisoners and left no other choice to the jurors with the hit "Love Shine a Light". The British victory was one of the most glorious in the history of the ESC in general and of the United Kingdom in particular: 10 Douze Points, points from all countries, only five times being awarded less than 8 points and 227 points, which were almost eighty per cent of the possible votes, an amazing balance. Far behind Katrina, local Marc Roberts reached the second place with "Mysterious Woman". Before another long-term retirement from European contest, Italy came pretentious with "Fiumi di parole" by the "Jalisse" duo. A victory or close competition with the British did not seem improbable (eventually only a disappointing fourth place for a beloved and remembered song from that year). Turkey made history, celebrating its historic third place as if it had won the grand prize. Şebnem Paker who represented her country for the second successive year proved that she is a trump card and gave the Turkish people a spectacular achievement with 121 points, following which she was accepted in Istanbul and Ankara as a national hero. For the second time in the history of the current points method and for the first time since 1983, this wonder enabling a participant to get zero points and not be last occurred: it was the consolation of Norway and Portugal that hung side by side, with an awkward and empty balance in the last place. Ralph Siegel wrote the entry "Zeit" especially for the Israeli singer Esther Ofarim who was in Germany. He offered her the song, proposed Ofarim to represent the Germans at the Eurovision but was quite offended when she informed him through his representative about her financial demands (150,000 marks for the task). Fate destined this excellent entry to Bianca Shomburg, but Europe failed to appreciate the quality, and Germany was rightly disappointed with the 18th place. Poland's Anna Maria Jopek struck with "Aie jestem", which was the song of the year in Poland and is still considered one of the notable classics of the contest. Russia sent the most prominent name it could offer: superstar Alla Pugacheva, who wrote, composed and wholeheartedly performed

"Primadonna", a big hit in the country that was slightly less successful in Dublin. Icelander Paul Oscar took the free spirit that started to rise in the contest a step further and performed "Minn hinsti dans" sitting on a couch surrounded by dancing maidens. In the voting, Oscar collapsed to the 20th place. Austria, Switzerland, Germany, Sweden and the UK were the pioneers of the telephone vote that allowed the audience at home to decide the score their country would award, instead of the traditional jury. This was a modern, very tempting venture that was also economically viable but made the decision on the winner more popular and less professional. This led to a reminder of a few seconds from each entry at the end of the show, to encourage the audience at home to vote over the phone. This graded transition to televoting, was certainly a choice of attractions over a purely musical one. A sign of this could be seen in the fact that the Icelandic Paul Oscar received 16 points from the five telephone voting countries and only two from the rest! France broke a small record when, in addition to Frédéric Ferrer, Marie Myriam — France's last Eurovision winner (as of this writing), also read the local voting's results. Already after four votes, The UK led, gaining a considerable margin that only cultivated to the end, while winning five consecutive Douze Points and thus equalling Izhar Cohen's record from 1978. Katrina and "The Waves" proudly went on to receive their award, granting The UK a fifth unquestionably justified victory. Two years after the football returned home in the 1996 Euro tournament, the Eurovision Song Contest also came back to England.

1998 – Birmingham, United Kingdom

The Eurovision returned to The UK After 16 years, and the British certainly missed it. Birmingham was chosen to host the event, and 25 countries took part in the fascinating contest. Ulrika Johnson (the Swedish television figure who did well in the broadcast) and the British Mr Eurovision, Terry Wogan, presented the event. Until the 1998 Eurovision, the connection between the gay community and the European song contest was hidden beneath the surface, but afterwards, the smouldering embers became a fait accompli, and the Eurovision grew most identified with the LGBTQ community. Love it or hate it, Dana International's breakthrough win at the event in Birmingham has changed the contest forever. In the four Eurovisions before 1998, Israel participated only once, and the 1990s seemed to be the worst period for the country that won twice (1978 and 1979). It appeared that Dana saved not only Israel's honour but also the future of the ESC that was utterly in doubt. In fact, since 1995, the IBA had hoped that the intriguing Dana, with her unusual life story, would come to the European stage and wreak havoc. Once, she achieved second place in the pre-selection, a second time, she avoided the local pre process, and a third time — lucky. Yoav Ginay joined Svika pick, and the two created "Diva" that suited Dana perfectly and sounded like a winning song from the get-go. Europe embraced "Diva", the brilliant entry, in addition to Dana's personality and appearance, which made Israel a candidate to win the contest after a long time. Dana International was under tremendous pressure throughout the week of preparations, and the fear was that she would arrive exhausted and nervous for the decisive moment. A day before, in an impatient interview with Channel 1's "Diary", Dana called her interviewers "geeks". Dana's nervousness made sense, as much tension and intrigue took place within the Israeli delegation. There was some bad blood between Svika pick and Dana and her team — Pick wanted to conduct the orchestra, but Ofer Nissim (Dana's manager) thought that if a full musical playback is used, there is no place for Pick to conduct. Of course, Pick did not agree and operated independently in Birmingham, even when the rehearsals did not go smoothly. Despite everything, Dana overcame the problems and performed Diva with all her might and pride, all the way to her incredible victory. But like the rest of Israel's winnings (except for the first one), it only came after a difficult and arduous birth.

The rehearsal week was not easy and characterised by quite a few confrontations between the British production team (led by Kevin Bishop and Jeff Posner) and some of the participants. Most of the complaints came from the Greek delegation, which was not satisfied with the shooting angles and blamed the organisers for their failure and 20th place. Incidentally, the Greeks were the first country in the contest's history to receive only a single Douze Points (from Cyprus of course ...) and nothing else. On the evening of the show, the Greek band "Thalassa" threatened to quit the contest due to the substantive disagreements but eventually recanted. The composer of the entry Yiannis Valvis claimed that Israel got the angles of shooting that the British refused to give Greece because "Diva" was the song favoured by the organisers ... Turkey also had quite a few problems with "Unutamazsın", one of the best entries in the contest musically. The excellent performer Tüzmen had to deal with the time constraints (3 minutes) that his entry had deviated from, but in the end, everything went well, and the Turks stood up, leaving behind a fantastic song that deserved much better than 14th place. For the first time, eight competitors competed with playback instead of a live orchestra. This was the prelude to the decision by the producer of the 1999 Eurovision, Amnon Barkai, to cancel the live orchestra altogether. The orchestra's end was also the parting point from the conductor and a musical style that many misses. Germany and Slovenia presented their conductors, even though their songs were in full playback and the conductors had nothing to do. After the successful pilot of the previous year, another crucial decision was that all countries would give their votes according to an open telephone vote by the viewers. This fantastic income source opened the appetite and space for making the Eurovision a lucrative commercial business. Turkey, Romania, Hungary and Slovakia have refused to use the Televoting system and have stayed with their jurors. North Macedonia made its debut at the Eurovision, while Russia expressed a unique protest that it was not allowed to participate in Birmingham (due to low average results in recent years): It did not broadcast the event, thus violating the EBU's guidelines, what prevented it from participating in the next year's contest. The Russians will return, in a big way, to the first Eurovision of the next millennium. Except for Dana International, which aroused great curiosity because she was the first transgender person to participate in the Eurovision, the British Imaani was also an earnest candidate to win the contest at home with "Where are you?". This great pop song, which was successful before and after the contest (even outside the UK), was the only one to receive points from all countries (The UK is the only one in history to receive points from all the participating countries in two consecutive years, apart of France). It also won 4 Douze Points but failed to produce a British winning streak and reached the second place that is so familiar to the British, for the 15th time, and the last one so far.

Another contestant treated favourably by the gambling agencies was Mélanie Cohl of Belgium with the song "Dis oui", which reached sixth place. Four artists returned to the Eurovision: José Cid of Portugal (1980) was the co-writer of "Se eu te pudesse abraçar" and accompanied the singer Alma Lusa. Paul Harrington of Ireland (the other half in a duo with Charlie McGettigan who won in 1994) accompanied Dawn Martin. Croatia's Danijela (who was part of "Magazin" with Lydia in 1995) marvelled with "Neka mi ne svane" and gave her country one of its most significant achievements of all time — the 5th place with 132 points. Egon Egemann, the singing violinist from Switzerland (1990), was part of the duo who wrote and composed "Lass ihn" and accompanied the performer Gunvor, but this was an evening he will certainly want to erase from his memories, as the country that hosted and won the first Eurovision, ended the night with placed last and zero points. The surprise of the contest came from Malta: Chiara, arrived without pretensions with a tender entry that received many compliments in rehearsals: "The One That I Love." In Malta, they did not believe Chiara could win, but it turned out that the spectators thought otherwise, and the Maltese performer realised that she would run head-to-head with Israel until the very last moment, only to be disappointed in the cruellest way, to finish in the third place. Another surprise was Edsilia from the Netherlands with "Hemel en aarde". 151 points and a place in the final 4, were the Dutch's biggest achievement since winning in 1975, a feat that went against expectations, with the Netherlands clinging to first place in the first part of the voting. The older, balding Guildo Horn of Germany, which seemed to many pathetic and amusing to others, appeared to be an outsider in Bermingham. The writer of the entry "Guildo hat euch lieb!", Stefan Raab, knew exactly what he was doing and contributed to turning the Eurovision from a singing contest to a show in which songs are only incidental. Three Douze Points (just like the winner!) made it clear that the spectators loved Horn's wandering and hilarity, which ended in the seventh place to everyone's astonishment. There was no dull moment during the voting which moved like a rollercoaster and included suspense and humour. Croatia, which was the first to vote, skipped Israel and awarded all the points to the host, but Dana International gained 44 points from the next four countries, with France and Spain giving her one Douze Points after the other.

Finished? Definitely not. Slovakia and Hungary also did not give a single point to Israel, behind which the UK, the Netherlands, Croatia, and sometimes Belgium, sprang up. But Malta was the biggest problem, leading five times during the evening and clinging to Dana throughout the voting's final stages. An unforgettable moment was when Ulrika Johnson turned to the Dutch announcer Conny Vandenbos, who represented her country at the 1965 Eurovision. The 61-year-old Conny was proud of her past and said that she had participated in the contest a few years ago. "This was a lot of years ago," Johnson said and the audience burst into laughter that lasted a while. Terry Wogan, the second presenter who accompanied the vote from the BBC's broadcast position, did not spare his co-announcer and said: "You have to get out of this fast... wait until I get back on stage." Back to the suspenseful Voting: Malta continued to erode Israel's lead until it completely closed the lead in perfect timing, with North Macedonia remaining to vote and the two leaders tied together with 166 points, and The UK behind with 157 points and a low chance of eliminating the margin. The breath was taken when North Macedonia awarded 8 points to Israel, which immediately eliminated Imaani's chances and ruled that any points for Malta would bring the next Eurovision to Valletta. Ten points went to the UK, and the hall held its breath to hear from Evgenija Teodosievska who the victor would be. Every name aside from Malta will bring the Eurovision back to Jerusalem after 20 years, and indeed the prayers of Dana International were answered. The 12 points from North Macedonia went to its neighbour Croatia. There were roars of joy from every house in Israel, and in Birmingham, the Israeli delegation jumped onto the stage. Interestingly, shortly after the contest ended, it became clear to the EBU that a mistake had been made in the Spanish vote: Germany received 12 points, Israel lost two points, and one point was reduced from each country getting points from Spain, including the United Kingdom and Malta. The source of the error was never revealed, nor is speculation about what would have happened if these were the crucial points of the race ... In the end, the Spanish score correction did not affect the scoreboard in any way. Another anecdote: Malta awarded 12 points to Israel while the winner gave only 7 points to Chiara.

The first to arrive at the stage were the backing singers and of course the songwriters Yoav Ginay and Svika pick. Ginay received the prize but Pick ("Let me hold it") snatched it from his hands ... Yoav did not give in and pulled the figurine back... Dana International came on stage with the unique parrot dress designed by Jean-Paul Gautier. She took centre stage, with the hosts rushing to finish the broadcast, before Katrina, who won the previous year, managed to embrace her successor. "Diva" is the first winner in the Eurovision history to be performed with full musical playback. "See you next year in Jerusalem, I want to thank you for everything, see you next year in Israel," said Dana during the replay of Diva, at an unforgettable moment. A second later, her life will be changed forever. Israel wins the ESC for the third time and the last contest of the millennium will be held in Jerusalem. Dana International was welcomed as a national hero in Israel, received a festive reception in Prime Minister Benjamin Netanyahu's office and declared that her victory was "my gift for Israel's 50th Independence Day celebrations."

1999 – Jerusalem, Israel

The 1999 Eurovision landed on the IBA as a thunderstorm. Although Dana International's chances of winning in Birmingham were high, with the many disappointments over the years, the Israel television bosses doubted that this would happen and found themselves on the morning of May 10th, 1998, with a substantial task.

Uri Porath, Director General of the IBA, and Yair Stern, Managing Director of Israel Television, understood that first a producer should be appointed for the event. Despite the heavy pressure to appoint Aharon Goldfinger and Yossi Meshulam, the choice was the talented Amnon Barkai, who, like his predecessor in 1979, had experience in the IBA's sports department and proved was successful in orchestrating elaborate productions.

Barkai minded the matter seriously and took off for a meeting with Kevin Bishop of the BBC who had that same job in 1998. He continued to meetings at the RTÉ offices in Dublin, a network that hosted no less than four (!) Eurovision events in the 90's. His motto was: "Everything must run smoothly, without mishaps."

Jerusalem was chosen without any hesitation as the host city, in an order by Prime Minister Benjamin Netanyahu and the mayor of the Israeli capital, Ehud Olmert. Thus, for the second time in 20 years, the International Convention Centre was chosen to host the ESC, probably for the last time (the theatre does not meet the EBU standards anymore). In general, this was the last time the Eurovision was held in an auditorium and not in an arena.

Yigal Ravid, a veteran radio and television personality and a great Eurovision expert, received the prestigious nomination to be the contest presenter. Alongside, Dafna Dekel was chosen for her knowledge of the French language. And where did Sigal Shachmon come from? Uri Porath exercised his authority and a pressurised the production team to include Shachmon as a presenter, making it the first time there were three presenters on stage. Ravid did it with great professionalism, Dafna Dekel was quite lukewarm, while Shachmon was indeed beautiful, but the event seemed to be a little too much for her.

Barkai began working on the technical details: 22 cameras were imported (some from the Netherlands — courtesy of Ralph Inbar), a broadcasting truck was rented from Belgium, sophisticated lighting equipment was brought in from Germany and broadcasting stations from Spain. At the beginning of January, Barkai submitted his resignation due to the IBA's decision to choose the artist Yaakov Agam as a stage designer for the contest, in place of Maya Hanoch. Two weeks later, the IBA recanted their decision, Barkai retracted his resignation, and thus one of the most unique stage designs in the Eurovision was born.

Barkai is also the one who led the decision to give up on live orchestra as a time saver because most countries were already using playback. It was not a simple decision, although it saved a lot of time, headaches and logistical coordination, but at the same time aroused criticism, including Johnny Logan, the man who won the Eurovision twice as a performer and once as the writer of a song who commented — "This is karaoke contest".

Another major decision was that for the first time since 1977, each country would be able to sing in any language it wishes, leading to a flood of entries in English (with a majority of over 12 countries choosing it). As a result of the change, the English language will completely dominate the Eurovision.

The contest was broadcast in stereo to the entire world, but in Israel, devil's luck, due to improper handling of the sound on one of the satellites — the transmission was faulty. A special but incomplete compilation of the contest's songs was released for sale by the EBU, which became a permanent tradition.

Two days before the dress rehearsal, the Rebbe of Gur announced that there would be no Shabbat desecration so no rehearsals on Friday or the day of the event ... Major General Arieh Yitzhaki of the Israeli Police, came to the rescue regarding a rare agreement with the Rebbe to relinquish the Friday rehearsal and hold it before the end of the Sabbath. On the one hand, there was a monetary loss (tickets were sold for the Friday event), but on the other hand, the threat of a large ultra-Orthodox demonstration in front of Binyanei Ha'uma was eliminated, which would have cast a very heavy shadow on the peaceful existence of the event.

While in other contests the broadcasters use the time slots between entries to talk about the next song, special video clips were screened. The clips combined animation by Yossi Abulafia, depicting Biblical stories, with video photography (starring real actors), illustrating the story's connection to the present time. Later, the IBA regretted spending a large amount of money on the clips.

The number of participants was reduced to 23, when Latvia was due to make its debut but did not register on time, allowing Hungary to participate but their local television gave up the option. Portugal became the 23rd country to take part in the Jerusalem 1999 Contest.

One favourite candidate, Selma of Iceland, undertook the many expectations of a historic victory for her country. "All out of luck" sounds like a winning entry and the Icelanders came to Jerusalem proud and ready for the win. The press conference held for Selma before the contest itself spoke in its own right. One of the journalists said: "Assuming you win this Eurovision…. and you will win this Eurovision ..."

After the press conference, the Icelandic press officer distributed Selma's merchandise. The way people went after the merchandise resembled the distribution of food packages to the needy... In less than a minute, everything was gone ... For those familiar with the Eurovision, it was clear that being a favourite for the win would actually harm Selma because the jurors and the audience do not usually like favourites. On the other hand, it was clear that Iceland would rank high. Finally, despite Selma's glamorous appearance, a tight vote and 146 points, Iceland did not win and was forced to settle on the second place, which is its best ever.

Far away in another corner sat Gert Langstrand, the Swedish songwriter, whom nobody approached or considered. He said: "We will win, we have a better song than Iceland, they tell me we have a song with an excellent chance." A journalist who listened to the conversation later commented sarcastically: "No one told him anything, it's only himself ... They have no chance ..." The entry "Take me to your heaven" sounds like a classic imitation of "ABBA", but with the enthusiastic performer Charlotte Nilsson, apparently included the ingredients that appealed to the juries and the audience. By the time of the dress rehearsal, Sweden was already noticeable, and Langstrand could have been proud of his feelings: Charlotte had given Sweden a fourth win, sweeping 163 points and getting points from every country but Croatia.

Ralph Siegel was not supposed to return to the Eurovision after losing the German battle with his German-Turkish band "Surpriz", to the blind singer Corrina May. But a smart man like Siegel was not ready to give up the opportunity to return to Jerusalem, and he found illegal cracks in May's entry, which led to its disqualification and paved the way for the participation of "Journey to Jerusalem" in the 1999 Eurovision. The Germans were the fans of the audience in Israel, thanks to the engaging performance and the rhythmic song with ethnic touches. It was essential to Siegel to win in Jerusalem: "I want to win and dedicate my victory to the wonderful State of Israel and the Jewish people. I think of the hardships they have gone through. I do not understand how my people could do such a thing," said Ralph in one of the evenings in the lobby of the Crown Plaza Hotel next to Binyanei Ha'uma and burst into tears. The Germans received 5 Douze Points (equal to the winner, Sweden), but in terms of gathering points they always remained a step or two behind the Sweden and Norway, settled for third place. Ralph and his band could take comfort because the host, Israel, gave Germany the full mark (12 points).

The Croatian Doris Dragović was back in shape and stronger, 13 years after she represented

Yugoslavia in Bergen. "Marija Magdalena" brought Croatia its most remarkable achievements with the fourth place and is considered one of the most favourite songs in this contest.

The first time Israel hosted the Eurovision (1979), it also completed a rare double win (only three other countries did so throughout history — Spain won 1969, Luxembourg and, of course, Ireland) but this time the hurdle was too high. Producer Shlomo Zach wanted to close the circle with his band "Eden", which consisted of the brothers Butler, Doron Oren and Rafael Dahan, who managed to break out of their anonymity in Israel and starred in the preparations for the Eurovision. The band performed a festive entry that still holds up — the song "Happy birthday". Secretly, the band members might have hoped that they would succeed in recreating Dana's win, and after the dress rehearsal some echoed this feeling, but on the night of the contest, "Happy birthday" only managed to reach the top 5.

Norway, led by the head of its delegation, Jon Ola Sand (now the chief supervisor of the Eurovision), wanted the young van Eijk to represent it and get a second chance to perform "Living my life without you" after he claimed that audio failures accompanied his performance. But as in the case of Carola in 1991, these faults were local only and had no effect on the transmission and therefore the request was disregarded. Sand also decided to deal with Croatia, which used its playback in masculine background voices. Norway appealed to the EBU, which chose not to touch the Croatian score on the one hand but to subtract it from the weighting of Croatia's calculating places over the next five years.

Three who saw themselves as great favourites for the contest ended extremely disappointed: The Netherlands was sure of Marlayne's right to "One good reason," but was pushed to ninth place; France with Nayah was convinced that as in those beautiful days "Je veux donner ma voix" in the slow French style, will easily take the lead, but the times have changed, and Nayah returned to Paris after finished 19th; Cyprus was convinced that this time it was with "It will be love" performed by Marlen Angelidou, who climbed to second place in the betting tables on the eve of the event and indeed finished the second place, but from the bottom ...

The major surprise came from Bosnia: as in the case of Germany, the "passengers" by Dino & Béatrice replaced the original entry that Bosnia chose and "starred" in the bets for the last place. The Bosnian duo thought differently and easily reached the seventh place with 12 points from Austria.

The video of Dana International against the backdrop of the Old City was a considerable success. Apropos Dana, she was invited to award Yaacov Agam's sculpture — a prestigious but hefty prize — to the Swedish winners. Dana stumbled with the statue on the stage, but she was lucky and was not hurt (it is said that the statue was a little twisted), thanks to the Swedish songwriter Gert Langstrand's resourcefulness who crouched down and softened her fall.

Earlier, there was a close and intriguing vote, with Sweden and Iceland swapping the first place, and Germany in the background trying to get closer. In the penultimate vote, Bosnia was the tipping point of the race, with a 3-point advantage for Sweden over Iceland, giving no point to Selma, but a Douze to Charlotte and Sweden.

The event ended with an impressive performance by all the Eurovision singing participants singing "Hallelujah" (winner of the 1979 Contest) in honour of the Balkans, who, due to the war there, could not watch the contest. The 1999 Eurovision broke the viewing record in Israel and climbed at its peak to 50% (an unprecedented rating in the country's inter-channel contest).

1990

Hosting Country: Yugoslavia

Hosting City: Zagreb

Date: 5.5.1990

Location: Vatroslav Lisinski Concert Hall

Presenters: Helga Vlahović Brnobić, Oliver Mlakar

Orchestra Conductor: Igor Kuljerić

Chief Executive: Frank Naef

Director: Nenad Puhovski

Executive Producer: Goran Radman

Participating Countries: 22

Every participating country has a jury (16 members) that gives 1-8 points and then 10 and 12 points to its favourite song

Broadcaster: Yugoslav Radio Television (JRT) / Radiotelevision Zagreb (RTZ)

Intermediate performance: Yugoslav Changes — a film about tourism in the country.

Duration: 2 hours and 50 minutes

Broadcast: To all participating countries and to Australia, Bulgaria, Canada, China, Czechoslovakia, Hungary, Japan, Poland, Romania, South Korea and the Soviet Union.

No.	Country	Song	Performing Artist	Lyrics	Composer	Conductor	Language	Commentator	Spoker of Results	Points	Place
01	Spain	"Bandido"	Azúcar Moreno (Antonia Salazar Encarnación Salazar)	José Luis Abel	Raúl Orellana, Jaime Stinus	Eduardo Leyva	Spanish	Luis Cobos	Matilde Jarrín	96	5
02	Greece	"Horis skopo"	Christos Callow & Wave	Yiorgos Papayiannakis	Yiorgos Papayiannakis	Michalis Rozakis	Greek	Dafni Bokota	Fotini Giannou-latou	11	19
03	Belgium	"Macédomienne"	Philippe Lafontaine	Philippe Lafontaine	Philippe Lafontaine	Rony Brack	French	Claude Delacroix and Luc Appermont	Jacques Olivier	46	12
04	Turkey	"Gözlerinin Hapsindeyim"	Kayahan	Kayahan	Kayahan	Ümit Eroglu	Turkish	Başak Doğru	Korhan Abay	21	17
05	The Netherlands	"Ik wil alles met je delen"	Maywood (Alice May, Caren Wood)	Alie de Vries	Alie de Vries	Harry van Hoof	Dutch	Willem van Beusekom	Joop van Os	25	15
06	Luxembourg	"Quand je te rêve"	Céline Carzo	Thierry Delianis	Jean-Charles France	Thierry Durbet	French	Valérie Sarn	Jean-Luc Bertrand	38	13
07	United Kingdom	"Give a Little Love Back to the World"	Emma	Paul Curtis	Paul Curtis	Alyn Ainsworth	English	Terry Wogan	Colin Berry	87	6
08	Iceland	"Eitt lag enn"	Stjórnin (Grétar Örvarsson, Sigríður Beinteinsdóttir)	Aðalsteinn Ásberg Sigurðsson	Hörður G. Ólafsson	Jon Kjell Seljeseth	Icelandic	Arthúr Björgvin Bollason	Árni Snævarr	124	4
09	Norway	"Brandenburger Tor"	Ketil Stokkan	Ketil Stokkan	Ketil Stokkan	Pete Knutsen	Norweigen	Leif Erik Forberg	Sverre Christophersen	8	21
10	Israel	"Shara Barchovot"	Rita	Tzruya Lahav	Rami Kleinstein	Rami Levin	Hebrew	-	Yitzhak Shimoni	16	18
11	Denmark	"Hallo Hallo"	Lonnie Devantier	Keld Heick	John Hatting, Torben Lendager	Henrik Krogsgaard	Danish	Jørgen de Mylius	Bent Henius	64	8
12	Switzerland	"Musik klingt in die Welt hinaus"	Egon Egemann	Cornelia Lackner	Cornelia Lackner	Bela Balint	German	Bernard Thurnheer, Thierry Masselot, Emanuela Gaggini	Michel Stocker	51	11
13	Germany	"Frei zu leben"	Chris Kempers & Daniel Kovac	Michael Kunze	Ralph Siegel	Rainer Pietsch	German	Fritz Egner	Gabi Schnelle	60	9
14	France	"White and Black Blues"	Joëlle Ursull	Serge Gainsbourg	Georges Ougier de Moussac	Régis Dupré	French	Richard Adaridi	Valérie Maurice	132	2
15	Yugoslavia	"Hajde da ludujemo"	Tajči	Alka Vuica	Zrinko Tutić	Stjepan Mihaljinec	Croatian	Branko Uvodić and Saša Gerdej	Drago Čulina	81	7
16	Portugal	"Há sempre alguém"	Nucha	Francisco Pereira, Frederico Pereira	Luís Filipe, Jan van Dijck	Carlos Alberto Moniz	Portuguese	Ana do Carmo	João Abel Fonseca	9	20
17	Ireland	"Somewhere in Europe"	Liam Reilly	Liam Reilly	Liam Reilly	Noel Kelehan	English	Jimmy Greeley and Clíona Ní Bhuachalla	Eileen Dunne	132	3
18	Sweden	"Som en vind"	Edin-Ådahl (Frank Ådahl, Simon Ådahl, Bertil Edin, Lasse Edin)	Mikael Wendt	Mikael Wendt	Curt-Eric Holmquist	Swedish	Jan Jingryd	Jan Ellerås	24	16
19	Italy	"Insieme: 1992"	Toto Cutugno	Salvatore Cutugno	Salvatore Cutugno	Gianni Madonini	Italian	Peppi Franzelin	Paolo Frajese	149	1
20	Austria	"Keine Mauern mehr"	Haris Anastasiou	Mario Botazzi	Marc Berry, Nanna Berry	Richard Österreicher	German	Barbara Stöckl	Tilia Herold	58	10
21	Cyprus	"Milas poli"	Haris Anastasiou	Haris Anastasiou	John Vickers	Stanko Selak	Greek	Neophytos Taliotis	Anna Partelidou	36	14
22	Finland	"Fri?"	Beat (Janne Engblom, Kim Engblom, Tina Petersson, Tina Krause)	Stina Engblom	Kim Engblom, Tina Krause, Janne Engblom	Olli Ahvenlaht	Finland	Erkki Pohjanheimo and Ossi Runne	Solveig Herlin	8	22

	Spain	Greece	Belgium	Turkey	The Netherlands	Luxembourg	United Kingdom	Iceland	Norway	Israel	Denmark	Switzerland	Germany	France	Yugoslavia	Portugal	Ireland	Sweden	Italy	Austria	Cyprus	Finland	
Spain	■	8	1	10	2	-	1	4	5	-	-	6	12	5	3	5	-	-	8	8	8	10	Spain
Greece	-	■	-	-	5	-	-	-	-	-	-	-	-	-	-	-	-	-	-	-	6	-	Greece
Belgium	-	-	■	-	7	4	-	-	1	-	-	4	8	8	-	2	1	7	-	4	-	-	Belgium
Turkey	-	-	-	■	3	-	-	2	4	-	-	-	5	-	7	-	-	-	-	-	-	-	Turkey
The Netherlands	-	1	-	3	■	1	4	-	-	2	-	3	-	6	-	1	-	-	2	-	2	-	The Netherlands
Luxembourg	-	4	-	-	-	■	3	-	-	-	-	-	3	12	2	3	-	-	1	5	5	-	Luxembourg
United Kingdom	7	5	12	-	-	3	■	-	-	10	3	10	1	10	10	-	6	-	6	1	3	-	United Kingdom
Iceland	4	3	10	1	-	8	12	■	10	8	10	7	-	-	4	12	7	8	3	10	-	7	Iceland
Norway	-	-	-	-	-	-	-	-	■	4	1	-	-	-	-	-	3	-	-	-	-	-	Norway
Israel	-	-	-	-	4	-	-	-	-	■	-	2	4	-	1	-	-	-	-	-	-	5	Israel
Denmark	6	-	3	2	-	-	-	7	7	7	■	1	-	-	-	7	4	3	7	6	4	-	Denmark
Switzerland	1	12	-	6	-	2	-	-	-	-	12	■	-	1	5	8	-	-	-	-	1	3	Switzerland
Germany	8	-	6	-	-	12	7	1	-	-	4	-	■	-	-	-	10	4	5	3	-	-	Germany
France	5	-	4	4	12	-	-	12	12	6	5	12	10	■	12	4	8	5	-	2	7	12	France
Yugoslavia	3	-	-	12	-	-	5	10	3	12	7	-	-	2	■	-	5	1	10	-	10	1	Yugoslavia
Portugal	-	-	-	-	-	7	2	-	-	-	-	-	-	-	-	■	-	-	-	-	-	-	Portugal
Ireland	10	7	7	5	10	6	10	8	8	-	8	5	7	7	-	6	■	12	-	12	-	4	Ireland
Sweden	2	2	-	-	6	-	6	-	6	-	-	-	2	-	-	-	-	■	-	-	-	-	Sweden
Italy	12	10	8	8	8	10	-	3	-	1	6	8	6	4	6	10	12	10	■	7	12	8	Italy
Austria	-	-	2	7	1	5	8	6	-	-	-	-	-	3	8	-	2	2	12	■	-	2	Austria
Cyprus	-	6	5	-	-	-	-	-	2	5	2	-	-	-	-	-	-	6	4	-	■	6	Cyprus
Finland	-	-	-	-	-	-	-	5	-	3	-	-	-	-	-	-	-	-	-	-	-	■	Finland

Hosting Country: Italy

Hosting City: Rome

Date: 4.5.1991

Location: Studio 15 di Cinecittà

Presenters: Gigliola Cinquetti, Toto Cutugno

Orchestra Conductor: Bruno Canfora

Chief Executive: Frank Naef

Director: Riccardo Donna

Executive Producer: Silvia Salvetti

Participating Countries: 22

Every participating country has a jury (16 members) that gives 1-8 points and then 10 and 12 points to its favourite song

Broadcaster: Radiotelevisione Italiana (RAI)

Intermediate performance: Arturo Brachetti

Duration: 3 hours and 13 minutes

Broadcast: To all participating countries and Australia, Bulgaria, Canada, China, Czechoslovakia, Hungary, Japan, Poland, Romania and Soviet Union.

1991

No.	Country	Song	Performing Artist	Lyrics	Composer	Conductor	Language	Commentator	Spoker of Results	Points	Place
01	Yugoslavia	"Brazil"	Baby Doll (Dragana Šarić)	Dragana Šarić	Zoran Vracević	Slobodan Marković	Serb	Mladen Popović, Ksenija Urličić, Miša Molk	Mebrura Topolovac	1	21
02	Iceland	"Draumur um Nínu"	Stefán & Eyfi (Eyjólfur Kristjánsson, Stefán Hilmarsson)	Eyjólfur Kristjánsson	Eyjólfur Kristjánsson	Jón Ólafsson	Icelandic	Arthúr Björgvin Bollason	Guðríður Ólafsdóttir	26	15
03	Malta	"Could It Be"	Georgina & Paul Giordimaina	Raymond Mahoney	Paul Abela	Paul Abela	English	Toni Sant	Dominic Micallef	106	6
04	Greece	"I anixi"	Sophia Vossou	Andreas Mikroutsikos	Andreas Mikroutsikos	Haris Andreadis	Greek	Dafni Bokota	Fotini Giannou-latou	36	13
05	Switzerland	"Canzone per te"	Sandra Simó	Renato Mascetti	Renato Mascetti	Flaviano Cuffari	Italian	Bernard Thurnheer, Lolita Morena, Emanuela Gaggini	Michel Stocker	118	5
06	Austria	"Venedig im Regen"	Thomas Forstner	Robby Musenbichler, Hubert Moser, Wolfgang Eltner	Robby Musenbichler, Hubert Moser, Wolfgang Eltner	Richard Österreicher	German	Herbert Dobrovolny	Gabriele Haring	0	22
07	Luxembourg	"Un baiser volé"	Sarah Bray	Mick Wersant, Linda Lecomte	Patrick Hippert	Francis Goya	French	Valérie Sarn	Jean-Luc Bertrand	29	14
	Sweden	"Fångad av en stormvind"	Carola	Stephan Berg	Stephan Berg	Anders Berglund	Swedish	Harald Treutiger	Bo Hagström	146	1
09	France	"C'est le dernier qui a parlé qui a raison"	Amina	Amina Annabi Wasis Diop	Amina Annabi Wasis Diop	Jérôme Pillement	French	Léon Zitrone	Marie-France Brière	146	2
10	Turkey	"İki Dakika"	İzel Çeliköz, Reyhan Karaca & Can Uğurluer	Aysel Gürel	Şevket Uğurluer	Turhan Yükseler	Turkish	Başak Doğru	Canan Kumbasar	44	12
11	Ireland	"Could It Be That I'm In Love"	KJackson	Liam Reilly	Liam Reilly	Noel Kelehan	English	Pat Kenny	Eileen Dunne	47	11
12	Portugal	"Lusitana paixão"	Dulce Pontes	Fred Micaelo, José Da Ponte	Jorge Quintela, José Da Ponte	Fernando Correia Martins	Portuguese	Ana do Carmo	Maria Margarida Gaspar	62	8
13	Denmark	"Lige der hvor hjertet slår"	Anders Frandsen	Michael Elo	Michael Elo	Henrik Krogsgaard	Danish	Camilla Miehe-Renard	Bent Henius	8	19
14	Norway	"Mrs. Thompson"	Just 4 Fun (Marianne Antonsen, Jan Groth, Eirikur Hauksson, Hanne Krogh)	Dag Kolsrud	P.G. Roness, Kaare Skevik Jr.	Pete Knutsen	Norweigen	John Andreassen and Jahn Teigen	Sverre Chris-tophersen	14	17
15	Israel	"Kan"	Duo Datz (Orna and Moshe Datz)	Uzi Chitman	Uzi Chitman	Kobi Oshrat	Hebrew	-	Yitzhak Shimoni	139	3
16	Finland	"Hullu yö"	Kaija Kärkinen	Jukka Välimaa	Ile Kallio	Olli Ahvenlahti	Finish	Erkki Pohjanheimo	Heidi Kokki	6	20
17	Germany	"Dieser Traum darf niemals sterben"	Atlantis 2000 (Alfons Weindorf, Jutta Niedhardt, Helmut Frey, Eberhard Wilhelm, Klaus Propper, Clemens Weindorf)	Alfons Weindorf	Helmut Frey	Herman Weindorf	German	Max Schautzer	Christian Eckhardt	10	18
18	Belgium	"Geef het op"	Clouseau (Kris Wauters, Koen Wauters, Bob Savenberg)	Kris Wauters, Koen Wauters, Bob Savenberg, Jan Leyers	Kris Wauters, Koen Wauters, Bob Savenberg, Jan Leyers	Roland Verloven	Flemish	André Vermeulen and Claude Delacroix	An Ploegaerts	23	16
19	Spain	"Bailar pegados"	Sergio Dalma	Luis Gómez Escobar	Julio Seijas	Eduardo Leiva	Spanish	Tomás Fernando Flores	María Ángeles Balanac	119	4
20	United Kingdom	"A Message to Your Heart"	Samantha Janus	Paul Curtis	Paul Curtis	Ronnie Hazlehurst	English	Terry Wogan	Colin Berry	47	10
21	Cyprus	"SOS"	Elena Patroklou	Andreas Christou	Kypros Charalambus	Alexandros Kyros Zografou	Greek	Evi Papamichail	Anna Partelidou	60	9
22	Italy	"Comme è ddoce 'o mare"	Peppino di Capri	Giampiero Artegiani	Marcello Marocchi	Bruno Canfora	Italian (Nea-politan)	-	Rosanna Vaudetti	89	7

	Yugoslavia	Iceland	Malta	Greece	Switzerland	Austria	Luxembourg	Sweden	France	Turkey	Ireland	Portugal	Denmark	Norway	Israel	Finland	Germany	Belgium	Spain	United Kingdom	Cyprus	Italy	
Yugoslavia	■	–	1	–	–	–	–	–	–	–	–	–	–	–	–	–	–	–	–	–	–	–	Yugoslavia
Iceland	–	■	–	–	4	–	–	10	–	–	–	–	–	–	–	–	5	–	–	–	–	7	Iceland
Malta	1	–	■	2	6	4	10	12	2	7	12	7	–	6	–	–	10	4	6	7	–	10	Malta
Greece	4	–	5	■	–	2	–	–	–	–	1	–	–	1	4	1	–	1	5	–	10	2	Greece
Switzerland	5	5	–	7	■	8	12	8	4	2	2	6	5	3	8	5	6	12	–	8	8	4	Switzerland
Austria	–	–	–	–	–	■	–	–	–	–	–	–	–	–	–	–	–	–	–	–	–	–	Austria
Luxembourg	–	4	–	–	–	5	■	1	–	3	–	2	4	–	–	–	3	2	–	3	2	–	Luxembourg
Sweden	6	12	–	–	10	10	7	■	–	6	3	10	12	8	10	8	12	10	4	12	6	–	Sweden
France	10	7	3	8	7	12	–	5	■	–	7	5	–	12	12	10	8	7	8	6	7	12	France
Turkey	–	–	7	–	–	–	–	–	7	■	–	–	8	–	7	–	–	–	2	5	–	8	Turkey
Ireland	3	–	4	–	3	1	8	–	–	4	■	–	7	–	1	2	2	5	–	4	–	3	Ireland
Portugal	–	8	–	4	1	–	2	7	10	5	–	■	1	2	–	7	–	–	10	–	4	1	Portugal
Denmark	–	–	–	–	–	–	–	3	–	–	–	–	■	5	–	–	–	–	–	–	–	–	Denmark
Norway	–	6	–	–	–	–	1	–	–	1	–	–	2	■	–	–	4	–	–	–	–	–	Norway
Israel	12	10	8	5	8	–	5	6	3	12	8	4	10	7	■	6	–	8	12	10	5	–	Israel
Finland	–	1	–	1	–	–	–	–	–	–	4	–	–	–	–	■	–	–	–	–	–	–	Finland
Germany	–	–	–	–	–	–	–	–	–	–	–	–	6	–	–	–	■	–	1	–	3	–	Germany
Belgium	–	–	–	–	–	3	–	2	5	–	–	–	–	–	–	3	–	■	3	2	–	5	Belgium
Spain	8	2	6	10	12	7	6	4	6	8	6	8	–	4	2	4	7	6	■	1	12	–	Spain
United Kingdom	–	–	10	3	5	6	3	–	1	–	–	1	3	–	5	–	–	3	–	■	1	6	United Kingdom
Cyprus	2	3	12	12	–	–	4	–	12	–	5	3	–	–	6	–	1	–	–	–	■	–	Cyprus
Italy	7	–	2	6	2	–	–	–	8	10	10	12	–	10	3	12	–	–	7	–	–	■	Italy

1992

Hosting Country: Sweden

Hosting City: Malmo

Date: 9.5.1992

Location: Malmö Isstadion

Presenters: Lydia Cappolicchio

Harald Treutiger

Orchestra Conductor: Anders Berglund

Chief Executive: Frank Naef

Director: Kåge Gimtell

Executive Producer: Ingvar Ernblad

Participating Countries: 23

Every participating country has a jury (16 members) that gives 1-8 points and then 10 and 12 points to its favourite song

Broadcaster: Sveriges Television (SVT)

Intermediate performance: A Century of Dance

Duration: 3 hours and 3 minutes

Broadcast: To all participating countries and to Australia, Bulgaria, Canada, China, Czechoslovakia, Hungary, Japan, Poland, Romania, Russia, North Macedonia and Slovenia.

No.	Country	Song	Performing Artist	Lyrics	Composer	Conductor	Language	Commentator	Spoker of Results	Points	Place
01	Spain	"Todo esto es la música"	Serafín	Luis Miguélez	Luis Miguélez, Alfredo Valbuena	Javier Losada	Spanish	José Luis Uribarri	María Ángeles Balañac	37	14
02	Belgium	"Nous, on veut des violons"	Morgane	Anne-Marie Gaspard	Claude Barzotti	Frank Fiévez	French	Claude Delacroix and André Vermeulen	Jacques Olivier	11	20
03	Israel	"Ze Rak Sport"	Dafna Dekel	Ehud Manor	Kobi Oshrat	Kobi Oshrat	Hebrew	-	Daniel Peer	85	6
04	Turkey	"Yaz Bitti"	Aylin Vatankoş	Aylin Uçanlar	Aldoğan Şimşekyay	Aydin Özari	Turkish	Bülend Özveren	Korhan Abay	17	19
05	Greece	"Olou tou kosmou i Elpida"	Cleopatra	Hristos Lagos	Hristos Lagos	Haris Andreadis	Greek	Dafni Bokota	Fotini Giannoulatou	94	5
06	France	"Monté la riviè"	Kali	Jean-Marc Monnerville (Kali)	Jean-Marc Monnerville (Kali)	Magdi Vasco Novarrez	Antillean Creole	Thierry Beccaro	Olivier Minne	73	8
07	Sweden	"I morgon är en annan dag"	Christer Björkman	Niklas Strömstedt	Niklas Strömstedt	Anders Berglund	Swedish	Jesper Aspegren and Björn Kjellman	Jan Jingryd	9	22
08	Portugal	"Amor d'água fresca"	Dina	Rosa Lobato de Faria	Ondina Veloso	Carlos Alberto Moniz	Portuguese	Eládio Clímaco	Ana Zanatti	26	17
09	Cyprus	"Teriazoume"	Evridiki	Giorgos Theophanous, Leonidas Malenis	Giorgos Theophanous, Leonidas Malenis	Giorgos Theophanous	French	Evi Papamichail	Anna Partelidou	57	11
10	Malta	"Little Child"	Mary Spiteri	Raymond Mahoney	Georgina Abela	Paul Abela	English	-	Anna Bonanno	123	3
11	Iceland	"Nei eða já"	Heart 2 Heart (Sigga Beinteins Sigrún Eva Ármannsdóttir Grétar Örvarsson Stefán Hilmarsson)	Stefán Hilmarsson	Friðrik Karlsson, Grétar Örvarsson	Nigel Wright	Icelandic	Árni Snævarr	Guðrún Skúladóttir	80	7
12	Finland	"Yamma, yamma"	Pave Maijanen	Heikki Harma	Pave Maijanen	Olli Ahvenlahti	Finish	Erkki Pohjanheimo and Kati Bergman	Solveig Herlin	4	23
13	Switzerland	"Mister Music Man"	Daisy Auvray	Gordon Dent	Gordon Dent	Roby Seidel	French	Mariano Tschuor, Ivan Frésard, Emanuela Gaggini	Michel Stocker	32	15
14	Luxembourg	"Sou fräi"	Marion Welter & Kontinent	Jang Linster, Ab van Goor	Jang Linster, Ab van Goor	Christian Jakob	Luxembourgish	Maurice Molitor	Unknown	10	21
15	Austria	"Zusammen geh'n"	Tony Wegas	Joachim Horn-Bernges	Dieter Bohlen	Leon Ives	German	Ernst Grissemann	Andy Lee	63	10
16	United Kingdom	"One Step Out of Time"	Michael Ball	Paul Davies, Tony Ryan, Victor Stratton	Paul Davies, Tony Ryan, Victor Stratton	Ronnie Hazlehurst	English	Terry Wogan	Colin Berry	139	2
17	Ireland	"Why Me?"	Linda Martin	Seán Sherrard (Johny Logan)	Seán Sherrard (Johny Logan)	Noel Kelehan	English	Pat Kenny	Eileen Dunne	155	1
18	Denmark	"Alt det som ingen ser"	Kenny Lübcke & Lotte Nilsson	Carsten Warming	Carsten Warming	Henrik Krogsgaard	Danish	Jørgen de Mylius	Bent Henius	47	12
19	Italy	"Rapsodia"	Mia Martini	Giancarlo Bigazzi	Giuseppe Dati	Marco Falagiani	Italian	Peppi Franzelin	Nicoletta Orsomando	111	4
20	Yugoslavia	"Ljubim te pesmama"	Extra Nena	Gale Janković	Radivoje Radivojević	Anders Berglund	Serb	Mladen Popović	Veselin Mrđen	44	13
21	Norway	"Visjoner"	Merethe Trøan	Andreas Christou	Kypros Charalambus	Alexandros Kyros Zografou	Greek	John Andreassen	Sverre Christophersen	23	18
22	Germany	"Träume sind für alle da"	Wind (Petra Scheeser, Albert Oberloher, Stefan Maro, Tina Hierstetter, Sami Kalifa, Oliver Hahn)	Bernd Meinunger	Ralph Siegel	Norbert Daum	German	Jan Hofer	Carmen Nebel	27	16
23	The Netherlands	"Wijs me de weg"	Humphrey Campbell	Edwin Schimscheimer	Edwin Schimscheimer	Harry van Hoof	Dutch	Willem van Beusekom	Herman Slager	67	9

	Spain	Belgium	Israel	Turkey	Greece	France	Sweden	Portugal	Cyprus	Malta	Iceland	Finland	Switzerland	Luxembourg	Austria	United Kingdom	Ireland	Denmark	Italy	Yugoslavia	Norway	Germany	The Netherlands	
Spain	■	1	–	1	4	6	–	–	–	2	–	3	–	3	2	1	–	1	7	–	5	–	1	Spain
Belgium	3	■	–	4	–	3	–	–	–	–	–	–	–	1	–	–	–	–	–	–	–	–	–	Belgium
Israel	10	–	■	2	–	8	4	7	4	7	–	–	4	8	1	7	–	2	–	12	2	4	3	Israel
Turkey	–	–	–	■	–	–	–	–	–	8	–	–	–	–	–	–	3	–	–	6	–	–	–	Turkey
Greece	–	–	7	8	■	7	3	5	12	–	2	5	10	–	4	–	–	–	12	7	8	–	4	Greece
France	6	–	12	3	–	■	–	–	3	–	–	7	12	–	–	–	5	–	6	–	10	3	6	France
Sweden	–	–	–	–	–	1	■	–	–	–	–	–	–	–	–	–	–	4	–	4	–	–	–	Sweden
Portugal	–	–	8	–	2	–	–	■	–	–	–	2	–	–	–	–	–	–	1	5	–	8	–	Portugal
Cyprus	–	–	3	–	10	2	–	2	■	1	–	8	2	–	–	–	6	–	4	8	3	–	8	Cyprus
Malta	12	10	–	–	7	–	12	12	1	■	8	–	5	12	8	–	10	8	3	10	–	–	5	Malta
Iceland	8	4	4	–	6	–	6	6	–	–	■	–	3	5	7	12	–	5	5	–	1	6	2	Iceland
Finland	–	–	1	–	–	–	–	–	–	–	–	■	–	–	–	–	–	–	–	3	–	–	–	Finland
Switzerland	–	5	–	–	–	–	–	–	–	–	12	–	■	–	–	4	1	–	10	–	–	–	–	Switzerland
Luxembourg	–	–	–	–	–	–	–	–	–	10	–	–	–	■	–	–	–	–	–	–	–	–	–	Luxembourg
Austria	2	8	–	–	8	–	1	3	8	4	–	–	–	–	■	10	12	7	–	–	–	–	–	Austria
United Kingdom	5	12	2	10	–	10	5	–	6	6	4	6	8	7	12	■	7	12	8	–	–	12	7	United Kingdom
Ireland	1	7	–	12	12	–	10	4	5	12	7	10	6	10	10	8	■	10	2	2	7	10	10	Ireland
Denmark	4	–	6	–	–	–	7	1	–	–	6	–	–	6	3	3	–	■	–	–	6	5	–	Denmark
Italy	–	–	–	5	3	12	8	8	10	5	10	12	7	–	6	–	–	–	■	–	12	1	12	Italy
Yugoslavia	–	–	10	6	1	5	–	–	2	3	5	4	–	2	–	–	4	–	–	■	–	2	–	Yugoslavia
Norway	–	3	–	–	–	–	2	–	–	–	1	1	–	4	–	5	–	6	–	1	■	–	–	Norway
Germany	–	6	–	–	–	–	–	10	–	–	–	–	–	–	–	–	6	2	3	–	–	■	–	Germany
The Netherlands	7	2	5	7	5	4	–	–	7	–	3	–	1	–	5	2	8	–	–	–	4	7	■	The Netherlands

1993

Hosting Country: Ireland
Hosting City: Millstreet
Date: 15.5.1993
Location: Green Glens Arena
Presenter: Fionnuala Sweeney
Orchestra Conductor: Noel Kelehan
Chief Executive: Christian Clausen
Director: Anita Notaro
Executive Producer: Liam Miller
Participating Countries: 25
Every participating country has a jury (16 members) that gives 1-8 points and then 10 and 12 points to its favourite song
Broadcaster: Raidió Teilifís Éireann (RTÉ)
Intermediate performance: Linda Martin, Johnny Logan
Duration: 3 hours and 4 minutes
Broadcast: To all participating countries and to North Macedonia, Hungary, Romania, Poland, Slovakia, Russia, Yugoslavia and Australia.

No.	Country	Song	Performing Artist	Lyrics	Composer	Conductor	Language	Commentator	Spoker of Results	Points	Place
01	Italy	"Sole d'Europa"	Enrico Ruggeri	Enrico Ruggeri	Enrico Ruggeri	Vittorio Cosma	Italian	Ettore Andenna	Peppi Franzelin	45	12
02	Turkey	"Esmer Yarim"	Burak Aydos	Burak Aydos	Burak Aydos	Mete Artun	Turkish	Bülend Özveren	Ömer Önder	10	21
03	Germany	"Viel zu weit"	Münchener Freiheit (Stefan Zauner, Alex Grünwald, Aron Strobel, Reniie Hatzke, Michael Kunzi)	Stefan Zauner	Stefan Zauner	Norbert Daum	German	Jan Hofer	Carmen Nebel	18	18
04	Switzerland	"Moi, tout simplement"	Annie Cotton	Jean-Jacques Egli	Christophe Duc	Marc Sorrentino	French	Bernard Thurnheer, Jean-Marc Richard, Emanuéla Gaggini	Michel Stocker	148	3
05	Denmark	"Under stjernerne på himlen"	Tommy Seebac	Keld Heick	Tommy Seebac	Georg Keller	Danish	Jørgen de Mylius	Bent Henius	9	22
06	Greece	"Ellada, hora tou fotos"	Katerina Garbi	Dimosthenis Stringlis	Dimosthenis Stringlis	Charis Andreadis	Greek	Dafni Bokota	Fotini Giannou-latou	64	9
07	Belgium	"Iemand als jij"	Barbara Dex	Tobana (Marc Dex)	Marc Vliegen	Bert Candries	Flemish	André Vermeulen and Claude Delacroix	An Ploegaerts	3	25
08	Malta	"This Time"	William Mangion	William Mangion	William Mangion	Paul Abela	English	-	Kevin Drake	69	8
09	Iceland	"Þá veistu svarið"	Inga (Ingibjörg Stefánsdóttir)	Friðrik Sturluson	Jon Kjell Seljeseth	Jon Kjell Seljeseth	Icelandic	Jakob Frímann Magnússon	Guðrún Skúladóttir	42	13
10	Austria	"Maria Magdalena"	Tony Wegas	Thomas Spitzer	Christian Kolonovits, Johann Bertl	Christian Kolonovits	German	Ernst Grissemann	Andy Lee	32	14
11	Portugal	"A cidade (até ser dia)"	Anabela	Pedro Abrantes, Marco Quelhas, Paulo de Carvalho	Pedro Abrantes, Marco Quelhas, Paulo de Carvalho, Fernando Abrantes	Armindo Neves	Portuguese	Isabel Bahia	Margarida Mercês de Mello	60	10
12	France	"Mama Corsica"	Patrick Fiori	François Valéry	François Valéry	Christian Cravero	French	Patrice Laffont	Olivier Minne	121	4
13	Sweden	"Eloise"	Arvingarna (Casper Janebrink, Kim Carlsson, Tommy Carlsson, Lars Larsson)	Gert Lengstrand	Lasse Holm	Curt-Eric Holmquist	Swedish	Jan Jingryd and Kåge Gimtell	Gösta Hanson	89	7
14	Ireland	"In Your Eyes"	Niamh Kavanagh	Jimmy Walsh	Jimmy Walsh	Noel Kelehan	English	Pat Kenny	Eileen Dunne	187	1
15	Luxembourg	"Donne-moi une chance"	Modern Times (Simone Weis, Jimmy Martin)	Patrick Hippert, Jimmy Martin	Patrick Hippert, Jimmy Martin	Francis Goya	French, Luxem-bourgish	Maurice Molitor	Unknown	11	20
16	Slovenia	"Tih deževen dan"	1X Band (Cole Moretti, Andrej Bedjanič, Brane Vidan, Tomaž Kosec, Sandra Županc, Barbara Sinigo)	Tomaž Kosec	Cole Moretti	Jože Privšek	Slovenian	Tajda Lekše	Miša Molk	9	22
17	Finland	"Tule luo"	Katri Helena	Jukka Saarinen	Matti Puurtinen	Olli Ahvenlahti	Finish	Erkki Pohjanheimo and Kirsi-Maria Niemi	Solveig Herlin	20	17
18	Bosnia Herzegovina	"Sva bol svijeta"	Fazla (Muhamed Fazlagić, Edina Salkanović, Amir Bjelanović, Enver Milišić, Izo Kolečić)	Fahrudin Pecikoza, Edin Dervišhalidovic	Edin Dervišhalidović	Noel Kelehan	Serbo-Croatian	Ismeta Dervoz-Krvavac	Senad Hadžife-jzovic	27	16
19	United Kingdom	"Better the Devil You Know"	Sonia	Brian Teasdale, Dean Collinson	Brian Teasdale, Dean Collinson	Nigel Wright	English	Terry Wogan	Colin Berry	164	2
20	The Nether-lands	"Vrede"	Ruth Jacott	Henk Westbroek	Eric van Tijn, Jochem Fluitsma	Harry van Hoof	Dutch	Willem van Beusekom	Joop van Os	92	6
21	Croatia	"Don't Ever Cry"	Put (Vivien Galletta, Olja Dešić, Melita Sedić, Naim Alfa, Petar Cicak, Anđela Jeličić)	Đorđe Novković	Andrej Baša	Andrej Baša	Croatian	Aleksandar "Aco" Kostadinov	Veljko Đuretić	31	15
22	Spain	"Hombres"	Eva Santamaría	Carlos Toro	Carlos Toro	Eduardo Leiva	Spanish	José Luis Uribarri	María Ángeles Balanac	58	11
23	Cyprus	"Mi stamatas"	Kyriakos Zympoulakis and Dimos Van Beke	Rodoula Papalambrianou	Aristos Moskovakis	Giorgos Theoph-anous	Greek	Evi Papamichail	Anna Partelidou	17	19
24	Israel	"Shiru"	Saraleh Sharon and "Shiru" (Benny Nadler, Rache-li Haim, Guy Bracha, Yulia Preitor, Varda Zamir)	Yoram Tahar-Lev	Shaike Paikov	Amir Frohlich	Hebrew	-	Danny Roup	4	24
25	Norway	"Alle mine tankar"	Silje Vige	Bjørn-Erik Vige	Bjørn-Erik Vige	Rolf Løvland	Norweigen	Leif Erik Forberg	Sverre Chris-tophersen	120	5

	Italy	Turkey	Germany	Switzerland	Denmark	Greece	Belgium	*Malta	Iceland	Austria	Portugal	France	Sweden	Ireland	Luxembourg	Slovenia	Finland	Bosnia Herzegovina	United Kingdom	The Netherlands	Croatia	Spain	Cyprus	Israel	Norway	
Italy	■	–	–	1	–	–	–	7	–	–	10	5	–	–	10	–	8	–	–	2	–	2	–	–	–	Italy
Turkey	–	■	–	–	–	–	–	–	1	–	–	–	–	–	–	–	–	2	–	–	1	6	–	–	–	Turkey
Germany	8	–	■	2	3	–	–	–	–	–	–	–	–	4	–	–	–	–	–	1	–	–	–	–	–	Germany
Switzerland	10	–		■	10	7	8	5	4	6	1	12	6	7	12	8	4	–	10	8	2	3	6	4	3	Switzerland
Denmark	–	–	–	–	■	–	–	–	–	–	–	–	1	–	3	–	–	5	–	–	–	–	–	–	–	Denmark
Greece	2	2	2	–	–	■	–	6	–	–	–	7	–	–	–	–	6	–	–	5	–	8	12	7	7	Greece
Belgium	–	–	3	–	–	–	■	–	–	–	–	–	–	–	–	–	–	–	–	–	–	–	–	–	–	Belgium
Malta*	7	5	4	7	5	5	–	■	–	4	2	2	4	2	–	–	–	4	6	–	4	4	1	3	–	Malta*
Iceland	–	–	–	–	4	4	–	–	■	1	–	–	7	1	–	5	–	–	2	7	5	–	2	2	2	Iceland
Austria	–	4	–	–	–	1	3	–	–	■	–	3	–	6	–	–	–	12	3	–	–	–	–	–	–	Austria
Portugal	–	–	1	–	1	2	–	–	2	5	■	8	2	–	4	–	2	–	1	12	–	12	3	–	5	Portugal
France	–	7	–	4	12	3	–	–	8	7	12	■	8	10	6	4	1	–	4	3	8	–	10	8	6	France
Sweden	–	–	8	8	7	–	10	–	7	10	4	–	■	–	5	6	7	–	7	–	–	–	–	10	–	Sweden
Ireland	12	1	5	12	6	6	2	12	3	8	6	10	12	■	7	12	3	8	12	10	6	10	7	5	12	Ireland
Luxembourg	–	–	–	–	–	–	–	10	–	–	–	–	–	–	■	1	–	–	–	–	–	–	–	–	–	Luxembourg
Slovenia	4	–	–	–	–	–	–	1	–	–	–	–	3	–	–	■	–	1	–	–	–	–	–	–	–	Slovenia
Finland	–	3	–	–	–	8	–	2	5	–	–	–	–	–	2	–	■	–	–	–	–	–	–	–	–	Finland
Bosnia Herzegovina	3	12	–	–	–	–	1	4	–	–	–	4	–	3	–	–	–	■	–	–	–	–	–	–	–	Bosnia Herzegovina
United Kingdom	1	8	6	5	8	–	12	–	12	12	7	6	10	8	8	10	5	3	■	4	10	5	4	12	8	United Kingdom
The Netherlands	6	6	7	–	–	–	7	3	6	3	–	–	5	12	–	7	–	10	–	■	3	7	–	–	10	The Netherlands
Croatia	–	–	–	3	–	–	4	–	–	–	5	–	–	–	–	–	–	–	8	–	■	1	–	6	4	Croatia
Spain	5	–	–	6	–	–	5	8	–	2	–	–	–	–	–	2	10	6	–	–	7	■	5	1	1	Spain
Cyprus	–	–	–	–	2	10	–	–	–	–	–	–	–	–	–	–	–	–	5	–	–	–	■	–	–	Cyprus
Israel	–	–	–	–	–	–	–	–	–	–	3	1	–	–	–	–	–	–	–	–	–	–	–	■	–	Israel
Norway	–	10	10	10	–	12		–	10	–	8	–	–	5	1	3	12	7	–	6	12	–	8	–	■	Norway

*Because of technical problem, the Maltese vote was heard last in order.

1994

Hosting Country: Ireland
Hosting City: Dublin
Date: 30.4.1994
Location: Point Theatre
Presenters: Cynthia Ní Mhurchú, Gerry Ryan
Orchestra Conductor: Noel Kelehan
Chief Executive: Christian Clausen
Director: Patrick Cowap
Executive Producer: Moya Doherty
Participating Countries: 25
Every participating country has a jury (16 members) that gives 1-8 points and then 10 and 12 points to its favourite song
Broadcaster: Raidió Teilifís Éireann (RTÉ)
Intermediate performance: Riverdance
Duration: 3 hours and 3 minutes
Broadcast: To all participating countries and to Belgium, Denmark, Israel, Slovenia, Turkey, Yugoslavia, North Macedonia and Australia.
Broadcast: To all participating countries and to Belgium, Denmark, Israel, Slovenia, Turkey, Yugoslavia, North Macedonia and Australia.

No.	Country	Song	Performing Artist	Lyrics	Composer	Conductor	Language	Commentator	Spoker of Results	Points	Place
01	Sweden	"Stjärnorna"	Marie Bergman & Roger Pontare	Mikael Littwold	Peter Bertilsson	Anders Berglund	Swedish	Pekka Heino	Marianne Anderberg	48	13
02	Finland	"Bye Bye Baby"	CatCat (Virpi Kätkä, Katja Kätkä)	Kari Salli, Make Lentonen	Kari Salli, Markku Lentonen	Olli Ahvenlahti	Finish	Erkki Pohjanheimo and Kirsi-Maria Niemi	Solveig Herlin	11	22
03	Ireland	"Rock 'n' Roll Kids"	Paul Harrington & Charlie McGettigan	Brendan Graham	Brendan Graham	-	English	Pat Kenny	Eileen Dunne	226	1
04	Cyprus	"Ime anthropos ki ego"	Evridiki	Giorgos Theophanous	Giorgos Theophanous	Giorgos Theophanous	Greek	Evi Papamichail	Anna Partelidou	51	11
05	Iceland	"Nætur"	Sigga (Sigríður einteinsdótti)	Stefán Hilmarsson	Friðrik Karlsson	Frank McNamara	Icelandic	Jakob Frímann Magnússon	Sigríður Arnardóttir	49	12
06	United Kingdom	"We Will Be Free (Lonely Symphony)"	Frances Ruffelle	George De Angelis, Mark Dean	George De Angelis, Mark Dean	Michael Reed	English	Terry Wogan	Colin Berry	63	10
07	Croatia	"Nek' ti bude ljubav sva"	Tony Cetinski	Željko Krznarić	Željen Klašterka	Miljenko Prohaska	Croatian	Aleksandar "Aco" Kostadinov	Helga Vlahović	27	16
08	Portugal	"Chamar a música"	Sara Tavares	Rosa Lobato de Faria	João Carlos Campos de Sousa Mota Oliveira	Thilo Krassmann	Portuguese	Eládio Clímaco	Isabel Bahia	73	8
09	Switzerland	"Sto pregando"	Duilio	Giuseppe Scaramello	Giuseppe Scaramello	Valeriano Chiaravalle	Italian	Bernard Thurnheer, Jean-Marc Richard, Wilma Gilardi	Sandra Studer	15	19
10	Estonia	"Nagu merelaine"	Silvi Vrait	Leelo Tungal	Ivar Must	Urmas Lattikas	Estonish	Vello Rand	Urve Tiidus	2	24
11	Romania	"Dincolo de nori"	Dan Bittman	Antonio Furtuna, Dan Bittman	Antonio Furtuna	Noel Kelehan	Romanian	Gabriela Cristea	Cristina Topescu	14	21
12	Malta	"More than Love"	Chris and Moira	Moira Stafrace	Christopher Scicluna	Anthony Chircop	English	Charles Arrigo	John Demanuele	97	5
13	The Netherlands	"Waar is de zon"	Willeke Alberti	Coot van Doesburgh	Edwin Schimscheimer	Harry van Hoof	Dutch	Willem van Beusekom	Joop van Os	23	4
14	Germany	"Wir geben 'ne Party"	MeKaDo (Dorkas Kiefer, Kati Karney, Melanie Bender)	Bernd Meinunger	Ralph Siegel	Norbert Daum	German	Jan Hofer	Carmen Nebel	128	3
15	Slovakia	"Nekonečná pieseň"	Tublatanka (Martin Ďurinda, Juraj Topor, Jožef Duban, Juraj Černy)	Martin Sarvaš	Martin Ďurinda	Vladimir Valović	Slovakian	Martin Sarvaš	Juraj Čurný	15	19
16	Lithuania	"Lopšinė mylimai"	Ovidijus Vyšniauskas	Gintaras Zdebskis	Ovidijus Vyšniauskas	Tomas Leiburas	Lithuanian	-	Gitana	0	25
17	Norway	"Duett"	Elisabeth Andreassen & Jan Werner Danielsen	Hans Olav Mørk	Rolf Løvland	Pete Knutsen	Norweigen	Jostein Pedersen	Sverre Christophersen	76	6
18	Bosnia Herzegovina	"Ostani kraj mene"	Alma & Dejan (Alma Čardžić, Dejan Lazarević)	Edo Mulahalilović	Adi Mulahalilović	Sinan Alimanović	Serbo-Croatian	Ismeta Dervoz-Krvavac	Diana Grković-Foretić	39	15
19	Greece	"To trehandiri"	Kostas Bigalis & The Sea Lovers	Kostas Bigalis	Kostas Bigalis	Noel Kelehan	Greek	Dafni Bokota	Fotini Giannoulatou	44	14
20	Austria	"Für den Frieden der Welt"	Petra Frey	Karl Brunner, Johann Brunner	Alfons Weindorf	Herman Weindorf	German	Ernst Grissemann	Tilia Herold	19	17
21	Spain	"Ella no es ella"	Alejandro Abad	Alejandro Abad	Alejandro Abad	Josef Llobell	Spanish	José Luis Uribarri	María Ángeles Balañac	17	18
22	Hungary	"Kinek mondjam el vétkeimet?"	Friderika Bayer	Szilveszter Jenei	Szilveszter Jenei	Péter Wolf	Hungarian	István Vágó	Iván Bradányi	122	4
23	Russia	"Vechny strannik"	Youddiph (Maria Lvovna Katz)	Pilgrim (Maria Katz)	Lev Zemlinski	Lev Zemlinski	Russian	Vadim Dolgachev	Irina	70	9
24	Poland	"To nie ja!"	Edyta Górniak	Jacek Cygan	Stanisław Syrewicz	Noel Kelehan	Polish	Artur Orzech	Jan Chojnacki	166	2
25	France	"Je suis un vrai garçon"	Nina Morato	Nina Morato	Bruno Maman	Alain Goraguer	French	Patrice Laffont	Laurent Romejko	74	7

	Sweden	Finland	Ireland	Cyprus	Iceland	United Kingdom	Croatia	Portugal*	Switzerland	Estonia	Romania	Malta	The Netherlands	Germany	Slovakia	Lithuania	Norway	Bosnia Herzegovina	Greece	Austria	Spain	Hungary	Russia	Poland	France
France	-	-	8	3	4	-	-	6	5	-	-	-	-	-	-	-	-	10	-	-	2	7	1	12	■
Poland	-	-	8	5	4	3	-	1	-	-	-	-	-	7	-	-	-	-	2	-	-	12	10	■	6
Russia	-	-	12	2	1	5	-	4	-	-	-	-	-	7	-	-	8	-	-	-	-	3	■	6	10
Hungary	2	-	10	-	-	3	-	7	-	-	-	-	-	12	-	-	5	1	4	-	-	■	6	8	-
Spain	1	-	10	4	6	3	-	12	2	-	-	-	-	8	-	-	5	7	-	-	■	-	-	-	-
Austria	5	-	10	-	3	1	-	-	-	-	-	-	4	2	-	-	-	-	-	■	-	8	6	12	7
Greece	-	10	-	12	-	-	5	-	-	2	6	7	-	-	3	-	1	-	■	-	8	-	4	-	-
Bosnia Herzegovina	-	1	10	-	-	-	4	-	-	-	-	12	-	7	-	-	6	■	-	5	-	3	-	8	2
Norway	10	-	12	5	-	2	-	-	-	-	-	-	-	1	-	-	■	-	4	-	-	8	3	6	7
Lithuania	5	-	10	-	3	-	-	-	-	-	2	7	-	4	-	■	1	-	-	-	-	-	6	12	8
Slovakia	-	-	6	-	1	3	12	-	-	-	-	10	-	7	■	-	-	8	5	-	2	-	-	4	-
Germany	5	-	12	-	-	4	-	-	-	-	-	3	-	■	-	-	2	-	1	-	-	7	6	10	8
The Netherlands	6	-	12	-	-	2	-	3	-	-	-	1	■	4	-	-	7	-	-	-	-	10	5	8	-
Malta	-	6	5	-	-	-	10	1	8	-	3	■	-	-	12	-	-	7	4	-	-	-	-	2	-
Romania	-	-	8	-	-	-	-	-	-	-	■	10	-	12	-	-	4	-	6	1	5	2	3	7	-
Estonia	2	-	10	-	-	5	-	-	-	■	-	7	-	3	-	-	8	-	-	-	-	4	1	12	6
Switzerland	7	-	12	2	3	8	-	5	■	-	-	6	-	-	-	-	1	-	-	-	-	4	-	10	-
*Portugal	-	-	12	5	3	8	-	■	-	-	-	4	-	10	-	-	-	-	-	-	-	1	2	7	6
Croatia	-	-	12	-	-	6	■	-	-	-	-	7	-	10	-	-	3	4	-	2	-	5	1	8	-
United Kingdom	-	-	10	-	6	■	-	3	-	-	-	1	-	7	-	-	4	-	-	8	-	2	5	12	-
Iceland	2	-	12	3	■	-	-	8	-	-	-	-	-	7	-	-	1	-	-	-	-	10	4	6	5
Cyprus	-	-	8	■	-	-	-	-	-	-	-	2	-	6	-	-	10	-	12	7	-	-	3	1	4
Ireland	-	-	■	-	6	1	-	8	-	-	-	10	-	5	-	-	3	-	-	-	-	12	4	7	2
Finland	-	■	7	10	1	-	-	5	-	-	-	-	-	3	-	-	6	2	4	-	-	12	-	8	-
Sweden	■	-	10	-	8	-	-	5	-	-	-	-	-	6	-	-	7	-	2	4	1	12	-	-	3

1995

Hosting Country: Ireland
Hosting City: Dublin
Date: 13.5.1995
Location: Point Theatre
Presenter: Mary Kennedy
Orchestra Conductor: Noel Kelehan, Proinnsías Ó Duinn
Chief Executive: Christian Clausen
Director: John Comiskey
Executive Producer: John McHugh
Participating Countries: 23
Every participating country has a jury (16 members) that gives 1-8 points and then 10 and 12 points to its favourite song
Broadcaster: Raidió Teilifís Éireann (RTÉ)
Intermediate performance: Lumen
Duration: 2 hours and 52 minutes
Broadcast: To all participating countries and to Estonia, North Macedonia, Finland, The Netherlands, Lithuania, Australia, Switzerland and Yugoslavia.

No.	Country	Song	Performing Artist	Lyrics	Composer	Conductor	Language	Commentator	Spoker of Results	Points	Place
01	Poland	"Sama"	Justyna	Wojciech Waglewski	Mateusz Pospieszalski, Wojciech Waglewski	Noel Kelehan	Polish	Artur Orzech	Jan Chojnacki	15	18
02	Ireland	"Dreamin'"	Eddie Friel	Richard Abbott, Barry Woods	Richard Abbott, Barry Woods	Noel Kelehan	English	Pat Kenny	Eileen Dunne	44	14
03	Germany	"Verliebt in Dich"	Stone & Stone (Cheyenne Stone, Glen Penniston)	Cheyenne Stone	Cheyenne Stone	Hermann Weindorf	German	Horst Senker	Carmen Nebel	1	23
04	Bosnia Herzegovina	"Dvadeset prvi vijek"	Davorin Popović	Zlatan Fazlić	Zlatan Fazlić	Sinan Alimanović	Serbo-Croatian	Ismeta Dervoz-Krvavac	Diana Grkovic-Foretić	14	19
05	Norway	"Nocturne"	Secret Garden (Fionnuala Sherry, Rolf Løvland) and Gunnhild Tvinnereim, Åsa Jinder, Hans Fredrik Jacobsen	Petter Skavlan	Rolf Løvland	Geir Langslet	Norweigen	Annette Groth	Sverre Christophersen	148	1
06	Russia	"Kolybelnaya dlya vulkana"	Philipp Kirkorov	Ilya Resnik	Ilya Bershadskiy	Michael Finberg	Russian	-	Marina Danielian	17	17
07	Iceland	"Núna"	Bo Halldórsson	Jón Örn Marinósson	Björgvin Halldórsson, Ed Welch	Frank McNamara	Icelandic	Jakob Frímann Magnússon	Áslaug Dóra Eyjolfsdottir	31	15
08	Austria	"Die Welt dreht sich verkehrt"	Stella Jones	Mischa Krausz	Mischa Krausz	Michael Kienzl	German	Ernst Grissemann	Tilia Herold	67	13
09	Spain	"Vuelve conmigo"	Anabel Conde	José María Purón	José María Purón	Eduardo Leiva	Spanish	José Luis Uribarri	Belén Fernández de Henestrosa	119	2
10	Turkey	"Sev"	Arzu Ece	Zeynep Talu Kurşuncu	Melih Kibar	Melih Kibar	Turkish	Bülend Özveren	Ömer Önder	21	16
11	Croatia	"Nostalgija"	Magazin & Lidija. (Danijela Martinović, Tonči Huljić, Zeljko Baričić, Ante Miletić, Nenad Vesanović Lidija Horvat-Dunjko)	Vjekoslava Huljić	Tonči Huljić	Stipica Kalogjera	Croatian	Aleksandar "Aco" Kostadinov	Daniela Trbović	91	6
12	France	"Il me donne ren-dez-vous"	Nathalie Santamaria	Didier Barbelivien	François Bernheim	Michel Bernholc	French	Olivier Minne	Thierry Beccaro	94	4
13	Hungary	"Új név a régi ház falán"	Csaba Szigeti	Attila Horváth	Ferenc Balázs	Miklós Malek	Hungarian	István Vágó	Katalin Bogyay	3	22
14	Belgium	"La voix est libre"	Frédéric Etherlinck	Pierre Theunis	Pierre Theunis	Alec Mansion	French	Jean-Pierre Hautier and André Vermeulen	Marie-Françoise Renson "Soda"	8	20
15	United Kingdom	"Love City Groove"	"Love City Groove" (MC Reason, Paul Hardy, Beanz, Jay Williams).	Paul Hardy, Jay Williams, Tatsiana Mais, Stephen Rudden	Paul Hardy, Jay Williams, Tatsiana Mais, Stephen Rudden	Mike Dixon	English	Terry Wogan	Colin Berry	76	11
16	Portugal	"Baunilha e chocolate"	Tó Cruz	António Vitorino d'Almeida, Rosa Lobato de Faria	António Vitorino d'Almeida	Thilo Krassmann	Portuguese	Ana do Carmo	Serenella Andrade	5	21
17	Cyprus	"Sti fotia"	Alexandros Panayi	Alexandros Panayi	Alexandros Panayi	Giorgos Theoph-anous	Greek	Neophytos Taliotis	Andreas Iakovidis	79	7
18	Sweden	"Se på mig"	Jan Johansen	Ingela Forsman	Håkan Almqvist, Bobby Ljunggren	Anders Berglund	Swedish	Pernilla Månsson and Kåge Gimtell	Björn Hedman	100	3
19	Denmark	"Fra Mols til Skagen"	Aud Wilken	Lise Cabble	Lise Cabble	Frede Ewert	Danish	Jørgen de Mylius	Bent Henius	92	5
20	Slovenia	"Prisluhni mi"	Darja Švajger	Primož Peterca	Primož Peterca, Sašo Fajon	Jože Privšek	Slovenian	Damjana Golavšek	Miša Molk	84	7
21	Israel	"Amen"	Liora Fadlon-Simon	Hamutal Ben-Zeev	Moshe Datz	Gadi Goldman	Hebrew	-	Daniel Peer	81	8
22	Malta	"Keep Me in Mind"	Mike Spiteri	Alfred C. Sant	Ray Agius	Ray Agius	English	Enzo Gusman	Stephanie Farrugia	76	10
23	Greece	"Pia prosefhi"	Elina Konstantopoulou	Antonis Pappas	Nikos Terzis	Haris Andreadis	Greek	Dafni Bokota	Fotini Giannou-latou	68	12

	Poland	Ireland	Germany	Bosnia Herzegovina	Norway	Russia	Iceland	Austria	Spain	Turkey	Croatia	France	Hungary	Belgium	United Kingdom	Portugal	Cyprus	Sweden	Denmark	Slovenia	Israel	Malta	Greece	
Poland	■	–	–	–	4	–	6	–	–	–	–	–	1	–	–	1	–	–	–	–	–	–	3	Poland
Ireland	–	■	1	5	1	5	3	–	3	5	–	1	–	–	–	–	–	10	1	5	–	–	4	Ireland
Germany	–	–	■	–	–	–	–	–	–	–	–	–	–	–	–	–	–	–	–	–	–	1	–	Germany
Bosnia Herzegovina	–	–	–	■	–	–	–	–	–	3	8	–	–	–	–	–	–	–	3	–	–	–	–	Bosnia Herzegovina
Norway	12	10	4	1	■	12	12	–	4	12	–	10	6	5	4	12	7	–	2	7	10	6	12	Norway
Russia	–	–	–	–	10	■	–	–	–	–	6	–	–	–	–	–	1	–	–	–	–	–	–	Russia
Iceland	–	6	–	–	2	3	■	4	–	–	–	2	–	–	–	–	–	6	8	–	–	–	–	Iceland
Austria	2	–	–	–	3	–	–	■	6	4	–	8	4	10	5	2	–	4	10	–	2	–	7	Austria
Spain	8	2	6	8	–	–	5	–	■	8	10	7	2	12	8	7	10	–	–	–	12	8	6	Spain
Turkey	–	–	–	–	–	–	–	–	2	■	5	–	–	1	2	–	–	–	–	3	1	7	–	Turkey
Croatia	–	3	–	10	7	–	10	–	12	7	■	–	–	–	–	4	5	–	–	12	4	12	5	Croatia
France	7	5	8	–	6	–	8	10	–	2	3	■	10	6	1	–	2	3	6	8	7	–	2	France
Hungary	–	–	–	–	–	2	–	–	1	–	–	–	■	–	–	–	–	–	–	–	–	–	–	Hungary
Belgium	–	–	–	–	–	–	–	1	7	–	–	–	–	■	–	–	–	–	–	–	–	–	–	Belgium
United Kingdom	5	1	–	4	–	1	–	12	–	–	–	12	7	7	■	10	–	5	7	–	5	–	–	United Kingdom
Portugal	–	–	–	–	–	–	–	–	–	–	–	4	–	–	–	■	–	–	–	–	–	–	1	Portugal
Cyprus	1	–	3	–	5	4	2	–	5	–	1	–	12	8	3	–	■	8	5	4	6	4	8	Cyprus
Sweden	10	12	12	2	8	6	4	8	–	1	–	3	–	–	6	8	4	■	12	1	–	3	–	Sweden
Denmark	3	7	7	3	12	10	7	7	–	6	–	–	3	3	–	6	–	12	■	6	–	–	–	Denmark
Slovenia	4	8	5	6	–	7	1	3	–	–	2	–	8	–	10	5	3	7	–	■	3	2	10	Slovenia
Israel	–	–	10	7	–	8	–	6	–	–	4	–	5	4	12	–	8	2	–	10	■	5	–	Israel
Malta	–	4	2	12	–	–	–	2	10	10	12	6	–	–	7	–	6	1	4	–	–	■	–	Malta
Greece	6	–	–	–	–	–	–	5	8	–	7	5	–	2	–	3	12	–	–	2	8	10	■	Greece

1996

Hosting Country: Norway
Hosting City: Oslo
Date: 18.5.1996
Location: Oslo Spektrum
Presenters: Ingvild Bryn
Morten Harket
Orchestra Conductor: Frode Thingnæs
Chief Executive: Christine Marchal-Ortiz
Director: Pål Veiglum
Executive Producer: Odd Arvid Strømstad
Participating Countries: 23
Every participating country has a jury (16 members) that gives 1-8 points and then 10 and 12 points to its favourite song
Broadcaster: Norsk rikskringkasting (NRK)
Intermediate performance: Nils Gaup & Runar Borge feat. Aamil Paus-Beacon Burning
Duration: 3 hours and 8 minutes
Broadcast: To all participating countries and to Denmark, North Macedonia, Germany, Hungary, Israel, Romania, Russia and Australia.

No.	Country	Song	Performing Artist	Lyrics	Composer	Conductor	Language	Commentator	Spoker of Results	Points	Place
01	Turkey	"Beşinci Mevsim"	Şebnem Paker	Selma Çuhacı	Levent Çoker	Levent Çoker	Turkish	Bülend Özveren	Ömer Önder	57	12
02	United Kingdom	"Ooh Aah... Just a Little Bit"	Gina G	Simon Tauber	Steve Rodway	Ernie Dunstall	English	Terry Wogan	Colin Berry	77	8
03	Spain	"¡Ay, qué deseo!"	Antonio Carbonell	Antonio Carmona, Josemi Carmona, Juan Carmona	Antonio Carmona, Josemi Carmona, Juan Carmona	Eduardo Leiva	Spanish	José Luis Uribarri	Belén Fernández de Henestrosa	17	20
04	Portugal	"O meu coração não tem cor"	Lúcia Moniz	José Fanha	Pedro Osório	Pedro Osório	Portuguese	Maria Margarida Gaspar	Cristina Rocha	92	6
05	Cyprus	"Mono gia mas"	Constantinos	Rodoula Papalambrianou	Andreas Giorgallis	Stavros Lantsias	Greek	Evi Papamichail	Marios Skordis	72	9
06	Malta	"In a Woman's Heart"	Miriam Christine	Alfred C. Sant	Paul Abela	Paul Abela	English	Charles Saliba	Ruth Amaira	68	10
07	Croatia	"Sveta ljubav"	Maja Blagdan	Zrinko Tutić	Zrinko Tutić	Alan Bjelinski	Croatian	Aleksandar "Aco" Kostadinov	Daniela Trbović	98	4
08	Austria	"Weil's dr guat got"	George Nussbaumer	Mischa Krausz, George Nussbaumer	Mischa Krausz, George Nussbaumer	Mischa Krausz	German	Ernst Grissemann	Martina Rupp	68	11
09	Switzerland	"Mon cœur l'aime"	Kathy Leander	Soren Mounir	Soren Mounir	Rui Filipe Reis	French	Sandra Studer, Pierre Grandjean, Joanne Holder	Yves Ménestrier	22	16
10	Greece	"Emis forame to himona anixiatika"	Marianna Efstratiou	Iro Trigoni	Kostas Bigalis	Michalis Rozakis	Greek	Dafni Bokota	Niki Venega	36	14
11	Estonia	"Kaelakee hääl"	Maarja-Liis Ilus & Ivo Linna	Kaari Sillamaa	Priit Pajusaar	Tarmo Leinatamm	Estonish	Jüri Pihel	Annika Talvik	94	5
12	Norway	"I evighet"	Elisabeth Andreassen	Torhild Nigar	Torhild Nigar	Frode Thingnæs	Norweigen	Jostein Pedersen	Ragnhild Sælthun Fjørtoft	114	2
13	France	"Diwanit Bugale"	Dan Ar Braz & l'Héritage des Celtes	Dan Ar Braz	Dan Ar Braz	Fiachra Trench	Breton	Olivier Minne	Laurent Broomhead	18	19
14	Slovenia	"Dan najlepših sanj"	Regina	Aleksander Kogoj	Aleksander Kogoj	Jože Privšek	Slovenian	Miša Molk	Mario Galunič	16	21
15	The Netherlands	"De eerste keer"	Maxine & Franklin Brown	Piet Souer	Piet Souer, Peter van Asten	Dick Bakker	Dutch	Willem van Beusekom	Marcha	78	7
16	Belgium	"Liefde is een kaartspel"	Lisa del Bo	Daniël Ditmar	John Terra, Silrak Brogden	Bob Porter	Flemish	Michel Follet, Johan Verstreken, Jean-Pierre Hautier, Sandra Kim	An Ploegaerts	22	16
17	Ireland	"The Voice"	Eimear Quinn	Brendan Graham	Brendan Graham	Noel Kelehan	English	Pat Kenny	Eileen Dunne	162	1
18	Finland	"Niin kaunis on taivas"	Jasmine	Timo Niemi	Timo Niemi	Olli Ahvenlahti	Finish	Erkki Pohjanheimo and Sanna Kojo	Solveig Herlin	9	23
19	Iceland	"Sjúbídú"	Anna Mjöll	Anna Mjöll Ólafsdóttir, Ólafur Gaukur Þórhallsson	Anna Mjöll Ólafsdóttir, Ólafur Gaukur Þórhallsson	Olafur Gaukur	Icelandic	Jakob Frímann Magnússon	Svanbildur Konraðsdóttir	51	13
20	Poland	"Chce znać swój grzech..."	Kasia Kowalska	Kasia Kowalska	Robert Amirian	Wiesław Pieregorolka	Polish	Dorota Osman	Jan Chojnacki	31	15
21	Bosnia Herzegovina	"Za našu ljubav"	Amila Glamočak	Adnan Bajramović	Sinan Alimanović, Adnan Bajramović, Aida Frljak	Sinan Alimanović	Serbo-Croatian	Sead Bejtović	Segmedina Srna	13	22
22	Slovakia	"Kým nás máš"	Marcel Palonder	Jozef Urban	Juraj Burian	Juraj Burian	Slovakian	Stanislav Ščepán	Alena Heribanová	19	18
23	Sweden	"Den vilda"	One More Time (Maria Rådsten, Nanne Grönvall, Peter Grönvall)	Nanne Grönvall	Peter Grönvall	Anders Berglund	Swedish	Björn Kjellman	Ulla Rundqvist	100	3

	Turkey	United Kingdom	Spain	Portugal	Cyprus	Malta	Croatia	Austria	Switzerland	Greece	Estonia	Norway	France	Slovenia	The Netherlands	Belgium	Ireland	Finland	Iceland	Poland	Bosnia Herzegovina	Slovakia	Sweden	
Turkey	■	6	8	–	–	10	1	–	6	–	–	–	4	–	7	5	–	5	–	–	5	–	–	Turkey
United Kingdom	3	■	–	12	1	6	7	3	4	–	2	–	8	–	–	12	3	–	4	–	–	6	6	United Kingdom
Spain	–	–	■	–	2	5	4	–	–	6	–	–	–	–	–	–	–	–	–	–	–	–	–	Spain
Portugal	5	2	–	■	12	–	10	1	10	5	–	12	5	–	6	6	–	3	10	–	1	–	4	Portugal
Cyprus	–	12		3	■	2	8	2	5	12	–	–	2	–	–	–	1	6	–	–	–	10	2	Cyprus
Malta	10	–	10	–	–	■	12	–	–	8	–	1	–	4	–	–	–	–	–	6	–	12	5	Malta
Croatia	8	4	5	10	8	7	■	–	1	1	6	7	–	3	5	4	6	–	5	2	10	5	1	Croatia
Austria	4	–	–	5	–	12	–	■	–	2	7	–	12	1	–	–	8	–	–	8	6	3	–	Austria
Switzerland	–	3	–	–	–	–	–	–	■	–	–	–	–	2	4	2	4	4	3	–	–	–	–	Switzerland
Greece	–	7	–	–	10	1	–	–	2	■	–	3	–	–	1	–	–	–	–	1	–	8	3	Greece
Estonia	–	10	4	–	7	–	–	5	–	–	■	8	1	8	3	–	2	12	12	10	–	–	12	Estonia
Norway	2	8	–	2	3	–	5	8	7	–	5	■	7	10	10	8	7	7	8	4	3	–	10	Norway
France	–	1	–	1	–	–	–	–	–	–	3	4	■	–	–	7	–	2	–	–	–	–	–	France
Slovenia	–	–	1	–	–	–	6	–	–	–	–	–	–	■	–	–	–	–	1	–	8	–	–	Slovenia
The Netherlands	1	–	6	7	5	–	–	12	3	–	4	–	10	5	■	1	5	–	2	7	2	–	8	The Netherlands
Belgium	–	5	12	–	–	–	2	–	–	–	1	–	–	–	2	■	–	–	–	–	–	–	–	Belgium
Ireland	12	–	–	8	6	4	–	7	12	10	12	10	6	12	12	3	■	10	–	12	12	7	7	Ireland
Finland	–	–	–	–	–	–	–	–	–	–	–	2	–	–	–	–	–	■	7	–	–	–	–	Finland
Iceland	–	–	3	6	–	–	–	6	–	3	8	5	–	6	–	–	10	–	■	3	–	1	–	Iceland
Poland	7	–	–	–	4	–	–	4	–	7	–	–	–	–	–	–	–	–	–	■	7	2	–	Poland
Bosnia Herzegovina	6	–	–	–	–	3	3	–	–	–	–	–	–	–	–	–	–	1	–	–	■	–	–	Bosnia Herzegovina
Slovakia	–	–	2	–	–	8	–	–	–	4	–	–	–	–	–	–	–	–	–	5	–	■	–	Slovakia
Sweden	–	–	–	4	–	–	–	10	8	–	10	6	3	7	8	10	12	8	6	–	4	4	■	Sweden

1997

Hosting Country: Ireland
Hosting City: Dublin
Date: 3.5.1997
Location: Point Theatre
Presenters: Carrie Crowley & Ronan Keating
Orchestra Conductor: Frank McNamara
Chief Executive: Marie-Claire Vionnet
Director: Ian McGarry
Executive Producer: Noel Curran
Participating Countries: 25
Every participating country has a jury (16 members) that gives 1-8 points and then 10 and 12 points to its favourite song
Broadcaster: Raidió Teilifís Éireann (RTÉ)
Intermediate performance: "Let The Message Run Free" performed by Ronan Keating & Boyzone
Duration: 3 hours and 11 minutes
Broadcast: To all participating countries and to Israel, Yugoslavia, Slovakia, North Macedonia, Belgium, Finland and Australia.

No.	Country	Song	Performing Artist	Lyrics	Composer	Conductor	Language	Commentator	Spoker of Results	Points	Place
01	Cyprus	"Mana mou"	Hara & Andreas Konstantinou	Constantina Konstantinou	Constantina Konstantinou	Stavros Lantsias	Greek	Evi Papamichail	Marios Skordis	98	5
02	Turkey	"Dinle"	Şebnem Paker & Grup Ethnic	Mehtap Alnıtemiz	Levent Çoker	Levent Çoker	Turkish	Bülend Özveren	Ömer Önder	121	3
03	Norway	"San Francisco"	Tor Endresen	Tor Endresen	Tor Endresen, Arne Myksvoll	Geir Langslet	Norweigen	Jostein Pedersen	Ragnhild Sælthun Fjørtoft	0	24
04	Austria	"One Step"	Bettina Soriat	Mark Berry, Martina Siber	Mark Berry	-	German	Ernst Grissemann	Adriana Zartl	12	21
05	Ireland	"Mysterious Woman"	Marc Roberts	John Farry	John Farry	-	English	Pat Kenny	Eileen Dunne	157	2
06	Slovenia	"Zbudi se"	Tanja Ribič	Zoran Predin	Saša Lošić	Mojmir Sepe	Slovenian	Miša Molk	Mojca Mavec	60	10
07	Switzerland	"Dentro di me"	Barbara Berta	Barbara Berta	Barbara Berta	Pietro Damiani	Italian	Sandra Studer, Pierre Grandjean, Jonathan Tedesco	Sandy Altermatt	5	23
08	The Netherlands	"Niemand heeft nog tijd"	Mrs. Einstein (Linda Snoeij, Marjolein Spijkers, Saskia van Zutphen, Suzanne Venneker, Paulette Willemse)	Ed Hooijmans	Ed Hooijmans	Dick Bakker	Dutch	Willem van Beusekom	Corry Brokken	5	22
09	Italy	"Fiumi di parole"	Jalisse (Alessandra Drusian, Fabio Ricci)	Carmen Di Domenico, Alessandra Drusian	Fabio Ricci	Lucio Fabbri	Italian	Ettore Andenna	Peppi Franzelin	114	4
10	Spain	"Sin rencor"	Marcos Llunas	Marcos Llunas	Marcos Llunas	Toni Xuclà	Spanish	José Luis Uribarri	Belén Fernández de Henestrosa	96	6
11	Germany	"Zeit"	Bianca Shomburg	Bernd Meinunger	Ralph Siegel	-	German	Peter Urban	Christina Mänz	22	18
12	Poland	"Ale jestem"	Anna Maria Jopek	Magda Czapińska	Tomasz Lewandowski	Krzesimir Dębski	Polish	Jan Wilkans	Jan Chojnacki	54	11
13	Estonia	"Keelatud maa"	Maarja-Liis Ilus	Kaari Sillamaa	Harmo Kallaste	Tarmo Leinatamm	Estonish	Jüri Pihel	Helene Tedre	82	8
14	Bosnia Herzegovina	"Goodbye"	Alma Čardžić	Milić Vukašinović	Milić Vukašinović, Sinan Alimanović	Sinan Alimanović	Serbo-Croatian	Diana Grković Foretić	Segmedina Srna	22	18
15	Portugal	"Antes do adeus"	Célia Lawson	Rosa Maria de Bettencourt Rodrigues Lobato de Faria	Thilo Krassman, Rosa Lobato de Faria	Thilo Krassman	Portuguese	Carlos Ribeiro	Cristina Rocha	0	24
16	Sweden	"Bara hon älskar mig"	Blond (Jonas Karlhager, Gabriel Forss, Patrick Lundström)	Stephan Berg	Stephan Berg	Curt-Eric Holmquist	Sweden	Jan Jingryd	Gösta Hanson	36	14
17	Greece	"Horepse"	Marianna Zorba	Manolis Manousselis	Manolis Manousselis	Anacreon Papageorgiou	Greek	Dafni Bokota	Niki Venega	39	12
18	Malta	"Let Me Fly"	Debbie Scerri	Ray Agius	Ray Agius	Ray Agius	English	Gino Cauchi	Anna Bonanno	66	9
19	Hungary	"Miért kell, hogy elmenj?"	V.I.P. (Józsa Alex, Rácz Gergő Rakonczai Imre, Rakonczai Viktor)	Krisztina Bokor Fekete	Viktor Rakonczai	Péter Wolf	Hungarian	István Vágó	Györgyi Albert	39	12
20	Russia	"Primadonna"	Alla Pugacheva	Alla Pugacheva	Alla Pugacheva	Rutger Gunnarsson	Russian	Philip Kirkorov and Sergei Antipov	Arina Sharapova	33	15
21	Denmark	"Stemmen i mit liv"	Kølig Kaj (Thomas Lægård, Christina Juul Hansen)	Thomas Lægård	Lars Pedersen	Jan Glæsel	Danish	Jørgen de Mylius	Bent Henius	25	16
22	French	"Sentiments songes"	Fanny	Jean-Paul Dréau	Jean-Paul Dréau	Régis Dupré	French	Frédéric Ferrer and Marie Myriam	Olivier Minne	95	7
23	Croatia	"Probudi me"	E.N.I. (Elena Tomeček, Nikolina Tomljanović, Iva Močibob, Ivona Maričić)	Alida Šarar	Davor Tolja	-	Croatian	Aleksandar "Aco" Kostadinov	Davor Meštrović	24	17
24	United Kingdom	"Love Shine a Light"	Katrina and the Waves (Katrina Leskanich, Kimberley Rew, Vince de la Cruz, Alex Cooper, Miriam Stockley)	Kimberley Rew	Kimberley Rew	Don Airey	English	Terry Wogan	Colin Berry	227	1
25	Iceland	"Minn hinsti dans"	Paul Oscar	Páll Óskar Hjálmtýsson	Páll Óskar Hjálmtýsson, Trausti Haraldsson	Szymon Kuran	Icelandic	Jakob Frímann Magnússon	Svanhildur Konráðsdóttir	18	20

	Cyprus	Turkey	Norway	Austria	Ireland	Slovenia	Switzerland	The Netherlands	Italy	Spain	Germany	Poland	Estonia	Bosnia Herzegovina	Portugal	Sweden	Greece	Malta	Hungary	Russia	Denmark	France	Croatia	United Kingdom	Iceland
Cyprus	■	–	2	–	3	4	4	10	4	10	5	–	1	–	3	–	12	7	–	1	7	4	4	5	12
Turkey	–	■	–	7	2	–	6	2	7	12	12	–	6	12	5	6	7	10	6	4	–	6	–	4	7
Norway	–	–	■	–	–	–	–	–	–	–	–	–	–	–	–	–	–	–	–	–	–	–	–	–	–
Austria	–	–	–	■	–	–	–	3	–	–	–	1	–	–	–	–	–	–	5	3	–	–	–	–	–
Ireland	8	6	3	10	■	1	7	4	10	6	8	7	8	8	10	10	–	–	8	5	10	10	6	12	–
Slovenia	2	10	–	–	–	■	–	–	–	–	–	2	4	7	4	–	3	5	–	10	–	7	3	–	3
Switzerland	–	–	–	–	–	–	■	–	2	3	–	–	–	–	–	–	–	–	–	–	–	–	–	–	–
The Netherlands	–	1	–	–	–	–	–	■	–	–	–	–	–	–	–	–	–	4	–	–	–	–	–	–	–
Italy	6	5	–	1	1	10	10	7	■	8	4	8	–	6	12	3	5	–	3	7	4	–	10	3	1
Spain	10	4	–	–	6	5	8	6	3	■	2	4	–	–	8	–	6	12	10	8	2	2	–	–	–
Germany	–	–	–	3	–	–	5	–	5	–	■	–	–	–	–	–	–	3	1	–	–	–	5	–	–
Poland	–	–	4	8	–	7	–	1	1	2	6	■	3	4	2	–	1	–	7	–	5	3	–	–	–
Estonia	1	–	–	6	8	3	–	–	12	4	7	6	■	1	1	1	–	–	4	–	8	8	–	10	2
Bosnia Herzegovina	–	8	–	4	–	–	2	–	–	–	3	–	–	■	–	4	–	–	–	–	–	–	1	–	–
Portugal	–	–	–	–	–	–	–	–	–	–	–	–	–	–	■	–	–	–	–	–	–	–	–	–	–
Sweden	–	–	8	–	5	6	–	–	–	–	–	–	–	–	–	■	–	–	–	–	6	–	–	7	4
Greece		–	5	–	–	–	–	–	–	7	–	–	–	–	–	–	■	6	–	2	–	–	7	–	–
Malta	5			–	7	–	–	–	6	1	–	–	–	5	–	–	8	■	–	–	3	1	8	–	–
Hungary	–	3	–	–	4	–	–	–	–	–	5	5	–	–	–	–	–	2	■	–	–	5	2	8	5
Russia	–	–	1	5	–	12	–	8	–	–	–	–	7	–	–	–	–	–	–	■	–	–	–	–	–
Denmark	–	–	7	–	–	–	1	–	–	–	–	–	–	–	–	7	2	–	–	–	■	–	–	2	6
France	3	2	12	–	10	2	3	5	–	–	–	12	12	3	6	2	4	–	2	6	1	■	–	–	10
Croatia	4	–	–	–	–	–	–	–	–	–	1	3	–	2	–	5	–	8	–	–	–	–	■	1	–
United Kingdom	7	7	6	12	12	8	12	12	8	5	10	10	10	10	7	12	10	1	12	12	12	12	12	■	8
Iceland	–	–	–	2	–	–	–	–	–	–	–	–	2	–	–	–	8	–	–	–	–	–	–	6	■

*Countries with grey background used the televoting system.

1998

Hosting County: United Kingdom
Hosting City: Bermingham
Date: 9.5.1998
Place: National Indoor Arena, Bermingham
Presenters: Terry Wogan, Ulrika Johnson
Chief Conductor: Martin Koch
Executive Supervisor: Christine Marchal-Ortiz
Directed by: Geoff Posner
Executive Producer: Jonathan King, Kevin Bishop
Participating Countries: 25
Voting System: Televoting, the results given by 1-8, 10 and 12 points to the most popular song
Broadcaster: British Broadcasting Corporation (BBC)
Intermediate performance: Jupiter, The Bringer of Joviality
Duration: 3 hours and 4 minutes
Broadcast: All participating countries and to Austria, Denmark, Iceland, Yugoslavia and Australia

No.	Country	Song	Performing Artist	Lyrics	Composer	Conductor	Language	Commentator	Spoker of Results	Points	Place
01	Croatia	"Neka mi ne svane"	Danijela	Petar Grašo, Stjepan Kalogjera, Remi Kazinotti	Petar Grašo, Stjepan Kalogjera, Remi Kazinotti	Stipica Kalogjera	Croatian	Aleksandar "Aco" Kostadinov	Davor Meštrović	131	5
02	Greece	"Mia Krifi Evesthisia"	Thalassa (Dionisia Karoki, Yiannis Valvis)	Yiannis Malachias	Yiannis Valvis	-	Greek	Giorgos Mitropoulos	Alexis Kostalas	12	20
03	France	"Où aller"	Marie Line	Jean-Philippe Dary, Marie Line, Moïse Crespy, Micaël Sené	Jean-Philippe Dary, Marie Line, Moïse Crespy, Micaël Sené	Martin Koch	French	Chris Mayne & Laura Mayne	Marie Myriam	3	24
04	Spain	"¿Qué voy a hacer sin ti?"	Mikel Herzog	Mikel Herzog	Alberto Estébanez	Alberto Estébanez	Spanish	José Luis Uribarri	Belén Fernández de Henestrosa	21	16
05	Switzerland	"Lass ihn"	Gunvor	Gunvor Guggisberg, Egon Egemann	Gunvor Guggisberg, Egon Egemann	-	German	Roman Kilchsperger and Heinz Margot, Jean-Marc Richard, Jonathan Tedesco	Regula Elsener	0	25
06	Slovakia	"Modlitba"	Katarína Hasprová	Anna Wepperyová	Gabriel Dušík	Vladimir reerValović	Slovak	Rastislav Sokol	Alena Heribanová	8	21
07	Poland	"To takie proste"	Sixteen I Renata Dabkowska, Jarosław Pruszkowski, Tomasz Stryczniewicz, Janusz Witaszek, Mirosław Hodun)	Olga Pruszkowska	Jarosław Pruszkowski	Wiesław Piere-gorolka	Polish	Artur Orzech	Jan Chojnacki	19	17
08	Israel	"Diva"	Dana International	Yoav Ginay	Svika Pick	-	Hebrew	-	Yigal Ravid	172*	1
09	Germany	"Guildo hat euch lieb!"	Guildo Horn	Stefan Raab	Stefan Raab	Stefan Raab	German	Peter Urban	Nena	86*	7
10	Malta	"The One That I Love"	Chiara	Sunny Aquilina	Jason Cassar	-	English	Gino Cauchi	Stephanie Farrugia	166	3
11	Hungary	"A holnap már nem lesz szomoru"	Charlie	Attila Horváth	István Lerch	Miklós Malek	Hungarian	Gábor Gundel Takács	Barna Héder	4	23
12	Slovenia	"Naj bogovi slišijo"	Vili Resnik	Urša Vlašič	Matjaž Vlašič	Mojmir Sepe	Slovenian	Miša Molk	Mojca Mavec	17	18
13	Ireland	"Is Always Over Now?"	Dawn Martin	Gerry Morgan	Gerry Morgan	Noel Kelehan	English	Pat Kenny	Eileen Dunne	64	9
14	Portugal	"Se eu te pudesse abraçar"	Alma Lusa	José Cid	José Cid	Mike Seargent	portuguese	Rui Unas	Lúcia Moniz	36	12
15	Romania	"Eu cred"	Mălina Olinescu	Liliana Ştefan	Adrian Romcescu	Romcescu	Romanian	Leonard Miron	Anca Ţurcaşiu	6	22
16	United Kingdom	"Where Are You?"	Imaani	Scott English, Phil Manikiza, Simon Stirling	Scott English, Phil Manikiza, Simon Stirling	James McMillan	English	Terry Wogan	Ken Bruce	166	2
17	Cyprus	"Genesis"	Michael Hajiyanni	Zenon Zindilis	Michalis Hatzigiannis	Costa Cacoyiannis	Greek	Evi Papamichail	Marina Maleni	37	11
18	Netherlands	"Hemel en aarde"	Edsilia	Eric van Tijn, Jochem Fluitsma	Eric van Tijn, Jochem Fluitsma	Dick Bakker	Dutch	Willem van Beusekom	Conny Vandenbos	150	4
19	Sweden	"Kärleken är"	Jill Johnson	Ingela Forsman	Håkan Almqvist, Bobby Ljunggren	Anders Berglund	Swedish	Pernilla Mânsson and Christer Björkman	Björn Hedman	53	10
20	Belgium	"Dis oui"	Mélanie Cohl	Philippe Swan	Philippe Swan	-	French	Jean-Pierre Hautier, André Vermeulen and Andrea Croonenberghs	Marie-Hélène Vanderborght	122	6
21	Finland	"Aava"	Edea (Marika Krook, Ralph van Manen, Abdissa Assefa, Alexi Ahoniemi, Samuli Kosminen, Tommy Mansikka-Aho)	Tommy Mansikka-Aho	Alexi Ahoniemi	Olli Ahvenlahti	Finish	Maria Guzenina and Sami Aaltonen	Marjo Wilska	22	15
22	Norway	"Alltid sommer"	Lars Fredriksen	Linda Andernach Johansen	David Eriksen	Geir Langslet	Norweigen	Jostein Pedersen	Ragnhild Sælthun Fjørtoft	79	8
23	Estonia	"Mere lapsed"	Koit Toome	Peeter Pruuli	Maria Rahula, Tomi Rahula	Heiki Vahar	Estonish	Reet Linna	Urve Tiidus	36	12
24	Turkey	"Unutamazsın"	Tüzmen	Canan Tunç	Erdinç Tunç	Ümit Eroglu	Turkish	Ömer Önder	Osman Erkan	25	14
25	North Macedonia	"Ne zori, zoro"	Vlado Janevski	Vlado Janevski	Grigor Koprov	Alexandar Dzam-bazov	North Mace-donian	Milanka Rašik	Evgenija Teodosievska	16	19

Spain awarded 12 points to Israel, but it turned out that Germany won them. Israel was only left with 10 points, and thus, Germany jumped to 7th place. Israel's victory was not affected.

	Croatia	Greece	France	Spain	Switzerland	Slovakia	Poland	Israel	Germany	Malta	Hungary	Slovenia	Ireland	Portugal	Romania	United Kingdom	Cyprus	The Netherlands	Sweden	Belgium	Finland	Norway	Estonia	Turkey	North Macedonia	
Croatia	■	5	8	1	5	10	6	10	10	10	–	12	3	2	–	2	7	4	3	5	3	6	3	4	12	Croatia
Greece	–	■	–	–	–	–	–	–	–	–	–	–	–	–	–	–	12	–	–	–	–	–	–	–	–	Greece
France	–	–	■	–	–	–	–	–	–	–	–	–	–	–	–	–	1	–	–	–	–	–	–	–	2	France
Spain	1	–	4	■	6	–	–	3	–	–	–	–	–	–	–	–	4	–	–	3	–	–	–	–	–	Spain
Switzerland	–	–	–	–	■	–	–	–	–	–	–	–	–	–	–	–	–	–	–	–	–	–	–	–	–	Switzerland
Slovakia	8	–	–	–	–	■	–	–	–	–	–	–	–	–	–	–	–	–	–	–	–	–	–	–	–	Slovakia
Poland	–	–	2	–	–	–	■	–	5	–	2	–	–	–	10	–	–	–	–	–	–	–	–	–	–	Poland
Israel	–	10	12	10	10	–	10	■	7	12	–	7	6	12	7	5	10	6	5	10	10	3	7	5	8	Israel
Germany	–	3	–	12	12	–	–	–	■	–	–	8	8	10	6	6	–	12	–	7	1	–	1	–	–	Germany
Malta	7	6	6	5	8	12	8	7	8	■	7	3	12	5	–	12	5	8	6	8	5	12	5	10	–	Malta
Hungary	–	–	1	–	–	–	–	–	–	–	■	–	–	–	1	–	–	–	–	–	–	2	–	–	–	Hungary
Slovenia	3	2	–	–	–	–	–	–	–	–	–	■	–	–	5	–	–	–	–	–	4	–	–	3	–	Slovenia
Ireland	2	–	–	–	2	4	2	–	2	6	6	1	■	1	8	8	–	–	1	–	–	4	2	8	7	Ireland
Portugal	–	1	10	6	–	2	–	2	–	2	–	–	–	■	–	–	2	–	–	1	–	–	–	6	4	Portugal
Romania	–	–	–	–	–	–	–	6	–	–	–	–	–	–	■	–	–	–	–	–	–	–	–	–	–	Romania
United Kingdom	12	7	3	3	3	1	7	12	1	8	10	5	5	6	12	■	8	7	7	6	8	5	8	12	10	United Kingdom
Cyprus	4	12	–	–	–	5	–	1	–	1	1	–	–	4	4	3	■	–	–	2	–	–	–	–	–	Cyprus
The Netherlands	10	8		4	7	6	5	8	6	7	12	–	10	7	–	10	–	■	8	12	7	8	–	7	3	The Netherlands
Sweden	–	–	–	–	–	–	3	–	–	4	8	–	2	–	–	1	–	5	■	–	6	10	12	2	–	Sweden
Belgium	–	4	7	7	4	7	12	5	4	3	3	6	7	8	–	7	6	10	2	■	–	7	6	1	6	Belgium
Finland	–	–	–	–	–	–	–	–	–	–	–	–	–	–	–	–	–	–	10	–	■	1	10	–	1	Finland
Norway	–	–	–	8	1	–	4	4	3	5	5	10	4	3	–	4	3	3	12	4	2	■	4	–	–	Norway
Estonia	–	–	–	2	–	8	1	–	–	–	4	2	1	–	–	–	–	2	4	–	12	–	■	–	–	Estonia
Turkey	5	–	–	–	–	–	–	–	12	–	–	–	–	–	2	=	=	1	=	=	=	=	=	■	5	Turkey
North Macedonia	6	–	–	–	–	3	–	–	–	–	–	4	–	–	3	–	–	–	–	–	–	–	–	–	■	North Macedonia

1999

Country Hosting: Israel

City Hosting: Jerusalem

Date: 29.5.1999

Location: International Convention Center

Presenters: Yigal Ravid, Sigal Shachmon and Dafna Dekel

Executive Supervisor: Christine Marchal-Ortiz

Directed By: Hagai Mautner

Executive Producer: Amnon Barkai

Participating Countries: 23

Voting System: Televoting, the results given by 1-8, 10 and 12 points to the most popular song

Broadcaster: Israel Broadcasting Authority (IBA)

Intermediate performance: "Freedom Calling", with the song "Free" performed by Dana International

Duration: 3 hours and 15 minutes

Broadcast: All participating countries and to Finland, Greece, North Macedonia, Romania, Switzerland and Australia.

No.	Country	Song	Performing Artist	Lyrics	Composer	Language	Commentator	Spoker of Results	Points	Place
01	Lithuania	"Strazdas"	Aistė	Sigitas Geda	Linas Rimša	Lithuanian-Samogitian	-	Andrius Tapinas	13	20
02	Belgium	"Like the Wind"	Vanessa Chinitor	Ilia Beyers, John Terra, Emma Philippa Hjalmas, Wim Claes	Ilia Beyers, John Terra, Emma Philippa Hjalmas, Wim Claes	English	André Vermeulen and Bart Peeters, Jean-Pierre Hautier	Sabine De Vos	38	12
03	Spain	"No quiero escuchar"	Lydia	Carlos López González, Adolfo Carmona Zamarreño, Fernando Rodríguez Fernández, Alejandro Piqueras Ramírez	Fernando Rodríguez Fernández, Alejandro Piqueras Ramírez	Spanish	José Luis Uribarri	Hugo de Campos	1	23
04	Croatia	"Marija Magdalena"	Doris Dragović	Vjekoslava Huljić	Tonči Huljić	Croatian	Aleksandar "Aco" Kostadinov	Marko Rašica	118	4
05	United Kingdom	"Say It Again"	Precious (Louise Rose, Anya Lahiri, Kalli Clark-Stemberg, Jenny Frost, Sophie McDonnell)	Paul Varney	Paul Varney	English	Terry Wogan	Colin Berry	38	13
06	Slovenia	"For a Thousand Years"	Darja Švajger	Primož Peterca	Sašo Fajon	English	Miša Molk	Mira Berginc	50	11
07	Turkey	"Dön Artık"	Tuğba Önal & Grup Mistik	Canan Tunç	Erdinç Tunç	Turkish	Gülşah Banda	Osman Erkan	21	16
08	Norway	"Living My Life Without You"	Stig Van Eijk	Stig Van Eijk, Sem	Stig Van Eijk, Sem	English	Jostein Pedersen	Ragnhild Sælthun Fjørtoft	35	14
09	Denmark	"This Time I Mean It"	Trine Jepsen & Michael Teschl	Ebbe Ravn	Ebbe Ravn	English	Keld Heick	Kirsten Siggaard	71	8
10	France	"Je veux donner ma voix"	Nayah	Gilles Arcens, Luigi Rutigliano	Pascal Graczyk, René Colombies	French	Julien Lepers	Marie Myriam	14	19
11	Netherlands	"One Good Reason"	Marlayne	Tjeerd van Zanen, Alan Michael	Tjeerd van Zanen, Alan Michael	English	Willem van Beusekom	Edsilia Rombley	71	9
12	Poland	"Przytul mnie mocno"	Mietek Szcześniak	Wojciech Ziembicki	Seweryn Krajewski	Polish	Artur Orzech	Jan Chojnacki	17	18
13	Iceland	"All Out of Luck"	Selma	Þorvaldur Bjarni Þorvaldsson	Selma Björnsdóttir, Sveinbjörn I. Baldvinsson, Þorvaldur Bjarni Þorvaldsson	English	Gísli Marteinn Baldursson	Áslaug Dóra Eyjolfsdottir	146	2
14	Cyprus	"Tha'nai Erotas"	Marlain	Andreas Karanicolas	Yiorgos Kallis	Greek	Evi Papamichail	Marina Maleni	2	22
15	Sweden	"Take Me to Your Heaven"	Charlotte Nilsson	Gert Lengstrand, Marcos Ubeda	Lars Diedricson	English	Pekka Heino and Anders Berglund	Pontus Gårdinger	163	1
16	Portugal	"Como tudo começou"	Rui Bandeira	Tó Andrade	Jorge do Carmo	portuguese	Rui Unas	Manuel Luís Goucha	12	21
17	Ireland	"When You Need Me"	The Mullans (Bronagh Mullan, Karen Mullan)	Bronagh Mullan	Bronagh Mullan	English	Pat Kenny	Clare McNamara	18	17
18	Austria	"Reflection"	Bobbie Singer	Dave Moskin	Dave Moskin	English	Andi Knoll	Dodo Roščić	65	10
19	Israel	"Yom Huledet"	"Eden" (Rafael Dahan, Doron Oren, Eddie Butler and Gabriel Butler)	Moshe Datz, Ya'akov Lamai, Jacky Oved, Gabriel Datz	Moshe Datz, Ya'akov Lamai, Jacky Oved, Gabriel Datz	Hebrew	-	Yoav Ginai	93	5
20	Malta	"Believe 'n Peace"	Times Three (Philippa Farrugia Randon, Diane Stafrace, Francesca Tabone)	Moira Stafrace	Moira Stafrace	English	Charlo Bonnici	Nirvana Azzopardi	32	15
21	Germany	"Reise nach Jerusalem — Kudüs'e seyahat"	Sürpriz (Zeyno Filiz, Deniz Filizmen, Bülent Ural, Yasemin Akkar, Savas Ucar, Chicco Özden)	Bernd Meinunger	Ralph Siegel	German-Turkish	Peter Urban	Renan Demirkan	140	3
22	Bosnia and Herzegovina	"Putnici"	Dino & Béatrice	Edin Dervišhalidović	Edin Dervišhalidović	Serbo-Croatian/French	Ismeta Dervoz-Krvavac	Segmedina Srna	86	7
23	Estonia	"Diamond of Night"	Evelin Samuel & Camille	Maian-Anna Kärmas	Priit Pajusaar, Glen Pilvre	English	Marko Reikop	Mart Sander	90	6

	Lithuania	Belgium	Spain	Croatia	United Kingdom	Slovenia	Turkey	Norway	Denmark	France	The Netherlands	Poland	Iceland	Cyprus	Sweden	Portugal	Ireland	Austria	Israel	Malta	Germany	Bosnia and Herzegovina	Estonia	
Lithuania	■	–	–	2	–	–	–	–	–	–	–	–	–	5	–	–	–	–	3	1	–	–	2	Lithuania
Belgium	–	■	–	4	–	–	–	–	–	2	10	2	–	–	–	–	10	–	5	–	–	–	5	Belgium
Spain	–	–	■	1	–	–	–	–	–	–	–	–	–	–	–	–	–	–	–	–	–	–	–	Spain
Croatia	6	5	12	■	–	12	8	–	–	7	1	7	4	2	1	6	6	8	7	5	10	8	3	Croatia
United Kingdom	5	–	4	5	■	2	4	–	1	–	–	–	–	4	–	–	–	–	4	8	–	1	–	United Kingdom
Slovenia	10	2	2		–	■	–	–	–	1	6	–	–	–	–	–	12	–	–	–	–	5	–	Slovenia
Turkey	–	–	–	–	–	–	■	4	–	5	–	–	–	–	–	–	–	–	–	–	12	–	–	Turkey
Norway	–	–	–	7	–	–	–	■	6	–	–	–	7	7	5	–	3	–	–	–	–	–	–	Norway
Denmark	–	–	5	–	5	5	–	–	■	–	–	1	12	8	8	3	7	5	2	4	–	–	6	Denmark
France	2	–	–	–	–	–	2	8	–	■	–	–	–	–	–	–	2	–	–	–	–	–	–	France
The Netherlands	4	12	3	–	8	3	5	–	7	–	■	–	6	–	4	2	1	4	6	2	–	4	–	The Netherlands
Poland	7	–	–	–	–	–	–	–	–	–	–	■	–	–	–	–	–	–	–	–	4	6	–	Poland
Iceland	8	8	10	–	10	–	10	10	12	–	7	4	■	12	12	4	4	2	10	10	3	–	10	Iceland
Cyprus	–	–	–	–	2	–	–	–	–	–	–	–	–	■	–	–	–	–	–	–	–	–	–	Cyprus
Sweden	3	7	6	–	12	7	6	12	10	3	8	6	10	6	■	10	5	6	8	12	2	12	12	Sweden
Portugal	–	–	–	–	–	–	–	–	–	12	–	–	–	–	–	■	–	–	–	–	–	–	–	Portugal
Ireland	12	–	–	–	4	–	1	1	–	–	–	–	–	–	–	–	■	–	–	–	–	–	–	Ireland
Austria	–	6	–	–	7	4	–	6	3	–	2	3	8	1	7	5	–	■	–	–	5	–	8	Austria
Israel	–	3	8	8	–	1	3	2	2	10	4	10	1	10	3	8	–	1	■	6	7	2	4	Israel
Malta	–	–	–	6	6	–	–	–	–	–	–	–	–	3	–	1	–	7	–	■	1	7	1	Malta
Germany	–	10	7	3	1	6	12	3	5	8	12	12	5	–	2	12	–	10	12	3	■	10	7	Germany
Bosnia and Herzegovina	–	1	–	10	–	10	7	7	8	6	3	5	3	–	6	–	–	12	–	–	8	■	–	Bosnia and Herzegovina
Estonia	1	4	1	–	3	8	–	5	4	4	5	8	2	–	10	7	8	3	1	7	6	3	■	Estonia

*The countries with the grey background used the old Juries System

2000–2009

THE BIG EAST

The first decade of the new millennium brought a unique phenomenon: Ten different winners, with the historic premieres of old Greece, Finland and Turkey — as well as Estonia, Latvia, Russia and Serbia, the newcomers. Norway, Finland and Denmark brought a glory to Scandinavia. Five female singers won in this decade, but the greatest success rate was actually for a male singer (Norway's Alexander Rybak, 2009). Compared to the previous millennium's last decade, the first of the 2000s was varied with hosts from all corners of the European map.

2000 – Stockholm, Sweden

The 45th Eurovision, the first for the new millennium, certainly renewed and rejuvenated the contest. It was decided to open the event to a lot more viewers and hold it in a large arena, creating a different atmosphere from the traditional concert halls that characterised the Eurovision in the previous decades.

Being the 1999 winner, Sweden took it one step further. The Globe Arena in the capital Stockholm, was filled with 16,000 enthusiastic spectators who created a unique atmosphere adding teen spirit to the Eurovision.

For the first time, the contest was also broadcasted on the Internet and could be watched in the United States, Canada, Australia and Japan. Six years after joining the Eurovision, Estonia was the main favourite to win with Ines' "Once in a lifetime", but reached only the disappointing fourth place.

Nicki French from the UK hoped to take her country back to the top, but "Don't Play That Song Again" was surprisingly the song that ended in the lowest place (16) in the glorious British history at the contest. The consolation of the British: the future will be much worse...

This time too, the English language had almost entirely dominated the contest: no less than 17 (!) of the 24 participants chose to use it. One of them, Russia, who returned to the event after a three-year absence, took the second place, which was excellent for Alsou's "Solo".

Israel created a huge controversy with its representative, "Ping Pong". It is impossible to know what the committee were thinking when they decided to send the tactless band, that performed the terrible entry "Sameach," which miraculously escaped the last place, by getting 7 points, 6 of which came from France. The provocative and rude band behaved outrageously, gave controversial interviews, made unorthodox statements, and even waved the Syrian flags (an enemy state to Israel) during the performance, causing the Israeli delegation to warn the band that they will withdraw from the contest (which they did not). Following the shameful episode, the IBA director, Uri Porath, sharpened the procedures to ensure that such a disgrace will not repeat itself and concluded with harsh words: "The Broadcasting Authority fell victim to a bunch of reckless, this is a band of crooks who deceived us".

The "Ping Pong" case also led to a clarification by the EBU: No more songs with a clear political message will participate. Latvia made an amazing debut — an excellent third place with one of the best and most valued entries in the contest, "My star," performed by Renārs Kauper of "Brainstorm". Like the winning entry, and like all the first 17 places (except for the ninth — Croatia), this song was in English.

A major fire in the city of Enschede in the Netherlands caused the broadcast to be taken off the air after the first half the contest and a recording of the contest was broadcast later. The unexpected winners from Denmark, the Olsen brothers, were the absolute opposite of the contest's youthful trend. Jurgen (50) and Niels (46) captured everyone with "Fly on the wings of love", that won clearly and definitively to join the rare group of winners' that led the vote from its first moment until the sweet end. Russia tried to challenge the Danes' claim that they used technical means to add an electronic dimension to the Olsen brothers' voice but was rejected outright.

2001 – Copenhagen, Denmark

For the first time, the Eurovision Song Contest was held in an open stadium — the "Parken" of Copenhagen, home of the Danish national football team. A record number of 35,000 spectators brought the Eurovision to new horizons, which was undoubtedly the contest with the homeliest atmosphere ever. This option was made possible thanks to the construction of a roof in the stadium. But it did not happen without issues: Many of the tens of thousands of spectators could not see the stage and quite a few performers claimed that the number of spectators and the way they were seated, made it exceedingly difficult for them. The legendary Terry Wogan has managed to insult the duo of presenters Søren Pilmark and Natasja Crone Back, quite rightly so, due to a rather childish manner of presentation. The Danes, who were deeply hurt by the comments, made an official protest to the BBC and Wogan was forced to apologise. Another confrontation was around the Swedish entry "Listen to Your Heartbeat", which sounded like a replica of the 1996 Belgian song "Liefde is een kaartspel". The Belgian songwriters filed a lawsuit against the Swedes, but it was ultimately ruled that there was no plagiarism and the "Friends" band achieved fifth place in Copenhagen with 100 points. Slovenia, France (with a global hit that crossed continents) and especially Greece (the only one to get points from all the countries and reach the highest position in its history in the contest so far) were the hot favourites to win. The last two met expectations when they finished in 3-4 places, but the duel for the victory took place between the host Denmark and surprising Estonia. "Never Ever Let You Go" by "Rollo & King", was awfully close to completing a second consecutive win for the host. Every time Denmark got the full points (it happened six times during the evening), the feeling was that the roof in "Parken" was about to collapse from the roars of joy. Second place and 177 points are an achievement that no Eurovision host has been able to reach in the 20 years to come. Tanel Padar and Dave Benton from Estonia were overly optimistic thanks to "Everybody", delivering an astonishing performance in the decisive moment and bringing their country a surprising and historic victory. In fact, Estonia led almost throughout the whole voting session, waged a desperate battle with host Denmark and the home crowd, but eventually laughed all the way to the first-ever win for the Baltic and ex-Soviet country in the Eurovision.

2002 - Tallinn, Estonia

The EBU had many concerns about Estonia's victory, the first ex-Soviet country to win the ESC. Many remembered what happened the last time an Eastern European country won and hosted the following year the biggest music show in the world: Yugoslavia's fiasco from 1990 is remembered to this day as a lousy production. For the first time, a unique 'board' was established consisting of past producers of the contest, including the Israeli Amnon Barkai, who considerably helped the Estonian television withstand the burden and with profound respect... A little history that lasts to this day: the selection of a slogan for the Eurovision, which in 2002 was called "A Modern Fairytale". The "Saku" hall, which hosted the contest, was built especially for the occasion, in double and triple shifts, at the end of which the venue was put on display, available to the Eurovision production company. Once again, the presenters were tastefully chosen: Annely Peebo and Marko Matvere, who did a flawless job and marvelled at their musical skills. Slovenia caused a stir when the boys' band that represented it performed in completely feminine attire, including all the accessories, with the entry "Samo ljubezen", which expressed support for the LGBTQ community. The country itself opposed vehemently to the song and the appearance of the "Sestre" trio. They may have been ahead of their time, but the noise they made was far beyond the 13th place they reached at the end of the evening. Sarit Hadad represented Israel in an exceedingly difficult period for the Middle East, with the second 'intifada' at its peak and the hate of some European countries towards Israel crossing borders. Hadad decided to send congratulatory letters to all contestants. Danish singer Malene Mortensen spat at Sarit Hadad's letter and said she did not want to receive anything from Israelis. Absurdly, Malene (the hot favourite to win this Eurovision) finished, amazingly, in the last place, when four of her seven points were given to her by... Israel. The hostility towards Sarit Hadad continued on both Swedish and Belgian television, with their broadcasters urging viewers not to vote for the Israeli entry. Under these conditions, 12th place was like a victory for Hadad and "Light a Candle" written by Svika Pick. However, this was not the end of the Israeli tribulations: after the contest, the writers of the Swedish children's song "Teddybjörnen Fredriksson" claimed that Pick's entry was copied from them... The prolific Israeli composer responded with ridicule to this claim, even though there is a minimal resemblance in the two songs' choruses. Apart from the Danes, Germany and Malta were also strong candidates for the victory. Germany connected the blind singer Corinna May and Mr Eurovision Ralph Siegel (the two finally blamed each other for May's inferior performance), which brought the poor 21st place. Only Ira Losco from Malta met expectations, led in the first half of the voting and gave a fair fight for the prize until surrendering to the winner.

Marija Naumova from Latvia was nominated as a potential winner, much thanks to the stage performance and choreography, in which she begins with a long-tailored suit and ends with a tight-fitting red evening dress and of course — a catchy song, "I Wanna", which won only 5 Douze Points, but was enough for a historic Latvian who kept the contest in the Baltic Sea.

The Swiss vote made a turnaround, which left Malta behind, trying to ger closer to the leading Latvian. The margin was getting smaller, until the last vote, in which Marija Naumova led Losco by just 3 points, but with optimism, as good neighbour Lithuania was the last to award its points. Indeed, the Lithuanians did not disappoint: they gave only 3 points to Malta and for dessert — a winning Douze Points for Marija, bringing the next year's event to Riga.

2003 - Riga, Latvia

After the relative success in Estonia, the Eurovision naturally moved to Latvia. The former Soviet Union countries took over the contest to some extent, and the "Skonto" arena in the capital Riga was the stage for an interesting and exciting event. The government of Latvia and the town of Riga set a high budget for the contest — 3.6 million euros, which was unquestionably enough to produce a good show. Twenty-six countries, the largest number ever, participated in the Eurovision as Ukraine makes its debut, with a song written by Svika Pick and Mirit Shem Or and reaching only 14th place. The substantial number of countries that took or wanted to take part in the contest led the EBU to the conclusion that there is no escape from splitting the competition into two evenings:

a semi-final and a final. Later, the number will increase to three evenings, of which two are semi-finals, so Eurovision 2003 was the last to be held in the old and familiar format. Another history was made when all the 26 participating artists where first timers in the contest and there were no returning artists. The two presenters were the ones who brought Latvia its two most impressive achievements in just three years (2002 winner Marija Naumova and "Brainstorm" lead singer Renārs Kaupers who came in third in 2000). The opening of the contest was surprising and intriguing with the presenters brought on screen the first Eurovision winner, Lys Assia, who was in Cyprus at the time. They went on to visit a space station and finished off with a video interview with music icon Elton John who wished luck to all contestants. The main contender for the victory was Russia with the provocative girl duo "t.A.T.u" and the entry "Ne ver ', ne boysia". The Russian girls were not ashamed to display bold behaviour and were marked as almost clear winners, even though they were frowned upon in their country for their non-politically correct behaviour, to put it mildly... The Russian girls caused trouble from the moment they arrived in Riga:

they criticised the "poor" production at a press conference, threatened to kiss naked on stage (which made the production get ready with an alternative recording of the Russian entry in case needed...) and promised everywhere that they will be the winners when no other song approaches their level. Overall, they missed the win by just 3 points after suspenseful voting and finished only in third place with 164 points, one less than second place, three less than first. The Russians appealed the result, claiming a malfunction in Ireland's telephone voting system made the latter use of a back-up panel of jurors, which allegedly robbed the Russians of essential points that could have given them the victory. The EBU ruled that there was no defect in the Irish conduct and dismissed the appeal.

Belgium first used an imaginary language with the entry "Sanomi" by the "Urban Trad" and managed to amaze by leading in most voting stages, being closer than ever to a second Eurovision win. It led by a significant advantage that shrank towards the end and right at the last minute following only 3 points it got from Slovenia, it was eliminated from the first place, in one of the most bitter and cruel losses in the history of the Eurovision. Austrian Alf Poier, with one of the strangest and most entertaining songs in the contest, brought his country the sixth place (Austria's best in 14 years); Host Latvia crashed to the 24th place with just five points (the worst position for a host so far). Many claims have accumulated over the years against the tribal and political voting between neighbouring countries. With the accession of the former Soviet states and the disintegration of Yugoslavia, this trend became unbearable. The one who paid the price was the UK, which after all its historical achievements, finished the 2003 Eurovision with nul points and a shameful unprecedented last place (the result caused a crisis of confidence in the kingdom towards the European singing contest). If 28 years before, after finishing last in the first Eurovision in which it participated (1975), Turkey was told that a day would come and it would win the contest and The UK would finish last, they would have surely thought this is an unrealistic prophecy. But it was realised in Riga 2003:

Sertab Erener did it with the ethnic and rhythmic "Everyway That I Can", which was not a really surprising victory. The voting was one of the tensest of all time, with the surprising Norway opening in the lead, which moved briefly to Turkey, after which Belgium took the first place, with Russia constantly in the picture. When the last three countries were about to vote, Belgium led by a large margin and was about to secure its victory, but the big advantage diminished until the very last minute when Slovenia was about to prevail, and so it did: Belgium got only 3 points, Russia received 12 points that did not help it, and Turkey jumped to the top with 10 points that gave it a turnaround and a first historic victory in the Eurovision.

2004 – Istanbul, Turkey

The Abdi İpekçi Arena, Istanbul's basketball temple, was festive for the 2004 Eurovision hosting. For the first time, the contest was split into two evenings, with the semi-final introduction, out of which 22 participants qualified for the final, joined by host Turkey, the five sponsoring countries and the eight countries that finished first in Riga. A record number of 36 participants, all of whom gave scores in the final, a number that will even increase over the years. A special animated tribute was screened on the eve of the semi-finals, honouring the legendary band "ABBA" on the 30th anniversary of its Eurovision victory. The semi-final did not rise to a particularly elevated level, although it included the three favourites, which were finally on the list of the ten appeased countries that joined the rest in the final. David D'Or from Israel, despite a considerable international record, failed in his attempt to be included in the big evening, as did Maryon from Monaco (who returned to the contest after a 25-year hiatus). Cyprus qualified and its presence at the international event on Turkish soil was sensitive, but overall, there were no clashes between the parties. The crowd itself reacted with scathing contempt when Greece awarded Cyprus the full points and vice versa when before the Greek vote, presenters Korhan Abay and Meltem Cumbul greeted Alexis Kostalas in the Greek language, and the latter rewarded them with a few words in Turkish: It was an icebreaker that should not be taken lightly due to the strained relations between the two countries.

Several significant glitches occurred in the semi-finals when Turkish television switched to commercials at the Slovenian entry's expense, which obviously did not get any point from the hosts... There were many issues with other countries that voted, which became known to the EBU only after the semi-final broadcast. The final itself was not errorless either, when the previous Eurovision winner's dress, Sertab Erener, was caught on one of the devices at the end of the stage, which prevented her from continuing to step forward... Turkey's eternal Prime Minister, Recep Tayyip Erdoğan, was the guest of honour in the final. Sakis Rouvas from Greece was the favourite with "Shake It" and what a sweet win it could have been for the Greeks on Turkish soil... Rouvas finished in the third place at the end of the evening and stepped down for an intriguing duel between Ukraine's Ruslana ("Wild Dances") and Serbia and Montenegro's Željko Joksimović, who was the runner-up (in his country's debut in the contest). In an exotic and memorable performance, Ruslana brought the third ex-Soviet victory and first for the proud Ukraine.

2005 – Kyiv, Ukraine

Ruslana's victory put Ukraine on the map. The country hoped that hosting the Eurovision would promote its image, tourism and, of course, its integration into the European continent. The stage design was praised, but the production was not errorless. It started with the Bulgarian flag's embedment in the Hungarian entry, continued with sound issues from which mainly damaged the Norwegian song and ended in an extremely long 39-nation voting process (Which got a typical protest from Terry Wogan during the UK broadcast: "How more countries we got? What time is it?"). The EBU drew the required conclusions, and from 2006, voting representatives from all countries will only provide the names of the participants who received 8, 10 and 12 points, with the rest of the scores appearing on the screen. Ruslana, the winner of the previous year, was supposed to be one of the presenters, but her little English language knowledge prevented it. Lebanon first asked to take part in the Eurovision Song Contest (due to its membership in the EBU), but as the contest approached and it became clear to the members from Beirut that they would be obliged to broadcast the Israeli entry and, god forbid, open the possibility for Lebanese citizens to vote for it, they sought and found a way out of participating in the contest.

Hats off to the EBU that did not blink and compromise in the face of this childish behaviour. The Israeli representative, Shiri Maimon, became the surprise of the contest when, contrary to expectations and thanks to a wonderful performance accompanied by the brothers Eyal and Guy Mazig, she managed to qualify for the final and bring Israel to the fourth place on the big evening, with "Hasheket Shenishar". Chiara from Malta returned to the Eurovision after seven years, and although she was far from first place compared to the drama of 1998, she managed to upgrade her position and equal her country's greatest achievement at the ESC — runner-up. This time, uncommonly, the favourite also won: Helena Paparizou from Greece arrived as the main favourite and did it sharply and clearly with "My Number One". After 31 years of participation with mostly disappointments, the European Singing Contest will finally take place in Athens.

2006 – Athens, Greece

Greece hosted a glorious Eurovision two years after the Athens Olympics, at the Nikos Galis Olympic Indoor Hall — named after the greatest Greek basketball player of all time. The popular Sakis Rouvas and Maria Menounos succeeded in the role of presenters. Armenia participated for the first time while Serbia and Montenegro's dissolution prevented them from taking part in the contest in Athens. Cyprus, on Greek soil, failed in its attempt to qualify for the final. In the semi-finals, the 1,000th song in the Eurovision Song Contest history was played, an honour that fell to the Irish Brian Kennedy (who managed to qualify for the final). The most prominent name came from Spain — "Las Ketchup" (which drove the world crazy at the beginning of the millennium with "The Ketchup Song –Aserejé-"), which failed in the final and finished 21st. Host Greece was the favourite to win with "Everything" sung by Anna Vissi (who returned to the contest for the third time in 24 years, hoping to close the circle and win it), but despite an invested tour and a great aura around her, the Greeks did not complete a back-to-back victory, and the disappointed Vissi reached only the ninth place. Many viewers liked the most memorable entry from the contest, "We Are the Winners" performed by the Lithuanian band "LT United". After years of disappointments and bitter results, finally, a sweet victory for Finland, thanks to the masked monster band "Lordi" and the metal song (a rare thing in the Eurovision) "Hard Rock Hallelujah". One of the band members, the Egyptian Samer el Nahhal, who was born and who lives in Finland, is the first Arab singer to win the contest. In a rare occurrence, the Finns got the same number of points in both the semi-finals and the final — 282.
Here goes to Helsinki.

2007 – Helsinki, Finland

42 countries and 13 million Euros were the enormous numbers behind the 2007 Eurovision. Finland's victory led to the country's first hosting of the European Singing contest. Turku and Espoo aspired to hold the event, but the capital Helsinki finally won the great honour. Israel (who competed in the semi-finals) made a big headache for the organisers when they chose the entry "Push the Button" performed by "Teapacks" (the song hinted at the Iranian nuclear problem). The EBU recognised the song's political affiliation and the heated discussions between the Israeli delegation and the production led to a threat of disqualifying the entry. The Israeli band was finally allowed to perform it but was harassed by the Finnish production, which sidestepped request regarding shooting angles, sound, etc. Ultimately, the rather weak song that was not really connected to the event did not even come close to being a finalist and finished in the 24th shameful place for Israel. Ukraine was the big favourite thanks to Verka Serduchka's entry "Dancing Lasha Tumbai", which gained countless plays before the contest and was claimed by many to be a kind of political protest against Russia. But the Grand Prix was taken by Serbian Marija Šerifović with "Molitva", which closed the circle with the first Yugoslavian Eurovision victory since 1989 (after the state's dissolution). The moving ballad brought musical sanity back to the European contest and the country that had been ostracised for most of the previous decade due to the brutal war in the Balkans became the most beautiful swan of the lake for one night and will proudly host the prominent show in Belgrade.

2008 - Belgrade, Serbia

The Eurovision in Belgrade once again broke the record number of participants: 43 with almost all of Europe taking part in the largest music show in the world. Changes in the semi-final format: As of this year, there were two semi-finals, of which 20 participants advanced to the grand final (9 from each end plus a free ticket for an additional entry from each semi-final, according to the juries' decision). These joined the four founding countries and the host, completing the picture of 25 entries that taking part in the final. The EBU also sought to fight the phenomenon of tribalism and prevent a lack of interest on the part of western European countries, which protested the points ruses between the eastern participants and found a unique way: Before the semi-finals, the 38 participants were divided into six pots, considering their geographical location and voting history. On the eve of the semi-finals, only the participating countries of each evening could vote rather than all the nations as has been the case until then. This effectiveness has undoubtedly led to some change, but it seemed that the Eastern European tribalism was back in the final.

Croatia's performance with the "75 Cents" band and Kraljevi Ulice aroused a lot of curiosity. There is deep animosity between the Croats and the Serbs due to the bitter war in Yugoslavia and any meeting between the two in any area, requires vigilance. To the pleasant surprise, the Croats received a warm and loving welcome from the hosts and an extremely high score from the Serbs. There were no surprises this time: Dima Bilan was the favourite, and he did it with "Believe", accompanied by a violinist and the Russian Olympic figure skater Evgeni Plushenko. In the first semi-final, he finished only third (behind Greece and Armenia), but in the final, he had a clean sweep and brought his country Russia its premier Eurovision victory, for the first time since joining the contest in 1994.

2009 - Moscow, Russia

The conflict between Armenia and Azerbaijan, the two countries in a state of war over the territory of Nagorno-Karabakh, was the most talked-about topic at the ESC held in Moscow, the capital of the former two countries — the Soviet Union. The Czech Republic set an all-time low when it became the first participant in the contest's history to finish the semi-finals with zero points. Ahinoam Nini and Mira Awad represented Israel (which introduced for the first time a song performed in Arabic), passed the semi-finals and failed to reach the top places in the final, despite the intriguing political story behind their entry and the participation of Nini, which was extremely popular in European Mediterranean countries. Once again, there were no surprises on the winning side: Norwegian Alexander Rybak (of Russian descent) gave his country a brilliant and unprecedented victory in his success rates: 387 points, 16 Douze Points, a confident lead from the start of the voting and points from all countries. "Fairytale", with the gipsy violin, was a legendary victory, third for the Nordic country, which had its share of suffering at the Eurovision over the years.

2000

Country Hosting: Sweden

City Hosting: Stockholm

Date: 13.5.2000

Location: Globe Arena

Presenters: Kattis Ahlström, Anders Lundin

Executive Supervisor: Christine Marchal-Ortiz

Directed By: Marius Bratten

Executive Producer: Svante Stockselius

Participating Countries: 24

Voting System: Televoting, the results given by 1-8, 10 and 12 points to the most popular song

Broadcaster: Sveriges Television (SVT)

Intermediate performance: "Once Upon a Time Europe Was Covered With Ice" film

Duration: 2 hours and 59 minutes

Broadcast: All participating countries and to Bosnia, Japan, Greece, Lithuania, Poland, Portugal and Slovenia.

No.	Country	Song	Performing Artist	Lyrics	Composer	Language	Commentator	Spoker of Results	Points	Place
01	Israel	"Sameach"	"Ping Pong" (Guy Assif, Roy Arad, Yifat Giladi and Ahal Eden)	Guy Assif, Roy Arad	Guy Assif, Roy Arad	Hebrew	-	Yova Ginai	7	22
02	Netherlands	"No Goodbyes"	Linda Wagenmakers	Ellert Driessen	John O'Hare	English	Willem van Beusekom	Marlayne	40	13
03	United Kingdom	"Don't Play That Song Again"	Nicki French	John Springate, Gerry Shephard	John Springate, Gerry Shephard	English	Terry Wogan	Colin Berry	28	16
04	Estonia	"Once in a Lifetime"	Ines	Jana Hallas	Alar Kotkas, Ilmar Laisaar, Pearu Paulus	English	Marko Reikop	Evelin Samuel	98	4
05	France	"On aura le ciel"	Sofia Mestari	Pierre Legay, Benoît Heinrich	Pierre Legay, Benoît Heinrich	French	Julien Lepers	Marie Myriam	5	23
06	Romania	"The Moon"	Taxi (Dan Teodorescu, Georgiana Pană, Lucian Cioargă, Adrian Borțun, George Pătrahoiu)	Dan Teodorescu	Dan Teodorescu	English	Leonard Miron	Andreea Marin	25	17
07	Malta	"Desire"	Claudette Pace	Gerard James Borg	Philip Vella	English	Charlo Bonnici	Valerie Vella	73	8
08	Norway	"My Heart Goes Boom"	Charmed	Tore Madsen, Morten Henriksen	Tore Madsen, Morten Henriksen	English	Jostein Pedersen	Marit Åslein	57	11
09	Russia	"Solo"	Alsou	Andrew Lane, Brandon Barnes	Andrew Lane, Brandon Barnes	English	Alexey Zhuravlev, Tatiana Godunova	Zhanna Agalakova	155	2
10	Belgium	"Envie de vivre"	Nathalie Sorce	Silvio Pezzuto	Silvio Pezzuto	French	Jean-Pierre Hautier, André Vermeulen, Anja Daems	Thomas Van Hamme	2	24
11	Cyprus	"Nomiza"	Voice (Christina Argyri, Alexandros Panayi)	Alexandros Panayi, Silvia M. Klemm	Alexandros Panayi	Greek, Italian	Evi Papamichail	Loukas Hamatsos	8	21
12	Iceland	"Tell Me!"	August & Telma (Telma Ágústsdóttir, Einar Ágúst Víðisson)	Örlygur Smári, Sigurður Örn Jónsson	Örlygur Smári	English	Gísli Marteinn Baldursson	Ragnheiður Elín Clausen	45	12
13	Spain	"Colgado de un sueño"	Serafín Zubiri	José María Purón	José María Purón	Spanish	José Luis Uribarri	Hugo de Campos	18	18
14	Denmark	"Fly on the Wings of Love"	Olsen Brothers (Jørgen Olsen, Niels Olsen)	Jørgen Olsen	Jørgen Olsen	English	Keld Heick	Michael Teschl	195	1
15	Germany	"Wadde hadde dudde da?"	Stefan Raab	Stefan Raab	Stefan Raab	German, English	Peter Urban	Axel Bulthaupt	96	5
16	Switzerland	"La vita cos'è?"	Jane Bogaert	Thomas Marin	Bernie Staub	Italian	Sandra Studer, Jean-Marc Richard, Jonathan Tedesco	Astrid Von Stockar	14	20
17	Croatia	"Kad zaspu anđeli"	Goran Karan	Zdenko Runjić, Neno Ninčević, Nikša Bratoš	Zdenko Runjić, Neno Ninčević, Nikša Bratoš	Croatian	Aleksandar "Aco" Kostadinov	Marko Rašica	70	9
18	Sweden	"When Spirits Are Calling My Name"	Roger Pontare	Peter Dahl, Linda Jansson, Thomas Holmstrand	Peter Dahl, Linda Jansson, Thomas Holmstrand	English	Pernilla Månsson Colt, Christer Lundh	Malin Ekander	88	7
19	North Macedonia	"100% te ljubam"	XXL (Marija Nikolova, Ivona Džamtovska, Rosica Nikolovska and Verica Karanfilovska)	Orče Zafirovski, Vlado Janevski	Dragan Karanfilovski Bojs	North Macedonian, English	Milanka Rašik	Sandra Todorovska	29	15
20	Finland	"A Little Bit"	Nina Åström	Gerrit aan 't Goor	Luca Genta	English	Jani Juntunen	Pia Mäkinen	18	19
21	Latvia	"My Star"	Brainstorm (Renārs Kaupers, Jānis Jubalts, Kaspars Roga, Gundars Mauševics, Māris Mihelsons)	Renārs Kaupers	Renārs Kaupers	English	Kārlis Streips	Lauris Reiniks	136	3
22	Turkey	"Yorgunum Anla"	Pınar Ayhan & The SOS	Pınar Ayhan, Orkun Yazgan	Sühan Ayhan	Turkish, English	Ömer Önder	Osman Erkan	59	10
23	Ireland	"Millennium of Love"	Eamonn Toal	Raymond J. Smyth	Gerry Simpson	English	Marty Whelan	Derek Mooney	92	6
24	Austria	"All to You"	The Rounder Girls (Christine Kainrath, Lynne Kieran, Kim Cooper)	Dave Moskin	Dave Moskin	English	Andi Knoll	Dodo Roščić	34	14

	Israel	The Netherlands	United Kingdom	Estonia	France	Romania	Malta	Norway	Russia	Belgium	Cyprus	Iceland	Spain	Denmark	Germany	Switzerland	Croatia	Sweden	North Macedonia	Finland	Latvia	Turkey	Ireland	Austria	
Israel	■	–	–		6	–	–	–	–	–	–	–	–	–	–	–	–	–	1	–	–	–	–	–	Israel
The Netherlands	8	■	–	–	2	–	5	–	–	8	5	1	4	–	1	–	2	–	–	–	–	3	1	–	The Netherlands
United Kingdom	1	–	■	2	–	3	6	–	–	–	3	–	–	–	–	–	4	–	–	–	3	6	–	–	United Kingdom
Estonia	6	7	4	■	–	6	7	4	–	2	6	5	–	4	5	–	6	6	–	8	10	2	7	3	Estonia
France	–	2	–	–	■	–	–	–	3	–	–	–	–	–	–	–	–	–	–	–	–	–	–	–	France
Romania	–	–	–	–	–	■	–	–	6	–	–	–	–	–	–	–	7	–	12	–	–	–	–	–	Romania
Malta	3	1	2	1	–	7	■	2	8	1	8	–	1	3	3	–	8	3	8	–	4	5	3	2	Malta
Norway	7	–	3	3	–	–	3	■	–	–	–	7	–	7	–	–	–	7	–	–	6	10	4	–	Norway
Russia	10	–	8	10	5	12	12	8	■	7	12	8	5	6	4	2	12	5	7	5	–	–	10	7	Russia
Belgium	–	–	–	–	–	–	–	–	–	■	–	–	–	–	–	–	–	2	–	–	–	–	–	–	Belgium
Cyprus	–	–	–	–	–	–	1	–	–	–	■	–	–	–	–	–	3	–	4	–	–	–	–	–	Cyprus
Iceland	5	–	–	6	–	–	–	7	–	–	–	■	–	12	–	–	–	8	–	–	7	–	–	–	Iceland
Spain	–	–	–	–	–	5	–	–	2	–	10	–	■	–	–	1	–	–	–	–	–	–	–	–	Spain
Denmark	12	10	12	8	7	1	8	10	12	10	4	12	10	■	12	10	–	12	–	10	12	1	12	10	Denmark
Germany	–	8	5	–	10	–	–	3	4	6	–	6	12	2	■	12	1	–	–	2	8	–	5	12	Germany
Switzerland	–	6	–	–	–	–	–	–	5	–	–	–	–	–	–	■	–	–	–	–	2	–	–	1	Switzerland
Croatia	–	–	–	–	8	8	–	–	10	–	–	–	2	–	6	6	■	–	10	6	–	8	–	6	Croatia
Sweden	–	–	6	5	1	–	4	5	–	5	–	4	6	10	8	3	–	■	6	7	–	12	6	–	Sweden
North Macedonia	–	–	–	–	–	10	–	–	7	–	2	–	–	–	–	–	10	–	■	–	–	–	–	–	North Macedonia
Finland	–	5	–	7	–	4	–	–	–	–	–	–	–	–	–	–	–	2	–	■	–	–	–	–	Finland
Latvia	4	4	7	12	3	–	–	12	1	12	1	10	7	8	7	7	–	10	3	12	■	–	8	8	Latvia
Turkey	–	12	–	–	12	–	–	1	–	3	–	–	–	1	10	5	–	1	5	4	–	■	–	5	Turkey
Ireland	2	3	10	4	4	2	10	6	–	4	7	2	3	5	–	8	5	4	–	1	1	7	■	4	Ireland
Austria	–	–	1	–	–	–	2	–	–	–	–	3	8	–	2	4	–	–	–	3	5	4	2	■	Austria

*The countries with the grey background used the old Juries System.

Country Hosting: Denmark
City Hosting: Copenhagen
Date: 12.5.2001
Location: Parken Stadium
Presenters: Natasja Crone Back, Søren Pilmark
Executive Supervisor: Christine Marchal-Ortiz
Directed By: Jan Frifelt
Executive Producer: Jørgen Ramskov
Participating Countries: 23
Voting System: Televoting, the results given by 1-8, 10 and 12 points to the most popular song
Broadcaster: Danmarks Radio (DR)
Intermediate performance: Medley of Aqua hits performed by Aqua feat. Safri Duo
Duration: 3 hours
Broadcast: All participating countries and to Australia, Austria, Belgium, Belarus, Cyprus, Finland, North Macedonia, Romania, Switzerland And Yugoslavia.

No.	Country	Song	Performing Artist	Lyrics	Composer	Language	Commentator	Spoker of Results	Points	Place
01	Netherlands	"Out on My Own"	Michelle	André Remkes	André Remkes, Dirk-Jan Vermeij	English	Willem van Beusekom	Marlayne	16	18
02	Iceland	"Angel"	Two Tricky	Einar Bardarson	Einar Bardarson, Magnús Thor Sigmundsson	English	Gísli Marteinn Baldursson	Eva María Jónsdóttir	3	22
03	Bosnia and Herzegovina	"Hano"	Nino Pršeš	Nino Pršeš	Nino Pršeš	Serbo-Croatian, English	Ismeta Dervoz-Krvavac	Segmedina Srna	29	14
04	Norway	"On My Own"	Haldor Lægreid	Tom-Steinar Hanssen, Ole Henrik Antonsen, Ole Jørgen Olsen	Tom-Steinar Hanssen, Ole Henrik Antonsen	English	Jostein Pedersen	Roald Øyen	3	23
05	Israel	"Ein Davar"	Tal Sondak	Shimrit Or	Yair Klinger	Hebrew	-	Yoav Ginai	25	16
06	Russia	"Lady Alpine Blue"	Mumiy Troll	Ilia Lagutenko	Ilia Lagutenko	English	Alexandr Anatolievich, Konstantin Mikhailov	Larisa Verbitskaya	37	12
07	Sweden	"Listen to Your Heartbeat"	Friends (Thomas G:son, Henrik Sethsson)	Thomas G:son, Henrik Sethsson	Thomas G:son, Henrik Sethsson	English	Henrik Olsson	Josefine Sundström	100	5
08	Lithuania	"You Got Style"	SKAMP (Erica Quinn Jennings, Vilius Alesius, Viktoras Diawara)	Viktoras Diawara, Erica Quinn Jennings, Vilius Alesius	Viktoras Diawara	Lithuanian, English	Darius Užkuraitis	Loreta Tarozaitė	35	13
09	Latvia	"Too Much"	Arnis Mednis	Arnis Mednis, Gustavs Terzens	Arnis Mednis	English	Kārlis Streips	Renārs Kaupers	16	18
10	Croatia	"Strings of My Heart"	Vanna	Vjekoslava Huljić	Tonči Huljić	English	Ante Batinović	Daniela Trbović	42	10
11	Portugal	"Só sej ser feliz assim"	MTM (Marco Quelhas, Tony Jackson)	Marco Quelhas	Marco Quelhas	portuguese	Eládio Clímaco	Margarida Mercês de Mello	18	17
12	Ireland	"Without Your Love"	Gary O'Shaughnessy	Pat Sheridan	Pat Sheridan	English	Marty Whelan	Bláthnaid Ní Chofaigh	6	21
13	Spain	"Dile que la quiero"	David Civera	Alejandro Abad	Alejandro Abad	Spanish	José Luis Uribarri	Jennifer Rope	76	6
14	France	"Je n'ai que mon âme"	Natasha St-Pier	Jill Kapler	Jill Kapler	French, English	Marc-Olivier Fogiel,Dave	Corinne Hermès	142	4
15	Turkey	"Sevgiliye Son"	Sedat Yüce	Nurdan Güneri, Figen Çakmak	Semih Güneri	Turkish, English	Ömer Önder	Meltem Ersan Yazgan	41	11
16	United Kingdom	"No Dream Impossible"	Lindsay Dracass	Russ Ballard, Chris Winter	Russ Ballard, Chris Winter	English	Terry Wogan	Colin Berry	28	15
17	Slovenia	"Energy"	Nuša Derenda	Lucienne Lončina	Matjaž Vlašič	English	Andrea F	Mojca Mavec	70	7
18	Poland	"2 Long"	Piasek (Andrzej Piaseczny)	Andrzej Piaseczny	Robert Chojnacki	English	Artur Orzech	Maciej Orłoś	11	20
19	Germany	"Wer Liebe lebt"	Michelle	Eva Richter	Gino Trovatello, Matthias Stingl	German, English	Peter Urban	Axel Bulthaupt	66	8
20	Estonia	"Everybody"	Tanel Padar, Dave Benton & 2XL	Maian-Anna Kärmas	Ivar Must	English	Marko Reikop	Ilomai Küttim "Elektra"	198	1
21	Malta	"Another Summer Night"	Fabrizio Faniello	Georgina Abela	Paul Abela	English	Alfred Borg	Marbeck Spiteri	48	9
22	Greece	"Die for You"	Antique (Elena Paparizou Nikos Panagiotidis)	Antonis Pappas	Nikos Terzis	English	Dafni Bokota	Alexis Kostalas	147	3
23	Denmark	"Never Ever Let You Go"	Rollo & King (Søren Poppe, Stefan Teilmann Laub Nielsen, Signe Svendsen)	Stefan Teilmann Laub Nielsen, Thomas Brekling	Søren Poppe	English	Hans Otto Bisgaard, Hilda Heick	Gry Johansen	177	2

2001

	The Netherlands	Iceland	Bosnia and Herzegovina	Norway	Israel	Russia	Sweden	Lithuania	Latvia	Croatia	Portugal	Ireland	Spain	France	Turkey	United Kingdom	Slovenia	Poland	Germany	Estonia	Malta	Greece	Denmark
The Netherlands	■	–	–	–	5	1	–	–	–	–	6	–	–	–	–	–	4	–	–	–	–	–	–
Iceland	–	■	–	1	–	–	–	–	–	–	–	–	–	–	–	–	–	–	–	–	–	–	2
Bosnia and Herzegovina	–	–	■	–	–	–	4	–	–	10	–	–	–	–	–	–	7	–	–	–	1	–	7
Norway	–	–	–	■	–	–	–	–	–	–	3	–	–	–	–	–	–	–	–	–	–	–	–
Israel	–	–	6	–	■	–	–	–	–	–	–	–	–	10	7	–	–	–	–	–	–	2	–
Russia	–	5	–	–	3	■	–	10	8	–	–	–	–	–	–	–	–	–	–	4	2	5	–
Sweden	–	7	3	2	8	2	■	2	6	4	5	8	5	2	8	8	–	5	–	7	8	–	10
Lithuania	5	1	2	–	4	10	1	■	5	–	–	1	–	–	–	4	2	–	–	–	–	–	–
Latvia	–	–	–	–	–	–	–	8	■	–	–	–	–	–	–	–	–	–	–	8	–	–	–
Croatia	–	–	7	–	–	–	–	–	–	■	–	–	–	–	10	–	5	–	3	–	10	7	–
Portugal	–	–	–	–	–	–	–	–	–	–	■	–	6	12	–	–	–	–	–	–	–	–	–
Ireland	–	–	–	–	–	–	–	–	–	–	1	■	–	–	–	5	–	–	–	–	–	–	–
Spain	7	2	5	4	12	–	5	–	4	–	7	3	■	5	6	3	1	1	–	3	–	8	–
France	8	4	12	7	2	12	6	7	7	6	12	7	3	■	1	6	6	10	6	10	–	4	6
Turkey	3	–	–	–	–	–	–	–	–	7	–	–	–	7	■	–	–	–	7	–	4	10	3
United Kingdom	2	–	–	–	–	3	–	3	3	3	2	4	1	–	–	■	–	2	2	–	3	–	–
Slovenia	4	6	10	6	1	4	7	4	–	8	–	2	2	1	–	–	■	6	4	5	–	–	–
Poland	–	–	–	–	–	–	2	–	–	–	–	–	–	–	–	–	3	■	5	–	–	–	1
Germany	1	–	–	3	–	8	–	–	1	1	10	6	10	6	3	2	–	4	■	1	5	1	4
Estonia	12	10	4	10	6	6	8	12	12	2	–	10	8	8	12	12	12	12	10	■	12	12	8
Malta	–	3	1	5	–	7	3	1	–	–	–	–	4	–	2	1	–	3	1	2	■	3	12
Greece	6	8	8	8	10	5	12	5	2	5	4	5	12	3	5	7	8	8	8	6	7	■	5
Denmark	10	12	0	12	7	–	10	6	10	12	8	12	7	4	4	10	10	7	12	12	6	6	■

*The countries with the grey background used the old Juries System, the countries with green background mixed equally the old jury's system and the televoting.

2002

Country Hosting: Estonia
City Hosting: Talin
Date: 25.5.2002
Location: Saku Suurhall
Presenters: Annely Peebo, Marko Matvere
Executive Supervisor: Christine Marchal-Ortiz
Directed By: Marius Bratten
Executive Producer: Juhan Paadam
Participating Countries: 24
Voting System: Televoting, the results given by 1-8, 10 and 12 points to the most popular song
Broadcaster: Eesti Televisioon (ETV)
Intermediate performance: Dance performance directed and choreographed by Teet Kask
Duration: 3 hours
Broadcast: All participating countries and to Ukraine, Portugal, Poland, Norway, Netherlands, Ireland and Iceland.

No.	Country	Song	Performing Artist	Lyrics	Composer	Language	Commentator	Spoker of Results	Points	Place
01	Cyprus	"Gimme"	One (Constantinos Christoforou, Panos Tserpes, Dimitris Koutsavlakis, Philippos Constantinos, Argyris Nastopoulos)	Giorgos Theofanous	Giorgos Theofanous	English	Evi Papamichail	Melani Steliou	85	6
02	United Kingdom	"Come Back"	Jessica Garlick	Martyn Baylay	Martyn Baylay	English	Terry Wogan	Colin Berry	111	4
03	Austria	"Say a Word"	Manuel Ortega	Robert Pfluger	Alexander Kahr	English	Andi Knoll	Dodo Roščić	26	18
04	Greece	"S.A.G.A.P.O."	Michalis Rakintzis	Michalis Rakintzis	Michalis Rakintzis	English	Dafni Bokota	Alexis Kostalas	27	17
05	Spain	"Europe's Living a Celebration"	Rosa	Xasqui Ten	Toni Ten	Spanish	José Luis Uribarri	Anne Igartiburu	81	7
06	Croatia	"Everything I Want"	Vesna Pisarović	Milana Vlaović	Milana Vlaović	English	Oliver Mlakar	Duško Ćurlić	44	11
07	Russia	"Northern Girl"	Prime Minister (Jean Grigoviev-Milimerov, Peter Jason, Vyacheslav Bodolika, Marat Chanyshev)	Karen Kavaleryan, Evgene Fridlyand, Irina Antonyan	Kim Breitburg	English	Yuri Aksyuta, Yelena Batinova	Arina Sharapova	55	10
08	Estonia	"Runaway"	Sahlene	Jana Hallas	Alar Kotkas, Ilmar Laisaar, Pearu Paulus	English	Marko Reikop	Ilomai Küttim Elektra	111	3
09	North Macedonia	"Od nas zavisi"	Karolina	Vladimir Krstevski, Diran Tavitjan	Nikola Perevski	North Macedonian	Milanka Rašik	Biljana Debarlieva	25	19
10	Israel	"Light a Candle"	Sarit Hadad	Yova Ginai	Svika Pick	English, Hebrew	-	Michal Zuaretz	37	12
11	Switzerland	"Dans le jardin de mon âme"	Francine Jordi	Francine Jordi	Francine Jordi	French	Sandra Studer, Phil Mundwiller, Jonathan Tedesco, Claudio Lazzarino	Diana Jörg	15	22
12	Sweden	"Never Let It Go"	Afro-dite (Blossom Tainton, Gladys del Pilar, Kayo Shekoni)	Marcos Ubeda	Marcos Ubeda	English	Claes Åkesson, Christer Björkman	Kristin Kaspersen	72	8
13	Finland	"Addicted to You"	Laura	Janina Frostell, Tracy Lipp	Maki Kolehmainen	Finish	Maria Guzenina and Asko Murtomäki	Marion Rung	24	20
14	Denmark	"Tell Me Who You Are"	Malene Mortensen	Michael Ronson	Michael Ronson	English	Keld Heick	Signe Svendsen	7	24
15	Bosnia and Herzegovina	"Na jastuku za dvoje"	Maja	Ružica Ćavić	Dragan Mijatović	Serbo-Croatian, English	Ismeta Dervoz-Krvavac	Segmedina Srna	33	14
16	Belgium	"Sister"	Sergio & The Ladies (Serge Quisquater, Ibernice Macbean Jody Pijper, Ingrid Simons)	Dirk Paelinck	Marc Paelinck	English	André Vermeulen and Bart Peeters	Geena Lisa Peeters	33	13
17	France	"Il faut du temps"	Sandrine François	Patrick Bruel, Marie-Florence Gros	Rick Allison, Patrick Bruel	French	Marc-Olivier Fogiel, Dave	Marie Myriam	104	5
18	Germany	"I Can't Live Without Music"	Corinna May	Bernd Meinunger	Ralph Siegel	English	Peter Urban	Axel Bulthaupt	17	21
19	Turkey	"Leylaklar Soldu Kalbinde"	Buket Bengisu & Group Safir	Sami Hodara, Figen Çakmak	Fani Hodara	Turkish, English	Bülend Özveren	Meltem Ersan Yazgan	29	16
20	Malta	"7th Wonder"	Ira Losco	Gerard James Borg	Philip Vella	English	John Bundy	Yvette Portelli	164	2
21	Romania	"Tell Me Why"	Monica Anghel & Marcel Pavel	Mirela Fugaru	Ionel Tudor	English	Andreea Demirgian	Leonard Miron	71	9
22	Slovenia	"Samo ljubezen"	Sestre (Tomaž Mihelič, Damjan Levec, Srečko Blas)	Barbara Pešut	Robert Pešut	Slovenian	Andrea F	Nuša Derenda	33	13
23	Latvia	"I Wanna"	Marie N	Marija Naumova, Marats Samauskis	Marija Naumova	English	Kārlis Streips	Ēriks Niedra	176	1
24	Lithuania	"Happy You"	Aivaras	Aivaras	Aivaras	English	Darius Užkuraitis	Loreta Tarozaitė	12	23

	Cyprus	United Kingdom	Austria	Greece	Spain	Croatia	Russia	Estonia	North Macedonia	Israel	Switzerland	Sweden	Finland	Denmark	Bosnia and Herzegovina	Belgium	France	Germany	Turkey	Malta	Romania	Slovenia	Latvia	Lithuania
Lithuania	4	8	-	-	-	-	6	7	-	-	-	10	-	1	-	2	5	-	-	3	-	-	12	■
Latvia	8	5	-	-	-	-	10	12	-	3	1	4	-	-	-	-	2	-	-	7	-	-	■	6
Slovenia	4	8	-	-	-	12	-	6	-	-	1	7	-	-	2	-	3	-	-	10	-	■	5	-
Romania	8	-	-	6	-	-	10	2	12	5	3	-	-	-	-	4	1	7	-	-	■	-	-	-
Malta	12	10	-	-	-	-	8	2	5	-	-	-	-	1	3	-	-	4	-	■	6	-	7	-
Turkey	-	2	12	-	-	-	-	8	-	-	-	4	-	1	-	10	-	3	■	5	7	-	6	-
Germany	-	8	-	-	7	3	-	4	-	5	2	-	-	-	-	-	6	■	-	10	1	-	12	-
France	-	1	-	-	12	-	-	-	-	10	3	-	-	-	-	2	■	-	7	6	4	5	8	-
Belgium	3	6	5	-	12	-	-	4	-	2	-	1	-	-	-	■	10	-	-	7	-	-	8	-
Bosnia and Herzegovina	-	7	-	-	6	2	-	10	-	-	-	12	3	-	■	-	8	-	-	4	-	1	5	-
Denmark	-	6	-	-	-	-	-	8	-	1	-	10	3	■	2	4	5	-	-	12	-	-	7	-
Finland	4	8	-	-	-	-	3	10	1	5	-	7	■	-	-	-	12	-	-	2	-	-	6	-
Sweden	1	2	-	-	7	-	-	12	-	-	-	■	10	-	6	3	8	-	-	4	-	-	5	-
Switzerland	-	6	7	-	12	5	-	-	-	1	■	-	-	-	-	-	10	3	-	4	-	2	8	-
Israel	-	5	-	-	6	-	1	2	-	■	-	3	-	4	-	-	7	-	-	10	8	-	12	-
North Macedonia	-	4	-	-	-	5	-	6	■	-	-	-	1	-	3	-	-	-	8	10	12	2	7	-
Estonia	4	6	-	-	-	-	10	■	-	-	-	8	5	-	-	-	3	1	-	7	-	-	12	2
Russia	6	-	1	8	-	-	■	3	-	-	-	-	-	-	7	-	2	-	-	5	12	-	10	4
Croatia	10	-	-	1	6	■	-	5	4	-	-	-	-	-	7	-	-	-	3	12	-	8	2	-
Spain	6	-	-	-	■	-	-	-	-	-	-	-	-	-	3	1	8	2	4	10	5	7	12	-
Greece	12	7	-	■	4	5	2	-	-	-	-	1	-	-	-	-	3	-	-	6	8	-	10	-
Austria	-	12	■	-	-	6	-	3	-	-	5	4	-	-	7	-	-	1	-	8	-	2	10	-
United Kingdom	3	■	-	-	2	-	-	7	-	5	-	1	-	-	-	4	10	-	-	12	-	-	6	8
Cyprus	■	-	1	12	7	6	5	-	3	-	-	-	2	-	-	-	-	-	-	10	8	-	4	-

*The countries with the grey background used the old Juries System, the countries with green background mixed equally the old jury's system and the televoting.

Country Hosting: Latvia
City Hosting: Riga
Date: 24.5.2003
Location: Skonto Hall
Presenters: Marie N, Renārs Kaupers
Executive Supervisor: Sarah Yuen
Directed By: Sven Stojanovic
Executive Producer: Brigita Rozenbrika
Participating Countries: 26
Voting System: Televoting, the results given by 1-8, 10 and 12 points to the most popular song
Broadcaster: Latvijas Televīzija (LTV)
Intermediate performance: Iļģi, Brainstorm, Marie N and Raimonds Pauls
Duration: 3 hours and 11 minutes
Broadcast: All participating countries and Albania, Armenia, Andora, Australia, Belarus, Denmark, Finland, Italy, Lithuania, North Macedonia, Puerto Rico, Switzerland, Serbia and Montenegro.

No.	Country	Song	Performing Artist	Lyrics	Composer	Language	Commentator	Spoker of Results	Points	Place
0	Iceland	"Open Your Heart"	Birgitta	Sveinbjörn I. Baldvinsson, Birgitta Haukdal	Hallgrímur Óskarsson	English	Gísli Marteinn Baldursson	Eva María Jónsdóttir	81	8
02	Austria	"Weil der Mensch zählt"	Alf Poier	Alf Poier	Alf Poier	German and Austro-Bavarian	Andi Knoll	Dodo Roščić	101	6
03	Ireland	"We've Got the World"	Mickey Harte	Martin Brannigan, Keith Molloy	Martin Brannigan, Keith Molloy	English	Marty Whelan, Phil Coulter	Pamela Flood	53	11
04	Turkey	"Everyway That I Can"	Sertab Erener	Demir Demirkan	Demir Demirkan, Sertab Erener	English	Bülend Özveren	Meltem Ersan Yazgan	167	1
05	Malta	"To Dream Again"	Lynn Chircop	Cynthia Sammut	Alfred Zammit	English	John Bundy	Sharon Borg	4	25
06	Bosnia and Herzegovina	"Ne brini"	Mija Martina	Arjana Kunštek	Ines Prajo	English, Serbo-Croatian	Dejan Kukrić	Ana Vilenica	27	16
07	Portugal	"Deixa-me sonhar"	Rita Guerra	Paulo Martins	Paulo Martins	portuguese, English	Margarida Mercês de Mello	Helena Ramos	13	22
08	Croatia	"Više nisam tvoja"	Claudia Beni	Andrej Babić	Andrej Babić	Croatian, English	Daniela Trbović	Davor Meštrović	29	15
09	Cyprus	"Feeling Alive"	Stelios Constantas	Stelios Konstantas	Stelios Konstantas	English	Evi Papamichail	Loukas Hamatsos	15	20
10	Germany	"Let's Get Happy"	Lou	Bernd Meinunger	Ralph Siegel	English	Peter Urban	Axel Bulthaupt	53	11
11	Russia	"Ne ver', ne boysia"	t.A.T.u. (Lena Katina, Julia Volkova)	Mars Lasar	Valeriy Polienko	Russian	Yuri Aksyuta, Yelena Batinova	Yana Churikova	164	3
12	Spain	"Dime"	Beth (Elisabeth Rodergas)	Jesús María Pérez, Amaya Martínez	Jesús María Pérez, Amaya Martínez	Spanish	José Luis Uribarri	Anne Igartiburu	81	8
13	Israel	"Milim shel Ahava"	Lior Narkis	Yosi Gispan	Yoni Roeh	Hebrew, English	-	Michal Zuaretz	17	19
14	Netherlands	"One More Night"	Esther Hart	Tjeerd van Zanen, Alan Michael	Tjeerd van Zanen, Alan Michael	English	Willem van Beusekom	Marlayne	45	13
15	United Kingdom	"Cry Baby"	Jemini	Martin Isherwood	Martin Isherwood	English	Terry Wogan	Lorraine Kelly	0	26
16	Ukraine	"Hasta la Vista"	Olexandr	Mirit Shem-Or	Svika Pick	English	Pavlo Shylko	Lyudmyla Hariv	30	14
17	Greece	"Never Let You Go"	Mando	Teri Siganos	Mando	English	Dafni Bokota	Alexis Kostalas	25	17
18	Norway	"I'm Not Afraid to Move On"	Jostein Hasselgård	Arve Furset, VJ Strøm	Arve Furset, VJ Strøm	English	Jostein Pedersen	Roald Øyen	123	4
19	France	"Monts et merveilles"	Louisa Baïleche	Hocine Hallaf	Hocine Hallaf	French	Laurent Ruquier and Isabelle Mergault	Sandrine François	19	18
20	Poland	"Keine Grenzen,—Żadnych granic"	Ich Troje (Michał Wiśniewski, Justyna Majkowska, Jacek Łągwa)	Joachim Horn-Bernges, Michał Wiśniewski, Jacek Łągwa	André Franke	Polish, German, Russian	Artur Orzech	Maciej Orłoś	90	7
21	Latvia	"Hello from Mars"	F.L.Y. (Mārtiņš Freimanis, Lauris Reiniks, Yana Kay)	Mārtiņš Freimanis, Lauris Reiniks	Mārtiņš Freimanis, Lauris Reiniks	English	Kārlis Streips	Ģirts Līcis	5	24
22	Belgium	"Sanomi"	Urban Trad (Yves Barbieux, Veronica Codesal, Soetkin Collier, Didier Laloy, Philip Masure, Dirk Naessens, Marie-Sophie Talbot, Cedric Waterschoot)	Yves Barbieux	Yves Barbieux	?	André Vermeulen, Anja Daems, Jean-Pierre Hautier	Corinne Boulangier	165	2
23	Estonia	"Eighties Coming Back"	Ruffus (Vaiko Eplik, Margus Tohver, Ivo Etti, Siim Mäesalu, Jaan Pehk)	Vaiko Eplik	Vaiko Eplik	English	Marko Reikop	Ines	14	21
24	Romania	"Don't Break My Heart"	Nicola	Nicola	Mihai Alexandru	English	Andreea Demirgian	Leonard Miron	73	10
25	Sweden	"Give Me Your Love"	Fame (Jessica Andersson, Magnus Bäcklund)	Carl Lösnitz, Calle Kindbom	Carl Lösnitz, Calle Kindbom	English	Pekka Heino	Kattis Ahlström	107	5
26	Slovenia	"Nanana"	Karmen	Karmen Stavec	Martin Štibernik	English	Andrea F	Peter Poles	7	23

	Iceland	Austria	Ireland	Turkey	Malta	Bosnia and Herzegovina	Portugal	Croatia	Cyprus	Germany	Russia	Spain	Israel	The Netherlands	United Kingdom	Ukraine	Greece	Norway	France	Poland	Latvia	Belgium	Estonia	Romania	Sweden	Slovenia	
Iceland	■	–	7	8	12	–	–	6	5	1	–	–	–	6	–	4	–	12	1	1	3	3	1	–	7	4	Iceland
Austria	10	■	–	6	–	5	10	5	4	2	–	8	–	8	8	–	2	8	–	–	4	2	6	–	6	7	Austria
Ireland	2	–	■	5	5	–	7	4	7	–	–	–	–	–	12	1	–	6	–	–	1	1	–	–	–	2	Ireland
Turkey	3	12	–	■	4	12	8	10	8	10	–	3	7	12	7	2	7	10	10	2	–	12	–	10	8	10	Turkey
Malta	–	–	3	–	■	–	1	–	–	–	–	–	–	–	–	–	–	–	–	–	–	–	–	–	–	–	Malta
Bosnia and Herzegovina	–	7	–	12	–	■	–	8	–	–	–	–	–	–	–	–	–	–	–	–	–	–	–	–	–	–	Bosnia and Herzegovina
Portugal	–	–	2	–	–	–	■	–	–	–	–	2	–	–	–	3	–	–	6	–	–	–	–	–	–	–	Portugal
Croatia	–	5	6	3	–	6	–	■	–	–	–	–	2	–	–	–	3	–	–	6	–	–	–	–	–	–	Croatia
Cyprus	–	–	–	–	2	–	–	–	■	–	–	–	1	–	–	–	12	–	–	–	–	–	–	–	–	–	Cyprus
Germany	8	1	4	–	3	–	–	–	–	■	7	4	–	2	4	–	–	–	–	5	2	–	2	1	10	–	Germany
Russia	4	8	–	10	1	3	4	12	10	8	■	6	10	1	–	12	10	2	7	4	12	7	12	7	2	12	Russia
Spain	6	–	–	2	–	–	12	7	6	–	6	■	12	5	–	–	5	–	–	–	–	10	–	5	4	1	Spain
Israel	–	–	–	–	–	–	–	–	–	–	5	1	■	–	–	–	3	–	8	–	–	–	–	–	–	–	Israel
The Netherlands	–	–	5	–	7	2	–	–	–	–	10	–	2	■	1	–	–	5	–	–	–	8	–	–	5	–	The Netherlands
United Kingdom	–	–	–	–	–	–	–	–	–	–	–	–	–	–	■	–	–	–	–	–	–	–	–	–	–	–	United Kingdom
Ukraine	–	–	–	–	–	–	–	–	–	–	8	–	4	–	–	■	–	–	–	10	5	–	3	–	–	–	Ukraine
Greece	–	–	1	4	–	–	–	–	12	5	1	–	–	–	–	–	■	–	–	–	–	–	–	2	–	–	Greece
Norway	12	2	12	–	6	–	5	–	–	7	4	–	3	7	6	7	–	■	3	6	7	6	10	3	12	5	Norway
France	–	–	–	–	–	8	2	–	–	–	–	–	–	–	–	–	–	–	■	3	–	–	–	6	–	–	France
Poland	–	10	–	–	10	–	–	–	–	12	–	5	–	4	2	8	6	4	5	■	8	5	4	4	3	–	Poland
Latvia	–	–	–	–	–	–	–	–	–	–	–	–	–	–	–	–	–	–	–	–	■	–	5	–	–	–	Latvia
Belgium	7	4	10	7	–	10	6	–	3	6	3	12	8	10	5	10	8	3	12	12	10	■	8	8		3	Belgium
Estonia	1	–	8	–	–	–	–	–	–	–	2	–	–	–	3	–	–	–	–	–	–	–	■	–	–	–	Estonia
Romania	–	6	–	1	–	7	–	1	2	4	12	10	6	–	–	6	4	1	4	8	–	–	–	■	1	–	Romania
Sweden	5	3	–	–	8	1	3	2	1	3	–	7	5	3	10	5	–	7	2	7	6	4	7	12	■	6	Sweden
Slovenia	–	–	–	–	–	4	–	3	–	–	–	–	–	–	–	–	–	–	–	–	–	–	–	–	–	■	Slovenia

*The countries with the grey background used the old Juries System.

2004

Under the Sky

Country Hosting: Turkey
City Hosting: Istanbul
Date: 12.5.2004 (Semi Final), 15.5.2004 (The Final)
Location: Abdi İpekçi Arena
Presenters: Meltem Cumbul, Korhan Abay
Executive Supervisor: Svante Stockselius
Directed By: Sven Stojanovic
Executive Producer: Bülent Osma
Participating Countries: 36
Voting System: Televoting, the results given by 1-8, 10 and 12 points to the most popular song
Broadcaster: Turkish Radio and Television Corporation (TRT)
Intermediate performance: "ABBA: The last Video" (Semi Final), "Fire of Anatolia" (Final)
Duration: 2 hours and 3 minutes (Semi Final), 3 hours and 17 minutes (The Final)
Broadcast: All participating countries and Australia.

Semi Final, 12.5.2004

10 marked grey countries qualified to the Final

No.	Country	Song	Performing Artist	Language	Points	Place
1	Finland	"Takes 2 to Tango"	Jari Sillanpää	English	51	14
2	Belarus	"My Galileo"	Aleksandra and Konstantin	English	10	19
3	Switzerland	"Celebrate"	Piero Esteriore & The MusicStars	English	0	22
4	Latvia	"Dziesma par laimi"	Fomins and Kleins	Latvian	23	17
5	Israel	"Believe"	David D'eor	Hebrew, English	57	12
6	Andora	"Jugarem a estimar-nos"	Marta Roure	Catalan	12	18
7	Portugal	"Foi magia"	Sofia Vitória	portuguese	38	15
8	Malta	"On Again... Off Again"	Julie and Ludwig	English	74	8
9	Monaco	"Notre planète"	Maryon	French	10	19
10	Greece	"Shake It"	Sakis Rouvas	English	238	3
11	Ukraine	"Wild Dances"	Ruslana	English	256	2
12	Lithuania	"What's Happened to Your Love?"	Linas and Simona	English	26	16
13	Albania	"The Image of You"	Anjeza Shahini	English	167	4
14	Cyprus	"Stronger Every Minute"	Lisa Andreas	English	149	5
15	North Macedonia	"Life"	Toše Proeski	English	71	10
16	Slovenia	"Stay Forever"	Platin	English	5	21
17	Estonia	"Tii"	Neiokõsõ	Estonish	57	11
18	Croatia	"You Are the Only One"	Ivan Mikulić	English	72	9
19	Denmark	"Shame on You"	Tomas Thordarson	English	56	13
20	Serbia and Montenegro	"Lane moje"	Željko Joksimović & Ad-Hoc Orchestra	Serbian	263	1
21	Bosnia and Herzegovina	"In the Disco"	Deen	English	133	7
22	Netherlands	"Without You"	Re-Union	English	146	6

No.	Country	Song	Performing Artist	Lyrics	Composer	Language	Commentator	Spoker of Results	Points	Place
01	Spain	"Para llenarme de ti"	Ramón	Kike Santander	Kike Santander	Spanish	Beatriz Pécker	Anne Igartiburu	87	10
02	Austria	"Du bist"	Tie Break (Tommy Pegram, Stefan di Bernardo, Thomas Elzenbaumer)	Peter Zimmermann	Peter Zimmermann	German	Andi Knoll	Dodo Roscic	10	19
03	Norway	"High"	Knut Anders Sørum	Dan Attlerud	Thomas Thörnholm, Lars Andersson	English	Jostein Pedersen	Ingvild Helljesen	3	24
04	France	"À chaque pas"	Jonatan Cerrada	Jonatan Cerrada	Ben "Jammin" Robbins, Steve Balsamo	French, Spanish	Ben "Jammin" Robbins, Steve Balsamo	Alex Taylor	40	15
05	Serbia Montenegro	"Lane moje"	Željko Joksimović	Leontina Vukomanović	Željko Joksimović	Serbian	Duška Vučinić-Lučić, Dražen Bauković, Tamara Ivankovic	Nataša Miljković	263	2
06	Malta	"On Again... Off Again"	Julie anc Ludwig	Gerard James Borg	Philip Vella	English	Eileen Montesin	Claire Agius	50	12
07	Netherlands	"Without You"	Re-Union (Paul de Corte, Fabrizio Pennisi)	Angeline van Otterdijk	Ed van Otterdijk	English	Willem van Beusekom and Cornald Maas	Esther Hart	11	20
08	Germany	"Can't Wait Until Tonight"	Max	Udo Schild	Udo Schild	German, Turkish	Peter Urban	Thomas Anders	93	8
09	Albania	"The Image of You"	Anjeza Shahini	Agim Doçi	Edmond Zhulali	English	Leon Menkshi	Zhani Ciko	106	7
10	Ukraine	"Wild Dances"	Ruslana	Ruslana Lyzhychko, Oleksandr Ksenofontov	Ruslana Lyzhychko	English, Ukraine	Rodion Pryntsevsky	Pavlo Shylko (DJ Pascha)	280	1
11	Croatia	"You Are the Only One"	Ivan Mikulić	Duško Gruborović	Ivan Mikulić, Vedran Ostojić	English	Aleksandar "Aco" Kostadinov	Barbara Kolar	50	12
12	Bosnia and Herzegovina	"In the Disco"	Deen	Vesna Pisarović	Vesna Pisarović	English	Dejan Kukric	Mija Martina	91	9
13	Belgium	"1 Life"	Xandee	Dirk Paelinck	Marc Paelinck	English	André Vermeulen, Bart Peeters, Jean-Pierre Hautier	Martine Prenen	7	22
14	Russia	"Believe Me"	Julia Savicheva	Brenda Loring	Maxim Fadeev	English	Yuri Aksyuta and Yelena Batinova	Yana Churikova	67	11
15	North Macedonia	"Life"	Toše Proeski	Ilija Nikolovski	Jovan Jovanov	English	Milanka Rasic	Karolina Petkovska	47	14
16	Greece	"Shake It"	Sakis Rouvas	Nektarios Tirakis	Nikos Terzis	English	Dafni Bokota	Alexis Kostalas	252	3
17	Iceland	"Heaven"	Jónsi	Magnús Thor Sigmundsson	Sveinn Rúnar Sigurðsson	English	Gísli Marteinn Baldursson	Sigrún Ósk Kristjánsdóttir	16	19
18	Ireland	"If My World Stopped Turning"	Chris Doran	Jonathan Shorten	Bryan McFadden	English	Marty Whelan	Johnny Logan	7	22
19	Poland	"Love Song"	Blue Café (Tatiana Okupnik, Paweł Rurak-Sokal)	Tatiana Okupnik	Paweł Rurak-Sokal	English, Spanish	Artur Orzech	Maciej Orłoś	27	17
20	United Kingdom	"Hold on to Our Love"	James Fox	Tim Woodcock	Gary Miller	English	Terry Wogan	Lorraine Kelly	29	16
21	Cyprus	"Stronger Every Minute"	Lisa Andreas	Mike Connaris	Mike Connaris	English	Evi Papamichail	Loukas Hamatsos	170	6
22	Turkey	"For Real"	Athena (Hakan Özoğuz, Gökhan Özoğuz, Burak Gürpinar, Ozan Musluoğlu)	Gökhan Özoğuz, Hakan Özoğuz	Gökhan Özoğuz, Hakan Özoğuz	English	Bülend Özveren and Didem Tolunay	Meltem Ersan Yazgan	195	4
23	Romania	"I Admit"	Sanda	Irina Gligor	George Popa	English	Andreea Demirgian	Andreea Marin	18	18
24	Sweden	"It Hurts"	Lena Philipsson	Thomas "Orup" Eriksson	Thomas "Orup" Eriksson	English	Pekka Heino	Jovan Radomir	170	5

	Andora	Albania	Austria	Bosnia and Herzegovina	Belgium	Belarus	Switzerland	Serbia Montenegro	Cyprus	Germany	Denmark	Estonia	Spain	Finland	France	United Kingdom	Greece	Croatia
Andora	■																	
Albania	–	■	5	4	1	–	7	8	–	5	4	–	–	3	1	1	10	6
Austria	–	–	■	–	–	–	–	–	–	–	–	–	–	–	4	–	5	–
Bosnia and Herzegovina	–	10	7	■	–	–	5	6	–	–	8	–	–	–	–	–	–	10
Belgium	1	–	–	–	■	–	–	–	1	–	–	–	–	–	–	–	–	–
Belarus						■												
Switzerland							■											
Serbia Montenegro	2	7	12	12	3	7	12	■	10	10	7	1	6	10	10	3	8	12
Cyprus	4	–	6	–	4	8	2	3	■	8	6	7	3	7	5	10	12	4
Germany	–	2	10	3	–	–	10	–	–	■	–	2	12	–	7	4	–	1
Denmark											■							
Estonia												■						
Spain	12	–	–	–	7	2	6	–	7	2	–	–	■	–	8	–	3	–
Finland														■				
France	7	1	–	–	10	–	–	–	–	–	–	–	4	–	■	–	–	–
United Kingdom	–	–	–	–	–	1	–	–	–	–	–	4	–	–	–	■	–	–
Greece	8	12	2	5	8	6	4	7	12	7	3	5	7	6	6	12	■	7
Croatia	–	–	3	10	–	5	3	5	–	1	–	–	–	1	–	–	–	■
Ireland	–	–	–	–	–	–	–	–	–	–	–	–	–	–	–	7	–	–
Israel																		
Iceland	–	–	–	–	–	–	–	–	–	–	2	–	–	2	–	–	–	–
Lithuania																		
Latvia																		
Monaco																		
North Macedonia	–	6	–	8	–	–	1	12	–	–	–	–	–	–	–	–	–	5
Malta	6	3	–	1	–	–	–	–	–	–	1	6	–	–	–	2	1	2
The Netherlands	–	–	–	–	6	–	–	–	–	–	–	3	–	–	–	–	–	–
Norway	–	–	–	–	–	–	–	–	–	–	–	–	–	–	–	–	–	–
Poland	–	–	–	–	–	–	–	–	2	4	–	–	1	–	–	–	4	–
Portugal																		
Romania	–	–	–	–	–	–	–	–	3	–	–	–	10	–	–	–	–	–
Russia	–	–	–	–	–	12	–	1	6	–	–	8	–	4	–	–	2	–
Sweden	5	4	1	2	2	4	–	4	5	3	12	10	5	12	3	8	–	–
Slovenia																		
Turkey	3	8	8	7	12	3	8	2	4	12	10	–	2	5	12	6	6	3
Ukraine	10	5	4	6	5	10	–	10	8	6	5	12	8	8	2	5	7	8

Ireland	Israel	Iceland	Lithuania	Latvia	Monaco	North Macedonia	Malta	The Netherlands	Norway	Poland	Portugal	Romania	Russia	Sweden	Slovenia	Turkey	Ukraine	
																		Andora
2	–	4	–	1	–	12	10	1	3	–	–	1	–	7	4	6	–	Albania
–	–	–	–	–	–	–	–	–	–	–	–	–	–	–	–	–	–	Austria
–	–	–	–	–	4	4	–	2	10	–	–	–	–	8	10	7	–	Bosnia and Herzegovina
–	–	–	–	–	–	–	–	5	–	–	–	–	–	–	–	–	–	Belgium
																		Belarus
																		Switzerland
		7	2	5	1	10	6	10	6	5	7	8	10	12	12	8	12	Serbia Montenegro
10	3	10	5	4	2	–	7	8	4	4	3	3	6	6	1	1	4	Cyprus
4	–	–	1	–	7	–	–	3	1	6	8	4	–	–	3	5	–	Germany
																		Denmark
																		Estonia
–	8	1	–	–	3	1	3	4	–	1	12	5	–	–	–	2	–	Spain
																		Finland
–	–	–	–	–	12	–	–	–	–	–	2	–	4	–	–	–	–	France
8	–	2	–	3	–	–	4	–	–	2	–	2	1	2	–	–	–	United Kingdom
5	10	6	10	7	10	7	12	6	2	7	6	12	7	4	6	10	8	Greece
–	–	–	–	–	–	5	–	–	–	–	–	–	5	–	5	–	7	Croatia
■	–	–	–	–	–	–	–	–	–	–	–	–	–	–	–	–	–	Ireland
	■																	Israel
–	–	■	–	–	5	–	–	–	5	–	–	–	2	–	–	–	–	Iceland
			■															Lithuania
				■														Latvia
					■													Monaco
–	–	–	–	–	–	■	1	–	–	–	–	–	–	–	7	4	3	North Macedonia
6	4	–	4	6	–	3	■	–	–	3	1	–	–	–	–	–	1	Malta
–	–	–	–	–	–	–	2	■	–	–	–	–	–	–	–	–	–	The Netherlands
–	–	–	–	–	–	–	–	–	■	–	–	–	–	3	–	–	–	Norway
–	–	3	7	–	–	–	–	–	–	■	–	–	–	1	–	–	5	Poland
											■							Portugal
–	1	–	–	–	–	–	–	–	–	–	4	■	–	–	–	–	–	Romania
–	6	–	8	10	–	–	–	–	–	–	–	–	■	–	–	–	10	Russia
12	5	8	6	8	–	2	5	–	12	10	5	7	3	■	2	3	2	Sweden
															■			Slovenia
1	2	5	3	2	8	6	–	12	8	8	–	10	8	5	–	■	6	Turkey
7	12	12	12	12	6	8	8	7	7	12	10	6	12	10	8	12	■	Ukraine

*The marked grey countries did not participate in the final but gave points to the final entries.

2005

Awakening

Country Hosting: Ukraine

City Hosting: Kyiv

Date: 19.5.2005 (Semi Final), 21.5.2005 (The Final)

Location: Palace of Sports

Presenters: Maria Efrosinina, Pavlo Shylko

Executive Supervisor: Svante Stockselius

Directed By: Sven Stojanovic

Executive Producer: Pavlo Grytsak

Participating Countries: 39

Voting System: Televoting, the results given by 1-8, 10 and 12 points to the most popular song

Broadcaster: National Television Company of Ukraine (NTU)

Intermediate performance: Kiev Percussion Ensemble ARS NOVA, Anatoliy Zalevskiy and Ruslana performing "The Same Star"

Duration: 2 hours and 19 minutes (Semi Final), 3 hours and 27 minutes (The Final)

Broadcast: All participating countries and Australia.

Semi Final, 19.5.2005

10 marked grey countries qualified to the Final

No.	Country	Song	Performing Artist	Language	Points	Place
1	Austria	"Y así"	Global.Kryner	English, Spanish	30	21
2	Lithuania	"Little by Little"	Laura & The Lovers	English	17	25
3	Portugal	"Amar"	2B	portuguese, English	51	17
4	Moldova	"Boonika bate doba"	Zdob și Zdub	English, Romanian	207	2
5	Latvia	"The War Is Not Over"	Walters & Kazha	English	85	10
6	Monaco	"Tout de moi"	Lise Darly	French	22	24
7	Israel	"Hasheket Shenishar"	Shiri Maimon	Hebrew, English	158	7
8	Belarus	"Love Me Tonight"	Angelica Agurbash	English	67	13
9	Netherlands	"My Impossible Dream"	Glennis Grace	English	53	14
10	Iceland	"If I Had Your Love"	Selma	English	52	16
11	Belgium	"Le grand soir"	Nuno Resende	French	29	22
12	Estonia	"Let's Get Loud"	Suntribe	English	31	20
13	Norway	"In My Dreams"	Wig Wam	English	164	6
14	Romania	"Let Me Try"	Luminița Anghel & Sistem	English	235	1
15	Hungary	"Forogj, világ!"	NOX	Hungarian	167	5
16	Finland	"Why?"	Geir Rönning	English	50	18
17	North Macedonia	"Make My Day"	Martin Vučić	English	97	9
18	Andora	"La mirada interior"	Marian van de Wal	Catalan	27	23
19	Switzerland	"Cool Vibes"	Vanilla Ninja	English	114	8
20	Croatia	"Vukovi umiru sami"	Boris Novković feat. Lado Members	Croatian	169	4
21	Bulgaria	"Lorraine"	Kaffe	English	49	19
22	Ireland	"Love?"	Donna and Joe	English	53	14
23	Slovenia	"Stop"	Omar Naber	Slovenian	69	12
24	Denmark	"Talking to You"	Jakob Sveistrup	English	185	3
25	Poland	"Czarna dziewczyna"	Ivan & Delfin	Polish, Russian	81	11

FINAL21.5.2005

No.	Country	Song	Performing Artist	Lyrics	Composer	Language	Commentator	Spoker of Results	Points	Place
01	Hungary	"Forogj, világ!"	NOX (Szilvia Peter Szabó, Tamás Nagy)	Attila Valla	Szabolcs Harmath	Hungarian	Zsuzsa Demcsák, András Fáber, Dávid Szántó	Zsuzsa Demcsák	97	12
02	United Kingdom	"Touch My Fire"	Javine	Javine Hylton	John Themis	English	Terry Wogan	Cheryl Baker	18	22
03	Malta	"Angel"	Chiara	Chiara Siracusa	Chiara Siracusa	English	Eileen Montesin	Valerie Vella	192	2
04	Romania	"Let Me Try"	Luminiţa Anghel & Sistem	Cristian Faur	Cristian Faur	English	Andreea Demirgian	Berti Barbera	158	3
05	Norway	"In My Dreams"	Wig Wam (Åge Sten Nilsen, Trond Holter, Øystein Andersen, Bernt Jansen)	Trond Holter	Trond Holter	English	Jostein Pedersen	Ingvild Helljesen	125	9
06	Turkey	"Rimi Rimi Ley"	Gülseren	Göksan Arman	Erdinç Tunç	Turkish	Bülend Özveren	Meltem Ersan Yazgan	92	13
07	Moldova	"Boonika bate doba"	Zdob şi Zdub (Roman Iagupov, Mihai Gîncu, Sveatoslav Starus, Andrei Cebotari, Valeriu Mazilu, Victor Dandeş)	Roman Iagupov	Mihai Gîncu	English	Vitalie Rotaru	Elena Camerzan	148	6
08	Albania	"Tomorrow I Go"	Ledina Çelo	Pandi Laço, Sidorela Risto	Adrian Hila	English	Leon Menkshi	Zhani Ciko	53	16
09	Cyprus	"Ela Ela"	Constantinos Christoforou	Constantinos Christoforou	Constantinos Christoforou	English	Evi Papamichail	Melani Steliou	46	18
10	Spain	"Brujería"	Son de Sol (María Dolores García de Soria, Esperanza García de Soria, Soledad García de Soria	Alfredo Panebianco	Alfredo Panebianco	Spanish	Beatriz Pécker	Ainhoa Arbizu	28	21
11	Israel	"Hasheket Shenishar"	Shiri Maimon	Ben Green	Pini Aronbaev	Hebrew, English	-	Dana Harman	154	4
12	Serbia Montenegro	"Zauvijek moja"	No Name (Marko Prentić, Danijel Alibabić, Dragoljub Purlija, Marko Perić, Branko Nedovic, Bojan Jovović)	Milan Perić	Slaven Knezović	Serbian	Duška Vučinić-Lučić, Danijel Popović	Nina Radulović	137	7
13	Denmark	"Talking to You"	Jakob Sveistrup	Andreas Mørck, Jacob Launbjerg	Andreas Mørck, Jacob Launbjerg	English	Jørgen de Mylius	Gry Johansen	125	9
14	Sweden	"Las Vegas"	Martin Stenmarck	Tim Larsson, Tobias Lundgren, Johan Fransson, Niklas Edberger	Tim Larsson, Tobias Lundgren, Johan Fransson, Niklas Edberger	English	Pekka Heino	Annika Jankell	30	19
15	North Macedonia	"Make My Day"	Martin Vučić	Branka Kostić	Dragan Vučić	English	Milanka Rasic	Karolina Gočeva	52	17
16	Ukraine	"Razom nas bahato"	GreenJolly	Roman Kalyn, Roman Kostyuk, Mikola Kulmich	Roman Kalyn, Roman Kostyuk, Mikola Kulinich	Ukraine, English	Yaroslav Chornenkyi	Maria Orlova	30	19
17	Germany	"Run and Hide"	Gracia	John O'Flynn	David Brandes, Jane Tempest;	English	Peter Urban	Thomas Hermanns	4	24
18	Croatia	"Vukovi umiru sami"	Boris Novković feat. Lado Members	Boris Novković	Franjo Valentić	Croatian	Aleksandar "Aco" Kostadinov	Barbara Kolar	115	11
19	Greece	"My Number One"	Helena Paparizou	Christos Dantis, Natalia Germanou	Manolis Psaltakis	English	Alexandra Pascalidou	Alexis Kostalas	230	1
20	Russia	"Nobody Hurt No One"	Natalia Podolskaya	Jussi-Pekka Järvinen, Mary Susan Applegate	Victor Drobysh	English	Yuri Aksyuta, Yelena Batinova	Yana Churikova	57	15
21	Bosnia and Herzegovina	"Call Me"	Feminnem (Neda Parmać Pamela Ramljak Ivana Marić)	Andrej Babić	Andrej Babić	English	Dejan Kukric	Ana Mirjana Račanović	79	14
22	Switzerland	"Cool Vibes"	Vanilla Ninja	John O'Flynn	David Brandes, Jane Tempest	English	Sandra Studer, Jean-Marc Richard, Marie-Thérèse Porchet, Daniela Tami, Claudio Lazzarino	Cécile Bähler	128	8
23	Latvia	"The War Is Not Over"	Walters & Kazha (Valters Fridenbergs, Kārlis Būmeisters)	Mārtiņš Freimanis	Mārtiņš Freimanis	English	Kārlis Streips	Marija Naumova	153	5
24	France	"Chacun pense à soi"	Ortal Malka	Ortal Malka, Saad Tabainet	Ortal Malka, Saad Tabainet	French	Julien Lepers and Guy Carlier	Marie Myriam	11	23

	Austria	Lithuania	Portugal	Monaco	Belarus	The Netherlands	Iceland	Belgium	Estonia	Finland	Andora	Bulgaria	Ireland	Slovenia	Poland	Hungary	United Kingdom	Malta	Romania
Austria	■																		
Lithuania		■																	
Portugal			■																
Monaco				■															
Belarus					■														
The Netherlands						■													
Iceland							■												
Belgium								■											
Estonia									■										
Finland										■									
Andora											■								
Bulgaria												■							
Ireland													■						
Slovenia														■					
Poland															■				
Hungary	–	–	2	–	2	–	6	2	3	–	6	5	–	–	10	■	–	–	8
United Kingdom	–	–	–	–	–	–	–	–	–	–	–	–	8	–	–	–	■	4	–
Malta	5	2	–	5	5	5	4	8	4	8	–	–	10	1	–	5	10	■	2
Romania	6	–	12	4	1	3	5	7	–	–	7	8	5	–	7	10	–	7	■
Norway	–	5	–	–	4	1	12	3	8	12	2	1	4	4	8	–	5	5	–
Turkey	7	–	–	–	–	12	–	10	–	–	–	3	–	–	–	–	1	–	3
Moldova	2	10	10		7	–	8	1	6	–	–	6	–	3	3	4	2	2	12
Albania	3	–	–	–	–	–	–	–	–	–	–	–	–	–	–	–	–	–	–
Cyprus	–	–	–	–	–	–	–			–	–	10	–	–	–	–	3	12	1
Spain	–	–	8	–	–	–	–	–	–	–	12	–	–	–	–	–	–	–	–
Israel	1	3	5	12	8	7	–	6	1	5	8		6	–	–	8	7	8	7
Serbia Montenegro	12	–	–	6	3	4	–	–	–	–	–	4	–	10	–	2	–	–	6
Denmark	–	4	1	10	–	8	10	4	5	2	3	–	7	–	5	6	8	3	4
Sweden	–	–	–	3	–	–	–	–	–	6	–	–	–	–	–	–	–	–	–
North Macedonia	–	–	–	1	–	–	–	–	–	–	–	–	7	–	5	–	–	–	–
Ukraine	–	–	7	–	–	–	–	–	–	–	–	–	–	–	12	–	–	–	–
Germany	–	–	2	–	–	–	–	–	–	–	–	–	–	–	–	–	–	–	–
Croatia	8	6	–	7	–	2	1	–	2	1	–	2	–	12	2	7	–	–	5
Greece	4	1	3	–	–	10	2	12	–	3	4	12	2	2	1	12	12	6	10
Russia	–	7	–	–	12	–	–	–	7	7	–	–	–	–	–	–	–	–	–
Bosnia and Herzegovina	10	–	–	–	–	6	–	–	–	–	–	–	1	8	–	–	4	–	–
Switzerland	–	8	4	8	10	–	7	–	12	10	1	–	3	6	6	3	–	1	–
Latvia	–	12	6	–	6	–	3	5	10	4	10	–	12	7	4	1	6	10	–
France	–	–	–	–	–	–	–	–	–	–	5	–	–	–	–	–	–	–	–

Norway	Turkey	Moldova	Albania	Cyprus	Spain	Israel	Serbia Montenegro	Denmark	Sweden	North Macedonia	Ukraine	Germany	Croatia	Greece	Russia	Bosnia and Herzegovina	Switzerland	Latvia	France	
																				Austria
																				Lithuania
																				Portugal
																				Monaco
																				Belarus
																				The Netherlands
																				Iceland
																				Belgium
																				Estonia
																				Finland
																				Andora
																				Bulgaria
																				Ireland
																				Slovenia
																				Poland
–	6	–	–	7	5	8	6	–	–	1	2	–	6	2	3	1	–	3	3	Hungary
–	1	–	–	5	–	–	–	–	–	–	–	–	–	–	–	–	–	–	–	United Kingdom
10	8	–	4	6	7	10	–	10	6	–	10	8	4	8	12	–	3	5	7	Malta
6	4	7	5	8	12	12	3	3	2	2	–	–	–	5	–	2	–	–	5	Romania
■	–	3	–	3	3	1	2	12	8	–	6	–	–	4	–	3	–	6	–	Norway
–	■	–	8	–	–	–	–	8	–	4	–	10	–	–	–	8	6	–	12	Turkey
–	7	■	–	2	4	4	5	–	–	5	12	1	1	7	10	4	–	8	2	Moldova
–	2	–	■	–	–	–	8	–	–	12	–	–	2	10	–	5	10	–	1	Albania
–	–	–	7	■	–	–	1	–	–	–	–	–	–	12	–	–	–	–	–	Cyprus
–	–	–	–	–	■	–	–	–	–	–	–	–	–	–	–	–	4	–	4	Spain
5	3	6	3	–	6	■	–	5	1	–	7	5	–	–	8	–	1	2	10	Israel
–	–	1	6	10	–	–	■	–	4	10	3	3	12	6	6	10	12	1	6	Serbia Montenegro
12	–	–	–	–	10	3	–	■	10	–	–	6	–	–	–	–	–	4	–	Denmark
1	–	5	–	–	2	–	–	7	■	6	–	–	–	–	–	–	–	–	–	Sweden
–	5	–	10	–	–	–	7	–	–	■	–	–	8	–	–	7	2	–	–	North Macedonia
–	–	8	–	–	1			–	–	–	■	–	–	–	2	–	–	–	–	Ukraine
–	–	2	–	–	–	–	–	–	–	–	–	■	–	–	–	–	–	–	–	Germany
2	–	–	2	–	–	–	10	–	–	8	8	2	■	–	1	12	8	7	–	Croatia
4	12	4	12	12	8	7	12	2	12	7	–	12	5	■	4	6	7	–	8	Greece
–	–	10	–	–	–	–	–	–	–	–	4	–	–	–	■	–	–	10	–	Russia
7	10	–	–	–	–	–	4	4	7	3	–	–	10	–	–	■	5	–	–	Bosnia and Herzegovina
3	–	–	–	4	–	2	–	1	5	–	5	4	3	3	7	–	■	12	–	Switzerland
8	–	12	–	1	–	6	–	6	3	–	1	7	7	1	5	–	–	■	–	Latvia
–	–	–	1	–	–	5	–	–	–	–	–	–	–	–	–	–	–	–	■	France

*The marked grey countries did not participate in the final but gave points to the final entries.

2006

Feel The Rhythm

Semi Final, 18.5.2006

10 marked grey countries qualified to the Final

No.	Country	Song	Performing Artist	Language	Points	Place
1	Armenia	"Without Your Love"	André	English	150	6
2	Bulgaria	"Let Me Cry"	Mariana Popova	English	36	17
3	Slovenia	"Mr Nobody"	Anžej Dežan	English	49	16
4	Andora	"Sense tu"	Jenny	Catalan	8	23
5	Belarus	"Mum"	Polina Smolova	English	10	22
6	Albania	"Zjarr e ftohtë"	Luiz Ejlli	Albanian	58	14
7	Belgium	"Je t'adore"	Kate Ryan	English	69	12
8	Ireland	"Every Song Is a Cry for Love"	Brian Kennedy	English	79	9
9	Cyprus	"Why Angels Cry"	Annet Artani	English	57	15
10	Monaco	"La Coco-Dance"	Séverine Ferrer	French, Tahitian	14	21
11	North Macedonia	"Ninanajna"	Elena Risteska	English, North Macedonian	76	10
12	Poland	"Follow My Heart"	Ich Troje feat. Real McCoy	English, Polish, German, Russian	70	11
13	Russia	"Never Let You Go"	Dima Bilan	English	217	3
14	Turkey	"Süper Star"	Sibel Tüzün	Turkish, English	91	8
15	Ukraine	"Show Me Your Love"	Tina Karol	English	146	7
16	Finland	"Hard Rock Hallelujah"	Lordi	English	292	1
17	Netherlands	"Amambanda"	Treble	English, Imaginary Language	22	20
18	Lithuania	"We Are the Winners"	LT United	English	163	5
19	Portugal	"Coisas de nada"	Nonstop	portuguese, English	26	19
20	Sweden	"Invincible"	Carola	English	214	4
21	Estonia	"Through My Window"	Sandra Oxenryd	English	28	18
22	Bosnia and Herze-govina	"Lejla"	Hari Mata Hari	Bosnian	267	2
23	Iceland	"Congratulations"	Silvia Night	English	62	13

Country Hosting: Greece

City Hosting: Athens

Date: 18.5.2006 (Semi Final), 20.5.2006 (The Final)

Location: Nikos Galis Olympic Indoor Hall

Presenters: Maria Menounos, Sakis Rouvas

Executive Supervisor: Svante Stockselius

Directed By: Volker Weicker

Executive Producer: Fotini Yannoulatou

Participating Countries: 37

Voting System: Televoting, the results given by 1-8, 10 and 12 points to the most popular song

Broadcaster: Hellenic Broadcasting Corporation (ERT)

Duration: 2 hours and 22 minutes (Semi Final), 3 hours and 1 minute (The Final)

FINAL

20.5.2006

No.	Country	Song	Performing Artist	Lyrics	Composer	Language	Commentator	Spoker of Results	Points	Place
01	Switzerland	"If We All Give a Little"	six4one (Liel Colette, Claudia D'Addio, Tinka Milinović, Marco Matias, Andreas Lundstedt, Keith Camilleri)	Bernd Meinunger	Ralph Siegel	English	Sandra Studer, Jean-Marc Richard and Alain Morisod, Sandy Altermatt and Claudio Lazzarino	Jubaira Bachmann	30	17
02	Moldova	"Loca"	Arsenium feat. Natalia Gordienko	Arsenium	Arsenium	English	Vitalie Rotaru	Svetlana Cocoş	22	20
03	Israel	"Together We Are One"	Eddie Butler	Eddie Butler, Osnat Tzabag, Orly Borg	Eddie Butler	Hebrew, English	-	Dana Harman	4	23
04	Latvia	"I Hear Your Heart"	Vocal Group Cosmos (Reinis Sējāns, Andris Sējāns, Juris Lisenko, Jānis Strazdiņš, Jānis Šipkēvics, Jānis Ozols)	Molly-Ann Leikin, Guntars Račs	Reinis Sējāns, Andris Sējāns	English	Kārlis Streips	Mārtiņš Freimanis	30	16
05	Norway	"Alvedansen"	Christine Guldbrandsen	Kjetil Fluge, Atle Halstensen, Christine Guldbrandsen	Kjetil Fluge, Atle Halstensen, Christine Guldbrandsen	Norweigen	Jostein Pedersen	Ingvild Helljesen	36	14
06	Spain	"Un Blodymary"	Las Ketchup	Manuel Ruiz Gómez "Queco"	Manuel Ruiz Gómez "Queco"	Spanish	Beatriz Pécker	Sonia Ferrer	18	21
07	Malta	"I Do"	Fabrizio Faniello	Aldo Spiteri, Fabrizio Faniello	Aldo Spiteri, Fabrizio Faniello	English	Eileen Montesin	Moira Delia	1	24
08	Germany	"No No Never"	Texas Lightning (Jane Comerford, Markus Schmidt, Olli Dittrich, Jon Hemming Olsen, Uwe Frenzel)	Jane Comerford	Jane Comerford	English	Peter Urban	Thomas Hermanns	36	15
09	Denmark	"Twist of Love"	Sidsel Ben Semmane	Niels Drevsholt	Niels Drevsholt	English	Mads Vangsø and Adam Duvå Hall	Jørgen de Mylius	26	18
10	Russia	"Never Let You Go"	Dima Bilan	Karen Kavaleryan, Irina Antonyan	Alexandr Lunyov	English	Yuri Aksyuta, Tatiana Godunova	Yana Churikova	248	2
11	North Macedonia	"Ninanajna"	Elena Risteska	Rade Vrčakovski	Darko Dimitrov	North Macedonian, English	Karolina Petkovska	Martin Vučić	56	12
12	Romania	"Tornerò"	Mihai Trăistariu	Cristian Hriscu, Mihaela Deac, Eduard Circotă	Cristian Hriscu, Mihaela Deac, Eduard Circotă	English, Romanian	Andreea Demirgian	Andreea Marin Bănică	172	4
13	Bosnia and Herzegovina	"Lejla"	Hari Mata Hari (Hari Varešanović, Nihad Voloder, Izudin Kolečić, Karlo Martinović)	Fahrudin Pecikoza, Dejan Ivanović	Željko Joksimović	Serbo-Croatian	Dejan Kukrić	Vesna Andree-Zaimović	229	3
14	Lithuania	"We Are the Winners"	LT United (Andrius Mamontovas, Marijonas Mikutavičius, Viktoras Diawara, Saulius Urbonavičius, Arnoldas Lukošius, Eimantas Belickas)	Andrius Mamontovas, Victor "Vee" Diawara	Andrius Mamontovas, Saulius "Samas" Urbonavičius	English, French	Darius Užkuraitis	Lavija Šurnaitė	162	6
15	United Kingdom	"Teenage Life"	Daz Sampson	John Matthews, Daz Sampson	John Matthews, Daz Sampson	English	Terry Wogan	Feame Cotton	25	16
16	Greece	"Everything"	Anna Vissi	Anna Vissi	Nikos Karvelas	English	Giorgos Kapoutzidis and Zeta Makrypoulia	Alexis Kostalas	128	9
17	Finland	"Hard Rock Hallelujah"	Lordi (Tomi Petteri Putaansuu – Mr. Lordi, Jussi Artero Sydänmaa – Amen, Samer al-Nahhal – Ox, Henna Riikka Paakkola – Hella, Antto Nikolai Tuomainen – Mana)	Tomi Petteri Putaansuu – Mr. Lordi	Tomi Petteri Putaansuu – Mr. Lordi	English	Heikki Paasonen, Jaana Pelkonen, Asko Murtomäki	Nina Tapio	292	1
18	Ukraine	"Show Me Your Love"	Tina Karol	Pavlo Shylko	Michael Nekrasov, Tina Karol	English	Pavlo Shylko	Igor Posypaiko	145	7
19	France	"Il était temps"	Virginie Pouchain	Corneille	Corneille	French	Michel Drucker, Claudy Siar	Sophie Jovillard	5	22
20	Croatia	"Moja štikla"	Severina	Severina Vučković	Boris Novković, Franjo Valentić	Croatian	Duško Čurlić	Mila Horvat	56	12
21	Ireland	"Every Song Is a Cry for Love"	Brian Kennedy	Brian Kennedy	Brian Kennedy	English	Marty Whelan	Eimear Quinn	93	10
22	Sweden	"Invincible"	Carola	Thomas G:son, Carola Häggkvist	Thomas G:son, Bobby Ljunggren, Henrik Wikström	English	Pekka Heino	Jovan Radomir	170	5
23	Turkey	"Süper Star"	Sibel Tüzün	Sibel Tüzün	Sibel Tüzün	Turkish, English	Bülend Özveren	Meltem Yazgan	91	11
24	Armenia	"Without Your Love"	André	Catherine Bekian	Armen Martirosyan	English	Gohar Gasparyan and Phelix Khachatryan	Gohar Gasparyan	129	8

	Slovenia	Andora	Romania	Denmark	Latvia	Portugal	Sweden	Finland	Belgium	Croatia	Serbia Montenegro	Norway	Estonia	Ireland	Malta	Lithuania	Cyprus	The Netherlands	Switzerland
Slovenia	■																		
Andora		■																	
Romania	5	3	■	6	2	10	6	6	2	5	4	4	4	6	10	1	10	–	1
Denmark	–	–	–	■	–	–	8	3	–	–	–	6	1	–	–	–	–	–	–
Latvia	–	–	–	–	■	–	–	–	–	–	–	–	3	4	–	8	–	–	–
Portugal						■													
Sweden	7	8	5	10	7	8	■	7	5	3	1	10	7	7	6	5	–	–	2
Finland	8	10	4	12	8	6	12	□	8	10	7	12	12	10	7	10	5	6	7
Belgium									■										
Croatia	10	–	–	–	–	–	–	–	–	■	10	–	–	–	–	–	–	–	6
Serbia Montenegro											■								
Norway	–	–	–	1	6	–	2	5	–	–	–	■	–	–	–	–	–	–	–
Estonia													■						
Ireland	1	4	2	5	4	5	5	4	–	2	–	7	6	■	4	6	–	4	3
Malta	–	–	–	–	–	–	–	–	–	–	–	–	–	–	■	–	–	–	–
Lithuania	3	7	–	7	10	4	3	8	4	6	3	5	8	12	1	■	4	6	–
Cyprus																	■		
The Netherlands																		■	
Switzerland	–	–	–	–	–	1	–	–	–	–	–	–	–	–	12	–	3	–	■
Ukraine	2	5	3	–	5	12	1	2	–	4	2	–	5	1	2	7	6	1	–
Russia	4	6	8	2	12	7	7	12	3	7	5	3	10	5	5	12	8	2	–
Poland																			
United Kingdom	–	2	–	4	1	–	–	–	–	1	–	2	2	8	3	–	1	–	–
Armenia	–	–	1	–	–	–	–	–	12	–	–	–	–	–	–	2	7	10	–
France	–	–	–	–	–	–	–	–	–	–	–	–	–	–	–	–	–	–	–
Belarus																			
Germany	–	–	–	3	3	–	–	–	1	–	–	1	–	3	–	–	–	3	7
Spain	–	12	–	–	–	–	–	–	–	–	–	–	–	–	–	–	–	–	–
Moldova	–	–	12	–	–	3	–	–	–	–	–	–	–	–	–	–	–	–	–
Bosnia and Herzegovina	12	–	7	8	–	2	10	10	6	12	12	8	–	2	–	4	2	8	12
Iceland																			
Monaco																			
Israel	–	–	–	–	–	–	–	–	–	–	–	–	–	–	–	–	–	–	–
Albania																			
Greece	–	1	10	–	–	–	4	1	10	–	6	–	–	–	8	3	12	5	5
Bulgaria																			
North Macedonia	6	–	–	–	–	–	–	–	–	8	8	–	–	–	–	–	–	–	4
Turkey	–	–	6	–	–	–	–	–	7	–	–	–	–	–	–	–	–	12	10

*The marked grey countries did not participate in the final but gave points to the final entries.

Ukraine	Russia	Poland	United Kingdom	Armenia	France	Belarus	Germany	Spain	Moldova	Bosnia and Herzegovina	Iceland	Monaco	Israel	Albania	Greece	Bulgaria	North Macedonia	Turkey	
																		–	Slovenia
																			Andora
1	4	3	6	4	7	3	5	12	12	2	2	–	10	2	7	2	2	3	Romania
–	–	–	–	–	–	–	–	–	–	–	8	–	–	–	–	–	–	–	Denmark
4	1	–	2	–	–	–	–	–	–	–	–	8	–	–	–	–	–	–	Latvia
																			Portugal
6	2	7	4	6	3	5	–	6	2	3	7	5	5	10	–	–	1	–	Sweden
6	7	12	12	–	8	7	10	10	6	7	12	–	7	–	12	5	6	7	Finland
																			Belgium
–	–	–	–	–	–	–	2	–	–	12	–	4	–	–	–	–	10	2	Croatia
																			Serbia Montenegro
3	7	–	–	1	–	1	–	–	3	–	4	1	–	–	2	–	–	–	Norway
																			Estonia
2	–	2	8	3	1	–	4	–	–	–	1	10	–	–	–	–	–	–	Ireland
–	–	–	–	–	–	–	–	–	–	–	–	–	–	1	–	–	–	–	Malta
5	5	8	10	–	–	6	1	4	4	–	10	7	3	–	4	1	3	–	Lithuania
																			Cyprus
																			The Netherlands
–	–	–	–	–	–	–	–	–	–	4	–	6	4	–	–	–	–	–	Switzerland
■	10	6	–	10	–	10	–	3	8	5	6	2	6	–	5	3	5	8	Ukraine
12	■	10	1	12	2	12	6	7	10	6	5	–	12	4	8	10	8	5	Russia
		■																	Poland
–	–	1	■	–	–	–	–	–	–	–	–	–	–	–	–	–	–	–	United Kingdom
8	12	5	–	■	10	8	3	8	7	–	–	–	8	–	10	8	–	10	Armenia
–	–	–	–	2	■	–	–	–	–	–	–	3	–	–	–	–	–	–	France
						■													Belarus
–	–	–	5	–	–	–	■	5	–	–	–	–	–	5	–	–	–	–	Germany
–	–	–	–	–	–	–	–	■	–	–	–	–	–	6	–	–	–	–	Spain
–	3	–	–	–	–	–	–	2	■	–	–	–	–	–	1	–	–	1	Moldova
10	6	4	–	5	6	4	7	1	5	■	3	12	2	12	6	7	12	12	Bosnia and Herzegovina
								–	–	▴	■	–	–						Iceland
												■	–						Monaco
–	–	–	–	–	4	–	–	–	–	–	–	–	■	–	–	–	–	–	Israel
														■					Albania
–	–	–	7	8	5	2	8	–	1	1	–	–	–	8	■	12	7	4	Greece
																■			Bulgaria
–	–	–	–	7	–	–	–	–	–	8	–	–	–	3	–	6	■	6	North Macedonia
–	–	–	3	–	12	–	12	–	–	10	–	–	1	7	3	4	4	■	Turkey

** Serbia Montenegro did not take part in this Eurovision but gave points to the final entries.

2007

True Fantasy

Country Hosting: Finland

City Hosting: Helsinky

Date: 10.5.2007 (Semi Final), 12.5.2007 (The Final)

Location: Hartwall Areena

Presenters: Mikko Leppilampi, Jaana Pelkonen

Executive Supervisor: Svante Stockselius

Directed By: Timo Suomi

Executive Producer: Heikki Seppälä

Participating Countries: 42

Voting System: Televoting, the results given by 1-8, 10 and 12 points to the most popular song

Broadcaster: Yleisradio (Yle)

Duration: 2 hours and 41 minutes (Semi Final), 3 hours and 13 minutes (The Final)

Semi Final, 10.5.2007
10 marked grey countries qualified to the Final

No.	Country	Song	Performing Artist	Language	Points	Place
1	Bulgaria	"Water"	Elitsa Todorova & Stoyan Yankoulov	Bulgarian	146	6
2	Israel	"Push the Button"	"Tippex"	Hebrew, English, French	17	24
3	Cyprus	"Comme ci, comme ça"	"Comme ci, comme ça"	French	65	15
4	Belarus	"Work Your Magic"	Koldun	English	176	4
5	Iceland	"Valentine Lost"	Eiríkur Hauksson	English	77	13
6	Georgia	"Visionary Dream"	Sopho	English	123	8
7	Montenegro	"'Ajde, kroči"	Stevan Faddy	Serbian	33	22
8	Switzerland	"Vampires Are Alive"	DJ BoBo	English	40	20
9	Moldova	"Fight"	Natalia Barbu	English	91	10
10	Netherlands	"On Top of the World"	Edsilia Rombley	English	38	21
11	Albania	"Hear My Plea"	Frederik Ndoci	Albanian, English	49	17
12	Denmark	"Drama Queen"	DQ	English	45	19
13	Croatia	"Vjerujem u ljubav"	Dragonfly feat. Dado Topić	Croatian, English	54	16
14	Poland	"Time to Party"	The Jet Set	English	75	14
15	Serbia	"Molitva"	Marija Šerifović	Serbian	298	1
16	Czech Republic	"Malá dáma"	Kabát	Czech	1	28
17	Portugal	"Dança comigo"	Sabrina	portuguese, English	88	11
18	North Macedonia	"Mojot svet"	Karolina	North Macedonian, English	97	9
19	Norway	"Ven a bailar conmigo"	Guri Schanke	English	48	18
20	Malta	"Vertigo"	Olivia Lewis	English	25	15
21	Andora	"Salvem el món"	Anonymous	Catalan, English	80	12
22	Hungary	"Unsubstantial Blues"	Magdi Rúzsa	English	224	2
23	Estonia	"Partners in Crime"	Gerli Padar	English	33	22
24	Belgium	"Love Power"	The KMG's	English	14	26
25	Slovenia	"Cvet z juga"	Alenka Gotar	Slovenian	140	7
26	Turkey	"Shake It Up Şekerim"	Kenan Doğulu	English	197	3
27	Austria	"Get a Life —— Get Alive"	Eric Papilaya	English	27	4
28	Latvia	"Questa notte"	Bonaparti.lv	Italian	168	5

<table><tr><td colspan="11">FINAL</td><td colspan="2">12.5.2007</td></tr></table>

No.	Country	Song	Performing Artist	Lyrics	Composer	Language	Commentator	Spoker of Results	Points	Place
01	Bosnia and Herzegovina	"Rijeka bez imena"	Marija Šestić	Aleksandra Milutinović	Aleksandra Milutinović, Goran Kovačić	Serbian	Dejan Kukrić	Vesna Andree Zaimović	106	11
02	Spain	"I Love You Mi Vida"	D'NASH (Francisco Javier Álvarez Colinet, Esteban Piñero Camacho, Antonio Martos Ortiz, Michael Hennet Sotomayor)	Tony Sánchez-Ohlsson, Rebeca Pous del Toro	Thomas G:son, Andreas Rickstrand	Spanish, English	Beatriz Pécker	Ainhoa Arbizu	43	20
03	Belarus	"Work Your Magic"	Dmitry Koldun	Karen Kavaleryan	Philip Kirkorov, Dimitris Kontopoulos	English	Denis Kurian	Juliana	145	6
04	Ireland	"They Can't Stop the Spring"	Dervish (Cathy Jordan, Liam Kelly, Brian McDonagh, Shane Mitchell, Michael Holmes, Tom Morrow)	John Waters, Tommy Moran	John Waters, Tommy Moran	English	Marty Whelan	Linda Martin	5	24
05	Finland	"Leave Me Alone"	Hanna Pakarinen	Martti Vuorinen, Hanna Pakarinen	Martti Vuorinen, Miikka Huttunen	English	Asko Murtomäki, Ellen Jokikunnas, Heikki Paasonen	Laura Voutilainen	53	17
06	North Macedonia	"Mojot svet"	Karolina	Ognen Nedelkovski	Grigor Koprov	North Macedonian	Milanka Rašić	Elena Risteska	73	14
07	Slovenia	"Cvet z juga"	Alenka Gotar	Andrej Babić	Andrej Babić	Slovenian	Mojca Mavec	Peter Poles	66	15
08	Hungary	"Unsubstantial Blues"	Magdi Rúzsa	Imre Mózsik	Magdi Rúzsa	English	Gábor Gundel Takács	Éva Novodomszky	128	9
09	Lithuania	"Love or Leave"	4Fun (Julija Ritčik, Justas Jasenka, Laimonas Staniulionis, Andžej Zujevič)	Julija Ritčik	Julija Ritčik	English	Darius Užkuraitis	Lavija Šurnaitė	28	21
10	Greece	"Yassou Maria	Sarbel	"Mack"	Alex Papakonstantinou, Marcus Englöf	English	Fotis Sergoulopoulos	Alexis Kostalas	139	7
11	Georgia	"Visionary Dream"	Sopho Khalvashi	Bibi Kvachadze	Beqa Jafaridze	English	Sandro Gabisonia, Sopho Altunashvili	Neli Agirba	97	12
12	Sweden	"The Worrying Kind"	The Ark (Ola Salo, Lars Ljungberg, Mikael Jepson, Sylvester Schlegel, Martin Axén, Jens Andersson)	Ola Salo	Ola Salo	English	Josef Sterzenbach	André Pops	51	18
13	France	"L'amour à la française"	Les Fatals Picards (Ivan Callot, Paul Léger, Jean-Marc Sauvagnargues, Laurent Honel, Yves Giraud)	Ivan Callot, Paul Léger, Jean-Marc Sauvagnargues, Laurent Honel, Yves Giraud	Ivan Callot, Paul Léger, Jean-Marc Sauvagnargues, Laurent Honel, Yves Giraud	French, English	Julien Lepers	Vanessa Dolmen	19	22
14	Latvia	"Questa notte"	Bonaparti.lv (Roberto Meloni, Andris Abelite, Normunds Jakušonoks, Kaspars Timanis, Zigfrids Muktupāvels, Andris Ērglis)	Kjell Jennstig	Francesca Russo, Torbjörn Wassenius, Kjell Jennstig	Italian	Kārlis Streips	Jānis Šipkevics	54	16
15	Russia	"Song #1"	Serebro (Marina Lizorkina, Elena Temnikova, Anastasia Karpova, Dasha Shashina, Polina Favorskaya, Olga Seryabkina)	Daniil Babichev	Maxim Fadeev	English	Yana Churikova	Yuri Aksyuta, Andreea Demirglan	207	3
16	Germany	"Frauen regier'n die Welt"	Roger Cicero	Frank Ramond, Matthias Hass	Frank Ramond, Matthias Hass	German, English	Thomas Mohr	Thomas Hermanns	49	19
17	Serbia	"Molitva"	Marija Šerifović	Saša Milošević Mare	Vladimir Graić	Serbian	Duška Vučinić-Lučić	Maja Nikolić	268	1
18	Ukraine	"Dancing Lasha Tumbai"	Verka Serduchka	Andriy Danylko	Andriy Danylko	Ukraine, German, English, Russian	Timur Miroshnychenko	Katya Osadcha	235	2
19	United Kingdom	"Flying the Flag (For You)"	Scooch (Russ Spencer, Natalie Powers, Caroline Barnes, David Ducasse)	Andrew Hill, Morten Schjolin, Russ Spencer, Paul Tarry	Andrew Hill, Morten Schjolin, Russ Spencer, Paul Tarry	English	Terry Wogan	Fearne Cotton	19	22
20	Romania	"Liubi, Liubi, I Love You"	Todomondo (Andrei Stefănescu, Ciro De Luca, Ghedi, Taşcău, Valeriu Raileanu, Crețu)	Taşcău, Crețu, Ghedi	Taşcău	Romanian, English, French, Spanish, Italian, Russian	Yuri Aksyuta	Andreea Marin Bănică	84	13
21	Bulgaria	"Water"	Elitsa Todorova & Stoyan Yankoulov	Elitsa Todorova	Elitsa Todorova, Stoyan Yankoulov	Bulgarian	Georgi Kushvaliev, Elena Rosberg	Mira Dobreva	157	5
22	Turkey	"Shake It Up Şekerim"	Kenan Doğulu	Kenan Doğulu	Kenan Doğulu	English	Hakan Urgancı	Meltem Ersan Yazgan	163	4
23	Armenia	"Anytime You Need"	Hayko	Karen Kavaleryan, Hayko	Hayko	Armenian, English	Gohar Gasparian	Sirusho	138	8
24	Moldova	"Fight"	Natalia Barbu	Elena Buga	Alexandru Brașoveanu	English	Vitalie Rotaru	Andrei Porubin	109	10

	Montenegro	Belarus	Armenia	Andora	Austria	France	Denmark	Greece	Spain	Serbia	Finland	Turkey	Bosnia and Herzegovina	Belgium	Portugal	Albania	Romania	Cyprus	Croatia	Slovenia	Israel
Montenegro	■																				
Belarus	3	■	10	–	–	–	–	5	–	2	–	–	4	–	1	2	1	6	–	–	12
Armenia	–	5	■	–	5	10	–	6	8	–	–	12	–	10	–	–	–	8	–	–	5
Andora				■																	
Austria					■																
France	–	–	2	8	–	■	–	–	–	–	–	–	–	–	–	4	–	–	–	–	–
Denmark							■														
Greece	–	3	8	–	–	3	1	■	2	4	–	4	3	8	–	7	10	12	–	–	1
Spain	4	–	–	–	–	6	–	1	■	–	–	–	–	3	8	12	–	–	–	–	2
Serbia	12	7	7	–	12	8	6	4	1	■	12	–	12	7	5	1	6	3	12	12	3
Finland	–	1	–	7	–	–	4	–	–	–	■	–	–	–	–	–	–	–	–	–	–
Turkey	1	–	–	–	10	12	10	–	–	–	4	■	10	12	–	10	7	–	–	–	–
Bosnia and Herzegovina	7	–	1	–	8	1	7	–	–	8	–	10	■	–	–	8	–	–	10	8	–
Belgium														■							
Portugal															■						
Albania																■					
Romania	–	–	–	10	3	7	–	2	12	–	–	2	–	–	7	–	■	5	–	–	7
Cyprus																		■			
Croatia																			■		
Slovenia	8	4	–	–	–	–	–	–	3	5	–	–	7	2	3	–	–	–	7	■	–
Israel																					■
Germany	–	–	–	5	7	–	5	–	5	–	1	–	–	–	–	6	–	–	–	–	–
Lithuania	–	2	–	1	–	–	–	–	–	–	–	–	–	–	–	–	–	–	–	–	–
Norway																					
Switzerland																					
Czech Republic																					
The Netherlands																					
Ireland	–	–	–	–	–	–	–	–	–	–	–	–	–	–	–	5	–	–	–	–	–
Malta																					
Estonia																					
Georgia	–	6	5	–	–	–	–	3	–	–	7	5	1	6	–	–	–	1	2	2	6
Bulgaria	5	–	4	–	6	5	–	12	10	6	5	6	6	4	6	–	5	10	6	7	–
Sweden	–	–	–	2	–	–	12	–	–	–	8	–	–	–	–	–	–	–	–	–	–
Ukraine	2	10	6	12	4	4	3	7	7	3	6	3	5	1	12	–	4	4	5	4	10
Russia	6	12	12	3	–	2	2	8	4	7	3	8	2	–	4	–	3	7	3	3	8
Latvia	–	–	–	–	–	–	–	–	–	–	–	–	–	–	–	–	2	–	1	6	–
Iceland																					
Poland																					
Moldova	–	8	3	4	–	–	–	10	6	1	2	7	–	–	10	–	12	2	–	1	4
United Kingdom	–	–	–	–	–	–	–	–	–	–	–	–	–	–	–	–	–	–	–	–	–
North Macedonia	10	–	–	–	1	–	–	–	–	10	–	1	8	–	–	3	–	–	8	10	–
Hungary	–	–	–	6	2	–	8	–	–	12	10	–	–	5	2	–	8	–	4	5	–

Germany	Lithuania	Norway	Switzerland	Czech Republic	The Netherlands	Ireland	Malta	Estonia	Georgia	Bulgaria	Sweden	Ukraine	Russia	Latvia	Iceland	Poland	Moldova	United Kingdom	North Macedonia	Hungary	
																–					Montenegro
–	7	–	–	2	–	–	10	7	8	1	–	12	12	8	4	7	10	–	7	4	Belarus
2	–	–	–	10	10	–	–	–	12	8	–	5	10	–	–	10	2	–	–	–	Armenia
																					Andora
																					Austria
–	3	–	–	–	–	–	–	2	–	–	–	–	–	–	–	–	–	–	–	–	France
																					Denmark
10	–	–	4	3	5	–	–	–	4	12	4	–	–	–	5	–	6	10	3	7	Greece
–	–	–	5	–	–	–	2	–	–	–	–	–	–	–	–	–	–	–	–	–	Spain
8	–	10	12	8	8	4	8	–	6	6	10	6	5	3	7	8	5	–	12	12	Serbia
1	5	4	1	–	–	–	–	6	–	–	12	–	–	–	12	–	–	–	–	–	Finland
12	–	7	10	–	12	–	–	–	2	7	7	1	2	–	3	–	1	12	10	1	Turkey
3	–	6	8	4	7	–	–	–	–	–	6	–	–	–	–	–	–	–	4	–	Bosnia and Herzegovina
																					Belgium
																					Portugal
																					Albania
–	–	–	–	–	–	3	–	–	–	2	–	2	1	1	–	–	12	–	–	8	Romania
																					Cyprus
																					Croatia
–	1	–	–	–	–	–	5	–	–	–	–	4	3	4	–	4	–	–	6	–	Slovenia
																					Israel
■	–	–	7	–	6	–	–	3	–	–	1	–	–	–	2	–	–	1	–	–	Germany
–	■	–	–	–	–	12	–	–	–	–	–	–	–	10	–	–	–	3	–	–	Lithuania
		■																			Norway
			■																		Switzerland
				■																	Czech Republic
					■																The Netherlands
–	–	–	–	–	–	■	–	–	–	–	–	–	–	–	–	–	–	–	–	–	Ireland
							■														Malta
								■													Estonia
–	12	–	–	1	2	1	–	5	■	–	–	8	7	6	–	5	4	–	–	2	Georgia
4	–	–	–	7	–	–	7	1	–	■	–	3	4	2	–	–	3	5	8	10	Bulgaria
–	–	12	–	–	–	–	–	–	–	–	■	–	–	–	10	–	–	7	–	–	Sweden
5	8	2	2	12	1	8	3	8	10	3	3	■	8	12	6	12	7	8	2	3	Ukraine
6	6	5	–	6	–	6	6	12	7	5	5	10	■	7	1	3	8	6	5	6	Russia
–	10	3	–	–	3	10	4	10	–	–	–	–	–	■	–	1	–	4	–	–	Latvia
															■						Iceland
																■					Poland
–	2	1	–	–	–	2	–	–	3	4	2	7	6	–	–	6	■	–	1	5	Moldova
–	–	–	–	–	–	7	12	–	–	–	–	–	–	–	–	–	–	■	–	–	United Kingdom
–	–	–	6	5	–	–	–	–	1	10	–	–	–	–	–	–	–	–	■	–	North Macedonia
7	4	8	3	–	4	5	1	4	5	–	8	–	–	5	8	2	–	2	–	■	Hungary

*The marked grey countries did not participate in the final but gave points to the final entries.

Country Hosting: Serbia

City Hosting: Belgrade

Date: 20.5.2008 (First Semi Final), 22.5.2008 (Second Semi Final), 24.5.2008 (The Final)

Location: Belgrade Arena

Presenters: Željko Joksimović, Jovana Janković

Executive Supervisor: Svante Stockselius

Directed By: Sven Stojanović

Executive Producer: Sandra Šuša

Participating Countries: 43

Voting System: Televoting, the results given by 1-8, 10 and 12 points to the most popular song

Broadcaster: Radio Television of Serbia (RTS)

2008

Confluence of Sound

First Semi Final 20.5.2008
9 marked grey countries and the wild card (gave by jury's decision)
qualified to the Final
(Germany and Spain were allowed to vote this semi-final)

No.	Country	Song	Performing Artist	Language	Points	Place
1	Montenegro	"Zauvijek volim te"	Stefan Filipović	Serbian	23	14
2	Israel	"The Fire in Your Eyes"	Boaz Mauda	English, Hebrew	104	5
3	Estonia	"Leto svet"	Kreisiraadio	Serbian, German, Finish	8	18
4	Moldova	"A Century of Love"	Geta Burlacu	English	36	12
5	San Marino	"Complice"	Miodio	Italian	5	19
6	Belgium	"O Julissi"	Ishtar	Language Imaginary	16	17
7	Azerbaijan	"Day After Day"	Elnur and Samir	English	96	6
8	Slovenia	"Vrag naj vzame"	Rebeka Dremelj	Slovenian	36	11
9	Norway	"Hold on Be Strong"	Maria Haukaas Storeng	English	106	4
10	Poland	"For Life"	Isis Gee	English	42	10
11	Ireland	"Irelande Douze Pointe"	Dustin the Turkey	English, French	22	15
12	Andora	"Casanova"	Gisela	Catalan, English	22	15
13	Bosnia Herzegovina	"Pokušaj"	Laka	Serbo-Croatian	72	9
14	Armenia	"Qélé, Qélé"	Sirusho	English, Armenian	139	2
15	Netherlands	"Your Heart Belongs to Me"	Hind	English	27	13
16	Finland	"Missä miehet ratsastaa"	Teräsbetoni	Finish	79	8
17	Romania	"Pe-o margine de lume"	Nico and Vlad	Romanian, Italian	94	7
18	Russia	"Believe"	Dima Bilan	English	135	3
19	Greece	"Secret Combination"	Kalomira	English	156	1

Second Semi Final 22.5.2008
9 marked grey countries and the wild card (gave by jury's decision)
qualified to the Final
(United Kingdom, France and Serbia were allowed to vote this semi-final)

No.	Country	Song	Performing Artist	Language	Points	Place
1	Iceland	"This Is My Life"	Euroband	English	68	8
2	Sweden	"Hero"	Charlotte Perrelli	English	54	12
3	Turkey	"Deli"	Mor ve Ötesi	Turkish	85	7
4	Ukraine	"Shady Lady"	Ani Lorak	English	152	1
5	Lithuania	"Nomads in the Night"	Jeronimas Milius	English	30	16
6	Albania	"Zemrën e lamë peng"	Olta Boka	Albanian	67	9
7	Switzerland	"Era stupendo"	Paolo Meneguzzi	Italian	47	13
8	Czech Republic	"Have Some Fun"	Tereza Kerndlová	English	9	18
9	Belarus	"Hasta la Vista"	Ruslan Alekhno	English	27	17
10	Latvia	"Wolves of the Sea"	Pirates of the Sea	English	86	6
11	Croatia	"Romanca"	Kraljevi ulice and 75 cents	Croatian	112	4
12	Bulgaria	"DJ, Take Me Away"	Deep Zone and Balthazar	English	56	11
13	Denmark	"All Night Long"	Simon Mathew	English	112	3
14	Georgia	"Peace Will Come"	Diana Gurtskaya	English	107	5
15	Hungary	"Candlelight"	Csézy	Hungarian, English	27	13
16	Malta	"Vodka"	Morena	English	38	14
17	Cyprus	"Femme Fatale"	Evdokia Kadi	Greek	36	15
18	North Macedonia	"Let Me Love You"	Tamara, Vrčak & Adrian	English	64	10
19	Portugal	"Senhora do mar (Negras águas)"	Vânia Fernandes	portuguese	120	2

FINAL

24.5.2008

No.	Country	Song	Performing Artist	Lyrics	Composer	Language	Commentator	Spoker of Results	Points	Place
01	Romania	"Pe-o margine de lume"	Nico and Vlad	Andreea Andrei, Anton Șuteu	Andrei Tudor	Romanian, Italian	Leonard Miron	Alina Sorescu	45	20
02	United Kingdom	"Even If"	Andy Abraham	Andy Watkins, Paul Wilson, Andy Abraham	Andy Watkins, Paul Wilson, Andy Abraham	English	Terry Wogan	Carrie Grant	14	25
03	Albania	"Zemrën e lamë peng"	Olta Boka	Pandi Laço	Adrian Hila	Albanian	Leon Menkshi	Leon Menkshi	55	17
04	Germany	"Disappear"	No Angels (Nadja Benaissa, Lucy Diakovska, Sandy Mölling, Jessica Wahls)	Remee, Hanne Sørvaag, Thomas Troelsen	Remee, Hanne Sørvaag, Thomas Troelsen	English	Thomas Mohr	Thomas Hermanns	14	23
05	Armenia	"Qélé, Qélé"	Sirusho	Sirusho	H.A. Der-Hovagimian	Armenian, English	Felix Khacatryan, Hrachuhi Utmazyan	Hrachuhi Utmazyan	53	17
06	Bosnia and Herzegovina	"Pokušaj"	Laka	Elvir Laković Laka	Elvir Laković Laka	Serbo-Croatian	Dejan Kukrić	Melina Garibović	110	10
07	Israel	"The Fire in Your Eyes"	Boaz Mauda	Dana International, Shay Kerem	Dana International	Hebrew, English	-	Noah Barak-Veshler	124	9
08	Finland	"Missä miehet ratsastaa"	Teräsbetoni (Jarkko Ahola, Arto Järvinen Viljo Fantanen, Jari Kuokkanen)	Jarkko Ahola	Jarkko Ahola	Finish	Jaana Pelkonen, Mikko Peltola, Asko Murtomäki	Mikko Leppilampi	35	22
09	Croatia	"Romanca"	Kraljevi Ulice and 75 cents (Miran Hadži Veljković, Zlatko Petrović Pajo, Ladislav Demeterffy a.k.a. Laci)	Miran Hadži Veljković	Miran Hadži Veljković	Croatian	Duško Čurlić	Barbara Kolar	44	21
10	Poland	"For Life"	Isis Gee	Isis Gee	Isis Gee	English	Artur Orzech	Radek Brzózka	14	24
11	Iceland	"This Is My Life"	Euroband (Friðrik Ómar, Regína Ósk)	Paul Oscar, Peter Fenner	Örlygur Smári	English	Sigmar Guðmundsson	Brynja Þorgeirsdóttir	64	14
12	Turkey	"Deli"	Mor ve Ötesi (Harun Tekin, Kerem Kabadayı, Burak Güven, Kerem Özyeğen)	Harun Tekin, Kerem Kabadayı, Burak Güven, Kerem Özyeğen	Harun Tekin, Kerem Kabadayı, Burak Güven, Kerem Özyeğen	Turkish	Bülend Özveren	Meltem Ersan Yazgan	138	7
13	Portugal	"Senhora do mar (Negras águas)"	Vânia Fernandes	Carlos Coelho	Andrej Babić	Portuguese	Isabel Angelino	Sabrina	69	13
14	Latvia	"Wolves of the Sea"	Pirates of the Sea (Roberto Meloni Aleksandra Kurusova)	Jonas Liberg	Jonas Liberg, Johan Sahlen, Claes Andreasson, Torbjörn Wassenius	English	Kārlis Streips	Kristine Virsnite	83	12
15	Sweden	"Hero"	Charlotte Perrelli	Fredrik Kempe	Bobby Ljunggren, Fredrik Kempe	English	Kristian Luuk, Josef Sterzenbach	Björn Gustafsson	47	18
16	Denmark	"All Night Long"	Simon Mathew	Jacob Launbjerg, Svend Gudiksen, Nis Bøgvad	Jacob Launbjerg, Svend Gudiksen, Nis Bøgvad	English	Nikolaj Molbech	Maria Montell	60	15
17	Georgia	"Peace Will Come"	Diana Gurtskaya	Karen Kavaleryan	Kim Breitburg	English	Bibi Kvachadze	Tika Patsatsia	83	11
18	Ukraine	"Shady Lady"	Ani Lorak	Karen Kavaleryan	Philipp Kirkorov, Dimitris Kontopoulos	English	Timur Miroshnychenko	Marysya Horobets	230	2
19	France	"Divine"	Sébastien Tellier	Amandine de La Richardière, Sébastien Tellier	Sébastien Tellier	French, English	Julien Lepers	Cyril Hanouna	47	19
20	Azerbaijan	"Day After Day"	Elnur and Samir	Zahra Badalbeyli	Govhar Hasanzadeh	English	Isa Melikov, Hüsniyyə Məhərrəmova	Leyla Aliyeva	132	8
21	Greece	"Secret Combination"	Kalomira	Poseidonas Giannopoulos	Konstantinos Pantzis	English	Maggira Sisters	Alexis Kostalas	218	3
22	Spain	"Baila el Chiki-chiki"	Rodolfo Chikilicuatre	Rodolfo Chikilicuatre and Friends	Rodolfo Chikilicuatre and Friends	Spanish, English	José Luis Uribarri	Ainhoa Arbizu	55	16
23	Serbia	"Oro"	Jelena Tomašević feat. Bora Dugić	Dejan Ivanović	Željko Joksimović	Serbian	Mladen Popović, Dragan Ilić	Dušica Spasić	160	6
24	Russia	"Believe"	Dima Bilan	Dima Bilan, Jim Beanz	Dima Bilan, Jim Beanz	English	Olga Shelest, Dmitry Guberniev	Oxana Fedorova	272	1
25	Norway	"Hold on Be Strong"	Maria Haukaas Storeng	Mira Craig	Mira Craig	English	Per Sundnes	Stian Barsnes Simonsen	182	5

	United Kingdom	North Macedonia	Ukraine	Germany	Estonia	Bosnia and Herzegovina	Albania	Belgium	San Marino	Latvia	Bulgaria	Serbia	Israel	Cyprus	Moldova	Iceland	France	Romania	Portugal	Norway	Hungary	Andora
United Kingdom	■	–	–	–	–	–	–	–	6	–	–	–	–	–	–	–	–	–	–	–	–	–
North Macedonia		■																				
Ukraine	5	4	■	–	4	3	8	1	–	10	7	6	10	6	7	5	–	3	12	–	6	6
Germany	–	–	–	■	–	–	–	–	–	–	12	–	–	–	–	–	–	–	–	–	–	–
Estonia					■																	
Bosnia and Herzegovina	–	5	–	5	–	■	–	–	–	–	–	12	–	–	–	–	2	–	–	10	–	–
Albania	–	12	–	–	–	1	■	–	3	–	–	–	–	–	–	–	–	–	–	–	–	–
Belgium								■														
San Marino									■													
Latvia	10	–	–	–	7	–	–	–	–	■	–	–	–	–	–	4	–	–	8	–	–	2
Bulgaria											■											
Serbia	–	10	–	8	–	12	5	–	–	–	4	■	–	5	1	2	7	7	–	6	7	–
Israel	–	–	5	3	–	5	4	5	10	–	2	7	■	2	6	–	6	6	–	3	3	–
Cyprus														■								
Moldova															■							
Iceland	6	–	–	–	–	–	–	–	–	2	–	–	4	–	–	■	–	–	7	8	–	–
France	2	–	–	–	6	–	–	–	–	3	–	–	–	–	–	8	■	–	–	1	–	3
Romania	–	–	–	–	–	–	–	–	1	–	–	–	6	3	12	–	4	■	4	–	–	–
Portugal	–	–	3	4	–	–	–	6	5	–	–	1	–	–	–	6	8	–	■	–	–	10
Norway	7	–	6	–	8	2	7	2	7	6	1	4	7	–	5	10	–	5	2	■	4	1
Hungary																					■	
Andora																						■
Poland	4	–	–	–	–	–	–	–	–	–	–	–	–	–	–	–	–	–	–	–	–	–
Slovenia																						
Armenia	–	1	7	6	–	6	2	12	8	–	8	5	8	10	2	1	12	4	–	–	–	–
Czech Republic																						
Spain	1	–	–	–	–	–	1	4	–	–	–	–	–	4	–	–	5	–	10	–	–	12
The Netherlands																						
Turkey	8	7	4	10	–	8	10	10	4	–	5	–	–	–	–	–	10	8	–	2	5	–
Malta																						
Ireland																						
Switzerland																						
Azerbaijan	–	8	10	1	–	–	–	7	–	4	3	–	3	–	8	–	–	2	–	–	12	7
Greece	12	3	2	12	1	7	12	8	12	–	10	8	5	12	4	–	3	12	–	–	8	8
Finland	–	–	–	–	10	–	–	–	–	1	–	–	–	–	–	7	–	–	–	4	–	4
Croatia	–	2	1	2	–	10	–	–	–	5	–	3	–	–	–	–	–	1	3	–	–	–
Sweden	–	–	–	–	2	–	3	–	–	–	–	2	1	1	–	3	–	–	–	7	1	–
Belarus																						
Lithuania																						
Russia	–	6	12	7	12	4	6	3	–	12	6	10	12	8	10	–	1	10	6	5	10	5
Montenegro																						
Georgia	–	–	8	–	5	–	–	–	–	8	–	–	2	7	3	–	–	–	1	–	–	–
Denmark	3	–	–	–	3	–	–	–	2	7	–	–	–	–	–	12	–	–	5	12	2	–

Poland	Slovenia	Armenia	Czech Republic	Spain	The Netherlands	Turkey	Malta	Ireland	Switzerland	Azerbaijan	Greece	Finland	Croatia	Sweden	Belarus	Lithuania	Russia	Montenegro	Georgia	Denmark	
–	–	–	–	–	–	–	–	8	–	–	–	–	–	–	–	–	–	–	–	–	United Kingdom
																					North Macedonia
10	2	5	8	7	–	8	10	6	–	10	6	3	7	–	10	6	8	4	10	7	Ukraine
–	–	–	–	–	–	–	–	–	2	–	–	–	–	–	–	–	–	–	–	–	Germany
																					Estonia
–	10	–	1	–	7	6	–	2	7	3	–	6	12	10	–	–	–	10	–	2	Bosnia and Herzegovina
–	4	–	–	–	–	1	–	–	8	1	10	–	8	–	–	–	–	7	–	–	Albania
																					Belgium
																					San Marino
–	–	–	3	2	–	–	7	12	–	–	–	–	4	3	–	10	–	3	2	6	Latvia
																					Bulgaria
4	12	3	6	–	8	–	1	–	12	2	5	–	10	6	1	–	4	12	–	–	Serbia
5	3	6	–	–	3	–	–	–	1	7	1	8	2	–	4	3	6	5	3	–	Israel
																					Cyprus
																					Moldova
–	–	–	–	4	–	–	6	–	–	–	–	7	–	8	–	–	–	–	–	12	Iceland
1	–	4	–	–	–	–	–	–	–	–	–	2	–	4	–	8	–	–	–	5	France
–	–	–	–	12	–	–	–	3	–	–	–	–	–	–	–	–	–	–	–	–	Romania
–	–	–	–	8	5	–	–	–	10	–	–	–	3	–	–	–	–	–	–	–	Portugal
8	–	7	–	6	4	2	3	7	–	5	2	12	1	12	5	4	5	–	5	10	Norway
																					Hungary
																					Andora
■	–	–	–	–	–	–	–	10	–	–	–	–	–	–	–	–	–	–	–	–	Poland
	■																				Slovenia
12	5	■	12	10	12	10	–	–	–	–	12	–	–	2	7	–	12	1	12	–	Armenia
			■																		Czech Republic
–	–	1	–	■	–	3	–	–	4	–	8	1	–	–	–	–	–	–	–	1	Spain
					■																The Netherlands
–	–	–	–	–	10	■	–	–	6	12	–	4	–	–	3	–	2	–	6	4	Turkey
							■														Malta
								■													Ireland
									■												Switzerland
7	1	–	10	–	2	12	–	–	–	■	3	–	–	–	8	7	10	–	7	–	Azerbaijan
3	6	8	5	3	6	7	2	4	5	6	■	–	5	1	2	–	3	6	4	3	Greece
2	–	–	–	–	–	–	–	–	–	–	–	■	–	7	–	–	–	–	–	–	Finland
–	8	2	–	–	–	–	–	–	3	–	–	–	■	–	–	–	1	2	1	–	Croatia
–	–	–	1	–	–	12	–	–	–	–	–	5	–	■	–	1	–	–	–	8	Sweden
															■						Belarus
																■					Lithuania
6	7	12	7	5	1	5	8	5	0	8	7	10	6	–	12	12	□	8	8	–	Russia
																		■			Montenegro
–	–	10	4	–	–	4	5	–	–	4	4	–	–	–	6	5	7	–	■	–	Georgia
–	–	–	2	–	–	–	4	1	–	–	–	–	–	5	–	2	–	–	–	■	Denmark

*The marked grey countries did not participate in the final but gave points to the final entries.

Country Hosting: Russia

City Hosting: Moscow

Date: 12.5.2009 (First Semi Final), 14.5.2009 (Second Semi Final), 16.5.2009 (The Final)

Location: SC Olimpiyskiy

Presenters: Natalia Vodianova, Andrey Malakhov (The Semi finals), Ivan Urgant, Alsou Abramova

Executive Supervisor: Svante Stockselius

Directed By: Andrei Boltenko

Executive Producer: Yury Aksyuta

Participating Countries: 42

Voting System: Televoting, the results given by 1-8, 10 and 12 points to the most popular song

Broadcaster: Channel One (C1R)

2009
We Are One

First Semi Final 12.5.2009
9 marked grey countries and the wild card (gave by jury's decision) qualified to the Final
(United Kingdom and Germany were allowed to vote this semi-final)

No.	Country	Song	Performing Artist	Language	Points	Place
1	Montenegro	"Just Get Out of My Life"	Andrea Demirović	English	44	11
2	Czech Republic	"Aven Romale"	Gipsy.cz	English, Romani	0	18
3	Belgium	"Copycat"	Copycat	English	1	17
4	Belarus	"Eyes That Never Lie"	Petr Elfimov	English	25	13
5	Sweden	"La voix"	Malena Ernman	French, English	105	4
6	Armenia	"Jan Jan"	Inga and Anush	Armenian, English	99	5
7	Andora	"La teva decisió (Get a Life)"	Susanne Georgi	Catalan, English	8	15
8	Switzerland	"The Highest Heights"	Lovebugs	English	15	14
9	Turkey	"Düm Tek Tek"	Hadise	English	172	2
10	Israel	"There Must Be Another Way"	Ahinoam Nini (Noa) and Mira Awad	Hebrew, English, Arabic	75	7
11	Bulgaria	"Illusion"	Krassimir Avramov	English	7	16
12	Iceland	"Is It True?"	Yohanna	English	174	1
13	North Macedonia	"Nešto što kje ostane"	Next Time	North Macedonian	45	10
14	Romania	"The Balkan Girls"	Elena	English	67	9
15	Finland	"Lose Control"	Waldo's People	English	42	12
16	Portugal	"Todas as ruas do amor"	Flor-de-Lis	portuguese	70	8
17	Malta	"What If We"	Chiara	English	86	6
18	Bosnia and Herzegovina	"Bistra voda"	Regina	Serbo-Croatian	125	3

Second Semi Final, 14.5.2009
9 marked grey countries and the wild card (gave by jury's decision) qualified to the Final
(France and Russia were allowed to vote this semi-final)

No.	Country	Song	Performing Artist	Language	Points	Place
1	Croatia	"Lijepa Tena"	Igor Cukrov feat. Andrea	Croatian	33	13
2	Ireland	"Et Cetera"	Sinéad Mulvey and Black Daisy	English	52	11
3	Latvia	"Probka"	Intars Busulis	Russian	7	19
4	Serbia	"Cipela"	Marko Kon and Milaan	Serbian	60	10
5	Poland	"I Don't Wanna Leave"	Lidia Kopania	English	43	12
6	Norway	"Fairytale"	Alexander Rybak	English	201	1
7	Cyprus	"Firefly"	Christina Metaxa	English	32	14
8	Slovakia	"Leť tmou"	Kamil Mikulčík and Nela Pociskova	Slovak	8	18
9	Denmark	"Believe Again"	Brinck	English	69	8
10	Slovenia	"Love Symphony"	Quartissimo feat. Martina	English, Slovenian	14	16
11	Hungary	"Dance with Me"	Zoli Ádok	English	16	15
12	Azerbaijan	"Always"	AySel and Arash	English	180	2
13	Greece	"This Is Our Night"	Sakis Rouvas	English	110	4
14	Lithuania	"Love"	Sasha Son	Russian, English	66	9
15	Moldova	"Hora din Moldova"	Nelly Ciobanu	Romanian, English	106	5
16	Albania	"Carry Me in Your Dreams"	Kejsi Tola	English	73	7
17	Ukraine	"Be My Valentine"	Svetlana Loboda	English	80	6
18	Estonia	"Rändajad"	Urban Symphony	Estonish	115	3
19	Netherlands	"Shine"	The Toppers	English	11	17

FINAL

16.5.2009

No.	Country	Song	Performing Artist	Lyrics	Composer	Language	Commentator	Spoker of Results	Points	Place
01	Lithuania	"Love"	Sasha Son	Sasha Son	Sasha Son	English	Darius Užkuraitis	Ignas Krupavičius	23	23
02	Israel	"There Must Be Another Way"	Ahinoam Nini (Noa) and Mira Awad	Ahinoam Nini (Noa), Mira Awad, Gil Dor	Ahinoam Nini (Noa), Mira Awad, Gil Dor	Hebrew, English, Arabic	-	Ofer Nachshon	53	16
03	France	"Et s'il fallait le faire"	Patricia Kaas	Anse Lazio, Fred Blondin	Anse Lazio, Fred Blondin	French	Julien Courbet, Cyril Hanouna	Yann Renoard	107	8
04	Sweden	"La voix"	Malena Ernman	Fredrik Kempe, Malena Ernman	Fredrik Kempe	English, French	Shirley Clamp, Edward af Sillén	Sarah Dawn Finer	33	21
05	Croatia	"Lijepa Tena"	Igor Cukrov feat. Andrea	Vjekoslava Huljić	Tonči Huljić	Croatian	Duško Čurlić	Mila Horvat	45	18
06	Portugal	"Todas as ruas do amor"	Flor-de-Lis	Paulo Pereira, Pedro Marques	Pedro Marques	portuguese	Hélder Reis	Helena Coelho	57	15
07	Iceland	"Is It True?"	Yohanna	Óskar Páll Sveinsson, Tinatin Japaridze, Chris Neil	Óskar Páll Sveinsson, Tinatin Japaridze, Chris Neil	English	Sigmar Guðmundsson	Þóra Tómasdóttir	218	2
08	Greece	"This Is Our Night"	Sakis Rouvas	Craig Porteils, Cameron Giles-Webb	Dimitris Kontopoulos	English	Maggira Sisters	Alexis Kostalas	120	7
09	Armenia	"Jan Jan"	Inga and Anush	Vardan Zadoyan, Avet Barseghyan	Mane Hakopyan	Armenian, English	-	Sirusho	92	10
10	Russia	"Mamo"	Anastasiya Prikhodko	Konstantin Meladze, Diana Golde	Konstantin Meladze	English	Yana Churikova, Philipp Kirkorov	Ingeborga Dapkūnaitė	91	11
11	Azerbaijan	"Always"	AySel and Arash	Arash Labaf, Robert Uhlmann, Elin Wrethov, Anderz Wrethov	Arash Labaf, Robert Uhlmann, Johan Bejerholm, Marcus Englof, Alex Papaconstantinou	English	Leyla Aliyeva, Isa Melikov	Hüsniyya Maharramova	207	3
12	Bosnia and Herzegovina	"Bistra voda"	Regina	Aleksandar Čović	Aleksandar Čović	Serbo-Croatian	Dejan Kukrić	Laka	106	9
13	Moldova	"Hora din Moldova"	Nelly Ciobanu	Andrei Hadjiu, Nelly Ciobanu, Aristotelis Kalimeris	Veaceslav Daniliu	Romanian, English	Rosalina Rusu, Andrei Sava	Sandu Leancă	69	14
14	Malta	"What If We"	Chiara	Gregory Bilsen	Marc Paelinck	English	Valerie Vella	Pauline Agius	31	22
15	Estonia	"Rändajad"	Urban Symphony	Sven Lõhmus	Sven Lõhmus	Estonish,	Marko Reikop	Laura Põldvere	129	6
16	Denmark	"Believe Again"	Niels Brinck	Lars Halvor Jensen, Martin Michael Larsson, Ronan Keating	Lars Halvor Jensen, Martin Michael Larsson, Ronan Keating	English	Nikolaj Molbech	Felix Smith	74	13
17	Germany	"Miss Kiss Kiss Bang"	Alex Swings Oscar Sings!	Alex Christensen/Steffen Häfelinger	Alex Christensen/Steffen Häfelinger	English	Ina Müller	Thomas Anders	35	20
18	Turkey	"Düm Tek Tek"	Hadise	Sinan Akçıl, Hadise, Stefan Fernande	Sinan Akçıl	English	Bülend Özveren	Meltem Ersan Yazgan	177	4
19	Albania	"Carry Me in Your Dreams"	Kejsi Tola	Agim Doçi	Edmond Zhulali	English	Leon Menkshi	Leon Menkshi	48	17
20	Norway	"Fairytale"	Alexander Rybak	Alexander Rybak	Alexander Rybak	English	Synnøve Svabø	Stian Barsnes Simonsen	387	1
21	Ukraine	"Be My Valentine"	Svetlana Loboda	Yevgeny Matyushenko	Svetlana Loboda	English	Timur Miroshnychenko	Marysya Horobets	76	12
22	Romania	"The Balkan Girls"	Elena	Alexandru Pelin, Duţă	Duţă, Daris Mangal, Ovidiu Bistriceanu	Spanish, English	Ioana Isopescu, Alexandru Nagy	Alina Sorescu	40	19
23	United Kingdom	"It's My Time"	Jade Ewen	Andrew Lloyd Webber, Diane Warren	Andrew Lloyd Webber	English	Grah`am Norton,	Duncan James	173	5
24	Finland	"Lose Control"	Waldo's People	A. Lehtonen, Karima, Waldo, A. Kratz Gutå	A. Lehtonen, Karima	English	Tobias Larsson, Jaana Pelkonen, Mikko Peltola, Asko Murtomäki	Jari Sillanpää	22	25
25	Spain	"La noche es para mí"	Soraya Arnelas	Felipe Pedroso	Irini Michas, Dimitri Stassos, Jason Gill	Spanish, English	Joaquín Guzmán	Iñaki del Moral	23	24

	Spain	Belgium	Belarus	Malta	Germany	Czech Republic	Sweden	Iceland	France	Israel	Russia	Latvia	Montenegro	Andora	Finland	Switzerland	Bulgaria	Lithuania	United Kingdom	North Macedonia	Slovakia
Spain	■	–	–	–	–	–	–	–	–	–	–	–	–	12	–	3	–	–	–	–	–
Belgium		■																			
Belarus			■																		
Malta	–	–	–	■	4	–	–	–	–	–	–	1	–	1	3	–	–	1	6	–	–
Germany	–	2	–	–	■	–	–	–	3	–	–	–	–	–	–	–	–	–	7	–	–
Czech Republic						■															
Sweden	–	–	–	4	–	–	■	3	2	–	–	–	–	2	7	–	–	–	–	–	–
Iceland	–	–	2	12	7	2	10	■	–	10	3	8	5	8	10	5	5	8	8	2	6
France	3	1	7	–	3	–	–	6	■	5	10	5	1	3	4	7	–	6	1	–	–
Israel	–	8	–	–	–	4	–	–	10	■	–	–	4	7	–	1	–	–	–	–	5
Russia	–	–	8	–	5	8	–	–	–	7	■	6	–	–	–	–	–	7	–	–	–
Latvia												■	–								
Montenegro													■								
Andora														■							
Finland	–	–	–	3	–	–	4	8	–	–	–	–	–	–	■	–	3	–	–	–	–
Switzerland																■					
Bulgaria																	■				
Lithuania	–	–	–	–	–	–	–	–	–	–	7	–	–	–	–	–	1	■	4	–	–
United Kingdom	10	–	3	10	8	6	–	–	4	4	6	2	–	4	–	–	7	3	■	6	7
North Macedonia																				■	
Slovakia																					■
Greece	1	5	5	7	6	–	2	–	–	–	4	–	2	–	–	2	12	–	5	–	–
Bosnia and Herzegovina	–	–	–	–	2	–	5	2	–	–	–	–	12	–	6	4	4	–	–	10	8
Ukraine	6	–	6	2	–	5	–	–	–	2	2	–	–	–	–	–	–	4	2	–	1
Turkey	2	12	–	5	10	1	6	–	12	3	–	–	3	–	5	12	10	–	12	12	–
Albania	–	–	–	–	–	–	1	–	–	–	–	–	7	–	–	6	–	–	–	7	–
Serbia																					
Cyprus																					
Poland																					
The Netherlands																					
Estonia	–	–	4	–	1	–	7	10	–	–	8	10	–	–	12	–	–	10	–	–	12
Croatia	–	–	–	–	–	–	–	1	–	–	–	–	8	–	–	–	–	–	–	4	–
Portugal	8	6	–	–	–	7	–	7	7	–	–	–	–	6	–	10	–	–	–	–	2
Romania	7	–	–	–	–	–	–	–	–	–	–	–	–	–	–	–	–	–	–	5	–
Ireland																					
Denmark	–	–	–	6	–	–	–	4	5	–	–	3	–	5	–	–	–	2	–	–	–
Moldova	5	4	–	–	–	–	–	–	–	1	1	–	–	–	–	–	–	–	–	–	–
Slovenia																					
Armenia	4	7	1	–	–	12	3	5	6	8	5	–	–	–	1	–	6	–	–	1	3
Hungary																					
Azerbaijan	–	3	10	1	–	10	8	–	1	6	7	4	6	–	2	–	8	5	3	3	4
Norway	12	10	12	8	12	3	12	12	8	12	12	12	10	10	8	8	2	12	10	8	10

	Greece	Bosnia and Herzegovina	Ukraine	Turkey	Albania	Serbia	Cyprus	Poland	The Netherlands	Estonia	Croatia	Portugal	Romania	Ireland	Denmark	Moldova	Slovenia	Armenia	Hungary	Azerbaijan	Norway
Spain	1	–	–	–	–	–	–	–	–	–	–	7	–	–	–	–	–	–	–	–	–
Belgium																					
Belarus																					
Malta	–	–	–	–	–	7	–	–	–	–	–	–	3	5	–	–	–	–	–	–	–
Germany	–	2	–	1	3	–	–	–	2	–	–	1	–	1	7	–	–	–	–	–	6
Czech Republic																					
Sweden	–	–	–	–	1	–	–	–	–	6	–	–	–	–	4	–	–	–	–	–	4
Iceland	4	–	–	2	6	–	5	1	7	8	2	8	10	12	10	3	5	5	7	–	12
France	6	6	3	–	2	3	–	–	6	–	–	–	–	3	2	–	7	6	–	–	1
Israel	–	8	1	–	–	–	–	–	–	5	–	–	–	–	–	–	–	–	–	–	–
Russia	–	–	8	4	–	–	1	3	–	10	–	–	–	–	–	6	–	12	–	6	–
Latvia																					
Montenegro																					
Andora																					
Finland	–	–	–	–	–	–	–	–	–	4	–	–	–	–	–	–	–	–	–	–	–
Switzerland																					
Bulgaria																					
Lithuania	–	–	–	–	–	–	–	–	–	2	–	–	–	7	1	–	–	–	–	1	–
United Kingdom	12	4	6	–	8	8	7	4	3	–	4	10	–	10	3	1	3	7	1	–	2
North Macedonia																					
Slovakia																					
Greece	■	5	–	–	12	6	12	–	1	–	7	–	8	–	–	–	4	10	4	–	–
Bosnia and Herzegovina	–	■	–	8	5	12	–	–	4	–	12	–	–	–	–	–	–	10	–	2	–
Ukraine	–	–	■	–	–	–	–	10	–	–	–	6	–	–	–	4	–	3	8	10	5
Turkey	3	7	–	■	10	–	–	–	8	–	1	3	6	–	6	–	–	4	5	12	7
Albania	7	–	–	10	■	–	–	–	–	1	5	–	–	–	–	–	2	–	2	–	–
Serbia						■															
Cyprus							■														
Poland								■													
The Netherlands									■												
Estonia	5	–	4	–	–	–	3	8	–	■	6	–	1	6	5	7	–	–	6	4	–
Croatia	2	12	–	–	–	5	–	–	–	–	■	–	–	–	–	2	6	–	–	5	–
Portugal	–	1	–	–	–	–	–	–	–	3	–	■	–	–	–	–	–	–	–	–	–
Romania	–			5	–	2	2	–	–	–	–	2	■	2	–	12	–	–	–	3	–
Ireland														■							
Denmark	–	–	5	–	–	1	6	7	–	–	–	–	2	4	■	5	8	–	3	–	8
Moldova	–	–	7	7	–	–	–	5	–	–	3	12	12	–	–	■	–	2	–	7	3
Slovenia																	■				
Armenia	–	–	2	6	–	–	4	2	5	–	–	4	7	–	–	–	–	■	–	–	–
Hungary																			■		
Azerbaijan	8	3	10	12	4	4	8	6	10	7	10	–	4	–	8	10	1	1	10	■	10
Norway	10	10	12	3	7	10	10	12	12	12	8	5	5	8	12	8	12	8	12	8	■

*The marked grey countries did not participate in the final but gave points to the final entries.

...oogy" representing Israel in the 1974 contest >> Photo by: Uri Aloni, in courtesy of Ilan Ben Shachar and the "Lahiton" archive

Atilla Şereftuğ, Céline Dion and Nella Martinetti in Dublin 1988

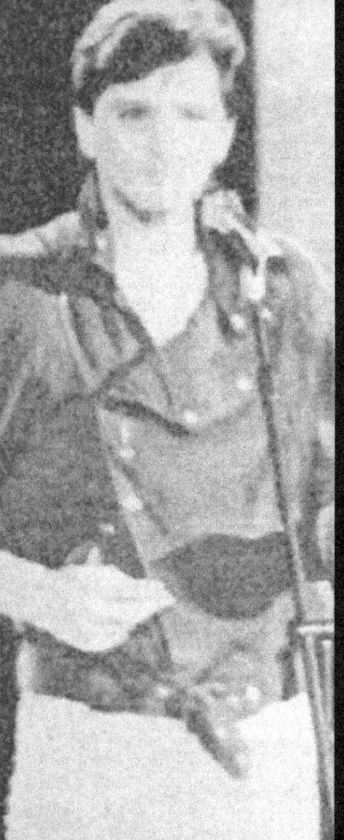

Daniel Popović from Yugoslavia, led the way to the contest's top places for his country in Munich (1983) >> P Uri Aloni, in courtesy of Ilan Ben Shachar and the "Lahiton" archive

The first to sing in Arabic on the Eurovision stage — Morocan Samira Bensaïd (1980) >> Photo by: Uri Aloni, in courtesy of Ilan Ben Shachar and the "Lahiton" archive

Israel's Ilanit with Anne-Marie David, both singers of the 1973 top four >> Photo by: Uri Aloni, in courtesy of Ilan Ben Shachar and the "Lahiton" archive

Peter, Sue and Marc performing their hit "Djambo, Djambo" in the Hague 1976 >> Photo by: Uri Aloni, in courtesy of Ilan Ben Shachar and the "Lahiton" archive

The ending of 1981 Eurovision, with the glitching scoreboard

Betty Missiego being noble in the end of the 1979 Eurovision, taking a photo with Gali Atari and Kobi Oshrat >> Photo by: Uri Aloni, in courtesy of Ilan Ben Shachar and the "Lahiton" archive

>> Photo by: Bruno Torricelli

Nicole captivating the European crowd in Harrogate 1982 >> Photo by: David Paz, in courtesy of Ilan Ben Shachar and the "Lahiton" archive

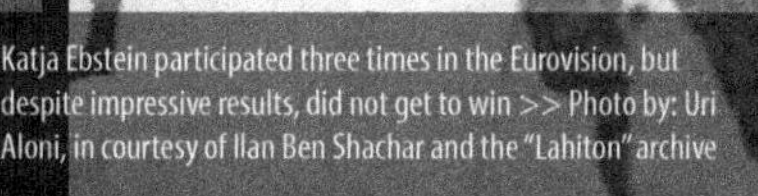

Katja Ebstein participated three times in the Eurovision, but despite impressive results, did not get to win >> Photo by: Uri Aloni, in courtesy of Ilan Ben Shachar and the "Lahiton" archive

Switzerland's Paola impressed with "Cinéma", which was only enough for the fourth place in 1980 >> Photo by: Uri Aloni, in courtesy of Ilan Ben Shachar and the "Lahiton" archive

Catherine Ferry reaching the second place with a tremendous performance in 1976 >> Photo by: Uri Aloni in courtesy of Ilan Ben Shachar and the "Lahiton" archive

Mary Christy with an impressing performance in The Hague 1976 >> Photo by: Uri Aloni, in courtesy of Ilan Ben Shachar and the "Lahiton" archive

>> Photo by: Uri Aloni, in courtesy of Ilan Ben Shachar and the "Lahiton" archive

Belgium's "Dream Express" that were favourites in the 1977 contest >> Photo by: Uri Aloni, in courtesy of Ilan Ben Shachar and the "Lahiton" archive

2010-2019

FIRST AND FOREMOST — THE SHOW

Two Swedish victories in the second decade of the new millennium, place the Scandinavian Empire a step away from the title of all-time queen of wins (Ireland). Five female singers won first place (not including Conchita Wurst...), with three of the last five winners being men. Sweden hosted the event twice this decade and Israel continued to maintain, since 1979, hosting in clusters of 20 years...

2010 – Oslo, Norway

For the third time and as per tradition, Norway hosted the Eurovision in splendour, with an invested stage and state of the art lighting and pyrotechnics, as expected from a production with a virtually unlimited budget. But all this did not prevent one of the biggest embarrassments contest's history when a spectator burst onto the stage during the Spanish entry in the grand finale. Performer Daniel Diges was given a replay after the Danes which were the last to perform. A major setback for Irish Niamh Kavanagh, the 1993 Eurovision winner who came with an invested team and dreamed of a second victory, but despite qualifying for the final (and that too with great difficulty in retrospect), finished in 23rd place out of 25 participants. The German Lena, one of the favourites, won easily, sweeping 246 points and leading by a considerable margin ahead of Turkey's surprising band "maNga". It was the first victory for one of the countries sponsoring the contest since the UK won in 1997 and is currently also the only in the current millennium. Overall, it was just the second win of the largest country in Europe, Germany, since Nicole in 1982.

2011 – Dusseldorf, Germany

Germany hosted the event for the third time, this time in Düsseldorf. In an unusual decision, for the first time since the fifties of the last century, a singer who won the contest represented her country the year after, which undoubtedly proves that Lena is a brave girl that also exceedingly loves the Eurovision... Finally, the host failed to reach the top again, and even Lena could not change the statistics (ranked 11th). Israel's Dana International, the winner of the 1998 contest, hoped that "Ding Dong" would do the trick and ring the bell once again for Israel, but she did not even make it to the final. Italy stormed the Eurovision after 14 years of absence and was considered the big favourite, but Azerbaijan stole the thunder with the duo Ell & Nikki, assisted by outside writers, and the entry "Running Scared" won the contest, bringing the 2012 Eurovision to the former Soviet state.

2012 – Baku, Azerbaijan

Azerbaijan, one of the most advanced and wealthiest countries in the eastern part of Europe, not only met the challenge of hosting the Eurovision but also left behind extremely lofty standards that brought the contest to new heights in terms of production and design. The Israeli "Time" by the "Izabo" band was one of the most played songs in the Holy Land, much more than any other Eurovision entry in Israel for decades, but this did not help it pass the semi-finals. The favourites were the "Buranovskiye Babushki" from Russia with a "Party for Everybody", which undoubtedly stole the show and got rave reviews, but musically the Swedish Loreen with "Euphoria" was much better, swept the final with 273 points and 18 Douze Points, when only Italy did not award anything to the winning entry. Ironically, in the year that Sweden wins (in English), the song that represented Finland in Swedish (one of the country's official languages) failed in the semi-finals... Sweden's fifth Eurovision win brought it to second place in the all-time table alongside France and Luxembourg.

2013 – Malmö, Sweden

For the second time, Malmö was the host city of the 58th Eurovision. The scenery was awe-inspiring, especially the bright stage and engaging decentralisation of the audience. Azerbaijan maintained its impressive line of positions when it finished second. The show was stolen by the well-known Bonnie Tyler who represented the UK, but even she failed to bring the United Kingdom back to its glory days, achieving only 19th place. The one who did live up to expectations was Emmelie de Forest from Denmark with "Only Teardrops", which became the Danes' 3rd victory at the contest and the 2nd in the current millennium (after the Olsen brothers in 2000).

2014 – Copenhagen, Denmark

The Danish hosts chose a unique shoreline in Copenhagen that became the 'Eurovision Island', where all the shows and events related to the big singing contest, which came to the Scandinavian country for the third time. After almost 40 years, the Netherlands returned to fight for the first place and finished as the runner-up. But with all due respect, the thunder was stolen by the Austrian Conchita Wurst, which is actually Thomas Neuwirth — a drag singer who was even diagnosed as an AIDS carrier in 2018. Wurst's appearance at the Eurovision led to enormous controversy in Austria and the other participating countries, that did not know what to make of her performance. Many protests (including on the social network) broke out against Conchita. There was a shocking surprise in the semi-finals when one of the hot favourites to win the entire contest, Mei Finegold from Israel, failed in her attempt to qualify for the finals. Despite the random order of announcement, Austria was the last country to be announced for the finals and Conchita was relieved ... "Rise Like a Phoenix" is maybe a song that in another constellation would not have even made it to the finals, but the Wurst's performance and the story behind it, brought Austria its second Eurovision victory (what a difference compared to Udo Jürgens who did it in 1966...). The Austrian win provoked protests, one of them by a Russian diplomat who said: "This is the future of Europe — a woman with a beard wins the Eurovision Song Contest", but there was also a great support for Wurst, some comparing her to a pioneer like Dana International.

2015 – Vienna, Austria

The Eurovision in Vienna broke records and added milestones to the history curve of the European contest: Australia made its debut after numerous years in which the ESC was considerably popular in the country. According to the agreement with the EBU, the Australians, if they win the contest, will not be able to host it due to the substantial distance between the continents. Sadly, for Austria, it was the first host in the Eurovision history to finish the night with nul points... Surprisingly, it was rescued from the last place thanks to the neighbour Germany which also did not receive any points, but since according to the rules Austria appeared in the final before Germany, the host finished in the penultimate place, if that is any comfort... Scandinavia recorded its 13th victory thanks to Måns Zelmerlöw and the song "Heroes", which gave Sweden its sixth win in the history of the contest and made it Ireland's runner-up (7 wins) in the all-time winners' table. In the grand final, Italy led with confidence, until in the last part the lead went to the Swedes who advanced to an impressive first place (365 points), with Russia finishing as runner-up.

2016 – Stockholm, Sweden

Turbulence at the third Eurovision held in Stockholm and the sixth on Swedish soil: A new scoring method supposed to keep everyone in suspense until the end was launched. First, the juries' score from each country was given, as usual, but at the end of the voting, additional results were presented (all in a 50-50 ratio), constituting the audience's choice, in ascending order of total points, from low to high, which should cause intriguing revolutions and glorify the drama. Indeed, it did the trick and big time. None other than Australia was the candidate to win the contest — although it was a victory that could not have led to hosting the event. It did win the juries' voting by a considerable margin, and it seemed that nothing could take the win away from it (leading by more than 100 points over second-placed Ukraine). However, an incredible turnaround in the crowd voting (323 points for the Ukrainians versus 191 points for the Australians, while Russia with 361 points wins the audience voting and reaches third place), gave Jamala the victory with "1944," a defiant political entry towards Russia, following the outbreak of the bitter conflict between the two over the Crimea. Were it not for the anti-Russian atmosphere and empathy for the Ukrainians, it is doubtful whether this entry could have come this far, but at the ESC of the 2000s, music is only one element among many others. This was a second win for Ukraine, for whom another hosting of the contest is like Opium of the masses.

2017 – Kyiv, Ukraine

Even before the first rehearsals of the second Eurovision in Kyiv, a major scandal occurred as the hosts refused to confirm the entry of the Russian performer into Ukraine. Surprisingly, the EBU did not intervene, and thus the European singing contest was launched, without the great and angry neighbour Russia, with whom Ukraine was as stated in an ongoing political conflict. This time there was no real drama when Salvador Sobral from Portugal delivered the goods as the favourite with "Amar pelos dois", a quiet Portuguese ballad, in a style that seems to have been forgotten in today's Eurovision. It was a first and impressive win for Portugal with 758 points (a record that has not been broken to date), with Bulgaria reaching its record achievement with second place and 615 points. After all the stunts and gimmicks, a beautifully simple ballad came on stage — as if it had been borrowed from other ESC periods. Sobral, whose health is fragile, managed to win a contest that he does not appreciate so much professionally, but in the test of time have possibly managed to revive the meaning of the contest's songs quality.

2018 – Lisbon, Portugal

It is doubtful whether the Portuguese prime minister bothered to pick up the phone and call Salvador Sobral minutes after winning the Eurovision in Kyiv. But in Israel, the ESC, it turns out, has been and remains a National craze of immense importance for the international image of the Jewish state, which is not even located in Europe and participates in the contest by virtue of being a member of the EBU. The roller coaster on which Netta Barzilai rode had many ups and downs from the tight battles in "Rising Star", through the crazy race to Lisbon, until the relaxed and exciting conversation with Prime Minister Benjamin Netanyahu, who called to congratulate on her victory at 2 AM. Host Portugal received great compliments from the participating countries for the cordial hospitality and obedient production. Even before the other participants finished choosing the entries that would represent them in Lisbon, Israel was one of the most significant favourites in the current millennium to win the Eurovision. Yet, all this put the unique performer Netta Barzilai under almost impossible pressure. After a week of rehearsals and before the action began, Netta dropped to fifth place in the betting tables but managed to get through the semi-finals safely despite all the pressure. Rumour had it that her rival Eleni Foureira, who was ranked first in the betting, managed to defeat her in the semi-finals, but these were only rumours since as the results became clear, Netta was first. The second semi-final was won by the Norwegian Alexander Rybak, who returned to the contest after winning in 2009. In the final, there was a surprising contrast between the juries' votes and the spectators' choice. Austria, which finished first in the juries' vote to the wonder of all, seemed to be in a fantastic opening position for victory with 271 points — but the spectators surprisingly gave it only 71... this was nothing compared to Sweden that breathed down Austria's neck, but fell in the popular vote with only 21 points! From there, it was clear that it would be Israel (212 points in the juries' vote) or Cyprus (183). Indeed, the most dramatic and exciting moment in which the presenters announced Cyprus' second place left the Grand Prix to Netta Barzilai who scooped 317 points from the spectators and won a huge victory. "Toy", which highlights the talent of Netta's unique performance, along with her unconventional appearance, was crafted by the skilled hands of Doron Medalie, a renowned songwriter with an impressive resume in the Eurovision contests, and Stav Beger, a brilliant musician. For Medalie, the experience was a thrilling full-circle moment, as he went from being a devoted Eurovision enthusiast and scholar to becoming a winning songwriter who made it into the history books. Netta was under a lot of pressure to win, and despite two slightly tense performances in the semi-finals and the grand final, she did it big-time and brought Israel its fourth Eurovision win. The Greek Foureira could be comforted by the fact that she gave Cyprus the greatest of its achievements – runner-up.

2019 – Tel Aviv, Israel

The Israeli Broadcasting Corporation "Kan" faced the biggest economic and production challenge in the year and a half since its inception. Madonna's guest appearance in the final was an excellent example of a million and a half dollars that could have been used more usefully for the Eurovision production, rather than for the international pop star's bad moment singing off-key and coming impatiently to a show that was too small for her. The choice of the Israeli entry was kind of arrogant: "Home" looked like a kind of assassination in the sympathetic performer Kobi Marimi, who did his best to represent the host country, but an anaemic song could not get beyond the 23rd place, which also seemed like kind of a sigh of relief (Israel finished the juries' score with zero points — last place and was saved only thanks to the viewers' vote). The guest appearance of the "Shalva" band in the second semi-final only increased the feeling of the local miss: Had the Israeli Broadcasting Corporation dared more to overcome the problem of Sabbath observance by some of the band members, Israel would have had an excellent chance of recreating the 1979 double win. The Netherlands was considered a hot favourite from the outset, but its path to the first place was more challenging than expected: It was the first Eurovision winner in the new system that did not win first place in the jury (Sweden) nor in the public voting (Norway). The two Scandinavian representatives that reached the first place in both categories did not even finish in the top four. Australia, which very much impressed with "Zero Gravity" and climbed to the second place in the betting tables was greatly disappointed when even as it seemed that the momentum was on its side, and despite a brilliant performance in the final, the juries and crowd left Kate Miller-Heidke in the eighth place only.

Sweden's John Lundvik was also among the favourites, receiving no less than 11 Douze Points (three more than the winner), but he eventually found himself only in the fifth place. North Macedonia was the final's major surprise, leading in most of the voting session, but the public voting put Tamara Todevska's nice entry into perspective (eighth place, which is also quite surprising). The Icelandic members of the "Hatari" were the Eurovision's 'bad boys', who searched and found the slot for provocation in the form of waving PLO scarves when the cameras were on them during the reading of the public results in the final. This time, the announcement of the public votes was in ascending order, from the state that finished last in the juries' voting to the one that finished first, and it seems that this change was also for the best. The lovable 25-year-old Dutchman Duncan Laurence (who achieved the lowest number of points for a winner since the scoring system was upgraded) with "Arcade", brought his country its first victory in the Eurovision 44 years after the "Teach-In". Thus, and symbolically, the Netherlands passed the host Israel in the number of wins (4) and clung to France, Luxembourg and the United Kingdom (5 titles per each)

2010

Share the Moment

Country Hosting: Norway
City Hosting: Oslo
Date: 25.5.2010 (First Semi Final), 27.5.2010 (Second Semi Final), 29.5.2010 (The Final)
Location: Telenor Arena
Presenters: Erik Solbakken, Haddy N'jie Nadia Hasnaoui,
Executive Supervisor: Svante Stockselius
Directed By: Ole Jørgen Grønlund, Kim Strømstad
Executive Producer: Jon Ola Sand
Participating Countries: 39
Voting System: Televoting, the results given by 1-8, 10 and 12 points to the most popular song
Broadcaster: Norsk rikskringkasting (NRK)

First Semi Final, 25.5.2010
10 marked grey countries qualified to the Final
(Spain, Germany and France were allowed to vote this semi-final)

No.	Country	Song	Performing Artist	Language	Points	Place
1	Moldova	"Run Away"	SunStroke Project and Olia Tira	English	52	10
2	Russia	"Lost and Forgotten"	Peter Nalitch and Friends	English	74	7
3	Estonia	"Siren"	Malcolm Lincoln and Manpower 4	English	39	14
4	Slovakia	"Horehronie"	Kristina	Slovak	24	16
5	Finland	"Työlki ellää"	Kuunkuiskaajat	Finish	49	11
6	Latvia	"What For?"	Aisha	English	11	17
7	Serbia	"Ovo je Balkan"	Milan Stanković	Serbian	79	5
8	Bosnia and Herzegovina	"Thunder and Lightning"	Vukašin Brajić	English	59	8
9	Poland	"Legenda"	Marcin Mroziński	Polish, English	44	13
10	Belgium	"Me and My Guitar"	Tom Dice	English	167	1
11	Malta	"My Dream"	Thea Garrett	English	45	12
12	Albania	"It's All About You"	Juliana Pasha	English	76	6
13	Greece	"OPA"	Giorgos Alkaios and Friends	Greek	133	2
14	Portugal	"Há dias assim"	Filipa Azevedo	Portuguese	89	4
15	North Macedonia	"Jas ja imam silata"	Gjoko Taneski	North Macedonian	37	15
16	Belarus	"Butterflies"	3+2 feat Robert Wells	English	59	9
17	Iceland	"Je ne sais quoi"	Hera Björk	English	123	3

Second Semi Final, 27.5.2010
10 marked grey countries qualified to the Final
(Norway and United Kingdom were allowed to vote this semi-final)

No.	Country	Song	Performing Artist	Language	Points	Place
1	Lithuania	"Eastern European Funk"	InCulto	English	44	12
2	Armenia	"Apricot Stone"	Eva Rivas	English	83	6
3	Israel	"Milim"	Harel Skaat	Hebrew	71	8
4	Denmark	"In a Moment Like This"	Chanée and N'evergreen	English	101	5
5	Switzerland	"Il pleut de l'or"	Michael von der Heide	French	2	17
6	Sweden	"This Is My Life"	Anna Bergendahl	English	62	11
7	Azerbaijan	"Drip Drop"	Safura	English	113	2
8	Ukraine	"Sweet People"	Alyosha	English	77	7
9	Netherlands	"Ik ben verliefd (Sha-la-lie)"	Sieneke	Dutch	29	14
10	Romania	"Playing with Fire"	Paula Seling and Ovi	English	104	4
11	Slovenia	"Narodnozabavni rock"	Ansambel Žlindra and Kalamari	Slovenian	6	16
12	Ireland	"It's for You"	Niamh Kavanagh	English	67	9
13	Bulgaria	"Angel si ti"	Miro	Bulgarian, English	15	19
14	Cyprus	"Life Looks Better in Spring"	Jon Lilygreen and The Islanders	English	67	10
15	Croatia	"Lako je sve"	Feminnem	Croatian	33	13
16	Georgia	"Shine"	Sofia Nizharadze	English	106	3
17	Turkey	"We Could Be the Same"	maNga	English	118	1

FINAL

25.5.2010

No.	Country	Song	Performing Artist	Lyrics	Composer	Language	Commentator	Spoker of Results	Points	Place
01	Azerbaijan	"Drip Drop"	Safura	Sandra Bjurman, Piotr Wass, Stefan Orn, Anders Bagge	Sandra Bjurman, Piotr Wass, Stefan Orn, Anders Bagge	English	Hüsniyyə Məhərrəmova	Tamilla Shirinova	145	5
02	Spain	"Algo Pequeñito"	Danie Diges	Jesús Cañadilla, Luis Miguel de la Varga, Alberto Jodar, Daniel Diges	Jesús Cañadilla, Luis Miguel de la Varga, Alberto Jodar, Daniel Diges	Spanish	José Luis Uribarri	Ainhoa Arbizu	68	15
03	Norway	"My Heart Is Yours"	Didrik Solli-Tangen	Hanne Sørvaag, Fredrik Kempe	Hanne Sørvaag, Fredrik Kempe	English	Olav Viksmo-Slettan	Anne Rimmen	35	20
04	Moldova	"Run Away"	SunStroke Project and Olia Tira	Alina Galetskaya	Anton Ragoza, Sergey Stepanov	English	Marcel Spătari	Tanya Cerga	27	22
05	Cyprus	"Life Looks Better in Spring"	Jon Lilygreen and The Islanders	Nasos Lambrianides	Nasos Lambrianides, Melis Konstantinou	English	Nathan Morley	Christina Metaxa	27	21
06	Bosnia and Herzegovina	"Thunder and Lightning"	Vukašin Brajić	Edin-Dino Šaran, Ulvija Tanović, Vukašin Brajić	Edin-Dino Šaran	English	Dejan Kukrić	Ivana Vidmar	51	17
07	Belgium	"Me and My Guitar"	Tom Dice	Tom Eeckhout, Jeroen Swinnen, Ashley Hickin	Tom Eeckhout, Jeroen Swinnen, Ashley Hickin	English	Jean-Pierre Hautier, Jean-Louis Lahaye, Andre Vermeulen, Bart Peeters	Katja Retsin	143	6
08	Serbia	"Ovo je Balkan"	Milan Stanković	Goran Bregović, Marina Tucaković, Ljiljana Jorgovanović	Goran Bregović	Serbian	Duška Vučinić-Lučić	Maja Nikolić	72	13
09	Belarus	"Butterflies"	3+2 feat Robert Wells	Malka Chaplin	Maxim Fadeev, Robert Wells	English	Denis Kurian	Aleksei Grishin	18	24
10	Ireland	"It's for You"	Niamh Kavanagh	Niall Mooney, Mårten Eriksson, Jonas Gladnikoff & Lina Eriksson	Niall Mooney, Mårten Eriksson, Jonas Gladnikoff & Lina Eriksson	English	Marty Whelan	Derek Mooney	25	23
11	Greece	"OPA"	Giorgos Alkaios and Friends	Gjannis Antoniou, Dimitris Hortarias, Manos Hortarias, Dionisis Sxoinas, Tolis sxoinas, Kassiani Karagioule, Stauros Apostolou	Giorgos Alkaios	Greek, English	Rika Vagiani	Alexis Kostalas	140	8
12	United Kingdom	"That Sounds Good to Me"	Josh Dubovie	Pete Waterman, Mike Stock, Steve Crosby	Pete Waterman, Mike Stock, Steve Crosby	English	Graham Norton	Scott Mills	10	25
13	Georgia	"Shine"	Sofia Nizharadze	Hanne Sørvaag, Harry Sommerdahl, Christian Leuzzi	Hanne Sørvaag, Harry Sommerdahl, Christian Leuzzi	English	Sopho Altunashvili	Mariam Vashadze	136	9
14	Turkey	"We Could Be the Same"	maNga (Ferman Akgül, Yağmur Sarıgül, Cem Bahtiyar, Özgür Can Öney)	Yağmur Sarıgül, Ferman Akgül, Evren Özdemir, Fiona Movery Akinci	Yağmur Sarıgül, Ferman Akgül, Evren Özdemir	English	Bülend Özveren	Meltem Ersan Yazgan	170	2
15	Albania	"It's All About You"	Juliana Pasha	Ardit Gjebrea, Pirro Çako	Ardit Gjebrea	English	Leon Menkshi	Leon Menkshi	62	16
16	Iceland	"Je ne sais quoi"	Hera Björk	Örlygur Smári, Hera Björk	Örlygur Smári, Hera Björk	English	Sigmar Guðmundsson	Yohanna	41	19
17	Ukraine	"Sweet People"	Alyosha	Olena Kucher	Olena Kucher, Borys Kukoba, Vadim Lisitsa	English	Timur Miroshnychenko	Iryna Zhuravska	108	10
18	France	"Allez Ola Olé"	Jessy Matador	Hugues Ducamin, Jacques Ballue	Hugues Ducamin, Jacques Ballue	French	Cyril Hanouna, Stéphane Bern	Audrey Chauveau	82	12
19	Romania	"Playing with Fire"	Paula Seling and Ovi	Ovidiu Cernăuțeanu	Simen M. Eriksrud	English	Leonard Miron	Malvina Cservenschi	162	3
20	Russia	"Lost and Forgotten"	Peter Nalitch and Friends	Peter Nalitch	Peter Nalitch	English	Olga Shelest, Dmitry Guberniev	Oxana Fedorova	90	11
21	Armenia	"Apricot Stone"	Eva Rivas	Karen Kavaleryan	Armen Martirosyan	English	Hrachuhi Utmazyan, Khoren Levonyan	Nazeni Hovhannisyan	141	7
22	Germany	"Satellite"	Lena	Julie Frost	Julie Frost John Gordon	English	Thomas Mohr	Hape Kerkeling	246	1
23	Portugal	"Há dias assim"	Filipa Azevedo	Augusto Madureira	Augusto Madureira	Portuguese	Sérgio Mateus	Ana Galvão	43	18
24	Israel	"Milim"	Harel Skaat	Tomer Hadadi	Noam Horev	Hebrew, English	-	Ofer Nachshon	71	14
25	Denmark	"In a Moment Like This"	Chanée and N'evergreen	Thomas G:son, Henrik Sethsson, Erik Bernholm	Thomas G:son, Henrik Sethsson, Erik Bernholm	English	Nikolaj Molbech	Bryan Rice	149	4

	Romania	Ireland	Germany	Serbia	Albania	Turkey	Croatia	Poland	Bosnia and Herzegovina	Finland	Slovenia	Estonia	Russia	Portugal	Azerbaijan	Greece	Iceland	Denmark	France	Spain
Romania	■	7	–	6	5	2	–	6	2	–	7	–	3	10	7	4	5	8	–	10
Ireland	–	■	2	–	–	–	1	–	–	1	–	2	–	–	–	–	–	–	–	–
Germany	3	8	■	8	10	10	6	7	8	12	10	12	6	1	1	2	3	12	3	12
Serbia	–	–	5	■	3	–	8	–	12	–	8	–	–	–	–	–	–	–	10	–
Albania	1	–	1	–	■	7	5	2	5	–	–	–	–	–	–	10	7	–	–	–
Turkey	8	1	10	3	8	■	12	–	10	3	2	6	–	–	12	–	–	6	12	3
Croatia							■													
Poland								■												
Bosnia and Herzegovina	–	–	–	12	6	8	10	–	■	–	4	–	–	–	–	–	–	–	5	–
Finland										■										
Slovenia											■									
Estonia												■								
Russia	–	–	–	–	–	4	–	–	–	–	–	10	■	2	3	–	–	–	–	–
Portugal	–	–	6	2	–	–	–	–	–	–	–	–	–	■	–	–	1	4	8	6
Azerbaijan	–	3	–	–	–	12	–	8	7	–	–	–	8	–	■	1	4	2	–	7
Greece	7	–	8	10	12	3	–	1	6	7	–	–	–	8	–	■	8	–	4	5
Iceland	–	–	4	–	–	–	–	–	–	5	–	4	–	–	–	3	■	3	–	–
Denmark	12	12	–	–	2	–	2	12	–	2	12	5	1	4	4	–	12	■	–	4
France	–	6	3	4	–	–	3	–	3	8	3	1	–	7	–	8	6	7	■	2
Spain	2	–	–	–	7	–	–	–	–	4	5	–	4	12	–	–	–	–	–	■
Slovakia																				
Bulgaria																				
Ukraine	5	–	–	7	–	1	–	3	–	–	–	–	7	–	10	–	–	–	2	–
Latvia																				
Malta																				
Norway	–	2	–	–	–	–	–	–	–	–	–	7	–	3	–	–	–	5	–	–
Cyprus	–	–	–	–	–	–	4	–	–	–	–	–	–	–	–	12	–	1	–	–
Lithuania																				
Belarus	–	–	–	–	–	–	–	–	–	–	–	–	2	–	–	–	–	–	–	–
Switzerland																				
Belgium	4	10			–	–	–	10	–	6	–	3	5	5	–	6	10	10	7	–
United Kingdom	–	4	–	–	1	–	–	–	–	–	–	–	–	–	2	–	–	–	–	–
The Netherlands																				
Israel	–	–	–	–	4	–	–	–	1	10	6	–	–	–	5	–	–	–	1	–
North Macedonia																				
Moldova	10	–	–	–	–	–	–	–	–	–	–	–	–	6	6	–	–	–	–	–
Georgia	–	5	–	–	–	5	7	4	4	–	1	8	10	–	8	5	2	–	–	1
Sweden																				
Armenia	6	–	7	1	–	6	–	5	–	–	–	–	12	–	–	7	–	–	6	8

Slovakia	Bulgaria	Ukraine	Latvia	Malta	Norway	Cyprus	Lithuania	Belarus	Switzerland	Belgium	United Kingdom	The Netherlands	Israel	North Macedonia	Moldova	Georgia	Sweden	Armenia	
1	–	2	3	5	10	8	2	1	4	–	8	5	8	–	12	–	10	1	Romania
–	–	–	–	–	–	–	–	–	6	–	7	–	6	–	–	–	–	–	Ireland
12	3	5	12	4	12	4	10	–	12	10	4	4	–	8	–	–	12	–	Germany
–	–	–	–	–	–	1	–	–	10	–	–	1	–	7	–	–	7	–	Serbia
–	–	–	–	–	–	–	–	–	8	3	1	–	–	12	–	–	–	–	Albania
–	10	8	–	–	2	–	4	3	3	6	10	8	–	10	–	5	5	–	Turkey
																			Croatia
																			Poland
–	–	–	–	–	–	–	–	–	–	–	–	–	–	6	–	–	–	–	Bosnia and Herzegovina
																			Finland
																			Slovenia
																			Estonia
6	–	10	8	–	–	–	5	12	–	–	–	–	10	–	10	–	–	10	Russia
–	–	–	6	1	–	–	–	–	5	–	–	–	–	–	–	–	–	4	Portugal
–	12	12	2	12	7	10	–	6	2	5	–	–	7	3	7	8	–	–	Azerbaijan
5	5	–	–	7	–	12	–	–	–	12	12	3	–	–	2	–	–	3	Greece
–	–	–	–	6	6	–	–	2	–	8	–	–	–	–	–	–	–	–	Iceland
7	–	–	10	8	8	–	3	–	–	2	6	2	4	2	–	–	8	5	Denmark
–	–	–	–	2	4	3	–	–	–	–	2	–	3	1	–	–	–	6	France
–	2	4	5	–	–	–	8	–	–	1	–	–	1	–	4	2	–	7	Spain
■																			Slovakia
	■																		Bulgaria
–	7	■	7	–	–	6	6	10	–	–	5	7	2	–	8	7	–	8	Ukraine
			■																Latvia
				■															Malta
3	–	–	–	3	■	–	–	–	–	–	–	–	–	–	–	6	4	2	Norway
2	4	–	–	–	–	■	1	–	–	–	–	–	–	–	–	–	3	–	Cyprus
							■												Lithuania
–	1	–	–	–	–	–	–	■	–	–	–	–	–	–	3	12	–	–	Belarus
									■										Switzerland
10	–	1	4	10	3	–	7	–	7	■	–	6	–	–	–	–	2	–	Belgium
–	–	–	–	–	–	–	–	–	–	–	■	–	–	–	–	3	–	–	United Kingdom
												■							The Netherlands
8	–	3	–	–	5	2	–	8	–	–	3	10	■	–	1	4	–	–	Israel
														■					North Macedonia
–	–	–	–	–	–	–	–	4	–	–	–	–	–	–	■	1	–	–	Moldova
–	6	7	–	–	1	5	12	7	1	4	–	–	5	5	5	■	6	12	Georgia
																	■		Sweden
4	8	6	1	–	–	7	–	5	–	7	–	12	12	4	6	10	1	■	Armenia

*The marked grey countries did not participate in the final but gave points to the final entries.

2011

Country Hosting: Germany
City Hosting: Dusseldorf
Date: 10.5.2011 (First Semi Final), 12.5.2011 (Second Semi Final), 14.5.2011 (The Final)
Location: Esprit Arena
Presenters: Anke Engelke, Judith Rakers Stefan Raab,
Executive Supervisor: Jon Ola Sand
Directed By: Ladislaus Kiraly
Executive Producer: Thomas Schreiber, Ralf Quibeldey
Participating Countries: 43
Voting System: Televoting, the results given by 1-8, 10 and 12 points to the most popular song
Broadcaster: Arbeitsgemeinschaft Rundfunkanstalten Deutschland (ARD)

Feel your heart beat!

First Semi Final, 10.5.2011
10 marked grey countries qualified to the Final
(United Kingdom and Spain were allowed to vote this semi-final)

No.	Country	Song	Performing Artist	Language	Points	Place
1	Poland	"Jestem"	Magdalena Tul	Polish	18	19
2	Norway	"Haba Haba"	Stella Mwangi	Norweigen, Swahili	30	17
3	Albania	"Feel the Passion"	Aurela Gaçe	Albanian, English	47	14
4	Armenia	"Boom Boom"	Emmy	English	54	12
5	Turkey	"Live It Up"	Yüksek Sadakat	English	47	13
6	Serbia	"Čaroban"	Nina	Serbian	67	8
7	Russia	"Get You"	Alexey Vorobyov	Russian, English	64	9
8	Switzerland	"In Love for a While"	Anna Rossinelli	English	55	10
9	Georgia	"One More Day"	Eldrine	English	74	6
10	Finland	"Da Da Dam"	Paradise Oskar	English	103	3
11	Malta	"One Life"	Glen Vella	English	54	11
12	San Marino	"Stand By"	Senit	English	34	16
13	Croatia	"Celebrate"	Daria	English	41	15
14	Iceland	"Coming Home"	Sjonni's Friends	English	100	4
15	Hungary	"What About My Dreams?"	Kati Wolf	Hungarian, English	72	7
16	Portugal	"A luta é alegria"	Homens da Luta	Portuguese	22	18
17	Lithuania	"C'est ma vie"	Evelina Sašenko	English	81	5
18	Azerbaijan	"Running Scared"	Ell & Nikki	English	122	2
19	Greece	"Watch My Dance"	Loukas Giorkas feat. Stereo Mike	Greek, English	133	1

Second Semi Final, 12.5.2011
10 marked grey countries qualified to the Final
(France, Germany and Italy were allowed to vote this semi-final)

No.	Country	Song	Performing Artist	Language	Points	Place
1	Bosnia and Herzegovina	"Love in Rewind"	Dino Merlin	Serbo-Croatian, English	109	5
2	Austria	"The Secret Is Love"	Nadine Beiler	English	69	7
3	Netherlands	"Never Alone"	3JS	English	13	19
4	Belgium	"With Love Baby"	Witloof Bay	English	53	11
5	Slovakia	"I'm Still Alive"	TWiiNS	English	48	13
6	Ukraine	"Angel"	Mika Newton	English	81	6
7	Moldova	"So Lucky"	Zdob și Zdub	English	54	10
8	Sweden	"Popular"	Eric Saade	English	155	1
9	Cyprus	"San Aggelos S'agapisa"	Christos Mylordos	English	16	18
10	Bulgaria	"Na inat"	Poli Genova	Bulgarian	48	12
11	North Macedonia	"Rusinka"	Vlatko Ilievski	North Macedonian, English	36	16
12	Israel	"Ding Dong"	Dana International	Hebrew, English	38	15
13	Slovenia	"No One"	Maja Keuc	English	112	3
14	Romania	"Change"	Hotel FM	English	111	4
15	Estonia	"Rockefeller Street"	Getter Jaani	English	60	9
16	Belarus	"Love Belarus"	Anastasia Vinnikova	English	45	14
17	Latvia	"Angel in Disguise"	Musiqq	English	25	17
18	Denmark	"New Tomorrow"	A Friend in London	English	135	2
19	Ireland	"Lipstick"	Jedward	English	68	8

<table><tr><td>FINAL</td><td>14.5.2011</td></tr></table>

No.	Country	Song	Performing Artist	Lyrics	Composer	Language	Commentator	Spoker of Results	Points	Place
01	Finland	"Da Da Dam"	Paradise Oskar	Axel Ehnström	Axel Ehnström	English	Tarja Närhi, Asko Murtomäki	Susan Aho	57	21
02	Bosnia and Herzegovina	"Love in Rewind"	Dino Merlin	Dino Merlin	Dino Merlin	English	Dejan Kukrić	Ivana Vidmar	125	6
03	Denmark	"New Tomorrow"	A Friend in London (Aske Damm Bramming, Esben Svane, Sebastian Vinther Olsen, Tim Schou)	Lise Cabble, Jakob Glæsner	Lise Cabble, Jakob Glæsner	English	Ole Tøpholm	Lise Rønne	134	5
04	Lithuania	"C'est ma vie"	Evelina Sašenko	Andrius Kairys	Paulius Zdanavičius	English	Darius Užkuraitis	Giedrius Masalskis	63	19
05	Hungary	"What About My Dreams?"	Kati Wolf	Johnny K. Palmer, Péter Geszti	Viktor Rakonczai, Gergő Rácz	Hungarian, English	Gábor Gundel Takács	Éva Novodomszky	53	22
06	Ireland	"Lipstick"	Jedward	Dan Priddy, Lars Halvor Jensen, Martin M. Larsson	Dan Priddy, Lars Halvor Jensen, Martin M. Larsson	English	Marty Whelan	Derek Mooney	119	8
07	Sweden	"Popular"	Eric Saace	Fredrik Kempe	Fredrik Kempe	English	Hélène Benno, Edward af Sillén	Danny Saucedo	185	3
08	Estonia	"Rockefeller Street"	Getter Jaani	Sven Lõhmus	Sven Lõhmus	English	Marko Reikop	Piret Järvis	44	24
09	Greece	"Watch My Dance"	Loukas Giorkas feat. Stereo Mike	Eleana Vrahali	Giannis Christodoulopoulos	Greek, English	Maria Kozakou	Lena Aroni	18	24
10	Russia	"Get You"	Alexey Vorobyov	Jack Lucien, RedOne	Alexei Vorobjov, RedOne, AJ Junior, Bilal Hajji, Eric Sanicola	Russian, English	Yana Churikova, Yuriy Aksyuta, Kirill Nabutov	Dima Bilan	77	16
11	France	"Sognu"	Amaury Vassili	Jean-Pierre Marcellesi, Julie Miller	Daniel Moyne, Quentin Bachelet	Corsican	Laurent Boyer, Catherine Lara	Cyril Féraud	82	15
12	Italy	"Madness of Love"	Raphael Gualazzi	Raphael Gualazzi	Raphael Gualazzi	Italian, English	Raffaella Carrà, Bob Sinclar	Raffaella Carrà	189	2
13	Switzerland	"In Love for a While"	Anna Rossinelli	David Klein	David Klein	English	Sven Epiney, Nicolas Tanner, Jonathan Tedesco	Cécile Bähler	19	25
14	United Kingdom	"I Can"	Blue	Duncan James, Lee Ryan, Ciaron Bell, Ben Collier, Ian Hope, Liam Keenan, StarSign	Duncan James, Lee Ryan, Ciaron Bell, Ben Collier, Ian Hope, Liam Keenan, StarSign	English	Graham Norton	Alex Jones	100	11
15	Moldova	"So Lucky"	Zdob şi Zdub	Andy Shuman, Marc Elsner	Roman Yagupov, Mihai Gincu, Marc Elsner	English	Marcel Spătari	Geta Burlacu	97	12
16	Germany	"Taken by a Stranger"	Lena	Monica Birkenes, Nicole Morier, Gus Seyffert	Monica Birkenes, Nicole Morier, Gus Seyffert	English	Thomas Mohr, Steffi Neu, Tim Frühling	Ina Müller	107	10
17	Romania	"Change"	HotelFM (David Bryan, Gabriel Băruţă, Alex Szüz, Darius Neagu, Vicky Sava, Vlady Săteanu)	Alexandra Ivan, Băruţă	Gabriel Băruţă	English	Liana Stanciu, Bogdan Pavlică	Malvina Cservenschi	77	17
18	Austria	"The Secret Is Love"	Nadine Beiler	Nadine Beiler	Thomas Rabitsch	English	Benny Hörtnagl	Kati Bellowitsch	64	18
19	Azerbaijan	"Running Scared"	Ell & Nikki	Stefan Örn, Sandra Bjurman	Stefan Örn, Sandra Bjurman, Iain Farquharson	English	Leyla Aliyeva	Safura Alizadeh	221	1
20	Slovenia	"No One"	Maja Keuc	Urša Vlašič	Matjaž Vlašič	English	Andrej Hofer	Klemen Slakonja	96	13
21	Iceland	"Coming Home"	Sjonni's Friends	Þórunn Erna Clausen	Sigurjón Brink	English	Hrafnhildur Halldorsdóttir	Ragnhildur Steinunn Jónsdóttir	61	20
22	Spain	"Que me quiten lo bailao"	Lucía Perez	Rafael Artesero	Rafael Artesero	Spanish	José María Íñigo	Elena S. Sánchez	50	23
23	Ukraine	"Angel"	Mika Newton	Maryna Skomorohova	Ruslan Kvinta	English	Timur Miroshnychenko, Tetiana Terekhova	Ruslana	159	4
24	Serbia	"Čaroban"	Nina	Kristina Kovač	Kristina Kovač	Serbian	Duška Vučinić-Lučić	Dušica Spasić	85	14
25	Georgia	"One More Day"	Eldrine	DJ BESS, Mikheil Chelidze	Beso Tsikhelashvili	English	Sopho Altunishvili	Sofia Nizharadze	110	9

	RU	BG	NL	IT	CY	UA	FI	NO	AM	MK	IS	SK	GB	DK	AT	PL	SE	SM	DE	AZ	SI	TR
RU	■	4	-	-	2	8	-	-	8	-	1	-	-	-	-	-	-	-	5	4	-	-
BG		■																				
NL			■																			
IT	-	-	-	■	1	-	3	-	6	1	3	-	7	-	6	10	-	12	3	1	3	-
CY					■																	
UA	10	8	-	7	5	■	-	-	12	7	-	12	-	-	-	2	2	-	-	12	6	7
FI	-	-	-	-	-	-	■	12	-	-	10	-	-	5	-	5	7	-	2	-	-	-
NO								■														
AM									■													
MK										■												
IS	-	-	-	5	-	-	8	8	-	-	■	-	4	6	-	-	1	-	-	-	-	-
SK												■										
GB	4	12	-	10	4	3	-	1	2	5	2	-	■	3	-	-	-	2	-	5	1	6
DK	-	7	12	-	3	-	-	7	-	-	12	6	5	■	-	3	10	4	6	-	8	-
AT	-	5	1	-	-	-	1	-	3	2	-	3	2	1	■	-	4	-	12	-	5	1
PL																■						
SE	1	-	10	-	10	1	6	10	4	6	7	10	3	10	-	-	■	6	-	3	4	4
SM																		■				
DE	-	-	7	6	-	-	-	5	-	-	6	-	-	8	10	4	6	-	■	-	7	3
AZ	12	-	6	-	8	10	5	-	-	-	8	7	-	-	8	8	3	10	-	■	-	12
SI	5	-	2	-	6	-	-	-	-	10	-	1	-	7	3	-	-	1	1	-	■	2
TR																						■
CH	-	-	-	-	-	-	-	-	-	-	-	-	4	10	-	-	-	-	-	-	-	-
GR	8	10	-	2	12	6	-	-	7	3	-	-	-	-	-	-	-	8	10	8	-	-
GE	6	1	-	-	-	12	-	-	10	-	-	-	-	-	-	7	-	7	-	10	-	8
FR	3	-	-	1	7	5	4	-	5	-	-	-	-	-	-	-	-	3	-	-	-	-
RS	-	-	3	3	-	-	2	6	1	8	-	-	-	-	7	6	-	5	-	-	10	-
HR																						
BY																						
RO	-	6	4	12	-	-	-	-	-	-	-	-	-	-	4	1	-	-	-	6	-	5
AL																						
MT																						
PT																						
HU	-	-	-	-	-	4	12	-	-	-	5	-	-	-	2	-	5	-	-	2	-	-
LT	2	-	-	-	-	-	-	3	-	-	-	-	6	-	-	12	-	2	-	-	-	-
BA	-	2	8	4	-	-	-	4	-	12	-	-	-	-	12	-	8	-	7	-	12	10
IE	-	3	5	-	-	-	10	-	-	-	4	8	12	12	4	1	12	-	8	-	-	-
ES	-	-	-	-	-	-	-	-	-	4	-	2	1	-	-	-	-	-	-	-	2	-
IL																						
EE	-	-	-	-	-	2	7	2	-	-	-	-	-	2	-	-	-	-	-	-	-	-
MD	7	-	-	8	-	7	-	-	-	-	-	5	8	-	5	-	-	-	4	7	-	-
BE																						
LV																						

CH	GR	GE	FR	RS	HR	BY	RO	AL	MT	PT	HU	LT	BA	IE	ES	IL	EE	MD	BE	LV	
–	1	4	–	4	–	5	–	4	–	–	3	6	–	–	–	8	5	5	–	–	RU
																					BG
																					NL
4	10	7	8	2	–	3	6	12	10	10	4	10	6	5	12	–	6	–	6	12	IT
																					CY
–	7	10	–	6	5	10	2	3	4	7	–	–	–	–	–	7	–	8	–	–	UA
5	–	–	–	–	–	–	–	–	–	–	–	1	–	3	–	–	7	–	–	–	FI
																					NO
																					AM
																					MK
10	–	–	–	–	–	–	–	–	–	4	12	–	1	–	2	–	–	–	–	–	IS
																					SK
–	2	–	1	–	–	2	–	6	7	3	–	3	–	6	–	1	–	4	–	5	GB
–	–	–	7	–	–	1	–	–	5	–	–	–	–	12	–	10	10	–	–	6	DK
7	–	3	–	–	3	–	–	–	2	–	2	–	7	–	–	–	–	–	–	–	AT
																					PL
–	6	1	10	1	4	4	3	–	6	–	10	–	5	4	5	12	12	3	4	–	SE
																					SM
8	4	–	3	–	1	8	–	–	–	–	–	2	3	–	3	–	–	–	5	8	DE
1	5	8	6	–	10	6	10	8	12	8	7	8	8	–	–	4	8	10	3	2	AZ
–	–	–	–	10	12	–	4	–	3	1	6	–	12	2	–	3	2	–	–	3	SI
																					TR
■	–	–	–	5	–	–	–	–	–	–	–	–	–	–	–	–	–	–	–	–	CH
2	■	6	–	3	–	–	8	10	–	–	8	–	–	–	–	–	–	1	8	–	GR
–	8	■	–	–	–	12	–	–	–	–	5	12	–	–	–	2	3	7	–	–	GE
–	12	2	■	–	6	–	–	2	1	2	–	–	4	–	10	–	–	2	12	1	FR
6	–	–	–	■	8	–	–	1	–	–	–	5	10	–	4	–	–	–	–	–	RS
					■																HR
						■															BY
–	–	–	–	–	–	–	■	–	–	–	1	–	–	1	8	6	1	12	10	–	RO
								■													AL
									■												MT
										■											PT
–	–	–	2	8	–	–	7	–	–	–	■	–	–	–	6	–	–	–	–	–	HU
–	–	12	–	7	2	–	1	–	–	–	–	■	–	10	1	–	–	–	–	7	LI
12	3	–	5	12	7	–	–	7	–	–	–	–	■	–	–	–	–	–	–	–	BA
–	–	–	–	–	–	–	–	–	8	6	–	–	2	■	7	–	–	–	7	10	IE
3	–	–	12	–	–	–	5	5	–	12	–	–	–	–	■	–	4	–	–	–	ES
																■					IL
–	–	–	–	–	–	–	–	–	–	–	–	7	–	7	–	5	■	6	2	4	EE
–	–	5	4	–	–	7	12	–	–	5	–	4	–	8	–	–	–	■	1	–	MD
																			■		BE
																				■	LV

*The marked grey countries did not participate in the final but gave points to the final entries.

2012

Light your fire

Country Hosting: Azerbaijan
City Hosting: Baku
Date: 22.5.2012 (First Semi Final), 24.5.2012 (Second Semi Final), 26.5.2012 (The Final)
Location: Baku Crystal Hall
Presenters: Leyla Aliyeva, Eldar Gasimov Nargiz Birk-Petersen,
Executive Supervisor: Jon Ola Sand
Directed By: Ladislaus Kiraly
Executive Producer: Adil Kerimli
Participating Countries: 42
Voting System: Televoting, the results given by 1-8, 10 and 12 points to the most popular song
Broadcaster: İctimai Television (İTV)

First Semi Final, 22.5.2012
10 marked grey countries qualified to the Final
(Spain, Italy and Azerbaijan were allowed to vote this semi-final)

No.	Country	Song	Performing Artist	Language	Points	Place
1	Montene-gro	"Euro Neuro"	Rambo Amadeus	English	20	15
2	Iceland	Never Forget""	Greta Salóme and Jónsi	English	75	8
3	Greece	"Aphrodisiac"	Eleftheria Eleftheriou	English	116	4
4	Latvia	"Beautiful Song"	Anmary	English	17	16
5	Albania	"Suus"	Rona Nishliu	Albanian	146	2
6	Romania	"Zaleilah"	Mandinga	Spanish	120	3
7	Switzerland	"Unbreakable"	Sinplus	English	45	11
8	Belgium	"Would You?"	Iris	English	16	17
9	Finland	"När jag blundar"	Pernilla Karlsson	Swedish	41	12
10	Israel	"Time"	"Izabo"	Hebrew, English	33	13
11	San Marino	"The Social Network Song (Oh Oh – Uh — Oh Oh)"	Valentina Monetta	English	31	14
12	Cyprus	"La La Love"	Ivi Adamou	English	91	7
13	Denmark	"Should've Known Better"	Soluna Samay	English	63	9
14	Russia	"Party for Everybody"	Buranovskiye Babushki	English, Udmurt	152	1
15	Hungary	"Sound of Our Hearts"	Compact Disco	English	52	10
16	Austria	"Woki mit deim Popo"	Trackshittaz	German	18	8
17	Moldova	"Läutar"	Pasha Parfeny	English	100	5
18	Ireland	"Waterline"	Jedward	English	92	6

Second Semi Final, 24.5.2012
10 marked grey countries qualified to the Final
(United Kingdom, Germany and France were allowed to vote this semi-final)

No.	Country	Song	Performing Artist	Language	Points	Place
1	Serbia	"Nije ljubav stvar"	Željko Joksimović	Serbian	159	2
2	North Macedonia	"Crno i belo"	Kaliopi	North Macedonian	53	9
3	Netherlands	"You and Me"	Joan Franka	English	35	15
4	Malta	"This Is the Night"	Kurt Calleja	English	70	7
5	Belarus	"We Are the Heroes"	Litesound	English	35	16
6	Portugal	"Vida minha"	Filipa Sousa	portuguese	39	13
7	Ukraine	"Be My Guest"	Gaitana	English	64	8
8	Bulgaria	"Love Unlimited"	Sofi Marinova	Bulgarian	45	11
9	Slovenia	"Verjamem"	Eva Boto	Slovenian	31	17
10	Croatia	"Nebo"	Nina Badrić	Croatian	42	12
11	Sweden	"Euphoria"	Loreen	English	181	1
12	Georgia	"I'm a Joker"	Anri Jokhadze	Georgian, English	36	14
13	Turkey	"Love Me Back"	Can Bonomo	English	80	5
14	Estonia	"Kuula"	Ott Lepland	Estonish	100	4
15	Slovakia	"Don't Close Your Eyes"	Max Jason Mai	English	22	18
16	Norway	"Stay"	Tooji	English	45	10
17	Bosnia and Herzegovina	"Korake ti znam"	Maya Sar	Serbo-Croatian	77	6
18	Lithuania	"Love Is Blind"	Donny Montell	English	104	3

FINAL — 26.5.2012

No.	Country	Song	Performing Artist	Lyrics	Composer	Language	Commentator	Spoker of Results	Points	Place
01	United Kingdom	"Love Will Set You Free"	Engelbert Humperdinck	Martin Terefe and Sacha Skarbek	Martin Terefe and Sacha Skarbek	English	Graham Norton	Scott Mills	12	25
02	Hungary	"Sound of Our Hearts"	Compact Disco (Behnam Lotfi, Gábor Pál, Csaba Walkó)	Behnam Lotfi, Gábor Pál, Csaba Walkó	Behnam Lotfi, Gábor Pál, Csaba Walkó	English	Gábor Gundel Takács	Éva Novodomszky	19	24
03	Albania	"Suus"	Rona Nishliu	Rona Nishliu	Florent Boshnjaku	Albanian	Andri Xhahu	Andri Xhahu	146	5
04	Lithuania	"Love Is Blind"	Donny Montell	Jodie Rose, Brandon Stone	Brandon Stone	English	Darius Užkuraitis	Ignas Krupavičius	70	14
05	Bosnia and Herzegovina	"Korake ti znam"	Maya Sar	Maya Sar	Maya Sar	Serbo-Croatian	Dejan Kukrić	Elvir Laković Laka	55	18
06	Russia	"Party for Everybody"	Buranovskiye Babushki, Granya Baysarova, Galina Koneva, Natalya Pugachyova, Valentina Pyatchenko, Olga Tuktareva, Ekaterina Shklyaeva)	Olga Tuktaryova, Marry S. Applegate	Viktor Drobych, Timofei Leontiev	Udmurt, English	Olga Shelest, Dmitry Guberniev	Oxana Fedorova	259	2
07	Iceland	"Never Forget"	Greta Salóme and Jónsi	Greta Salóme	Greta Salóme	English	Hrafnhildur Halldorsdóttir	Matthías Matthíasson	46	20
08	Cyprus	"La La Love"	Ivi Adamou	Alex Papaconstantinou, Björn Djupström, Alexandra Zakka, Viktor Svensson	Alex Papaconstantinou, Björn Djupström, Alexandra Zakka, Viktor Svensson	English	Melina Karageorgiou	Loucas Hamatsos	65	16
09	France	"Echo (You and I)"	Anggun	William Rousseau, Anggun	William Rousseau, Jean-Pierre Pilot	French, English	Cyril Féraud, Mireille Dumas	Amaury Vassili	21	22
10	Italy	"L'amore è femmina (Out of Love)"	Nina Zilli	Nina Zilli, Christian Rabb, Kristoffer Sjökvist, Frida Molander, Charlie Mason	Christian Rabb, Kristoffer Sjökvist, Frida Molander, Charlie Mason	Italian, English	Filippo Solibello, Marco Ardemagni	Ivan Bacchi	101	9
11	Estonia	"Kuula"	Ott Lepland	Aapo Ilves	Ott Lepland	Estonish	Marko Reikop	Getter Jaani	120	6
12	Norway	"Stay"	Tooji	Tooji, Peter Boström and Figge Boström	Tooji, Peter Boström and Figge Boström	English	Olav Viksmo-Slettan	Nadia Hasnaoui	7	26
13	Azerbaijan	"When the Music Dies"	Sabina Babayeva	Anders Bagge, Sandra Bjurman, Stefan Örn, Johan Kronlund	Anders Bagge, Sandra Bjurman, Stefan Örn, Johan Kronlund	English	Konul Arifgizi, Saleh Baghirov	Safura Alizadeh	150	4
14	Romania	"Zaleilah"	Mandinga (Barbara Isasi, Alex, Chupi, Zach (Vale), El Niño, Omar, Tony)	Omar Secada, Ioniţă, Elena Ionescu	Costi Ioniţă, Dimitriu Silviu	Spanish, English	Leonard Miron	Paula Seling	71	12
15	Denmark	"Should've Known Better"	Soluna Samay	Chief 1	Remee, Chief 1, Amir Sulaiman, Isam Bachiri	English	Ole Tøpholm	Louise Wolff	21	23
16	Greece	"Aphrodisiac"	Eleftheria Eleftheriou	Dimitri Stassos, Mikaela Stenström, Dajana Lööf	Dimitri Stassos, Mikaela Stenström, Dajana Lööf	English	Maria Kozakou	Adriana Magania	64	17
17	Sweden	"Euphoria"	Loreen	Peter Boström, SeventyEight	Thomas G:son, Peter Boström	English	Edward af Sillén, Gina Dirawi	Sarah Dawn Finer	372	1
18	Turkey	"Love Me Back"	Can Bonomo	Can Bonomo	Can Bonomo	English	Bülend Özveren	Ömer Önder	112	7
19	Spain	"Quédate conmigo"	Pastora Soler	Tony Sánchez-Ohlsson	Thomas G:son, Tony Sánchez-Ohlsson, Erik Bernholm	Spanish	José María Íñigo	Elena S. Sánchez	97	10
20	Germany	"Standing Still"	Roman Lob	Wayne Hector, Steve Robson, Jamie Cullum	Wayne Hector, Steve Robson, Jamie Cullum	English	Thomas Mohr	Anke Engelke	110	8
21	Malta	"This Is the Night"	Kurt Calleja	Johan Jämtberg, Kurt Calleja and Mikael Gunheras	Johan Jämtberg, Kurt Calleja and Mikael Gunheras	English	Elaine Saliba, Ronald Briffa	Keith Demicoli	41	21
22	North Macedonia	"Crno i belo"	Kaliopi	Kaliopi	Romeo Grill	North Macedonian	Karolina Petkovska	Kristina Talevska	71	13
23	Ireland	"Waterline"	Jedward (John Grimes, Edward Grimes)	Nick Jarl, Sharon Vaughn	Nick Jarl, Sharon Vaughn	English	Marty Whelan	Gráinne Seoige	46	19
24	Serbia	"Nije ljubav stvar"	Željko Joksimović	Marina Tucaković, Miloš Roganović	Željko Joksimović	Serbian	Duška Vučinić-Lučić	Maja Nikolić	214	3
25	Ukraine	"Be My Guest"	Gaitana	Gaitana	Gaitana	English	Timur Miroshnychenko, Tetiana Terekhova	Oleksiy Matias	65	15
26	Moldova	"Lăutar"	Pasha Parfeny	Pavel Parfeni	Pavel Parfeni, Alex Braşoveanu	English	Marcel Spătari	Olivia Fortuna	81	11

	Albania	Montenegro	Romania	Austria	Ukraine	Belarus	Belgium	Azerbaijan	Malta	San Marino	France	United Kingdom	Turkey	Greece	Bosnia and Herzegovina	Moldova	Bulgaria	Switzerland	Slovenia	Cyprus	Croatia
Albania	■	10	1	8	–	–	10	–	1	12	–	–	5	10	6	–	4	12	3	4	5
Montenegro		■																			
Romania	–	–	■	–	–	–	3	6	–	–	2	–	4	7	–	12	–	–	–	3	–
Austria				■																	
Ukraine	–	–	–	–	■	10	–	3	7	–	–	–	–	1	–	8	–	–	–	–	–
Belarus						■															
Belgium							■														
Azerbaijan	4	5	–	–	12	7	–	■	12	4	–	2	12	5	7	10	10	–	–	8	–
Malta	–	–	–	–	7	3	–	8	■	2	–	5	2	–	–	–	–	–	–	–	–
San Marino										■											
France	–	–	–	2	–	–	–	–	–	–	■	–	–	–	2	–	–	6	–	–	–
United Kingdom	–	–	–	–	–	–	1	–	–	–	–	■	–	–	–	–	–	–	–	–	–
Turkey	10	–	3	3	–	–	7	12	8	5	5	1	■	–	4	–	7	3	–	–	–
Greece		–	8	–	5	–	2	5	–	–	–	–	3	■	1	4	1	–	–	12	–
Bosnia and Herzegovina	–	6	–	7	–	–	–	–	–	–	–	–	10	–	■	–	–	1	7	–	10
Moldova	–	3	12	1	8	5	–	–	–	8	–	–	–	2	–	■	–	2	1	–	1
Bulgaria																	■				
Switzerland																		■			
Slovenia																			■		
Cyprus	6	–	2	–	–	–	–	2	–	–	–	–	–	12	–	–	–	–	–	■	–
Croatia																					■
Slovakia																					
North Macedonia	8		–	–	3	2	–	–	–	–	–	–	8	–	12	–	2	–	6	–	8
The Netherlands																					
Portugal																					
Iceland	–	–	–	–	–	–	–	–	–	–	–	–	–	–	–	–	–	–	4	1	–
Sweden	5	7	10	12	6	6	12	7	6	3	12	12	6	6	8	7	8	7	10	10	7
Norway	–	–	–	–	–	–	–	–	–	–	–	–	–	–	–	–	–	–	–	–	–
Lithuania	–	1	–	–	–	8	–	4	4	–	3	7	–	–	–	–	5	–	–	–	–
Estonia	–	–	–	–	1	4	–	–	–	–	10	4	–	–	–	2	–	–	–	–	–
Denmark	–	–	–	–	–	–	–	–	–	–	–	–	–	–	–	–	–	–	–	–	–
Latvia																					
Spain	–	–	6	6	–	–	6	–	–	1	6	8	–	–	5	–	3	8	–	6	–
Finland																					
Georgia																					
Italy	7	2	–	–	4	–	–	–	10	7	1	–	–	3	–	5	–	5	5	2	2
Serbia	1	12	5	10	2	–	5	–	5	6	8	–	–	8	10	3	12	10	12	7	12
Germany	2	–	–	4	–	–	–	–	2	–	7	6	–	–	–	–	–	4	2	–	4
Russia	3	4	4	5	10	12	8	10	3	10	4	3	7	4	3	6	6	–	8	5	6
Hungary	–	–	7	–	–	–	–	–	–	–	–	–	1	–	–	1	–	–	–	–	–
Israel																					
Ireland	–	–	–	–	–	1	4	1	–	–	–	10	–	–	–	–	–	–	–	–	3

Slovakia	North Macedonia	The Netherlands	Portugal	Iceland	Sweden	Norway	Lithuania	Estonia	Denmark	Latvia	Spain	Finland	Georgia	Italy	Serbia	Germany	Russia	Hungary	Israel	Ireland	
–	12	–	–	–	1	–	–	–	5	1	–	6	3	12	1	6	–	8	–	–	Albania
																					Montenegro
–	–	–	4	–	–	–	–	–	1	–	10	–	–	7	–	–	1	–	6	5	Romania
																					Austria
–	3	–	1	–	–	1	2	1	–	6	2	–	6	3	–	–	8	–	–	3	Ukraine
																					Belarus
																					Belgium
6	2	–	–	–	–	–	12	–	–	–	–	–	10	–	3	–	10	–	8	1	Azerbaijan
–	1	–	–	–	–	–	7	–	–	–	–	–	–	–	6	–	–	–	–	–	Malta
																					San Marino
–	–	–	–	6	2	–	–	–	–	3	–	–	–	–	–	–	–	–	–	–	France
–	–	–	–	–	–	–	–	5	–	2	–	–	–	–	–	–	–	–	–	4	United Kingdom
–	8	8	–	–	6	–	1	–	2	–	–	–	7	–	–	8	–	3	1	–	Turkey
–	–	–	–	–	–	–	–	–	–	–	–	–	1	–	4	1	3	–	2	–	Greece
2	7	–	–	–	–	–	–	–	–	–	–	–	–	5	–	–	–	–	–	–	Bosnia and Herzegovina
–	–	–	6	–	–	–	–	–	7	–	7	–	–	4	–	–	7	2	5	–	Moldova
																					Bulgaria
																					Switzerland
																					Slovenia
–	–	–	–	8	12	–	–	–	–	–	5	–	–	5	8	–	2	–	3	–	Cyprus
																					Croatia
■																					Slovakia
1	■	–	–	–	–	–	–	–	–	–	–	–	–	1	12	–	–	–	–	–	North Macedonia
		■																			The Netherlands
			■																		Portugal
4	–	–	–	■	–	5	–	6	6	–	4	7	–	–	–	3	–	6	–	–	Iceland
12	6	12	3	12	■	12	10	12	12	12	12	12	8	–	10	12	12	12	12	12	Sweden
–	–	3	–	1	3	■	–	–	–	–	–	–	–	–	–	–	–	–	–	–	Norway
–	–	1	–	–	–	6	■	3	–	4	–	–	12	–	–	–	5	–	–	7	Lithuania
10	–	7	7	10	8	7	8	■	–	8	6	10	–	–	–	4	6	–	–	8	Estonia
–	–	–	–	5	–	2	–	2	■	–	–	5	–	2	–	5	–	–	–	–	Denmark
										■											Latvia
–	–	6	12	2	4	–	–	4	–	–	■	3	–	–	–	–	–	1	10	–	Spain
												■									Finland
													■								Georgia
5	5	–	2	–	–	4	4	7	3	–	1	–	4	■	–	2	–	5	4	2	Italy
7	10	10	5	3	10	10	5	–	–	–	–	2	–	6	■	10	4	4	–	–	Serbia
–	–	2	10	–	–	3	3	10	10	7	3	1	2	8	–	■	–	10	–	10	Germany
3	4	4	8	7	7	8	6	8	8	10	8	8	5	10	7	7	■	7	7	6	Russia
8	–	–	–	–	–	–	–	–	–	–	–	–	–	–	–	2	–	■	–	–	Hungary
																			■		Israel
–	–	5	–	4	5	–	–	–	4	5	–	4	–	–	–	–	–	–	–	■	Ireland

*The marked grey countries did not participate in the final but gave points to the final entries.

2013

We Are One

Country Hosting: Sweden
City Hosting: Malmo
Date: 14.5.2013 (First Semi Final), 16.5.2013 (Second Semi Final), 18.5.2013 (The Final)
Location: Malmö Arena
Presenters: Petra Mede
Executive Supervisor: Jon Ola Sand
Directed By: Daniel Jelinek, Robin Hofwander, Sven Stojanovic
Executive Producer: Martin Österdahl
Participating Countries: 39
Voting System: Televoting, the results given by 1-8, 10 and 12 points to the most popular song
Broadcaster: Sveriges Television (SVT)

First Semi Final, 14.5.2013
10 marked grey countries qualified to the Final
(United Kingdom, Italy and Sweden were allowed to vote this semi-final)

No.	Country	Song	Performing Artist	Language	Points	Place
1	Austria	"Shine"	Natália Kelly	English	27	14
2	Estonia	"Et uus saaks alguse"	Birgit	Estonish	52	10
3	Slovenia	"Straight into Love"	Hannah	English	8	16
4	Croatia	"Mižerja"	Klapa s Mora	Croatian	38	13
5	Denmark	"Only Teardrops"	Emmelie de Forest	English	167	1
6	Russia	"What If"	Dina Garipova	English	156	2
7	Ukraine	"Gravity"	Zlata Ognevich	English	140	3
8	Netherlands	"Birds"	Anouk	English	75	6
9	Montenegro	"Igranka"	Who See	Serbian	41	12
10	Lithuania	"Something"	Andrius Pojavis	English	53	9
11	Belarus	"Solayoh"	Alyona Lanskaya	English	64	7
12	Moldova	"O mie"	Aliona Moon	Romanian	95	4
13	Ireland	"Only Love Survives"	Ryan Dolan	English	54	8
14	Cyprus	"An me thimasai"	Despina Olympiou	Greek	11	15
15	Belgium	"Love Kills"	Roberto Bellarosa	English	75	5
16	Serbia	"Ljubav je svuda"	Moje 3	Serbian	46	11

Second Semi Final, 16.5.2013
10 marked grey countries qualified to the Final
(Spain, Germany and France were allowed to vote this semi-final)

No.	Country	Song	Performing Artist	Language	Points	Place
1	Latvia	"Here We Go"	PeR	English	13	17
2	San Marino	"Crisalide (Vola)"	Valentina Monetta	Italian	47	11
3	North Macedonia	"Pred da se razdeni"	Esma & Lozano	North Macedonian, Romanian	28	16
4	Azerbaijan	"Hold Me"	Farid Mammadov	English	139	1
5	Finland	"Marry Me"	Krista Siegfrids	English	64	9
6	Malta	"Tomorrow"	Gianluca	English	118	4
7	Bulgaria	"Samo shampioni"	Elitsa Todorova & Stoyan Yankoulov	Bulgarian	45	12
8	Iceland	"Ég á líf"	Eythor Ingi	Iceland	72	6
9	Greece	"Alcohol Is Free"	Koza Mostra feat. Agathon Iakovidis	Greek	121	2
10	Israel	"Rak Bishvilo"	Moran Mazor	Hebrew	40	14
11	Armenia	"Lonely Planet"	Dorians	English	69	7
12	Hungary	"Kedvesem"	ByeAlex	Hungarian	66	8
13	Norway	"I Feed You My Love"	Margaret Berger	English	120	3
14	Albania	"Identitet"	Adrian Lulgjuraj & Bledar Sejko	Albanian	31	15
15	Georgia	"Waterfall"	Nodi Tatishvili & Sophie Gelovani	English	63	10
16	Switzerland	"You and Me"	Takasa	English	41	13
17	Romania	"It's My Life"	Cezar	English	83	5

FINAL   18.5.2013

No.	Country	Song	Performing Artist	Lyrics	Composer	Language	Commentator	Spoker of Results	Points	Place
01	France	"L'enfer et moi"	Amandine Bourgeois	Boris Bergman	David Salkin	French	Cyril Féraud, Mireille Dumas	Marine Vignes	14	23
02	Lithuania	"Something"	Andrius Pojavis	Andrius Pojavis	Andrius Pojavis	English	Darius Užkuraitis	Ignas Krupavičius	17	22
03	Moldova	"O mie"	Aliona Moon	Iuliana Scutaru	Pasha Parfeny	Romanian	Liana Stanciu	Sonia Argint	71	11
04	Finland	"Marry Me"	Krista Siegfrids	Krista Siegfrids, Erik Nyholm, Kristofer Karlsson, Jessika Lundström	Krista Siegfrids, Erik Nyholm, Kristofer Karlsson, Jessika Lundström	English	Aino Töllinen, Juuso Mäkilähde	Kristiina Wheeler	13	24
05	Spain	"Contigo hasta el final"	ESDM (Raquel del Rosario, David Feito, Juan Luis Suárez)	David Feito, Raquel del Rosario, Juan Luis Suárez	David Feito, Raquel del Rosario, Juan Luis Suárez	Spanish	José María Íñigo	Inés Paz	8	25
06	Belgium	"Love Kills"	Roberto Bellarosa	Jukka Immonen, Iain Farquharson	Jukka Immonen, Iain Farquharson	English	Maureen Louys, André Vermeulen	Barbara Louys	71	12
07	Estonia	"Et uus saaks alguse"	Birgit	Mihkel Mattisen, Silvia Soro	Mihkel Mattisen, Silvia Soro	Estonish	Marko Reikop	Rolf Roosalu	19	20
08	Belarus	"Solayoh"	Alyona Lanskaya	Martin King	Marc Paelinck	English	Evgeny Perlin	Darya Domracheva	48	16
09	Malta	"Tomorrow"	Gianluca	Boris Cezek, Dean Muscat	Boris Cezek, Dean Muscat	English	Gordon Bonello, Rodney Gauci	Emma Hickey	120	8
10	Russia	"What If"	Dina Garipova	Gabriel Alares, Joakim Björnberg, Leonid Gutkin	Gabriel Alares, Joakim Björnberg, Leonid Gutkin	English	Yana Churikova, Yuriy Aksuuta	Alsou	174	5
11	Germany	"Glorious"	Cascada	Yann Peifer, Manuel Reuter, Andres Ballinas, Tony Cornelissen	Yann Peifer, Manuel Reuter, Andres Ballinas, Tony Cornelissen	English	Peter Urban	Lena	18	21
12	Armenia	"Lonely Planet"	Dorians	Vardan Zadoyan	Tony Iommi	English	Erik Antaranyan, Anna Avanesyan	André	41	18
13	Netherlands	"Birds"	Anouk	Anouk Teeuwe	Tore Johansson, Martin Gjerstad	English	Jan Smit, Daniël Dekker	Cornald Maas	114	9
14	Romania	"It's My Life"	Cezar	Cristian Faur	Cristian Faur	English	Liana Stanciu	Sonia Argint	65	13
15	United Kingdom	"Believe in Me"	Bonnie Tyler	Desmond Child, Lauren Christy, Christopher Braide	Desmond Child, Lauren Christy, Christopher Braide	English	Graham Norton	Scott Mills	23	19
16	Sweden	"You"	Robin Stjernberg	Robin Stjernberg, Linnea Deb, Joy Deb, Joakim Harestad Haukaas	Robin Stjernberg, Linnea Deb, Joy Deb, Joakim Harestad Haukaas	English	Josefine Sundström, Björn Kjellman	Yohio	62	14
17	Hungary	"Kedvesem"	ByeAlex	Alex Márta	Alex Márta, Zoltán Palásti Kovács Zoohacker	Hungarian	Gábor Gundel Takács	Éva Novodomszky	84	10
18	Denmark	"Only Teardrops"	Emmelie de Forest	Lise Cabble, Julia Fabrin Jakobsen, Thomas Stengaard	Lise Cabble, Julia Fabrin Jakobsen, Thomas Stengaard	English	Ole Tøpholm	Sofie Lassen-Kahlke	281	1
19	Iceland	"Ég á líf"	Eythor Ingi	Örlygur Smári, Pétur Örn Gudmundsson	Örlygur Smári, Pétur Örn Gudmundsson	Iceland	Felix Bergsson	María Sigrún Hilmarsdóttir	47	17
20	Azerbaijan	"Hold Me"	Farid Mammadov	John Ballard, Ralph Charlie	Dimitris Kontopoulos	English	Konul Arifgizi	Tamilla Shirinova	234	2
21	Greece	"Alcohol Is Free"	Koza Mostra feat. Agathon Iakovidis	Stathis Pahidis	Ilias Kozas	Greek, English	Maria Kozakou, Giorgos Kapoutzidis	Adriana Magania	152	6
22	Ukraine	"Gravity"	Zlata Ognevich	Karen Kavaleryan	Mikhail Nekrasov	English	Timur Miroshnychenko, Tetiana Terekhova	Matias	214	3
23	Italy	"L'essenziale"	Marco Mengoni	Marco Mengoni, Casalino, De Benedettis	Roberto Casalino, Francesco De Benedettis	Italian	Filippo Solibello, Marco Ardemagni, Natascha Lusenti	Federica Gentile	126	7
24	Norway	"I Feed You My Love"	Margaret Berger	MachoPsycho, Karin Park	MachoPsycho, Karin Park	English	Olav Viksmo-Slettan	Tooji	191	4
25	Georgia	"Waterfall"	Nodi Tatishvili and Sophie Gelovani	Thomas G:son	Thomas G:son, Erik Bernholm	English	Temo Kvirkvelia	Liza Tsiklauri	50	15
26	Ireland	"Only Love Survives"	Ryan Dolan	Wez Devine and Ryan Dolan	Wez Devine and Ryan Dolan	English	Marty Whelan	Nicky Byrne	5	26

	San Marino	Sweden	Albania	The Netherlands	Austria	United Kingdom	Israel	Serbia	Ukraine	Hungary	Romania	Moldova	Azerbaijan	Norway	Armenia	Italy	Finland	Spain	Belarus	Latvia
San Marino	■																			
Sweden	–	■	–	3	–	–	–	1	–	–	–	5	–	12	–	–	4	–	–	4
Albania			■																	
The Netherlands	–	8	4	■	8	6	–	–	–	5	2	–	–	8	–	–	8	–	–	–
Austria					■															
United Kingdom	–	1	–	–	–	■	–	–	–	–	3	–	–	–	–	–	–	4	–	–
Israel							■													
Serbia								■												
Ukraine	–	–	–	5	1	5	10	10	■	7	4	12	12	1	12	5	–	10	12	7
Hungary	6	3	8	7	–	–	–	2	–	■	–	–	–	2	–	3	10	–	–	–
Romania	–	4	5	–	4	4	–	–	–	–	■	10	6	6	–	1	–	–	–	–
Moldova	–	–	–	–	2	–	1	6	8	–	12	■	1	–	–	4	–	2	4	–
Azerbaijan	2	–	7	2	12	–	12	5	10	12	10	8	■	–	–	–	–	7	10	3
Norway	7	12	2	6	–	–	6	7	3	2	8	2	2	■	3	8	12	5	3	8
Armenia	1	–	–	–	–	–	–	–	6	3	–	1	–	–	■	–	–	–	2	–
Italy	4	–	12	–	10	–	–	4	–	–	1	–	–	–	1	■	–	12	–	–
Finland	3	–	–	–	–	–	4	–	–	–	–	–	–	–	–	–	■	–	–	–
Spain	–	–	6	–	–	–	–	–	–	–	–	–	–	–	–	2	–	■	–	–
Belarus	–	–	–	–	–	–	3	–	12	–	–	4	7	–	5	–	–	–	■	–
Latvia																				■
Bulgaria																				
Belgium	5	7	–	12		3	–	3	–	4	–	–	–	3	–	–	3	–	–	2
Russia	–	5	–	4	–	10	7	8	4	–	–	7	–	–	7	–	2	6	8	12
Malta	10	–	–	8	–	7	–	–	2	8	5	–	8	10	6	10	–	1	7	5
Estonia	–	–	–	–	–	–	–	–	–	–	–	–	–	–	–	–	–	6	–	10
Germany	–	–	3	–	6	–	5	–	–	–	–	–	–	–	–	–	–	3	–	–
Iceland	–	6	–	–	–	2	–	–	–	6	–	–	–	4	–	–	5	–	–	–
France	8	–	–	–	–	–	–	–	–	–	–	–	–	–	2	–	–	–	–	–
Greece	12	–	10	1	7	8	2	–	–	1	7	–	4	5	8	7	1	–	6	1
Ireland	–	2	–	–	–	1	–	–	–	–	–	–	–	–	–	–	–	–	–	–
Denmark	–	10	1	10	5	12	8	12	5	10	6	6	5	7	4	12	7	8	1	6
Montenegro																				
Slovenia																				
Georgia	–	–	–	–	–	–	–	–	7	–	–	3	10	–	10	–	–	–	–	–
North Macedonia																				
Cyprus																				
Croatia																				
Switzerland																				
Lithuania	–	–	–	–	–	–	–	–	1	–	–	–	3	–	–	6	–	–	5	–

Bulgaria	Belgium	Russia	Malta	Estonia	Germany	Iceland	France	Greece	Ireland	Denmark	Montenegro	Slovenia	Georgia	North Macedonia	Cyprus	Croatia	Switzerland	Lithuania	
																			San Marino
4	1	–	–	1	3	4	–	–	5	8	–	6	–	–	–	1	–	–	Sweden
																			Albania
–	12	3	–	7	–	8	–	–	6	10	–	7	–	2	–	2	4	4	The Netherlands
																			Austria
–	–	–	5	–	–	–	–	–	7	–	–	1	–	–	–	–	2	–	United Kingdom
																			Israel
																			Serbia
10	8	1	10	10	–	3	–	8	8	3	–	–	8	–	10	12	–	10	Ukraine
6	–	–	–	4	12	–	–	2	–	–	–	–	–	–	–	4	10	5	Hungary
–	–	–	7	–	–	6	1	10	–	–	1	–	–	–	–	–	–	–	Romania
3	3	6	–	–	–	–	4	–	3	–	5	–	–	7	–	–	–	–	Moldova
12	5	12	12	–	4	7	8	12	2	–	12	3	12	–	8	7	6	12	Azerbaijan
1	7	7	3	3	7	10	–	4	–	12	4	5	4	8	4	3	7	6	Norway
8	–	2	1	–	–	–	7	–	–	–	–	–	10	–	–	–	–	–	Armenia
–	6	–	8	–	–	–	10	6	–	–	6	8	2	10	6	8	12	–	Italy
–	–	–	–	–	1	–	3	–	–	2	–	–	–	–	–	–	–	–	Finland
–	–	–	–	–	–	–	–	–	–	–	–	–	–	–	–	–	–	–	Spain
–	–	–	2	–	–	–	–	1	–	–	3	–	5	5	–	–	–	1	Belarus
																			Latvia
■																			Bulgaria
–	■	8	–	2	–	–	5	–	4	5	–	2	–	–	–	–	–	–	Belgium
5	4	■	–	12	2	1	6	–	10	7	7	10	6	6	5	6	–	7	Russia
–	–	–	■	5	5	5	2	3	–	4	–	–	3	3	3	–	–	–	Malta
–	–	–	–	■	–	–	–	–	–	–	–	–	–	–	–	–	–	3	Estonia
–	–	–	–	–	■	–	–	–	–	–	–	–	–	–	–	–	1	–	Germany
–	–	–	–	6	8	■	–	–	–	1	–	4	–	–	–	–	5	–	Iceland
–	–	–	–	–	–	2	■	–	–	–	–	–	–	1	1	–	–	–	France
7	2	10	4	–	6	–	–	■	–	6	8	–	–	4	12	5	8	–	Greece
–	–	–	–	–	–	–	–	–	■	–	–	–	–	–	2	–	–	–	Ireland
2	10	4	6	8	10	12	12	7	12	■	10	12	7	12	7	10	3	2	Denmark
											■								Montenegro
												■							Slovenia
–	–	5	–	–	–	–	–	5	–	–	2	–	■	–	–	–	–	8	Georgia
														■					North Macedonia
															■				Cyprus
																■			Croatia
																	■		Switzerland
–	–	–	–	–	–	–	–	–	1	–	–	–	1	–	–	–	–	■	Lithuania

*The marked grey countries did not participate in the final but gave points to the final entries.

2014

#Join US

Country Hosting: Denmark
City Hosting: Copenhagen
Date: 6.5.2014 (First Semi Final), 8.5.2014 (Second Semi Final), 10.5.2014 (The Final)
Location: B&W Hallerne
Presenters: Lise Rønne, Nikolaj Koppel, Pilou Asbæk
Executive Supervisor: Jon Ola Sand
Directed By: Per Zachariassen
Executive Producer: Pernille Gaardbo
Participating Countries: 37
Voting System: Televoting, the results given by 1-8, 10 and 12 points to the most popular song
Broadcaster: Danmarks Radio (DR)

First Semi Final, 6.5.2014
10 marked grey countries qualified to the Final
(Spain, Denmark and France were allowed to vote this semi-final)

No.	Country	Song	Performing Artist	Language	Points	Place
1	Armenia	"Not Alone"	Aram MP3	English	121	4
2	Latvia	"Cake to Bake"	Aarzemnieki	English	33	13
3	Estonia	"Amazing"	Tanja	English	36	12
4	Sweden	"Undo"	Sanna Nielsen	English	131	2
5	Iceland	"No Prejudice"	Pollapönk	English	61	8
6	Albania	"One Night's Anger"	Hersi	English	22	15
7	Russia	"Shine"	Tolmachevy Sisters	English	63	6
8	Azerbaijan	"Start a Fire"	Dilara Kazimova	English	57	9
9	Ukraine	"Tick-Tock"	Mariya Yaremchuk	English	118	5
10	Belgium	"Mother"	Axel Hirsoux	English	28	14
11	Moldova	"Wild Soul"	Cristina Scarlat	English	13	16
12	San Marino	"Maybe"	Valentina Monetta	English	40	10
13	Portugal	"Quero ser tua"	Suzy	portuguese	39	11
14	Netherlands	"Calm After the Storm"	The Common Linnets	English	150	1
15	Montenegro	"Moj svijet"	Sergej Ćetković	Serbian	63	7
16	Hungary	"Running"	András Kállay-Saunders	English	127	3

Second Semi Final, 8.5.2014
10 marked grey countries qualified to the Final
(United Kingdom, Germany and Italy were allowed to vote this semi-final)

No.	Country	Song	Performing Artist	Language	Points	Place
1	Malta	"Coming Home"	Firelight	English	63	9
2	Israel	"Same Heart"	Mei Finegold	Hebrew, English	19	14
3	Norway	"Silent Storm"	Carl Espen	English	77	6
4	Georgia	"Three Minutes to Earth"	The Shin and Mariko	English	15	15
5	Poland	"My Słowianie — We Are Slavic"	Donatan & Cleo	Poland, English	70	8
6	Austria	"Rise Like a Phoenix"	Conchita Wurst	English	169	1
7	Lithuania	"Attention"	Vilija	English	36	11
8	Finland	"Something Better"	Softengine	English	97	3
9	Ireland	"Heartbeat"	Can-Linn feat. Kasey Smith	English	35	12
10	Belarus	"Cheesecake"	Teo	English	87	5
11	North Macedonia	"To the Sky"	Tijana	English	33	13
12	Switzerland	"Hunter of Stars"	Sebalter	English	92	4
13	Greece	"Rise Up"	Freaky Fortune feat. RiskyKidd	English	74	7
14	Slovenia	"Round and Round"	Tinkara Kovač	Slovenian, English	52	10
15	Romania	"Miracle"	Paula Seling & Ovi	English	125	2

FINAL

10.5.2014

No.	Country	Song	Performing Artist	Lyrics	Composer	Language	Commentator	Spoker of Results	Points	Place
01	Ukraine	"Tick-Tock"	Mariya Yaremchuk	Mariya Yaremchuk, Sandra Bjurman	Mariya Yaremchuk	English	Timur Miroshnychenko, Tetiana Terekhova	Zlata Ognevich	113	6
02	Belarus	"Cheesecake"	Teo	Dmitry Novik	Yuri Vashchuk	English	Evgeny Perlin	Alyona Lanskaya	43	16
03	Azerbaijan	"Start a Fire"	Dilara Kazimova	Stefan Örn, Johan Kronlund, Alessandra Günthardt	Stefan Örn, Johan Kronlund, Alessandra Günthardt	English	Konul Arifgizi	Sabina Babayeva	33	22
04	Iceland	"No Prejudice"	Pollapönk (Heiðar Örn Kristjánsson, Haraldur Freyr Gíslason, Guðni Þórarinn, Finnsson Arnar Þór Gíslason)	Heiðar Örn Kristjánsson, Haraldur F. Gíslason, John Grant.	Heiðar Örn Kristjánsson	English	Felix Bergsson	Benedict Valsson	58	15
05	Norway	"Silent Storm"	Carl Espen	Josefin Winther	Josefin Winther	English	Olav Viksmo-Slettan	Margrethe Røed	88	8
06	Romania	"Miracle"	Paula Seling & Ovi	Beyond 51, Frida Amundsen, Cernauțeanu, Philip Halloun	Beyond 51	English	Bogdan Stănescu	Sonia Argint-Ionescu	72	12
07	Armenia	"Not Alone"	Aram MP3	Garik Papoyan	Aram Sargsyan	English	Tigran Danielyan, Arevik Udumyan	Anna Avanesyan	174	4
08	Montenegro	"Moj svijet"	Sergej Ćetković	Sergej Ćetković, Emina Jahović	Sergej Ćetković,	Serbian	Dražen Bauković, Tamara Ivanković	Tijana Mišković	37	9
09	Poland	"My Słowianie – We Are Slavic"	Donatan & Cleo	Cleo	Cleo	Polish, English	Artur Orzech	Paulina Chylewska	62	14
10	Greece	"Rise Up"	Freaky Fortune feat. RiskyKidd	Freaky Fortune, RiskyKidd	Freaky Fortune	English	Maria Kozakou	Andrianna Maggania	35	20
11	Austria	"Rise Like a Phoenix"	Conchita Wurst	Charlie Mason, Joey Patulka, Ali Zuckowski, Julian Maas	Charlie Mason, Joey Patulka, Ali Zuckowski, Julian Maas	English	Andi Knoll	Kati Bellowitsch	290	1
12	Germany	"Is It Right"	Elaiza	Elżbieta Steinmetz, Adam Kesselhaut	Elżbieta Steinmetz, Adam Kesselhaut	English	Peter Urban	Helene Fischer	39	18
13	Sweden	"Undo"	Sanna Nielsen	Fredrik Kempe, David Kreuger, Hamed "K-One" Pirouzpanah	Fredrik Kempe, David Kreuger, Hamed "K-One" Pirouzpanah	English	Malin Olsson, Edward af Sillén	Alcazar	218	3
14	France	"Moustache"	TWIN TWIN (Lorent Idir, François Djemel, Patrick Biyik)	Lorent Idir, François Ardouvin	Pierre Beyres, Kim N'Guyen	French	Cyril Féraud, Natasha St-Pier	Elodie Suigo	2	26
15	Russia	"Shine"	Tolmachevy Sisters	John Ballard, Ralph Charlie, Gerard James Borg	Philipp Kirkorov, Dimitris Kontopoulos	English	Olga Shelest, Dmitriy Guberniev	Alsou	89	7
16	Italy	"La mia città"	Emma	Emma Marrone	Emma Marrone	Italian	Linus, Nicola Savino	Linus	33	21
17	Slovenia	"Round and Round"	Tinkara Kovač	Tinkara Kovač, Hannah Mancini, Tina Piš	Raay	Slovenian, English	Andrej Hofer	Ula Furlan	9	25
18	Finland	"Something Better"	Softengine (Topi Latukka, Ossi Mäkelä, Tuomo Alarinta)	Topi Latukka, Henri Oskár	Topi Latukka	English	Jorma Hietamäki, Sanna Pirkkalainen	Redrama	72	11
19	Spain	"Dancing in the Rain"	Ruth Lorenzo	Ruth Lorenzo, Jim Irvin, Julian Emery	Ruth Lorenzo, Jim Irvin, Julian Emery	Spanish, English	José María Íñigo	Carolina Casado	74	10
20	Switzerland	"Hunter of Stars"	Sebalter	Sebastiano Paù-Lessi	Sebastiano Paù-Lessi	English	Sven Epiney, Sandy Altermatt, Alessandro Bertoglio, Jean-Marc Richard and Valérie Ogier	Kurt Aeschbacher	64	13
21	Hungary	"Running"	András Kállay-Saunders	András Kállay-Saunders, István Tabár	András Kállay-Saunders, Krisztián Szakos	English	Gábor Gundel Takács	Éva Novodomszky	143	5
22	Malta	"Coming Home"	Firelight (Michelle Mifsud, Richard Edward Micallef, Tony Polidano, Daniel Micallef, Wayne Williams, Leslie Decesare)	Richard Micallef	Richard Micallef	English	Carlo Borg Bonaci	Valentina Rossi	32	23
23	Denmark	"Cliché Love Song"	Basim	Basim, Lasse Lindorff, Kim Novak-Zorde, Daniel Fält	Basim, Lasse Lindorff, Kim Novak-Zorde, Daniel Fält	English	Anders Bisgaard	Sofie Lassen-Kahlke	74	9
24	Netherlands	"Calm After the Storm"	The Common Linnets	Lise DeLange, JB Meijers, Rob Crosby, Matthew Crosby, Jake Etheridge	Lise DeLange, JB Meijers, Rob Crosby, Matthew Crosby, Jake Etheridge	English	Cornald Maas, Jan Smit	Tim Douwsma	238	2
25	San Marino	"Maybe"	Valentina Monetta	Mauro Balestri	Ralph Siegel	English	Lia Fiorio, Gigi Restivo	Michele Perniola	14	24
26	United Kingdom	"Children of the Universe"	Molly	Molly Smitten-Downes, Anders Hansson	Molly Smitten-Downes, Anders Hansson	English	Graham Norton	Scott Mills	40	17

	Azerbaijan	Greece	Poland	Albania	San Marino	Denmark	Montenegro	Romania	Russia	The Netherlands	Malta	France	United Kingdom	Latvia	Armenia	Iceland	North Macedonia	Sweden	Belarus
Azerbaijan	■	–	–	–	12	–	–	–	10	–	–	–	–	–	–	–	–	–	3
Greece	4	■	–	2	–	–	–	–	4	–	1	–	2	–	7	–	–	–	6
Poland	2	1	■	–	–	–	4	–	–	–	–	5	–	–	–	3	5	2	7
Albania				■															
San Marino	3	–	–	3	■	–	–	–	–	–	–	–	–	–	3	–	–	–	–
Denmark	–	–	6	–	1	■	–	4	–	1	–	3	3	–	1	8	–	8	–
Montenegro	–	–	–	6	–	–	■	–	–	–	–	–	–	–	12	–	12	–	–
Romania	6	–	–	–	–	–	–	■	–	–	8	–	–	–	–	–	4	–	1
Russia	12	10	–	–	–	–	–	–	■	–	5	–	–	2	10	–	6	–	12
The Netherlands	–	8	12	–	2	10	–	3	3	■	–	8	8	12	4	12	7	10	2
Malta	5	–	–	1	4	–	–	–	–	5	■	–	10	–	–	–	–	–	–
France	–	–	–	–	–	–	–	–	–	–	–	■	–	–	–	–	–	1	–
United Kingdom	–	–	–	–	5	7	–	–	–	–	4	–	■	–	–	4	–	–	–
Latvia														■					
Armenia	–	7	1	–	6	2	10	7	8	7	6	12	–	10	■	2	8	5	10
Iceland	–	–	–	–	8	5	–	–	1	6	–	7	4	–	–	■	–	4	–
North Macedonia																	■		
Sweden	–	2	4	7	10	12	3	12	2	8	7	4	7	8	–	7	–	■	–
Belarus	7	–	–	–	–	–	1	–	12	–	–	–	–	–	8	–	–	–	■
Germany	–	–	8	4	–	–	–	2	–	–	–	–	–	–	6	–	–	–	–
Israel																			
Portugal																			
Norway	–	3	7	–	–	6	–	1	–	10	2	2	–	5	–	1	–	3	4
Estonia																			
Hungary	8	6	–	8	7	3	12	10	6	4	–	–	–	1	–	6	10	7	5
Moldova																			
Ireland																			
Finland	–	–	3	–	3	4	–	–	–	2	–	–	6	3	–	5	–	6	–
Lithuania																			
Austria	1	12	–	5	–	8	2	8	5	12	10	10	12	6	–	10	3	12	–
Spain	–	–	2	12	–	–	–	5	–	–	–	6	5	4	2	–	–	–	–
Belgium																			
Italy	–	–	–	10	–	–	6	–	–	–	12	1	–	–	–	–	2	–	–
Ukraine	10	5	5	–	–	1	7	–	7	–	–	–	–	7	–	–	–	–	8
Switzerland	–	4	10	–	–	–	5	6	–	3	3	–	1	–	5	–	–	–	–
Georgia																			
Slovenia	–	–	–	–	–	–	8	–	–	–	–	–	–	–	–	–	1	–	–

Germany	Israel	Portugal	Norway	Estonia	Hungary	Moldova	Ireland	Finland	Lithuania	Austria	Spain	Belgium	Italy	Ukraine	Switzerland	Georgia	Slovenia	
–	–	–	–	–	–	–	–	–	–	–	–	–	–	1	–	7	–	Azerbaijan
–	2	–	–	–	–	–	–	–	–	–	–	–	3	–	–	4	–	Greece
10	–	–	2	–	3	2	–	–	–	–	–	–	8	7	–	–	1	Poland
																		Albania
–	–	–	–	–	4	1	–	–	–	–	–	–	–	–	–	–	–	San Marino
8	–	5	1	–	–	–	–	6	1	–	3	6	–	–	3	–	6	Denmark
–	–	–	–	–	–	–	–	–	–	–	–	–	–	–	–	–	7	Montenegro
–	8	1	4	–	–	12	2	–	–	8	8	5	5	–	–	–	–	Romania
–	3	2	–	1	–	8	–	–	6	–	–	–	–	4	–	8	–	Russia
12	–	10	12	12	12	–	10	8	12	10	7	8	4	–	10	–	10	The Netherlands
–	–	–	–	–	–	–	3	3	–	–	–	–	1	–	–	–	–	Malta
–	–	–	–	–	–	–	–	1	–	–	–	–	–	–	–	–	–	France
–	–	–	3	–	–	–	8	–	–	–	5	1	–	–	–	3	–	United Kingdom
																		Latvia
6	6	4	–	5	7	3	–	4	–	12	4	–	–	10	–	12	–	Armenia
2	–	–	6	–	5	–	–	–	–	2	1	–	7	–	–	–	–	Iceland
																		North Macedonia
–	10	8	8	10	8	6	4	10	7	6	10	10	–	12	6	2	8	Sweden
–	1	–	–	–	–	5	–	–	3	–	–	–	–	6	–	–	–	Belarus
■	–	–	–	–	–	–	–	–	–	–	–	–	–	5	7	5	2	Germany
	■																	Israel
		■																Portugal
5	–	3	■	3	–	–	7	7	8	1	–	–	–	–	5	–	5	Norway
				■														Estonia
–	7	6	–	7	■	4	1	5	–	7	2	7	–	3	1	–	–	Hungary
						■												Moldova
							■											Ireland
4	–	–	7	6	6	–	–	■	–	4	–	3	6	–	4	–	–	Finland
																		Lithuania
7	12	12	10	4	10	7	12	12	10	■	12	12	12	8	12	10	12	Austria
1	4	–	5	2	–	–	6	–	4	–	■	2	–	2	8	–	4	Spain
												■						Belgium
–	–	–	–	–	–	–	–	–	–	–	–	–	■	–	2	–	–	Italy
–	5	–	–	8	2	10	–	2	5	5	6	4	10	■	–	–	–	Ukraine
3	–	7	–	–	1	–	5	–	2	3	–	–	2	–	■	1	3	Switzerland
																■		Georgia
–	–	–	–	–	–	–	–	–	–	–	–	–	–	–	–	–	■	Slovenia

*The marked grey countries did not participate in the final but gave points to the final entries.

2015

Building Bridges

Country Hosting: Austria
City Hosting: Vienna
Date: 19.5.2015 (First Semi Final), 21.5.2015 (Second Semi Final), 23.5.2015 (The Final)
Location: Wiener Stadthalle
Presenters: Arabella Kiesbauer, Alice Tumler, Mirjam Weichselbraun, Conchita Wurst (green room)
Executive Supervisor: Jon Ola Sand
Directed By: Kurt Pongratz
Executive Producer: Edgar Böhm
Participating Countries: 40
Voting System: Televoting, the results given by 1-8, 10 and 12 points to the most popular song
Broadcaster: Österreichischer Rundfunk (ORF)

First Semi Final, 19.5.2015
10 marked grey countries qualified to the Final
(Austria, Australia and France were allowed to vote this semi-final)

No.	Country	Song	Performing Artist	Language	Points	Place
1	Moldova	"I Want Your Love"	Eduard Romanyuta	English	41	11
2	Armenia	"Face the Shadow"	Genealogy	English	77	7
3	Belgium	"Rhythm Inside"	Loïc Nottet	English	149	2
4	Netherlands	"Walk Along"	Trijntje Oosterhuis	English	33	14
5	Finland	"Aina mun pitää"	Pertti Kurikan Nimipäivät	Finish	13	16
6	Greece	"One Last Breath"	Maria Elena Kyriakou	English	81	6
7	Estonia	"Goodbye to Yesterday"	Elina Born & Stig Rästa	English	105	3
8	North Macedonia	"Autumn Leaves"	Daniel Kajmakoski	English	28	15
9	Serbia	"Beauty Never Lies"	Bojana Stamenov	English	63	9
10	Hungary	"Wars for Nothing"	Boggie	English	67	8
11	Belarus	"Time"	Uzari & Maimuna	English	39	12
12	Russia	"A Million Voices"	Polina Gagarina	English	182	1
13	Denmark	"The Way You Are"	Anti-Social Media	English	33	13
14	Albania	"I'm Alive"	Elhaida Dani	English	62	10
15	Romania	"De la capăt"	Voltaj	Romanian, English	89	5
16	Georgia	"Warrior"	Nina Sublatti	English	98	4

Second Semi Final, 21.5.2015
10 marked grey countries qualified to the Final
(United Kingdom, Italy, Australia and Germany were allowed to vote this semi-final)

No.	Country	Song	Performing Artist	Language	Points	Place
1	Lithuania	"This Time"	Monika Linkytė & Vaidas Baumila	English	67	7
2	Ireland	"Playing with Numbers"	Molly Sterling	English	35	12
3	San Marino	"Chain of Lights"	Anita Simoncini & Michele Perniola	English	11	16
4	Montenegro	"Adio"	Knez	Serbian	57	9
5	Malta	"Warrior"	Amber	English	43	11
6	Norway	"A Monster Like Me"	Mørland & Debrah Scarlett	English	123	4
7	Portugal	"Há um mar que nos separa"	Leonor Andrade	portuguese	19	14
8	Czech Republic	"Hope Never Dies"	Marta Jandová & Václav Noid Bárta	English	33	13
9	Israel	"Golden Boy"	Nadav Guedj	English	151	3
10	Latvia	"Love Injected"	Aminata	English	155	2
11	Azerbaijan	"Hour of the Wolf"	Elnur Huseynov	English	53	10
12	Iceland	"Unbroken"	Maria Olafs	English	14	15
13	Sweden	"Heroes"	Måns Zelmerlöw	English	217	1
14	Switzerland	"Time to Shine"	Mélanie René	English	4	17
15	Cyprus	"One Thing I Should Have Done"	John Karayiannis	English	87	6
16	Slovenia	"Here for You"	Maraaya	English	92	5
17	Poland	"In the Name of Love"	Monika Kuszyńska	English	57	8

FINAL

23.5.2015

No.	Country	Song	Performing Artist	Lyrics	Composer	Language	Commentator	Spoker of Results	Points	Place
01	Slovenia	"Here for You"	Maraaya (Aleš "Raay" Vovk Marjetka Vovk)	Raay, Charlie Mason	Raay, Marjetka Vovk	English	Andrej Hofer	Tinkara Kovač	39	14
02	France	"N'oubliez pas"	Lisa Angell	M. Albert, Laure Izon	Michel Illouz, M. Albert	French	Stéphane Bern, Marianne James	Virginie Guilhaume	4	25
03	Israel	"Golden Boy"	Nadav Guedj	Doron Madali	Doron Madali	English	-	Ofer Nachshon	97	9
04	Estonia	"Goodbye to Yesterday"	Elina Born & Stig Rästa	Stig Rästa	Stig Rästa	English	Marko Reikop	Tanja	106	7
05	United Kingdom	"Still in Love with You"	Electro Velvet	David Mindel, Adrian Bax Grey	David Mindel, Adrian Bax Grey	English	Ken Bruce	Nigella Lawson	5	24
06	Armenia	"Face the Shadow"	Genealogy (Essaï Altounjan, Inga Arshakyan, Tamar Kaprelian, Mary-Jean O'Doherty, Vahe Tilbian, Stephanie Topalian)	Inna Mkrtchyan	Armen Martirosyan	English	Avet Barseghyan, Arevik Udumyan	Lilit Muradyan	34	16
07	Lithuania	"This Time"	Monika Linkytė & Vaidas Baumila	Vytautas Bikus, Monika Liubinaitė	Vytautas Bikus, Monika Liubinaitė	English	Darius Užkuraitis	Ugnė Galadauskaitė	30	18
08	Serbia	"Beauty Never Lies"	Bojana Stamenov	Charlie Mason	Vladimir Graić	English	Duška Vučinić	Maja Nikolić	53	10
09	Norway	"A Monster Like Me"	Mørland & Debrah Scarlett	Kjetil Mørland	Kjetil Mørland	English	Olav Viksmo-Slettan	Margrethe Røed	102	8
10	Sweden	"Heroes"	Måns Zelmerlöw	Anton Malmberg Hård af Segerstad, Joy Deb, Linnea Deb	Anton Malmberg Hård af Segerstad, Joy Deb, Linnea Deb	English	Sanna Nielsen, Edward af Sillén	Mariette Hansson	365	1
11	Cyprus	"One Thing I Should Have Done"	John Karayiannis	Mike Connaris, Giannis Karagiannis	Mike Connaris, Giannis Karagiannis	English	Melina Karageorgiou	Loukas Hamatsos	11	22
12	Australia	"Tonight Again"	Guy Sebastian	Guy Sebastian, David Ryan Harris, Lodis Schoorl	Guy Sebastian, David Ryan Harris, Lodis Schoorl	English	Julia Zemiro, Sam Pang	Lee Lin Chin	196	5
13	Belgium	"Rhythm Inside"	Loïc Nottet	Loic Nottet, Beverly Jo Scott	Luuk Cox	English	Peter Van de Veire, Eva Daeleman, Jean-Louis Lahaye, Maureen Louys	Walid	217	4
14	Austria	"I Am Yours"	The Makemakes (Dominic "Dodo" Muhrer, Markus Christ, Florian Meindl)	Jimmy Harry, Dominic Muhrer, Paul Estrela, Florian Meindl, Markus Christ	Jimmy Harry, Dominic Muhrer, Paul Estrela, Florian Meindl, Markus Christ	English	Andi Knoll	Kati Bellowitsch	0	26
15	Greece	"One Last Breath"	Maria Elena Kyriakou	Vangelis Konstantinidis, Evelina Tziora	Efthivoulos Theocharous, Maria Elena Kyriakou	English	Maria Kozakou, Giorgos Kapoutzidis	Helena Paparizou	23	19
16	Montenegro	"Adio"	Knez	Željko Joksimović, Marina Tucaković, Dejan Ivanović, English version: Nicole Bodriguez, Tamj Rodriguez, Milica Fajgelj, Dunja Vujadinović	Željko Joksimović	Serbian	Dražen Bauković, Tijana Mišković	Andrea Demirović	44	13
17	Germany	"Black Smoke"	Ann Sophie	Michael Harwood, Ella McMahon, Tonino Speciale	Michael Harwood, Ella McMahon, Tonino Speciale	English	Peter Urban	Barbara Schöneberger	0	27
18	Poland	"In the Name of Love"	Monika Kuszyńska	Monika Kuszyńska	Jakub Raczyński	English	Artur Orzech	Ola Ciupa	10	23
19	Latvia	"Love Injected"	Aminata	Aminata Savadogo	Aminata Savadogo	English	Valters Fridenbergs	Markus Riva	186	6
20	Romania	"De la capăt"	Voltaj (Călin Goia, Gabriel Constantin, Adrian Cristescu, Valeriu Ionescu, Oliver Sterian)	Călin Goia, Gabriel Constantin, Adrian Cristescu, Silviu Marian Păduraru, Victor Răzvan Alstani	Călin Goia, Gabriel Constantin, Adrian Cristescu, Silviu Marian Păduraru, Victor Răzvan Alstani	Romanian, English	Bogdan Stănescu	Sonia Argint Ionescu	35	15
21	Spain	"Amanecer"	Edurne	Tony Sánchez-Ohlsson	Thomas G:son, Peter Boström, Tony Sánchez-Ohlsson	Spanish	José María Íñigo, Julia Varela	Lara Siscar	15	21
22	Hungary	"Wars for Nothing"	Boggie	Sára Hélène Bori	Áron Sebestyén, Boglárka Csemer	English	Gábor Gundel Takács	Csilla Tatár	19	20
23	Georgia	"Warrior"	Nina Sublatti	Nina Sublatti	Nina Sublatti, Thomas G:son	English	Lado Tatishvili, Tamuna Museridze	Natia Bunturi	51	11
24	Azerbaijan	"Hour of the Wolf"	Elnur Huseynov	Sandra Bjurman, Nicolas Rebscher, Nicklas Lif, Lina Hansson	Nicolas Rebscher, Nicklas Lif, Lina Hansson	English	Kamran Guliyev	Tural Asadov	49	12
25	Russia	"A Million Voices"	Polina Gagarina	G. Alares, J. Björnberg, K. Noorbergen, L. Gutkin, V. Matetsky	G. Alares, J. Björnberg, K. Noorbergen, L. Gutkin, V. Matetsky	English	Yana Churikova, Yuriy Aksyuta	Dmitry Shepelev	303	2
26	Albania	"I'm Alive"	Elhaida Dani	Sokol Marsi	ZzapnChriss, Darko Dimitrov	English	Andri Xhahu	Andri Xhahu	34	17
27	Italy	"Grande amore"	Il Volo (Piero Barone, Ignazio Boschetto, Gianluca Ginoble)	Francesco Boccia, Ciro "Tommy" Esposito	Francesco Boccia, Ciro "Tommy" Esposito	Italian	Federico Russo, Valentina Correani	Federico Russo	292	3

	Montenegro	Malta	Finland	Greece	Romania	Belarus	Albania	Moldova	Azerbaijan	Latvia	Serbia	Denmark	Switzerland	Belgium	France	Armenia	Ireland	Sweden	Germany	Australia
Montenegro	■	-	-	-	-	-	6	-	2	-	12	-	-	-	-	8	-	2	-	-
Malta		■																		
Finland			■																	
Greece	-	-	-	■	-	-	10	-	-	-	-	-	-	-	-	5	-	-	-	-
Romania	-	-	-	-	■	-	-	12	-	-	-	2	-	5	-	-	-	-	-	-
Belarus						■														
Albania	10	-	-	6	-	-	■	-	-	-	-	-	-	6	-	-	-	-	-	-
Moldova								■												
Azerbaijan	8	8	-	-	3	-	-	3	■	-	-	-	-	-	-	-	-	-	-	-
Latvia	-	4	6	3	5	5	-	2	5	■	1	4	4	7	7	2	12	5	6	7
Serbia	12	-	-	-	-	-	2	-	-	-	■	-	5	-	-	-	-	-	-	5
Denmark												■								
Switzerland													■							
Belgium	-	-	7	7	7	8	1	6	-	4	4	7	2	■	12	4	2	10	8	6
France	-	-	-	-	-	-	-	-	-	-	-	-	-	-	■	3	-	-	-	-
Armenia	-	-	-	1	-	4	-	-	-	-	-	-	-	3	3	■	-	-	-	-
Ireland																	■			
Sweden	5	10	12	4	8	10	7	8	6	12	8	12	12	12	8	7	10	■	10	12
Germany	-	-	-	-	-	-	-	-	-	-	-	-	-	-	-	-	-	-	■	-
Australia	-	6	5	5	2	6	3	4	-	5	3	8	8	4	2	1	5	12	7	■
Czech Republic																				
Spain	2	-	-	-	-	-	-	1	1	-	-	-	1	-	5	-	-	-	-	-
Austria	-	-	-	-	-	-	-	-	-	-	-	-	-	-	-	-	-	-	-	-
North Macedonia																				
Slovenia	4	-	1	-	-	-	-	-	3	3	5	-	-	-	-	-	-	1	-	-
Hungary	-	-	-	-	4	-	-	-	-	-	-	-	-	-	1	-	-	-	1	-
United Kingdom	-	1	-	-	-	-	-	-	-	-	-	-	-	-	-	-	-	-	1	-
Lithuania	-	-	-	-	-	-	-	-	-	7	-	1	-	-	-	-	-	7	-	-
The Netherlands																				
Poland	-	-	-	-	-	-	-	-	-	-	-	-	-	-	4	-	3	-	-	-
Israel	3	5	3	-	1	2	5	-	7	1	6	-	3	-	-	-	-	4	5	2
Russia	7	7	8	8	10	12	8	10	12	10	10	10	7	10	10	12	8	6	12	10
San Marino																				
Italy	6	12	2	12	12	1	12	7	8	8	7	5	6	8	6	6	6	8	3	8
Iceland																				
Cyprus	-	-	-	10	-	-	-	-	-	-	-	-	-	-	-	-	-	-	-	-
Norway	-	2	4	-	6	-	-	-	-	2	-	3	10	-	-	-	4	7	4	4
Portugal																				
Estonia	1	3	10	-	-	7	4	-	4	6	2	6	-	2	-	-	-	3	2	3
Georgia	-	-	-	2	-	3	-	5	10	-	-	-	1	-	10	-	-	-	1	4

Czech Republic	Spain	Austria	North Macedonia	Slovenia	Hungary	United Kingdom	Lithuania	The Netherlands	Poland	Israel	Russia	San Marino	Italy	Iceland	Cyprus	Norway	Portugal	Estonia	Georgia	
–	–	–	4	10	–	–	–	–	–	–	–	–	–	–	–	–	–	–	–	Montenegro
																				Malta
																				Finland
–	–	–	–	–	–	–	–	–	–	–	–	–	–	–	8	–	–	–	–	Greece
–	5	–	–	–	1	–	–	–	–	5	–	–	–	–	1	–	4	–	–	Romania
																				Belarus
–	–	–	12	–	–	–	–	–	–	–	–	–	–	–	–	–	–	–	–	Albania
																				Moldova
12	–	–	–	–	–	–	2	–	–	–	3	–	–	–	–	–	–	–	10	Azerbaijan
5	4	1	–	7	5	7	12	2	10	–	2	12	4	7	3	8	2	6	4	Latvia
3	–	3	10	6	–	1	–	1	–	2	–	–	3	–	–	–	–	–	–	Serbia
																				Denmark
																				Switzerland
6	6	5	1	3	12	3	7	12	5	4	10	5	7	4	7	7	5	7	5	Belgium
–	–	–	–	–	–	–	–	–	–	–	–	1	–	–	–	–	–	–	–	France
2	–	–	3	–	–	–	–	–	–	–	6	–	–	–	–	–	–	–	12	Armenia
																				Ireland
10	8	7	5	12	10	12	10	10	12	10	8	7	12	12	10	12	8	10	7	Sweden
–	–	–	–	–	–	–	–	–	–	–	–	–	–	–	–	–	–	–	–	Germany
–	7	12	–	2	8	10	3	8	8	7	4	8	6	8	4	10	–	5	–	Australia
■																				Czech Republic
–	■	–	–	–	–	–	–	–	–	1	1	–	–	–	–	–	3	–	–	Spain
–	–	■	–	–	–	–	–	–	–	–	–	–	–	–	–	–	–	–	–	Austria
			■																	North Macedonia
–	–	–	8	■	–	–	4	–	1	6	–	–	–	2	–	1	–	–	–	Slovenia
1	–	–	–	–	■	–	–	–	–	–	4	–	–	–	–	–	–	8	–	Hungary
–	–	–	–	–	–	■	–	–	–	–	3	–	–	–	–	–	–	–	–	United Kingdom
–	–	–	–	–	–	4	■	–	–	–	–	–	–	–	–	6	–	2	3	Lithuania
								■												The Netherlands
–	–	–	–	–	–	2	–	–	■	–	–	–	1	–	–	–	–	–	–	Poland
–	1	2	–	–	–	5	–	5	4	■	–	2	8	5	6	4	7	–	1	Israel
8	10	8	6	5	6	6	–	6	6	8	■	–	10	3	5	2	10	12	5	Russia
												■								San Marino
7	12	10	7	8	2	8	1	7	7	12	12	10	■	6	12	5	12	3	8	Italy
														■						Iceland
–	–	–	–	1	–	–	–	–	–	–	–	–	–	–	■	–	–	–	–	Cyprus
–	2	4	–	4	4	–	5	3	3	–	–	6	5	10	–	■	6	4	–	Norway
																	■			Portugal
–	3	6	2	–	7	–	8	4	2	3	7	–	2	1	2	3	1	■	2	Estonia
–	–	–	–	3	–	6	–	–	–	5	–	–	–	–	–	–	–	1	■	Georgia

2016

Come Together

Country Hosting: Sweden
City Hosting: Stockholm
Date: 10.5.2016 (First Semi Final), 12.5.2016 (Second Semi Final), 14.5.2016 (The Final)
Location: Ericsson Globe
Presenters: Måns Zelmerlöw, Petra Mede
Executive Supervisor: Jon Ola Sand
Directed By: Daniel Jelinek, Robin Hofwander, Sven Stojanovic
Executive Producers: Johan Bernhagen, Martin Österdahl
Participating Countries: 42
Voting System: Juries voting and televoting (50-50), points are given by the regular system
Broadcaster: Sveriges Television (SVT)

First Semi Final, 10.5.2016
10 marked grey countries qualified to the Final
(Sweden, Spain and France were allowed to vote this semi-final)

No.	Country	Song	Performing Artist	Language	Points	Place
1	Finland	"Sing It Away"	Sandhja	English	51	15
2	Greece	"Utopian Land"	Argo	Greek, English	44	16
3	Moldova	"Falling Stars"	Lidia Isac	English	33	17
4	Hungary	"Pioneer"	Freddie	English	197	4
5	Croatia	"Lighthouse"	Nina Kraljić	English	133	10
6	Netherlands	"Slow Down"	Douwe Bob	English	197	5
7	Armenia	"LoveWave"	Iveta Mukuchyan	English	243	2
8	San Marino	"I Didn't Know"	Serhat	English	68	12
9	Russia	"You Are the Only One"	Sergey Lazarev	English	342	1
10	Czech Republic	"I Stand"	Gabriela Gunčíková	English	161	9
11	Cyprus	"Alter Ego"	Minus One	English	164	8
12	Austria	"Loin d'ici"	Zoë	French	170	7
13	Estonia	"Play"	Jüri Pootsmann	English	24	18
14	Azerbaijan	"Miracle"	Samra	English	185	6
15	Montenegro	"The Real Thing"	Highway	English	60	13
16	Iceland	"Hear Them Calling"	Greta Salóme	English	51	14
17	Bosnia and Herze-govina	"Ljubav je"	Dalal & Deen feat. Ana Rucner and Jala	Bosnian	104	11
18	Malta	"Walk on Water"	Ira Losco	English	209	3

Second Semi Final, 12.5.2016
10 marked grey countries qualified to the Final
(United Kingdom, Italy and Germany were allowed to vote this semi-final)

No.	Country	Song	Performing Artist	Language	Points	Place
1	Latvia	"Heartbeat"	Justs	English	132	8
2	Poland	"Color of Your Life"	Michał Szpak	English	151	6
3	Switzerland	"The Last of Our Kind"	Rykka	English	28	18
4	Israel	"Made of Stars"	Hovi Star	English	147	7
5	Belarus	"Help You Fly"	Ivan	English	84	12
6	Serbia	"Goodbye (Shelter)"	Sanja Vučić ZAA	English	105	10
7	Ireland	"Sunlight"	Nicky Byrne	English	46	15
8	North Macedonia	"Dona"	Kaliopi	North Mace-donian	88	11
9	Lithuania	"I've Been Waiting for This Night"	Donny Montell	English	222	4
10	Australia	"Sound of Silence"	Dami Im	English	330	1
11	Slovenia	"Blue and Red"	ManuElla	English	57	14
12	Bulgaria	"If Love Was a Crime"	Poli Genova	Bulgarian, English	220	5
13	Denmark	"Soldiers of Love"	Lighthouse X	English	34	17
14	Ukraine	"1944"	Jamala	English, Tatar	287	2
15	Norway	"Icebreaker"	Agnete	English	63	13
16	Georgia	"Midnight Gold"	Nika Kocharov & Young Georgian Lolitaz	English	123	9
17	Albania	"Fairytale"	Eneda Tarifa	English	45	16
18	Belgium	"What's the Pressure"	Laura Tesoro	English	274	3

FINAL

14.5.2016

No.	Country	Song	Performing Artist	Lyrics	Composer	Language	Commentator	Spoker of Results	Points	Place
01	Belgium	"What's the Pressure"	Laura Tesoro	Sanne Putseys, Louis Favre, Birsen Uçar	Sanne Putseys, Louis Favre, Birsen Uçar	English	Peter Van de Veire, Jean-Louis Lahaye, Maureen Louys	Umesh Vangaver	181	10
02	Czech Republic	"I Stand"	GabrielaGunčíková	Sara Biglert, Aidan O'Connor	Christian Schneider, Sara Biglert	English	Libor Bouček	Daniela Písařovicová	41	25
03	Netherlands	"Slow Down"	Douwe Bob	Douwe Bob, Jan Peter Hoekstra, Jeroen Overman, Matthijs van Duijvenbode	Douwe Bob, Jan Peter Hoekstra, Jeroen Overman, Matthijs van Duijvenbode	English	Jan Smit, Cornald Maas	Trijntje Oosterhuis	153	11
04	Azerbaijan	"Miracle"	Samra	Amir Aly, Jakob "Jakke" Erixson, Henrik Wikström, Don Amir	Amir Aly, Jakob "Jakke" Erixson, Henrik Wikström, Don Amir	English	Azer Suleymanli	Tural Asadov	117	17
05	Hungary	"Pioneer"	Freddie	Borbála Csarnai	Zé Szabó	English	Gábor Gundel Takács	Csilla Tatár	108	19
06	Italy	"No Degree of Separation"	Francesca Michielin	Federica Abbate, Francesca Michielin, Norma Jean Martine	Cheope, Fabio Gargiulo, Federica Abbate	Italian, English	Flavio Insinna, Federico Russo	Claudia Andreatti	124	16
07	Israel	"Made of Stars"	Hovi Star	Doron Madali	Doron Madali	English	-	Ofer Nachshon	135	14
08	Bulgaria	"If Love Was a Crime"	Poli Genova	Borislav Milanov, Sebastian Arman, Joachim Persson, Poli Genova	Borislav Milanov, Sebastian Arman, Joachim Persson, Poli Genova	Bulgarian, English	Elena Rosberg, Georgi Kushvaliev	Anna Angelova	307	4
09	Sweden	"If I Were Sorry"	Frans	Fredrik Andersson, Michael Saxell, Frans Jeppsson-Wall, Oscar Fogelström	Fredrik Andersson, Michael Saxell, Frans Jeppsson-Wall, Oscar Fogelström	English	Lotta Bromé	Gina Dirawi	261	5
10	Germany	"Ghost"	Jamie-Lee	Anna Leyne	Thomas Burchia, Anna Leyne, Conrad Hensel	English	Peter Urban	Barbara Schöneberger	11	26
11	France	"J'ai cherché"	Amir	Amir Haddad, Johan Errami, Nazim Khaled	Nazim Khaled, Silvio Lisbonne, Skydancers	French, English	Marianne James, Stéphane Bern	Élodie Gossuin	257	6
12	Poland	"Color of Your Life"	Michał Szpak	Kamil Varen	Andy Palmer	English	Artur Orzech	Anna Popek	229	8
13	Australia	"Sound of Silence"	"Sound of Silence"	Anthony Egizii, David Musumeci	Anthony Egizii, David Musumeci	English	Julia Zemiro, Sam Pang	Lee Lin Chin	511	2
14	Cyprus	"Alter Ego"	Minus One (Andreas Kapatais, Constantinos Americanos, Christoffer Ioannides, Chris J, Harrys Pari, Maxim Theofanides)	Minus One, Thomas Gason	Minus One, Thomas Gason	English	Melina Karageorgiou	Loukas Hamatsos	96	21
15	Serbia	"Goodbye (Shelter)"	Sanja Vučić ZAA	Ivana Peters	Ivana Peters	English	Duška Vučinić	Dragana Kosjerina	115	18
16	Lithuania	"I've Been Waiting for This Night"	Donny Montell	Jonas Thander, Beatrice Robertsson	Jonas Thander, Beatrice Robertsson	English	Darius Užkuraitis	Ugnė Galadauskaitė	200	9
17	Croatia	"Lighthouse"	Nina Kraljić	Andreas Grass, Nikola Paryla	Andreas Grass, Nikola Paryla	English	Duško Ćurlić	Nevena Rendeli	73	23
18	Russia	"You Are the Only One"	Sergey Lazarev	John Ballard, Ralph Charlie	Philipp Kirkorov, Dimitris Kontopoulos	English	Dmitry Guberniev, Ernest Mackevičius	Nyusha	491	3
19	Spain	"Say Yay!"	Barei	Bárbara Reyzábal, Rubén Villanueva, Víctor Púa Vivó	Bárbara Reyzábal, Rubén Villanueva, Víctor Púa Vivó	English	José María Íñigo, Julia Varela	Jota Abril	77	22
20	Latvia	"Heartbeat"	Justs	Aminata Savadogo	Aminata Savadogo	English	Valters Fridenbergs	Toms Grēviņš	132	15
21	Ukraine	"1944"	Jamala	Art Antonyan, Jamala	Jamala	English, Tatar	Timur Miroshnychenko, Tetiana Terekhova	Verka Serduchka	534	1
22	Malta	"Walk on Water"	Ira Losco	Lisa Desmond, Tim Larsson, Tobias Lundgren, Molly Pettersson Hammar, Ira Losco	Lisa Desmond, Tim Larsson, Tobias Lundgren, Molly Pettersson Hammar, Ira Losco	English	Arthur Caruana	Ben Camille	153	12
23	Georgia	"Midnight Gold"	Nika Kocharov & Young Georgian Lolitaz	Kote Kalandadze	Kote Kalandadze, Thomas Gason	English	Tuta Chkheidze, Nika Katsia	Nina Sublatti	104	20
24	Austria	"Loin d'ici"	Zoë	Zoë Straub, Christof Straub	Zoë Straub, Christof Straub	French	Andi Knoll	Kati Bellowitsch	151	13
25	United Kingdom	"You're Not Alone"	Joe and Jake	Schwartz, Justin J. Benson, S. Kanes	Schwartz, Justin J. Benson, S. Kanes	English	Graham Norton	Richard Osman	62	24
26	Armenia	"LoveWave"	Iveta Mukuchyan	Iveta Mukuchyan, Stephanie Crutchfield	Lilith Navasardyan, Lewon Navasardyan	English	Avet Barseghyan	Arman Margaryan	249	7

2017

Celebrate Diversity

Country Hosting: Ukraine
City Hosting: Kyiv
Date: 9.5.2017 (First Semi Final), 11.5.2017 (Second Semi Final), 13.5.2017 (The Final)
Location: International Exhibition Centre
Presenters: Volodymyr Ostapchuk, Oleksandr Skichko, Timur Miroshnychenko
Executive Supervisor: Jon Ola Sand
Directed By: Troels Lund, Alexander Kolb, Ladislaus Kiraly
Executive Producer: Pavlo Grytsak
Participating Countries: 42
Voting System: Juries voting and televoting (50-50), points are given by the regular system
Broadcaster: National Public Broadcasting Company of Ukraine (UA:PBC)

First Semi Final, 9.5.2017

10 marked grey countries qualified to the Final
(United Kingdom, Italy and Spain were allowed to vote this semi-final)

No.	Country	Song	Performing Artist	Language	Points	Place
1	Sweden	"I Can't Go On"	Robin Bengtsson	English	227	3
2	Georgia	"Keep the Faith"	Tamara Gachechiladze	English	99	11
3	Australia	"Don't Come Easy"	Isaiah	English	160	6
4	Albania	"World"	Lindita	English	76	14
5	Belgium	"City Lights"	Blanche	English	165	4
6	Montenegro	"Space"	Slavko Kalezić	English	56	16
7	Finland	"Blackbird"	Norma John	English	92	12
8	Azerbaijan	"Skeletons"	Dihaj	English	150	8
9	Portugal	"Amar pelos dois"	Salvador Sobral	Portuguese	370	1
10	Greece	"This Is Love"	Demy	English	115	10
11	Poland	"Flashlight"	Kasia Moś	English	119	9
12	Moldova	"Hey, Mamma!"	Sunstroke Project	French	291	2
13	Iceland	"Paper"	Svala	English	60	15
14	Czech Republic	"My Turn"	Martina Bárta	English	83	13
15	Cyprus	"Gravity"	Hovig	English	164	5
16	Armenia	"Fly with Me"	Artsvik	English	152	7
17	Slovenia	"On My Way"	Omar Naber	English	36	17
18	Latvia	"Line"	Triana Park	English	21	18

Second Semi Final, 11.5.2017

10 marked grey countries qualified to the Final
(Ukraine, France and Germany were allowed to vote this semi-final)

No.	Country	Song	Performing Artist	Language	Points	Place
1	Serbia	"In Too Deep"	Tijana Bogićević	English	98	11
2	Austria	"Running on Air"	Nathan Trent	English	147	7
3	North Macedonia	"Dance Alone"	Jana Burčeska	English	69	15
4	Malta	"Breathlessly"	Claudia Faniello	English	55	16
5	Romania	"Yodel It!"	Ilinca ft. Alex Florea	English	174	6
6	Netherlands	"Lights and Shadows"	O'G3NE	English	200	4
7	Hungary	"Origo"	Joci Pápai	Hungarian	231	2
8	Denmark	"Where I Am"	Anja	English	101	10
9	Ireland	"Dying to Try"	Brendan Murray	English	86	13
10	San Marino	"Spirit of the Night"	Valentina Monetta and Jimmie Wilson	English	1	18
11	Croatia	"My Friend"	Jacques Houdek	English, Italian	141	8
12	Norway	"Grab the Moment"	JOWST	English	189	5
13	Switzerland	"Apollo"	Timebelle	English	97	12
14	Belarus	"Story of My Life"	Naviband	Russian	110	9
15	Bulgaria	"Beautiful Mess"	Kristian Kostov	English	403	1
16	Lithuania	"Rain of Revolution"	Fusedmarc	English	42	17
17	Estonia	"Verona"	Koit Toome and Laura	English	85	14
18	Israel	"I Feel Alive"	Imri Ziv	English	207	3

No.	Country	Song	Performing Artist	Lyrics	Composer	Language	Commentator	Spoker of Results	Points	Place
01	Israel	"I Feel Alive"	Imri Ziv	Dolev Ram, Pan Hazut	Dolev Ram, Pan Hazut	English	-	Ofer Nachshon	39	23
02	Poland	"Flashlight"	Kasia Moś	Kasia Moś, Pete Baringger, Rickard Bonde Truumeel	Kasia Moś, Pete Baringger, Rickard Bonde Truumeel	English	Artur Orzech	Anna Popek	64	22
03	Belarus	"Story of My Life"	Naviband	Arciom Lukjanienka	Arciom Lukjanienka	Russian	Evgeny Perlin	Alyona Lanskaya	83	17
04	Austria	"Running on Air"	Nathan Trent	Nathan Trent, Bernhard Penzias	Nathan Trent, Bernhard Penzias	English	Andi Knoll	Kristina Inhof	93	16
05	Armenia	"Fly with Me"	Artsvik	Avet Barseghyan, David Tserunyan	Lilith Navasardyan, Levon Navasardyan	English	Avet Barseghyan, Gohar Gasparyan	Iveta Mukuchyan	79	18
06	Netherlands	"Lights and Shadows"	O'G3NE (Lisa Vol, Amy Vol, Shelley Vol)	Rick Vol	Rory de Kievit	English	Cornald Maas, Jan Smit	Douwe Bob	150	11
07	Moldova	"Hey, Mamma!"	Sunstroke Project (Pasha Parfeny, Aleksei Myslitsky, Anton Ragoza)	Alina Galetskaya	SunStroke Project, Mihail Cebotarenco	English	Galina Timuş	Gloria Gorceag	374	3
08	Hungary	"Origo"	Joci Pápai	József Pápai	József Pápai	Hungarian	Krisztina Rátonyi, Freddie	Csilla Tatár	200	8
09	Italy	"Occidentali's Karma"	Francesco Gabbani	Francesco Gabbani, Fabio Ilacqua, Luca Chiaravalli	Francesco Gabbani, Fabio Ilacqua, Luca Chiaravalli	Italian	Flavio Insinna, Federico Russo	Giulia Valentina Palermo	334	6
10	Denmark	"Where I Am"	Anja	Anja Nissen, Angel Tupai, Michael D'Arcy	Anja Nissen, Angel Tupai, Michael D'Arcy	English	Ole Tøpholm	Ulla Essendrop	77	20
11	Portugal	"Amar pelos dois"	Salvador Sobral	Luísa Sobral	Luísa Sobral	Portuguese	José Carlos Malato, Nuno Galopim	Filomena Cautela	758	1
12	Azerbaijan	"Skeletons"	Dihaj	Sandra Bjurman	Isa Melikov	English	Azər Süleymanlı	Tural Asadov	120	14
13	Croatia	"My Friend"	Jacques Houdek	Jacques Houdek, Arjana Kunštek, Fabrizio Laucella, Ines Prajo	Jacques Houdek, Tony Roberth Malm, Siniša Reljić	English, Italian	Duško Ćurlić	Uršula Tolj	128	13
14	Australia	"Don't Come Easy"	Isaiah	Anthony Egizii, David Musumeci, Michael Angelo	Anthony Egizii, David Musumeci, Michael Angelo	English	Myf Warhurst, Joel Creasey	Lee Lin Chin	173	9
15	Greece	"This Is Love"	Demy	Romy Papadea, John Ballard	Dimitris Kontopoulos	English	Giorgos Kapoutzidis, Maria Kozakou	Constantinos Christoforou	77	19
16	Spain	"Do It for Your Lover"	Manel Navarro	Manel Navarro, Antonio Rayo "Rayito"	Manel Navarro, Antonio Rayo "Rayito"	Spanish, English	José María Íñigo, Julia Varela	Nieves Álvarez	5	26
17	Norway	"Grab the Moment"	JOWST	Joakim With Steen, Jonas McDonnell	Joakim With Steen, Jonas McDonnell	English	Olav Viksmo-Slettan	Marcus & Martinus	158	10
18	United Kingdom	"Never Give Up on You"	Lucie Jones	Emmelie de Forest, Daniel Salcedo, Lawrie Martin	Emmelie de Forest, Daniel Salcedo, Lawrie Martin	English	Graham Norton	Katrina Leskanich	111	15
19	Cyprus	"Gravity"	Hovig	Thomas G:son	Thomas G:son	English	Tasos Tryfonos, Christiana Artemiou	John Karayiannis	68	21
20	Romania	"Yodel It!"	· Ilinca ft. Alex Florea	Alexandra Niculae	Mihai Alexandru	English	Liana Stanciu, Radu Andrei Tudor	Sonia Argint-Ionescu	282	7
21	Germany	"Perfect Life"	Levina	Lindsey Ray, Lindy Robbins, Dave Bassett	Lindsey Ray, Lindy Robbins, Dave Bassett	English	Peter Urban	Barbara Schöneberger	6	25
22	Ukraine	"Time"	O.Torvald	Yevhen Halych, Yevhen Kamenchuk	Yevhen Halych, Yevhen Kamenchuk	English	Tetiana Terekhova, Andriy Horodyskyi	Zlata Ognevich	36	24
23	Belgium	"City Lights"	Blanche	Pierre Dumoulin, Blanche	Pierre Dumoulin	English	Maureen Louys, Jean-Louis Lahaye, Peter Van de Veire	Fanny Gillard	363	4
24	Sweden	"I Can't Go On"	Robin Bengtsson	David Kreuger, Hamed "K-One" Pirouzpanah, Robin Stjernberg	David Kreuger, Hamed "K-One" Pirouzpanah, Robin Stjernberg	English	Måns Zelmerlöw, Edward af Sillén	Wiktoria	344	5
25	Bulgaria	"Beautiful Mess"	Kristian Kostov	Borislav Milanov, Sebastian Arman, Joacim Bo Persson, Alex Omar, Alexander V. Blay	Borislav Milanov, Sebastian Arman, Joacim Bo Persson, Alex Omar, Alexander V. Blay	English	Elena Rosberg, Georgi Kushvaliev	Boryana Gramatikova	615	2
26	France	"Requiem"	Alma	Nazim Khaled	Nazim Khaled	French, English	Marianne James, Stéphane Bern, Amir Haddad	Élodie Gossuin	135	12

2018

All Aboard

Country Hosting: Portugal
City Hosting: Lisbon
Date: 8.5.2018 (First Semi Final), 10.5.2018 (Second Semi Final), 12.5.2018 (The Final)
Location: Altice Arena
Presenters: Sílvia Alberto, Catarina Furtado, Filomena Cautela, Daniela Ruah
Executive Supervisor: Jon Ola Sand
Directed By: Tores Lund, Paula Macedo, Pedro Miguel
Executive Producer: João Nuno Nogueira
Participating Countries: 43
Voting System: Juries voting and televoting (50-50), points are given by the regular system
Broadcaster: Rádio e Televisão de Portugal (RTP)

First Semi Final, 8.5.2018

10 marked grey countries qualified to the Final
(United Kingdom, Spain and Portugal were allowed to vote this semi-final)

No.	Country	Song	Performing Artist	Language	Points	Place
1	Azerbaijan	"X My Heart"	Aisel	English	94	11
2	Iceland	"Our Choice"	Ari Ólafsson	English	15	19
3	Albania	"Mall"	Eugent Bushpepa	Albanian	162	8
4	Belgium	"A Matter of Time"	Sennek	English	91	12
5	Czech Republic	"Lie to Me"	Mikolas Josef	English	232	3
6	Lithuania	"When We're Old"	Ieva Zasimauskaitė	English	119	9
7	Israel	"Toy"	Netta	English, Hebrew	283	1
8	Belarus	"Forever"	Alekseev	English	65	16
9	Estonia	"La forza"	Elina Nechayeva	Italian	201	5
10	Bulgaria	"Bones"	Equinox	English	177	7
11	North Macedonia	"Lost and Found"	Eye Cue	English	24	18
12	Croatia	"Crazy"	Franka	English	63	17
13	Austria	"Nobody but You"	Cesár Sampson	English	231	4
14	Greece	"Oniro mou"	Yianna Terzi	Greek	81	14
15	Finland	"Monsters"	Saara Aalto	English	108	10
16	Armenia	"Qami"	Sevak Khanagyan	Armenian	79	15
17	Switzerland	"Stones"	ZiBBZ	English	86	13
18	Ireland	"Together"	Ryan O'Shaughnessy	English	179	6
19	Cyprus	"Fuego"	Eleni Foureira	English	262	2

Second Semi Final, 10.5.2018

10 marked grey countries qualified to the Final
(Italy, France and Germany were allowed to vote this semi-final)

No.	Country	Song	Performing Artist	Language	Points	Place
1	Norway	"That's How You Write a Song"	Alexander Rybak	English	266	1
2	Romania	"Goodbye"	The Humans	English	107	11
3	Serbia	"Nova deca"	Sanja Ilić & Balkanika	Serbian	117	9
4	San Marino	"Who We Are"	Jessika feat. Jenifer Brening	English	28	17
5	Denmark	"Higher Ground"	Rasmussen	English	204	5
6	Russia	"I Won't Break"	Julia Samoylova	English	65	15
7	Moldova	"My Lucky Day"	DoReDoS	English	235	3
8	Netherlands	"Outlaw in 'Em"	Waylon	English	174	7
9	Australia	"We Got Love"	Jessica Mauboy	English	212	4
10	Georgia	"For You"	Ethno-Jazz Band Iriao	Georgian	1	18
11	Poland	"Light Me Up"	Gromee feat. Lukas Meijer	English	81	14
12	Malta	"Taboo"	Christabelle	English	101	13
13	Hungary	"Viszlát nyár"	AWS	Hungarian	111	10
14	Latvia	"Funny Girl"	Laura Rizzotto	English	106	12
15	Sweden	"Dance You Off"	Benjamin Ingrosso	English	254	2
16	Montenegro	"Inje"	Vanja Radovanović	Serbian	40	16
17	Slovenia	"Hvala, ne!"	Lea Sirk	Slovenian	132	8
18	Ukraine	"Under the Ladder"	Mélovin	English	179	6

FINAL

12.5.2018

No.	Country	Song	Performing Artist	Lyrics	Composer	Language	Commentator	Spoker of Results	Points	Place
01	Ukraine	"Under the Ladder"	Mélovin	Mike Ryals	Mélovin	English	Serhiy Prytula	Natalia Zhyzhchenko	130	17
02	Spain	"Tu canción"	Amaia & Alfred	Raúl Gómez, Sylvia Santoro	Raúl Gómez, Sylvia Santoro	Spanish	Tony Aguilar, Julia Varela	Nieves Álvarez	61	23
03	Slovenia	"Hvala, ne!"	Lea Sirk	Lea Sirk	Lea Sirk, Tomy DeClerque	Slovenian	Andrej Hofer	Maja Keuc	64	22
04	Lithuania	"When We're Old"	Ieva Zasimauskaitė	Vytautas Bikus	Vytautas Bikus	English	Darius Užkuraitis, Gerūta Griniūtė	Eglė Daugėlaitė	181	12
05	Austria	"Nobody but You"	Cesár Sampson	Cesár Sampson, Boris Milanov, Sebastian Arman, Joacim Persson, Johan Alkenäs	Cesár Sampson, Boris Milanov, Sebastian Arman, Joacim Persson,	English	Andi Knoll	Kati Bellowitsch	342	3
06	Estonia	"La forza"	Elina Nechayeva	Ksenia Kuchukova, Mihkel Mattisen, Elina Nechayeva, Timo Vendt	Ksenia Kuchukova, Mihkel Mattisen, Elina Nechayeva, Timo Vendt	Italian	Marko Reikop	Ott Evestus	245	8
07	Norway	"That's How You Write a Song"	Alexander Rybak	Alexander Rybak	Alexander Rybak	English	Olav Viksmo-Slettan	Aleksander Walmann, JOWST	144	15
08	Portugal	"O jardim"	Cláudia Pascoal	Isaura	Isaura	portuguese	Nuno Galopim, Hélder Reis	Pedro Fernandes	39	26
09	United Kingdom	"Storm"	SuRie	Nicole Blair, Gil Lewis, Sean Hargreaves	Nicole Blair, Gil Lewis, Sean Hargreaves	English	Graham Norton	Mel Giedroyc	48	24
10	Serbia	"Nova deca"	Sanja Ilic & Balkanika	Sanja Ilić, Tanja Ilić, Danica Krstajić	Sanja Ilić, Tanja Ilić, Danica Krstajić, Darko Dimitrov	Serbian	Duška Vučinić	Dragana Kosjerina	113	19
11	Germany	"You Let Me Walk Alone"	Michael Schulte	Michael Schulte, Thomas Stengaard, Nisse Ingwersen, Nina Müller	Michael Schulte, Nina Müller, Thomas Stengaard, Nisse Ingwersen	English	Peter Urban	Barbara Schöneberger	340	4
12	Albania	"Mall"	Eugent Bushpepa	Eugent Bushpepa	Eugent Bushpepa	Albanian	Andri Xhahu	Andri Xhahu	184	11
13	France	"Mercy"	Madame Monsieur	Émilie Satt, Jean-Karl Lucas	Émilie Satt, Jean-Karl Lucas	French	Stéphane Bern, Christophe Willem, Alma	Élodie Gossuin	173	13
14	Czech Republic	"Lie to Me"	Mikolas Josef	Mikolas Josef	Mikolas Josef	English	Libor Bouček	Radka Rosická	281	6
15	Denmark	"Higher Ground"	Rasmussen	Niclas Arn, Karl Eurén	Niclas Arn, Karl Eurén	English	Ole Tøpholm	Ulla Essendrop	226	9
16	Australia	"We Got Love"	Jessica Mauboy	Anthony Egizii, David Musumeci, Jessica Mauboy	Anthony Egizii, David Musumeci, Jessica Mauboy	English	Myf Warhurst, Joel Creasey	Ricardo Gonçalves	99	20
17	Finland	"Monsters"	Saara Aalto	Saara Aalto, Joy Deb, Linnea Deb, Ki Fitzgerald	Saara Aalto, Joy Deb, Linnea Deb, Ki Fitzgerald	English	Mikko Silvennoinen	Anna Abreu	46	25
18	Bulgaria	"Bones"	Equinox (Zhana Bergendorff, Georgi Simeonov, Vlado Mihailov, Trey Campbell, Johnny Manuel)	Borislav Milanov, Trey Campbell, Joacim Persson, Dag Lundberg,	Borislav Milanov, Trey Campbell, Joacim Persson, Dag Lundberg	English	Elena Rosberg, Georgi Kushvaliev	Joanna Dragneva	166	14
19	Moldova	"My Lucky Day"	DoReDos (Marina Djundyet, Eugeniu Andrianov, Sergiu Mița)	John Ballard	Philipp Kirkorov	English	Doina Stimpovschii	Djulieta Ardovan	209	10
20	Sweden	"Dance You Off"	Benjamin Ingrosso	MAG, Louis Schoorl, K Nita, Benjamin Ingrosso	MAG, Louis Schoorl, K Nita, Benjamin Ingrosso	English	Sanna Nielsen, Edward af Sillén	Felix Sandman	274	7
21	Hungary	"Viszlát nyár"	AWS (Bence Brucker, Dániel Kökényes, Örs Siklósi, Aron Veress, Soma Schiszlér)	Örs Siklósi	Dániel Kökényes, Bence Brucker, Aron Veress, Soma Schiszler	Hungarian	Krisztina Rátonyi, Freddie	Bence Forró	93	21
22	Israel	"Toy"	Netta	Stav Beger	Doron Madali	Hebrew, English	Erez Tal, Itit Hershkowitz	Lucy Ayoub	529	1
23	Netherlands	"Outlaw in 'Em"	Waylon	Jim Beavers, Waylon, Ilya Toshinskiy	Jim Beavers, Waylon, Ilya Toshinskiy	English	Cornald Maas, Jan Smit	O'G3NE	121	18
24	Ireland	"Together"	Ryan O'Shaughnessy	Ryan O'Shaughnessy, Mark Caplice, Laura Elizabeth Hughes	Ryan O'Shaughnessy, Mark Caplice, Laura Elizabeth Hughes	English	Marty Whelan	Nicky Byrne	136	16
25	Cyprus	"Fuego"	Eleni Foureira	Alex Papaconstantinou, Geraldo Sandell, Viktor Svensson, Anderz Wrethov, Didrick	Alex Papaconstantinou, Geraldo Sandell, Viktor Svensson, Anderz Wrethov, Didrick	English	Costas Constantinou, Vaso Komninou	Hovig	436	2
26	Italy	"Non mi avete fatto niente"	Ermal Meta & Fabrizio Moro	Andrea Febo, Ermal Meta, Fabrizio Moro	Ermal Meta, Fabrizio Moro	Italian	Serena Rossi, Federico Russo	Giulia Valentina Palermo	308	5

2019

Dare To Dream

Country Hosting: Israel
City Hosting: Tel Aviv
Date: 14.5.2019 (First Semi Final), 16.5.2019 (Second Semi Final), 18.5.2019 (The Final)
Location: Expo Tel Aviv
Presenters: Erez Tal, Bar Refaelli, Assi Azar, Lucy Ayoub
Executive Supervisor: Jon Ola Sand
Directed By: Sivan Magazanik, Amir Ukrainitz
Executive Producer: Zivit Davidovich
Participating Countries: 41
Voting System: Juries voting and televoting (50-50), points are given by the regular system
Broadcaster: Israeli Public Broadcasting Corporation (IPBC)

1st Semi Final, 14.5.2019
10 marked grey countries qualified to the Final
(Israel. France and Spain were allowed to vote this semi-final)

No.	Country	Song	Performing Artist	Language	Points	Place
1	Cyprus	"Replay"	Tamta	English	149	9
2	Montenegro	"Heaven"	D mol	English	46	16
3	Finland	"Look Away"	Darude feat. Sebastian Rejman	English	23	17
4	Poland	"Fire of Love (Pali się)"	Tulia	Polish, English	120	11
5	Slovenia	"Sebi"	Zala Kralj & Gašper Šantl	Slovene	167	6
6	Czech Republic	"Friend of a Friend"	Lake Malawi	English	242	2
7	Hungary	"Az én apám"	Joci Pápai	Hungarian	97	12
8	Belarus	"Like It"	ZENA	English	122	10
9	Serbia	"Kruna"	Nevena Božović	Serb	156	7
10	Belgium	"Wake Up"	Eliot	English	70	13
11	Georgia	"Keep on Going"	Oto Nemsadze	English	62	14
12	Australia	"Zero Gravity"	Kate Miller-Heidke	English	261	1
13	Iceland	"Hatrið mun sigra"	Hatari	Icelandic	221	3
14	Estonia	"Storm"	Victor Crone	English	198	4
15	Portugal	"Telemóveis"	Conan Osiris	Portuguese	51	15
16	Greece	"Better Love"	Katerine Duska	English	185	5
17	San Marino	"Say Na Na Na"	Serhat	English	150	8

2nd Semi Final, 16.5.2019
10 marked grey countries qualified to the Final
(United Kingdom, Germany and Italy were allowed to vote this semi-final)

No.	Country	Song	Performing Artist	Language	Points	Place
1	Armenia	"Walking Out"	Srbuk	English	49	16
2	Ireland	"22"	Sarah McTernan	English	16	18
3	Moldova	"Stay"	Anna Odobescu	English	85	12
4	Switzerland	"She Got Me"	Luca Hänni	English	232	4
5	Latvia	"That Night"	Carousel	English	50	15
6	Romania	"On a Sunday"	Ester Peony	English	71	13
7	Denmark	"Love Is Forever"	Leonora	English, French	94	10
8	Sweden	"Too Late for Love"	John Lundvik	English	238	3
9	Austria	"Limits"	PÆNDA	English	21	17
10	Croatia	"The Dream"	Roko	Croatian, English	64	14
11	Malta	"Chameleon"	Michela	English	157	8
12	Lithuania	"Run with the Lions"	Jurij Veklenko	English	93	11
13	Russia	"Scream"	Sergey Lazarev	English	217	6
14	Albania	"Ktheju tokës"	Jonida Maliqi	Albanian	96	9
15	Norway	"Spirit in the Sky"	KEiiNO	English	210	7
16	The Netherlands	"Arcade"	Duncan Laurence	English	280	1
17	North North Macedonia	"Proud"	Tamara Todevska	English	239	2
18	Azerbaijan	"Truth"	Chingiz	English	224	5

FINAL

18.5.2019

No.	Country	Song	Performing Artist	Lyrics	Composer	Language	Commentator	Spoker of Results	Points	Place
01	Malta	"Chameleon"	Michela	Joacim Persson, Paula Winger, Borislav Milanov, Johan Alkenäs	Joacim Persson, Paula Winger, Borislav Milanov, Johan Alkenäs	English	-	Ben Camille	107	14
02	Albania	"Ktheju tokës"	Jonida Maliqi	Eriona Rushiti	Eriona Rushiti	Albanian	Andri Xhahu	Andri Xhahu	90	17
03	Czech Republic	"Friend of a Friend"	Lake Malawi (Albert Černý, Jeroným Šubrt, Antonín Hrabal)	Jan Steinsdoerfer, Mikolaj Trybulec, Albert Cerny	Jan Steinsdoerfer, Mikolaj Trybulec, Albert Cerny	English	Libor Bouček	Radka Rosická	157	11
04	Germany	"Sister"	S!sters (Laurita Spinelli Carlotta Truman)	Laurell Barker, Marine Kaltenbacher, Tom Oehler, Thomas Stengaard	Laurell Barker, Marine Kaltenbacher, Tom Oehler, Thomas Stengaard	English	Peter Urban	Barbara Schöneberger	24	25
05	Russia	"Scream"	Sergey Lazarev	Sharon Vaughn, Dimitris Kontopoulos	Sharon Vaughn, Dimitris Kontopoulos	English	Dmitry Guberniev, Olga Shelest	Ivan Bessonov	370	3
06	Denmark	"Love Is Forever"	Leonora	Lise Cabble, Melanie Wehbe, Emil Rosendal Lei	Lise Cabble, Melanie Wehbe, Emil Rosendal Lei	English, French	Ole Tøpholm	Rasmussen	120	12
07	San Marino	"Say Na Na Na"	Serhat	Serhat, Mary Susan, Applegate	Serhat	English	Lia Fiorio, Gigi Restivo	Monica Fabbri	77	19
08	North Macedonia	"Proud"	Tamara Todevska	Kosta Petrov, Sanja Popovska	Darko Dimitrov, Robert Bibliov, Lazar Cvetkoski	English	-	Nikola Trajkovski	305	7
09	Sweden	"Too Late for Love"	John Lundvik	John Lundvik, Anderz Wrethov, Andreas "Stone" Johansson	John Lundvik, Anderz Wrethov, Andreas "Stone" Johansson	English	Charlotte Perrelli, Edward af Sillén	Eric Saade	334	5
10	Slovenia	"Sebi"	Zala Kralj & Gašper Šantl	Zala Kralj, Gašper Šantl	Zala Kralj, Gašper Šantl	Slovene	-	Lea Sirk	105	15
11	Cyprus	"Replay"	Tamta	Alex Papaconstantinou, Geraldo Sandell, Viktor Svensson, Albin Nedler, Kristoffer Fogelmark	Alex Papaconstantinou, Geraldo Sandell, Viktor Svensson, Albin Nedler, Kristoffer Fogelmark	English	Evridiki, Tasos Trifonos	Hovig	109	13
12	The Netherlands	"Arcade"	Duncan Laurence	Duncan de Moor, Joel Sjöö, Wouter Hardy	Duncan de Moor, Joel Sjöö, Wouter Hardy	English	Jan Smit, Cornald Maas	Emma Wortelboer	498	1
13	Greece	"Better Love"	Katerine Duska	Katerine Duska, David Sneddon	Katerine Duska, Leon of Athens, David Sneddon	English	Giorgos Kapoutzidis, Maria Kozakou	Gus G	74	21
14	Israel	"Home"	Kobi Marimi	Ohad Shragai, Inbar Weitzman	Ohad Shragai, Inbar Weitzman	English	Sharon Taicher, Eran Zarachowicz	Izhar Cohen	35	23
15	Norway	"Spirit in the Sky"	KEiiNO (Tom Hugo Hermansen, Fred-René Buljo, Alexandra Rotan)	Tom Hugo Hermansen, Fred-René Buljo, Alexandra Rotan, Henrik Tala, Alexander N Olsson, Rüdiger Schramm	Tom Hugo Hermansen, Fred-René Buljo, Alexandra Rotan, Henrik Tala, Alexander N Olsson, Rüdiger Schramm	English	Olav Viksmo-Slettan	Alexander Rybak	331	6
16	United Kingdom	"Bigger than Us"	Michael Rice	Laurell Barker, Anna-Klara Folin, John Lundvik, Jonas Thander	Laurell Barker, Anna-Klara Folin, John Lundvik, Jonas Thander	English	Graham Norton	Rylan Clark-Neal	11	26
17	Iceland	"Hatrið mun sigra"	Hatari (Klemens Nikulásson Hannigan, Matthías Tryggvi Haraldsson, Einar Hrafn Stefánsson)	Einar Hrafn Stefánsson, Klemens Nikulásson, Hannigan, Matthías Tryggvi Haraldsson	Einar Hrafn Stefánsson, Klemens Nikulásson, Hannigan, Matthías Tryggvi Haraldsson	Icelandic	Gísli Marteinn Baldursson	Jóhannes Haukur Jóhannesson	232	10
18	Estonia	"Storm"	Victor Crone	Stig Rästa, Victor Crone, Fred Krieger	Stig Rästa, Vallo Kikas, Victor Crone, Sebastian Lestapier	English	Aleksandr Hobotov, Julia Kalenda	Kelly Sildaru	76	20
19	Belarus	"Like It"	ZENA	Yulia Kireeva	Yulia Kireeva, Viktor Drobysh, Zinaida Kupriyanovic	English	Evgeny Perlin	Maria Vasilevich	31	24
20	Azerbaijan	"Truth"	Chingiz	Borislav Milanov, Trey Campbell, Pablo Dinero, Hostess, Joacim Persson	Borislav Milanov, Chingiz Mustafayev, Trey Campbell, Pablo Dinero, Hostess, Joacim Persson	English	Murad Arif	Faig Agayev	302	8
21	France	"Roi"	Bilal Hassani	Bilal Hassani, Madame Monsieur	Bilal Hassani, Madame Monsieur, Medeline	French, English	Stéphane Bern, André Manoukian	Julia Molkhou	105	16
22	Italy	"Soldi"	Mahmood	Charlie Charles, Dario "Dardust" Faini, Alessandro Mahmoud	Charlie Charles, Dario "Dardust" Faini, Alessandro Mahmoud	Italian, Arabic	Federico Russo, Flavio Insinna	Ema Stokholma	472	2
23	Serbia	"Kruna"	Nevena Božović	Nevena Božović	Nevena Božović	Serb	Duška Vučinić	Dragana Kosjerina	89	18
24	Switzerland	"She Got Me"	Luca Hänni	Laurell Barker, Frazer Mac, Luca Hänni, Jenson Vaughan, Jon Hallgren, Lukas Hallgren	Laurell Barker, Frazer Mac, Luca Hänni, Jenson Vaughan, Jon Hallgren, Lukas Hallgren	English	Sven Epiney, Bastian Baker, Clarissa Tami, Sebalter	Sinplus	364	4
25	Australia	"Zero Gravity"	Kate Miller-Heidke	Kate Miller-Heidke, Nuttall	Kate Miller-Heidke, Keir Nuttall, Julian Hamilton	English	Myf Warhurst, Joel Creasey	Electric Fields	284	9
26	Spain	"La Venda"	Miki	Adrià Salas	Adrià Salas	Spanish	Tony Aguilar, Julia Varela	Nieves Álvarez	54	22

2016				
Country	12 Points	Juries voting	Popular voting	Total points
Ukraine	17	211	323	534
Australia	12	320	191	511
Russia	14	130	361	491
Bulgaria	2	127	180	307
Sweden	5	122	139	162

2017				
Country	12 Points	Juries voting	Popular voting	Total points
Portugal	30	382	376	758
Bulgaria	11	278	337	615
Moldova	5	110	264	374
Belgium	5	108	255	363
Sweden	4	218	126	344

2018				
Country	12 Points	Juries voting	Popular voting	Total points
Israel	13	212	317	529
Cyprus	9	183	253	436
Austria	9	271	71	342
Germany	6	204	136	340
Italy	4	59	249	308

2019				
Country	12 Points	Juries voting	Popular voting	Total points
The Netherlands	8	237	261	489
Italy	10	219	235	472
Russia	12	126	244	370
Switzerland	1	152	212	364
Sweden	8	241	93	334

2020-2024

WARS AND PANDEMICS

The decade began with an unsettling event: the COVID-19 pandemic led to the postponement of Eurovision 2020 to 2021. During the latter year, Italy achieved a remarkable victory for the first time in 31 years. In 2022, Ukraine secured its third Eurovision win, but was unable to host the event. Consequently, the contest was relocated to Liverpool. This relocation marked a historic moment for Loreen, who became the first female performer (alongside Johnny Logan) to achieve first place twice. Additionally, her country, Sweden, tied with Ireland for the highest number of wins in the contest's history.

Eurovision 2024 was won by Switzerland, the first-ever Eurovision winner, marking their third victory, this time with Nemo.

2020 – The Coronavirus Eurovision

Apparently, this beat can be stopped... Enough has been written and spoken about the coronavirus that is still raging in the world as of this writing, and the end of this nightmare is not in sight. What is almost certain is that the world will no longer be as it was before the pandemic outbreak. Everything was ready for Eurovision 2020 in Rotterdam, but in early March, the global storm of corona infections started and did not spare Europe (and the Netherlands in particular). The new and unfamiliar rules of health dictated a strict reality: isolation, distance, and the elimination of large events. After the shock and digestion also came the inevitable news: the Eurovision, like many other big events — will be postponed and held next year. The EBU produced a replacement programme for this year. The same participants will be able to take part next year, but not with the same entry. There were many controversies around this decision. Was it possible to keep the tradition and hold the Eurovision in isolation? Arguably, despite the lack of crowds and the festive atmosphere.

On the other hand, why should the performers and the host suffer from a limited, isolated and sad Eurovision on their shift? Indeed, it was not an easy decision for the EBU. The consequences of the cancellation are interrupting a 64-year-old sequential history.

And again, the Netherlands is facing a fault line in which it is supposed to elevate the Eurovision Song Contest: in 1970, after the Scandinavian countries' retirement and the contest in Madrid, the Dutch hosted the first event of the early 1970s in Amsterdam and did a great job within limits: An amazing stage designed by De Groot, the invention of the "postcard" videos and an exciting win for the Irish Dana. Ten years later, the ESC was in extremis: Practically at the last minute, Israel decided to withdraw from hosting the contest for budgetary reasons, and the contest's permanent cancellation was on the table. Once again, the Netherlands took on the task, on a tight budget, with noticeably brief time to get organised, and excelled yet again with creative ideas and an event that brought the all-time successful Eurovision star, Johnny Logan. Now, for the third time, the Dutch will face a huge challenge: to preserve the event's tradition, which was interrupted due to force majeure, to make the world forget the dark year of 2020 and create a contest that will get the Eurovision train back on track.

Let it be.

2021 - Rotterdam, The Netherlands

The 2021 Eurovision was a great challenge for the Netherlands, which faced a huge hurdle once again - organising and producing the ESC in adverse conditions following a year-long layoff due to the Coronavirus. It is fair to say that the Dutch have done a commendable job in tackling the arduous task. The Coronavirus symptoms: Australia's performance was pre-recorded rather than performed live on stage like the other countries, which may have influenced the fact that the Eurovision aliens ended their journey in the semi-finals.

The event in Rotterdam was not exciting enough, and the entertaining production lacked new ideas (despite the spectacular concept and performance of counting down before the voting lines closed to the audience). A word of praise goes to the contest's new supervisor, Martin Österdahl, who operated modestly, efficiently, and without drawing attention to himself.

This year's slogan was, of course, OPEN UP, a reference to the continent's reopening after the coronavirus nearly entirely closed it down.

The favourites to win this time were Italy and France (which finally lived up to expectations and finished first and second), implying that there is a longing for the old days, and for the first time since the law allowed each country to sing in any desired language - no English song reached the top three (to cap off a particularly dismal evening for this language, the UK finished with 0 points for the first time in the new scoring system's history).

The first semi-final resulted in an unsurprising victory for Malta, which settled for 7th place in the grand final after a fantastic performance by the passionate Destiny. The greatest surprise of the first semi-final came from Israel: Eden Alene's "Set Me Free" was not among the candidates to qualify for the finals. Yet, thanks to a well-executed performance that transcended the song's quality - the Israeli singer of Ethiopian origin achieved the fifth and outstanding place, which did not help her two days later (only 17th place in the final).

The second semi-final included another potential winner, Switzerland, courtesy of Gjon's Tears's emotional performance of the ballad "Tout l'univers." The Swiss won the juries' vote in the final, but as seen in recent years, the audience vote nearly invariably reversed the outcome, sending the devastated Swiss to third place, the best achievement for the country that won the inaugural Eurovision since Céline Dion in 1988.

On the eve of the final, it appeared that France was ready to break the jinx and that Barbara Pravi would finally become the latest French artist to win Eurovision for her country, succeeding Marie Myriam (1977). "Voilà," another tranquil and intriguing ballad, led the voting at times and came close to winning the grand prize before finishing second in the juries' vote. The audience's vote set France in the top three, but it was not enough to place higher than runner-up - a very respectable ending to a spectacular evening for the French (for virtually the whole jury's vote, two quiet entries in French competed for first place).

Italy and the "Måneskin" band eventually swept to victory with a riotous performance of "Zitti e buoni." The Italians led the betting tables virtually the entire time, what may have been the spark for the drift in the public vote, which awarded the Italians 318 points, compared to a lesser score of France, Switzerland, and Malta, which were ahead of them in the jury vote. A minor uproar erupted when the band's lead vocalist was supposedly spotted sniffing a drug during the vote, but a sweeping denial and a voluntary drug test he took rendered the story a storm in a teacup, and the only thing Damiano David sniffed was the intoxicating taste of victory.

Italy wins the Eurovision Song Contest again, 31 years after Toto Cutugno, with France finishing second like it did in Zagreb 1990.

2022 – Turin, Italy

The (nearly) final exit from the corona crisis that engulfed the European continent served as the backdrop for
Eurovision 2022, which also took place amid the Russia-Ukraine war.
The European singing contest, established in order to bring its members together and prevent conflicts, evolved into a different sort of battlefield. The Ukrainian delegation was welcomed with open arms, and the latter's victory was already assured long before the first rehearsal.
Although this cannot be confirmed conclusively, the Russian Federation was suspected of carrying out cyberattacks during the contest's preparations.
Italy cannot be detached from its historic musical heritage, and the organisers did well to include one of the country's best singers, Laura Pausini, on the presenting team.
Eurovision in Italy is usually a source of amusing mini-scandals, and this year was no exception, as the organisers sought to build a "kinetic sun" to recreate the Eurovision stage from 1999. Unfortunately, when it came time to
conduct the intricate technological operation, the organisers faced several malfunctions, leaving them with no choice but to maintain the facility static, and nations that chose to become dynamic did so at their own responsibility.
At one of the contest's receptions, Andrea, North Macedonia's representative, threw her country's flag on the carpet before arriving to take a photo. The unusual conduct shocked the proud Balkan country, and as a result,
Macedonians will be missing from the Eurovision Song Contest in the United Kingdom.
The real "scandal," at least in the eyes of the European Broadcasting Union, was the disqualification of juries' votes from no fewer than six (!) countries (Azerbaijan, Georgia, Montenegro, Poland, Romania and San Marino). The EBU refused to provide further information beyond the official, terse explanation of "irregular voting patterns." Due to the disqualification, the points were distributed based on voting patterns in comparable nations.
The discrepancies in the jury and audience results serve as evidence that there is professional disagreement over the quality of the entry "Stefania" by the band "Kalush Orchestra". Even in the first semi-final, the jurors only awarded the Ukrainians a third-place finish; nevertheless, the audience's vote propelled it to the top spot. A lot was anticipated of Greece, The Netherlands, and Portugal when they joined this round's winner and even hoped to make the top five, but on the night of the finals, they fell short of these positions.
The favourites for the second semi-final were Sweden, Australia, and Serbia, and they delivered by placing in the top three. The Australians, as usual, failed to impress and came in just 15th place, while Sweden and Serbia both maintained their promises on the final night and earned decent positions on the top five.
The United Kingdom, Spain, and Italy also competed in the grand final and were seen to be strong favourites to win; Although there won't be a repeat victory by a host nation at Eurovision this year, Mahmood & Blanco's performance was great. With yet another second-place finish, Sam Ryder brought back the glory of the United Kingdom, much as in the joyous 1980s and 1990s. "Space Man" was the jurors' favourite, but with the impact of the Russia-Ukraine war, it appears that even Paul McCartney could not have secured a British victory that evening...

2023 – Liverpool, United Kingdom

During the week of the contest, the entire kingdom was immersed in ceremonies to honour the inauguration of King Charles, and music took a backseat. However, despite this, Eurovision 2023 emerged as one of the most significant and highest-quality events of the millennium's start. The event showcased a plethora of stars, songs, and attractions. The list of potential victors was extensive and captivating. Leading the contenders was Sweden's Loreen, poised to achieve a double victory like Ireland's Johnny Logan. Following closely was Finland's Kaarija. Israel's Noa Kirel garnered attention not just for her music but also for her "Unicorn" persona, which captured the betting world. Ukraine, amidst ongoing conflict, garnered sympathy and Norway was seen as a dark horse. Even the Czech female performers secured a favourable position. France, United Kingdom, and Italy added intrigue to the multifaceted race.

Liverpool, hometown of the "Beatles", won the hosting rights, solidifying the BBC's reputation as Eurovision's most prolific broadcaster. The partnership between the host and the previous year's winner underscored the collaborative nature of the event. Local directors and producers skilfully leveraged the situation for active participation from King Charles and Queen Camilla, adding a royal touch to Eurovision.

Tradition held its ground, as late Terry Wogan's hosting in 1998 was succeeded by his Irish compatriot Graham Norton, who carried forward their lighthearted approach.

37 nations vied for the 67th Grand Prix. The trend of foreign writers and composers contributing to multiple countries continued, highlighting the inclusive nature of the event.

The first semi-final had a mere 15 participants, with two-thirds of them advancing to the grand final. Despite its apparent ease, this semi-final was one of the most competitive ever, as four of the final's top five, including the top three, emerged from this round.

Loreen's Eurovision win was nearly certain after coming from the Swedish "Melodifestivalen". Betting agencies overwhelmingly crowned her the victor, and experts universally agreed on her impending success. However, a new trend arose leading up to the main event, as the live audience began to embrace the Finnish sensation Kaarija, who astounded the continent with his "Cha Cha Cha" entry. Though Loreen's "Tatoo" still held a significant lead in the stakes, the charismatic young Finn became the crowd favourite. Looking back, Kaarija outperformed Loreen in the semi-finals and claimed the top spot, with the Swede taking second place and Noa Kirel securing third—a remarkably similar outcome to the grand evening.

The second semi-final, featuring 16 participants, showcased notably lower quality. This is evident as Australia, the winner with "Promise," only secured ninth place in the final. Alongside Italy, United Kingdom, France, and Ukraine - the automatic final qualifiers - Saturday evening held much promise and indeed delivered.

The initial third of the evening served as a warm-up for the intense battles that followed. Loreen's polished ninth performance was impressive. "Tatoo" immediately proved its hit status, vindicating those who placed their bets on it.

Italy, since its Eurovision return, consistently achieved high positions. Marco Mangoni followed suit, landing in the top four with "Due Vita". Kaarija's performance nearly tore the roof off Liverpool Arena. The tremendous enthusiasm and uninterrupted applause, even during voting, suggested Finland might waltz to a second victory. This marked the rise of a new star, reading as Eurovision 2023's official highlight. The talented rapper's life story, coupled with battling a chronic disease, resonated with millions, significantly raising awareness.

Czech group "Vesna" anticipated a top 5 spot, but landed only in tenth place. Australia, the second semi-final winner, disappointedly received just 21 points from juries, relegating them to ninth place. Belgium's surprise seventh-place start was soon followed by another shocker - Alika from Estonia.

Norwegian Alessandra secured fifth place with "Queen of Kings", earning 216 audience points. The song remained a post-Eurovision hit. Germany's hopes were dashed, "Lord of the Lost" getting a mere 3 points from juries and 15 from the audience, placing last with "Blood & Glitter." United Kingdom's representative, Mae Muller, fared even worse, her playful "I Wrote a Song" landing second-to-last.

Noa Kirel, impressively, delivered an unforgettable performance with "Unicorn." Though a standout, Israel faced stiff competition in terms of hits and quality, resulting in a commendable third place finish. The swift initial voting deflated tension, as Sweden quickly amassed high scores. A substantial gap separated Loreen from second place, held interchangeably by Finland, Italy, and Israel. Israel emerged as runner-up following juries' votes. The incredibly slight margin fo nearly 2 points the runner-up secured Loreen's historic double victory after Johnny Logan, etching her name in Eurovision history.

Kaarija swept the voters, amassing an impressive 376 points and securing second place. Despite the resonating "cha cha cha" chants in the arena, victory eluded him. Finland's performance stood out, achieving 18 maximum scores, while Sweden failed to secure a single Douze Points from the public votes. This fuelled a significant protest among Eurovision fans, urging for an equal weighting of their votes alongside juries', a protest that gained traction.

Sweden's victory brought their total wins to 7, tying with Eurovision powerhouse Ireland. This marks Sweden's fourth victory since 1999, while Ireland continues to await its first win since 1994.

2024 - Malmö, Sweden

Past Eurovision contests have seen tensions between rival nations, but the hostility and hatred on display in Malmö were unprecedented. We can only pray such ugliness is never repeated. Boycotts, last-minute suspensions, and other challenges plagued those responsible for organising the event.

The events of Eurovision 2024 were directly impacted by the ongoing conflict in the Middle East, from which Israel, a long-time participant, emerged. Israel called for empathy following the brutal massacre of its citizens on October 7, 2023, which inspired the song the country sent to Sweden.

There is a basic rule that has remained unbroken throughout the years of the contest: Leaving politics off the Eurovision stage. Although there were politically charged decisions, it seems we did not encounter an audience tainted by vested interests, managers, producers, or, worst of all, artists and singers focused on boycotts, negativity, hatred, and division.

By the way, the winning song of the contest is titled "The Code." The Swiss performer, Nemo, aims to transcend genders, sects, sides, and choices, but the surrounding reality prevented the song's message from taking hold.

Becoming the queen of contest wins, alongside Ireland, led Sweden to select Malmö as the host city for Eurovision for the third time.

The first semi-final saw the favourite Croatia, alongside the much-discussed Ukraine and Ireland, which came with high ambitions after years of mediocrity. Indeed, these three secured top spots in the final, with Croatia's "Baby Lasagna" winning first place. Luxembourg, returning to the contest after a 31-year absence, shone with Israeli performer Tali, who finished in the top five, kicking off the principality's comeback on a positive note.

In the second semi-final, Israeli Eden Golan triumphed over loud boos, securing an impressive first place. Overnight, Golan emerged as a leading contender for victory, alongside Croatia. The most notable result from this round: Switzerland, the third favourite to win, finished only in fourth place, behind the Netherlands and Armenia.

The grand final was opened by local Björn Skifs, remembered for his Eurovision appearances in 1978 and 1981, where he did not achieve extraordinary success. However, in Sweden, he became a musical idol and one of the country's greatest artists.

After 54 years, since the Netherlands last did so, the Eurovision host is once again opening the contest: Marcus & Martinus did relatively well, finishing in 9th place—not bad.

Dutchman Joost Klein made negative history by being disqualified from the finals, along with his country, due to what was deemed inappropriate behaviour. This unconventional decision by the organisers reduced the number of participants to 25. After years of avoiding its negative reputation, Norway once again finished last at Eurovision... The "Gåte" band can take comfort in joining great Norwegian performers like Jahn Teigen and Finn Kalvik, who faced the same fate.

The Israeli Eden Golan stood in the eye of the storm: During her semi-final and grand final performances, she faced boos and disrespectful calls that could have toppled any other performer. Yet, Eden Golan amazed with polished and courageous performances that, on any other night, would likely have earned first place. The song "Hurricane" (originally titled "October Rain" and rejected due to claims of political connotations) and Eden Golan's stirring vocals stirred great excitement among every Israeli and Jew watching the event. The audience, free from threats and fear, awarded her 323 points. A similar and deserving score from the juries would have been enough for her to win, but, as noted, the impossible situation was clearly reflected in the juries' scores.

The curse of the favourite did not spare Croatia: The audience adored "Baby Lasagna" and awarded him a victory, but the juries defied the betting odds, leaving Croatia with 210 points—only enough for second place overall. France was the only major country to secure a top-five finish, thanks to Slimane's excellent performance. Meanwhile, Ukraine surprised with the song "Teresa & Maria," earning third place and proving that there are countries at war that can garner support and encouragement.

The Swiss Nemo struggled a bit in the semi-finals, but those present at the rehearsals, sensing the buzz around "The Code," understood something significant was brewing—and they were right: The juries voted overwhelmingly in favour of non-binary Nemo. The audience was less decisive, but the combined scores delivered Switzerland its third Eurovision victory in history: After Lys Assia and the legendary Céline Dion, Nemo secured their place in their country's Eurovision pantheon.

2021

Open Up

Country Hosting: The Netherlands
City Hosting: Rotterdam
Date: 18.5.2021 (1st Semi Final), 20.5.2021 (2nd Semi Final), 22.5.2021 (Final)
Location: Rotterdam Ahoy
Presenters: Chantal Janzen, Edsilia Rombley, Jan Smit, Nikkie de Jager
Executive Supervisor: Martin Österdahl
Directed By: Marnix Kaart, Marc Pos, Daniel Jelinek
Executive Producer: Sietse Bakker, Astrid Dutrénit
Participating Countries: 39
Voting System: Juries voting and televoting (50-50), points are given by the regular system
Broadcaster: Nederlandse Omroep Stichting (NOS), Nederlandse Publieke Omroep (NPO)

First Semi Final, 18.5.2021

10 marked grey countries qualified to the Final
(Germany, Italy and The Netherlands were allowed to vote this semi-final)

No.	Country	Song	Performing Artist	Language	Points	Place
1	Lithuania	"Discoteque"	The Roop	English	203	4
2	Slovenia	"Amen"	Ana Soklič	English	44	13
3	Russia	"Russian Woman"	Manizha	Russian, English	225	3
4	Sweden	"Voices"	Tusse	English	142	7
5	Australia	"Technicolour"	Montaigne	English	28	14
6	North Macedonia	"Here I Stand"	Vasil	English	23	15
7	Ireland	"Maps"	Lesley Roy	English	20	16
8	Cyprus	"El diablo"	Elena Tsagrinou	English	170	6
9	Norway	"Fallen Angel"	"Tix"	English	115	10
10	Croatia	"Tick-Tock"	Albina	English , Croatian	110	11
11	Belgium	"The Wrong Place"	Hooverphonic	English	117	9
12	Israel	"Set Me Free"	Eden Alene	English	192	5
13	Romania	"Amnesia"	Roxen	English	85	12
14	Azerbaijan	"Mata Hari"	Efendi	English	138	8
15	Ukraine	"Shum" (Шум)	Go_A	Ukrainian	267	2
16	Malta	"Je me casse"	Destiny	English	325	1

Second Semi Final, 20.5.2021

10 marked grey countries qualified to the Final
(United Kingdom, France and Spain were allowed to vote this semi-final)

No.	Country	Song	Performing Artist	Language	Points	Place
1	San Marino	"Adrenalina"	Senhit	English	118	9
2	Estonia	"The Lucky One"	Uku Suviste	English	58	13
3	Czech Republic	"Omaga"	Benny Cristo	English	23	15
4	Greece	"Last Dance"	Stefania	English	184	6
5	Austria	"Amen"	Vincent Bueno	English	66	12
6	Poland	"The Ride"	Rafał	English	35	14
7	Moldova	"Sugar"	Natalia Gordienko	English	179	7
8	Iceland	"10 Years"	Daði og Gagnamagnið	English	288	2
9	Serbia	"Loco Loco"	Hurricane	Serbian	124	8
10	Georgia	"You"	Tornike Kipiani	English	16	16
11	Albania	"Karma"	Anxhela Peristeri	Albania	112	10
12	Portugal	"Love Is on My Side"	The Black Mamba	English	239	4
13	Bulgaria	"Growing Up Is Getting Old"	Victoria	English	250	3
14	Finland	"Dark Side"	Blind Channel	English	234	5
15	Latvia	"The Moon Is Rising"	Samanta Tina	English	14	17
16	Switzerland	"Tout l'univers"	Gjon's Tears	French	291	1
17	Denmark	"Øve os på hinanden"	Fyr & Flamme	Danish	89	11

FINAL 22.5.2021

No.	Country	Song	Performing Artist	Lyrics	Composer	Language	Commentator	Spoker of Results	Points	Place
01	Cyprus	"El diablo"	Elena Tsagrinou	Jimmy "Joker" Thörnfeldt, Laurell Barker, Cleiton "OXA" Sia, Thomas Stengaard	Jimmy "Joker" Thörnfeldt, Laurell Barker, Cleiton "OXA" Sia, Thomas Stengaard	English	Louis Patsalides	Loukas Hamatsos	94	16
02	Albania	"Karma"	Anxhela Peristeri	Kledi Bahiti	Raúl Gómez, Sylvia Santoro	Albanian	Tony Aguilar, Julia Varela	Nieves Álvarez	57	21
03	Israel	"Set Me Free"	Eden Alene	Lea Sirk	Lea Sirk, Tomy DeClerque	English	Andrej Hofer	Maja Keuc	93	17
04	Belgium	"The Wrong Place"	Hooverphonic	Alex Callier, Charlotte Forêt	Alex Callier, Charlotte Forêt	English	Fanny Jandrain, Jean-Louis Lahaye	Danira Boukhriss	74	19
05	Russia	"Russian Woman"	Manizha	Manizha	Ori Avni, Ori Kaplan, Manizha	English, Russian	Yuri Aksyuta , Yana Churikova	Polina Gagarina	204	9
06	Malta	"Je me casse"	Destiny	Amanuel Dermont, Malin Christin, Nicklas Eklund, Pete Barringer	Amanuel Dermont, Malin Christin, Nicklas Eklund, Pete Barringer	English	-	Stephanie Spiteri	255	7
07	Portugal	"Love Is on My Side"	"The Black Mamba" (Pedro Tatanka, Miguel Casais, Marco Pombinho, Rui Pedro "Pity" Vaz, Guilherme "Gui" Salgueiro)	Pedro Tatanka, Caldeira	Pedro Tatanka, Caldeira	English	José Carlos Malato, Nuno Galopim	Elisa Maria Silva	153	12
08	Serbia	"Loco Loco"	"Hurricane" (Sanja Vučić, Ivana Nikolić, Ksenija Knežević)	Sanja Vučić	Nemanja Antonić, Darko Dimitrov	Serbian	Duška Vučinić	Dragana Kosjerina	102	15
09	United Kingdom	"Embers"	James Newman	James Newman, Conor Blake, Danny Shah, Tom Hollings, Samuel Brennan	James Newman, Conor Blake, Danny Shah, Tom Hollings, Samuel Brennan	English	Scott Mills, Sara Cox, Chelcee Grimes, Graham Norton	Amanda Holden	0	26
10	Greece	"Last Dance"	Stefania	Dimitris Kontopoulos, ARCADE, Sharon Vaughn	Dimitris Kontopoulos, ARCADE	English	Maria Kozakou, Giorgos Kapoutzidis	Manolis Gkinis	170	10
11	Switzerland	"Tout l'univers"	"Gjon's Tears" (Gjon Muharremaj)	Gjon Muharremaj, Nina Sampermans, Wouter Hardy, Xavier Michel	Gjon Muharremaj, Nina Sampermans, Wouter Hardy, Xavier Michel	French	Sven Epiney, Jean-Marc Richard, Nicolas Tanner, Joseph Gorgoni, Clarissa Tami and Sebalter	Angélique Beldner	432	3
12	Iceland	"10 Years"	Daði og Gagnamagnið	Daði Freyr Pétursson	Daði Freyr Pétursson	English	Gísli Marteinn Baldursson, Elsa G. Björnsdóttir	Hannes Óli Ágústsson	378	4
13	Spain	"Voy a quedarme"	Blas Cantó Moreno	Blas Cantó, Dan Hammond, Leroy Sanchez, Dangelo Ortega	Blas Cantó, Dan Hammond, Leroy Sanchez, Dangelo Ortega	Spanish	Tony Aguilar, Julia Varela , Víctor Escudero	Nieves Álvarez	6	24
14	Moldova	"Sugar"	Natalia Gordienko	Mikhail Gutseriev, Sharon Vaughn	Dimitris Kontopoulos, Philipp Kirkorov	English	-	Sergey Stepanov	115	13
15	Germany	"I Don't Feel Hate"	Jendrik Sigwart	Jendrik Sigwart, Christoph, Oswald	Jendrik Sigwart, Christoph, Oswald	English	Peter Urban	Barbara Schöneberger	3	25
16	Finland	"Dark Side"	"Blind Channel" (Joel Hokka, Niko Moilanen, Joonas Porko, Olli Matela, Tommi Lalli, Aleksi Kaunisvesi)	Aleksi Kaunisvesi, Joonas Porko, Joel Hokka, Niko Moilanen, Olli Matela	Aleksi Kaunisvesi, Joonas Porko, Joel Hokka, Niko Moilanen, Olli Matela	English	Mikko Silvennoinen	Katri Norrlin	301	6
17	Bulgaria	"Growing Up Is Getting Cld"	Victoria Georgieva	Helena Larsson, Maya Nalani, Oliver Björkvall, Victoria Georgieva	Helena Larsson, Maya Nalani, Oliver Björkvall, Victoria Georgieva	English	Elena Rosberg , Petko Kralev	Joanna Dragneva	170	11
18	Lithuania	"Discoteque"	"The Roop" (Vaidotas Valiukevičius, Robertas Baranauskas, Mantas Banisauskas)	Vaidotas Valiukevičius, Mantas Banisauskas, Kalle Lindroth	Vaidotas Valiukevičius, Robertas Baranauskas, Mantas Banisauskas, Laisvūnas Cernovas, Ilkka Wirtanen	English	Ramūnas Zilnys	Andrius Mamontovas	220	8
19	Ukraine	"Shum"	"Go_A" (Kateryna Pavlenko, Taras Shevchenko, Ihor Didenchuk, Ivan Hryhoriak)	Kateryna Pavlenko	Taras Shevchenko, Kateryna Pavlenko, Ihor Didenchuk	Ukrainian	Timur Miroshnychenko	Tayanna	364	5
20	France	"Voilà"	Barbara Pravi	Barbara Pravi, Lili Poe	Barbara Pravi, Antoine "Igit" Barrau	French	Stéphane Bern, Laurence Boccolini	Carla	499	2
21	Azerbaijan	"Mata Hari"	Samira Azer gizi Efendiyeva	Amy van der Wel, Josh Earl, Tony Cornelissen, Luuk van Beers	Amy van der Wel, Josh Earl, Tony Cornelissen, Luuk van Beers	English	Hüsniyyə Məhərrəmova	Ell & Nikki	105	16
22	Norway	"Fallen Angel"	Tix - Andreas Andresen Haukeland	Andreas Haukeland, Emelie Hollow, Mathias Haukeland	Andreas Haukeland	English	Marte Stokstad	Silje Skjemstad Cruz	75	18
23	Netherlands	"Birth of a New Age"	Jeangu Macrooy	Jeangu Macrooy , Pieter Perquin	Jeangu Macrooy , Pieter Perquin	English, Sranan Tongo	Cornald Maas , Sander Lantinga	Romy Monteiro	11	23
24	Italy	"Zitti e buoni"	"Måneskin" (Damiano David, Victoria De Angelis, Thomas Raggi, Ethan Torchio)	Damiano David, Ethan Torchio, Thomas Raggi, Victoria De Angelis	Damiano David, Ethan Torchio, Thomas Raggi, Victoria De Angelis	Italian	Gabriele Corsi , Cristiano Malgioglio	Carolina Di Domenico	524	1
25	Sweden	"Voices"	Tusse - Tousin Michael Chiza	Joy Deb, Linnea Deb, Jimmy "Joker" Thörnfeldt, Anderz Wrethov	Joy Deb, Linnea Deb, Jimmy "Joker" Thörnfeldt, Anderz Wrethov	English	Edward af Sillén, Christer Björkman	Carola	109	14
26	San Marino	"Adrenalina"	Senhit Zadik Zadik	Chanel Tukia, Tramar Dillard, Jimmy "Joker" Thörnfeldt, Joy Deb, Kenny Silverdique, Linnea Deb, Malou Linn, Eloïse Ruotsalainen, Senhit Zadik Zadik, Suzi Pancenkov, Thomas Stengaard	Chanel Tukia, Tramar Dillard, Jimmy "Joker" Thörnfeldt, Joy Deb, Kenny Silverdique, Linnea Deb, Malou Linn, Eloïse Ruotsalainen, Senhit Zadik Zadik, Suzi Pancenkov, Thomas Stengaard	English	Lia Fiorio and Gigi Restivo	Lia Fiorio and Gigi Restivo	50	22

Country Hosting: Italy
City Hosting: Turin
Date: 10.5.2022 (1st Semi Final), 12.5.2022 (2nd Semi Final), 14.5.2022 (Final)
Location: ParaOLimpico
Presenters: Alessandro Cattelan, Mika, Laura Pausini
Executive Supervisor: Martin Österdahl
Directed By: Christian Biondani, Duccio Forzano
Executive Producer: Claudio Fasulo, Simona Martorelli
Participating Countries: 40
Voting System: Juries voting and televoting (50-50), points are given by the regular system
Broadcaster: RAI (Radioetelevisione Italian)

2022
The Sound of Beauty

First Semi Final, 10.5.2022
10 marked grey countries qualified to the Final
(France and Italy were allowed to vote this semi-final)

No.	Country	Song	Performing Artist	Language	Points	Place
1	Albania	"Sekret"	Ronela Hajati	English, Albanian	58	12
2	Latvia	"Eat Your Salad"	Citi Zēni	English	55	14
3	Lithuania	"Sentimentai"	Monika Liu	Lithuanian	159	7
4	Switzerland	"Boys Do Cry"	Marius Bear	English	118	9
5	Slovenia	"Disko"	LPS	Slovene	15	17
6	Ukraine	"Stefania"	Kalush Orchestra	Ukrainian	337	1
7	Bulgaria	"Intention"	Intelligent Music Project	English	29	16
8	Netherlands	"De diepte"	S10	Dutch	221	2
9	Moldova	"Trenulețul"	Zdob și Zdub and Advahov Brothers	Romanian, English	154	8
10	Portugal	"Saudade, saudade"	Maro	English, Portuguese	208	4
11	Croatia	"Guilty Pleasure"	Mia Dimšić	English, Croatian	75	11
12	Denmark	"The Show"	Reddi	English	55	13
13	Austria	"Halo"	Lumix feat. Pia Maria	English	42	15
14	Iceland	"Með hækkandi sól"	Systur	Icelandic	103	10
15	Greece	"Die Together"	Amanda Georgiadi Tenfjord	English	211	3
16	Norway	"Give That Wolf a Banana"	Subwoolfer	English	177	6
17	Armenia	"Snap"	Rosa Linn	English	187	5

Second Semi Final, 12.5.2022
10 marked grey countries qualified to the Final
(United Kingdom, Germany and Spain were allowed to vote this semi-final)

No.	Country	Song	Performing Artist	Language	Points	Place
1	Finland	"Jezebel"	The Rasmus	English	162	7
2	Israel	"I.M"	Michael Ben David	English	61	13
3	Serbia	"In corpore sano"	Konstrakta	Serbian, Latin	237	3
4	Azerbaijan	"Fade to Black"	Nadir Rustamli	English	96	10
5	Georgia	"Lock Me In"	Circus Mircus	English	22	18
6	Malta	"I Am What I Am"	Emma Muscat	English	47	16
7	San Marino	"Stripper"	Achille Lauro	Italian, English	50	14
8	Australia	"Not the Same"	Sheldon Riley	English	243	2
9	Cyprus	"Ela"	Andromache	English, Greek	63	12
10	Ireland	"That's Rich"	Brooke	English	47	15
11	North Macedonia	"Circles"	Andrea	English	76	11
12	Estonia	"Hope"	Stefan	English	209	5
13	Romania	"Llámame"	WRS	English, Spanish	118	9
14	Poland	"River"	Ochman	English	198	6
15	Montenegro	"Breathe"	Vladana	English, Italian	33	17
16	Belgium	"Miss You"	Jérémie Makiese	English	151	8
17	Sweden	"Hold Me Closer"	Cornelia Jakobs	English	396	1
18	Czech Republic	"Lights Off"	We Are Domi	English	227	4

FINAL

14.5.2022

No.	Country	Song	Performing Artist	Lyrics	Composer	Language	Commentator	Spoker of Results	Points	Place
01	Czech Republic	"Lights Off"	We Are Domi (Dominika Hašková, Casper Hatlestad, Benjamin Rekstad)	Einar Eriksen Kvaløy, Abigail Frances Jones, Dominika Hašková Casper Hatlestad, Benjamin Rekstad	Einar Eriksen Kvaløy, Abigail Frances Jones, Dominika Hašková Casper Hatlestad, Benjamin Rekstad	English	Jan Maxián	Taťána Kuchařová	38	22
02	Romania	"Llámame"	WRS (Andrei-Ionuț Ursu)	Andrei Ursu, Cezar Gună	Andrei Ursu, Cezar Gună, Alexandru Turcu, Costel Dominteanu	English, Spanish	Bogdan Stănescu	-	65	18
03	Portugal	"Saudade, saudade"	Maro (Mariana Brito da Cruz Forjaz Secca)	Mariana Secca	Mariana Secca, John Blanda	English, Portugûes	Nuno Galopim	Pedro Tatanka	207	9
04	Finland	"Jezebel"	The Rasmus (Lauri Ylönen, Eero Heinonen, Aki Hakala, Emilia "Emppu" Suhonen)	Lauri Ylönen, Desmond Child	Lauri Ylönen, Desmond Child	English	Mikko Silvennoinen	Aksel	38	21
05	Switzerland	"Boys Do Cry"	Marius Bear	Marius Hugli, Martin Gallop	Marius Hugli, Martin Gallop	English	Sven Epiney, Jean-Marc Richard , Gjon's Tears, Clarissa Iami, Francesca Margiotta, Boris Piffaretti	Julie Berthollet	78	17
06	France	"Fulenn"	Alvan (Alexs Moryan Rosius) & Ahez (Marine Lavigne, Sterenn Diridollou, Sterenn Le Guillou)	Alvan, Ahez, Alexandra Redde-Amiel	Alvan, Ahez, Alexandra Redde-Amiel	Breton	Stéphane Bern, Laurence Boccolini	Élodie Gossuin	17	24
07	Norway	"Give That Wolf a Banana"	Subwoolfer (Keith Jim DJ Astronaut)	DJ Astronaut, Jim, Keith	DJ Astronaut, Jim, Keith	English	Marte Stokstad	Tix	182	10
08	Armenia	"Snap"	Rosa Linn	Rosa Linn, Larzz Principato, Jeremy Dusoulet, Allie Crystal, Tamar Kaprelian, Courtney Harrell	Rosa Linn, Larzz Principato, Jeremy Dusoulet, Allie Crystal, Tamar Kaprelian, Courtney Harrell	English	Garik Papoyan , Hrachuhi Utmazyan	Garik Papoyan	61	20
09	Italy	"Brividi"	Mahmood & Blanco	Mahmood, Blanco	Michelangelo, Mahmood, Blanco	Italian	Gabriele Corsi ,Cristiano Malgioglio, Carolina Di Domenico	Carolina Di Domenico	268	6
10	Spain	"SloMo"	Chanel	Leroy Sanchez, Keith Harris, Ibere Fortes, Maggie Szabo, Arjen "SWACQ" Thonen	Leroy Sanchez, Keith Harris, Ibere Fortes, Maggie Szabo, Arjen "SWACQ" Thonen	English, Spanish	Tony Aguilar , Julia Varela	Nieves Álvarez	450	3
11	Netherlands	"De diepte"	S10	Arno Krabman, Stien den Hollander	Arno Krabman, Stien den Hollander	Dutch	Cornald Maas, Jan Smit	Jeangu Macrooy	171	11
12	Ukraine	"Stefania"	Kalush Orchestra (Oleh Psiuk, Ihor Didenchuk, Vlad Kurochka)	Ivan Klymenko, Oleh Psiuk	Ihor Didenchuk, Tymofii Muzychuk, Vitalii Duzhyk	Ukrainian	Timur Miroshnychenko	Kateryna Pavlenko	631	1
13	Germany	"Rockstars"	Malik Harris	Malik Harris, Marie Kobylka, Robin Karow	Malik Harris, Marie Kobylka, Robin Karow	English	Peter Urban	Barbara Schöneberger	6	25
14	Lithuania	"Sentimentai"	Monika Liu	Monika Liubinaitė	Monika Liubinaitė	Lithuanian	Ramūnas Zilnys	Vaidotas Valiukevičius	128	14
15	Azerbaijan	"Fade to Black"	Nadir Rustamli	Andreas Stone Johansson, Anderz Wrethov, Sebastian Schub, Thomas Stengaard	Andreas Stone Johansson, Anderz Wrethov, Sebastian Schub, Thomas Stengaard	English	Murad Arif	-	106	16
16	Belgium	"Miss You"	Jérémie Makiese	Jérémie Makiese, Mike BGRZ, Manon Romiti, Paul Ivory, Silvio Lisbonne	Jérémie Makiese, Mike BGRZ, Manon Romiti, Paul Ivory, Silvio Lisbonne	English	Peter Van de Veire, Jean-Louis Lahaye , Maureen Louys	David Jeanmotte	64	19
17	Greece	"Die Together"	Amanda Georgiadi Tenfjord	Amanda Georgiadis , Tenfjord Bjørn, Helge Gammelsæter	Amanda Georgiadis , Tenfjord Bjørn, Helge Gammelsæter	English	Maria Kozakou , Giorgos Kapoutzidis	Stefania	215	8
18	Iceland	"Með hækkandi sól"	Systur (Sigríður Eyþórsdóttir, Elísabet Eyþórsdóttir, Elín Eyþórsdóttir)	Lovísa Elísabet, Sigrúnardóttir	Lovísa Elísabet, Sigrúnardóttir	Icelandic	Gísli Marteinn Baldursson	Árný Fjóla Ásmundsdóttir	20	23
19	Moldova	"Trenuleţul"	Zdob și Zdub (Roman Iagupov, Mihai Gîncu, Sveatoslav Starus, Andrei Cebotari, Valeriu Mazîlu, Victor Dândeș) & Advahov Brothers	Zdob și Zdub, Frații Advahov	Zdob și Zdub, Frații Advahov	English, Romanian	Ion Jalbă, Daniela Crudu	Elena Băncilă	253	7
20	Sweden	"Hold Me Closer"	Cornelia Jakobs	Cornelia Jakobsdotter, David Zandén, Isa Molin	Cornelia Jakobsdotter, David Zandén, Isa Molin	English	Edward af Sillén , Linnea Henriksson	Dotter	438	4
21	Australia	"Not the Same"	Sheldon Riley	Sheldon Riley, Cam Nacson, Timi Temple	Sheldon Riley, Cam Nacson, Timi Temple	English	Myf Warhurst , Joel Creasey	Courtney Act	125	15
22	United Kingdom	"Space Man"	Sam Ryder	Sam Ryder, Amy Wadge, Max Wolfgang	Sam Ryder, Amy Wadge, Max Wolfgang	English	Graham Norton	AJ Odudu	466	2
23	Poland	"River"	Ochman	Ochman, Ashley Hicklin	Ochman, Ashley Hicklin, Adam Wiśniewski, Mikołaj Trybulec	English	Aleksander Sikora, Marek Sierocki	Ida Nowakowska	151	12
24	Serbia	"In corpore sano"	Konstrakta	Ana Đurić	Ana Đurić. Milovan Bošković	English, Serbian	Silvana Grujić	Dragana Kosjerina	312	5
25	Estonia	"Hope"	Stefan	Stefan Airapetjan, Karl-Ander Reismann	Stefan Airapetjan, Karl-Ander Reismann	English	Marko Reikop	Tanel Padar	141	13

2023
United by Music

Country Hosting: United Kingdom
City Hosting: Liverpool
Date: Date: 9.5.2023 (1st Semi Final), 11.5.2023 (2nd Semi Final), 13.5.2023 (Final)
Location: Liverpool Arena
Presenters: Alesha Dixon, Hannah Waddingham, Julia Sanina, Graham Norton
Executive Supervisor: Martin Österdahl
Directed By: Nikki Parsons, Richard Valentine, Ollie Bartlett
Executive Producer: Andrew Cartmell
Participating Countries: 37
Voting System: Juries voting and televoting (50-50), points are given by the regular system
Broadcaster: BBC (British Broadcasting Corporation)

First Semi Final, 9.5.2023
10 marked grey countries qualified to the Final
(France, Germany and Italy were allowed to vote this semi-final)

No.	Country	Song	Performing Artist	Language	Points	Place
1	Norway	"Queen of Kings"	Alessandra	English	102	6
2	Malta	"Dance (Our Own Party)"	The Busker	English	3	15
3	Serbia	"Samo mi se Spava"	Luke Black	Serbian, English	37	10
4	Latvia	"Aija"	Sudden Lights	English	34	11
5	Portugal	"Ai coracao"	Mimicat	Portuguese	74	9
6	Ireland	"We are one"	Wild Youth	English	10	12
7	Croatia	"Mama SC!"	Let 3	Croatian	76	8
8	Switzerland	"Watergun"	Remo Forrer	English	97	7
9	Israel	"Unicorn"	Noa Kirel	English, Hebrew	127	3
10	Moldova	"Soarele si luna"	Pasha Pafeni	Romanian	109	5
11	Sweden	"Tatoo"	Loreen	English	135	2
12	Azerbaijan	"Tell me more"	TuralTuranX	English	4	14
13	Czech Republic	"My sister's Crown"	Vesna	English, Ukrainian, Czech, Bulgarian	110	4
14	Netherlands	"Burning Daylight"	Mia Nicolai & Dion Cooper	English	7	13
15	Finland	"Cha Cha Cha"	Kaarija	Finnish	177	1

Second Semi Final, 11.5.2023
10 marked grey countries qualified to the Final
(United Kingdom, Ukraine and Spain were allowed to vote this semi-final)

No.	Country	Song	Performing Artist	Language	Points	Place
1	Denmark	"Breaking my heart"	Reiley	English	6	14
2	Armenia	"Future Lover"	Brunette	English, Armenian	99	6
3	Romania	"D.G.T. (Off and on)	Theodor Andrei	Romanian, English	0	15
4	Estonia	"Bridges"	Alika	English	74	10
5	Belgium	"Because of you"	Gustaph	English	90	8
6	Cyprus	"Break a Broken Heart"	Andrew Lambrou	English	94	7
7	Iceland	"Power"	Dilja	English	44	11
8	Greece	"What they say"	Victor Vernicos	English	14	13
9	Poland	"Solo"	Blanka	English	124	3
10	Slovenia	"Carpe Diem"	Joker Out	Slovenian	103	5
11	Georgia	"Echo"	Iru	English	33	12
12	San Marino	"Like an Animal"	Piqued Jacks	English	0	15
13	Austria	"Who the Hell is Edgar?"	Teya and Salena	English	137	2
14	Albania	"Duje"	Albina and Familija Kalmendi	Albanian	83	9
15	Lithuania	"Stay"	Monika Linkyte	English	110	4
16	Australia	"Promise"	Voyager	English	149	1

FINAL 13.5.2023

No.	Country	Song	Performing Artist	Lyrics	Composer	Language	Commentator	Spoker of Results	Points	Place
01	Austria	"Who the hell is Edgar?"	Teya & Salena	Selina-Maria Edbauer, Ronald Janecek, Pele Loriano, Teodora Spiric	Selina-Maria Edbauer, Ronald Janecek, Pele Loriano, Teodora Spiric	English	Jan Bohmermann, Olli Schulz	Philipp Hansa	120	16
02	Portugal	"Ai Coracao"	Mimicat (Marisa Isabel Lopes Mena)	Marisa Isabel Lopes Mena	Marisa Isabel Lopes Mena, Luis Pereira	Portuguese	Josa Carlos, Malato & Nuno Galopim	Ben Adams	59	23
03	Switzerland	"Watergun"	Remo Forrer	Argyle Singh, Ashley Hicklin, Mikolaj Trybulec	Argyle Singh, Ashley Hicklin, Mikolaj Trybulec	English	Jean-Marc Richard, Nicolas Tanner, Priscilla Formaz, Ellis Cavallini, Gian-Andrea Costa	Chiara Dubey	92	20
04	Poland	"Solo"	Blanka (Stajkow)	Blanka Stajkow, Maria Broberg, Julia Sundberg	Blanka Stajkow, Maciej Puchalski, Mikolaj Trybulec, Bartlomiej Rzeczycki, Martin Gorecki	English	Aleksander Sikora, Marek Sierocki	Ida Nowakowska	93	18
05	Serbia	"Samo mi se spava"	Luke Black	Luke Black	Luke Black	Serbian, English	Duska Vucinic	Dragana Kosjerina	30	24
06	France	"Evidemment"	La Zarra	Fatima Zahra Hafdi, Ahmed Saghir	Fatima Zahra Hafdi, Ahmed Saghir, Yannick Rastogi, Zacharie Raymond	French	Laurence Boccolini, Stephane Bern	Anggun	104	17
07	Cyprus	"Brake a Broken Heart"	Andrew Lambrou	Jimmy Jansson, Jimmy "Joker" Thornfeldt, Marcus Winther-John, Thomas Stengaard	Jimmy Jansson, Jimmy "Joker" Thornfeldt, Marcus Winther-John, Thomas Stengaard	English	Melina Karageorgiou, Alexandros Taramountas	Loukas Hamatsos	126	12
08	Spain	"Eaea"	Blanca Paloma	Blanca Paloma Ramos, Jose Pablo Polo, Alvaro Tato	Blance Paloma Ramos, Jose Pablo Polo	Spanish	David Asensio, Imanol Duran, Irene Vaquero, Angela Fernandez	Ruth Lorenzo	100	18
09	Sweden	"Tattoo"	Loreen	Jimmy "Joker" Thornfeldt, Jimmy Jansson, Lorine Talhaoui, Moa Carlebecker, Peter Bostrom, Thmoas G:son	Jimmy "Joker" Thornfeldt, Jimmy Jansson, Lorine Talhaoui, Moa Carlebecker, Peter Bostrom, Thmoas G:son	English	Edward af Sillen, Mans Zelmerlow	Farah Abadi	583	1
10	Albania	"Duje"	Albina & Familija Kelmendi	Eriona Rushiti	Enis Mullaj	Albanian	Andri Xhahu	Andri Xhahu	76	22
11	Italy	"Due Vita"	Marco Mangoni	Marco Mangoni, Davide Petrella, Davide Simonetta	E.D.D., Davide Simonetta	Italian	Gabriele Corsi, Mara Maionchi	Kaze	350	4
12	Estonia	"Bridges"	Alika	Alika Milova, Wouter Hardy, Nina Sampermans	Alika Milova, Wouter Hardy	English	Marko Reikop, Aleksandr Hobotov, Julia Kalenda	Ragner Klavan	168	8
13	Finland	"Cha cha cha"	Kaarija	Johannes Naukkarinen, Jere Poyhonen, Aleksi Nurmi, Jukka Sorsa	Johannes Naukkarinen, Aleksi Nurmi, Jukka Sorsa	Finnish	Eva Frantz, Johan Lindroos, Heli Huovinen, Aslak Paltto	Bess	526	2
14	Czech Republic	"My Sister's Crown"	Vesna (Patricie Kanok Fuxova, Bara Sustkova, Olesya Ochepovskaya, Marketa Jerdalova, Tanita Yankova, Tereza Cepkova)	Patricie Kanok Fuxova, Tanita Yankova, Kateryna Vatchenko	Adam Albrecht, Michal Jiran, Patricie Kanok Fuxova, Simon Martinek, Tanita Yankova	English, Czech, Bulgarian, Ukrainian	Jan Maxian	Radka Rosicka	129	10
15	Australia	"Promise"	Voyager (Daniel "Danny" Estrin, Simone Dow, Scott Kay, Ashley Doodkorte, Alex Canion)	Daniel Estrin	Alex Canion, Ashley Doodkorte, Daniel Estrin, Scott Kay, Simone Dow	English	Myf Warhurst, Joel Creasey	Catherine Martin	151	9
16	Belgium	"Because of you"	Gustaph	Stef Caers, Jaouad Alloul	Stef Caers, Jaouad Alloul	English	Peter Van de Veire, Jean-Louis Lahaye, Maureen Louys	Bart Cannaerts	182	7
17	Armenia	"Future Lover"	Brunette	Elen Yeremyan	Elen Yeremyan	English, Armenian	Hrachuni Utmazyan, Hamlet Arakelyan	Malena	122	15
18	Moldova	"Soarele si luna"	Pasha Parfeni	Iuliana Pafeni	Pavel Pafeni, Andrei Vulpe	Romanian	Ion Jalba	Doina Stimpovschi	96	19
19	Ukraine	"Heart of Steel"	Tvorchi (Andrii Hutsuliak, Jimoh Augustus Kehinde)	Andrii Hutsuliak, Jimoh Augustus Kehinde	Andrii Hutsuliak, Jimoh Augustus Kehinde	Ukrainian, English	Timur Miroshnychenko, Oleksandra Franko, Oleksander Barbelen	Zlata Ognevich	243	6
20	Norway	"Queen of Kings"	Alessandra	Henning Olerud, Stanley Ferdinandez, Allessandra Mele, Linda Dale	Henning Olerud, Stanley Ferdinandez, Allessandra Mele, Linda Dale	English	Arian Engebo, Egil Skurdal, Adelina Ibishi, Nate Kahungu	Ben Adams	268	5
21	Germany	"Blood & Glitter"	Lord of the Lost (Chris "Lord" Harms, Class Grenayde, Gared Dirge, Pi Stoffers, Niklas Kahl)	Anthony J. Brown, Chris Harms, Pi Stoffers, Rupert Keplinger	Chris Harms, Rupert Keplinger	English	Peter Urban	Elton	18	26
22	Lithuania	"Stay"	Monika Linkyte	Monika Linkyte, Krists Indrisonoks, Arturas Plume	Monika Linkyte, Krists Indrisonoks, Arturas Plume	English	Ramunas Zilnys	Monika Liu	127	13
23	Israel	"Unicorn"	Noa Krel	Doron Madalie, May Sfadia, Yinon Yahel, Noa Kirel	Doron Madalie, May Sfadia, Yinon Yahel, Noa Kirel	English, Hebrew	Assaf Liberman, Akiva Novick, Doron Madalie	Ilanit	362	3
24	Slovenia	"Carpe Diem"	Joker Out (Bojan Cvjeticanin, Jure Maces, Kris Gustin, Jan Peteh, Nace Jordan)	Bojan Cvjeticanin	Bojan Cvjeticanin, Jan Peteh, Jure Maces, Kris Gustin, Nace Jordan, Zarko Pak	Slovene	Maja Stepancic, Miha Salehar, Ursula Zaletelj	Melani Mekicar	78	21
25	Croatia	"Mama SC!"	Let 3 (Damir Martinovic, Zoran Prodanovic, Ivan Bojcic, Drazen Baljak, Matej Zec)	Damir Martinovic	Damir Martinovic, Zoran Prodanovic	Croatian	Dusko Curlic	Maja Ciglenecki	123	14
26	United Kingdom	"I wrote a Song"	Mae Muller	Holly Mae Muller, Keren Poole, Lewis Thompson	Holly Mae Muller, Keren Poole, Lewis Thompson	English	Graham Norton, Mel Giedroyc	Catherine Tate	24	25

Country Hosting: Sweden
City Hosting: Malmö
Date: 7.5.2024 (1st Semi Final), 9.5.2024 (2nd Semi Final), 11.5.2024 (Final)
Location: Malmö Arena
Presenters: Petra Mede, Malin Akerman
Executive Supervisor: Martin Österdahl
Directed By: Robin Hofwander, Daniel Jelinek, Fredrik Backlund
Executive Producer: Ebba Adielsson, Christel Tholse Willers
Participating Countries: 37
Voting System: Juries voting and televoting (50-50), points are given by the regular system
Broadcaster: Sveriges Television (SVT)

2024

United by Music

Second Semi Final, 9.5.2024

10 marked grey countries qualified to the Final

(France, Italy, Spain and the 'Rest of the World' were allowed to vote this semi-final)

No.	Country	Song	Performing Artist	Language	Points	Place
1	Malta	"Loop"	Sarah Bonnici	English	13	16
2	Albania	"Titan"	Besa	English	14	15
3	Greece	"Zari"	Marina Satti	Greek	86	5
4	Switzerland	"The Code"	Nemo	English	132	4
5	Czech Republic	"Pedestal"	Aiko	English	38	11
6	Austria	"We Will Rave"	Kaleen	English	46	9
7	Denmark	"Sand"	Saba	English	36	12
8	Armenia	"Jako"	Ladaniva	Armenian	137	3
9	Latvia	"Hollow"	Dons	English	72	7
10	San Marino	"11:11"	Megara	Spanish	16	14
11	Georgia	"Firefighter"	Nutsa Buzaladze	English	54	8
12	Belgium	"Before the party's Over"	Mustii	English	18	13
13	Estonia	"(Nendest) narkootikumidest ei tea me (kull) midagi"	5miinust & Puuluup	Estonian	79	6
14	Israel	"Hurricane"	Eden Golan	Hebrew, English	194	1
15	Norway	"Ulveham"	Gate	Norweigen	43	10
16	Netherlands	"Europapa"	Joost Klein	Dutch	182	2

First Semi Final, 7.5.2024

10 marked grey countries qualified to the Final

(United Kingdom, Germany, Sweden and the 'Rest of the World' were allowed to vote this semi-final)

No.	Country	Song	Performing Artist	Language	Points	Place
1	Cyprus	"Liar"	Silia Kapsis	English	67	6
2	Serbia	"Ramonda"	Teya Dora	Serbian	47	10
3	Lithuania	"Luktelk"	Silvester Belt	Lithuanian	119	4
4	Ireland	"Doomsday Blue"	Bambie Thug	English	124	3
5	Ukraine	"Teresa & Maria"	Alyona Alyona & Jerry Heil	Ukrainian, English	173	2
6	Poland	"The tower"	Luna	English	35	12
7	Croatia	"Rim Tim Tagi Dim"	'Baby Lasagna'	English	177	1
8	Iceland	"Scared of Heights"	Hera Bjork	English	3	15
9	Slovenia	"Veronika"	Raiven	Slovene	51	9
10	Finland	"No Rules!"	'Windows95man'	English	59	7
11	Moldova	"In the Middle"	Natalia Barbu	English	20	13
12	Azerbaijan	"Ozunle apar"	Fahree feat. Ilkin Dovlatov	English, Azerbaijani	11	14
13	Australia	"One Milkali (One Blood)"	'Electric Fields'	English, Yankunytjatjara	41	11
14	Portugal	"Grito"	Iolanda	Portuguese	58	8
15	Luxembourg	"Fighter"	Tali	French, English	117	5

FINAL

11.5.2024

No.	Country	Song	Performing Artist	Lyrics	Composer	Language	Commentator	Spoker of Results	Points	Place
01	Sweden	"Unforgetable"	Marcus & Martinus	Linnea Deb, Marcus Gunnarsen, Martinus Gunnarsen	Jimmy "Joker" Thornfeldt, Joy Deb	English	Tina Mehrafzoon, Edward af Sillen	Frans	174	9
02	Ukraine	"Teresa & Maria"	Alyona Alyona & Jerry Heil	Aliona Savranenko, Yana Shemaieva	Anton Chilibi, Ivan Klymenko	Ukrainian, English	Timur Miroshnychenko, Vasyl Baidak	Jamala	453	3
03	Germany	"Always on the run"	Isaak (Guderian)	Guderian, Lost, Jupiter, Taro	Isaak Guderian, Kevin Lehr, Leo Salminen, Greg Taro	English	Amelie Ernst, Max Spallek	Ina Muller	117	12
04	Luxembourg	"Fighter"	Tali (Golergant)	Ana Zimmer, Manon Romiti, Silvio Lisbonne	Ana Zimmer, Dario Faini, Manon Romiti	French, English	Raoul Roos, Roger Saurfeld	Desiree Nosbusch	103	13
05	Israel	"Hurricane"	Eden Golan	Avi Ohayon, Keren Peles	Avi Ohayon, Keren Peles, Stav Beger	English, Hebrew	Asaf Liberman, Akiva Novick, Yoav Tzafir	Maya Alkulumbre	375	5
06	Lithuania	"Luktelk"	Silvester Belt	Dzesika Syyokaite, Elena Jurgaityte, Silvestras Belte	Dzesika Syyokaite, Elena Jurgaityte, Silvestras Belte	Lithuanian	Ramunas Zilnys	Monika Linkyte	90	14
07	Spain	"Zorra"	Nebulossa (Mery Bas & Mark Dasousa)	Mery Bas, Mark Dasousa	Mery Bas, Mark Dasousa	Spanish	Julia Varela, Tony Aguilar	Soraya Arenas	30	22
08	Estonia	"(Nendest) Kaljjootikuumidest ei tea me"	Smilinust (Kristian Jakobson, Mihkel Tamm, Karl Kivastik, Priit Jantson, Mihkel "Paevakoer" Puulluup (Marko Veisson, Ramo Teder) Korea, Kivastik	Kristian "Paiver" Jakobson, Priit Lanteeipt, Jantson, Mihkel "Paevakoer" Tamm, Karl "Pohja Korea" Kivastik	Kim Wengerstrom, Marko Veisson, Ramo Teder	Estonian	Marko Reikop	Birgit	37	20
09	Ireland	"Doomsday Blue"	Bambie Thug	Bambie Ray Robinson, Olivia Cassy Brookingm Sam Matlock, Tylr Rydr	Bambie Ray Robinson, Olivia Cassy Brookingm Sam Matlock, Tylr Rydr	English	Zbyszek Zalinski, Neil Doherty	Paul Harrington	278	6
10	Latvia	"Hollow"	Dons (Arturs Singirejs)	Arturs Singirejs, Kate Northrop, Liam Geddes	Arturs Singirejs, Kate Northrop, Liam Geddes	English	Toms Grevins, Lauris Reiniks	Andrejs Reinis Zitmanis	64	16
11	Greece	"Zari"	Marina Satti	Vlospa, Oge, Marina Satti, Manolis Sollmeister Solidakis	Ginp "The Ghost" Borri, Jay Lewitt Stolar, Jordan Richard Palmer, Konstantin Plajmenov Beshkov, Marina Satti, Nick Kodonas, Oge	Greek	Thanasis Alveras, Jerome Kaluta	Helena Paparizou	126	11
12	United Kingdom	"Dizzy"	Olly Alexander	Olivier Alexander Thornton, Daniel Harle	Olivier Alexander Thornton, Daniel Harle	English	Graham Norton	Joanna Lumley	46	18
13	Norway	"Ulveham"	Gate (Gunphild, Magnus Bormark, Jon Even, Scharer, Mats Paulsen, John Stenersen)	Erlend Skjetne, Gunnhild Sundli, Magnus Bormark, Jon Even Scharer, Marit Jensen Lillebuen, Ronny Graff Janssen, Sveinung Ektoo Sundli	Erlend Skjetne, Gunnhild Sundli, Magnus Bormark, Jon Even Scharer, Marit Jensen Lillebuen, Ronny Graff Janssen, Sveinung Ektoo Sundli	Norweigian	Marte Stokstad	Ingvild Helljesen	16	25
14	Italy	"La Noia"	Angelina Mango	Angelina Mango, Francesca Calearo	Angelina Mango, Dario Faini, Francesca Calearo	Italian	Gabriele Corsi, Mara Maionchi	Mario Acampa	268	7
15	Serbia	"Ramonda"	Teya Dora	Teodora Pavlovska, Andrijano Kadovic	Teodora Pavlovska, Luka Jovanovic	Serbian	Duska Vucinic	Konstrakta	54	17
16	Finland	"No Rules"	Windows95man (Keisteri)	Henri Piispanen, Jussi Roine, Teemu Keisteri	Henri Piispanen, Jussi Roine, Teemu Keisteri	English	Mikko Silvennoinen, Eva Frantz, Johan Lindroos	Toni Laaksonen	38	19
17	Portugal	"Grito"	Iolanda	Iolanda Costa	Iolanda Costa, Alberto "Luar" Hernandez	Portuguese	Jose Carlos Malato, Nuno Galopim	Mimicat	152	10
18	Armenia	"Jako"	Ladaniva (Jaklin, Baghdasaryan, Louis Thomas)	Jaklin Baghdasaryan, Louis Thomas	Audrey Lederaq, Jaklin Baghdasaryan, Louis Thomas	Armenian	Hrachuhi Utmazyan, Sevak Hakobyan	Brunette	183	8
19	Cyprus	"Liar"	Silia Kapsis	Eike Tiel	Dimitris Kontopoulos	English	Melina Karageorgiou, Hovig Demirjian	Loukas Hamatsos	78	15
20	Switzerland	"The Code"	Nemo	Benjamin Alasu, Lasse Midtsjan Nymann, Linda Dale, Nemo Mettler	Benjamin Alasu, Lasse Midtsjan Nymann, Linda Dale, Nemo Mettler	English	Ellis Cavallini, Gian-Andrea Costa, Jean-Marc Richard, Nicolas Tanner, Sven Epiney	Jennifer Bosshard	591	1
21	Slovenia	"Veronika"	Raiven (Sara Briski Cirman)	Bojan Cvjeticanin, Klavdija Kopina, Sara Briski Cirman	Bojan Cvjeticanin, Danilo Kapel, Klavdija Kopina, Martin Bezjak, Peter Khoo, Sara Briski Cirman	Slovene	Mojca Mavec	Lorella Flego	27	23
22	Croatia	"Rim Tim Tagi Dim"	Baby Lasagna (Marko Purisic)	Marko Purisic	Marko Purisic	English	Dusko Curlic	Ivan Dorian Molnar	547	2
23	Georgia	"Firefighter"	Nutsa Buzaladze	Ada Satka, Darko Dimitrov	Ada Satka, Darko Dimitrov	English	Nika Lobiladze	Sopho Khalvashi	34	21
24	France	"Mon Amour"	Slimane	Silmane Nebchi	Silmane Nebchi, Yaacov Salah, Meir Salah	French	Stephane Bern, Laurence Boccolini	Natasha St-Pier	445	4
25	Austria	"We Will Rave"	Kaleen (Marie-Sophie Kreissl)	Anderz Wrethov, Jimmy "Joker" Thornfeldt, Julie Agaard, Thomas Stengaard	Anderz Wrethov, Jimmy "Joker" Thornfeldt, Julie Agaard, Thomas Stengaard	English	Andi Knoll	Philipp Hansa	24	24

The Netherlands was disqualified from the finals due to performer Joost Klein's misconduct.

2021				
Country	12 Points	Juries voting	Popular voting	Total points
Italy	9	206	318	524
France	12	248	251	499
Switzerland	9	267	165	432
Iceland	4	198	180	378
Ukraine	6	97	267	364

2022				
Country	12 Points	Juries voting	Popular voting	Total points
Ukraine	33	192	439	631
United Kingdom	9	283	183	466
Spain	9	231	228	459
Sweden	5	258	180	438
Serbia	7	87	225	312

2023				
Country	12 Points	Juries voting	Popular voting	Total points
Sweden	15	340	243	583
Finland	20	150	376	526
Israel	9	177	185	362
Italy	7	176	174	350
Norway	1	52	216	268

2024				
Country	12 Points	Juries voting	Popular voting	Total points
Switzerland	23	365	226	591
Croatia	11	210	337	547
Ukraine	9	146	307	453
France	5	218	227	445
Israel	15	52	323	375

The Eurovision in Numbers

AND THE WINNER IS

Ireland and Sweden lead in Eurovision victories, each with 7 wins (Ireland has not won in the current millennium, while Sweden boasts 3 victories and counting). The UK, Luxembourg, the Netherlands, and France follow closely with 5 wins each (and they, too, except for the Netherlands, did not get a taste of victory in the 2000s). Israel reached the first place four times (and wins every 20 years since 1978). Switzerland, Italy, Norway Denmark and Ukraine had three wins each. Spain, Germany, and Austria gained two titles.

While these reached the glorious win only once: Belgium, Monaco, Yugoslavia (which will no longer win...), Estonia, Latvia, Turkey, Greece, Finland, Serbia, Russia, Azerbaijan and Portugal. 35 entries that won, an overwhelming majority, were in English, 14 in French and the rest are shared among the other languages. The last time a song in the French language won was in... 1988, when Céline Dion brought Switzerland its second victory.

GENDER AND ORIGIN IN THE EUROVISION

To date, 38 solo female singers have won the Eurovision (excluding the Austrian Conchita Wurst), compared to only 11 solo male singers.

Six duos reached the first place: three male duos, two mixed and only one female pair ("BobbySocks!" In 1985). Twelve bands tasted the victory in the contest: Twelve bands tasted the victory in the contest: "ABBA" was the first in 1974 while "Maneskin" from Italy is the last band to win, in 2021. Luxembourg triumphed five times, but all of them were achieved by one French male singer, three French female singers and one Greek female singer... None of them was born, raised or had any relation in his life to Luxembourg. Talking about origins, ten French performers won the Eurovision with France, Luxembourg and Monaco.

GROUND ZERO

So far, 19 countries have had the dubious honour of finishing the Eurovision with nul points. Austria and Norway are the "zero" champions, experiencing this horrible feeling four times, followed by Finland, Germany, Switzerland and Spain — three times.

Four countries had the zero twice: Belgium, Turkey, United Kingdom and Portugal.

This embarrassing occurrence happened only once to the Netherlands, Sweden, Yugoslavia, Monaco, Italy, Luxembourg, Iceland and Lithuania.

Among the countries that won the contest in the previous millennium, only Israel, Denmark and France have a respectable balance sheet free of nul points in the Eurovision.

They are, naturally, joined by the queen of the contest, Ireland, which has also not yet experienced the zero trauma.

There are practically zero chances of finishing the contest with zero points due to the current scoring method...

But this negative miracle happened to the UK in 2021.

THE HOST

There is a belief that the host's chances of duplicating its victory from the previous year are slim since there is a desire to innovate and reform.

But the home advantage (crowd, atmosphere and local push) should not be underestimated.

Five hosts have so far won the Eurovision:

Switzerland (1956), Spain (1969), Luxembourg (1972), Israel (1979) and Ireland, which surpassed them all (1993, 1994).

Only three host countries were runners-up:

Ireland (1997), Denmark (2001) and The UK that was the sole host that was runner-up until 1997 and swept the second place in a total of five times (1960, 1968, 1972, 1977 and 1998).

Eight countries never gave up the possibility of hosting the ESC after winning, one of them is, of course, Ireland which has won the most times.

THE MOST IMPRESSIVE WINNERS

"Brotherhood of Man" from the UK has the highest success rate, 164 points at the 1976 Eurovision (which is 80.3%).

Salvador Sobral, the winner of 2017 Eurovision, scored the most points ever — 758.

Even before the contests in which the voting split and the points multiplied, Alexander Rybak managed to leave behind his opponent in the second place with an unimaginable margin of 169 points! Norway celebrated its first victory in 1985, but "BobbySocks!" scored only 123 points (a 56.9% success rate) — the lowest for a Eurovision winner since the renewal of the points method in 1975.

THE WINNERS

Thirty countries have won the Eurovision so far.

Between 2001 and 2008, there was an amazing streak in which the winning country's victory was the first in the history of its participation in the contest. Yugoslavia, which disintegrated in 1992 and went deep into a brutal civil war, won only in 1989.

Among the republics it consisted of, Serbia was the one that managed to replicate the success with a victory in 2007.

The countries that were in the Soviet Union, which never participated in the contest, were a remarkable success, when five of its countries won the contest six times, all of which in the 2000s, obviously.

Scandinavian countries are the most successful in the ESC, led by Sweden with six wins.

In fact, except for Iceland (which was close to doing so in 1999), all Scandinavian countries won the contest.

Among the winners, France has been waiting 44 years for a first place since its last Eurovision victory in 1977 (not considering Monaco that won in 1971 but withdrew from the contest).

Israel has a unique collection of wins: since 1978, it has won the Eurovision every twenty years (1998 with Dana International and 2018 with Netta Barzilai).

The country with the longest intermission between wins is Austria, which won in 1966 with Udo Jürgens and only after 48 years, in 2014, Conchita Wurst managed to reach the first place.

HOME SWEET HOME?

The UK hosted 9 Eurovisions (more than any other country so far) and has never managed to win when the contest was held on its soil (but, of course, came in second place five times...). In contrast, Ireland, which hosted 7 ESCs, won 2 of them.

Sweden, also hosting seven times, did slightly worse at home, with their best result being Kiki Danielsson's third-place finish in Gothenburg in 1985.

Luxembourg, Israel, Spain and Switzerland complete the list of the only five countries that managed to win in an event they hosted.

France, which hosted three contests, has never fallen beneath the fourth place at home.

Six countries have given up the possibility of hosting the contest:

Switzerland, Germany, France, the Netherlands, Monaco and Israel — which is currently the last to do so (1980).

Monaco is the only winner in the Eurovision history that the contest has never been held on its soil.

ALL-TIME RANKING

The ranking refers to the winning balance of the countries participating in the contest in the first five places. Of course, Ireland is currently leading in first place over Sweden, and although reaching the top five 17 times in its first 30 appearances in the contest, it failed to reach the top 5 in the last 27 Eurovisions.

Two particularly noticeable position statistics in the all-time table:

The UK, which achieved an unusual number of 'wins' in second place at the contest (15) and Sweden, with an equally unusual number (10) of reaching the fifth place. France reached the third place (7 times) and the fourth place (7 times as well) more than any other country. Luxembourg, which until 1993 was considered the queen of the contest, never reached the second place. Except for the latter, all 13 first countries in the all-time ranking reached at least once to one of the top five places. Among the new countries that joined the contest in the 2000s, Ukraine is the one that made the most impressive jump and is in the 11th place with a fine cluster of three wins and two runners-up. Its neighbour, Russia, also had a cluster of excellent results in the 2000s. The two last countries in the ranking, Portugal and Finland, were never in the top five, in any Eurovision, except for their wins (2006 and 2017) and yet, Portugal is last in the winning countries' ranking since the two countries reached the sixth place once, but Finland has more seventh place finishes...

The Winners

Ranking	Country	Number of Wins	Contests
1	Ireland	7	1970, 1980, 1987, 1992, 1993, 1994, 1996
2	Sweden	7	1974, 1984, 1991, 1999, 2012, 2015, 2023
3	Luxembourg	5	1961, 1965, 1972, 1973, 1983
	France	5	1958, 1960, 1962, 1969, 1977
	United Kingdom	5	1967, 1969, 1976, 1981, 1997
	The Netherlands	5	1957, 1959, 1969, 1975, 2019
7	Israel	4	1978, 1979, 1998, 2018
8	Italy	3	1964, 1990
	Norway	3	1986, 1995, 2009
	Denmark	3	1963, 2000, 2013
	Ukraine	3	2004, 2016, 2022
	Switzerland	3	1956, 1988, 2024
13	Spain	2	1968, 1969
	Germany	2	1982, 2010
	Austria	2	1966, 2014
16	Monaco	1	1971
	Belgium	1	1986
	Yugoslavia	1	1989
	Estonia	1	2001
	Latvia	1	2002
	Turkey	1	2003
	Greece	1	2005
	Finland	1	2006
	Serbia	1	2007
	Russia	1	2008
	Azerbaijan	1	2011
	Portugal	1	2017

All-Time Ranking

Ranking	Country	1st Place	2nd Place	3rd Place	4th Place	5th Place
1	Ireland	7	3	1	3	3
2	Sweden	7	1	6	3	10
3	United Kingdom	5	16	3	5	1
4	France	5	4	7	8	2
5	Luxembourg	5	-	2	5	1
6	The Netherlands	5	1	1	2	2
7	Israel	4	2	2	2	3
8	Italy	3	3	4	4	5
9	Denmark	3	1	3	2	5
10	Norway	3	1	1	3	4
11	Ukraine	3	2	2	1	-
12	Switzerland	3	3	3	5	2
13	Germany	2	4	5	4	2
14	Spain	2	4	2	2	1
15	Austria	2	-	1	1	4
16	Russia	1	4	4	-	2
17	Belgium	1	2	-	4	2
18	Monaco	1	1	3	3	2
19	Turkey	1	1	1	3	-
20	Azerbaijan	1	1	1	1	1
21	Serbia	1	1	1	-	1
22	Finland	1	1	-	-	-
23	Greece	1	-	3	-	2
24	Estonia	1	-	1	1	1
25	Latvia	1	-	1	-	1
26	Yugoslavia	1	-	-	3	-
27	Portugal	1	-	-	-	-

The Hosts

Ranking	Country	Contests	Contests	The winning countries respectively	The host's ranking respectively
1	United Kingdom	9	1960	France	2
			1963	Denmark	4
			1968	Spain	2
			1972	Luxembourg	2
			1974	Sweden	4
			1977	France	2
			1982	Germany	7
			1998	Israel	2
			2023	Sweden	25
2	Ireland	7	1971	Monaco	11
			1981	United Kingdom	5
			1988	Switzerland	8
			1993	Ireland	1
			1994	Ireland	1
			1995	Norway	14
			1997	United Kingdom	2
3	Sweden	7	1975	The Netherlands	8
			1985	Norway	3
			1992	Ireland	22
			2000	Denmark	7
			2013	Denmark	14
			2016	Ukraine	5
			2024	Switzerland	9
4	The Netherlands	5	1958	France	9
			1970	Ireland	7
			1976	United Kingdom	9
			1980	Ireland	5
			2021	Italy	23
5	Luxembourg	4	1962	France	3
			1966	Austria	10
			1973	Luxembourg	1
			1984	Sweden	10
6	Israel	3	1979	Israel	1
			1999	Sweden	5
			2019	The Netherlands	23
7	Denmark	3	1965	Italy	7
			2001	Estonia	2
			2014	Austria	9

Ranking	Country		Contests	The winning countries respectively	The host's ranking respectively
8	Norway	3	1986 1996 2010	Belgium Ireland Germany	12 2 20
9	France	3	1959 1961 1978	The Netherlands Luxembourg Israel	3 4 3
10	Germany	3	1957 1983 2011	The Netherlands Luxembourg Azerbaijan	4 5 10
11	Italy	3	1965 1991 2022	Luxembourg Sweden Ukraine	5 7 6
12	Switzerland	2	1956 1989	Switzerland Yugoslavia	1 13
13	Ukraine	2	2005 2017	Greece Portugal	19 24
14	Austria	2	1967 2015	United Kingdom Sweden	14 26
15	Spain	1	1969	Spain- United Kingdom- France- The Netherlands	1 (Alongside 3 more countries)
16	Estonia	1	2002	Latvia	3
17	Turkey	1	2004	Ukraine	4
18	Azerbaijan	1	2012	Sweden	4
19	Serbia	1	2008	Russia	6
20	Yugoslavia	1	1990	Italy	7
21	Greece	1	2006	Finland	9
22	Russia	1	2009	Norway	11
23	Belgium	1	1987	Ireland	11
24	Finland	1	2007	Serbia	17
25	Latvia	1	2003	Turkey	24
26	Portugal	1	2018	Israel	26

www.ingramcontent.com/pod-product-compliance
Lightning Source LLC
Chambersburg PA
CBHW081357130726
47998CB00011B/2987